## Praise for previous editions of
### *The Practical Nomad: How to Travel Around the World*

"Take something else out of your backpack and make room for this book — it answers all the questions you haven't even thought to ask yet. Hasbrouck gives indispensable advice to all travelers — male or female, solo or not, mainstream or otherwise — that the glossy travel magazines don't write for."
Thalia Zepatos, author of *A Journey of One's Own: Uncommon Advice for the Independent Woman Traveler*

"If you've decided to put your money where your fantasy is, and save for the trip of trips, Edward Hasbrouck is your travel guru."
Amazon.com, Travel Editor's Recommended Book

"To travelers around the world, Edward Hasbrouck is the Practical Nomad, the go-to authority on international travel, an expert on airfares, and how to get the best deals on the Internet."
*Business Week*

"A wealth of no-nonsense, hard-scrabble information."
*Islands* magazine

"Essential information on airfare strategies, travel documents, information sources, and more."
*Transitions Abroad*

"The bible when it comes to planning around-the-world trips."
BookIdeas.com

"Nowhere else will you find in a single volume such valuable information…. You may consider yourself a seasoned traveler, one who has read it all and seen most of it, but you'll still learn plenty from this guide. The references and resources listed in the book's appendix are worth the cover price alone."
Travel Reference Library

More praise for
*The Practical Nomad: How to Travel Around the World*

"Thank goodness for opinionated and informed writers like
Edward Hasbrouck.... For anyone who has always wanted to
take the trip of a lifetime without going near a package tour,
Hasbrouck wrote just the book."
Arthur Frommer's Budget Travel (Frommers.com)

"A wealth of information, tips and advice, equally applicable
to the novice and the experienced traveller. A must for the
independent traveller,"
*Conde Nast Traveller* [U.K.] online

"This chapter [on airfares] alone is... worth the price ofthe
book. Knowledge is power and little is left uncovered in
Hasbrouck's manifesto."
*Gourmet Traveller,* Australia

"The Practical Nomad is a must-read for anyone planning
or even considering extended international travel,
especially for do-it-yourselfers, and especially if you're
heading to an exotic locale."
IndependentTraveler.com

"If you're an independent traveler, eager to explore the
world and willing to make your way on your own, Edward
Hasbrouck's *The Practical Nomad* is a book for you....[It] will
put you years ahead in mastering the art of travel."
Barnesandnoble.com

"Well-written... Valuable information."
*Student World Traveler*

"Attention, travel lovers: Hasbrouck... has written the handbook for world travelers.... Smart travelers will make sure to
have this necessary guide in their backpacks."
*Library Journal*

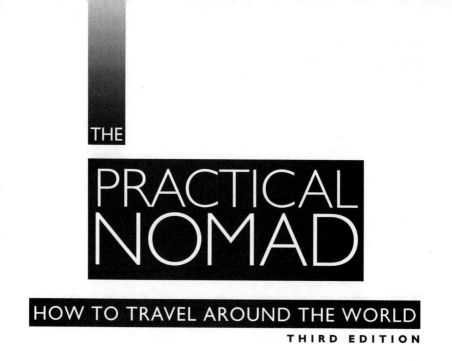

# THE
# PRACTICAL
# NOMAD

## HOW TO TRAVEL AROUND THE WORLD
### THIRD EDITION

## EDWARD HASBROUCK

AVALON
TRAVEL

THE PRACTICAL NOMAD
How to Travel Around the World
Third Edition
Edward Hasbrouck

Please send all feedback to:
The Practical Nomad
Avalon Travel Publishing
1400 65th Street, Suite 250
Emeryville, CA 94608, USA
atpfeedback@avalonpub.com
www.practicalnomad.com

Printing History
1st edition—1997
3rd edition—February 2004
5 4 3 2 1

ISBN: 1-56691-433-7
ISSN: 1088-6419

Editor: Kevin McLain
Copy Editor: Helen Sillett
Graphics Coordinator: Deb Dutcher
Design and Production: Jacob Goolkasian
Indexer: Laura Welcome

Front cover photo: © Woody Woodwroth/SuperStock

Printed in USA by Malloy
Distributed by Publishers Group West

# CONTENTS

## ABOUT THE AUTHOR

Edward Hasbrouck is the world's best-known authority on around-the-world travel and an expert in international air-fares, with a global reputation founded on his writing on the Internet and in the *Practical Nomad* book series. Winner of a Lowell Thomas Travel Journalism award for investigative reporting, Edward has been featured in a BBC-TV travel documentary and interviewed on CNN, PBS, NPR, and Pacifica Radio, and has given travel planning seminars throughout the USA, in Canada, and in the UK. In addition to his writing and speaking, Edward has been a full-time travel agent specializing exclusively in around-the-world travel and airline tickets since 1991. Currently, he is a travel consultant, industry analyst, and

the "Travel Guru" for AirTreks.com in San Francisco.

Before finding his niche in around-the-world travel, Edward worked as a bicycle courier, graphic artist, publications assistant, database maintainer, and volunteer paralegal, political organizer, lobbyist, and publicist. He has traveled around the world twice, visited all 50 states of the United States and 27 other countries, and worked with thousands of independent travelers to help them plan and organize their trips. His clients have included educational groups, environmental organizations, development NGOs, aid volunteers, and human rights workers. He is an evangelist for travel as a positive force for global understanding and change as well as personal growth and empowerment.

Edward is a member of numerous professional associations and peace and human rights groups, including the International Airlines Travel Agent Network, Tourism Concern, Guidebookwriters.com, Bay Area Travel Writers, the National Writers Union, the National Lawyers Guild, the War Resisters League, the National Association of Railroad Passengers, the Train Riders Association of California, and the San Francisco Bicycle Coalition. When he has time, he is an avid traveler; bicyclist; internationalist; and activist for youth and human rights and liberation, disarmament, peace, democracy, self-determination, and the decentralization of power. When he's not traveling, he lives in San Francisco with his partner of 22 years, Ruth Radetsky.

# PREFACE

## WHO IS THIS BOOK FOR?

If you've ever dreamed of a trip around the world, this book is for you. It is a unique, comprehensive "how-to" handbook of advice and tips for independent, on-your-own travel anywhere in the world. It's especially suitable for anyone planning—or dreaming about—the big trip: "gap year," "wander year," or "trip of a lifetime" around the world.

But this book isn't just for people whose journeys will take them all the way around the world. It's for *anyone* considering, planning, or preparing for long-term, complex, multistop, or multicountry international travel; first-time international travelers; travelers new to different regions of the world; and would-be travelers interested in learning more about travel planning than any guidebook to a specific destination can or does say. Even experienced travelers will find new and useful advice in the chapters that follow.

In writing this book and compiling this advice, I've drawn on the experiences of thousands of travelers I've worked with over the years as they planned their trips, as well as thousands more who've come to my seminars or sent me letters and e-mail messages after reading my online columns or the previous editions of this book. The opinions expressed here are my own, of course, but they are informed by the individual and collective experiences of an extended worldwide community of fellow travelers. This book gives tips that all travelers can use to enhance their next trips: about choosing destinations; obtaining visas and permits; money, budgeting, and finances; safety and health; what to bring; how to find your way around; rail, road, and water transportation; about the often-misunderstood inside world of international airline tickets, fares, and discounts; and much more to ease and enhance your travels and travel planning.

## WHY I WROTE THIS BOOK

I work as a travel agent. More than anything else, this book grew out of my dissatisfaction with my job; or, to be more precise, my dissatisfaction with the limitations of my job.

Throughout more than 10 years as a travel agent, I've specialized exclusively in around-the-world and other multicountry international trips for independent, do-it-yourself travelers. I'm not a peddler, much less a pusher, of cruises, tours, or package holidays. Rather, I do my best to encourage and empower people to travel independently and to make as many of their arrangements locally as is possible.

Nonetheless, even the most experienced and independent travelers often want and need advice about how to plan and prepare for their journey. Rarely do they have access to any independent source of professional travel advice other than that of guidebooks and travel agents.

Most travelers, even those planning extensive, long- term journeys, come to a travel agent primarily to buy airline tickets. And they tend to do so only after they have made (or failed to make) most of their other commitments and advance arrangements, when it is already too late to take advantage of whatever suggestions a travel agent might offer.

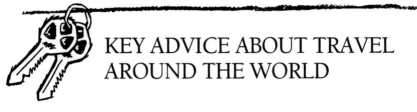

# KEY ADVICE ABOUT TRAVEL AROUND THE WORLD

- World travel is fun. World travel is sexy. World travel is the ultimate trip.
- Independent world travel is the world's best learning experience. It's the best possible investment of time and money you can make in your own career or your children's education.
- World travel will change you, and change your life, for the better.
- World travel is easier than you think.
- Getting time for travel is easier than you think.
- World travel is more affordable than you think.
- Traveling affordably doesn't take magic and doesn't require giving up comfort or convenience. The keys to affordable world travel are traveling independently and concentrating on more affordable regions of the world.
- Independent world travelers include women, men, and children of all ages, occupations, backgrounds, and careers.
- World travel can be for you if you want it to be. Making your travel dreams come true is mostly just a matter of deciding to do it.
- This book will hold your hand and help show you how you can explore the world easily, safely, and affordably

**For more information on the topics in this chapter, see the Resource Guide in the back of the book, and the links on the Practical Nomad Web site at http://www.practicalnomad.com.**

Although many travel agents call themselves, some more accurately than others, "travel consultants," they traditionally have been paid primarily as sellers of airline tickets (except for those who sell packages and tours, which is why some travel agents are so eager to sell tours and other overpriced extra services).

Like most travel agents, I simply can't afford to spend as much time with each traveler who consults me, or give them nearly as much advice and assistance, as I would like.

Of course, some of the most important questions are those that aren't asked at all, because people either don't realize they are important or assume they already know the answers, especially when the conventional wisdom is a myth.

Destination guidebooks focus on specific information about particular places or regions, not the things that are common to international or long-term travel in diverse places. Even most compendia of general travel advice are intended for short-term travelers on package tours or those who travel on their own, unescorted, only in wealthy, "Westernized" countries most like their homelands.

This book is my effort to fill that gap: to provide a how-to guide to independent world travel, to answer the most frequently asked questions about this sort of travel, to debunk the most widespread myths, and to share some advice compiled from my own trips, my colleagues, my clients, and other travelers. It's the desire to empower and facilitate independent travel—and the learning, communication, and understanding between different peoples and parts of the world that it leads to—that keeps me in the travel business despite the low pay, long hours, high stress, deadlines, and (contrary to myth) the limited time and opportunities it leaves me to travel myself.

This book began as a series of short answers to travel questions on the Internet—posted anonymously because my employer at the time thought my explanations of international airline ticket discounting revealed too many trade secrets! Later, when I changed employers and began answering questions in my own name, some of my tips came to be widely known and archived, prompting more people to call, write, and e-mail me with questions, suggestions, and issues on which they sought advice. (I continue to post the updated version of these answers to FAQs about airline ticket discounts every month on the "rec.travel.air" newsgroup, as well as at http://hasbrouck.org/faq.)

Later, I began leading seminars on how to plan and prepare for long-term and around-the-world travel at hostels, colleges and universities, travel gear and bookstores, and travel shows and events throughout the United States, Canada, and the UK. This has given me even more understanding of what travelers seek in the early stages of their preparations, long before they talk to a travel agent.

Eventually, all of this information came together, much revised and expanded, as this book. It's been thoroughly updated once again in 2003 for this third edition, incorporating feedback and suggestions from readers of the previous editions.

# "I COULDN'T TAKE A BIG TRIP LIKE THAT, BECAUSE…"

You say want to travel around the world, but you haven't done it? What's your excuse for not fulfilling your travel dreams?

### • "I couldn't get that much time off."

If you think, "No one in my situation could get six months off," you're wrong. Whatever your age, occupation, and stage in your career, people like you are finding time to travel. Once you really resolve to travel, you'll find a way to make the time.

### • "I have a job and a career."

Your job and career may be the best reasons for world travel: There's no better investment in your skills and future earning potential than a year or two of international travel.

### • "I have children."

Children are another great reason to take a trip around the world. Few other gifts you could give your children could match the lifelong value of international experience and exposure to global diversity as a child. No one I know who has traveled abroad as a child would think of trading a year of world travel for a year of conventional schooling. Experience living abroad as a child is the single best predictor of success in an international career as an adult.

### • "I don't have that much money."

You can't extrapolate from short vacations to long- term travel, or from package tours to independent travel.

## HOW TO USE THIS BOOK

This is not a menu, a list of choices, or a guide to specific routes around the world or anywhere else. There aren't many specific prices in this book, and those that appear are only examples. (Except as otherwise noted, prices are based on available information as of 2003, and all prices have been converted to US dollars.) This book is intended to direct you to resources, information, and advice that will help you prepare and plan the trip *you* want to take.

I'll discuss some things that can happen along the way, but mainly in terms of what you can do in advance to prepare for them. The emphasis is on what to do *before* you leave.

In the following sections I give some basic suggestions on how to plan your trip, answer some frequently asked questions, and suggest sources of answers to a variety of other questions. Although the stages of planning and preparation overlap and can vary from trip to trip, I've tried to present topics in the general sequence in which I recommend that you deal with them.

Most people who follow the principles in this book, find that their total costs, including airfare, for an extended international trip are less than their living costs were at home. If you can afford to spend a summer or a year sitting around your back yard doing nothing, you could afford to spend the same amount of time traveling around the world—for less than the cost of staying home.

## • "The places you talk about are too far away."

Europe isn't the closest other continent to North America. From San Francisco or Seattle, Tokyo is closer than London. From Miami, Sao Paulo or Santiago de Chile are closer than Madrid. From New York, Senegal is closer and a shorter flight than Switzerland. And the Third World is, of course, right next door to the United States in Mexico and much of the Caribbean.

## • "It would be too difficult and uncomfortable."

Because services are so much cheaper in poorer places, independent budget travel in the Third World can be much easier and more comfortable than in the First World. It's travel in wealthy, expensive places like the United States or Western Europe that's most difficult on a budget and takes the most travel savvy.

## • "I don't speak a foreign language."

Never before has any language had the truly global hegemony that English has today. You'll learn much more if you know more languages, but there is almost nowhere that you can't get around on English. You speak English: you're lucky and privileged. Make the most of it—you can go wherever in the world you want.

I begin with the most basic question""Where do you want to go?""and some sources of information (in print, on the Internet, and elsewhere) to help you choose.

Next, you're ready to start figuring out how to get there. I first survey the possibilities and limitations of rail, road, and water travel, with an emphasis on where they are and aren't feasible and affordable, and when you need to make decisions before you leave home. Then I'll explain how to get the best set of airline tickets for your trip, with a particular emphasis on international airline ticket discounting and how best to find and work with the travel agent who's right for you. (I include, of course, information about travel agents and other Internet ticket sellers, although I've also made the Internet and travel the subject of a separate book, *The Practical Nomad Guide to the Online Travel Marketplace*.)

Then I'll review some of the other essential things you'll need to do before you leave and how to go about them: obtaining necessary travel documents, making health and insurance preparations to protect yourself while traveling, deciding what to bring with you, planning your budget, and dealing with money.

Then I'll talk about some of the nitty-gritty of traveling life: accommodations, food, tours, guides, and sightseeing. Even if you plan to deal with these things on your own as you go, you may want to start thinking about them in advance.

To put it all in perspective, throughout the book I share general advice about what makes for good and bad trips, and what you can do both before and during your trip to improve your chances of having a good one.

Don't feel you have to read the whole book. I'll probably repeat some things that seem obvious, especially if you're an experienced international traveler. And I'll probably leave some of your questions unanswered, or raise new ones. Where I've deliberately left information out because it's already been compiled elsewhere and/or it changes too often to be kept up to date in a book like this. I've tried to include references to sources where this sort of information can be found. I'll be happy if each traveler who reads this book finds something in it of value.

I especially hope this book will serve the needs of people who don't like package tours, or can't find one they like, but who aren't confident that they can do what they want on their own, or just don't know how. If there is one thing I want to get across, it's that anyone can do it. Independent travel isn't for everyone, but it is *possible* for anyone.

# "Is This *For Me?*"

# AN INTRODUCTION TO TRAVEL AROUND THE WORLD

## INDEPENDENT WORLD TRAVELERS

Long-term, independent world travelers are a far more diverse lot than anyone would imagine. If you think this sort of travel is only for students, hippies, and other broke young people willing to put up with bad food and bed bugs, think again. I've seen everyone from gray-haired pensioners to middle-aged upper-class financiers to 30- something computer programmers take off around the world for a year or two at a time.

### Demographics
People who buy tickets around the world from me and my colleagues at AirTreks.com are far more diverse than most people would imagine. When last we checked, our customers' average age was 35, but 15 percent were younger than 20 (including children of all ages), 8 percent were in their 50s, and 5 percent (and rising) were older than 60. Women traveling alone made up 24 percent of all our customers.

### Independent Travel Defined
By "independent" travel, I mean travel that isn't done as part of a tour, and for which most accommodations and other services are arranged locally, on arrival, as you go along, rather than reserved in advance. It is travel on your own, by yourself or with only one or a few traveling companions (perhaps people met along the way), not with a group following a common itinerary. It's travel that involves direct, unmediated, daily interactions with local people and involvement with local ways of living and doing.

### Who Is Independent Travel For?
This sort of travel isn't for everyone. Impatient, intolerant, inflexible, or closed-minded people; worriers; and those without a sense of humor aren't likely to enjoy it unless they are transformed by this travel into people with different

# REASONS TO TRAVEL

Anthropologist and travel researcher Klaus Westerhausen, who studied long-term travelers in Asia, came up with this partial list of motives for extended international travel.

• **The Long-Held Dream** travel as the fulfillment of a lifelong aspiration

• **Journey into Adult Life** travel as a rite of passage, personal growth, and empowerment

• **The Final Fling** travel before "settling down" to career, family, or other involvements

• **The Escape** travel as part of, or as a response to, a career break or life transition

traits. Control freaks either love it or hate it, sometimes simultaneously. Be honest with yourself. Are you ready to learn new things and to experience the unexpected? Don't travel independently just to save money. Travel on your own only if you truly want to travel that way, and are open to the possibility and potential benefits of the unexpected, including the possibility that you will come home a different person. Take for granted that you don't know, and can't be sure, in advance what your trip will be like. If you don't like these possibilities, those ideas, or need to know in advance just how things will go, take a tour. That's what they are for.

What long-term independent travelers have in common is not their age, race, wealth, or social status but simply their taste in travel: they take more time to travel; they prefer to arrange things on their own as they go, leaving themselves maximum flexibility to change their plans en route; and they put a relatively low priority on money spent on accommodations as opposed to other travel activities. These tastes reinforce each other: it's hard to afford to travel for a long time unless you are careful about your budget, and the best way to cut the cost of travel is to stay in locally booked budget accommodations, making any tour arrangements locally.

### Stereotypes

The image of independent long-term travelers as undesirables is, fortunately, much less prevalent in the global South than travelers often expect, or than it was some years ago. "Starving" First World students are rich by local standards in the Second, Third, and Fourth Worlds, and their spending is the backbone of the economy in many places where few package tourists go. These days most poor countries welcome backpackers and their money.

Prejudice against independent travelers remains widespread in the First World, especially in the travel industry itself. When I mention "independent" travel to other travel agents, airlines, and government tourist promotion offices, they usually assume that I am talking about customized but prearranged inclusive tours ("FIT" travel, as this type of travel is called in industry jargon). They find it incomprehensible that people would prefer to arrange things for themselves, or that I would want to facilitate their doing so.

"They're going to stay somewhere," is the industry adage, "so why not make sure it's somewhere that gives you a commission?" The last thing most travel agents want travelers to realize is that cheaper places are cheaper *because* they don't take advance reservations from overseas or pay commissions to travel agents.

## Backpacker Facts

Factual research about independent travelers supports neither the demographic stereotypes of them as students and youth, nor the economic stereotype of them as poorer than other tourists. Those who bother to learn who backpackers really are find out what experienced travelers have always known: almost every type of person likes to travel. For example, Australia's Minister of Tourism, Michael Lee, described the results of that country's first serious study of international backpackers as follows: "Despite their reputation as travelers on a shoestring budget, backpackers actually pour more money into our economy than almost any other type of traveler."

The Australian Bureau of Tourism Research found that despite spending an average of only A$51 (approximately US$40) per day (compared with A$78/US$60 for all visitors to Australia), backpackers stayed so much longer (almost three times as long as the typical visitor) that the average backpacker spent almost twice as much in Australia as the average for all visitors.

Only one-fourth of "backpackers"—defined as tourists who spent at least one night of their stay in Australia in a hostel—were students. Fully one-third were employed in professional or technical occupations, and seven percent were executives and managers.

Contrary to the widespread presumption that long-term visitors take jobs away from locals, the Australian Department of Employment, Education, and Training estimated that backpackers—the category of tourists most likely to seek paid jobs while on holiday—generate two-thirds more jobs for locals per visitor than other tourists, both because of their greater total spending and because more of their spending on travel goes directly to local businesses as opposed to foreign tour operators and agents. In addition, "Backpackers spend much more than they earn, since they work only to supplement their funds and to travel further."

Further, the report recommended that visa restrictions be eased and procedures simplified, long-term visas made less expensive, and visa extensions made easier and cheaper. "Such changes could encourage travelers to stay longer and to spend more tourist dollars in Australia, instead of having to curtail their holidays simply because their visas have expired."

The Australian report was, according to Minister of Tourism Lee, "The first time any national government anywhere in the world has developed a specific strategy for this sector of the tourism industry." Implementation of that strategy has lagged even in Australia. Most tourism organizations ignore independent travel entirely.

A study of foreign backpackers in North America, or many other regions, would find similar figures. Perhaps countries such as the United States, where the government does the least to facilitate inbound international tourism, will eventually recognize their economic interest in making it easier for foreigners, especially independent travelers, to come here and spend their money.

# FINDING TIME TO TRAVEL

Don't rule out long-term travel just because you have a full-time job. I don't mean to make light of unemployment, job insecurity, and the credit-card debts that burden so many North Americans. Nonetheless, my impression is that the key reason more people don't get more time to travel is that would-be long-term travelers are afraid even to ask for additional time off for fear of losing their jobs.

I regularly ask my clients, "How did you get the time for this trip?" No one has ever answered, "I asked for time off, so they fired me."

**REAL LIFE**

Workers in the United States get very short paid vacations compared to those in Western Europe. Unlike a typical two-week USA vacation, a standard four- to eight- or even nine-week Western European vacation is long enough to give significant freedom for independent exploration within one region or large country, if not for a trip around the world. In the United States, only students and teachers and union members with a lot of seniority have annual vacations long enough for that sort of travel. But that doesn't mean other Americans have to feel limited to short-duration tours, or that workers anywhere in the First World can't get additional unpaid leave if they ask for it.

### Travel Is a Business Asset

Over the last decade, I've noticed that far more— and far more diverse—people are taking extended trips abroad. A variety of trends are making it easier for people to justify travel to themselves, their friends and families, and their employers: the trend from permanent to contingent employment; the globalization of the economy (one major corollary of which is the enormous demand in all economic sectors for workers with international experience); and the growing cultural and ethnic diversity of the United States (with its similar corollary of demand for cross-cultural communication and business skills). Travel—*especially* the sort of independent, international travel that necessitates interaction and communication with diverse local people— is increasingly recognized as a valuable experience, with cultural and educational immersion leading to personal growth and self-improvement. This kind of travel is no longer thought of as a frivolous, self-indulgent, or escapist vacation—not that this sort of trip isn't also the most fun and excitement you could ever hope for.

### Just Ask

Don't be afraid to ask for time off. Your boss may never have gotten such a request before, and may not know what to do. The most common response from management seems to be a mix of mild jealousy and "I wish that I'd had the courage to do that when I was your age." The most common answer is "Yes." Even if the boss says "No, I won't guarantee you a job when you get back," you haven't lost anything by asking.

### But What About My Résumé?

Some people are afraid to have a gap in their résumé. Don't worry about it; put your travels on your résumé. Having taken a trip around the world means far more than having taken the Grand Tour of Europe ever did. More and more, I hear from returned travelers who are putting their travel experience at the top of their résumé: "A year spent traveling the world, familiarizing myself with the diversity of world cultures, and learning how to understand and deal with people from backgrounds different from my own." Prospective employers may smile, they may laugh, they may be jealous— but they will offer you the job.

### Travel Becomes a Job Credential

Businesses today can't find enough qualified employees with international experience. International travel will teach you new skills and improve your ability to do almost any job. If your old job isn't waiting for you, travel will be a credential that will help you get another job.

"But I'm just going to travel, not work abroad. That's not the sort of international experience that businesses want." Maybe, but consider the competition: 85 percent of all USA citizens don't have a passport. That means they've never left North America—and couldn't even if a free ticket fell in their lap. If you've ever been overseas, you have more international experience than 85 percent of the people in the United States. If you've spent six months traveling around the world, you have more bona fide international experience than almost all competing job seekers.

Even in the shrinking number of industries where the global marketplace isn't yet perceived as relevant to job skills, "I quit my last job because I wanted to travel around the world" is a strong line to use in a job interview when you get back. It's a good opening for describing the things you've done that will set you apart from other candidates for the job.

I've come to the conclusion—one that has surprised me as much as it has surprised most of the people whose experiences have brought me to it—that the greatest barrier to long-term travel by American workers is the perceived

# "HOW COULD I GET THE TIME
# TO TRAVEL?"

I continue to be amazed at the diversity of people who come to me to plan months-long trips. How do they get the time? Here are some of the ways:

- **Educate, agitate, and organize for more time off.**

 Everywhere in the world, mandatory allowances of time for rest, and limits on working hours, have been the result of extended political struggle. Laws and union contracts entitling workers in Europe to four to eight weeks of vacation have come about through the same processes that led to the eight-hour day and the 40-hour week in the United States. North American workers will get the same vacation rights as Europeans only if the labor movement, individual workers, and voters make this an issue and demand.

- **Work as a temporary, freelancer, or contractor.**

 So-called "contingent" workers make up at least 10–15 percent of the workforce in the United States. It's now possible for people in almost

any occupation or career to reorganize their work—if they haven't been forced to already—on a freelance or contract basis that leaves them regular opportunities to travel, after finishing one job or assignment and before starting the next.

- **Work in a seasonal job or occupation.**

 Seasonal jobs may be more diverse than you think, including those in agriculture, the building trades, tourism, etc. Some seasonal jobs, such as those at resorts or in national parks and forests, include employer-provided housing. I've know ski-resort workers who travel every summer, and national park workers who travel every winter, without having to pay to maintain a home while they're on the road in the off-season.

- **Work for a school, college, or university.**

 Many jobs in educational institutions are seasonal. Part of the trade-off for teachers' low wages (although far from a sufficient one) is their long summer vacations. What many people don't think about is that schools, colleges, and universities employ all sorts of workers for the academic year. Academic-year jobs include everything from food service to word processing to computer support to building maintenance. For much of the time that I was growing up, my mother did office and administrative work for a college, rather than some other employer, in order to have long summers off with her children. Others do the same thing in order to have time to travel. And even nonacademic educational staff are often eligible for paid sabbaticals.

- **Take a sabbatical.**

Periodic year-long paid sabbaticals are standard for professors, and common for teachers even at the elementary and secondary level. But sabbaticals aren't limited to academia anymore. More and more employers have formal or informal programs for granting paid or unpaid extended leave. (See the Resource Guide for some surveys and examples of corporate sabbatical and leave programs.) Sabbaticals improve employee skills, productivity, morale, and loyalty. If your employer doesn't already have such a program, why not suggest it?

- **Take an unpaid leave of absence.**

Even if your employer doesn't have a formal leave program, you can always ask. Pitch it to your employer as a no-lose proposition: you are willing, entirely at your own expense, to take an unpaid leave to acquire some of the skills they need most to succeed in a global economy. If it's not going to cost them anything, why would they say no? Even if they think travel is irrelevant to your job, they'd probably rather you come back to work for them after your travels than go to work for someone else.

- **Quit your job. Get a better one when you get back.**

Even if you have to quit your job, there's a good chance you'll actually get it back—if you want it—when you return. If not, you'll have international travel experience under your belt and on your resumé. With that, you should be able to find a new job a step up the career and salary ladder from your old one.

disempowerment that leaves them unable to bring themselves even to ask for time off.

Just do it.

## HOW MUCH DOES A TRIP LIKE THIS COST?

Too many people abandon all hope of world travel because they assume that it must be very expensive. I'll return to the question of travel costs and budgeting in much more detail later on in the chapter, "The Bottom Line." But I want to give you a sense of just how affordable independent world travel can be.

So how much does it cost for a trip around the world? One way to predict your expenses is to look at how much other travelers have spent.

### Survey Data

The best data on international travelers from the United States comes from an annual survey by the U.S. Department of Commerce of several tens of thou-

---

## "HOW CAN I AFFORD TO TRAVEL?"

Lots of travelers seem to want a magic bullet for travel costs: "How can I go on fancy tours or cruises, or go to big cities or major tourist destinations in expensive countries like those in Western Europe, stay in five-star hotels, and have everything be cheaper?"

There are some money-saving tips that can cut the cost of this sort of travel to these sorts of places, but let's not lose the forest for the trees. Two things, above all else, will determine how expensive or how affordable your travel will be. Compared to these, other strategies for cutting costs, and their impact on your travel bottom line, are trivial.

• **Do you travel to rich, and therefore expensive, places? Or do you travel to poor, and therefore cheap places?**

Travel is a "service industry." When you travel, most of what you're paying for is for people to do things for you: cook and serve your food, clean the rooms and make the beds in the hotel, drive or guide you around, and so forth. Most of the cost of travel services is the cost of labor. What this means is that the cost of local travel services in a particular country is almost purely a function of local wage scales. And the differences between First World and Third World wages are so extreme that which world you travel in makes much, much more difference to your costs than how thriftily you travel.

• **Do you prearrange services through intermediaries in the First World? Or do you arrange as little as possible other than air tickets in advance, and**

sands of passengers on intercontinental flights departing from the United States. AirTreks.com commissioned an analysis of the trip cost data for those traveling overseas on coach-class tickets (excluding first- and business-class travelers) to compare the budgets of short-term and long-term travelers.

The average traveler taking a 60–100 night trip overseas from the United States budgeted a total of US$3,418, including airfare, prepaid tours and hotels or other services, and planned expenses on the road. Because longer trips are so much less expensive per day, that's less than 50 percent more than the cost of the typical two-week overseas trip. The average budget for a six-month trip was US$7,092, only about three times as much as for the typical two-week trip overseas.

Per diem cost declined steadily with increased trip length: the typical American overseas budgeted US$68 per person per day, but this fell to US$29 per person per day for trips of two months or more. And these figures would have been even lower if business travelers were excluded. It's important to note that, because the survey was conducted on outbound flights, the survey measured

---

**arrange and pay for accommodations and other services locally, as close as possible to the people and places where and by whom those services are actually provided?**

The premium you have to pay to arrange things in advance is highest for travel in countries where local services are cheapest. That's because the foreign intermediaries (tour operators, travel agents, etc.) in the First World have dollar or other hard-currency, high-wage, costs and expenses to cover: rent and overhead for an office in the United States, salaries for staff in the USA to handle your reservations, commissions in US dollars to travel agents in the USA to represent them, a guide based in the USA or Europe to accompany the tour, and so forth. These are real costs inherent in making it possible for you to make reservations in advance from the United

States. But these transaction costs far exceed the actual costs of services provided by local people at local wages in a Third World destination country.

In addition, only the more expensive local Third World tour companies and accommodations providers can afford to be connected to a computerized reservation system, maintain a foreign hard-currency bank account, or pay commissions to foreign travel agents. Even in wealthy First World countries there is usually an entire layer of local hostelries, guest houses, and freelance guides who aren't set up to take reservations through travel agencies or tour companies from abroad, and who have fundamentally lower costs and prices as a result. The cheapest hotel room in a major city that can be reserved from abroad may be five or fifty times the cost of the cheapest bed available locally.

expected—not actual—spending. In my experience, most people spend somewhat more than they expected. The numbers produced in this survey are averages: some travelers spent more and some spent less.

### Consider the Value

Your mileage may vary. Overall, though, these survey results show that people like you can and do travel for months for less than you might spend on a new entertainment system or the down payment (much less the monthly bills) for a new car or SUV. It's only a tiny fraction of the cost of a typical honeymoon. Think about other things you might spend this kind of money on, and compare the value.

### Packaged Travel Costs

If you don't want to travel independently, it's another story. Escorted around-the-world group tours come and go. Various tour operators have scheduled them from time to time, but they are infrequent. In the last decade, a couple of tour operators have offered month-long around-the-world packages: one by chartered private jet for about US$30,000 per person, and the other on scheduled airlines for about US$10,000 per person, inclusive of air and surface transportation, accommodations, sightseeing excursions, guides, and most meals. Each year several cruise ships steam around the world; prices in 2003 ranged upward from about US$25,000 (per person, double occupancy, not including any activities or excursions on land at ports of call) for three- to four-month cruises. Details vary, but these prices and durations are typical of what has been offered.

Most people, however, prefer to travel on their own without a group or escort. Most have smaller budgets than would be required for these tours. And many want to travel for much longer periods of time. Few happen to want exactly the itinerary of one of these tours.

## TYPES OF TRIPS

A trip around the world, or any long-term international trip, is, at the very least, a significant step on anyone's journey through life. Many (perhaps most) of those who take such a trip do so only once in a lifetime. It's a major undertaking, one in which you may be investing as much as a year of your life and on which you may be spending most of your accumulated savings or using all the vacation time you've accumulated at work. The check I wrote for my own first set of tickets around the world was the largest check I had written in my life. A trip like this means a lot to anyone who takes one.

There are different sorts of travelers, trips, and reasons for multistop and long-term journeys. You obviously have your own reasons or you wouldn't be reading this book.

## One Extreme—Short on Time

At one extreme are travelers who combine specific business trips or visits to friends and relations in different places that are more quickly and cheaply reached as multiple stops on a single trip than as separate roundtrips from home.

Trips like this tend to be shorter, and I've sent people around the world on business in as few as 10 days. Partly as a result, travelers like this also tend to have more specific requirements for their travel dates and the sequence in which they visit the cities in their itinerary. Moreover, those who are short on time tend to put a higher priority on direct flights and routings. They often prefer to travel by air whenever possible, to fix their exact travel dates in advance, and to have all their tickets in hand before they leave.

## The Other Extreme

At the other extreme are those whose trips are extended explorations, adventures, or even just very long vacations. These travelers tend to have more time than money, and some are traveling for more than a year at a time.

These sorts of travelers tend to be more flexible in choosing a set of destinations and a sequence in which to visit them, to be more willing to change their itinerary to save money, and to want to use surface transportation wherever possible. They often welcome the opportunity for additional stopovers or layovers en route, even in places they may not originally have thought to visit. They usually want tickets that will permit them to change their travel dates as they go. Finally, some of them deliberately buy tickets for only part of their trip so that they can change their onward routing and itinerary. They decide along the way whether to take optional side trips or to travel some sections by air, land, or water, or to extend their travel for more than a year.

## Between Extremes

Many trips combine several purposes and have aspects of both these extremes: "I'm going to my cousin's wedding in Delhi on September 5. I need to arrive by September 3 at the latest, and to stay for at least one full week. On the way there I want to stop for 2–3 business days to meet with my business contacts in Shanghai, and before returning home I'd like to spend about two weeks on vacation in Greece." Or whatever. Each trip is different, and each traveler has different priorities.

## Customizing Your Trip

Smart travelers and good travel agents customize each trip around the world. You should try to find the best route and tickets for what you want, not which "standard" package more-or-less approximates what you want.

When a travel agent questions you about your plans, they do so not to pry but in order to find the itinerary and the set of tickets that will best meet your needs. The more the agent understands your purposes, the better they can help you to fulfill them. And before you call a travel agent, you need to be clear in your own mind on your own goals and destinations. In the next chapter, I'll guide you through some of the major sources of information you can use to figure out where you want to go.

# "Where
## in the World ...?"

## CHOOSING DESTINATIONS

### IT'S A BIG WORLD AFTER ALL

It may seem obvious, but the first step in planning a trip is deciding where to go.

We're often told that we live in the Jet Age on a planet that modern technology has made a small world. There's a certain truth to all of that. By scheduled airliner, most major world cities are no more than two or three days' travel time apart, if money is no object, space is available, and you pick the right day of the week on which to leave. There aren't many countries where some people (if only the rulers) aren't watching CNN and exchanging e-mail. But information technology has a way of making physical distances seem shorter than they are. Earth is still as big a world as ever, and, fortunately, still a pretty varied one.

Six months, a year, two years, or a lifetime aren't long enough to "see it all." There's much more of the world that you won't see than that you will. Color in all the places you've seen with your own eyes on the largest map of the world you can find, and all you'll see is a few tiny dots for the broadest views from tall buildings and mountains, and intermittent hairlines marking routes you flew over in cloudless daylight while looking out the airplane window.

Some people seem (and claim) to have been everywhere. What does that mean? Has someone who once spent a day in New York or Miami "seen" the United States? Some people are country collectors, and there's a club exclusively for those who have visited at least 100 countries. Yet, even the rare globetrotter who reaches that threshold has been to fewer than half the world's sovereign nations.

I'd go a day out of my way to get a glimpse of any country I hadn't been in before. (Admittedly, I've also declined the chance to step across a border into a new country when it would have cost me US$100 for a visa.) But I try not to kid myself about the significance of merely setting foot somewhere. One of my conscious goals for my first trip around the world was to learn the meaning of my ignorance: to get a better sense of just how much allowance I should make, in drawing conclusions about things, for how little I knew about the world. I came back having been many places, and learned many things, but with a much-heightened sense of how much I don't know and never will.

No matter what the length of the trip, it's tempting to try to go too many places and to see and do too much. Paradoxically, people who realize that they'll never be able to see everything and who fear that they may never get back to a country or region again, are sometimes those who feel most driven to complete their mental "must-see" checklist on their first visit to an area. When I talk to travelers after a big trip, most of them say they wish they had chosen fewer places to try to visit, or that they had narrowed their explorations to smaller regions.

Even places that seem small in our conventionally Eurocentric North American worldview can be huge. (Getting a less distorted mental map of the world is one of the potential benefits of world travel.) If the trains are on time and you make the best possible connections, it's a journey of five days and nights across the full width of the territory governed by the People's Republic of China. It's

# KEY ADVICE ABOUT CHOOSING DESTINATIONS

- The world is big. You can't see it all in a lifetime, much less a few months or years. Narrow your choices. Most people try to do too much in too little time.

- Contrary to what you might think, the best way to start your planning may be to choose a list of specific destinations, not to draw lines on a map.

- Make your own choices. Don't go somewhere just because someone else liked it or told you to go there.

- Your daily activities and the people you meet have more influence on the quality of your travel experience than the sites you visit or sights you see.

- Travel in the present. Use the Internet and other resources to learn about contemporary life and current affairs in the places where you are going.

- Think about who is giving you advice and what their knowledge is based on. Many resources for travelers are propaganda, designed to sell travel "products" rather than to inform. Many of the most useful resources for choosing destinations aren't intended primarily for travelers.

- Look to resources from and by people in the places you are thinking of going for the most accurate picture of what travel in those places will really be like.

For more information on the topics in this chapter, see the Resource Guide in the back of the book, and the links on the Practical Nomad Web site at http://www.practicalnomad.com.

2–3 weeks by ship from one end of the Indonesian archipelago to the other, if you time your departure just right. It's 1300 kilometers (800 miles) from Capetown to Johannesburg, and South Africa is only a small piece of the tip of Africa. The entire distance across Europe from London to Istanbul is shorter than the distance across just a part of Brazil from Rio de Janeiro to Manaus in the center of the country.

Within the United States, we're accustomed to being able to travel long distances quickly and easily to places with wildly different landscapes (no other country is geographically more diverse then the United States, although China comes close), but with only minimal variation in culture, language, or way of life. Elsewhere in the world, be prepared to find much more extreme variations in lifestyle even within smaller countries or regions—which makes it important to research and choose specific destinations, not just general regions or countries.

## Choosing Destination Points

It's natural to start planning a trip around the world by drawing lines on a map. But my strong recommendation, unless your plans require otherwise, is to start planning any multistop trip by choosing a set of destination points, not a route. Or start with a set of experiences you want to have or activities you want to engage in, even if you don't yet know in what part(s) of the world you might best pursue those interests.

Once you know where you want to go, the ways to get there will follow, as will other incidental places that happen to be along the way. Think about points first, not lines. Resist the temptation to try to connect the dots until you've gotten airfare estimates from a specialty travel agent (as discussed in the "Air Transportation" chapter later on in the book) and thoroughly researched the expense, time, difficulty, and political feasibility of any overland travel (as discussed in the chapter that follows on "Surface Transportation"). Unless you really have to follow a particular route, it is the set of destinations you want to go to that will determine the best and cheapest route, not the other way around. Lots of lines you could draw on maps, on the other hand, don't correspond to any possible, much less affordable, travel routes.

## Reasons to Choose a Tour

If you have little time and a long agenda of specific sites, sights, and highlights that you'd be heartbroken if you didn't get to, especially a list derived from tour brochures, you may really be better off on a tour. Perhaps the biggest reason to travel on a tour, rather than independently, is that you can cover more ground in a short time. On your own, you'll spend a significant amount of your time arranging things that others arrange in advance for people on tours, and you won't be able to make as "efficient" use of your time for sightseeing. Try to remember this when you budget your time for independent travel, and don't plan a schedule as fast and busy as that of a tour.

# EFFICIENCY AND INDEPENDENCE

CHOOSING DESTINATIONS

## Capital vs. Labor

In the United States and many other Northern countries, we are rich in material possessions, while our very wealth (and restrictions on immigration) makes labor expensive. So we measure efficiency in terms of maximizing what can be done with a given amount of human labor, and regard labor-saving devices as improvements. Poor countries, where the greatest problems are often unemployment (a surplus of labor) and national debt (a shortage of capital), measure efficiency in how much can be accomplished with fixed material and capital inputs. These countries often regard more labor-intensive methods as improvements if they reduce the need for material and capital inputs.

Southerners regard us as wasteful of capital for using elaborate, gas-guzzling machines to do things that could be done by a sufficient number of people with hand tools, while we regard them as inefficient in labor expenditure for using so much human energy to keep old vehicles and machinery running.

Many Southern ways of doing things that Northerners are tempted to dismiss as backward look different when they are evaluated in terms of labor efficiency rather than capital efficiency. Worldwide, labor is a plentiful and all-too-rapidly self-renewing resource; metal and petroleum— the main constituents of capital goods—are not. Capital-intensive ways of living cannot be sustained. A large part of the definition of "appropriate" or "intermediate" technology is that it uses a more appropriate balance of capital and labor inputs than "high" technology.

Northerners may have something to teach Southerners about technology, but we also have a great deal to learn. The world's most skilled mechanics aren't the Northerners who can afford to throw something away and buy another if it's "too much trouble" to repair it. Southerners are—by necessity—the world champions of ingenuity, improvisation, repair,

## Pace

Different people prefer different paces. Some people are eager to go on after a few days in one place, always wanting to keep moving. Others would rather settle into each place they visit and are always reluctant to move on. Often, as people gain more travel experience and learn to travel more quickly, they begin to desire to travel more slowly. The most frequent mistakes of people planning their first long-term trip are either not planning at all (assuming that "We'll work it out as we go") or planning to do too much in too little time. If you are inexperienced or at all unsure, my recommendation is to err on the side of planning to visit fewer places more slowly.

rebuilding, scrounging, adapting, and mak-ing-do. These are all alternative names for recycling. Forced to make a long journey in an unreliable, randomly chosen old vehicle, with few tools or spare parts, I would unhesitatingly choose a team of Vietnamese or other Fourth World mechanics as most likely to get me where I wanted to go.

## Independence vs. Interdependence

Northerners, especially those from the United States and Australia, with our fron-tier settler cultures of self-reliance, tend to define "independence" as freedom from other people. So we think of driving our "own" car as more independent, an inter-pretation derived from the following, often unconscious, underlying cultural assumption: Machines are more reliable than people, and with them we can live our lives in splendid isolation from depen-dence on other people.

However, machines can't be relied on in most of the world. And "interdepen-dence"—a recent buzzword in the North—has always been taken for granted as a fact of life for those just barely getting by, whether they describe it in terms of ritual or religious obligation or as "the solidarity of the oppressed."

People who know this, and whose marginal survival depends upon other people's willingness to help them when they are in need, can often be relied on to a degree that surprises Northerners. In places where few people can afford machines, security and independence often depend more on human relation-ships. Southerners, in fact, may interpret the Northerners' desires for "indepen-dence" and "doing things for themselves" as a sign of distrust and disrespect. Why would you insist on doing it yourself unless you felt the local people couldn't be relied on to do it properly?

Insist on going it alone, and they will conclude you think them untrustworthy or incompetent, or that you are too snobbish or antisocial to associate with them. If things then go wrong, you can count on the minimum of sympathy and assistance, at the maximum price.

From the start you have to make choices; no one else can tell you where you should go. This chapter is about how to figure out where you want to go, and—together with the Resource Guide—about resources to help you decide.

# DIVISIONS OF THE WORLD

When thinking about where to travel, most people think in terms of a map or globe. So you might expect me to start by surveying the world in conti-nental or other physical regions. In the broadest terms, however, it makes more sense for purposes of overall travel planning to think first in terms of different economic, rather than cartographic, worlds. There is considerable cultural similarity within some continents and physical regions, of course, although far less than is generally assumed by inexperienced travelers. But there are even greater commonalties in the nature of travel, especially when it comes to logistics, within even physically distant parts of the same geopolitical region. Travel in interior Borneo may have more in common with travel on other continents—in the Amazon, say, or in Central Africa—than with travel elsewhere in Southeast Asia, such as in Singapore or even Peninsular Malaysia. There are continental patterns of wealth, but the world's most fundamental divisions are not between continents, per se, but between rich and poor.

The division of the world by political economists into the First, Second, Third, and Fourth Worlds, or the North and South, may require some explanation. This terminology is less familiar in the United States, where there is little discussion using these labels, than to the majority of the world's people, who live in other regions. And many Southerners would say that "North-South dialogue" between the world's peoples has largely been a Southern monologue ignored by the North. But I think that these crude categorizations of world regions are helpful for purposes of travel planning and budgeting. Since these terms may not be familiar to some readers, and are used in different ways by different writers, let me explain what I mean by them.

## First World

The "First World" refers to the "developed" (i.e., wealthy and industrialized) capitalist or market economies (including social democracies and most mixed economies): the United States, Canada, Western Europe, Israel, Japan, Australia, New Zealand. By most standards, the term would also include the less populous and more wealthy oil-exporting countries such as Saudi Arabia and the Gulf states, but few of them encourage or facilitate tourism, so it's not necessary for our purposes to worry about how to classify them. A few countries sometimes described as "middle income" are borderline First World states. For example, Singapore, South Korea, and Taiwan are moving into the category, while Argentina is falling out of it.

## Second World

The term "Second World" originated during the Cold War when the United States divided all the world into our side and their side. The "Second World" now refers to "developed," centrally planned (or formerly so) economies: Russia and the former Soviet Union—now referred to as the Community of Independent States (CIS)—and the rest of Eastern and Central Europe. Despite the changes and the increasing diversity among these countries, they retain a certain commonality in the nature of their tourist and other infrastructures, the appropriate and feasible modes of budget travel and types of budget accommodations, and the costs of travel relative to the other main world regions.

## Third World

The "Third World" was a term originally used to identify those countries neither in the First nor the Second World by virtue of political nonalignment with either the capitalist or communist "blocs." It has since come to mean those that are in neither of the first two worlds by virtue of not being "developed"—the "developing," or poor, countries. The Third World includes countries with capitalist, communist, and mixed economies as well as those trying to pursue independent economic paths.

## Fourth World

The "Fourth World" is the most recently coined and least precisely defined of these terms. As distinct from the "developing" Third World, Fourth World countries are those poor countries that are not "developing" economically. These are marginalized poor countries that have been deemed peripheral to the world's centers of power and trade, and have been written off by those centers of power.

While some Asian countries (Bangladesh, Afghanistan, Myanmar/Burma, Cambodia, and Laos are most often cited) are regarded as Fourth World, most of the Fourth World is in Africa, and almost all of sub-Saharan Africa is in the Fourth World. (Of the 41 countries categorized as least developed by the United Nations, 27 are in Africa). One reason for the dearth of flights to, from, and within Africa (especially other than between African cities and their former colonial capitals in Europe) is that airline routes follow trade routes, and less than one percent of the total value of international trade is to, from, or within Africa.

Prior to the adoption of the term Fourth World, there was much controversy over how to refer to these countries without stigmatizing them. Various euphemisms remain in use but are often disliked; the United Nations calls them "least developed countries" while the World Bank calls them "low-income" countries.

The differences between the Third and Fourth Worlds, and between Third and Fourth World travel, are mainly differences in degree. Fourth World infrastructure is, as a rule, bad to nonexistent. Unlike in the Third World, where almost anything is available for a price, many things we take for granted—from clean water to reliable motorized transport—are not available in much of the Fourth World at *any* price.

To confuse matters further, some people have begun using "Fourth World" to denote indigenous and "traditional" peoples and tribes. Though definitions are essentially arbitrary, and this concept does need a word to identify it, this alternate usage of "Fourth World" muddies the meaning of an already well-defined term, and I have declined to adopt it.

## East and West

During the Cold War, the First World was referred to as "the West," and the Second World was referred to as "the East." Nowadays "the West" is more often used to refer to Europe and the Eurocentric world of white-skinned people (including the United States, Canada, Australia, New Zealand, and Asian Russia), and "the East" is used to refer to those parts of Asia inhabited primarily by nonwhite people (i.e., Asia except Russia). But many people see the former usage as obsolete and the latter as Eurocentric and racist.

In any case, the two very different sets of meanings make any usage of the terms "the East" and "the West" hopelessly ambiguous and subject to misinterpretation. I try to avoid any use of these terms; if you want to be understood around the world, you will too.

Asians do not think of themselves as living in "the East." And, in relation to the Pacific Ocean, I live in the East in San Francisco, while Japan lies in the West. "The Orient," "the East," "the Far East," and "the Middle East" are labels that people in the regions thus referred to often find offensive, except in the Russian Far East, where people insist on using that label to distinguish their region from Siberia, which is farther west.

What Europeans and Eurocentrists call the Far East is a group of quite different, geographically separated regions, variously referred to locally as East or Northeast Asia, Southeast Asia, and South Asia. What Europeans call the Middle East is usually described by others as the Eastern Mediterranean, West Asia, or North Africa depending on their perspective.

## North and South

Use of the terms "North" and "South" has increased as use of the old Cold War labels "East" and "West" has declined. "North" is the term commonly used to describe the wealthy countries that dominate the world economy, most of which are located north of the world's poorer countries, the "South." Most of the people and countries of "the South" are in South America, sub-Saharan Africa, and South and Southeast Asia. Those who are represented on top of most standard maps (with north "up") also tend to be on top of the world's economic and power relationships. But the point of the terms is to describe the strata of economic, political, and military power, not cartography.

There are obvious exceptions to the geographical division between North and South. Australia and New Zealand are unambiguously Northern countries in the Southern Hemisphere. The most populous Southern countries are India and China, both in the Northern Hemisphere and the latter almost entirely north of the northern tropics. Some Northerners argue that the terms North and South are inaccurate or confusing, but some of the same people seem to have no problem using East and West in their traditional, nongeographic yet widely understood senses.

The term "North" has never been as widely used as "South," and both terms are heard much more in the South than the North. For purposes of talking about travel, North is a less useful concept than South, because travel in the First and Second Worlds is less similar than travel in the Third and Fourth Worlds. A distinction is not always made between the Third and Fourth Worlds, and in casual usage "the Third World," "the Third and Fourth Worlds" and "the South" are equivalent terms.

There is no consensus on which usage is best. Kofi Buenor Hadjor, in the essay on the meaning of "Third World" that forms the introduction to his *Dictionary of Third World Terms*, argues that, "To use the terminology of North-South...contains the danger of converting a social, economic, and political division into a geographic one." On the other hand, Paul Harrison said in his introduction to the updated edition of his *Inside the Third World*, that, "If this book were appearing for the first time today, it would be called *Inside the South.*"

Were this a book about politics rather than travel, my strong preference would be to use "South" except where making specific distinctions between the Third and Fourth Worlds. The danger of "South" being misunderstood by non-specialists in a geographic or directional sense has induced me to refer instead, in many cases, to "the Third and Fourth Worlds," and where I'm talking about something that is similar in both I have often, for conciseness, used "Third World" as shorthand for "Third and Fourth Worlds." I beg the indulgence of political scientists, economists, and other academics, offering in my defense that readers will undoubtedly hear all of these terms used somewhat interchangeably, without definition, in books, newspapers, and conversations throughout the regions thus described.

The former Soviet Union is sometimes said to have "become a collection of Third World nations." Little is meant by this, I think, except that Russia has lost most of its empire. Whatever the merits of the academic argument that the former Second World should now be considered Third World or Southern in view of politics or economics, such claims have little basis in travel conditions. In travel, much of the Second World is still its own world, with its own ways. When I say "the North" I mean both the First World and the Second World. Feel free to read this as, "the former Second World," if that makes you happier. There are some similarities to travel anywhere outside the First World; in such cases, I use the ungainly "the Second, Third, and Fourth Worlds" for want of any clear, concise alternative.

Finally, I must stress that these generalizations, while useful, all have their exceptions. In particular, keep in mind that variations within a country or region— between rich and poor, center and periphery, urban and rural, black and white—can be as great as those between regions. Life on Native American reservations in the United States and Canada is often reminiscent of the Third World, while urban elites in many a Third World capital have access to the latest First World consumer goods, health care, amenities, and services.

## Which World's for You?

The preceding categorizations may have struck some readers as irrelevant. Aside from defining terminology, what's the point?

The longer your trip, the more likely you are to be limited by your budget. Most employed middle-class North Americans, if they choose to make it their highest priority and have three weeks vacation once a year, could fly to almost any major city in the world and spend two weeks happily and comfortably there. But even if they had the time, most of the same people wouldn't want to spend what it would cost for two or three comfortable months, much less a year, in Western Europe, Japan, or Saudi Arabia, no matter how carefully they planned.

### Time vs. Money

Per day, as I've already mentioned, long-term travel is cheaper. As you spend more time in a place, you figure out how to do things more cheaply, and you can spread out the cost of getting there over more days. But the total expenses for a months-long trip tend to enforce constraints even on people who wouldn't have to pay much attention to prices in planning a two-week vacation.

So what does how much you spend have to do with which "world" you go to? Not everything, but a lot. Yes, there are lots of ways to save money on travel wherever you go. Staying in hostels or camping, and traveling around by train rather than by plane, can drastically reduce the price of travel in Western Europe, North America, or Japan. But as long as you don't insist on intercontinental standards of luxury and make a minimal effort to travel economically, the differences between travel costs in the different worlds are much greater than the differences between more and less expensive styles of travel in the same world.

So the longer your trip, the larger the proportion of it that you may need to spend in cheaper places if you are going to stay within your budget. Nothing wrong with that. Doesn't everyone like places where everything is cheap?

Occasionally everything is cheap for some artificial reason, such as that the exchange rate doesn't reflect the real buying power of the local currency. More often, travel in a place is cheap for a single, simple reason: the people there are poor. The all-too-often overlooked corollary to affordable, long-term travel is that it means spending the majority of your time in places where most people are poor.

**REAL LIFE**

Russia is currently one of the outstanding travel "best buys." Most Russians aren't poor, in Third World terms, but anyone with a salary in hard currency (e.g., dollars) is rich. Ruble prices of Soviet goods are absurdly low. But prices are increasing, as Russians figure out what they can get for things on the export market, so the way to see Russia on the cheap is to see it now. Prices in Central Europe are likewise rising quickly toward those in Western Europe, but aren't there yet in much of the region.

Nothing wrong with that either; most places are poor. The majority of the world's people make less than US$3 a day, and some of the most interesting, educational, beautiful, and enjoyable places in the world are among the poorest. But you need to be honest with yourself: if you aren't prepared to confront the reality of the world, you aren't prepared to try to travel around the world.

When people come home from a trip around the world, the most enduring memories are usually not of museums, monuments, or famous sights but of encounters with the reality of everyday life for the ordinary people of the Second, Third, and Fourth Worlds. This is the dominant reality of human life, and seeing it face-to-face is the aspect of world travel that most often changes people's lives.

This doesn't mean you need to live, or travel, like the poor to travel cheaply. It's often the reverse: in a rich country on a budget, you have to travel like the poor; in a poor country, you can live like a king (or at least like an upper middle-class local business traveler). Where people are poor, labor is cheap, and you may be able to afford labor-intensive services and ways of doing things that are considered great luxuries, or have disappeared entirely in the First World.

### Typical Itineraries

On the whole, around-the-world and other long-term travelers spend more time in Asia than any other continent, mostly in East and Southeast Asia (though the proportion of travelers' time spent in Latin America is growing rapidly). Those who stay in Africa for anything more than a weeklong safari or Nile cruise usually spend at least a couple of months. An overland trip entirely across Africa in either direction, if you can complete it, takes six months to a year or more. More and more travelers to Europe are going farther and farther East. As for trends within the First World, if you're curious, the biggest ones for independent travelers at the moment are away from Western Europe and toward North America, Australia, and New Zealand, where current prices are significantly lower.

**REAL LIFE**

If you so choose, you can travel around South and Southeast Asia in first-class sleeping cars, occasionally hiring a private guide for a tour of a city or a car and driver for an out-of town excursion, staying in comfortable hotels (not the best, but upper-class), having your laundry professionally cleaned and pressed, and eating catered meals at restaurants and food stands, for less than you'd spend to travel around Western Europe sitting up all night on second-class trains, staying in hostels, washing your clothes in the sink, and subsisting on bread and cheese.

Your fantasy of seeing the world may start out with the classic image of a months-long grand tour of a long list of cities in Western Europe, followed perhaps by a few weeks in Central or Eastern Europe, and ending with a week or less in each of a few more "exotic" places in Africa and "the East" to round out the trip:

perhaps Cairo to see the pyramids, somewhere in East Africa for a wildlife-viewing safari, India for the Taj Mahal, and Japan for some shrines and temples.

I don't mean to denigrate such a trip, if you want it and you can afford it. But trips that begin from this fantasy often end up consisting of a fast few weeks' glimpse of Western Europe, a more leisurely month or two in Central or Eastern Europe, and six months or more in Africa and Asia, ending with a few days in Japan. Or reversing the whole order, with Western Europe last.

### New World Order

Inexperienced travelers often think they aren't "ready" for the South, and defer Third World travel until after they have had a chance to gain experience at overseas travel within the First World, where they figure it will be easier. Depending on your budget, the best strategy may be the other way around.

In the first place, it takes much more skill and experience, if it is possible at all, to travel on the same budget in the First World as in the Third World. Traveling on the same budget, you may actually have to put up with lower standards of comfort and cleanliness of accommodations in a rich country where you have to stay in hovels and dives (or don't yet know how to find the few good, cheap places) than in a poor country where you can easily afford to stay in places catering to the local gentry.

In the second place, budget travelers in the First World have to figure out how to do things for themselves that they could afford to pay local people to do for them in the South. You have to be more self-sufficient in the First World. You can't afford to hire an English-speaking private translator and guide to show you around a city if you can't find your way on your own, or to pay someone else to go down to the train station and buy your tickets for you. Each of these might cost you only a couple of USA dollars, maybe only pennies, in the Third World.

In the third place, mistakes, misunderstandings, and misjudgments in the First World are apt to be expensive. Learning by experience is cheaper in cheaper places. Budget travelers can more easily afford to solve problems and rectify mistakes by throwing money at them in the South, where costs are lower.

All else being equal, I'd definitely put as much as possible of the First World traveling at the end of my first big trip, not at the beginning where it might

# POPULATION CENTERS

The most populous countries of the South, according to estimates as of 2000 from the United Nations, are:

- China (1.3 billion people)
- India (over 1 billion people, and likely to pass China as the world's most populous country sometime around 2020)
- Indonesia (210 million; next most populous country after the United States)
- Brazil (170 million)
- Pakistan (140 million)
- Bangladesh (140 million)
- Nigeria (110 million)
- Mexico (100 million)
- Vietnam (80 million)
- Philippines (75 million)
- Iran (70 million)
- Egypt (70 million)
- Turkey (65 million)
- Ethiopia (60 million)
- Thailand (60 million)
- Congo/Zaire (50 million)
- Myanmar/Burma (50 million)
- South Korea (45 million)

Together these 18 countries—10 percent of the membership of the United Nations—have about two-thirds of the world's population. The most populous six contain more than half the world's people. China (larger in area than the United States, including Alaska), Brazil, India, Congo, Mexico, and Indonesia are also among the world's dozen largest countries by area. Two-thirds of these most populous Southern countries are in Asia.

So there are more than just financial reasons why a journey around the world, is likely to be, more than anything else, a journey through the Third and Fourth Worlds—especially those parts of them in Asia. If you find yourself wondering why so many of the examples in this book are from Asia, and to a lesser extent Africa and Latin America, it's because that's where most of the world's people are and where most long-term independent budget travelers spend the most time.

blow my budget. I'd make Central America or Southeast Asia my shakedown trip to prepare for Western Europe, not the reverse.

### Try Before You Go
If you want to find out what independent travel is like in a place where it will be easier, consider a trip in your home country or region, where presumably you know the language and how things are done. I'm always surprised how few people in the United States have ever spent a few months or more exploring North America, a destination that draws tourists from around the world.

### Fourth World Travel

Fourth World, as opposed to Third World, travel sometimes requires more logistical self-sufficiency and skill. If my first trip abroad was a trip around the world, I wouldn't go first to New Guinea. But I wouldn't be too worried about planning to include it later in a first trip. After a few months in the Third World, you'll be as ready for the Fourth World—if you still want to go there—as you'll ever be. At the same time, don't kid yourself: as First World services follow the tourist money trail, Third World travel is getting easier all the time, but the hassles of truly Fourth World travel are changing much less.

# TRAVEL IN THE PRESENT

An important point to keep in mind, wherever you consider going, is that you will be traveling in the present, not the past. The farther you get from the First World, the smaller your budget, and the more you know about the history, traditions, or past of your destination, the more important this idea becomes.

You may be interested in a destination because of its "classical" history or culture, and the sights you want to see may be primarily ancient monuments or archaeological sites. These are all good and sufficient reasons to travel. But for every spine-tingling moment spent in a place whose history you've read and dreamed about, you'll also spend days or weeks dealing with the present-day reality of the place.

You may have learned a country's language to read its classical literature, but most people who speak that language may be illiterate, the most popular publications in that language may be film-star gossip magazines and soap-opera digests, and the most popular contemporary music in that language may be sung or rapped to a disco beat. You can ask locals if they have read the Ramayana, or where to find a concert of classical music, and they may even humor you. But they may be much more interested in asking you about American rap stars or World Bank structural adjustment programs, or finding out if you have the latest Hollywood movies (bootlegs of which are often available worldwide before they open in theaters, much less are released on video, in the United States).

In my experience, people who are ignorant, but who are aware of their ignorance, open-minded, and genuinely desire to learn, are less likely to suffer from "culture shock" than those who think they know the most about where they are going, but who know only or primarily about its past, and have paid inadequate attention to the present. Some extremely naive people are remarkably successful travelers. Other travelers, extremely knowledgeable about the past, are utterly disoriented by their inability to reconcile the modern reality of their traveling life with the context and setting they had imagined from the literature.

These latter are also some of the people who, because they fail to pay attention to their surroundings, do the most dangerous things, usually without even realizing the risks they are taking. The best insurance against getting into trouble is to keep your eyes open, keep thinking about what you see and what it means, read the newspapers, and talk to local people about what is going on.

## Sourcing Real-Life Information

For a variety of reasons (see the references on the world information order in the "Background Reading" section of the Resource Guide) we in the First World get very little information about contemporary Second, Third, and Fourth World life. English-language newspapers, magazines, and novels from these countries are published throughout the world, and many of them are available on the Internet. But few First Worlders are aware of them. Our impressions of the other worlds are shaped by the more accessible literature about them: classics, histories, travelogues (by foreigners), and tourist brochures. None of these focuses on, or gives much indication of, contemporary real life. It's well worth making an extra effort to seek out a reality check in Web sites and recent literature, fiction and nonfiction, *by*, not just about, people in the places you plan to visit.

### *Pitfalls of Tourism Propaganda*

Tourist literature, whether from tour operators or government tourist boards, often glosses over the less attractive aspects of contemporary reality, or avoids them entirely, for fear of scaring away potential tourists.

Even the attractive features of contemporary local culture and life—things that will be immediately apparent to any visitor—may not be mentioned in tourist propaganda if the people writing the brochures think this would conflict with the *image* of the country that attracts foreign visitors, no matter how distorted or out-of-date that image may be. The flip side of this is that you can always find what you expect, if you're willing to pay for it. The customer is always right: if people go somewhere in search of something, locals will (for a price) attempt to fulfill the tourists' fantasies, even if that means dressing in costumes and performing "rituals" or "traditional" music, arts, or other activities that have been created solely to satisfy the tourist market (perhaps even by copying pictures in tour brochures).

**REAL LIFE**

One extreme example of tourism propaganda is East Africa: it's difficult to find *any* pictures or even mention of Black African urban life. Presumably the tour operators think that tourists want to come to Africa to see animals, not Africans, and that enough of the potential tourists are racists, or scared of Southern cities, that it would be bad for business to remind people that the "big game" animals co-inhabit Africa with a billion (mostly nonwhite) humans. Sad to say, the brochure writers are probably all too correct in their assessment of the attitudes of too many tourists.

### The Trouble with Travelogues

Reading lists in guidebooks, even in otherwise-sensitive guidebooks for independent travelers, tend to be heavy on narratives by First World travelers about their visits to the destination. These are often entertaining reading, but don't take them too seriously as a guide to what your trip will be like. Travelogues are written to entertain, and a good deal of artistic license is permitted to spice up a narrative. You also need to pay attention to the authors' attitudes: did they dislike a place because of their racism or because the "natives" were insufficiently servile, for example.

One notable exception to all this is the excellent series of anthologies for travelers published by Whereabouts Press, which feature writing by people from different countries, selected in most cases by editors from those places. (See the Resource Guide for details.)

### The Pace of Change

It's obvious that things may have changed greatly since a Victorian travelogue was written. It may be less obvious, and must be stressed, that things may have changed completely since something was written 20, 10, or two years ago. In making allowances for dated information about other "worlds," it would be a mistake to apply the same standard that you would to information about the First World.

Northerners are taught to think of the South as "backward" (i.e., living in the past), "underdeveloped," or "developing" (as though they were somewhere "behind" us on a timeline of development). We compare aspects of Southern ways of life (such as subsistence agriculture) with those the North has "left behind" in our past, and we compare Southern averages of wealth and health with those of Northerners a century or more ago.

It's entirely natural, but entirely wrong, to infer from this (not all of which is true in the first place) that poor countries are traditional and "living in the past," and from there to jump to the conclusion they are "timeless" and unchanging, or that what was written about them in the past will still be true to a greater extent than would dated information about Northern places that are "making progress," "moving forward," "going places."

Nothing could be further from the truth. The world, and *especially* the Third World, is changing fast. Life is changing much

**REAL LIFE**

A dozen years ago, one could get a visa or a flight to Vietnam only in Bangkok or Moscow, and only by joining a tour or hiring a guide. Now you can get a visa to Vietnam without paying for a tour or guide and without leaving the United States, and you can fly to Vietnam by way of at least a dozen cities on as many airlines. Conversely, a dozen years ago an invitation from anywhere in the former USSR was sufficient to get a single visa valid throughout all the ex-Soviet republics. Today you would need separate invitations for each republic, each of which would have to be submitted to a separate embassy for a separate visa.

more rapidly in "developing" countries than it is in those that have already been highly "developed" for some time. The pace of change may be greater today in parts of the Third World than it has ever been in what is now the First World.

Travel-specific matters are not exempt from the winds of Second, Third, and Fourth World change. It would be easier to get to, or get around, New York or San Francisco with a guidebook 20 years old than to get around Vietnam or Russia with a guidebook five years old.

### Contemporary Local Life

The reality of contemporary local life matters much more to long-term, independent, and budget travelers than to escorted or group tourists, or to people with larger budgets. Travelers in groups interact mainly with each other and may scarcely speak with any local people. This holds true even for budget groups, such as overland group camping "expeditions." Escorted travelers, even "independent" ones (i.e., on personalized private tours) interact mainly with their guides and translators, who as speakers of English or another foreign language and in regular contact with foreigners (and their money) are almost by definition part of the local upper-middle class or elite. With enough money, you can insulate yourself from Third World reality in an Intercontinental Hotel or hire enough servants to travel in the same way as the gentlemen and ladies who wrote Victorian travelogues.

On your own, on a budget (long-term travel puts almost everyone on a budget, as I've mentioned already), you have to deal with local people, here and now, many times every day. Your life on the road will resemble the lives of local people, at least local travelers of similar means, except to the extent that you pay extra to have things done differently for you than they are for locals.

You won't have to live like the local poor. Southerners migrate North in the belief, confirmed by the judgments of their acquaintances who have gone before them, that they will be materially better off as poor people in the North than as middle class (those who have passports and can afford passage North are usually at least middle class) people in the South. Even as a "budget" First World traveler you can afford to travel more comfortably in any other world than you could for the same money in the First World. But neither can you entirely avoid experiencing the reality of the places you go. After all, that's the point of travel. I just recommend that you "Be prepared."

# EVALUATING TRAVEL ADVICE

A common problem with any set of sources is conflicting advice or information of uncertain reliability. Here are some general principles you can use to assess destination information and other travel advice. This advice is applicable to information in all media and from all sources, including books and word-of-mouth. But it's especially important on the Internet, where one often knows little or nothing about who has provided a particular piece of information.

## How Recently Did They Visit?

As I've already pointed out, things can change overnight. People often give undue weight to the experience of a friend, or someone from a place, even if they visited or emigrated some time ago. Ask someone what year they were there. Ask an immigrant when they emigrated, and when they last went "home" to visit. A further useful question in evaluating what an immigrant says about their "mother country" is, "Where is home now? Here or there?"

Disregard excessively vague answers. Obsolete advice, delivered in an authoritative tone and relied on, can lead to worse surprises than total ignorance. If the information is second (or third) hand, discount it heavily and don't assume it is current. "My friend was just there," may mean that they were there last week or five years ago; you won't find out which, or if the intermediary knows, unless you probe carefully.

## How Long Did They Stay?

This is kind of a trick question. You'd think that people who had been in a place longer would know more about it, and they generally do. On the other hand, people who spent a long time in a place—especially if they lived there, rather than just traveling through—may have lived very differently than you will as a transient. Things that were "no problem" for someone who knew at least some of a local language, had local connections, perhaps had their own car (and driver) and friends to stay with along the way might be very much harder for a new arrival to arrange. If they were there a long time, ask them how easy or difficult things were when they first arrived, and how long it took them to figure out how to get things done and get around.

Don't assume that travel writers (including guidebook writers) spend a lot of time getting to know each place they write about. Professional travel writers are experts at collecting the essential information about a place quickly, so that they can move on to the next. Someone who writes a book about a country or region probably spent at least several months there doing research. But they may only have spent a day in a provincial town, even a large provincial city if it's not especially popular with tourists. Some guidebook publishers seek to hire authors with destination expertise. But others (notably including Lonely Planet) prefer writers with little or no prior experience in the destinations they are writing about, so that they will describe them from the perspective of the first-time visitor who's the likely reader of the guidebook.

People who seem to have been everywhere probably weren't anywhere for very long. If their purpose in travel is to collect countries or sights, so as to be able to say, "Been there, done that," they probably don't make it a priority to hang around. Ask them specifically how long they spent in the particular place or country you are interested in. They may have very useful nuggets of practical information, but don't count on subtlety or depth of understanding.

## How Does Their Style of Travel Compare to Yours?

This is probably the most important question to ask in evaluating why someone else did or didn't like a place.

The experience of travel for someone in a group, or on a tour, has little in common with that of an independent traveler. How did they travel? If they liked or didn't like the hotels, are they talking about the US$200 a night hotels? The US$20 a night hotels? The US$2 a night hotels? The US$20 hotels are great value in some places where the US$2 and US$200 hotels are a terrible value. Did they stay in places you'd want to stay? Did they do things you'd want to do? What was the purpose of their trip?

If they thought there was nothing to do, was that because there were no beaches? No museums? No discotheques? No street markets and bazaars? No air conditioning? What is their picture of an ideal day of traveling? (If they take photographs while traveling, they can probably show you.) If they loved the place, was it because of the food? The conversations? The music? The scenery? The social structure? The

Every guidebook I've read describes Tashkent, Uzbekistan, as completely without touristic interest—a big, industrialized city. Too civilized. Too modern. Not quaint. Too fast-moving. Too aware of the rest of the world. Too much of an ethnic mix to give one a proper sense of "pure" Uzbek culture. All accurate descriptions. Most tourists don't like Tashkent, for just these reasons.

Reading the guidebooks' denunciations, I knew immediately that Tashkent was the place for me. I found it was everything I had hoped for. I didn't find a mythic past in Tashkent, but I wasn't looking for the past. Tashkent is the future of Central Asia, all brought together in one bustling, cosmopolitan, accessible mélange: an intellectual and ideological center; the largest and richest city north of the Himalayas between Beijing and Moscow; a magnet for the best, brightest, and most ambitious people of a dozen nationalities from a thousand miles around. And, as of this writing, USA citizens no longer need a sponsor (as they still do for Russia, Ukraine, or Kazakhstan) in order to obtain a visa for Uzbekistan.

pattern of daily life? Even independent budget travelers with similar travel styles may be interested in very different aspects of places, and find the same place exciting or boring, wonderful or awful.

The reasons some people would choose a destination are reasons other people would shun it, and vice versa. This is one of the strongest reasons not to rely on experts, no matter how well traveled and knowledgeable, in deciding where *you* should go. Travel writers often adopt a pseudo-objective voice that gives too little information about themselves for readers to judge whether they would prefer the places writers love or the ones they pan. The perfect trip is different for everyone, and there's nothing like travel itself for making one aware of the diversity of humanity, and our multiplicity of tastes and styles. It's your trip. Make your own choices.

# EDUCATING YOURSELF ABOUT DESTINATIONS

A wide variety of resources can help you decide where you want to go, and when: the Internet, libraries, bookstores, guidebooks, tourist boards, embassies and consulates, governments, immigrants, friends, other travelers, tour operators, and travel agents. Specific references and contact details are given in the Resource Guide at the back of this book, and on the *Practical Nomad* Web site. What follows is only a general introduction to some of the major types and sources of destination information.

## Tour Operators and Travel Agents

Tour brochures and travel agents are usually the first places people turn when figuring out where to go. In my opinion as a travel agent, they should be the last.

### Travel Agents

Every day travelers ask me, "I want to go around the world. Where should I go?" I refuse to give that sort of advice, not only because I don't want to be held responsible if people end up not liking a place I suggest but also, perhaps more importantly, because most people don't—and can't—preface the question with enough information about themselves, their goals, and their desired style of travel to provide a meaningful basis for a recommendation.

A good travel agent can be a great help in facilitating and organizing your trip and helping you to get places, once you have decided where you want to go. Trying to do it all yourself, particularly dealing with airlines directly, is likely to lead you to spend much more on transportation than you would have with the assistance of an agent. And a specialist agent, or one who happens to have a lot of knowledge or experience about a particular small country or region, may be able to refine your choices of precise places: "In which of these three cities am I likely to find fewer tourists?" "In which of these two neighboring countries will

**REAL LIFE**

"Where should I go for a month in Southeast Asia?" is not a question anyone can answer for you without a great deal more information about what you want. If you want a lazy, romantic beach holiday, maybe you should go to Ko Samui. If you want scenic landscapes and romantic cities, maybe you should go to Vietnam. If you want to sit around talking politics with the local intelligentsia, maybe you should go to Bandung. If you want a diversity of cultures, ethnicities, and cuisines in one country, or want to speak English with middle or lower-class people, maybe you should go to Malaysia. If you want sex with prostitutes, maybe you should go to Bangkok or Manila (but don't ask me for help if that's your goal). And if you are scared of Asia and are willing to prop up the local fascists to get a sanitized glimpse of Europeanized Asia with all the comforts of home (at the same prices), maybe you should go to Singapore.

it be easier to get out of the cities into the countryside, and talk to villagers?" Do see a travel agent, but do so *after* you decide, at least preliminarily, where you want to go.

Travel agents spend less time traveling than many of our clients. You can't expect any travel agent to have been to every country, much less city, that you are going to. But good travel agents solicit, and pass on, recommendations from their clients. It's worth at least asking whether they happen to know a place to recommend, of a particular type, in a particular price range.

The better agencies that specialize in around-the-world travel maintain libraries of visa applications and instructions, guidebooks, maps, tourist board literature, country and regional reference materials, background reading, and hotel directories. Travel agents get paid to sell tickets, not to do research, but you should be suspicious of the qualifications of an agent who can't or won't provide references for these sorts of basic tools.

### Tour Operators

Brochures from tour operators can sometimes be useful even if you plan to travel independently: they'll give you a quick idea of which are the most popular times to visit and the "must-see" attractions, so that you can either avoid them entirely or approach them with an awareness that they are certain to be more crowded, more expensive, and more dominated by foreign tourists than other places that aren't featured in tours, and times when the groups are gone.

The alternative to a tour is another tour. But the alternative to *all* tours is independent travel. For tour operators, the very possibility of do-it-yourself travel is the ultimate competition. All tour operators share a collective interest in persuading tourists that it is too difficult or dangerous to go it alone. They showcase in their brochures things you genuinely can't do by yourself, because they require special permits granted only to tour groups, admission is rationed with the quotas held by tour operators, or individual transportation is prohibitively expensive.

Don't look to brochure itineraries to give you *any* picture of what travel is like for independent travelers. "After breakfast, you will be transferred to the train station . . ." in a tour brochure might instead be summarized as follows for the independent traveler: "On the morning of day one, you start looking for the railway ticket office. It's moved, and by the time you get to the new location (after various interesting and educational sights and encounters along the way) it is closed. Eventually, you find someone who tells you that it is only open in the mornings. So you come back on the morning of day two, have a long conversation over several cups of tea with the stationmaster, and buy a ticket. After breakfast on day three, you board the train . . . ."

One of the worst mistakes you can make is to try to replicate an itinerary from a brochure or guidebook, day by day, on your own. If you actually want to follow that itinerary, take the tour. If you can follow a brochure itinerary on your own, you can expect it to take at least twice as much time, anywhere in the world, as it would on a tour. In the Third World, it will probably take longer. In the Fourth World, it may not affordably be possible at all. Budget your time accordingly. If you *must* see or do certain things in a certain time, either give yourself a generous additional allowance for delay (the more so the less experienced you are in that part of the world or type of country) or take a tour. Outside the First World, trying to travel independently on a fixed schedule that allows only a few days in each place is a recipe for frustration and disappointment.

On the whole, tour operators avoid giving out (much less including in their brochures) the sort of information that would enable you to replicate their tours on your own. Don't be discouraged if tour brochures imply that independent travel is impossible or prohibitively expensive, as that is rarely the case.

A more common situation is that there is no middle ground between an expensive and efficient tour and a challenging independent trip. In a fair number of countries (Russia is at present the outstanding example, and has changed surprisingly little in this regard since the early 1990s) there is very little infrastructure for independent travel. You can either travel more or less smoothly, quickly, comfortably, and expensively on an escorted tour—or you can find your own way, very cheaply but not without difficulty.

I've been in big cities where all the hotel rooms cost over US$100 or under US$10 a night, nothing in between. It's particularly common to find that only (relatively) expensive, "international" hotels can be reserved in advance from overseas, even in places where comfortable, midrange local hotels exist.

## Offices of Foreign Governments

### Tourist Boards
Most countries (except the USA, which considers the idea socialistic) have some sort of national tourist board or government ministry for the promotion of tourism, and many of these have offices in the USA and/or a presence on the Internet. Some are larger and better funded than others, but all of them exist precisely to serve potential visitors like you: to inform you about why you might want to visit their country and to give you information that will help you have an enjoyable trip.

Some of the less helpful tourist board offices do no more than refer you to operators of package tours, but the services of the tourist boards themselves are free. The best of them will send you, or provide online, mountains of useful free maps; weather tables; train, bus, and ferry schedules; hotel, restaurant, sightseeing and shopping guides; schedules of holidays, festivals, and special events; peculiarities of local modes of travel, accommodations, customs, religious practices, and taboos; cultural and historical background information; suggested itineraries; and practical tips for independent travelers.

It can be surprisingly hard to track down some tourist board offices, especially those that aren't on the Internet. In the United States, few tourist boards have toll-free numbers. The only quasi-comprehensive listings of them are in expensive specialized references for travel agents. A travel agent should be able to give you the telephone number and address or URL of a country's tourist board office, if there is one in your country.

Tourist boards that are represented in the United States (many African tourist boards aren't) almost always have an office in New York or Los Angeles, in addition to any offices in other cities. So you can try calling directory assistance ("enquiries," in British usage) in the nearest international gateway city or, failing that, in New York (+1-212-555-1212 or +1-718-555-1212), Los Angeles (start with +1-213-555-1212, but unfortunately the tourist offices might be in any of the many Southern California area codes: 323, 310, 714, or 818, with more to come soon), Miami (+1-305-555-1212), San Francisco (+1-415-555-1212), or Chicago (+1-312-555-1212). In other countries, check directories for listings in the capital or principal city. Or look for their Web sites on the Internet.

If you can't find a travel agent who knows, and you can't locate the tourist board office, try asking the national airline of the country (many airlines have offices even in countries to which they don't fly, and in the USA even these "offline" offices almost all have toll-free telephone numbers). If they don't know, or there's no such airline or office, ask any embassy or consulate of the country. Virtually every country in the world has either or both an embassy to the USA in Washington, DC (directory assistance +1-202-555-1212, or the list of accredited foreign embassies in the USA on the US State Department Web site) and/or a mission to the United Nations in New York. If there is a tourist board office, they will be able to refer you to it.

### National Airlines

Whether or not it's the airline on which you will fly, the national airline of the country you wish to visit can often provide literature promoting that country as a destination.

Airline literature tends to be more marketing and package-tour oriented and less objective and informational than that of tourist boards, but for some small countries the national airline is the only source (and may even share an office with, or be officially designated to represent, the national tourist board).

### Consulates and Embassies

Consulates and embassies of larger countries generally serve a purely diplomatic role, but ambassadors of smaller countries often interpret their role more broadly. If there isn't a separate tourist board office, try the embassy or a consulate.

Don't be too surprised if they aren't too helpful. Maintaining offices in the USA is expensive for poor countries, and consulates are often understaffed and overworked. Some countries have had particularly bad experiences with culturally insensitive foreign tourists, and many have official policies against "hippies."

Remember also that some countries get few visitors from the United States at all, and that independent travel in some places is genuinely difficult, or possible but quite unheard of by the embassy. Some countries try hard—sometimes with good reason—to steer would-be visitors toward organized, escorted, group tours.

But consular staff can be astonishingly helpful and supportive to independent travelers who are polite—not demanding—and who evince genuine interest and respect for their country. Ask for a visa, and you might get pages of handwritten notes from the ambassador on his favorite nooks and crannies of his country, as I once did (even without identifying myself as a travel agent)!

## U.S. Department of State Publications

Don't count on too much from the United States government. On the whole, State Department publications (and the government of the United States as a whole) are less helpful to travelers than most USA citizens expect. I list various State Department publications in some detail here, not because they are especially useful but because many travelers from the United States ask about some of them (not necessarily the most useful ones) and give them undue weight in deciding where to go. Except as noted below, all of these are available on the State Department's travel or general Web sites at either http://travel.state.gov or http://www.state.gov in addition to in print.

### Background Notes

A series of short but relatively up-to-date pamphlets of *Background Notes* on many countries of the world is produced for the use of soldiers, diplomats, and other USA government personnel or contractors who may be sent to a country on short notice, or as a starting point for Americans considering doing business in or with the country. While somewhat sketchy, they do focus on the most basic questions: "What is it most essential for an American to know before getting off a plane in Country X?" If you have to hurry off to some place you've never heard of, they are better than nothing. State Department Background Notes are available online at http://www.state.gov/r/pa/ei/bgn.

### Tips for Travelers

The most useful State Department publications are a series of pamphlets of *Tips for Travelers* to various regions of the world. These brochures include practical advice on visas, health, crime, safety, political instability, communications, banking, internal transportation, etc. While they are, perhaps, overly cautious, they do contain many useful "dos" and "don'ts." This series has been considerably expanded and improved in recent years, and while they still have their biases, I recommend consulting them for any region you're planning to visit. They're available at USA passport offices or at http://travel.state.gov/travel_pubs.html.

### Travel Advisories

The most commonly requested USA government publications for travelers are what used to be known as *Travel Advisories*. There are now two categories of State Department information: *Consular Information Sheets* and *Travel Warnings*.

Travelers from countries other than the United States often find themselves consulting USA travel advisories, even while they complain about their biases. (A favorite sport of foreigners, on the Internet and elsewhere, is writing parodies of what the travel advisory for travel to the United States would look like if there were one.) The United States is the world's superpower, with the world's largest diplomatic service and embassies in more countries than any other. Some other First World countries publish advisories or warnings for their citizens about selected countries where there are special hazards, but no other country publishes a complete set of advisories about travel to every world country.

Whether or not you're a USA citizen, USA travel advisories can be useful as long as you read them with an awareness of the perspective from which they are written. They have long been notorious for their ideological bias. They can be counted on to stress the hazards of countries whose governments are in disfavor with the USA government, and to minimize problems that would embarrass governments friendly or subservient to the USA government.

There has, however, been noticeable improvement in the overall accuracy of USA travel advisories in recent years. These days overseas consular and ambassadorial staff appear to have been given much more say in what goes into the travel advisories. If USA citizens routinely get into some particular kind of trouble in a country or seek help from the embassy or consulate about a particular sort of problem, the field staff who help them will eventually add a warning about the problem to the travel advisory for that country.

**Consular Information Sheets:** Available for every country of the world, *Consular Information Sheets* include the location of the USA embassy or consulate(s), unusual immigration practices, health conditions, political dangers, unusual currency and entry regulations, crime and security information, and drug penalties. They "generally do not include advice, but present information in a factual manner so the traveler can make his or her own decisions concerning travel to a particular country," says the State Department. All *Consular Information Sheets* and *Travel Warnings* are available at http://travel.state.gov/travel_warnings.html.

**Travel Warnings:** The State Department issues *Travel Warnings* when it recommends that USA citizens avoid travel to a certain country. Countries where avoidance of travel is recommended have a *Consular Information Sheet* as well as a *Travel Warning*. All USA passport offices, consulates, and embassies maintain copies of current *Travel Warnings*. The list of countries for which there are currently *Travel Warnings* is at http://travel.state.gov/warnings_list.html.

Many people decide where it is safe enough to go solely on the basis of *Travel Warnings* (or the absence thereof). You shouldn't ignore them: they provide much useful information on which countries, and which areas within them, may be less safe, and why. But most people traveling around the world travel quite happily through at least one country for which a *Travel Warning* is in effect. And the desire to protect itself against liability, as a rule, makes the State Department err on the side of caution.

For example, until 1995 the USA government forbade any USA travel agent to sell tickets to Lebanon, even to Lebanese citizens wishing to go home. This is not because Lebanon was the most dangerous country in the world—it wasn't—but because the USA government feared being held responsible should an American citizen be kidnapped or killed in Lebanon.

On the other hand, it's worth checking for warnings of hazards you may not have heard about. For example, many people who go to India plan to spend time in the Indian-occupied portion of the state of Kashmir, not realizing that 70,000 people have been killed in Kashmir since 1989 and most of the hotels have been converted into barracks and bunkers for the Indian army and paramilitary police.

## Books, Periodicals, Web Sites, and Videos

If it's worth spending US$1,000 on transportation and a month of your time on a trip somewhere, it's certainly worth spending a day before you leave home in a library or visiting bookstores and periodical dealers to learn about where you are going. You don't have to become an expert, and you shouldn't be intimidated into not traveling because you haven't prepared enough. But if you can, take the time to do some reading. These small investments in extra effort will be repaid with generous interest: request a few books on interlibrary loan or special-order them from the publisher, take out a subscription to a regional magazine from or about the place(s) you plan to go next year, visit a research library with a regional studies collection you can browse through, or take your own little "field trip" to an immigrant neighborhood to track down some immigrant or imported print publications or videos. Many specialized and local publications are available on the Internet, but enough aren't that the Internet is still not a complete substitute for books, periodicals, or libraries. (For more on using the Internet for travel research, including using the Internet to find offline travel resources, see *The Practical Nomad Guide to the Online Travel Marketplace*.)

Unfortunately, most people start their research too late, reading up on places only *after* they decide to go there. A little research earlier on can be crucial in helping you make choices of destinations that you'll be happy with when you get there. Doing your homework can also help you travel in a more culturally and politically responsible manner. It won't eliminate all the surprises: encounters with the unexpected are among the inevitable joys (and annoyances) of travel. If you could know in advance exactly what you'd find, you wouldn't need to travel to find it.

## Information Shelf Life

Feature articles in the travel sections of Sunday newspapers usually have a lead time of a month or two between acceptance of an article and publication. Articles about seasonal destinations and activities, however, are often held for publication in the same season, a full year after the research on which they are based, often without any serious updating. Lead times for glossy magazines are considerably longer, with the same problem of seasonal articles being published a year after they were researched.

## Search for Sources

Some of the publications in the Resource Guide may seem obscure, and you may be tempted to dismiss them out of hand as impossible to find. But the most obvious and accessible publications are sometimes the least useful. With a few exceptions, noted as such in the listings and included nonetheless because of their exceptional usefulness, all of the books in the Resource Guide should be readily available from any USA or other First World library. Your local library will probably have to request a few of them on interlibrary loan from a big-city or university research library, but don't let that hold you back. Interlibrary loan services are available, free, at almost all USA public libraries. Borrowing books this way is a simple process. Ask your local librarian.

I've tried to include information on publishers and distributors wherever possible (particularly for periodicals not stocked by ordinary newsstands and magazine dealers) to facilitate special and direct orders and subscriptions. Regular bookstores are sometimes reluctant to place special orders with obscure or foreign publishers, and may not be familiar with importers of books from

**REAL LIFE**

The Kashmir Valley has been unsuitable for tourism since the current phase of the Kashmiri struggle against Indian occupation began in 1989. But for more than a decade after that, the valley was still described as "idyllic" in some "current" guidebooks—despite martial law enforced by half a million Indian troops; 24-hour curfews; torture, "disappearances," and assassinations of suspected nationalists and sympathizers by Indian death squads; machine-gunning of nationalist street demonstrations; razing of inner-city neighborhoods suspected of harboring anti-Indian militants; attacks on Kashmiri religious shrines; and the murder, rape, and kidnapping of foreign tourists by Indian soldiers and renegade Kashmiris (condemned by mainstream Kashmiri nationalists) alike.

the South. For most of the imported books and most of the periodicals in the Resource Guide, you'll find it easier to order directly from the publishers or the listed specialty distributors.

### Guidebooks

Independent travelers tend to buy guidebooks only after they've chosen their general destination, and to use them primarily as directories of recommended places to stay (and perhaps secondarily for choosing specific places or routes to go within a country or region).

I use guidebooks very little for choosing specific hotels. In my opinion—and, I've discovered, in the opinion of most other guidebook writers—the greatest value of guidebooks intended for independent travel is in the early stages of deciding where to go.

Properly used, good guidebooks for independent travelers can be some of the best tools for getting a feel for what travel in a place will be like. Resist the temptation to skip the front matter. The first things I read in any guidebook are the introductory "how-to" sections. These things change less from edition to edition than hotel ratings, so it's a good idea to buy an inexpensive used or remaindered copy of the previous edition to help you decide if you want to go to a place, then a new copy of the latest edition just before you leave, if you do go. (If it's worth carrying a guidebook with you, it's worth paying for the latest edition, even if you have to order it specially.)

The guidebooks that have the least to say about the sights and attractions of a place—which churches, temples, or mosques to visit, when monuments were built, the literary or historical associations and significance of sites—sometimes have the most to say about what life is like for independent travelers. "Practicalities" aren't a side issue for independent travelers: they are daily life. As you read the descriptions of the things you'll have to deal with while traveling—how you'll get around, how you'll communicate, what you'll eat, where you'll sleep— try to visualize the sort of day that you might spend in such a place. When you get there, it will be real, not a fantasy. The more you can make the day-to-day reality of your destination real in your mind, before you leave, the more prepared you will be.

There's a fine line, of course, between being adequately prepared and being unable to adapt. Temper your expectations with an awareness of the possibility that things will be different. No amount of preparation can substitute for experience. (If it could, why travel?) The less you count on, the less disappointed you'll be, and the better able you'll be to enjoy, rather than be frustrated by, the inevitable surprises.

The better guidebooks are written in the hope that you'll read them well in advance, and they include extended bibliographies of suggested further reading about the countries or regions they cover. These booklists are rarely to my taste, I'm sorry to say. There are exceptions, but guidebook bibliographies tend to overemphasize travelogues by foreigners. It's rare to find listings or ordering information for contemporary publications from the destination, or by emigrants from it, even though these almost always exist and often are available on the Internet. This is a pity as this information can be difficult to track down, and guidebook writers and publishers would be the people best able to provide it.

### Imported and Immigrant Publications

If you can find them in English or a language you know, current publications from the place you are thinking of visiting, or by or for emigrants from there, are the single best window into current events in their home country. Scanning the headlines in a newspaper or reading a contemporary popular novel can give you a better picture of life than anything else. The greatest value of the World Wide Web for would-be world travelers is the access it gives to contemporary news, analysis, and other writing from and by people in even the most obscure parts of the world.

Most people assume that English-language publications don't exist in places where English isn't a major local language, or that they aren't available in First World countries. They are sometimes expensive (though by no means always) or hard to find in print, but they do exist. And even if they aren't on the Internet, they are worth great effort and cost to track down. I've gone on some wild goose chases looking for English-language books, and I've wasted some money on boring tracts, but I've never regretted having sought out local writing in English.

I have yet to visit a country where there was not at least one English-language newspaper or news magazine published at least monthly, where there were not at least some nonfiction books published in English, and where at least some fiction by local writers wasn't either written in English originally or available in English translation. Current English-language versions of local newspapers or newsmagazines from more than 100 countries, including ones from all seven continents (including the only Antarctican newspaper) and from all major world regions are available for free on the Internet.

No language has ever dominated the world the way English does today. Other languages—Spanish, French, Russian, Arabic, Chinese, Portuguese, Hindi/Urdu, Swahili— are widely used in particular regions, or groups of former colonies. You'll find some speakers of most of these languages almost anywhere you go. But no other language reaches the worldwide listenership or readership of English. Like it or not (most of the world doesn't like it, and English is not especially easy to learn as a foreign language), anything intended for a truly global audience perforce must be—and is—published in English. The Internet has greatly accelerated this trend, and some newspapers translate their entire daily content into English solely for posting on the Internet for international consumption.

Native speakers of English, and to a lesser extent anyone who has learned English, are the beneficiaries of this linguistic hegemony. English speakers can get away with speaking only English in most of the world. But if we don't learn the local languages—which isn't really possible for all but the most adept of short-term visitors—the least we can do to make up for making others speak to us in our language is to make some effort to read what they have to say to us in our language. In today's world, literacy in English is a privilege that opens windows into every part of the world. Take advantage of it. You'll shortchange yourself if you waste the opportunities a knowledge of English gives you.

Most long-term travelers spend most of their travel time outside the wealthy "developed" North, in part because poorer countries are usually cheaper to travel in for long periods of time. Regardless of your own perspective on North-South relations, it's important to understand the perspectives of those with whom you'll be dealing. Gandhian, Maoist, and Nehruvian analyses of imperialism and the history of the Non-Aligned Movement and the North-South conflict have been as central to political discourse in most of the world as anti-Communism, the history of the Cold War, and the East-West conflict have been in the United States. Editorials in Southern newspapers, for example, take for granted familiarity with Southern terminology, ideologies, and world views to which First World travelers may not have been exposed in mainstream schooling.

Fortunately, the kinds of materials of most relevance to travelers are among those most likely to be published in English. English speakers, much less readers, are the educated and internationalist elite. Southern publications in English are consciously directed to an international and educated audience, often going out of their way to clarify local terminology and ideas that might be unfamiliar to foreign readers; if they were intended for the local masses, they'd be published in the vernacular. In a country such as India, for example, of which it is often falsely said that "everyone speaks English," only a few percent of the population is literate in English, with publishing in Hindi, Urdu, and the so-called "regional" languages larger and faster growing than English-language publishing.

English is particularly used for academic materials and as a link language between native speakers of different languages from different world regions. Three of the most common kinds of nonfiction books to find in English in any country are all excellent starting points for a traveler wanting to learn about the country: histories of the country by local scholars, texts on the national culture and arts, and contributions by local thinkers to debates on global issues. Especially interesting are those publications directed to readers in other regions of the South, rather than to Northerners.

English fiction is less reliably useful. The most common fiction to find in English includes translations of national classics (sometimes ones that few locals actually read in any language, and not necessarily of much use in understanding current events) and short stories and novels by the foreign-educated elite. On the other hand, the standard of living of First World budget travelers, on the road in the South, may be most similar to that of the local upper-middle class; i.e., the sort of locals who are educated in English-medium schools and write in English. And foreign-educated local writers may be able to serve as cultural interpreters, in both directions, between local and First World points of view.

All this is interesting, you may say, but of little use in planning if you can't find these publications at home before you leave. True enough. But with some effort you can find English publications from all over the world. Places to look for them included ethnic and immigrant cultural, religious, and community centers and neighborhoods; academic departments of ethnic and regional studies and languages; and region-specific Internet sites.

Included in the "Background Reading" section of the Resource Guide, under the heading of "Southern Perspectives on the World," is a selection of pan-Southern publications and examples of some leading strains of Southern thought, all of which are available in First World libraries. Also included in this book's resource guide are some general world references from the South (*The World Guide* is the most outstanding), a few of the leading First World distributors of English-language books imported from the South, and regional English-language magazines, distributed in the First World, from and about each of the Southern continents (South America, Africa, and Asia).

Those newspapers printed in English from the South, and that aren't available on the Internet, are hard but not impossible to come by in the North. You'll find them in major academic libraries, especially those with regional studies centers or departments; in consulates and embassies (whenever I visit a consulate, I pause to browse the home-country papers in the waiting room or library); and sometimes in immigrant community centers.

An increasing number of foreign newspapers—to which print subscriptions by airmail would be prohibitively expensive—now publish online international editions in English translation. On the Internet, in English, you can read what was considered the top of the news in Tokyo, Rio de Janeiro, Taipei, Chennai (Madras), or Melbourne. You don't need the World Wide Web to read a newspaper that you could have delivered to your door for 50 cents. But it's a great way to browse through a sample copy of a paper from the other side of the globe.

Where you can't get an imported newspaper, you may be able to find a local periodical for emigrants from the place you are going. The smallest ethnic and immigrant communities have some sort of journal for networking and news from home. These are distributed anywhere immigrants congregate: ethnic and immigrant neighborhoods, restaurants, cafes and bars, sports clubs, places of worship, community centers, foreign-language video-rental shops, imported-food shops, businesses run by members of the immigrant group. Ask anyone you know who is from the place you are going where they get news from home, or ask around in appropriate ethnic neighborhoods or businesses, if you can find them.

Movies and videos don't even have to be in English to be useful. Consider renting or borrowing a few DVD's or videotapes of recent TV or movie hits from your destination. They are likely to include contemporary street scenes, interiors of homes and workplaces, and images of clothing, body language, and social interactions. The picture they give of ordinary life will probably be as distorted as the picture of ordinary American life that the world gets from Hollywood movies and TV shows. Still, movies and soap operas are in some respects more realistic in depicting ordinary life than CNN, which only shows pictures of the most extreme and unusual ("newsworthy") events.

Finding English books while you are traveling in a non-English-speaking country, is a hit or miss affair. Resign yourself to spending a lot of time searching through English textbooks (English as a foreign language, business and management, science and engineering) to find the locally written social science, humanities, and fiction books. Don't despair, and don't be put off by locals and expatriates alike who say they don't exist. But buy local books that interest you when you find them; you aren't likely to see the same book twice.

English-language newspapers are easy to find while traveling. In some cases they have a substantial local audience and are sold all over. There are more English-language daily newspapers in New Delhi, for example, than in any city in the USA. In other places English-language newspapers are read almost exclusively by expatriate foreigners and/or local people who are studying English. Look for them where such people might congregate: in the arrival area of the international airport (many publications give away free copies to arriving international airline passengers), in expensive hotels catering to foreign business travelers (where it's common to see backpackers reading either the local English-language paper or the foreign sports scores in the *International Herald Tribune* or *USA Today*), and/or local English language schools. Or ask any English-speaking expatriate or English language teacher.

## Word of Mouth

It scarcely needs mentioning that you can learn from any friends or acquaintances who hail from your expected destination. They'll probably be happy to give you advice. But be aware that things may have changed greatly in their home country since they emigrated. And remember that accepting invitations to visit their friends or relatives incurs an expectation of reciprocal hospitality should your hosts later come to your country.

Once you start talking about going around the world, or mention specific destinations, you'll probably get lots of suggestions from friends. You'll hear even more tales from fellow travelers along the way. Some will be firsthand, some fourthhand, some entirely unfounded rumor. Use common sense, a modicum of skepticism, and the guidelines for evaluating advice in the previous section.

## Travel Events

If you get a chance, go to events where you can meet other travelers, and people from the place(s) you are thinking of going, in person. Most travel trade shows are marketing events dominated by sales pitches for tours. But others, such as the annual Independent Traveller's World in London (http://www.itwshow.com), offer resources for do-it-yourself travelers. Nonprofit membership organizations such as Hostelling International affiliates worldwide and the REI cooperative in the United States are more likely to emphasize education and empowerment at their events. HI-USA sponsors a variety of "World Travel 101" workshops at hostels, as well as highly recommended "International Travel Day" events at which you can meet people who are from, or who have lived in, dozens of countries (a mix of tourist board representatives, diplomats, foreign students, returned Peace Corps volunteers and other former expatriates, etc.). See the Resource Guide for contact details.

## The Internet and Other Online Information Sources

Online information sources—especially Usenet newsgroups, Internet editions of local newspapers and magazines, and local portal sites for people from the places you are going—can be a great source of information on current conditions in other parts of the world, and a good way to make some advance contact with people in or from countries you are going to. If you don't have a computer or access to the Internet, you can skip this section and the references elsewhere in this book to online information. Or, if it sounds interesting, you could ask a friend to look some things up or post an Internet query for you, or show you how. Or you could let this be your cue to go to your local library or a cybercafé and learn how to get on the Internet yourself.

This section and those in other chapters of this book on the Internet are only an introduction to the uses of the Internet for travelers. For more detailed information and consumer advice on all aspects of how you can best use the Internet for travel planning, reservations, and purchasing, see my companion book in this same series, *The Practical Nomad Guide to the Online Travel Marketplace*. Links to all the Internet resources mentioned in the *Practical Nomad* series, as well as updates to the books, are on the *Practical Nomad* Web site at http://www.practicalnomad.com.

### Newsgroups

A posting to the appropriate "rec.travel.*" newsgroup (rec.travel.asia, rec.travel.usa-canada, rec.travel.europe, etc.) is a good way to get answers to specific questions about even obscure destinations. Don't waste the Internet's time if you can find the answer elsewhere, and try to find the most narrowly focused single newsgroup in which to ask your question. But if some detail is crucial to your trip, there is probably someone sitting at a computer somewhere who was there last month and who has just the information you need.

There are also a large number of "soc.culture.country name" newsgroups (e.g., "soc.culture.indonesia") which seem to be mainly populated by students from these countries living abroad. They tend to be quite welcoming to would-be travelers to their home countries, and quite generous with their time in corresponding with, and educating, them. Just reading one of these newsgroups can be an informative introduction to the country. These are also a good place to find out about immigrant newspapers or sources of imported books or other printed information about a country.

### Proprietary Online Information Services

Proprietary online information services (AOL,etc.) and bulletin boards have their own internal forums and conferences for discussion of travel topics. Stick with the Usenet newsgroups if you have access to them: they draw on the contributions of the Internet as well as all the major proprietary services, and have a more truly international audience and participation than any online service.

### Regional Web Portals

As in print, the more useful Web sites tend to be those that aren't intended primarily for travelers: English-language Web editions of local newspapers, and "portal" sites that cater to people in and/or from the places you are thinking of going. The latter include portal sites for people in other countries and regions like http://www.rediff.com in India, as well as portals for immigrants and expatriates looking for news from home (which are more likely to be in English than portals for locals).

If you can't find such Web sites or portals directly, look for ads for regional Web portals in print publications from or about the region. Check the list of FAQ's (Frequently Asked Questions) for the relevant newsgroup at http://www.faqs.org, or read the newsgroup for a few weeks and then post a query if you don't see references to such sites. Or look in a Web encyclopedia: in Yahoo, for example, they are listed in the "countries" menu in the directory, under "media by country".

### Browser Beware

Remember, though, to treat advice by newsgroup posting, electronic mail, or from any Web site without an identifiable source (a "*.gov" host is probably a real government agency, for example) as skeptically as any other advice from a stranger. Your respondent may have very different tastes and interests, a budget of a different order of magnitude, and may travel in a very different way from you. Or they may only be relaying a rumor or repeating a myth. The Internet is a powerful medium for the rapid global dissemination of information; it is also the most effective medium in history for the rapid global propagation of rumor, myth, and false information. Internet users are highly unrepresentative of the general population, even in the USA, and even more so in poor countries.

Most "travel" Web sites are basically online brochures: advertising and propaganda, with all the same problems as printed brochures. Many other travel Web sites about destinations are essentially self-published amateur guidebooks. Some are quite good. But many are not, so exercise caution when using these online tools. If a printed guidebook is no good, it likely won't stay in print for long. But on the Web, anyone can say anything and keep saying it, no matter how many other people tell them that it's wrong. There's no way for a browser to tell what's true, and very little way to tell the real source of the information on a Web site, or what hidden agenda it may have. Some Web sites are designed to appear to have been produced by someone other than their real sponsor. Some of the best-looking, best-written travel Web sites are full of false or misleading information: political propaganda, dangerous advice, third-hand rumors. Anyone can post anything to a newsgroup, but at least you'll know if it goes unchallenged or if other posters take issue with it.

Even Web sites from otherwise-reputable guidebook publishers sometimes mix excerpts, updates, and stories from their own writers with unverified information from readers' letters. The "Thorn Tree" section of the Lonely Planet Web site, in particular, is probably the largest single repository of travel rumor, misinformation, and bad advice on the Internet. Some reader contributions are useful news, some of it is misleading rumor or exaggerated boasting, some of it is simply inaccurate or incomplete, and there is little way to tell how knowledgeable any contributor was, or how careful the research and reporting.

## CLIMATE, WEATHER, AND WHEN TO GO

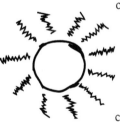

Most of the sources I've already mentioned include information on when to go as well as what to do. The best single reference on world weather is the *World Weather Guide* (see "Logistics" in the resource guide). Many Web sites give current weather, but few give good information on climate patterns and typical weather at different times of the year. See the resource guide for those I've found most useful. Keep in mind that variations in climate within the same country can be extreme, and that many countries are larger and more climatologically diverse than many Americans realize.

National tourist board offices and guidebooks have information on other seasonal factors that affect travel. It's particularly worth checking whether the dates you plan to visit correspond with a local holiday or festival (Diwali, Ramadan, Lunar New Year) that would either enhance or interfere with your other plans. If you're trying to do business on a tight schedule, remember that days as well as hours of business vary: are they closed for the local day of prayer on Friday, Saturday, Sunday, or even some other day? On the Internet, Holidayfestival.com does a superb job of compiling this sort of information.

Resist the temptation to try to arrange to be in each place at the time that the books say is best. Experienced travelers generally prefer to avoid peak season (August in Europe, October in Nepal, etc.) anywhere. Better weather is rarely enjoyable enough to offset the extra crowding and higher prices.

Most of the time, in most places, the weather isn't perfect. Most of the time, if you let your budget determine your schedule, you'll find yourself in places at sometime other than peak season. That's reality. If you want to engage in some specific activity that isn't possible all year-round, it's usually more important to avoid the worst weather than it is necessary to be there in the absolute best weather.

For a long, multistop trip, my advice is first to figure out which (if any) of the things you want to do absolutely must be done, or cannot be done, at certain times of the year. Let those requirements determine the overall direction of your trip, but let the timing and sequence of the rest of your stops be determined by whatever will make the airfare cheapest (or is necessary for visa purposes), with minor adjustments in your schedule to avoid any really intolerable seasons.

On a long-term trip around the world, airfare for the sequence of stops that will put you in each place at the "perfect" time of year is likely to be at least twice the airfare for the cheapest sequence of stops. Even if you like crowds and can afford to pay peak-season prices everywhere, it's rarely worth it. Once you've chosen your set of destinations, and perhaps a general direction, use information about local climates as a guide to what weather to expect at the times that you'll be in places rather than to determine exactly when to get there.

# "Can I Get There
## from Here?"

# SURFACE TRANSPORTATION

Even for those who prefer surface travel, air travel is usually the only realistic and affordable option for long- distance international travel. Even if you set out to travel around the world overland or by sea, you will probably end up covering 90 percent or more of the distance by air, assuming you have the typical budget of time, money, patience, and tolerance for delay, discomfort, danger, and uncertainty.

It remains possible, though, to travel entirely around the world without flying: A handful of people have done it recently, with considerable difficulty and great patience and commitment to their goal. They did it to prove it could be done, and at least one of them wrote a book about it. More people accomplish around-the-world surface travel on luxury cruises, for prices far beyond most of our budgets.

I happen to like airplanes; they are the fastest, safest, and, considering the shorter time one has to spend cooped up in them, most comfortable way to cover long distances. But airplanes have their drawbacks. They are incredibly un-ecological; they isolate you from the places you pass over; if you aren't really in a hurry, speed may be not be a good thing; and a lot of people are, irrationally, afraid of flying.

However, there is often no functional alternative to air travel. To understand why requires a survey of surface transportation options, with particular reference to where they are and aren't likely to be available and when they are likely to be good or bad choices.

That survey of surface transportation makes up the balance of this chapter. We'll return to a much more detailed discussion of air travel in the chapter that follows.

## RAIL TRANSPORTATION

Trains are the safest, most energy-efficient, and often the fastest and most comfortable motorized means of land transportation. Trains are almost always cheaper than planes, but can still constitute a sizable portion of your budget. Planning ahead is helpful, sometimes essential, in making the best use of the railways.

## Railroad History

Unfortunately, building and equipping a railroad on most terrain requires a larger initial investment than building a minimally passable road. Many poor countries—particularly those that don't produce their own locomotives, railroad cars (coaches), and other equipment—have found it hard to come up with enough capital to expand their rail systems or link them to those of neighboring countries.

# KEY ADVICE ABOUT SURFACE TRANSPORTATION

- Don't plan on any means of surface travel—or even assume it's possible—until you've carefully checked out conditions on the route, current services, and the rules for any border crossings or restricted areas. You could draw a lot of lines on maps that don't correspond to feasible surface travel routes.

- Don't try to convert distances into times without knowing something about local conditions and conveyances. Surface transportation in most of the world is slower, more difficult, and above all less reliable than in the First World.

- For safety's sake, travel by train rather than by road when you have a choice. The biggest difference between rail and road travel is the greater safety of rail travel.

- Never drive at night or take a night bus outside the First World if there is any alternative. Night road travel is overwhelmingly the most dangerous thing that ordinary travelers regularly do.

- Treat the journey as part of the experience and the adventure, not as an interruption in your trip. Thinking of a trip by rail, road, or boat as just a way to get from point A point B is an excellent recipe for impatience and frustration.

- Be prepared for surprises. Be prepared for delays. Be prepared to change your plans. Do your homework to get an idea of what to expect, but don't take schedules, prices, or other information in guidebooks or on the Internet as gospel. If you want things to be predictable, take a guided tour.

- Don't punish yourself or take unnecessary risks just to earn a merit badge for hard traveling. Overland travel isn't usually an expedition, but it isn't usually a picnic either. There's no shame in going first class if you can afford it; most local people would think you crazy not to. Bad trips may make for good stories, but that doesn't mean they're fun while they're happening, or worth the discomfort or danger.

For more information on the topics in this chapter, see the Resource Guide in the back of the book, and the links on the Practical Nomad Web site at http://www.practicalnomad.com.

Third World countries have often lacked the resources to extend or connect the railroads left behind by the colonialists. Most railroads in the South were originally intended and designed for military defense or to carry raw materials and other export commodities—minerals, agricultural products, slaves—to ports where they could be shipped to the ruling colonial country.

Local needs, internal commerce, and most of all regional ("South-South") linkages are typically ill-served by these ex-colonial railways, especially where neighboring countries had different colonial masters. Competing colonialists had every interest in not coordinating their railroads, and usually imported their equipment, and differing gauges and technical standards, from their different homelands.

So trains—my favorite way to cover distances too great for a bicycle—are mainly useful for transportation within certain countries, within certain international regions, and on certain particular transcontinental routes. Outside of Europe, relatively few trains cross continents or international borders. Many desirable rail links and routes just don't exist.

For planning purposes, it's important to work out whether a train can take you where you want to go; whether train information will be available locally, or what schedules you should bring with you; and whether you need to make reservations or buy tickets before you leave.

## Transcontinental Train Routes

There are many rail routes across Europe, five east-west routes across North America, one across southern South America, two across Eurasia, one across Australia, and none across Africa. There are no railroads in Antarctica, though there are some other things in Antarctica that you might not expect. (For a while the United States had a nuclear reactor there, for example, despite having signed a treaty making Antarctica a nuclear-free zone.)

### Europe

Railroads go everywhere in Europe. Where trains don't go, ferries and buses are integrated with the rail system, usually on the same tickets.

**Western Europe:** Unless you are touring by bicycle, or have a whole lot of money to rent and operate a car, I can't think of a good reason to travel in Western Europe by any means but train.

Americans are more likely to have heard of Japan's "bullet trains," but the pace-setters in fast rail service are the French Très Grande Vitesse ("Very Great Speed") trains, known by their acronym as the TGV. The name is appropriate. TGVs operate reliable scheduled services at over 300 km/h (185 mph). Minimally modified TGV locomotives and cars have been tested with carloads of dignitaries at sustained speeds exceeding 500 km/h (310 mph).

Two types of passenger trains now operate in the Chunnel under the English Channel. Automobiles are carried on special rail cars, while walk-on passengers are carried through the Chunnel on Eurostar trains using TGV technology. The TGV network is rapidly being extended into other neighboring countries. Eurailpasses are valid, without supplement, on the TGV (although not for passage through the Chunnel). Don't miss a chance to try the TGV.

**Central and Eastern Europe:** I recommend the choice of rail travel even more strongly in Central and Eastern Europe. Central and Eastern European roads are much worse, and the risks of automobile theft and vandalism are much higher, than in Western Europe. A car in most of this region is more hindrance and hazard than help.

Planners in the Second World of Central and Eastern Europe and the former USSR, and centrally planned Third World economies such as China, all made the same decision: railroads are the appropriate technology for long-distance passenger and freight transportation. Roads aren't. Railroads and associated industries (e.g., locomotive and passenger-car construction) were accordingly expanded and improved while roads languished in mud.

Long-distance trains in the former Second World are only a bit slower than in the First World, and much faster than Second World buses. Comparable classes of service may be slightly less comfortable than in Western Europe, perhaps more on a par with the oldest Amtrak cars; however, you can usually afford a much higher class, enabling you to travel in greater comfort on the same budget. For the price of a seat on a Western European or other First World train—sometimes much less—you can get a berth in a sleeping car, or even a private compartment, on a Second World train in Central or Eastern Europe or ex-Soviet Asia.

I've paid US$3 for a berth in a first-class compartment on a 12-hour overnight train from Kiev to Moscow. At prices like these, single foreign tourists or couples on ex-Soviet trains routinely buy all four tickets to a sleeping compartment for privacy and security. Prices are rising, but Second World trains are likely to remain a great value for some time.

Railroads are also useful in Second World cities. Quiet, energy-efficient, low-pollution subways and electric street railways were the Second World's chosen means of urban mass transportation. The world's best subways and the majority of the world's streetcar and trolley systems are in Eastern Europe and the former USSR. At the time of the breakup of the USSR, 88 percent of urban passenger trips in the USSR were by public transport, compared to 19 percent in the UK and 3 percent in the United States, putting Eastern and Central Europe in the enviable position (one that is now, unfortunately, being lost) of not being dependent upon the automobile.

### Asia

There is no clear geographic break between Europe and Asia—only in culture are they really two continents rather than one—and there are many routes across Eastern Europe and into Asia. But only two through routes cross the center of Asia, both of which require advance planning for visas to Russia.

**The Trans-Siberian Railway and Its Branches:** The most famous transcontinental train is of course the Trans-Siberian Railway. Since the 1991 opening of the city of Vladivostok it's been possible, as it hadn't been for 50 years, for foreigners to travel the full length of the Trans-Siberian between European Russia, Siberia, and the Russian Far East.

Some cities have little to recommend them but the allure of the formerly forbidden. Vladivostok is another story. It's a natural sister city to San Francisco, the other most-European city of the Pacific Rim, with splendid pre-revolutionary Victorian architecture. It includes the Trans-Siberian terminus, itself a monument to the czars' manifest destiny to extend their rule to the Pacific. All this, in a spectacular setting on steep hills overlooking the narrow mouth of the Golden Horn Bay.

Overnight, Vladivostok was transformed from a military city closed to even Soviet citizens without special permits to a "Wild East" free port and center of smuggling and black market trade. There are now direct international flights to Vladivostok, permitting air travel to or from the United States without having to go through European Russia. Trans-Siberian guidebooks are still only very slowly being updated to reflect the opening of Vladivostok and the trans-Pacific flight connections to and from the Russian Far East.

The "Russia," train #1 (westbound) and #2 (eastbound), is the train usually known outside the former USSR as the "Trans-Siberian Express." These through Vladivostok-Moscow expresses (7 days and nights' journey time, if you don't stop over anywhere along the way) operate daily in both directions. Many other expresses and local trains operate on shorter sections of the route, which is double-tracked and electrified for its entire 9,200 km (5,700 miles).

There are also branches from the middle of the Trans-Siberian south through Mongolia and Manchuria to Beijing. Fares on these branches are much higher, and service less frequent, than on the Russian main line. Only one Moscow-Beijing train each week operates over the respective Trans-Mongolian and Trans-Manchurian branches.

The longest continuous through train in the world is the weekly train on the least-known branch from the Trans-Siberian. Diverging from the main line less than 100 km (60 miles) north of Vladivostok, it continues for another day and a half into the Democratic People's Republic of Korea (DPRK), or North Korea, for which, I regret to say, USA citizens are not currently being given visas. Russia and the DPRK have a land border along the coast so short that it shows on only the most detailed maps. If you leave Moscow on day one, and the train is on time, you arrive in Pyongyang, North Korea, on day nine. Truly the end of the line.

I've enjoyed several three-to four-day train trips across both the United States and China. The diversity of scenery kept me enthralled each time, and I rarely felt the need to open a book or leave the window. The Trans-Siberian Railway is a longer route through less diverse scenery. Russian and other ex-Soviet railways were engineered for freight, and Russian and ex-Soviet passenger trains still move at speeds set by freight. Bring plenty of books and diversions for the long ride.

**The Central Asian Rail Route:** Fewer people have heard of it, and it's more recent—the last rails on the Northern Xinjiang Railway were only laid in 1990, and passenger service began in 1991—but there is now a more diverse and scenic through rail route all the way across Asia. It is well south of the Trans-Siberian, although it's possible to make connections between the two.

Some Chinese literature calls it the "Eurasian Railway," but this new route has no single consistently-used name, nor are there yet through passenger trains. You have to change, at a minimum, in Urumchi, East Turkestan (occupied by China as what it calls "Xinjiang Province") and Almaty, Kazakhstan. From Almaty there are connections on the Turkestan-Siberian (Turksib) Railway north to the Trans-Siberian mainline at Novosibirsk, and southwest to Tashkent, Uzbekistan, and thence to Samarkand, Bukhara, and on to European Russia. East from Urumchi there are direct trains east to Beijing and Shanghai or southwest to Kashgar, as well as connections to the entire Chinese rail network.

As with the Trans-Siberian, this is a route to take only if you are interested in and have appropriate visas for some of the intermediate stops. If you are just trying to get from eastern China to Europe, it makes more sense to fly. Kazakh visas are essential for this route and difficult to obtain. It's much easier to get permission to transit Kazakhstan from Russia to China (once you have Russian and Chinese visas) than vice versa, so I recommend traveling east rather than west on this route.

### North America

North America is the next best region for transcontinental train travel. Until World War II the United States had by far the world's largest passenger rail system. So dense was the USA rail network, you could get from New York to Chicago entirely by electric streetcars and interurban railways. American trains declined steadily after World War II until the creation of the National Railroad Passenger Corporation (Amtrak) in 1971. Since nationalization, service on USA railroads has steadily improved, with almost all Amtrak passenger cars being replaced or completely refurbished to modern standards.

Most Amtrak trains run at capacity, and one of Amtrak's biggest problems is getting funds to buy enough rolling stock (cars and locomotives) to handle peak-season demand. Currently, most long-distance trains operate daily, but Amtrak's future depends on whether the USA government will offer a more secure source of long-term funding or anything comparable to the government subsidies for air, road, and barge transportation.

Canadian trains were similarly but more recently nationalized as VIA Rail Canada. Despite drastic cutbacks in the extent and frequency of operations, Canadian train services remain first-rate and a justifiable point of national pride.

Speeds of trains in the United States and Canada lag behind Western European averages but usually exceed those of cars or buses, particularly on longer routes. Prices for sleeping car accommodations typically exceed airfares, but North American long-distance coach or economy (chair-car) accommodations are designed for overnight and multiday journeys. They have more spacious and comfortable seating than business class on an airplane, at prices often less than those of buses. It's sad that so many foreign visitors and locals alike overlook the opportunity to ride the railroads of North America. There is simply no comparison between the view from a train and the view from a highway, or the fast-food restaurants where buses stop versus the dining-car food on the railroad. There's no better or easier way to see the scenery of the continent than by train.

Amtrak and VIA don't go everywhere, but feeder buses, with coordinated schedules and guaranteed connections, greatly extend the utility of their networks. Major tourist destinations, such as Yosemite and Grand Canyon National Parks are linked to the rails by Amtrak buses and included in Amtrak ticketing and passes.

Limited routes do mean that touring North America by train is likely to require careful planning. There are surprisingly few connections between the USA and Canadian rail systems, for example, and no north-south routes in the United States between those along the Mississippi River and along the West Coast. Get timetables in advance, and start studying them early.

### Africa
No rail line, or even road, in any North American or European sense of the word, crosses Africa from south to north or west to east.

**East-West:** Operations on the Benguela Railway, which used to provide connections between the Atlantic coast and Zambia, eventually linking to Dar es Salaam on the Indian Ocean, by way of Angola and southern Congo, were interrupted more than a decade ago by the fighting in Angola. Even if local service resumes, it seems unlikely foreigners will be permitted to travel through that part of Angola anytime soon due to millions of land mines left buried along the road and railways.

**North-South:** From a map, it looks like one could cross the Sahara by rail from Alexandria or Cairo through Egypt and Sudan to within 500 km (310 miles) of the Ugandan railways. But southern Egypt is one of the few places in the world where, in an effort to drive them away and reduce revenue to the government from tourism, foreign tourists have been specifically targeted by terrorist attacks. Southern Sudan has only the roughest pathways for jeeps or trucks through areas of recent heavy fighting containing up to two million uncleared mines.

Between eastern and southern Africa, there is a single continuous north-south rail route from Kampala (Uganda) to Capetown (South Africa), by way of Kenya, Tanzania, Zambia, and Zimbabwe. The key link in this route is the Tazara railway, built with Chinese aid to provide the front-line southern African states with an alternative to dependence on South African ports. Now that it has lost that raison d'être, service on the Tazara (never known for comfort or speed) has declined even more. Railroads in Botswana and Namibia are linked to this system.

### South America

South and west of the Amazon, South America has a limited but, at one time, unusually well connected network of railroads. As in North America, the railroads have suffered from the diversion of wealthier passengers to planes, private cars, and even buses; service on many lines is being discontinued. Trains in most areas are slow and not always as comfortable as they might once have been.

As of this writing, all countries from Bolivia and Brazil south are joined by a continuous web of rails. There are even a surprising number of trans-Andean railroads traversing the world's highest and some of the most technically remarkable and scenic mountain sections. Services on many of these routes are infrequent or erratic, however, sometimes limited to certain seasons, one train a week, or only unscheduled special trains for tour groups.

As in North America, the ecological advantages of railroads will probably in time be rediscovered. But if you are interested in railroads for their own sake, go to South America soon, as trains there seem bound to get worse before they will get better.

### Australia

There is rail service across Australia, but the train costs as much as flying, and its route skips most of the attractions of the interior. The transcontinental trains run only twice a week, on a route noted for its monotony. Most independent travelers take the train only between Adelaide and Perth, and take buses elsewhere. The Australian government can't figure out why, because trains are potentially more useful in the more densely populated eastern and southeastern part of the country.

If you want to reach the outback, or the north, you'll have to fly, drive, or take a bus. Most people who want to see the whole country end up taking at least a few planes. Flights within Australia are cheaper when purchased in conjunction with your international ticket, before you leave for Australia. Minimal advance planning of your inter-Australian itinerary, before you leave home, can save you a substantial amount of money.

## Rail Travel Within Countries and Regions

Even if you aren't crossing a continent, there are many countries and regions within which trains are your best long-
distance transportation choice.

### Asia

Trains are the primary means of long-distance
passenger transportation in all the largest
countries of Asia.

*China and India:* Railroads in much
of the Third World have to import locomotives, signals, and other significant parts
from Europe or the United States. Much of the rolling stock taken out of service in the United States in the 1940s, '50s, and '60s remains in use by Third
World countries who bought it. Railroads take a lot of capital and tend to
receive low priority in the allocation of scarce hard currency for economic
development. India and China, however, have developed the capability to
produce everything their railroads need, including locomotives. This is not
surprising, as both countries also produce atomic bombs, satellites and
launchers, and intermediate-range missiles.

India and China continue to build new rail lines, electrify existing ones, and
increase speeds and capacity, unlike countries where whatever the colonialists
left behind is gradually rusting away, despite the best efforts to patch it up and
keep it running.

Railroads go pretty much everywhere within India and China. It is worth
noting that there is no railroad or road *between* India and China, or between
South Asia (India and the "Subcontinent") and Southeast Asia. With rare exceptions (the most important of which are the Karakoram Highway and the rail
links between China and Vietnam) travelers between India, China, and/or Southeast Asia have to fly at least part of the way. Land transit of Myanmar/Burma is
strictly forbidden, road transit of Laos is arduous and of Cambodia extremely
dangerous, and the border between Tibet and Nepal opens and closes unpre-
dictably, at the whim of the Chinese authorities.

A few areas under Indian or Chinese rule are inaccessible by rail, despite
their strategic and symbolic importance to their respective occupiers. There
aren't yet trains from China into Tibet; a railroad is actually under construction, but it will be many years before it is functioning . Don't doubt thegovern-
ment of China's willingness to spend money to complete it, though. In 2000,
China started service on a US$700 million new rail line to Kashgar, the center
of East Turkestan's resistance to Chinese rule, 1,000 km (620 miles) of unin-
habitable desert beyond the previous railhead at Urumchi. Neither can you
travel by train from India into the Kashmir Valley, as the only plausible route
for a railroad into the valley, and formerly the only road route, is through

India's arch-enemy Pakistan.

***Malaysia and Thailand:*** Two linked small and excellent national railroads frequently used by foreign travelers are those of Malaysia and Thailand. It costs about US$100 to go the 1,500-km (930-mile) length of the Malay Peninsula in an air-conditioned sleeper, depending on which route and trains you take, and how often and where you stop. Although expensive by Third World standards, the service is worth every penny. The equipment, on most lines in both countries, is clean, comfortable, and well maintained.

There are railroad tracks on the mile-long causeway between Johore Bahru, Malaysia (often referred to as J.B.), and Singapore, so one could technically include Singapore with the Thai and Malaysian railways. But prices for through train tickets to or from Singapore are almost 50 percent higher than those to or from Johore Bahru. For that matter, everything is cheaper, and should be bought, in Malaysia rather than Singapore. That's why downtown J.B. is dominated by malls catering to transborder shoppers. So spend a dollar or two on the bus between central Singapore and J.B., and get on or off the train in Malaysia. The J.B. train station is only 100 meters (100 yards) from the bus stop for customs and immigration at the Malaysian end of the causeway.

***Japan:*** Japan's railways are best known for the Shinkansen, or bullet trains, which signaled Japan's post-World War II return to world technological and industrial leadership. In 1964, the bullet trains began running start-to-stop scheduled service at 125 km/h (80 mph). Since then, the trains' speeds have doubled, although they have now been surpassed by the French TGV. Even the original, 30-year-old Shinkansen technology still compares favorably with any train outside Western Europe.

The larger engineering miracle is simply the existence of a truly national Japanese rail network: linking all the main Japanese islands by rail has involved the construction of the world's longest tunnel—53 km (33 miles) under a deepwater ocean shipping channel in an active earthquake fault zone—and the longest bridge—14 km (nine miles) with multiple high-level suspension and cable-stayed spans over deep-water channels.

Even the slowest Japanese trains aren't cheap, with highway buses costing about as much as the slowest local trains. Faster trains with fewer stops have progressively higher supplemental charges. Shinkansen fares are only slightly cheaper than domestic airfares, although if you include the time and expense of getting to the airport, the Shinkansen have a bigger edge, being somewhat cheaper, much easier, and almost as fast for all but the longest journeys. Traffic makes buses far slower and less reliable than trains, and everything about automobile travel in Japan— car rental, gasoline, parking, repairs, and tolls for roads, bridges, and tunnels—is prohibitively expensive. Japan probably has the world's highest density of passenger rail traffic. Most travelers, like most Japanese, travel by train. If you can't afford the trains, you probably can't afford to travel in Japan.

***Other Asian Countries:*** Some other Asian countries within which trains are particularly useful to travelers:

• **Pakistan:** Trains are safer than buses, although Pakistan's railroads cover less of the country than India's railroads.

• **Vietnam:** There is basically just one slow single-track narrow-gauge line (with a few short branches), which follows the main tourist route, but the roads and buses are appallingly slow, dangerous, and uncomfortable, so the train is still the best choice.

• **Taiwan:** It's a small island compared to continental Asia, but it's bigger than you might think, and the most scenic parts are away from the big cities. The train is the best bet for longer distances.

• **South Korea:** Likewise a bigger country than many people think, with an excellent, dense rail network.

• **Indonesia:** There is a remarkably good, insanely cheap rail system throughout the island of Java, although almost none anywhere else in the archipelago.

• **Myanmar/Burma:** The trains are bad, but the buses are worse. Where there is one, take a train.

Where not to take a train:

• **Cambodia:** Several foreign tourists have been kidnapped from trains, purely for ransom and not for any political reasons. I recommend against tourist travel in Cambodia in general, but if you must go, try to fly.

As for countries without railroads, it is perhaps worth noting, given the frequency with which people tell me they plan to travel to Nepal by train, that Nepal is far too mountainous, not to mention poor, for railway construction. You have to take a long, slow, uncomfortable bus on dangerous mountain roads, fly, or walk to get from India to Nepal, or to get anywhere within the country, although I've read there are 50 km (30 miles) of narrow-gauge railroad trackage somewhere in the Nepalese lowlands.

### Oceania
• **Australia:** The railroads of this continent-country-island are discussed above in the section on transcontinental routes.

• **Aotearoa/New Zealand:** One rail line runs the north-south length of the country, with a ferry connection between the rails of the North and South Islands.

### The Americas
Railroads in the United States and Canada are discussed in the sections above on transcontinental rail routes of North America.

In the Americas, the largest railway system I haven't mentioned is Mexico's, which covers the country pretty thoroughly—no small feat considering the topography. Mexico's railways are standard gauge, like those of the United

States. A lot of equipment taken out of service by USA railways— including historically interesting and once-elegant cars from some of their most prestigious trains —remains in service in Mexico.

There are no through trains between the United States and Mexico. The best connections between USA railways and Mexico are by foot or taxi across the Rio Grande between El Paso, Texas (USA), and Ciudad Juarez (Mexico). The El Paso and Ciudad Juarez train stations are about four km (2.5 miles) apart.

There are small, mostly disconnected but sometimes useful pieces of railroad in most countries of Central America and northern South America. As in some other regions, service tends to be deteriorating as money is invested in road-buiding rather than railroad maintenance.

### Africa

The extensive linked system I discussed earlier in the section on transcontinental routes also includes comprehensive domestic services in South Africa and the popular line from Nairobi to Mombasa. In addition, there are significant but isolated domestic rail systems in Egypt, Nigeria, Morocco, and Cameroon. Two useful but detached dead-end lines inland from the West African coast to the Sahel are between Abidjan (Côte d'Ivoire) and Ouagadougou (Burkina Faso), and between Dakar (Senegal) and Bamako (Mali).

## Timetables

Except in First World countries, rail timetables—even in local languages, much less in English—can be hard to find. It is frequently easier to find good local maps than local timetables. Train timings, frequencies, trip durations, and fares in even the best guidebooks are usually much less accurate than those in timetables, even much older ones. I pack the best rail timetables I can find, and I've never regretted their volume or weight in my luggage. Even in the First World, many national railroads have been broken up into separately-privatized pieces, making it harder and harder to find comprehensive, integrated timetables.

Don't be intimidated by timetables in a foreign language, such as Spanish or Portuguese in Central and South America or French or Portuguese in Africa. All you need to be able to understand are the station names, times, and codes for the days of the week (usually 1–7 for Monday-Sunday). On the other hand, a Chinese timetable without Pinyin transliterations will do you no good if you can't recognize any of the characters in the place-names. In such circumstances be grateful for any timetable in the Latin alphabet.

Treat all published timetables, especially those published other than by the railroads themselves, as no more than suggestions. The fine details, complex footnotes, and annotations of the Thomas Cook timetables—the standard reference, especially for more remote parts of the world—in particular look impressive. But these tables contain many, sometimes glaring, errors, and all schedules can change overnight.

Building a railroad takes a while, so you are unlikely to happen upon an entirely new major route. But you may find more or fewer trains. Allow room in your plans for the possibility a daily service has been cut back to weekly, a weekly service changed to a different day of the week, a night train changed to a day train, or vice versa.

Beware of train timetables posted on the Internet. If the site provides online reservations, the schedule is probably reasonably accurate (albeit subject to change between when you buy your ticket and when you plan to travel). Otherwise, the information was probably taken from a printed timetable collected by or sent to the webmaster, or from notes someone took at a station—possibly long ago, or badly translated. (Even the printed Thomas Cook timetables—generally considered the best available—are obtained from a network of itinerant correspondents who send them in from around the world, sometimes at long and irregular intervals.) Treat any timetable that doesn't specify its date and source with extreme skepticism. I've seen schedules at least 10 years out of date posted on otherwise authoritative-looking Web sites.

Even if you have reservations and tickets, always check the schedule of your next train locally, as soon as you get to the departure point. The most current, but still not guaranteed, schedule is usually posted in the station. If the lines aren't too long, try to confirm the posted schedule with the local railway staff as well.

Outside Western Europe and Japan, allow substantial time for any train to be late. If the journey is scheduled to take more than a day, or operates less often than daily, allow at least a couple of days for delays en route.

### North America

Amtrak and VIA Rail Canada (see the "Logistics" section of the Resource Guide) publish similar free complete pamphlet-sized national timetables for the United States and Canada, respectively. These are supposed to be available at all staffed Amtrak and VIA Rail stations (some stations are actually unattended flag stops), but they are often out of stock. Be sure to request a fare and pass guide at the same time, as the timetables have no information on fares. You can get schedules and fares for specific routes from the Amtrak or VIA Rail Web sites, but for overall planning the printed timetables are much more useful. VIA Rail's Web site has a downloadable system timetable, but Amtrak only has downloadable timetables for specific routes.

Whether or not you bring timetables with you to North America, it's worth looking at them in advance to get an idea of the routes. Routes are somewhat limited, requiring fairly careful itinerary planning if this is to be your primary means of exploring the continent, and travel times, like the distances, are long by European standards. The frequencies of the transcontinental United States and Canadian trains are particularly susceptible to change, and whether they operate twice a week or daily can be critical to the availability of summer seats and sleeping compartments.

## Western Europe

Eurailpass buyers are given the best English-language timetable, summarizing express trains between major cities, for Western European train travel. Even if you don't get a Eurailpass, try to find someone to give you a copy. Main-line European train schedules change surprisingly rarely, so even a two-year-old schedule can be valuable.

Complete Western European timetables are available only from private publishers; they are too big, heavy, detailed, and expensive for the needs of ordinary travelers. Locally available free European timetables are usually produced by national tourist boards or national railways, and are limited to single countries or at most regions such as Scandinavia or Benelux. You'll need a thick pile of these if you're crossing borders often, and it may be difficult to figure out routes and times of through international trains between regions (for which the Eurailpass timetable is best).

## Eastern Europe and the Former USSR

The USSR had the world's largest rail system, and Russia's remains among the world's three largest, along with those of India and China. Details are hard to come by, however, because all route and schedule information was considered a state secret of potential military value. The new private travel industry in Russia is targeting the richest travelers, who fly rather than take trains, and domestic customers, used to the Soviet system, don't expect printed schedules. So no private publisher has yet made it a priority to invest in producing a national timetable.

For now, the only printed schedules for Russian and other ex-Soviet and Eastern European railways are in the Thomas Cook timetables (see the "Logistics" section of the Resource Guide). Worse luck, you'll need portions of both the European and Overseas volumes, if you are traveling throughout Russia or the former USSR. Together they have fewer than 30 pages on the former USSR, so tear out and bring only the relevant pages. And you'll have to ask Thomas Cook how they came to define "overseas" as including all of Eurasia east of the Ural Mountains.

Railroads in Central Europe used to base their operations on Soviet models, but have been becoming much more "Westernized." Printed timetables are now available locally in most Central European countries. As of 2003 Hungary and the former East Germany have even joined the

Eurailpass program, and their mainline trains are included in the Eurailpass schedules.

## Asia

The Thomas Cook timetable is least accurate and useful in Asia. A few years ago they said they were making a special effort to improve their coverage of the Pacific Rim, but that hasn't happened. In their defense, Asian countries, especially China and India, have been among those where rail systems and services have been expanding most rapidly. It's hard for anyone to keep up with the changes.

Because there are few international trains in Asia, most of your train travel in Asia is likely to be within countries. And because these countries are mostly much larger than European countries, using separate timetables in different countries is less likely to be an inconvenience. The following are some suggestions for the Asian countries with the largest rail systems, except for the former USSR.

Note: I've included the former USSR above with Eastern Europe for conventional and cultural reasons, though geographically it's mostly in Asia.

**Japan:** The Japan National Tourist Organization (JNTO) distributes an excellent English-language guide to Japanese rail routes, timings, and fares. If you can't find a JNTO office, ask the Japanese embassy or any Japanese consulate in your country, or see their Web site.

**India:**There are two privately published English-language timetables of Indian trains. *Trains at a Glance* is a compact summary of mainline expresses, which are the only trains most foreigners ever take. The  *Indian Bradshaw* is a book the size of one of the Thomas Cook timetables listing every train in India. Both are sold cheaply at newsstands on railway platforms in major cities. Oddly, they are not available at ticket offices, even those for foreigners.

Neither of these books is available anywhere outside India. Indian government tourist offices have no information on train routes, schedules, or fares, except for the Palace on Wheels, an ultraluxury chartered train of former private cars of the maharajas that costs a minimum of almost US$300 per person per night in a double compartment.

**China:** Foreign-language train timetables are hard to find within China. You'll probably want to bring whatever you can find abroad, but the rapid pace of railroad improvement and construction of new rail lines in China makes most foreign publications based on second-hand information obsolete.

If you can't find a timetable, and can't read Chinese or speak Mandarin, at least equip yourself with a good bilingual map showing railroads. Like a bilingual timetable, it's a tool for communicating with ticket clerks and train attendants. You point at the English, they read the corresponding Chinese. And vice versa. Because one of the great accomplishments of Communism in China has been the achievement of near-universal literacy, this is a surprisingly effective, if limited, means of communication.

## Africa
Timetables are hard to come by anywhere in Africa except South Africa. For an extensive African trip, I'd invest in the Thomas Cook Overseas Timetable, tearing out and carrying the 60-odd pages on Africa. In much of Africa, schedules are sufficiently elastic that timetables are of limited usefulness, but anything is better than no schedule at all, at least in giving you a vague idea of the approximate frequency of trains on particular routes.

## Central and South America
Chances of finding timetables are a bit better in South America than in Africa, although where they exist they are likely to be limited to single countries. Here too I'd bring the relevant pages of the Thomas Cook Overseas Timetable. Mex-

# TOURIST CLASS

Foreign tourists often have to pay more for air and train tickets than locals, but they usually get treated differently as well, both when buying tickets and while traveling.

In India, foreigners who pay in hard currency (precluding buying on the black market, where they might save slightly on the price) get to buy train tickets in special air-conditioned offices, with guards at the door to keep out the pickpockets and touts. Instead of standing in line, you relax in comfortable upholstered armchairs while being waited on by the most expert few dozen of the Indian Railways' 1.6 million employees.

In China, foreigners have to buy train tickets with hard currency at special foreigners' prices, through CITS (China International Travel Service). But foreigners are spared the scrum at the ticket windows or the problems of communicating in Chinese. At the CITS office or desk in your hotel, you pay a service charge of US$1–2—well worth it, I think—for a messenger from CITS to spend a day fighting through the reservation and ticket lines at the station, while you go about your sightseeing. At the station, your soft-class ticket gives you entrée to the soft-class waiting room, with comfy couches, bright lighting, and refreshments available. Meanwhile, local passengers crowd each other for squatting space on the floor of the dim, cavernous, hard-class waiting hall.

Nowhere, though, were the differences more dramatic than on domestic flights in the USSR and (until the special foreigners prices were abolished) in post-Soviet Russia. Foreigners—whether or not they were on Intourist tours—checked in at the Intourist desk at the airport, where they got the sort of special service—even if they were flying in

ico and all of Central and South America take up about 70 pages.

### Australia

As of 2003 there is no single timetable for all trains in Australia. A good set of links to online timetables for the various regional and private railways, mostly from official sources, is at http://www.railpage.org.au/tt. The Australian Ministry of Tourism has been claiming for several years to have put a priority on publishing a unified train timetable. Check with the nearest office of the Australian Tourist Commission to see if they've made any progress by the time you read this.

## Passes, Tickets, and Reservations

The most important thing to find out about the trains you intend to take is whether you need to make reservations or buy tickets in advance, either to get

---

coach—that only business-and first-class passengers get in most countries.

You went to a separate check-in area (sometimes in a separate building), which was often air-conditioned, clean, and spacious with comfortable chairs or couches. An attendant came to your seat to collect your tickets, saving you from having to stand in any lines. When your flight was ready for boarding (in most cases, after all other passengers had boarded, so that you waited on the plane as little as possible before takeoff) an attendant came to your seat to tell you that your plane was ready and to escort you and any other foreigners onto the plane.

On arrival, you went not to the main arrivals area but, again, to the Intourist desk or building. (This could be actually be a bit hard to find if you were the only foreigner on the plane and Intourist, not expecting anyone on an Intourist tour, hadn't known to send a representative to meet the plane and escort you to its building or office.) Again, you waited in a separate, more comfortable area for your luggage to be delivered. In both arrival and departure areas you had access to foreigners-and-VIPs-only restaurants and bars.

When one of my flights was delayed, we were told that we could wait in the bar with US$1 bottles of champagne and 50-cent platters of bread and caviar. When the flight was ready, Intourist sent someone to the bar to fetch us.

Fewer people would complain about the higher fares for foreigners—even aside from the question of tax subsidies by locals—if they thought twice about the fact that the higher price got even coach-class foreigners dramatically higher quality VIP treatment and amenities on the ground. Too many foreigners, unfortunately, take such special privileges and amenities for granted (or never even notice that they are being treated differently from the locals), even while they demand to be allowed to travel for the local price.

seats on the schedule you want or to get a better price. Except within Europe, there is no standard form for train tickets, and unlike airline tickets there is no international payment clearinghouse to permit an agent in any country to issue tickets for travel in any other. Most train reservations and tickets are best obtained locally. But there are some significant exceptions that require advance booking or ticketing, particularly for train travel in Japan, Western Europe, or North America.

If advance reservations or ticketing are not required and if you are unsure of your plans, don't tie up your money or foreclose other options unless you have to. It's worth getting an idea, if you can, how much tickets for the trains you want to take are likely to cost. But for the Second, Third, and Fourth Worlds it's almost always easier and cheaper to make reservations and buy tickets locally. Arranging reservations and/or tickets for Second, Third, or Fourth World train travel in advance generally means paying an agent in your country to pay an agent in the destination country to send a person down to the local booking office or station in the city from which the train will depart to make reservations and buy you a ticket.

The countries where it is most difficult and expensive to do this tend to be the poorest countries or those where the currency has collapsed. Not coincidentally, this is also where tickets bought locally are likely to be cheapest. Communications, funds transfer, and other transaction costs (not to mention the agent's time) are likely to be expensive in relation to the ticket price. It wouldn't be unreasonable for an agent to charge US$50 or more to have a US$5 ticket waiting for you. Unless you are on a rushed and critical schedule, or you want to take a train that is likely to be sold out weeks in advance, that's not worth it.

First World rail travel is another story. All of the First World countries in which you are most likely to travel by train have special passes or fares for foreign visitors. These are often cheaper than tickets purchased locally. An unlimited travel pass may cost only a fraction of what you would pay locally for separate tickets, and it is often less restrictive. The common feature of these passes is that they can only be purchased outside the country in which they are to be used, so you have to decide in advance whether you will want them. The Canrailpass and the North American Rail Pass are exceptions; either can be purchased on arrival. But advance reservations (available through the Amtrak and VIA Rail Web sites, or through local agents in some countries overseas) are strongly recommended in both countries, especially for sleeping car, peak-season, or transcontinental travel.

You can often buy a rail pass even before you know your exact route, although the better sense you have of your plans the better you can judge which pass or ticket will be best for your trip. You also need to make a realistic assessment of the degree of uncertainty in your plans: if they are likely to change, getting cheaper fixed-route tickets, rather than a somewhat more expensive but flexible pass, may be a false economy.

### Rail Passes

Of the passes described below, all except the highest classes of Indian ("Indrail") rail passes are for coach or economy (chair-car) service. With any of the other passes, upgrades to various categories of "couchettes," berths, and private compartments may be available at additional, per-night charges. If you expect to travel in sleeping cars, be sure to check before you buy a pass how much extra this will cost.

In some countries there are supplements or surcharges in addition to the basic fare for travel on faster or more luxurious trains. Check whether the pass you are considering covers these.

Also check whether all trains have cars (coaches) of the class for which you are buying a pass. You can't use a second-class pass on a train that has only first-class cars. You can't use an economy-class pass, without paying sleeping car charges, on a train that has only sleepers and no chair cars. A notable exception is the French TGV. There are second-class as well as first-class cars on the TGV, and it is a point of French pride that the TGV be accessible to all. Holders of any type of Eurailpass can travel without supplement on any trains in the covered region, including the TGV.

### European Rail Passes and Tickets

The best-known of the rail passes is the Eurailpass. There is actually no one Eurailpass or single price. There is a confusing multiplicity of Eurailpasses at widely varying prices. The most expensive Eurailpasses allow unlimited travel for a certain period of time, by train and certain buses and ferries, such as those between Ireland and France and between Brindisi, Italy, and Patras, Greece. Note that they do not include any ferries to or from the United Kingdom. Eurailpasses may be used for unlimited travel within a specified validity period within Western Europe excluding the UK, the Chunnel, and Turkey.

A few Central European countries have joined the Eurailpass program. Most have not. Some separate passes are available for parts of Central Europe, but as of 2003, point-to-point tickets, purchased locally, remain cheaper than any of these passes. There are as yet no passes for rail travel in Eastern Europe or other parts of the former USSR.

For those traveling more slowly, there are Eurail Flexi-

> You can often find clerks in smaller European cities or suburbs who are less busy, equally competent, less jaded by tourists, and thus more helpful than those at the biggest stations or downtown offices most crowded with foreigners.

passes. If you aren't on a train every day, these are usually a better deal than the continuous-travel Eurailpasses. Flexipasses allow varying numbers of days of travel within a longer validity period. The Flexipass expires either when all the travel days have been used or the overall validity period expires, whichever comes first.

Both unlimited Eurailpasses and Eurail Flexipasses are available at different prices for travel in first and second class; for adults, youth, and children; and for groups of as few as two or three people traveling together. Prices and rules of some categories vary between peak season (April–Sept.) and off-season (the rest of the year). Pass rates are adjusted at the start of each Christian calendar year. Check approximate prices early in your planning. Eurailpasses are an excellent deal, but still cost more than many Americans expect.

There are a variety of other passes for specific countries and regions, as well as passes combining various numbers of days of train travel and car rental. It is also possible to mix-and-match combinations of specified numbers of countries from certain groups. See the "Logistics" section of the Resource Guide for sources of detailed Eurailpass information and pass selection advice.

Within the UK, British Rail offers a similar range of pass options under the Britrail pass scheme. These include passes for travel throughout the UK, for various regions, and for combinations of UK rail travel with ferries to and from the Irish Republic, rail travel in Ireland, and/or car rental.

Neither Eurail nor Britrail passes are valid for any means of transport between the UK and the Continent, across or beneath the English Channel.

The primary overseas agent for the competing Eurostar trains, Rail Europe (the Eurail consortium), represents none of the cross-channel ferries. British Rail represents a few of the many ferries. Both Rail Europe and British Rail can arrange the required reservations and tickets for the Eurostar passenger trains through the Chunnel Tunnel, more commonly known as the Chunnel.

The Eurostar trains carry passengers only. There are separate trains for transporting automobiles through the Chunnel, although they are more likely to be useful to Europeans than to overseas visitors. Unless you have a car on a long-term lease, it's not worth the expense to take a rental car across the channel by train or ferry.

High prices are the main reason the Chunnel has thus far attracted such a small share of the cross-channel market. Both Rail Europe and British Rail offer special fares on Eurostar services in conjunction with Britrail or Eurailpasses, with slightly lower prices and fewer restrictions than if tickets are purchased separately. But even the pass-holder prices are higher than ferry prices and not significantly less than some airfares.

All but the most expensive Eurostar tickets (which are more expensive than flying) and the special Eurostar fares for pass holders have fixed dates and change penalties that make them inappropriate for travelers without set schedules. By comparison, there are so many channel ferries that finding space, especially for walk-ons or bicycles as opposed to cars, is scarcely ever a problem.

All Eurail and Britrail passes must be used within six months of being issued. Eurailpasses are sold only in North America. If you will be traveling for many months before reaching Europe, and want a Eurailpass, you will probably need to arrange in advance to have one issued and sent to you. Some Eurail pass agents in the United States will send Eurail and British Rail passes to USA citizens overseas, if you make arrangements with them before you leave the United States and pay for shipping.

British Rail offices in the United States say their passes are available to North American passport holders in Paris and Brussels in addition to North America. If you will be stopping in one of these cities before you get to Britain, buying your Britrail pass there may be an option. But I haven't talked to anyone who has done it, and even British Rail strongly recommends buying your pass from British Rail or one of its agents in your home country. Similarly, it is possible, but difficult and not recommended, to buy a Eurailpass in London (if you have proof that you have arrived within less than a week from outside Europe) before you cross the Channel or the Irish Sea to start using it.

By now you should have gotten the message that there is no simple answer to the frequently asked question, "How much does a Eurailpass or Britrailpass cost?" Fortunately, Rail Europe publishes a fairly clear annual summary of pass options and prices, as does British Rail for the UK.

Adding up point-to-point fares in Western Europe may lead you immediately to conclude that some form of pass will be cheaper for any multistop long-distance rail journey. This isn't always so. A little-known fact is that full-fare one-way point-to-point tickets within Western Europe (and in some other places) allow unlimited stopovers within certain route restrictions. If you plan a continuous, more or less direct one-way journey across Europe, in whatever direction, a one-way ticket between your starting and ending points may permit all or most of the stops you want for less than the price of a pass.

Most Western European trains require advance reservations, for which, even if you have a Eurailpass, you have to pay a nominal fee. Most European services are frequent, and it's usually sufficient to reserve seats a day or two in advance for off-season travel. For holidays or other busy times, or if you want sleeping berths, allow more time. Holiday trains in Europe, like holiday flights in the United States, can be fully booked months in advance.

Unless you are extremely short on time or trying to cover many destinations very quickly, it's probably an unnecessary extra hassle to make reservations before you get to Europe. In marked contrast to the situation in most of the world, you can make reservations at any Western European train station or ticket office for trains throughout the region, even for trains leaving from other countries. So it often saves time and effort to book several legs of your trip at a time, particularly if you are spending only a few days in each city.

### Japan Rail Passes

Like point-to-point tickets on Japanese trains, Japan Rail Passes seem expensive but offer good value for the money. Prices are fixed in yen, unlike Eurail and other passes with fixed foreign-currency prices, so prices in your home currency will fluctuate with the yen.

Japan Rail Passes allow unlimited travel for 7, 14, or 21 days in second-class (ordinary car) or first-class (green car) seating. This includes travel to and from the train stations at all international airports. Ordinary class is more than adequate. The price of a seven-day ordinary-class Japan Rail Pass is comparable to the cost of a roundtrip domestic airfare or Shinkansen (bullet train) fare between Tokyo and Osaka.

Japan Rail Passes cannot be purchased on or after arrival in Japan, and must be used within 90 days of purchase. If you are traveling for a long time before getting to Japan you may have to buy yours along the way. This isn't as much of a problem as it is for Eurailpasses; passes can be purchased from designated agents in many countries. Check with the Japan National Tourism Office (JNTO) for a list of pass agents in your country, or wherever you will be within 90 days before arriving in Japan. If you have trouble finding the JNTO, check with the nearest Japanese embassy or consulate, or any Japan Air Lines (JAL) or All Nippon Airways (ANA) office. JAL itself also sells Japan Rail Passes, but in most cases only to passengers holding JAL tickets.

### Australian Rail Passes
Rail Australia offers several varieties of rail passes, including the nationwide rail-only Austrail Pass, regional rail-only passes, and combination passes for bus and train travel. The plethora of air, rail, and bus passes for Australian travel, most of which must be purchased outside the country, can be advantageous for travelers, but figuring out which variety of pass is right for you can be confusing.

Australia is one country where it pays to plan your route ahead and to enlist the help of a specialized travel agent in figuring out which transportation options will be best for you. Check with any office of the Australian Tourist Commission (ATC) for the latest information on pass options and prices. If you can't find the ATC, ask the nearest Australian embassy or consulate, or any office of Qantas or another airline serving Australia.

It's difficult to make reservations for most specific trains from outside Australia, but it's best to make them as far as possible in advance, or as soon as possible after your arrival. This is especially true for the twice-weekly Indian Pacific transcontinental service and the Adelaide-Alice Springs "Ghan."

### North American Rail Passes and Special Fares
**USA Rail Passes:** USA Rail Passes for 15 or 30 days of unlimited travel, either throughout the United States or only within certain regions, are available to foreign visitors, holders of non-USA passports, and USA citizens with proof of residence outside North America. Amtrak agents outside North America are few and often hard to find, especially outside the First World, so you may be

tempted to wait until you get to the United States. But a pass is useless if no space is available; it's worth the extra effort to find a local Amtrak agent, or to make reservations directly with Amtrak. Well in advance, call or write Amtrak for a system timetable, pass price guide, and list of their overseas agents (see the "Logistics" section of the Resource Guide).

The Internet would be an ideal way to serve customers overseas. (Foreign passports could be checked and eligibility for the fare verified when passes are picked up at Amtrak ticket offices after visitors arrive in the United States.) But USA Rail Passes are not available through Amtrak's Web site, although the site does have a (partial) list of agents abroad who sell them at http://www .amtrak.com/international.

Unfortunately, Amtrak still hasn't figured out quite what to do with visitors from countries where Amtrak doesn't have agents, or where the local agents try to sell passes without first making reservations for the desired trains. Even if you already have a pass, you can't make reservations to use it through Amtrak's Web site, for reasons Amtrak hasn't been able to explain.

Don't buy any Amtrak ticket or pass without first making reservations for all the trains you want to take that require them. Insist on reservations— through an overseas Amtrak agent, by e-mail to Amtrak customer service, or, if necessary, by an international phone call to one of Amtrak's reservation offices—for all reserved trains. All long-distance Amtrak trains require reservations. Amtrak's transcontinental trains, and to a lesser extent the other long-haul trains, fill the fastest. In the summer and around holidays, sleeping berths and compartments, sometimes even seats, on many trains sell out months in advance. The only Amtrak trains that don't require reservations are on shorter routes with more frequent service where you don't need to worry about finding space. If the train is unreserved, the timetable will show this in the "Services" notes.

If you can't get reservations in advance, don't risk the money on a pass you may not be able to use. Wait and make reservations and buy your pass as soon as you arrive in North America. Unlike Eurail and other passes that can only be purchased outside the region, USA Rail Passes *can* be purchased by foreign visitors after they arrive in the United States. If space turns out to be available, you can still buy a pass at the same price as if you had bought it abroad.

USA Rail Pass holders must pay a supplement for travel on the Metroliners and some Acela expresses (the fastest trains on the northeast corridor between Boston, New York City, and Washington, DC) or for sleeping compartments or berths. But there are plenty of conventional chair-car trains on the same corridor route, and you may find sleeping-car travel less essential than you had expected. Europeans, in particular, may be pleasantly surprised at the comfort level of North American long-haul chair cars. Most Americans can't afford sleepers. Amtrak and VIA Rail chair cars are about as well designed as possible for multiday rides.

**Canrailpasses:** The Canrailpass may be bought on arrival by Canadians and foreign visitors alike. However, it is subject to most of the same caveats as the Amtrak passes: difficulty in finding overseas agents, limited capacity, and the need to make reservations well in advance and before buying tickets.

SURFACE TRANSPORTATION

In my experience, there is a remarkable worldwide spirit of professionalism among railroad workers. Even in countries where nothing else seems to work, they take pride in doing their jobs well. Let them help you. They know the schedules better than you or I ever will. If the ticket clerk says, "There is a better train to where you want to go," they are probably right. Former Soviet railways, Intourist, and Amtrak telephone reservation agents are the exceptions that prove this rule. Intourist denies that any train exists unless Intourist has a quota of seats on it reserved for foreigners. As for Amtrak, plan your own Amtrak trip on the Internet, or go directly to an Amtrak station agent for help; don't waste your time with the people who answer the phones at their toll-free number.

Don't assume that a pass will be the cheapest ticket, especially for a one-way transcontinental journey with stopovers. A Canadian rail journey, even one with stops, is likely to follow a single continuous through route. A full one-way fare allows unlimited stopovers along the way. Full fare (the highest, least restricted, nondiscount price) isn't cheap, but it's usually cheaper than buying separate tickets for each leg of the journey and more economical than one-way plane fare. Good rail tariff agents are even harder to find than good air tariff agents; you'll probably have to go to a train station or VIA ticket office to get a ticket with multiple stopovers.

**North American Rail Pass:** The North American Rail Pass is more expensive than either the national USA Rail Pass or the Canrailpass. But it's valid throughput both the United States and Canada, and it's available to locals as well as foreign visitors. If your journey includes both countries, coast to coast, or if you can't arrange to purchase a USA Rail Pass before you arrive, this may be the best deal. The pass is available from either Amtrak or VIA Rail.

### Trans-Siberian Tickets and Reservations

I noted earlier that it is rarely necessary or desirable to make reservations for rail travel before leaving home for the Second, Third, or Fourth World. There is an important exception: the two branch lines between the Trans-Siberian Railway and China, one of which passes through Mongolia as well.

The only trains on these routes are the weekly through trains on each branch in each direction between Moscow and Beijing, and a few other trains on the

Trans-Mongolian branch that terminate at Ulan Bator and on which one is not allowed without a visitors visa (not just a transit visa) for Mongolia.

The trains to and from China were popular with foreigners who wanted to get a glimpse of Russia. But changes in Russia, and the opening of the full length of the true Trans-Siberian main line to foreigners, have made it unnecessary and indeed more costly to go through China just to ride part of the Trans-Siberian. There are now easier ways to see more of Russia. Many people erroneously think of the branch lines to China as being the Trans-Siberian. But more than 3,500 km (2,200 miles) of the Trans-Siberian main line, including some of the most interesting cities and scenery, lie east of where either of the branches to and from China diverge.

There are no chair cars on the through China trains, only sleeping cars. In the summer, all berths are often booked months ahead. Foreigners need foreign-price tickets, as passports are checked repeatedly. Ticket sales to foreigners are controlled by Intourist (from Russia) and CITS (in China), although other agencies can buy from them. The prices charged by both are higher than for other Russian or Chinese domestic trains.

So you have three options: pay an agent in your country a high price to arrange through train tickets between China and Russia, well in advance; risk a considerable wait (several weeks, possibly longer) in Beijing arranging tickets and transit visas; or take the Trans-Siberian within Russia. The last option does require a Russian visa, but it's worth it. Even at Intourist prices, or the prices scalpers charge foreigners, you'll pay less than you would for a ticket to or from China. (However you do it, in either direction, it's likely to cost more than it would to fly between the Pacific Rim and Europe. But the point of a week-long train trip isn't to save money.)

### Other Rail Passes and Tickets

**Indrail Passes:** For foreigners in India, the advantage of an Indrail Pass is not the price but the priority it gives you for otherwise unavailable space on sold-out trains. An Indrail Pass is extremely unlikely to be cheaper than separate tickets.

The Indian railways provide special foreigners' booking offices in Delhi, Mumbai (Bombay), Kolkata (Calcutta), and Chennai (Madras). (The official names for these cities were recently changed, but the older names remain recognized, and in widespread parallel use.) These offices are comfortable, air-conditioned (when the power is on), and relatively uncrowded—a near-miraculous respite from the norms of Indian bureaucracy and the hubbub and confusion of Indian train stations, which may have literally dozens of different windows for tickets in different classes on different rail lines, and where you may have to wait in half a dozen different queues to find out on which trains space is available, to make reservations, pay for tickets, collect your tickets, and reserve and pay for bedding. (Yes, in India you sometimes have to

I once wanted to take four overnight trains in little more than a week, during Diwali, a big Indian holiday. All the trains I wanted were sold out. What to do? "Buy an Indrail Pass," I was told. I did, and space materialized on every train. I didn't have to take any time out of the couple of days I spent at each stopover to arrange onward reservations; it had been taken care of all at once back in Bombay. I simply went down to the train stations in Ahmedabad, Abu Road, and Jaipur at the appointed hours, and there was my name on a berth-assignment list by the door of the car when the train pulled in. Quite a testament for those who think nothing works in India.

reserve bedding separately, or do without. It's a small additional charge and a large additional nuisance.)

Use the foreigners' booking offices whenever possible. If buying an Indrail Pass is the only way to get space on the trains you want, or that will be best for your desired itinerary, the staff at the foreigners' booking office will tell you so. Take their advice. In my experience, the staff at these offices are efficient, helpful, and knowledgeable. I've never heard of anyone being given bad advice, or asked for a bribe, at any of these offices.

The final reason to use the foreigners' booking offices is that they can arrange reservations even for trains leaving from other cities. Normally, in India (as in China, Russia, and most other countries in the Second, Third, and Fourth Worlds) you can confirm reservations only for journeys originating from wherever you make the reservations. So if you break your journey, you can't make reservations for your next onward leg until you reach each stopover point. The foreigners' booking offices in India provide the exception. Before you leave one of the four cities where they are located, book your trains as far ahead as you know your plans. You'll be spared a great deal of hassle and wasted time in each intermediate city from which you pre-arrange your departure.

The Indian Airlines Pass, which is far less of a bargain than the Indrail Pass, can also be purchased by foreign passport holders even within India. So whether you will use a pass or separate tickets, there is no need to commit yourself to either before you get to India and see what both are like.

The only reason to pre-pay transportation within India is if domestic flights can be included in your through international tickets for less than the likely price of transportation purchased on arrival.

### Other Second, Third, and Fourth World Rail Tickets

A few other Third World countries offer rail passes, but all the ones I know of can be bought once you are in the various countries. You can decide when you get there if they will be worthwhile or not.

Both Thailand and Malaysia offer passes for unlimited domestic rail travel, but almost no one but rail fans who spend all their time on trains would travel enough, within either country, in the allotted time, to make either pass pay off.

In the rest of the Second, Third, and Fourth World you will need to make your reservations and buy train tickets locally, in each place you stop, for the next leg of your journey. The easiest time to do so is as soon as you arrive, while you are still at the station, unless, as is not unknown, especially for ticket purchases by foreigners, you have to go to a ticket office at some remove from the station.

Whether or not you buy your onward tickets immediately upon arrival, at least try to do so as far as possible before your intended departure, up to several weeks ahead if you know when you will want to leave. In my experience, you have a much better chance of getting on the trains you want, in the class of service and accommodations you want, if you book each leg at least a few days in advance.

On shorter notice you may have no choice but to pay for a higher class of service or accommodations than you want or need, such as air-conditioning; to travel in a lower class of service than you want, such as sitting up overnight or for several days; or take a slower train than the one you want.

Truly local trains can be excruciatingly slow in countries where even the fastest expresses may go only 50 km/h (30 mph). Passengers on local trains routinely pull the emergency cord to stop the train wherever they want to get off, often every couple km. Slow trains may only have third-class (or 10th-class) cars; few foreign tourists willingly take such a train more than once.

### Urban Mass-Transportation Passes

Urban passenger rail systems—subways, elevated trains, streetcars, trams, and suburban and commuter trains—are more common in the rest of the world than they are in the United States. Most large world cities, from Beijing to Buenos Aires to Cairo, have some sort of intra-urban railroad. (Note that outside the United States the word "subway" is generally used only in its British sense of "pedestrian underpass." What is called a "subway" in the United States—an underground intracity railway—is more often called an "underground" or "metro" in the rest of the world.) You'll find excellent

Don't buy a through train ticket with stopovers—even if it is a cheaper and, in theory, allows stopovers—unless you can make seat or sleeping berth reservations beyond the stopover point(s). If you get off, and later get back on another train to continue your journey, you may have to stand for the rest of your trip. If "the rest of your trip" is several days, or even just overnight, the savings on the through ticket was probably a false economy.

subways/undergrounds/metros in some places you may not expect: the engineers of the San Francisco BART train systems took their lessons in how to build an earthquake-resistant subway from the engineers of the fine modern metro in Tashkent, Uzbekistan.

Especially where you don't speak the language, urban railways are almost always much easier to navigate, and harder to get truly lost on, than buses. Trains are more likely than buses to follow fixed routes and to be marked with their route or their final destination. Rail stations and stops are more likely to be marked, and easier to find, than bus stops. Even if there are no announcements, if you have even a crude schematic map you can usually tell how far to go, and when to get off, by counting stations or stops. Within urban areas, railways are invariably faster than buses, often faster even than taxis in big cities with slow-moving traffic. And electric trains are, of course, much less polluting than buses. For all these reasons, it makes sense to make urban rail transportation your first choice, and to take buses around town only where there are no trains or rail cars, or when you don't want to get anywhere particular but just want to sightsee on random streets.

Whether traveling by bus or local rail, mass-transit passes marketed to tourists are often more expensive than mass-transit passes for local commuters, and should be viewed with skepticism. Of course, the information given to tourists always emphasizes the special tourist passes to the exclusion of all others. You'll probably have to ask local commuters to get accurate information on such items as Travelcards in London, Cartes Orange in Paris, multiride transit ticket books, quantity discounts on token purchases, and their counterparts in other cities. Just look for people showing things that look like passes or coupons to conductors and ticket-takers or using special tokens at turnstiles, and ask the passengers how they got them and how much they cost.

A good example of this situation is the "Visitor's Travelcard," purchasable only outside Europe, for travel on the London Underground (subway or "tube") and London-area commuter trains. It also covers the local buses, but not the airport express buses that visitors are much more likely to use. The Visitor's Travelcard is valid in all six tube zones, but most visitors stay within the central one or two zones. Unless you are traveling daily to and from the outer suburbs, the Visitor's Travelcard is a lousy deal. A regular one-or two-zone Travelcard—the sort that Londoners use—is quite a bit cheaper, the more so the longer you stay.

If you're in a city for a week or more, there's a good chance you can save by using some sort of pass or multiride ticket. The Travelcard and the Carte Orange,

SURFACE TRANSPORTATION

among others of their ilk, require a visa photo to preclude several people from sharing one pass. Just another reason to always carry extra visa photos.

## Rail Ticket Prices

Pay no attention to the rail ticket prices in the Thomas Cook timetables. I've never figured out who makes them up. It doesn't help that they are updated only when schedules change, which they sometimes don't for years at a time. They are usually printed in local currencies which, in the Third and Fourth World, tend to decline with time against USA dollars or other First World currencies. Even the publisher tries to warn readers not to take the printed prices too seriously.

Don't be fooled by ticket prices in guidebooks, either. Expect them to have increased substantially with inflation. The poorer, more remote, and less visited a country is, the longer the lead time and the less frequent the revisions of guidebooks are likely to be, and the more you should expect prices to have increased from those in current guidebooks.

### Local vs. Foreigners' Prices

In some countries foreigners have to pay much more for train tickets (and sometimes other things) than locals. Foreign travelers in such countries spend a lot of their time complaining—to each other and to locals—that the higher prices for foreigners are unfair.

Rarely do foreigners take time to consider the rationale for the dual-price system. In communist and socialist countries, and even most "social democracies," local people subsidize transportation and other services with their labor. Whether they officially "pay" taxes, or whether these fringe benefits are simply reflected in low salaries, they receive only part of their earnings in take-home pay. The rest of their earnings goes to support public services such as transportation. It would be grossly unfair to local workers if foreigners—who haven't paid local income taxes or contributed labor—were allowed to travel for the same nominal ticket price as locals.

Foreigners who demand to be allowed to buy tickets at the local price are, in effect, demanding that local people subsidize tourists who are already many times richer than most of them can ever hope to be. To claim this as your right is to set yourself up for accusations of exploitation, imperialism, and, depending on your skin color and theirs, racism as well.

Foreigners' prices seem quite logical and fair to those who charge them. Arguing will only anger them, make you lose face, and reinforce their low opinions of rich capitalist foreigners.

My rule of thumb for guidebook prices is to add 20 percent to prices in a newly revised guidebook plus 10 percent for each year since the copyright date. It adds up fast: if in 2006 you're using a 2003 guidebook, expect prices to be 50 percent higher than in the book.

A first-class ticket the length of Vietnam (40–48 hours total travel time, 1,700 km, 1,060 miles) costs a foreign tourist about US$100, depending on what trains you take and what stops you make. That's several times the price Vietnamese pay. But it's slightly less than the price foreigners or locals pay for a journey of similar length along the Malay Peninsula through Thailand and Malaysia—the nearest and most comparable rail line in capitalist, one-price countries.

Part of what may tempt foreign travelers to argue is that a country doesn't generally set up a separate price schedule for foreigners unless the price difference is substantial. Where they exist, foreigners' prices are usually at least twice, often 10 times, local prices. Still, they are usually very cheap compared to the prices of similar services or goods in capitalist countries, even Third World capitalist countries.

It's hard to predict just where you'll find a "dual-price" system with higher prices for foreigners. Foreigners' prices are being phased out in the former Second World countries of Eastern and Central Europe. On the other hand, local prices in these countries, while still below Western European or other First World prices, rose sharply in the 1990s.

Since 1992, foreigners have been allowed to go almost anywhere in the former USSR (save the war zones) and to ride almost any trains. In theory, you can now buy your own tickets, for rubles, directly from the regular ticket windows. On the other hand, scalpers have often bought up all the tickets, and it can be easier or, in some cases, cheaper to pay the Intourist service charge than deal with the black marketeers. It's thus impossible to predict how much a train ticket in the former USSR will cost. Budget on the high side, hope for the low, and inquire locally.

## Life on Board

Some trains have only one sort of car for all passengers, while others have many different classes with several gradations even within each class. You may find second class more luxurious than necessary in some countries, and first class intolerably uncomfortable in others. As with hotels, the key to happiness is figuring out which of the available options best suits your particular standards and budget.

A good destination guidebook should explain the types of trains, classes of service and accommodations, and the surcharges for faster trains (fast, rapid, special express, or mail trains), higher classes, air-conditioning, sleeping berths, private compartments, meals, bedding, etc.

This is where you will learn that in India first class is actually the fourth-best of a great many classes, with three air-conditioned classes above it—only someone who grew up in a caste society can fully comprehend the nuances of the class system of the Indian railways. You will learn that a Japanese Kodama makes more stops than a Hikari; or that a mail train in India is faster than an express. But what all this means is hard to judge without some context.

It's hard to learn much about train classes from other travelers unless you can find some country in which you have both ridden the same class of train, as a basis of comparison. "First class here is a little more comfortable than second class in Country X" is only helpful if you know Country X. "I found second class intolerable" is of little use without a sense of the other person's standards. Also, don't count on people to remember accurately in which class they traveled.

The best way to learn about the different classes and types of equipment is actually to look at them. If you've already gone to the station to buy your tickets, it should be easy to inspect whatever trains are passing through. At most you'll have to pay a trivial price for a platform ticket to look at the trains.

Ticket clerks and other locals will often suggest the class that they think is appropriate for foreigners. Unless a lot of foreigners are traveling in lower classes, this is generally the highest class, the one that probably used to be exclusively for the former colonial masters.

You might find a lower class acceptable, but don't dismiss their advice out of hand. If they are seriously reluctant to sell you a lower-class ticket, there may be a good reason. Last-class Third World train travel, and anything but top-class Fourth World train travel, can be more than most First World travelers are prepared for. If you haven't ridden a rail line before, and haven't been able to inspect the cars, err on the side of a higher class.

Train-station restaurants are generally poor everywhere, and train passengers—a captive market—are generally overcharged severely for the fruit, drinks, and snacks offered

through the windows or on platforms by vendors at stations. If every vendor at a station is offering the same fruit or dish, give it a try. It's probably a distinctive local delicacy of the place or region that you're passing through. I didn't get off the train in Hami, but I'll never forget the taste of the Hami melons—renowned for a thousand kilometers—that were sold to us through the train windows when we stopped there for a few minutes.

Dining cars, where they exist, tend to overcharge even more. Good sleeping cars are common in the South, but good dining cars rare. Sometimes you'll get lucky and get a wonderful cheap meal on board, but don't count on it. Always bring enough food and water to see you through to your destination. Most trains have some sort of toilet, but don't expect much more than a hole in the floor. Bring your own toilet paper. Availability of washing up facilities, and of water for washing and drinking, varies greatly. Sometimes you'll be brought hot moist towels after every meal, and thermos bottles of boiled water. Sometimes there will be no water to drink or wash with unless you bring it yourself.

## International Trains

Procedures for crossing borders by train vary greatly. In some cases customs and immigration inspectors carry out their work on board while the train travels between the stops on either side of the border. This is true of all rail border crossings within Western Europe, and between the United States and Canada. In other places, the train stops for a car-by-car check at the border before it proceeds. In the worst cases, everyone has to disembark. This is unusual; one reason people pay more to take a through international train, rather than two domestic trains that connect on either side of a border, is precisely to avoid this delay. But it does happen, sometimes unexpectedly.

It's common to have to stop at a border, or even within a country, for a change of locomotive from diesel to electric, or vice versa, or between third-rail and overhead electric power, or between electric locomotives operated on different types of current (AC or DC), frequencies, or voltages.

There are no real standards of any of these things, although some electric locomotives, including those of the French TGVs, can operate on more than one type of power.

### Railway Gauges

The most common reason not to connect two adjacent railways is that they have been built to different gauges. The gauge is the width between the rails, specified as the distance between the outer flanges.

For travelers, variations in rail gauges could mean a transfer between trains, and perhaps between stations on different rail lines, even when the rails appear on a map to be seamlessly connected across a border or through a city. It's common for a single city to have many train stations, so always make sure to ask which station your train leaves from. On the other hand, within rail networks on the same gauge—such as within most of Western Europe—through cars can be switched from train to train as often as necessary. The same train often includes cars bound for different destinations, so that if you get on the wrong car, even if you're on the right train, you can wake up on the wrong branch line, or in the wrong country!

Train gauges are also one of the clearest and most conspicuous examples—set in steel—of how differing colonial legacies have hampered post-independence efforts to promote trade, travel, and cooperation between Third and Fourth World countries.

Most countries that could afford it have tried to convert their railroads to a single national gauge. Australia has invested particularly large amounts in converting from other gauges, both wider and narrower, to standard gauge. Where this hasn't been financially feasible or when crossing borders between countries with different standards, a change of gauge usually requires a change of train.

## ROAD TRANSPORTATION

Road travel has a seductive appeal: get on the road and you can go anywhere. But as the song goes, "It ain't necessarily so."

Roads themselves cover far more territory than railroads, although still not everywhere. No such elaborate geographic survey as I conducted in the previous section on railroads is needed here: pretty much anywhere you can go by rail, you can also go by road, and then some.

There are significant regional differences, however, in the desirability and (dis)advantages of road travel relative to other options. The appropriate mode of road travel differs from region to region as well.

In the following sections on private and public road vehicles, I'll try to give some sense of the factors to consider in choosing whether to go by road.

### Road or Rail: "Comfort, Safety, Speed"

Where there is a train, take it. Don't think twice about the choice. In comparison with rail travel, road travel is dangerous, polluting, and expensive.

"Comfort, Safety, Speed" was the slogan of the Pacific Electric Railway, the Los Angeles and Southern California streetcar and interurban system that was once, believe it or not, the world's largest. Comfort, safety, and speed are the advantages of trains over road vehicles. Even where cars or buses are faster, comfort and safety—especially safety—are the reasons I still travel by rail wherever I can.

### *Comfort*

With few exceptions, road travel is less comfortable than travel by rail. Don't be misled by the apparent comfort of the interiors of luxury buses. No matter how well-appointed their interiors, they are limited by the conditions of the roads on which they are operated. Even the best bus will bump and bounce painfully and slowly over an unpaved, potholed, rutted road.

Beware: The standard of luxury in Third World buses has become the video bus on which passengers are entertained by continuous high-volume, low-fidelity bootlegs of local pop music videos, movies, and TV shows. The novelty wears off quite early in your first day or night on such a bus. Video buses are symptoms and vectors alike of the cultural imperialism of USA television.

## Safety

Railroads use relatively mature and forgiving technology. Even human errors are less likely to be disastrous. If the engineer or motorman of a train falls asleep, he (female professional drivers are unknown in most of the world) will probably wake up before any damage is done. If a bus or truck driver, who may drive for 24 hours, or 72, with no more than brief meal breaks, falls asleep, the vehicle will probably run off the road within a few seconds.

> "Rail travel in the United States, per passenger-kilometer, is 18 times as safe as private car travel….The risk of being injured or killed in a road accident is 29 times as great as that for rail in the former West Germany and the Netherlands, and 80 times as great in France."
>
> —Worldwatch Institute

The safety advantages of trains over road travel are even greater in areas where both are less safe than they are in the United States. Countries (other than the United States) with a useful rail system invest far more heavily in railroads and railroad safety than in roads and road safety.

It may be obvious that Third and Fourth World countries with limited resources have put a lower priority on road than rail development, because the same investment in rail can build a system that can carry many times as many people as the same investment in roads. It may be less obvious that roads in even the most industrialized Second World countries are almost as bad as Third and Fourth World roads, central planners having decided that roads were not appropriate technology.

In most of the world rail travel is probably at least 100 times safer than road travel. Given that surface transportation is already the most dangerous aspect of almost any trip, this is a compelling reason to ride the rails, rather than the roads.

## Speed

Some bus rides are so difficult, dangerous, slow, or uncomfortable that even the stingiest travelers, if they can at all afford it, make it a monetary priority to fly or take a train. The cost for flying may be large in comparison with your daily budget in a poor country, but it may be a price worth paying to avoid two or three days on a bus through deserts, mountains, jungle, or mudholes. On the other hand, the scenery makes some truly scary bus trips worthwhile, if nothing goes wrong. Let both your budget and your tolerance for danger and discomfort be your guides in choosing whether to use road transport.

## North America vs. the Rest of the World

North Americans travel by road, rather than rail, more than anyone else in the world. North Americans are thus accustomed to an extreme imbalance between the availability and convenience of road and rail transport. Coming from the United States or Canada, your first instinct may be to rent a car or take a bus, even in a place where neither makes any sense.

Conversely, first-time visitors to North America typically expect such a wealthy country as the United States to have a modern public transportation system. Even if they are forewarned about the 20th-century decline of North American intercity trains they are often unprepared for the near-total abandonment of urban public transit by all but the poorest people in many major USA cities.

The difficulties this causes are compounded by the tendency of visitors from smaller countries to underestimate the scale of the United States. It's almost impossible for people who grew up in Western Europe, Japan, or Taiwan, and who haven't traveled to big countries before, to imagine just how far it is between different places in any of the largest countries. A bus trip across North America may seem less of a bargain when you realize that it will take 72 mostly sleepless hours.

## Road vs. Air

Where there is no railroad, you may have no choice but road travel. Don't rule out air travel, particularly if local roads are horrible. Domestic airfares in some countries, even fares for foreigners, are very cheap. Some international fares are quite low too, and customs and immigration formalities are usually less of a hassle at airports than at land borders.

The bottom line is that the appropriate mode of transportation depends greatly on local conditions. You can make life pretty hard for yourself by choosing the wrong way to get around.

## Where There Is No Road

Good or bad, roads are almost everywhere, so in a sense road travel is the most widely available choice. Other than Antarctica, there is no continent that can't be crossed (albeit with difficulty) by some sort of land vehicle on something called a "road."

Severe logistical difficulties, however, are presented by road travel across the Sahara, the Congo (Zaire) Basin, the Amazon Basin, and between Europe and East, South, or Southeast Asia. None of these crossings should be attempted without careful planning and preparation.

### The Sahara

There has never been any public transit across the Sahara. Even if a route opens up, you need to have your own vehicle or get a ride with another traveler or a tour operator with a vehicle. From west to east, there is a continuous band across the continent of countries posing problems for would-be north-south travelers.

***Western Sahara:*** Fighting continues between Morocco's army of occupation and the nationalist Polisario Front. Some overland tour companies send their trucks through, but only as parts of convoys escorted by Moroccan military vehicles. The Polisario Front's government-in-exile is recognized as the rightful government of the Saharan Democratic Arab Republic (RASD) by several dozen other countries, the International Court of Justice, and the Organization of African Union. But documents associating a traveler with the RASD, even if one of its offices-in-exile could be persuaded to issue a "visa," would only brand a traveler a subversive in the eyes of the Moroccan soldiers who wield power at gunpoint in most areas. It's indicative of the extreme difficulties of trans-Saharan travel that, as of 2003, the *easiest* way to get across the Sahara is the following: whenever enough vehicles accumulate heading through in one direction or the other, and military conditions permit, the Moroccan army escorts them through in a convoy.

***Algeria:*** Widespread assassinations of those accused of being agents of European secularism and cultural imperialism, including presumptively non-Muslim foreigners, make this an area to travel with extreme caution, if at all. It's probably still an okay route for Muslims, but only for those who are very sensitive and careful not to offend local sensibilities.

***Libya:*** The international trade and travel embargo against Libya was lifted in 1999, so it's no longer the USA government that stands in the way of travel through Libya. But visas and permits from the Libyan government remain hard to come by, especially for independent travel away from the coast and the cities.

***Sudan:*** There's a very serious danger of land mines, among other hazards, especially in the south.

### Congo

There are roads across the Congo (formerly Zaire), but they are among the world's worst. Going between East and West Africa, there is no way around Congo: go north or south, and you have to cross minefields and war zones of Sudan or Angola, respectively. No road across Congo is paved, and the only vehicles on many stretches are lumber trucks (or military vehicles). You have to pay for rides, when you can find them. When the trucks stop—whether for rest or because they have bogged or broken down—you have no choice but to stop where they do. If you're lucky, you'll be allowed to sleep under a truck, giving you some protection from the rain. Conditions were bad already, but got much worse during and after the civil war in 1999.

It's possible to get stuck in the middle of the jungle for weeks, and if you decide you want to give up it could be a long way to an airport, railhead, or major river port.

Domestic flights in Congo, when they operate at all, are also among the world's worst and most dangerous, so there's no readily available alternative if you give up on overland travel.

### Amazonia

There are east-west and north-south roads across Amazonia, although no bridge spans the Amazon itself or any of its major tributaries. I've heard from fewer people who have taken these roads than those across the Congo basin, but my impression is that they are a bit better. Certainly Brazil is spending more money than is Congo on building roads to open up, exploit, and clear-cut the land. On the other hand, crossing Amazonia between north and south requires a much longer distance by road than does crossing Congo. Not for the timid.

### Eurasia

Until 1979, it was possible to travel by road between Europe and Asia by way of Turkey, Iran, and Afghanistan. There were regular through "hippie buses" via Pakistan and India as far east as Nepal. The Iranian revolution in 1979 and the war in Afghanistan in the 1980's closed that route. Iran is welcoming tourists from the United States again, but so many land mines are scattered on roads and trails in Afghanistan (not to mention in cities, fields, pastures, and everywhere else) that travelers and residents alike will be endangered for the foreseeable future. Any through route passes through both Turkish-controlled and Iranian-controlled portions of Kurdistan, where the ruling powers are at war with Kurdish nationalist guerrillas. Tourists in Kurdistan are not welcomed by the authorities and are at risk of being caught in the crossfire.

It's theoretically possible to take buses across Central Asia via Russia, Kazakhstan, East Turkestan (Chinese-occupied "Xinjiang Province"), and China, following essentially the same route as the rail route described earlier. Buses as well as trains run between Almaty and Urumchi. But it's peculiarly difficult to get permission to bring foreign vehicles across Chinese borders, and given the conditions of roads in Russia and China, much less Central Asia, I can't think of any reason to forsake the comforts of the trains. *Red Odyssey* (see "Travel Narratives" in the Resource Guide) is the narrative of a well-connected Soviet citizen who tried to drive the Soviet section of this route and gave up halfway.

## Private Road Transport

It's not always easy, and rarely simple or cheap, to bring, buy, or rent any private vehicle larger or more elaborate than a bicycle. Before we get to the bicycle question, though, let's work down through some of the more grandiose possibilities, in descending order of power, independence, and expense: taking a car with you, buying a car locally, renting a self-drive car, hiring a chauffeured car, bringing or buying a motorized two-wheeler, and hiring a motorized two-wheeler.

### Bringing Your Own Vehicle

Taking a car with you makes sense if you either already have a car and are going to a nearby destination that you can get to by road (e.g., within North and Central America, or within Europe) or by relatively short and affordable ferries (e.g., from Europe to North Africa), or you are going to a more distant place where suitable vehicles are either utterly unobtainable or so much more expensive as to warrant the costs of shipping your own car from home (e.g., for trans-African travel).

If you are going to somewhere nearby, with a similar level of wealth and technology and similar cars and roads (such as between the United States and Canada, or within Western Europe), then the only things different from driving within your home country will be dealing with different legal and regulatory requirements and possibly different languages, signage, and driving on the opposite side of the road.

If you are going somewhere farther afield, you'll have to deal with additional costs and complications of shipping. Unless there's a ferry that carries both vehicles and passengers, as is the case across the Strait of Gibraltar, you'll have to send your vehicle by cargo ship.

Because you won't be there to expedite its arrival and passage through customs, it's important to triple-check all the papers and procedures before you consign your vehicle to the shipping line. Even so, you'll probably want to plan your own arrival for shortly before the ship with your vehicle is scheduled to dock and unload, to keep an eye on things. If you can't, you may have to hire a customs broker or shipping agent to push the papers and perhaps grease palms in your absence.

The minimum legal and regulatory requirements are registration of your vehicle in your home country, a driver's license in your home country, an international driver's license, and liability insurance valid in each country in which you operate the vehicle. If you are driving between very different countries, you'll need to be prepared for considerable, and perhaps unexpected, logistical hassles as well.

### Operator Licensing

To operate a motor vehicle in any country, you need either a valid local driving license or both a license to drive in your home country and an International Driving Permit (IDP).

An IDP is a certified translation of your driver's license in standard format, into English, French, Spanish, Italian, German, Swedish, Russian, Chinese, and Arabic.

An IDP is valid only in conjunction with your license to drive in your home country. The permit has no independent validity and should always be carried, and shown, with your local license. Most travelers, and even many traffic police, don't realize this. But if you carry only an IDP, and not your driving license from home, there's always a risk of being stopped by an officer who knows and enforces the requirement that you carry both documents.

International Driving Permits are issued either by local governments or by driving clubs or organizations designated and authorized by the government to perform this function. If you want an IDP, you have to get it before you leave home. An IDP is valid for one year from the date of issue, provided that the local license in conjunction with which it is issued and used remains valid.

In the United States, International Driving Permits are issued by the American Automobile Association (AAA) and its local affiliates. You don't have to be an AAA member to get an IDP from the AAA. Just bring your current driver's license and a passport photo to any AAA or affiliate office, and for a nominal fee they will issue you an IDP on the spot.

The permit is endorsed to be valid only for the class(es) of vehicle(s) for which your regular license is valid. If you want to be able to operate a truck, bus, or motorcycle, you must already have a license to operate such a vehicle in your home country before you apply for your IDP.

### Vehicle Licensing and Insurance

As I said above, the minimum requirement is that a vehicle you take abroad be legally registered in your home country (or the country you are coming from). Many countries have additional requirements, from minor fees and taxes to mandatory insurance, massive duties, or requirements for a *carnet de passage*.

At each border crossing you can expect to be asked for proof of ownership, registration, and insurance of your vehicle. Bring extra copies (if possible, notarized) of the title, registration, and insurance certificates, as you will have an extremely hard time if you lose them.

If the owner of the vehicle isn't traveling with you, you may also need to produce written permission from the owner (preferably notarized) to be using and crossing borders with their car. This is for good reason: many cars and trucks stolen in the United States end up in Mexico or Central America, and even more cars stolen in Western Europe end up in Central or Eastern Europe or ex-Soviet Asia.

Often you'll be required to display a standard emblem identifying what country your car is registered in. You're probably already familiar with these white oval stickers with a black border and a one-, two-, or three-letter abbreviation for the country of registration (i.e., the country that issued your license plates). You'll need one to cross most borders.

Many countries impose more-or-less minor taxes or fees on incoming vehicles of foreign registration. If they put a tax or registration sticker on your car when you pay the fee to take it into the country, at least you know the money went to the government, not in the tax collector's pocket.

Standard automobile insurance policies are valid only in the country in which the vehicle is registered and insured. Check with your regular automobile insurance agent and/or automobile association for the vehicle insurance rules of each country to which you might bring your vehicle.

You should get insurance valid wherever you are going, even if it's not required. Those who engage in activities as dangerous as driving have, I believe, a moral obligation to ensure that those whom they might injure will be provided for. If that doesn't move you, consider this: if you don't have insurance and are in a collision in many countries, you can be jailed until liability is determined and all claims are settled.

### Import Duties

A fair number of poor countries have decided that importing private cars is inappropriate and a waste of scarce foreign exchange. Either regarding a private car as inherently a luxury and deserving of being taxed as such, and/or trying to protect the development of an indigenous automobile manufacturing industry, they impose duties on imported cars. These duties may be as much as several times the value of the car.

Obviously, this is prohibitive for a tourist, especially one who wants to drive through a whole series of such countries, as one must do to cross Africa.

In theory, it is possible to pay the duty and to get it refunded after one can prove that one has taken the vehicle back out of the country ("re-exported" it). In practice, nobody in their right mind would pay thousands of dollars in duties to most of these governments and ever hope to see their money again.

### Carnets de Passage

The other way to avoid the automobile import duties is to have a *carnet de passage*. (It's a French term, but it's used worldwide, including in English-speaking countries.) A *carnet* is a sort of re-export performance bond: it's a document guaranteeing that you will pay the import duty if you fail to re-export the vehicle that you are bringing into the country. The point is to allow you to drive your vehicle *through* a country, while preventing you from evading the import duty by bringing a vehicle in as a tourist and then selling it or giving it away locally.

If you bring a vehicle in, then don't take it out again and don't pay the duty, the issuer of the *carnet* will pay the duty and collect it from you. If the issuer of the *carnet* has to pay duty for your vehicle, you are liable to them for the duty in addition to what you had to pay for the *carnet* in the first place. They can sue you, if necessary, to collect it from you.

Because few people take cars through countries that require a *carnet*, it can be quite hard to find someone to issue one. A bank or insurance company can issue them, but they are most often arranged through automobile organizations. You must get a *carnet* in advance; it isn't something you can arrange at the border.

Because a *carnet* is a financial commitment by the issuer, you have to pay something for it and provide your own guarantee to the issuer that you'll reimburse them if need be. Usually this means you have to post a bond or deposit equal to the possible duties, or buy a bond. If you post a deposit or bond, you can get it back when you've taken the vehicle out of any country that requires the *carnet* and have had the *carnet* canceled.

*Carnets* are most often needed for trans-African travel; most people planning to drive their own vehicles across Africa arrange for *carnets* in the UK or France before they leave for Africa. Insurance companies in the United States rarely are called upon to issue a *carnet de passage* and thus tend to be unfamiliar with the procedures.

Most countries in the Americas no longer require a *carnet* as long as you certify via specific paperwork that you are a tourist and will take your vehicle back out of the country when you leave. Even if they don't require a *carnet*, however, they can still charge you import duties if you fail to take the car back out of the country.

### Leaving Without Your Car

*Carnet* or no, it will be noted in your passport, visa, or other documents if you enter a country with a vehicle. Unless you leave the country with that vehicle, you are liable for duty.

If you sell the vehicle (most people who drive across Africa start from Europe and sell their vehicle in a distant part of Africa at the end of their trip, or when they decide to stop driving), make sure you have the purchaser pay the duty.

If the vehicle breaks down and has to be abandoned (common in the Sahara and elsewhere), or is stolen, or if you can't find a buyer for it at the end of your road and can't afford or find a way to ship or drive it back home, you are liable for duty for having imported it. This is a cost that can be hard to predict, and one more reason not to bring a vehicle. If you can't afford this risk, you can't afford to take your own vehicle abroad.

### Logistics

A surprising number of roads cross directly from the First World to the Third World, the outstanding examples being between the United States and Mexico. Or from the First World to the Second World, mainly between Western and Central Europe, through the former Iron Curtain. The ease of the crossing itself makes it all too easy to forget just how different things can be a short distance over a border. Learn as much as you can about the current conditions where you are going, and be prepared.

The Association for Safe International Road Travel (ASIRT), listed in the resource Guide, publishes country reports on local driving practices, peculiarities, and hazards in countries around the world. The largest number of Northerners driving their own vehicles into the South are those from the United States and Canada driving into Mexico; some of the best general advice on driving into the Third World is found in *The People's Guide to Mexico*. Fourth

World road trips, mainly across Africa, are the stuff of a whole sub-genre of travel books.

If you are bringing your own vehicle because suitable vehicles aren't available locally, that's a good indication that parts and repair services, maybe even fuel, won't be easy to find, either.

### Vehicle Types

Not all First World vehicles are suitable for extensive travel on rough or unpaved roads. It's one thing to drive a resilient American-model pickup truck to Mexico; it's quite another to drive a late-model subcompact car.

Most people planning extensive overland journeys in more remote areas, especially in the Second or Fourth World, start with a four-wheel-drive light truck or SUV and invest considerable time and money in modifications such as skid plates under the body; rock screens for the headlights, windshield, and perhaps other windows; extra fuel and water tanks; interior or secure rooftop luggage enclosures; enclosed sleeping accommodations; etc.

If you're buying a vehicle specifically for such a trip, it's worth considerable effort to find out what sort of suitable vehicle (if any) is in most common local use, and get one of that model. This will maximize your chance of finding parts and repairs, although parts for even the most common models may still be scarce and expensive. It would be foolish to buy a Range Rover for a trip through Mexico and Central America, for example, where American brands of pickup trucks and SUVs are the standard vehicles for those owning motor vehicles.

While you are at it, think about whether you'd be better off buying such a local vehicle on arrival, rather than trying to bring one with you. (See the next section.) Sometimes suitable vehicles, or ones that could be made suitable with locally available materials, are unlikely to be available, or are terribly overpriced because of import duties. In such cases, the only feasible way to have a vehicle may be to bring your own vehicle with you.

### Fuel

Try to get current information on what sort of motor fuel is most widely available: unleaded gasoline, leaded gasoline, diesel, or gasohol? Vehicles made for leaded gas require fuel additives if operated exclusively on unleaded gasoline. Gasohol (common only in Brazil) requires specially built or at least retuned engines.

Unleaded gasoline is entirely unavailable in some countries, while a single tank of leaded gasoline will irrevocably ruin the catalytic converter on any vehicle made for unleaded gasoline. You'll have to replace the catalytic converter if you ever want to operate the vehicle again in the USA, Canada, or another country with emission limits for vehicle licensing.

Diesel cars are uncommon in the United States, but common in many other places, including Western Europe. (Why? Diesel engines are more fuel-efficient than gasoline engines, but produce more of some types of air pollution. Government regulations in the United States have put a higher priority on low emissions than on high fuel efficiency. Some other countries have made the opposite choice, or don't have such regulations at all.) Don't put fuel in any motor vehicle, even a passenger car, without being sure if it needs gas or diesel.

There are diesel trucks even in places where there are no cars, so a diesel vehicle may be most versatile in the extreme back of beyond. But trucks have large fuel tanks, and a long range, so places to buy diesel can be spaced farther apart (especially in the back of beyond). If you are headed to such a place, you'll probably need to equip your vehicle with auxiliary fuel tanks.

Notice that I said "tanks," not "cans." Fuel is precious in the Third and Fourth Worlds, particularly in the back of beyond. Cans of gasoline (petrol) or diesel fastened to the exterior of your vehicle will swiftly be removed by thieves.

### Theft

Of course, your vehicle itself is vulnerable to thieves. Car theft, for example, is the most compelling reason not to drive a car from Western Europe into Central or Eastern Europe. Again, if you are bringing your own car because such cars are excessively expensive where you are going, that's strong evidence that cars such as yours will be prized by local thieves. Foreign makes and models of cars, foreign license plates and other insignia, and visibly foreign gear or accessories (not to mention foreign faces) all help to single you out as a target.

### Increased Costs

The kinds of vehicles favored by hard-core overland travelers with their own vehicles—Toyota Land Cruisers in Asia, large USA-brand SUV's or pickup trucks in Central and South America, Range Rovers and Land Rovers in Africa—tend to be the favorite vehicles of the highest levels of the local elite. Traveling in such a vehicle, you'll get plenty of attention—maybe more than you want. You'll be treated like a king, and you'll be charged a king's ransom for anything you need to buy along the way.

As a rule, outside the First World, people who arrive in a place by any sort of private car or truck will be charged more for everything, at least by people who see or hear about their vehicle, than people who arrive by any form of nonmotorized or public surface transportation. In the United States, where "everyone" has a car, it's easy to forget that in most of the world any sort of good or service related to automobiles—fuel, parts, repairs, towing out of mudholes—is, by definition, a luxury, and priced accordingly. Even elsewhere in the First World, such as in Western Europe and Japan, cars are often treated as a luxury, and things such as road tolls and parking are priced accordingly.

In places where officials and functionaries expect to supplement their income by fees, fines, or bribes, drivers are the first target. If you can afford a car, they think, you can obviously afford to share some of your great wealth with a soldier or village policeman whose life's dream may be to save enough to buy a bicycle. They may have a point, but that doesn't mean you'll be happy to pay them what they want.

### Buying a Car at Your Destination

By now you may have decided that I'm inflexibly anti-car. Not so. In a few countries, I'd even recommend buying a car. Buying a car locally may make sense for an extensive trip across a region where public transport is poor or nonexistent, but where foreign cars may be hard to repair or attract undue attention.

Another time to purchase a car is where a very high proportion of the local people have cars so there is no other effective mode of transportation. Be sure you are staying long enough for the cost savings of buying over renting to offset the much greater hassles of buying (and selling again when you leave). If you will be traveling away from places where there are hotels, especially if you are traveling with a small group of friends or family with a common itinerary, having a vehicle allows you to camp where the facilities and the climate permit it.

Where does this mean? Mostly, this means stays of at least a couple months in the United States, Canada, or Australia.

In Australia, in particular, some used-car dealers specialize in selling used cars to arriving travelers and buying them back at the ends of their trips. You have to watch out, of course, especially if you don't know a lot about cars or local conditions. Caveat emptor (let the buyer beware) is never so appropriate as when buying used cars. But at least these specialists are somewhat familiar with the special difficulties foreigners face in licensing, insurance, etc., and can offer at least some assistance, for a price, as well as a network of affiliates in other cities who will later buy back cars, suitably depreciated for wear and tear.

I know of no such specialists in the United States or Canada. Bureaucracies in the United States are set up with no consideration whatsoever for the needs of foreigners. If at all possible, get a local friend or acquaintance to assist you with the paperwork and formalities of purchase, registration, taxes, and insurance, or at least to refer you to their automobile insurance agent. If the agent values your friend's business, they may take more time to help you than would an agent who stood to sell you only a short-term policy.

Joining the American Automobile Association (AAA) may also be worthwhile. For the price of annual dues you get all the road maps you want; emergency road service and towing; helpful publications and advice on questions like insurance and international road travel; and hotel, campground, and sightseeing guides.

The AAA guidebooks are poor, but their campground guides are much better. That an organization for motorists publishes one of the most comprehensive sets of campground guides—they're better for most government campgrounds on public land than any publications from the government itself—is not surprising; most campgrounds in the United States can be reached only by private car. (Of course, AAA guides aren't the only privately published campground guides. Other campground guidebooks, such as those in the Foghorn Outdoors series also published by Avalon Travel, give more detail and list hike-in campgrounds not listed in the AAA guides.)

REAL LIFE

If you are intent on driving across Central or Eastern Europe, you'll probably get much farther, more easily, in a used car of local manufacture, than in a Western European car. Similarly, it may be better to buy a used car of a locally common variety on another continent than to have a foreign car shipped in by sea. Sure, a local car will break down more often. But it's much less likely to get stripped or stolen for parts, and when it breaks it'll be much easier to find a mechanic with the skills, tools, and parts to fix it.

One tow, or a complete set of maps of the United States and Canada, could cost you more than a year's AAA membership, currently priced at approximately US$50 per person. Unfortunately, the AAA uses a portion of each member's dues to support its lobbying in support of road-building and in opposition to railroads and mass transit. If you join the AAA, consider contributing an offsetting or larger amount to railroad or transit advocacy groups, such as the National Association of Railroad Passengers (900 2nd St. NE, Ste. 308, Washington, DC 20002, +1-202-408-8362, fax +1-202-408-8287, http://www.narprail.org, narp@narprail.org).

One alternative in the United States to buying or renting a car for a cross-country road trip is a "driveaway" company. These companies serve as intermediaries between car owners who are relocating long distances, but don't want to drive their own cars, and freelance drivers, often foreign tourists. The usual deal is that the owner (through the driveaway company), pays for insurance and sometimes gas, and the driver pays the rest of the expenses. As a driver, you don't get paid, but you get the equivalent of a free car rental with a specified allowable maximum of time and miles to get from where you pick the car up to where you deliver it.

In the United States, look for ads for these companies in hostels (a major source of their drivers), or under "auto transportation" in the phone book. Auto driveaway companies are a product of the peculiar transience and auto-dependence of life in the United States, however, and don't seem to exist on a large scale anywhere else.

### Choosing to Rent a Self-Drive Car

If you aren't in a country long enough to warrant buying and selling back a car, need a car in only some of the places you will visit, or don't want the time, work, or inconvenience of long-distance driving, it probably makes more sense to rent (hire) a car locally, where and when you need it.

**Western Europe and Japan:** It makes sense to rent a car in places with car-oriented transportation systems (if private cars can be called a "system") and poor public transit; good roads; readily available vehicle services; available and affordable parking (a strike against driving in Western Europe or Japan); free or low-toll roads (strike two); and affordable fuel prices (strike three).

Despite generally good roads and (unfortunately) increasingly automotive cultures, renting a car in Europe or Japan is rarely worth the expense and hassle, unless you have a carful of people traveling together, such as a family, and are experienced at driving in the region in question. Fortunately, good mass transit systems extend to even the rural parts of these regions.

**Australia and Aotearoa/New Zealand:** Both are reasonable places to rent cars, especially if you combine car rental with public transit for the longer legs in Australia. Don't underestimate the distances. If you are coming from the United States, be aware that Australian outback roads are mostly unpaved with an accompanying lack of roadside services and facilities; there is not yet a paved north-south or east-west highway across Australia. Driving across Australia is more like driving the Alaska Highway than like driving across the continental United States.

**North America:** Car rental is particularly likely to make sense on this car-crazy continent. It's possible to get around Miami or Los Angeles by public transit, but you'll spend as much time on buses as Lagos or Jakarta slum-dwellers spend commuting to their jobs. I hate cars and driving, but I'd get together a few fellow travelers to rent a car if I wanted to go sightseeing anywhere in the United States or Canada except the West Coast cities from San Francisco to Vancouver, and the largest and densest cities of the Northeast and Midwest (Chicago, New York, Boston, Philadelphia, Washington, Toronto, Montreal, and Québec).

Foreigners are, justifiably, afraid of the United States, and have probably heard of carjackings and murders of foreign tourists. These fears are to some extent well-founded: the United States is a violent country with an astonishingly heavily armed civilian population. Many ordinary-seeming Americans keep guns in their houses, cars, and offices, and carry concealed guns on their persons on public streets. All USA police carry guns; indeed, when I see guns being brandished on my street, they are usually in the hands of plainclothes police.

But fear of violence shouldn't be a reason not to rent a car in the United States. Because the upper and middle classes have abandoned public transit to the poor and the under-class, public buses (the only urban mass transit in most of the United States) may be even more dangerous than travel by rental car. Driving in most places in the United States is, as driving goes, extremely safe.

If anything, foreigners may be frustrated by how slowly and carefully North Americans (except Québecois) drive, especially by comparison with Europeans. That's not a slur against Québec, just a note that it has, in many respects including driving style, a distinctly European culture and way of life. If you drive at European autobahn speeds on USA Interstate highways you will quickly be arrested.

The most unpleasant surprise for foreign drivers in the United States is that not only are distances on road signs in English units (miles, yards, and feet) rather than metric, but USA road signs are in words only. English words. International-standard symbolic road signs are almost entirely unheard-of in the United States, greatly complicating life for non-English-speaking drivers. A profusion of peculiar abbreviations, unique to USA highway signage, makes the problem even worse.

Both the cause and effect of USA auto-mobility is that the danger of violence is largely confined to certain ghettoes of the urban, nonwhite poor. Wealthier people with cars simply never go near such areas, or whiz through on highways at 105 km/h (65 mph).

Your visit to the United States would be incomplete without a visit to such an area, but driving by yourself, especially in a conspicuously rented car, is an inappropriate way to do so. If you are going to explore a slum, do so with a local guide.

**South Africa:** With the continent's best roads, this is the only country in Africa where self-drive car hire makes any sense. Fuel isn't cheap, and there are other ways to get around. But renting a car gives you a chance that you won't get elsewhere in Africa to explore the countryside. Many of the scenic areas, particularly on the coast, are otherwise inaccessible except by hitchhiking. If you plan to drive into poor Black South African urban neighborhoods, bring a local guide, just as white peole driving into similar neighborhoods in US cities should. Anywhere else in Africa, if you hire a car, hire a driver too. (See the next section).

**Central and Eastern Europe:** Carjacking, car theft, vandalism, and assault or extortion of motorists are major reasons not to drive in Central or Eastern Europe. I'd hire a car and driver rather than driving myself. If you must drive yourself, find a company that will rent you a Lada, Moskvich, or other car of Soviet design and local manufacture, rather than a Mercedes, Fiat, or other Western make. Local cars often have higher clearance and are better suited for unpaved, bad, or ill-maintained roads; more importantly, they won't flag you nearly so much as a target for thieves.

### Costs of Renting a Self-Drive Car

When calculating the cost of renting a car, be sure that you consider the following costs:

- daily, weekly, or monthly rental fees

- additional per-mile or per-kilometer charges

- taxes: Value-added-tax (VAT) and other taxes may be 20 percent of the pre-tax price. Quoted prices usually do not include tax.

- insurance: Absolutely essential even if not legally required. Depending on the country, it can cost US$20–50/day or more. (The places where insurance is most expensive are the ones where it's most needed) USA minimum insurance requirements of US$200,000 to US$500,000 accurately reflect potential damage awards in that country in even nonfatal collisions.

- fuel: Gasoline can cost US$5/gallon or more in Western Europe or Japan; USA and Canadian gas prices are exceptionally low by world standards.

- road, bridge, and tunnel tolls: Japanese highway tolls often exceed train fares for similar distances; Western European road and bridge tolls are encountered more frequently, and are several times higher, than US tolls.

- parking: Especially in cities, finding parking can cost you time as well as money; once again, Western European and Japanese urban parking lots and garages often charge several times as much as their counterparts in even the densest US cities.

Make sure to get copies of all essential documents before you set off in a rented car. Don't leave them in the car when you aren't in it: keep them with you, with your most important papers, in your money belt at all times. Losing them could cost you thousands of dollars, especially if you have traveled across international borders, can't get back without proper papers, and have to pay for weeks of additional rental charges while proper replacement documentation is procured.

You'll need proof of the car's registration (licensing) with the proper governmental authorities, proof of ownership (title) by the rental company, proof of your permission to operate it (usually provided by the rental contract), and proof of insurance (sometimes in the rental contract, sometimes in a separate insurance contract and/or certificate).

Each person who will be driving a rented car must be listed on the rental and insurance contract, which usually means that all potential drivers must be personally present when the car is rented, and each must sign the contract. Don't ignore this rule. If an unauthorized driver gets in an accident, the renter who let that person drive could be liable not merely for damages (unprotected by insurance, which doesn't apply to unauthorized drivers) but also for breach of contract in allowing someone else to drive.

In addition to the general licensing and border-crossing requirements for privately owned vehicles discussed earlier, you'll need the permission of the car rental company (as the owner of the car) to take it across any international border.

### Crossing International Borders

It is imperative that the rental car contract explicitly give you permission to take the car into any country that you will pass through, no matter how briefly, and that the insurance policy explicitly cover operation of the car in each country.

If you plan to take a rented car across an international border, that should be the first thing you tell the car rental company or travel agent when you inquire about renting the car. Rates for international rentals may be much higher than domestic rates, and international rentals may be subject to very different rules.

For example, car rental companies generally allow their cars to be taken back and forth across the USA-Canadian border, although one-way transborder rentals may be prohibited or severely surcharged. But almost none will allow cars rented in the United States to be taken into Mexico, at any price.

Similarly, most car rentals in Western Europe have substantial surcharges, if not outright prohibitions, on travel into Central or Eastern Europe. Rental contracts in South Africa generally prohibit travel into any other country.

If there are restrictions like this, there's a reason, and you should think twice about what it might be. Are road conditions much worse or more dangerous across the border? Are repair services harder to find, or more expensive? Are cars (perhaps especially foreign cars) more likely to be stolen, vandalized, or stripped of easily removed but essential parts—like, say, wheels?

### Reasons to Hire a Car and Driver

In most of the Second, Third, and Fourth Worlds, it makes more sense to hire a chauffeured car rather than drive a car yourself. In many countries, it's the only way to hire a car, and if you ask to rent a car it will be assumed that you want to hire a driver as well.

This is a strange idea to many First Worlders. If you've never been in a chauffeured car other than a taxi, you might never even think of hiring one. Because this is actually the predominant form of car rental in most of the world, but seems so outlandish to those unfamiliar with it, a somewhat detailed explanation of its rationale is in order. "I know how to drive," you may be tempted to say. "Why would I want or need a chauffeur?" There are lots of reasons.

• *A Local Driver's Most Important Role May Be as Navigator.* They may already know the way, especially if yours is a nearby or a common destination. If not, they may be better able than you to read and interpret cryptic road signs, ask directions in local language(s) from passers-by, figure out which people are best to ask, and—perhaps most important—know how to interpret the directions they are given. They are more likely than you to know which routes are apt to be faster, less crowded, or more scenic, or which are apt to be impassable in the current season and weather.

In rich countries, there are detailed maps of even small streets and roads in less-traveled areas. In poor countries, there are usually fewer, less-detailed, and less-frequently updated maps—if you can find any maps at all. The best available maps may be the mental maps of local residents. A day's wages for a driver may be no more than you'd willingly pay in your home country for a good map.

In addition to navigating the roads, a local driver can navigate the local bureaucracy and deal with officials. Roadblocks, police and/or military check-points, and document checks are more common in countries other than in the First World. Private cars, being most rare (and thus most suspicious) are most likely to be stopped. A local driver is more likely than you to know the appropriate things to say and do in such situations, and to be able to maximize your chances of being allowed to proceed, without having to pay too much. In places where hijackers and extortionists often masquerade as officials, a driver is more likely than you to be able to recognize the real McCoy, and to know when it is best to stop, when and how much to pay, and when to drive on without stopping.

• **A Chauffeur Can Often Be Helpful as an Interpreter and Guide.** Presumably, you are driving around in a strange country because you want to experience it and learn about it. Why spend your time in a car in silence, or talking to yourself or fellow travelers, when you could spend it talking with a local informant? Even a chauffeur who doesn't speak a word of your language can point out things to look at, take you to places that you wouldn't have found or noticed on your own, or indicate places that you shouldn't go or things you shouldn't do.

A driver's less-carefully constructed presentation may give you a more accurate perspective on local opinion than that of a professional guide who is trained and paid to say what they think tourists want to hear. A driver gets paid to drive, no matter what they think or say, and taxi drivers the world over are rightly known for speaking their minds. Not for nothing are cabbies so often quoted by foreign journalists as the mouthpieces of local public opinion.

• **A Driver Buys Fuel and Arranges for Any Necessary Repairs or Services, Sparing You Much Work, Worry, and Responsibility.** In some countries (e.g., Russia) it is expected that professional drivers will also be professional mechanics, scroungers, and hoarders of scarce parts. Even in countries where "driver" and "mechanic" are distinct jobs, a local driver will probably be more knowledgeable than you at finding fuel, parts, and services, and knowing how much they ought to cost. And your driver may be able to take care of some of these tasks while you are sightseeing, so you don't have to waste your time on them.

If your self-drive car breaks down, you'll have to stay with it until it is fixed. With a driver to look after the vehicle, you can do other things while it is repaired, or settle your bill, abandon car and driver, and continue your travels without them.

Having a driver thus gives you, perhaps paradoxically, more freedom and flexibility. It's possible, for example (I've done it several times) to hire a car and driver for a one-way journey—provided you are willing to pay the cost for the driver to return without you—in many places where one-way self-drive car rental would be impossible.

• **Hiring a Driver Greatly Reduces Your Legal and Financial Liability.** Hiring a driver is thus, in a certain sense, the most effective and often the cheapest form of insurance. If you are driving a car, you are responsible for complying with all the local ownership, licensing, tax, and insurance requirements, and for having all the related paperwork in order.

In your own country, where you know the language and are familiar with the rules, this may be a straightforward task. In other countries, even your best efforts to comply with the law may be unsuccessful. If you are told that your vehicle's documents aren't in order, you may have no way of knowing whether or not you have actually committed a crime, or whether you are simply being shaken down for a bribe. Unfortunately, both inadvertent law-breaking and attempted extortion are common road hazards in most of the world—even if you are lucky enough never to be involved in a collision. You are far less vulnerable to fine, arrest, or extortion, whether for real or pretend violations, if you aren't driving.

If you are in a collision (assuming you survive unhurt), whether you are the driver can make all the difference in the world. In the United States, motor vehicle collisions are presumed to be accidents unless there is proof of negligence, drunkenness, or violation of the rules of the road. Hitting someone or something with a motor vehicle is not, per se, a crime.

In less automotive societies, where cars are a luxury, a nuisance, and a danger, people operating automobiles are responsible for any damage caused by their cars. Laws in many countries require fatal or injury car crashes to be treated like any other incidents of killing or wounding of people by other people. Suspects— that is, any surviving drivers—are automatically arrested on assault or murder charges. At the very least, you can expect to be held for questioning until the police have completed their investigation. You may be held until it is known if the injured people will survive or how extensive or permanent their injuries are. This could mean days, weeks, or months of incarceration, even if you are eventually acquitted. As a foreigner who is rich enough to afford a car, you are obviously likely to be motivated and able to flee, and thus are unlikely to be released on bail. This is no joke: I know more than one person who's been arrested in a foreign country for having been involved in a vehicle collision.

Drivers blamed for fatal crashes in some other countries are likely to be lynched, or at least severely beaten, by mobs of survivors, victims' families, and other passersby.

Passengers, on the other hand, are likely to have no liability, and (unless they are injured) little inconvenience in such cases. You may be delayed, even held briefly by the police for questioning, but if you aren't hurt it probably won't ruin your trip or delay you more than a few days, possibly not at all.

• **A Driver Will Look After the Vehicle When You Aren't in It.** You still can't be too cavalier about leaving valuables in a vehicle, or too unconcerned with where it is parked, but a driver is the best security for a vehicle and its contents that would otherwise be left unattended.

Security is the main reason hiring a car and driver can even be cheaper, as well as easier, than hiring a self-drive car. In a country where labor is cheap, it may be entirely reasonable for someone who hires out a car without an accompanying driver to charge more—on the basis of the justifiable expectation that renters on their own are more likely to get into costly trouble or to damage the car or allow it to be damaged.

Paying to protect a rented car shouldn't be an unusual concept. After all, we are accustomed to paying more per day for theft and vandalism insurance on a car rented in the First World than would equal the wages of a semi-skilled Third World worker. We are just accustomed to capital-intensive approaches to security—locks, alarms, garage doors—rather than labor-intensive ones like a full-time watchman, lookout, and vehicle guard. This is only one example of a much larger pattern of how things are done, and how people expect them to be done, in different worlds.

### How to Hire a Car and Driver

You can hire a car and driver by the hour, by the day, or for a specific journey. In places where chauffeurs' wages are very low and visitors rich enough to hire cars are relatively wealthy, the chauffeur's wages are usually included in prices quoted for the hire of a car. But it never hurts to ask.

The longer the journey or term of the rental, the more everything is negotiable. Be sure whether you will have exclusive use of the vehicle. If you charter a car to take you from point A to point B, there will typically be one price for a ride shared with as many other riders as the car's owner or driver can find, and a higher price to ride alone. Also settle whether you will be expected to pay for fuel (usually yes) and/or food and lodging for the driver (usually no) in addition to the agreed-upon price. Never get in any vehicle except a metered taxi without agreeing in advance on a precise price.

If need be, don't hesitate to tell the driver to slow down, or to drive more safely. You'll probably only be laughed at if you ask a reckless or speeding public bus driver to slow down, but if you've chartered the vehicle and hired the driver, you are perfectly entitled to insist that they satisfy your standards of safe driving. Don't assume that "they must know what they are doing" if you feel they are driving recklessly, or too fast.

"Self-sufficient" First Worlders think it a sign of incompetence to ask directions from people along the way. People in the rest of the world think it symptomatic of arrogant First Worlders' "superior" knowledge that they insist on following their map—even if ambiguous, potentially out of date, or simply wrong—when there are plenty of local people around who actually know exactly where local places are and would be happy to tell them if asked.

Drivers often make the assumption that you have chartered a car because you wanted to go faster than you could by bus. If this isn't the case, make that clear before you start. It can be hard to get across that you are willing to pay for the privilege of going more slowly, less directly, and stopping more often. If the driver doesn't speak your language, and you can communicate more easily through the person with whom you have arranged the rental, have that person explain this to the driver before you set off.

Private companies in Russia routinely offer bonuses to drivers if their foreign passengers don't complain about their speed or safety. Chartering a car on your own, you can take their example: if the driver knows they will be paid a few extra dollars at the end of the day if they don't exceed a certain speed, or simply if you are pleased with how they have driven, they will be much more willing to humor your desire to survive the ride.

Sometimes an archaeological, historical, or scenic site is accessible only by slow, painful, and unreliable buses, or a game park admits visitors only in enclosed motorized vehicles. If you can't afford to hire a vehicle on your own, a solution is to gather a group of travelers to share the rental of a car and driver for a few hours or days. At times like these "travelers' ghettos" come in handy: ask around at places where travelers hang out, or post notices on guesthouse bulletin boards. Put out the word that you'll give a small tip to anyone who finds you people to share a ride, and soon the word will be all over town.

### Motorized Two-and Three-Wheeled Vehicles
Most of the world's motorized vehicles are two-and three-wheeled: mopeds, scooters, and motorcycles. In the Third and even more the Fourth World, a

family bicycle is the mark of the middle class. A family Honda (the brand name has, almost everywhere, become a generic term for a motorized two-wheeler of any type, make, or model) is the mark of the elite. Three-wheelers are mostly used as taxis and cargo vehicles, not for private passenger use.

As with a car, you can bring such a vehicle with you, buy one locally, rent one, or even hire someone to drive you around on one. As with a car, each has its pitfalls. And two-wheelers have a few special dangers of their own, even aside from the intrinsically greater danger of riding them than riding in cars.

Licensing, registration, tax, and insurance requirements are fundamentally similar for two-wheelers and four-wheelers, although somewhat cheaper for two-wheelers. Not that much cheaper, though: even a moped, much less a four-stroke motorcycle, is still a great luxury in most of the world, and taxed and dutied as such. There's about the same amount of paperwork and bureaucracy regardless of the size or type of vehicle.

Transoceanic shipping charges are likewise not that much less for big motorcycles than for small cars. You can, however, sometimes bring a small motorbike or scooter in the baggage car of a passenger train. Some ships and ferries that won't carry cars will carry motorcycles.

Roads are a mixed bag. A car's higher wheels (especially compared to a small-wheeled scooter) can get through deeper mud and larger potholes. But many Third and Fourth World roads are too narrow for cars. And a motorbike is easier to carry or push through or over obstacles, or to carry on a raft or small boat across floods or waters that simply aren't bridged.

There's less reason to bring a motorbike with you (except perhaps if you want the largest of motorcycles) than to bring a car, since mopeds and scooters are in wider use in the South than the North. You're likely to find more types of mopeds and scooters available where you are going then at home. Vietnam takes the prize, with every conceivable variety of Russian, Chinese, Japanese, Indian, Western and Central European, and USA motorbike in use. Several large Southern countries, such as India, not only produce but export large numbers of motorized two-and three-wheelers. (You can even get Indian scooters in the United States, certified to meet California emissions limits!)

As with a locally purchased car, it's usually easiest to find parts and repairs for a locally purchased bike, especially a locally made one.

You are probably more likely to be tempted to rent a small moped or motor scooter than to bring, buy, or rent a big motorcycle. However, don't be lulled into complacency by the small size and weight, small engine, and relatively low speed of a moped or scooter. Even small motorbikes are much more dangerous than bicycles. Motorized two-wheeler crashes are the leading cause of death among Peace Corps workers, for example.

The legal requirements to own and/or operate any motorized vehicle are essentially the same, with the additional requirement that both your local and international driving licenses must be specially endorsed for motorcycles for them to be valid for any motorized two-wheeler. You probably wouldn't even think of renting a motorcycle unless you were an experienced rider already. But you might not realize that operating even a small scooter or moped legally requires, in most countries, both a regular license and a motorcycle endorsement. If you want to be able to rent a moped or scooter anywhere along the way, get a proper motorcycle license in your home country before you get your international driving permit. Even if you don't care about the law, do it for your own safety.

People who rent small scooters and mopeds to foreigners would lose most of their business if they rented only to riders with valid motorcycle licenses. So they don't check. But that doesn't mean the police won't check your license, either at routine roadblocks or traffic stops or if you're in any kind of crash. You can probably bribe your way out of a charge of riding without a license, but it could be expensive.

Outside the First World, I wouldn't ever drive more than a couple of miles at night, in any motor vehicle. The best book on Third World travel by car, Carl Franz's *The People's Guide to Mexico*, has this simple advice on night driving: "Don't." I'd say the same for riding motorbikes or buses at night.

Author Bill Dalton's comments in his *Moon Handbooks Indonesia* could be applied to anywhere in the Third or Fourth World:

"Indonesia is no place to learn to ride a motorcycle. Ride one with great caution as serious motorcycle accidents on Indonesia's madcap roads are common. Chickens, dogs, and children dart out unexpectedly into the road, there are giant potholes, big trucks lumber down the road straddling both lanes, and cars travel at night without using their headlights. Boulders, small rivers, and landslides on the road in the rainy season are other hazards.... You should possess at least a crude knowledge of motorcycle mechanics if you plan to rent a bike here. It's also advisable to bring a few simple tools."

It's all too easy to get in trouble on mopeds or scooters. We tend to think of them as just like bicycles: "child's play." But what is only a fender-bending crash in a car can leave a motorbike rider with scrapes, gashes, broken bones, and the possibility of serious infection from the wounds. Foreign travelers often use two-wheelers to get to remote or rural areas where medical treatment is a long way away. If you went by motorbike because cars can't get through (because the roads are too narrow or muddy, or the ferries or fords are too small to carry cars), getting back on the bike may be the only way out, no matter how badly you are hurt.

People who rent out motorbikes by the day in the Third or Fourth World don't usually even pretend to offer insurance. If you get hurt while operating a vehicle illegally, no insurance will cover you anyway. If someone else gets hurt, and you are operating your vehicle illegally (without a proper license) you will be presumptively at fault.

Keep a close eye on any motorbike, bought or rented, and always leave it securely locked and, if possible, guarded or watched. In rich countries, where there are more cars than motorbikes, thieves prefer cars. In a poor country, a stolen car is conspicuous and can be hard to sell or make use of. A stolen motorbike is easy to ride away, yet widely coveted. Even a small moped may still cost the average worker a couple of years' wages—enough to motivate thieves to pretty extreme measures. Don't count on collision or theft insurance for a rented motorbike. If you rent a bike, and it's stolen or destroyed in a crash, you'll have to buy the owner a new one. Find out before you rent one how much it will cost if it's stolen or wrecked. If you couldn't afford to pay for it if you had to, don't take the risk of renting it. Or rent something cheaper, like a nonmotorized bicycle.

### Which Side (of the Road) Are You On?

If you operate your own vehicle, of any sort, you may have to deal with doing so on the opposite side of the road. There is no world standard, but, at the risk of offending the British, I will say that the practice of the majority of the world is to ride and drive on the right-hand side of the road. For up-to-date country-by-country listings, see the article by Brian Lucas and other volunteer contributors at http://www.travel-library.com/general/driving/drive_which_side.html. (For more background on the issue than you probably want to know, see the definitive book, *The Rule of the Road,* by legal scholar and historian Peter Kincaid.)

Outside the First World, of course, roads are more often than not one lane or less wide, and any vehicle drives down the middle of the road. But when they pass, they keep to the right. They drive on the right in all of the Americas (except some former British colonies in the Caribbean and northern South America), continental Europe, northern and western Africa, Madagascar, and Asia north of the Himalayas except Japan and (as of 2003) Hong Kong. They drive on the left in the British Isles, South Asia, southern and most of eastern Africa, Australia, and Aotearoa/New Zealand.

Southeast Asia and Oceania are a complex patchwork. They drive on the right in Taiwan, the Philippines, Vietnam, Laos, Cambodia, and (rather strangely, given its history and neighbors) Myanmar/Burma. They drive on the left in Papua New Guinea, East Timor, Indonesia, Malaysia, Brunei, Singapore, and Thailand. The smaller Pacific Ocean island states and colonies are likewise a mix.

A long flight across time zones will leave you in no condition for your first attempt at driving on the left (or right) side of the road. I wouldn't think of doing so if I could possibly avoid it. You usually get a better rate on a rental car if you pick it up at an airport, but that needn't mean picking it up immediately on arrival. If you'll be driving on the opposite side for the first time, try to stay at the airport, or take public transportation to your hotel, and pick up your rental car later.

You won't usually find hostels or the cheapest accommodations near airports. But the price of a night's rest in an airport hotel is cheap compared to the potential cost—your life and those of the people in the other vehicles with which you may collide—of trying to learn to drive on the "wrong" side of the road while fresh off a plane, tired and jet lagged, dazed and confused.

If you really can't afford a hotel at the airport, you can probably still take public transportation to a cheap place to stay in the city and return to the airport the next day to rent a car. Yes, it's a hassle, and you'll be tempted to get the car right away. For safety's sake, please don't.

Sometimes you may feel you have no choice but to drive out of the aiport immediately upon your arrival. If you must get your first "wrong side drive" car when you are fresh off a long flight, go directly to the nearest affordable hotel and don't drive any farther until you have gotten a good night's sleep.

Your first experience of driving or riding on the opposite side of the road is not an easy situation. Use extreme caution. On a bicycle, go slowly and keep to the edge of the road. In a car, it can be harder to go more slowly than the rest of the traffic. Keep reminding yourself that your instinct in an emergency will be to swerve the wrong way, into the path of oncoming traffic. If you start to panic and don't know which path to follow through an intersection, which way to turn, or which lane to use, follow the vehicle in front of you. It is always better to take a wrong turn than to turn the wrong way down a one-way street, around a rotary/ roundabout/traffic circle, or onto a highway, and cause a head-on crash.

There are remarkably few roads across borders between left-and right-hand drive countries. Most of them are on extremely lightly traveled roads between central and eastern or southern Africa. You are unlikely ever to drive yourself across such a border. The busiest crossing is between Hong Kong and the rest of China, but it's mostly a crossing for local and professional drivers; few visitors drive themselves in China.

## Bicycles

Bicycles are the world's most common vehicles and most common form of mechanized transportation. With good reason: they are also the most energy-efficient form of human transportation now known, or likely to be developed in the foreseeable future. The whole point of a bicycle, after all, is to enable you to go farther, with more cargo, with less work, than you could on foot.

Bicycles are also the most environmentally friendly form of short-distance mechanized transportation. Except for protection against the weather, they are everything one could hope for. They produce very little chemical pollution, essentially only that required for their manufacture and occasional maintenance. And bicycles are essentially silent; the first thing most people used to notice on a city street in China, before motor vehicles began to dominate the traffic mix in the 1990's, was the absence of noise pollution.

Because bicycles make such efficient use of even narrow streets, they require very little land for roads. Bicycle roads also require smaller (or no) bridges and less elaborate engineering and construction of roads than for any other type of vehicle. We think of bicycles more as urban vehicles, but they are even more dominant in rural areas where there is little or no mass transportation and roads are little wider than paths. A family bicycle is the mechanical workhorse of the world's peasantry.

As the only land vehicle readily portaged by a single person, a bicycle can go almost anywhere a pedestrian can—only faster, and with less work. As for cargo, minimally modified bicycles or pedal tricycles can carry up to half a ton of cargo at jogging speed on smooth level pavement. Foreigners think of pedal tricycles as "bicycle rickshaws" for passengers, but local people use them more as light trucks for hire by the load. "In Bangladesh, trishaws . . . transport more tonnage than all motor vehicles combined," notes the Worldwatch Institute. In short, the bicycle is already the world's primary means of mechanized short-distance personal transportation and will be the primary medium-distance (between walking and trains) vehicle of any "green" or sustainable human future.

### Bicycling in All Weather

A bicycle rider is exposed to the weather, and I won't try to persuade you to emulate the millions of people who ride their bicycles through the heaviest snow-

storms in Beijing. But I will point out that in all but extreme
cold, exercise and a warm coat may keep you warmer on a
bicycle than riding the typical Third World unheated
but drafty bus. And it's difficult to imagine any circumstances in which bicycling could be less comfortable than some Fourth World buses, no matter
what the weather.

It's also worth noting, for those of you who
remain skeptical, that places far from the tropics, such as Copenhagen, Den-
mark, and Basel, Switzerland, have a year-round average of 20 percent of daily
passenger trips made by bicycle, with the figure climbing to as much as 50 percent in some Dutch cities.

In a hot climate, relaxed pedaling can create a pleasant breeze. I'm more
comfortable bicycling in the tropics than walking, especially if there's little or no
wind. If it's hot, rain can also be quite enjoyably cooling.

If it rains, you'll get wet, but so what? In tropical areas subject to heavy rain-
storms, it's better to dress for a soaking and enjoy the free shower if it happens,
rather than to make a futile attempt at dressing to stay dry that will only ensure
that you stay too hot. Any attempt to stay dry in a tropical downpour is futile,
no matter what means of transport you use.

### Bringing a Bicycle

As with cars and motorcycles, you can bring a bicycle with you, buy one locally,
or rent one. Given the cost and hassle of shipping a bike by air, and the greater
availability of parts for locally purchased models, bringing a bicycle from home
makes sense only if you'll be spending a long time in one place, or in a region
within which you won't need or want to travel much by air, but will still need to
cover as much distance as possible.

The main factor in the cost of bringing your bike with you by air is whether
your flights are governed by the "piece" or "weight" rule. (See the "Baggage"
chapter.)

Under the piece rule, you are allowed two pieces of luggage up to 27 kg (60
lb) each. Your bike will count as one of your two pieces, possibly subject to a
modest surcharge for being "oversize," as distinct from "overweight" or "excess."
You should be able to fit the rest of your stuff in your second piece of luggage.
No big problem, and no extra cost.

According to the weight rule, you are allowed a total of 20 kg (44 lb) for all
your luggage. A hard-core touring biker, with minimal survival gear, no camping equipment, and no clothes for anything but riding, might manage with 20
kg including the weight of their bike, but most people would find it a difficult
challenge. This also does not allow for the additional weight of spare parts or
specialized tools. Those are necessary items, and you can't count on finding
them in places where bikes like yours aren't common or available locally.

A snapshot I took in Shanghai shows a trishaw carrying two people and a full-size refrigerator. They went by faster than I could walk. None of the locals thought it an unusual sight. If they looked at anything, they looked at the electric refrigerator-freezer—a sign of considerable wealth—not the mode of its transport.

©Edward Hasbrouck

SURFACE TRANSPORTATION

If the bike and all your gear (including whatever clothes or other things you accumulate along the way) go over 20 kg on the weight rule, you're in for stiff fees for excess baggage. At one percent of the (unrestricted) first-class fare per excess kg (2.2 lb), these fees are apt to be prohibitive for intercontinental flights on the weight rule, or for more than one or two shorter flights.

Taking a bike from North America to Australia and back on the piece rule would cost little or nothing, while taking a bike even one-way between Europe and Australia, or on aseries of flights within Asia, Africa, or Latin America, might cost a large fortune.

If you plan to take many flights, it may make sense to take your bike only as far as you can on the piece rule, and then sell it, rather than trying to take it all the way around the world. The same principle applies for other heavy items such as surfboards, collapsible kayaks, or heavy camping or trekking gear.

Shipping such things home isn't usually much of an option. Unaccompanied air cargo costs even more than excess accompanied baggage—one reason for the use of air couriers to accompany express cargo on passenger flights. Sea-freight shipping is moderately expensive and an enormously time-consuming pain to arrange in most foreign countries.

Getting a bike through customs is generally no problem, except in places where *everyone* gets hassled at customs. If you are entering the country as a tourist, it's usually taken for granted that you will take the bike away with you when you leave. If you are considering or planning to sell the bike or give it way before leaving the country, don't say so. But be sure to take note of whether the bike is recorded in your customs declaration, or any other document you'll have to show when you leave the country. If it is, the game is up, and you'll probably have to pay some sort of duty or fee to leave the country without the bike.

As long as you say you intend to take the bike with you when you go, you'll rarely be charged duty or need a *carnet*, proof of ownership, or any documentation. Tourists are rarely forced to register their bikes with any government agency, even if bicycle registration requirements are strictly enforced on local people.

### Buying a Local Bike

Buying a bike locally makes sense if you're staying in one place for a while and are interested in local transportation rather than rapid cross-country touring. (Local bikes outside the First World are apt to be heavier and slower, but less and less so as the same bikes come to dominate the mid-range market worldwide, and as the quality of export-grade Chinese bikes improves.) Buying a bike may also be a good choice if you are traveling by train or bus through an area where, although bicycles are effective local transportation, bicycle rental is little-known and thus time-consuming to arrange in each town.

One way to look for a used bike is to ask around among shorter-term expatriate residents, such as teachers at language schools. Many buy new bicycles when they arrive, even for stays as short as a few months, and sell them when they leave. They may be able to help spread the word that you are looking for a used bike, suggest places you could post "wanted to buy" notices, advise you on how much to pay, or suggest bike dealers who speak your language and are accustomed to dealing with foreigners.

Don't count on getting much back, if anything at all, by selling your bike before you leave. Buyers will know you are leaving, can't take the bike with you, and have to take whatever you can get. Many foreigners simply give their bikes away when they move on, sometimes as a "tip" to someone who has been particularly helpful or generous to them during their stay.

### Renting a Bike

In the South, renting is usually the simplest way to get the use of a bicycle when you need one. If you are taking more than a few flights, and not staying more than a month in one place, renting will probably be cheaper than buying a bike or bringing one with you.

The ease of arranging to rent a bicycle varies enormously from place to place. In tourist centers in China and Vietnam, bikes are a standard means of transportation for foreign travelers as well as expatriates, and the rental of bikes to foreigners is a well-established trade. Elsewhere in Asia, except in the former USSR, bikes are common, and with a little effort you can always find someone willing to rent you a bike, even if there is no organized system of bicycle rental.

Bikes make perfect sense in smaller Second World cities, weather permitting. But Soviet people, like North Americans, are so infatuated with automobiles and so over-protective of foreigners that you may have trouble persuading them to let you travel by bicycle. It's certainly not the Intourist way to go. Fortunately, you may not need a bike in the cities. The Soviet Union had the world's best urban rail transportation systems, even in provincial cities. While streetcar and subway services in the former USSR have declined in the last decade, they are still superior to those in most other parts of the world.

# ALL IN A DAY'S RIDE

You never know just what will happen when you ask for a bike. Consider how it went for me in Ahmedabad, India (at the time the world's 52nd-largest city, population about 3.5 million—slightly more than Sydney, Australia). My traveling companion was sick in bed and wanted a room with a private, clean, flush toilet. So we stayed at a downtown hotel, more expensive than my norm. At 250 rupees (then about US$15) per night, it was insufficiently upscale for most foreigners, but a fairly high-class place by the standards of the domestic business travelers who seemed to make up most of its clientele.

When I told the desk clerk I wanted a bicycle, he first offered to arrange the hire of a car and driver for the day. This was a big city, he made clear, with roads wide enough for cars, where big-city services like cars for hire could be had. He took it for granted that no one would choose a bicycle if there were "better" options.

When I insisted I wanted a bicycle, he tried to hail a cycle rickshaw for me. Finally I got across that I wanted to pedal a bicycle myself.

Still trying to set me straight, he insisted that this just wouldn't do. As tactfully as possible, he warned me that pedaling a bicycle just wasn't appropriate for a sahib. He could have said, but didn't, that it violated the rules of the caste-like special status of a white person, and thus offended his sense of caste. He did say that I would be embarrassed and that people might mistake me for a commoner. He really felt that he was trying to help me, in my obvious ignorance, avoid an inadvertent faux pas and loss of face. Had I been traveling on business and trying to keep my face, I would have been grateful for his advice.

But it would have been impossible to get him to understand that I wanted to be able to talk to people that I met as an equal, not to have the conversation limited to, "Yes, sahib," "No, sahib," and "What you want, sahib?" I simply insisted that I wanted to pedal myself. Finally he gave up trying to dissuade me and gamely got to work getting me what I wanted.

He might have come to the conclusion that I was a crazy sahib, but I was still a sahib, and a rich one at that. As everywhere, rich lunatics are humored, and

Bicycles are a less-dominant transportation form in most countries in Africa and Central and South America than in Asia. People too poor to afford motorized transportation in these parts of the world are more likely to walk, except in a few countries—notably Cuba and Nicaragua—where central economic planners have decided to emphasize providing bicycles for the masses. That doesn't mean bikes are unknown—there are bicycles everywhere—but it does mean your request to rent a bike may be unusual. Most people will assume at first that you want a motorbike; be prepared to explain "no motor" and to pantomime pedaling.

SURFACE TRANSPORTATION

Indians, like most once-colonized peoples, have a long tradition of being forced to provide for the desire of rich white foreigners for bizarre-seeming styles of living. If I was willing to pay 250 rupees a night for a room, he was willing to do his best to accommodate my eccentricities. Just as, if you order a peanut-butter sandwiches from a US$250-a-night Ritz Hotel, the chefs will do their best, and the waiter will bring them with a smile.

The clerk summoned one of the hotel servants and gave him instructions in Gujarati. "You go with our man here," he said to me in English.

I followed him down a side street and through the maze of the bazaar to a bike shop I would never have found on my own, where he argued for a while with the man in charge. Neither the servant nor anyone in the shop spoke any English, but I assume that he was vouching for me on behalf of the hotel.

Presently I was shown a fine new bike and a sum to pay for the day (50 rupees, about US$3), asked to sign a chit (presumably acknowledging responsibility for the bike), and without having to hand over my passport or a deposit I was on my way. The hotel's man showed me the best way out of the bazaar before he left me, and the hotel never tried to charge me extra for their services.

It was a fine day full of experiences I wouldn't have had without the bike. I rode through the countryside to the museum and library at Gandhi's ashram, 6 km (4 miles) out of town, stopping to watch the bathing and laundry ghats by the river along the way. Returning, on the other side of the river, I kept stopping to watch the street life and shrines in a series of exceptionally diverse neighborhoods. My snapshots from that day include the roof lines, towers, and minarets of Muslim, Hindu, Sikh, Buddhist, Jain, and Parsi mosques, temples, and gurdwaras.

Few people paid me any special notice, or interrupted what they were doing to stare back at me. In local clothes, I was just another bicyclist. When I stopped to have a look at the exterior of one temple, however, I was noticed as a foreigner and good omen, invited in for tea (pressed upon me by a fasting acolyte), and not allowed to leave until I had joined them for the annual ritual blessing of the temple's financial account books.

Unfortunately, destination guidebooks tend to mention bicycle-rental services only in the few cities where many foreigners rent bikes, and where you'd have little trouble finding a bike to rent. They rarely include general information about bike rental rates or availability, or bicycling conditions, in their summaries of transportation options. You'll probably be on your own in finding a bike, or dependent on tips or help from local expatriates, other foreign travelers (if you see another foreigner on a bike, don't hesitate to stop her or him and inquire), or the staff of your hotel, hostel, or guest house.

Bike shops or people who rent bikes will usually demand some sort of deposit. Either they want cash equal to the replacement cost of the bike (i.e., the price of a new bike, even if you are renting an old one), typically US$50–200. Or they want your passport or some other essential document without which you wouldn't be able or willing to abscond if anything happens to the bike.

If the bike is wrecked or stolen while under your care, you're responsible. Unconditionally. Never mind that you don't consider yourself at fault for the wreck, or that you were careful to lock the bike. That won't repay the former owner, nor will it get her or him another bike. Nor is anyone in a poor country likely to have theft or accident insurance.

Get the damaged bike restored to as good condition as it was when you rented or borrowed it, or better. Or buy another bike, as good or better. Don't try to scrimp, even if it costs US$200 for a proper replacement. The value of the bike—perhaps someone's life's savings—means more to its owner than the money does to you. This is one more reason to rent a bicycle rather than a motorbike, as the cost of even the smallest motorbike can be much higher than that of the best bicycle.

Try to avoid having to leave a cash deposit. Having so much cash in hand creates a great temptation for even the most honest poor person to find some way—such as inventing or exaggerating a claim of damage to the bike—to hold onto some of it when you bring the bike back. If you have so much money for a deposit, you obviously can afford to lose a small part of it. Given a choice, I'd rather leave my passport than cash. But the best solution is to leave some other document that is less essential, but sufficiently official and important-looking to be acceptable as security. An International Driving Permit, printed in nine or more languages with your photograph and official-looking seals, fills the bill well. In fact, I've used my IDP more often as security for renting bicycles and other things than for actually driving motor vehicles. Airline frequent-flyer cards embossed with your name and identification number—easily mistaken for some sort of credit card—sometimes work as well. Be creative: I've sometimes used a library card.

The best place to start looking for a bike to rent is wherever you are staying. Renting a bike from, or arranging the rental through, the place you are staying usually obviates any need for a deposit. After all, they have your luggage as security for the safe return of the bike. Point this out if your hotel, hostel, guesthouse, or whatever asks for a deposit.

Some guesthouses and hostels keep bikes for the use of their guests, sometimes including bicycle usage in the services provided for the basic nightly or weekly room rate. In destinations where renting a bike can cost as much as a night's stay, it's worth searching out such a place to stay. Others add a small charge to their bill for bicycle use. Still others may loan or rent their personal bike, or that of one of their employees, relatives, friends, or neighbors.

Ask, "Do you have a bicycle I can use today? Do you know where I can find one?" There's a good chance you won't be charged anything if you don't mention "renting" or "hiring" a bike. If you aren't charged, give a tip when you return the bike, or when you leave. Try to give the tip to the person who actually loaned the bike, particularly if it wasn't the proprietor of the hotel.

If you do have to pay, rates in Southern cities vary from 50 cents to US$5 per day, depending on the place and the bicycle. Ask other travelers on bicycles what they have paid, or ask disinterested local people how much you should have to pay. You can bargain, as always, but if you push too hard for the cheapest price you're likely to get stuck with a lemon of a bike and come back the next day willing to pay the original asking price for a better one. Rates are usually specified by the day, but you can sometimes rent a bike for half a day, and you can usually negotiate a substantial discount for longer-term rentals.

### Choosing a Bike

In more bicycle-friendly places, you'll be offered several types for rent. Three-fourths of the world's bicycles, listed here in order of production volume, are made in China, Taiwan, Japan, the United States, the former USSR, and India. All these countries export bikes.

I've worked as a professional bicyclist for courier services in Boston and San Francisco, and I've ridden every common type of foreign bike while traveling. Japanese, Western European, and USA bikes are of high quality but so expensive as to be rare in the South. If you want one, bring it with you. Former Soviet bikes are typically the only choice in the Second World, but rare elsewhere. In most Third and Fourth World countries, the choice is between a more expensive Chinese export-grade or Taiwanese low-end lightweight multispeed mountain or road bike, or a cheaper Chinese domestic-style, Indian, or comparable locally-made heavy one-speed "cruiser."

Lightweight 10-speeds may seem more modern, but all else being equal, I'd choose heavy one-speeds. One-speeds are more versatile, more resistant to damage, and more easily repaired. They are more suitably equipped (wide low-pressure tires and padded spring seat for bad roads and trails, cargo rack and/or basket, etc.), and for most riders more comfortable, stable, and easy to ride. Their weight, for example, makes them track better over ruts and bumps. They are slower, but speed isn't usually the highest priority.

You may think of mountain bikes as best suited to mud, but on a wet or unpaved road you'll stay much cleaner and drier on a bike with mudguards and an enclosed chain, both rare on mountain or road touring models.

Never rent a bike without a lock. Never leave it unless it's locked. If there is a guarded parking area, use it, both for security and because parking a bicycle elsewhere may not be allowed. Watch where and how other people park their bikes, and be considerate of other users of the roads and sidewalks when you park a bike. In Asian cities, you can be ticketed and fined for parking a bike in a prohibited area, or obstructing passage.

All Chinese and most Indian and Russian one-speed bikes come with integral frame-mounted wheel locks. To lock one, push down the lever to bring a pair of steel fingers together through the spokes, preventing the wheel from turning. To unlock it, turn the key and a spring pulls the fingers out of the spokes and secures the key in the lock. You can't lose the key while you are riding, and you can't remove it unless the lock is locked. It doesn't look that secure, but I've never heard of anyone having their bike stolen while it was locked with one.

Some people prefer Chinese to Indian bikes, or vice versa, but between similar models the condition of the individual bike makes more difference than the manufacturer. Inspect a bicycle closely before you rent it. The first priority is working brakes. (The performance of caliper brakes can often be improved greatly by a quick adjustment to take the excess slack out of the cables, and by oiling the pivots, if oil is available.) The second is main bearings—headset, hubs, cranks, and pedals—that don't stick. The third is a working lock. In addition, there's no point renting a multispeed bike if it doesn't shift easily.

You can't count on finding a well-fitting frame, but at least check the seat and handlebar height, and insist that they be adjusted to fit you as well as possible. Don't be hasty. Check for broken spokes, cable housings, cables, other broken parts, or cables that are frayed close to the breaking point. Tighten any loose nuts and bolts. Pump up the tires. Not too far—they may be tires designed for a lower pressure than those to which you are accustomed, and you may want somewhat less pressure on bumpier roads than on smooth pavement.

Ride the bike up and down for a hundred meters (yards). Listen for unusual sounds, especially of anything rubbing against the tires. Swerve back and forth. Try a few panic stops. Lock the bike. Remove the key. (Sometimes a lock opens and closes but is useless because the key sticks and can't be removed.) Put the key back in and open the lock. If you're not satisfied with anything, ask to look at another bike, or to have better adjustments and lubrication done.

### Getting Around by Bike

If you plan on bicycling during your travels, and you don't already bicycle regularly in conditions similar to those where you are going, practice before you go. Try both to get in physical shape for riding (and walking) and to learn how to ride in heavy mixed city traffic and on unpaved paths.

Good practice for riding rented bikes in, or on excursions from, Southern cities would be to find or borrow a one-speed "clunker" and try riding it downtown in the nearest big city and on some mountain-bike trails or old dirt roads in the woods.

Don't be too intimidated by city traffic. Most of the danger to bikes in traffic comes from cars, and the more bikes there are the fewer cars there are likely to be. If you can bicycle through suburban USA strip-mall developments, where traffic is heavy and fast and the roads are planned with nil concern for bicycles, you can handle bicycling anywhere.

It surprises inexperienced riders to find that the most crowded USA cities—thought of as having the worst traffic—are actually the best USA cities for bicycling. Distances aren't large, and the traffic slows the cars down to a safe bicycling pace (or slower). City drivers, especially in the most traffic-choked downtown areas that depend on bicycle messengers for urgent deliveries, are more accustomed to bicycles and know to watch for them on the streets. Washington DC, seems as though it were designed for bicyclists. New York City (especially Manhattan) may be the next-best USA city for bicycling. Boston, San Francisco, and Seattle are pretty good as well. Bicycle-rental services, catering increasingly to foreign tourists, are springing up rapidly in all these cities.

In the South, day trips by bicycle are an excellent way to see the countryside while staying in the city. In the United States, we are accustomed to sprawling automotive cities where it takes at least an hour of driving, at 100 km/h (60 mph), to get beyond the city and its residential suburbs. Land use patterns are denser and different in poor cities where most people and goods move by nonmotorized means. Start in the center of a Southern city of a few million people, and a half day of bicycling may take you into villages of farms and market-gardens supplying produce to the city.

Bicycling makes you seem accessible. Other good ice-breakers include: squatting on your heels while eating, conversing, waiting, or resting (people who can't afford chairs and tables are accustomed to squatting and to using the floor or ground as their work surface); joining in pick-up football (soccer) games or other sports; flying a kite (you can get very small backpackers' parafoil kites without any sticks); washing and mending clothes (I save my sewing for trains, planes, and waiting rooms); playing with infants or children; and sharing food, especially foods known to be scorned by foreigners and/or the privileged (sometimes the best local food is looked down on by the local elite).

One of the greatest advantages of riding a bicycle is that it brings you closer to local people. "Most people in the Third World will never sit inside—let alone own—an automobile," according to the Worldwatch Institute. Most people honestly have no idea what they might have in common with someone who rides around in a car. Even when you have stopped, and gotten out of the car, it's hard to escape from being seen as an alien being from the foreign world of the automobile. Sure, some local people ride in cars—politicians, police, landlords, and the like. Friends of the peasantry or the slum-dwellers don't ride in cars, even if they could afford to, for exactly the same reasons I'm advising you not to if there's another way to get where you are going. Sightseeing by car introduces a major barrier to communication with ordinary people.

Riding a bicycle isn't enough for you to pass as a local. But it brings you into contact with local people while engaged in, or at least identified with (if they see you arriving by bike) an activity to which they can relate. It's amazing how much difference this can make. On a bicycle, you become a participant in things that you could only observe as external scenes from a car. On a bicycle, you will be perceived as a fellow human being before you're perceived as a foreigner or a tourist.

### Transporting Bikes on Trains, Buses, and Boats

It's possible to take a bicycle, at minimal cost, on almost any other means of surface transportation, including buses, trains, and boats. Procedures vary with the place and the conveyance; you'll have to ask and/or watch what other cyclists do.

In addition to checking my bike as airline luggage, I've been poled across a river in a canoe while holding my bicycle upright (with half a dozen other people and sundry animals), taken it on subways and long-distance trains, and seen hundreds of bikes tied on the roofs of long-distance buses in diverse countries.

Urban rail systems—subways, elevated trains, streetcars, and commuter trains—have erratic rules and procedures for bicycles, and some try to prohibit them entirely. No matter what the rules, a foreign tourist can usually get let off with only a lecture, once, by being apologetic and pleading ignorance.

On long-distance trains, bikes are almost always carried in the baggage car. Sometimes you ride your own bike up to the car and put it in yourself, or hand it over at trackside when the train arrives. In other places (including the United States), you have to check it in at the baggage office in advance. On arrival, you claim your bike the same way you checked it in.

You don't generally have to break your bike down or box it to take it on trains, but you should take all your panniers and gear off before you check it. You may not be allowed to lock it, as the baggage handlers need to be able to wheel it on the platform.

On ferries, you can usually just ride on and be directed to where to put your bike. On car ferries bikes are sometimes carried with the other vehicles and sometimes on the passenger deck. Securing your bike with bungee cords and even a bit of padding on each side (e.g., a couple of large scraps of cardboard) can help keep it from getting too badly scraped if a bunch of bikes are stacked in a heap, as they often are, or the crossing is rough. You can't usually stay within sight of your bike, so lock it and take everything portable away from it with you.

Whether you can take a bike on an intercity or long-distance bus depends on the bus, and where luggage is stored. On streamlined high-speed buses, such as those in the United States, luggage is stored in enclosed compartments below the passenger space. Cargo space is limited, and bikes are carried fully boxed, if at all, and with difficulty at best.

Most Third World and almost all Fourth World buses lack cargo holds. Luggage is piled and tied on to the roof. Passengers ride on the roof, too, often sitting on the luggage. On buses like these, you are welcome to put your bike on the roof. It's up to you, though, to carry it up the ladder to the roof and tie it on. Secure it well against the jolts from rocks, bumps, and potholes taken at too high a speed: pad it as best you can, and try to load it last, so it will be on the top of the pile. And keep a close eye on it whenever the bus stops and especially when other luggage is being loaded or unloaded.

Urban buses don't generally like to take bikes. But that's not a problem, because if you have a bike you don't generally need local buses.

### If Your Bike Breaks Down

If your bike breaks down, you may (with a fair amount of grumbling) be allowed to bring it on, or tie it on the roof of a bus. But you may be better off locking up the broken-down bike and going for help, tools, or parts by bus, or taking the bike away in a taxi or trishaw. I've seen a surprising number of bicycles being carried by trishaw, sometimes half a dozen or more at a time.

In a poor country, a bike mechanic may well be willing, for a minimal surcharge, to come back with you to where you locked up your broken bike. A bike mechanic in a poor country probably doesn't have an elaborate workshop, or too many tools to carry, anyway. In poor countries where bikes are common, you'll find bike mechanics and tire patchers everywhere, so you won't have far to look. In some countries, when you get a flat tire, you can be accosted by rival tire patchers before you've even figured out why your bike has come to a stop.

## Buses

Buses, of diverse sorts, are the most widespread form of public transportation. They are always dangerous, usually uncomfortable, often slow, sometimes an ordeal, and only rarely appropriate where there's any other mass transit choice. But in their many forms they go more places than any other form of mass transit.

As a general rule, the worse the transportation infrastructure is in a country, the greater difference it will make to your comfort to avoid long bus rides. Trains can be pretty bad, but they are almost never as bad as the worst buses. Use buses only where there's no other choice. If you can go partway by train, do so; take a bus only beyond the railhead.

## Conditions on Buses

Australia, the United States, and Canada differ from all other First World countries in being overwhelmingly larger in area and less densely populated. These are the only places in the First World where you are likely to take really long-distance buses. In these countries, there are many places where the only alternatives to buses are private cars or airplanes, either of which are much more expensive. This does mean that buses are regarded as the vehicles of the poor, especially in the United States, and bus services are often less frequent in the United States than between Third World cities of comparable size where few people have cars and more people ride the buses. But long-distance buses are reasonably comfortable (air-conditioned, with toilets, cushioned reclining seats, individual reading lights, overhead racks for carry-on luggage, etc.) and roads good, although even main highways in the Australian outback and the Canadian far north are sometimes unpaved.

Outside the First World, it's another story. You hear tales of bus rides from hell at any gathering of people who've traveled in the Third or Fourth Worlds. Second World buses can be as bad, but Second World trains are so good that bus travel is rarely necessary.

Some buses are the other extreme, which can be deceptive. It's easy to be fooled by high-class buses—if you forget about the roads. Ultra-deluxe *ejecutivo* buses in Mexico, or sleeper buses in Argentina, look far more more luxurious than Greyhound buses in the United States or Canada. First-class buses in many cheap-labor countries have onboard attendants to bring you hot towels and serve you meals (inlcuded in the ticket price) at your seat.

So where's the rub? The limiting factor in the comfort and safety of road travel is as likely to be the quality of the road itself as the condition of the vehicle. A ride on a truly bad road can be torture for the passengers (and, for that matter, the driver), even on the best of buses.

Your first long bus ride in the South can be a shock. I don't want to exaggerate—a bus ride isn't an expedition. Many things that look intolerable aren't. But you should do what you can to find out what you're in for, and prepare for it.

## Reservations

It amazes me how often people who insist on knowing what type of aircraft is usually used on a particular flight before they make reservations, and on reserving their preferred seats on planes in advance, will buy bus tickets without checking out the equipment and without asking for pre-assigned seats.

Variations in equipment, and in the comfort of different seats, are much greater on buses than planes. Because you are often on buses for longer than the longest flight, and since they are less comfortable than airplanes in the first place, it's much more important to choose your bus and seat carefully than to worry about which type of plane or which seat you have when you fly.

Don't buy a bus ticket from an agent without first looking at the company's buses. I always try to go down to the bus yard to check things out before I buy my ticket. There often are several companies and/or different types of buses operating between the same places, or other possible ways of getting there if the buses look intolerable. Southern buses are cheap and uncomfortable enough that I usually take first-class buses when there's a choice, even though I often take second-class trains and fly third class.

For people in the United States who haven't traveled outside the First World and want to know what to expect of buses elsewhere, start by thinking about a standard USA school bus. Lots of decommissioned USA school buses are, in fact, sold South and used as public buses in Mexico and Central America. Other Third and Fourth World buses are often similar, although generally a bit smaller overall, with harder seats and the addition of a rooftop luggage rack and a ladder welded onto the back to reach it. No, the seats aren't moved any farther apart for carrying adults than for carrying children in the United States, and there are often more adults on each seat. Many bus bodies are locally built onto truck chassis.

Unless you are really desperate, and can't wait for a better seat on the next bus, never take a seat behind the rear wheels. (Remember bouncing up and down in the back of the school bus?) Try to get a seat as far forward as possible. The farther forward your seat, the smoother the ride. The seats in the front row (behind or next to the driver and conductor) are the best because they are the least affected by road bumps and have the best view.

If tickets aren't sold in advance or seats aren't pre-assigned for a long bus trip, that's a tip-off that most people aren't taking the bus very far (and thus that it's a local bus that stops a great many times), that there are going to be more passengers than seats, and/or that all the seats, such as they are, will be equally excruciating. Be very suspicious of long-distance buses with open seating. Do yourself a favor and take a more expensive bus with reserved seats, if there is one.

If you care, check if videos will be shown on the bus. It gets harder and harder to find a "luxury" bus without a VCR or DVD player. If you haven't experienced a video bus before, and don't know if you'll like it, bring an eyeshade and earplugs (not a bad idea on any bus anyway).

### Bus Schedules and Routes

Outside the First World, I've rarely found much use for bus schedules or route maps. Bus routes, unlike railroads, can change overnight. Some buses don't even follow fixed routes. If buses are well-used, and thus frequent, there's little need for a schedule. If you want a schedule to know when a bus will run, that's generally because there is little traffic and buses are infrequent. But bus services under such conditions are unreliable anyway, prone to be suspended or changed, and may operate only "on demand," meaning they depart only when and if there is a full (overflowing) load of passengers and/or cargo.

Even a "schedule" may not be precise. If local people say, "There will be a bus here tomorrow," that may well mean —as it has in some places I've been—that you are expected to be waiting by the side of the road at dawn for a bus that may pass by any time between then and dusk—and quite possibly won't stop unless the driver sees you waving.

Guidebooks are even less use. If a guidebook says, "A bus leaves A for B every Tuesday and Thursday," that's a fair indication that it will be possible for you to get from A to B by bus, probably at least once a week. But you certainly shouldn't turn up in A on Monday, counting on there being a bus the next day. Nor should you blame the guidebook writer if there isn't.

One of the most useless things to say to anyone is, "But it says here in this guidebook that . . ." The outsider who argues with reality, on the basis of a book, will be interpreted only as stupid, closed-minded, unwilling to learn, and/or contemptuous of local people.

### Trip Duration

Try to find out in advance how long the bus trip normally takes. In most of the United States, "It's about 60 miles [100 km]" and "It's about an hour" are used as synonyms. It's assumed that one travels by car, that distance is measured along a highway, and that distance is converted into time, and vice versa, at or close to the highway speed limit (currently 65 mph in most states, equivalent to 105 km/h). This equivalence becomes deeply ingrained and unconscious, causing people from the United States automatically to underestimate the time required for road trips in other countries with less elaborately engineered highways.

Thirty km/h (20 mph) is good time for a bus on level dirt, exclusive of meal and rest stops and other delays. Speeds can be much slower on sand, mud, or hills, or where buses are underpowered and/or overloaded. In mountainous terrain, I've been on a 24-hour express through bus that averaged 25 km/h (15 mph) on smooth traffic-free pavement wide enough for other buses or trucks to pass.

So it's common for a trip across a country that looks small on the map to take several days by bus. For example, it takes more than 72 hours on the road (plus any stops) to go the approximately 1,500-km (930-mile) length of the trans-Sumatra highway in Indonesia. It's at least 36 hours by bus between Delhi and Kathmandu, even now that the road has been paved.

### Night Buses

Some buses travel straight through, day and night, or are scheduled to travel only at night. Because traffic is lighter at night, it is possible (albeit suicidal) to drive faster at night. If the road is smooth enough, and the bus comfortable enough, you can sometimes sleep. In hot climates, it cools down at least a little at night. Night buses, where they exist, are thus often the most luxuriously equipped "premium" choice, recommended by everyone including guidebook writers who ought to know better.

For safety's sake, avoid night buses and any other night road travel. There are all kinds of obstacles and hazards on Third and Fourth World roads: pedestrians, bicycles, herds of livestock, carts, and broken-down vehicles. They are as likely to be squarely in the middle of the road as to either side. Most of the roads and the vehicles are poorly lit, if at all. Poor countries can't afford elaborate markings of blind curves, hazards, potholes, rock slides and the like. Roads typically lack any shoulders or guardrails. Both collisions and single-vehicle accidents are far more common at night. If you must make a multiday journey by bus, try to find a bus that stops at night.

### Packing for Bus Trips

You need to pack with more care for a trip by bus than for one by plane. Unless you've seen that the bus has interior luggage compartments, assume that your luggage will be tied on the roof, exposed to the elements. Pack your bag to withstand having heavy boxes piled on top of it or people sitting on it.

If it might rain, pack everything you want to stay dry in waterproof bags. If you don't have one already, consider getting a nondescript canvas or lightweight cloth bag sewn to cover and protect your pack from dust, dirt, and scrapes. Even air travelers in many countries routinely sew cloth covers over their suitcases, or have them wrapped in multiple layers of plastic (harder to do yourself without special tools and materials), as added protection against damage and pilferage.

Unless your pack is extremely small, and you are prepared to hold it on your lap the whole way, what to carry onto a bus is a dilemma. No matter how long the trip lasts —even several days—you can't count on being able to get luggage down from the roof anywhere en route. You have to carry on everything you'll need for the ride and any night halts. On the other hand, you can't expect to have any room to put luggage inside the bus anywhere but in your lap, so you don't want to carry on any more than is essential. Organize your carry-on bag before you board: once you are on, you may be so crowded you can barely move.

### Facilities Along the Way

Provisions for meals and night halts vary. On luxury buses, attendants may bring boxed meals and drinks to your seat. Alternatively, road-house meals and beds for the night at intermediate stops may be included in the price of the bus ticket.

Ordinary buses stop periodically at places where some sort of meal (generally overpriced and from a limited menu) is available at your own expense. If you don't speak the language, just follow the lead of the other passengers when the bus stops.

You can't count on finding anything particularly edible at bus stops, so it's wise to bring your own food if you can, enough to get you through the entire trip if necessary. For a price, most hotels or guesthouses will pack box meals for you, if you ask a day in advance. At the very least bring plenty of water and some snacks.

Keep a close eye on when other passengers get back on the bus, but don't worry too much about being left behind as long as you stay in sight. As a foreigner, you're probably pretty conspicuous, and people will probably notice and yell or beckon if you're not back on the bus when it's ready to leave.

Very few buses in the South have toilets. Toilets at bus stops around the world are frequently among the filthiest of public toilets. As always, bring your own toilet paper.

Don't be surprised if a bus stops in the middle of nowhere for people to answer the call of nature. You can always ask the driver to stop—pantomiming the urgency of your need will help, and will usually be understood—but you'll have to be prepared to do your business in full view of everyone on the bus. In open country, when everyone on the bus gets off to relieve themselves, the usual custom is for men to go off on one side of the road and women on the other, pretending not to see each other.

## Other Public Road Transportation

### Long-Distance Taxis

Intercity or other long-distance shared taxis are a convenient alternative to buses. These often operate on fixed routes from a central taxi stand. If it's not far out of the way, they will usually drop you at the door of your destination before going to the taxi stand to pick up return riders. There is usually a standard price and number of passengers for a given route. A taxi leaves when there are enough passengers to fill it. If you want to leave sooner, or have the taxi to yourself, you can pay for any empty places and it will leave right away. If you don't want to pay extra, but no one else gets into the taxi with you, make sure there isn't a misunderstanding, and that you aren't going to be charged for chartering the entire vehicle.

Shared taxis are typically about twice the price of buses, often worth it for the extra comfort. A full carload starting for the same destination won't have to stop, so a bus trip that would take six to eight hours on a local bus, with frequent stops, may take only four hours by taxi. Unfortunately, taxi drivers often feel they are being paid extra for speed (in a sense they are, because the faster they go the more runs they can make in a day) and drive in an accordingly more dangerous fashion.

### Tourist Minibuses

In areas with lots of tourists, travel agencies and tour companies have been offering more and more private intercity minibus and van services specifically for foreigners. These seem attractive because tickets are sold by agents who speak foreign languages and have offices at or near tourist hotels—you don't have to go down to the bus station—and they usually leave from tourist hotel districts, or even pick passengers up at their hotels. They go straight from one tourist center to the next. They are air-conditioned. Sometimes they are cleaner and more comfortable than local buses. But they are much more expensive than local buses or even shared taxis. They ensure that your traveling companions will be other foreigners, not local people with whom you might pass the journey in conversation. And minibuses and vans—top-heavy and poorly protected in a crash—are the most dangerous of four-wheeled vehicles. I take these only as a last resort.

### City Buses

Bus travel within cities takes many forms, with two main flavors: full-size buses (again, visualize the vintage USA school bus), often run by public entities, and a plethora of private, often informal and unlicensed, smaller vehicles. Public buses are often easier to find and more likely to be marked with their route and/or destination. Private buses are much harder to deal with, especially if you don't speak the language of the bus conductors, but they are often faster, more frequent, and more direct. Outside the First World, all buses have both a driver and a conductor.

Private and informal bus lines make use of every conceivable sort of light vehicle: vans, open or closed large and small pickup trucks with benches or seats in the bed, jeeps, and custom bodies built on car or truck chassis. They go by an equal diversity of names: wagons, jeepneys, jitneys, matatus, bemos, tempos, etc., or often just the name of the make or model of vehicle locally used for the purpose, such as Suzukis or Colts.

Informal buses often have fixed routes but no fixed stops. You have to watch other passengers to see how they signal when they want to get off. In some places you shout to the conductor or driver. In others, such as when you're in the back of a closed truck out of their sight, you may need to stamp—hard—on the truck floor to get the driver's attention.

You can expect local buses of any sort to be cramped and hideously overcrowded. Getting a backpack on and off a bus can be a real challenge. Before you board, try to arrange your valuables and hold your luggage so that it will be difficult for pickpockets to take anything important, as you may not be able to move to stop them.

### Local Taxis

All sorts of vehicles are used as local taxis, from cars to motorized three-wheelers to pedal tricycles. The cardinal rule is to agree on a price and

make sure the driver understands where you want to go before you get in.

The most dangerous form of public transportation is the motorcycle taxi. This is just what it sounds like: you pay someone to carry you behind her or him on a motorcycle or moped. Don't try to carry too much luggage this way. This mode of travel is encountered in rural areas where roads are unfit for four-wheeled vehicles and in crowded cities without rail systems where it is the fastest way through gridlock. Motorcycle taxis in Bangkok, for example, charge as much as taxis, and are the fastest way to get across town. But it's more speed with less comfort and more danger.

### Beasts of Burden

Animal-drawn carts are still used for local public transportation in more remote places. I've been in a city of half a million people where the public buses were pulled by ponies and the taxis were chartered donkey carts. If you ride, you can rent horses in rural parts of the South for much less than they cost in the North, because much of the cost of maintaining animals is the cost of human labor to care for them. Likewise trekkers who don't want to carry all their own gear, or who want to have provisions for a longer stay in an area without villages, stores, or provisions, may be able to afford pack animals (mules, llamas, yaks, etc.) or porters that they couldn't afford at home. Human-pulled carts (rickshaws) are generally regarded as degrading to the rickshaw-pullers and an obsolete relic of colonialism, but are still encountered in some places.

### Hitchhiking

You might think that where there's a road, there's a bus. There's a certain truth to that, but it's not entirely so. You can't count on a bus to come along if you wait by just any road. If you need to get somewhere, and haven't been told by local people to expect a bus on a particular day, be prepared to ask for a ride from any vehicle that passes. Beggars can't be choosers. You may be crowded into an open truck full of livestock (one of my favorite snapshots is of some other riders wrestling with a truckload of goats trying to clear enough space to unload their bicycles) or expected to sit on top of other passengers or piles of cargo (a loose pile of coal, say) or on the roof of a truck's cab or bus. The poorer the place, the more likely you are to have to hitch rides with whomever passes, even on vehicles not designed for passengers.

Ask local people how you should signal to passing vehicles that you want a ride. In some places, all vehicles stop for anyone standing by the road. In Russia, you hold your arm out at a downward angle, palm down, with your fingers extended and waving as though beckoning passing traffic in toward you at the roadside. In North America, you either hold up a sign with your destination (or the big city nearest it) or you extend your arm with your fingers curled in and your thumb pointed up. Don't try this anywhere else unless you see others doing it: in many places this, and similar gestures (such as pointing or beckoning with a single extended finger), have obscene, rude, or insulting connotations. In a new place, it's safest not to point at all and to beckon Asian-style, with your fingers together, palm down. People everywhere will understand, even if they think you a little strange, and this gesture rarely gives the sort of offense that finger-up gestures often do.

### Paying for Rides

Outside the First World, riders are expected to pay. Agreeing to pay is implicit in soliciting a ride. If you accept a ride, you are morally and maybe legally obligated to pay the customary price for the ride. Most often this is what the fare would be for the same or a comparable trip by bus or shared taxi, although sometimes riders in private cars are expected to be willing to pay more for a faster, more comfortable ride than in a bus.

North Americans, accustomed to the presumption that people who stop for hitchhikers are offering free rides, unless they say otherwise, may feel uncomfortable initiating negotiations about prices with passing drivers (who, if they decide they don't like you, can always just drive off without you). But if you say nothing, you are agreeing to pay and will be assumed to know how much is normally expected from riders on that route.

### Trucks

In some locations there are no purely passenger vehicles, only trucks. In the Congo (Zaire) and Amazon River basins, Borneo, and New Guinea, for example, only the mining and logging companies are making enough money to afford to build roads. They build them no better than is necessary for their lumber and ore trucks, and they often have such deep ruts and mudholes as to make them impassable to smaller vehicles. Hitchhikers in such places are expected to be willing to pay for their rides on trucks.

Rides on trucks aren't necessarily cheaper for being less comfortable. As Geoff Crowther points out in *Africa on a Shoestring*, "The price of lifts often reflects the difficulty of getting there rather than the distance." In such places, you can count on nothing by way of accommodations at night. Mud, landslides, and the like can close a road for a week at a time, and there may be no other way around. You need to be pretty self-sufficiently equipped and prepared for delays. Once you start out into the bush by bus or truck, you are committed. There may be no way to turn back for days or weeks.

Most travelers never get this far off the beaten track, and don't really want to. Of course, there's a silver lining: cross a region like this on the ground, and you can impress people for years with your stories.

## Walking

In most places where you could take a bus, you could also walk, provided that water and places for lodging or camping are available at adequate intervals. Few people choose to walk across continents, of course, or even countries. But you could, if you have enough time and money and are physically up to it.

In some ways, it seems faddish that so many people include treks from village to village in Nepal and so few ever walk through the countryside or villages anywhere else, even in the Himalayas. Certainly there is more infrastructure for trekking in Nepal, but that doesn't mean it's not possible, or even that it's difficult, to arrange elsewhere.

But most people have other priorities. They don't want to work that hard, don't have enough time, don't have enough money, or prefer to travel more quickly through some regions in order to linger longer in others. Walking creates a unique immersion in a place, but it also enforces its own pace.

Walking to get from one place to another, rather than on sightseeing or recreational excursions, is actually most common to bridge small gaps in motorized transportation routes. But where there isn't a road, there's usually a reason, and you can't expect walking to be easy.

For example, there is no road, railroad, or ferry service between North and South America. A stretch of hilly, roadless jungle in southern Panama breaks the continuity of the Pan-American Highway. Foot travel might seem an obvious means across, and in some sense it is. But possible doesn't always mean practical, much less a good choice.

It is possible to trek across the Darien Gap between North and South America, particularly if you are in good physical condition, well equipped but only very lightly burdened, and can afford to hire a guide. But most people choose other routes and means once they realize what this overland trip entails, and how arduous it is likely to be. Every one of my clients who set out to cross the Darien Gap by land and/or water has changed his or her mind and turned back or decided to fly.

On the other hand, in many cases where there aren't through international trains or buses, it is nonetheless possible to take a train or bus to one side of the border, walk across, and catch another train or bus on the other side. I think I've crossed almost as many international borders on foot as by any other means except flying. Stepping from one country to the next, on my own two feet, gives me a satisfying feeling of accomplishment.

At such places there are often porters, bicyclists, or motorcyclists willing, for a price, to carry your luggage across the no-man's-land between the borders. At crossings with only light traffic you may have no choice but to carry all your belongings on your back. This is when you'll be most glad to have kept your luggage light and easily carried. I've encountered border posts and train or bus stations anywhere from 50 meters (50 yards) apart to 5 kilometers (3 miles).

You can expect to do a lot of walking, even if you plan no trekking. Most of the physical work ("exercise") of long-term budget travel is in walking around cities and towns, either seeing the sights, getting logistical things done, or getting to and from motorized transportation (often on the way to or from hotels or places where you are staying, and therefore often carrying all your luggage with you).

Try to be in the best physical condition for walking that you can be in before you leave, and try to get regular (or if need be irregular) exercise while traveling even when you are in situations where you don't have to do a lot of walking. You'll be glad you're in shape when you arrive in an interesting but sprawling town without a good bus system, or when you discover that the sight you came to see is a 3 km (2 mile) walk up a trail fit for only foot traffic. Every day in San Francisco, I see tourists whose visits have been ruined by their lack of preparedness for extensive walking on the city's hills.

# WATER TRANSPORTATION

If you have enough time, if the price is right, and if the ship is sufficiently comfortable and safe, most people would rather take a ship than fly. So why don't more people do it?

Sad to say, water transportation is less of an option than many people think or hope, particularly across oceans and other long distances. Long-distance water travel requires either good luck or careful planning and research to know what will be possible. Some things that look easy are impossible, yet there are other possibilities that have probably never occurred to you.

## Cruise Ships

Cruising may be an enjoyable vacation experience. But cruise ships aren't intended as pure transportation and aren't an affordable means of transportation for independent travelers.

Cruise ships do go around the world. Typically, these cruises last three to four months with minimum prices (per person, double occupancy, sharing one of the worst cabins) ranging from US$25,000 to US$50,000. If you don't have that much time or money it's possible to meet most of these ships for just part of one of their routes around the world. But you're still looking at a minimum of US$200–400 per day.

Around-the-world cruises schedule at most a day in each port, except perhaps for a couple of two-or three-day dockings for passengers to take added-cost excursions to inland points (e.g., two days in Mumbai so people can fly to Agra and back to see the Taj Mahal, three days in Mombasa so people can drive to a game preserve).

If you like cruising, like the route one of these ships will take, and have the money, one of these cruises may be for you. Plenty of people think so. These cruises are popular and generally are fully booked months in advance. There are more cruises around the world than escorted tours around the world by air.

Cruises are not for independent travelers. The appeal of cruises is precisely that everything is decided and arranged in advance—the ultimate package holiday. You know many months ahead exactly where you will be each day. You dine with the same fellow travelers every day. You sleep in the same bed in the same cabin every night. You have to pack and unpack only once, at the start and end of the cruise. You never have to arrange anything on your own with local people.

Whether this is your idea of a good time, much less of active, independent, or experiential travel, is probably irrelevant. Most around-the-world travelers simply don't have that much money to spend, and wouldn't choose to spend it that way if they did.

Even if you have the money and want to do it, the chances that there will be a cruise ship going where you want to go, when you want to go, are slim. And the chances that you'll be able and willing to commit to the cruise ship's schedule for that leg of your trip, months in advance, are probably even smaller.

I'm not a cruiser, as you might have guessed. If you want to do this sort of thing, you need expert advice. Imagine choosing your hotel room, months in advance, sight unseen, and committing yourself to stay there for three months. Plan far in advance; see a travel agent who specializes in cruises and really knows the ships.

## Freighters

Some transoceanic cargo ships have cabins for a few passengers in addition to those for their crew. Those that carry paying passengers generally provide a high standard of comfort, accommodations, and food, although not, of course, the diversity of entertainment that you'd find on a cruise ship.

Travel on cargo ships has advantages over cruising. Freighters spend more time in each port to load and unload cargo and tend to visit less touristed, although, of course, bigger, busier, and more industrial ports than cruise ships.

The market for long-distance freighter travel is mainly among retired or independently wealthy people with lots of time and ample means: people who could choose a cruise around the world, but who prefer a more personal and contemplative shipboard experience.

Unfortunately, the total passenger capacity of freighters is tiny compared to that of the world's cruise ship fleets. Cargo ships charge less than cruise ships, but they aren't cheap: almost none charge less than US$75–100 per person per day. Even at that, they are often fully booked many months in advance.

You have to make an advance commitment, but the shipping line doesn't. As a supernumerary, you are at the ship's mercy. A scheduled sailing can be canceled, advanced, delayed, or its ports of departure and arrival changed, at any time including while at sea, all without explanation or obligation to you. If you aren't willing to accept these conditions, shipping lines don't want you as a passenger. They can find plenty of other, more flexible, people to fill their cabins many times over.

The chances of finding a freighter willing to take you across the ocean, with space available when you want to go, are poor unless you can plan your dates long in advance. And your chances of finding all this for a price competitive with flying, even if you plan far ahead, are essentially nil.

If you want to take a freighter for one leg of a long trip, it probably makes the most sense to do so for your first transoceanic leg, because it's usually easier to fix the date of your initial departure than of any intermediate stages or your return. In this niche, demand far exceeds supply. You'll need to plan and commit yourself longer in advance than for almost any other form of common-carrier transportation. Several agencies, Web sites, and newsletters for passenger travel on cargo ships are listed in the Resource Guide. They can give you an idea of what's possible, on what routes, and at what prices.

As for "working your way" as a member of a ship's crew, forget it unless you already have seamen's papers to prove your qualifications and experience. Unskilled crewmembers are not hired on working oceangoing ships.

## Yachts

Hitching rides on yachts is sometimes possible but not to be relied on. Your chances are best if you have sailing experience (credentials, letters of reference, or names to drop will improve your chances) and have contacts in the yachting community to give you leads on times and places to look for rides.

To find rides, ask yachting friends where to look. If you are already at your intended port of departure, go down to the harbor and ask yachties or the harbormaster, "If you were looking for crew, where would you advertise? Who would you talk to?" Ask the staff and hangers-around and look for bulletin boards at yacht marinas, harbormasters' offices, and businesses serving yachts and yachties. Ask yachties what publications carry "crew wanted" ads.

Don't expect to find rides right away. Budget for the possibility that finding a ride may take a month or more even if you are qualified and know where to look, and that you may not find a yacht at all and may have to fly.

Crewmembers on pleasure yachts are expected to share in the work and the running expenses. Work out an explicit understanding, in advance, of what is and will be expected of you.

Space on yachts is always cramped; privacy ranges from limited to nonexistent. Personality conflicts are the bane of yachting. Take time to get to know everyone who will be traveling with you before you commit yourself to living with them for weeks in the middle of an ocean in a space smaller than a studio apartment.

A short shakedown and get-acquainted cruise will give you a chance to judge the ship's condition, the skipper's competence (and vice versa), and familiarize yourself with the people and routine on board. A ship at sea, even a yacht, is a paramilitary dictatorship, not a democracy. If you aren't ready to trust the skipper completely and take orders without question, don't go.

Even in this best of circumstances, be prepared to have potential rides fall through. The skipper changes plans at the last minute, the boat needs work, another member of the crew falls in love, falls out of love, doesn't show up, or decides to leave. Yachts are an incestuous little world, and anything can happen. Yachting isn't for people with a fixed agenda, itinerary, or schedule. As with cruising, the point is the experience and way of life more than the destination.

About the only people who can readily find rides on yachts, without boating experience, are young women (and sometimes men) willing to provide sexual services to yachtsmen in exchange for passage. Thinly veiled "female traveling companion wanted" ads abound in the classified pages and on bulletin boards. Similar ads for male companions show up regularly in the gay press. Expectations of sex aren't always explicit until you're at sea. If there's a shadow of doubt in your mind, ask point-blank before you sail if you're being taken along for sex.

## Seagoing Ferries

There are ferries across every significant channel, strait, sea, and narrows in Europe and the Mediterranean, although perhaps not as many trans-Mediterranean ferries as one might expect. European ferry services are so highly developed—in safety, speed, convenience, and comfort—that despite the completion of the English Channel tunnel far more people still go across the channel on ferries than go under it on trains through the Chunnel. Whether or not they actually carry rail cars (many do), European ferries are extremely well coordinated with the railroads. Ferries between railheads are timed to connect with trains, and many honor Eurailpasses.

In other parts of the world, it's hard to tell where you'll find ferries operating, or to get good information about prices, schedules, or services.

Japan, the world's richest archipelago, has invested extraordinary amounts of money and engineering skill in bridges and tunnels that obviate the need for ferries between any of the major islands. Excellent public ferries continue to operate, however, and provide the only alternative to air travel to the smaller islands of the Ryukyu chain in the south. Several international ferries operate between Japan and neighboring countries: Russia, South Korea, China, and Taiwan. It should be noted, however, that the cheapest and most-used of these, between Shimonoseki, Japan, and Pusan, South Korea, is something of a dead-end as a way out of Japan to anywhere else. South Korea has no open land borders and no international ferries to anywhere except back to Japan.

Indonesia and the Philippines are the most extensive and (along with Japan) most populous archipelagic nations. They also possess the world's most extensive interisland ferry services. Some of the ships are in terrible condition, uncomfortable, overloaded, and dangerous. Others are safe, modern, and comfortable, with air-conditioning, staterooms with private baths, and restaurant-quality dining rooms. These are some of the best chances you'll ever have anywhere for affordable ocean voyages.

It's typical of the disparity everywhere between domestic (common) and international (not) ferry services that there are no ferries *between* Indonesia and the Philippines, or Malaysia and the Philippines. There are ferries between Malaysia, Batam Island (Singapore), and Indonesia. But the international ferries to Indonesia land in Sumatra or the Riau Islands. It's a long tedious journey between any of these ports and the population and tourist centers of Java or Bali.

Most populated offshore islands—even in countries where water transportation is generally poor, such as the United States—have ferry service to somewhere on the mainland. Multi-island countries may or may not be linked by ferries, depending on how wealthy and how far apart the islands are. There are ferries between the Australian mainland and Tasmania, between the North and South Islands of Aotearoa/New Zealand, and between West Malaysia (on the Malay Peninsula) and East Malaysia (on Borneo), for example. But there are no ferries between Australia and Aotearoa/New Zealand (flights aren't cheap, either), and no ferries link many poorer, more spread out Pacific island nations.

Good destination-specific guidebooks for low-budget independent travelers are the best source of information on domestic ferry services. Many reliable and well-established domestic ferry services are omitted from the Thomas Cook timetables. If service, comfort, or amenities are anything less than international-class, the national tourist board or guidebooks for up-market travelers may gloss over, or not even mention, ships and ferries. Moon Handbooks, Footprint Handbooks, Rough Guides, and Lonely Planet all make a particular effort to give information on public water transport, but no guidebook can have complete or up-to-date information.

Routes operated by sizable ships, once established, don't suddenly change without strong reason (such as that the ship breaks down or sinks). As a rule of thumb, I wouldn't plan a trip, without a backup plan, that depends on a ferry or shipping service so new that it hasn't made it into a guidebook yet. If a guidebook says that service on a route is "uncertain," "erratic," "endangered," or the like, heed the warning. If it was on its last legs when the book was researched, it may well be gone by now. Have a more reliable alternative worked out in case it is. Don't just assume that you will fly if there is no ferry. If the reasons for the absence of ferry service are political, there may be no flights either. You may have to backtrack for hundreds of kilometers to get a flight, and a short flight on an obscure route flown by only a single airline can cost as much as a discounted flight across a large ocean between major air hubs.

International ocean ferry services are much less common than domestic ones.

Oddly, their very rarity makes them conspicuous by their mere existence. Most of them are listed in the relevant sections of the Thomas Cook timetables (see the Resource Guide).

Unless I had a recent printed timetable, schedule, or brochure from the shipping company in hand, or had spoken directly with someone who had personally traveled on (not merely heard of) the ship in question within the last few months, I would evaluate with great skepticism rumors of international passenger shipping services not listed in the Thomas Cook timetables. Abandoned and unmaintained Web sites can linger for years, so a Web site describing a ferry service can't be relied on unless you are *sure* it is both authoritative and up to date.

In particular, there are persistent false rumors—seen most recently on the Internet—of ships carrying passengers between Australia and Indonesia (don't get me wrong: this would be a good thing, and may someday happen, but it hasn't yet) and between South and Southeast Asia (there apparently once was a ferry from Penang to Chennai (Madras), but no such service has operated for many years). There are less frequent rumors of ships between India and eastern or southern Africa (Mumbai-Dar Es Salaam-Durban or the like). As of 2003 there was no truth to any of these rumors. You have to fly or get lucky and get a ride on a yacht (unlikely, as discussed above) to travel between these places.

The Greater and Lesser Antilles islands of the Caribbean Sea appear to form an almost-continuous chain between North and South America. This is among the most popular cruise routes, and some islands make most of their money from cruise ships' port calls. One might expect to find a passenger ferry, plying the same through route, more cheaply, for island-hopping local traffic. Alas, there are no through ferries around the Antilles, and not even local ferries between many of the adjacent islands. The flights between these islands cost more than direct flights across the Caribbean between Miami and Caracas or other cites on the north coast of South America.

## Coastal Ships and Ferries

Coastal shipping or ferry services along the edges of, rather than across, bodies of water have become rare. The usual reason for their existence is that the coastline is either too steep or too swampy for a road or railroad; in the former case they are invariably highly scenic. Some of the outstanding remaining ones are along the Norwegian coast, between Hong Kong and Shanghai, and in northwest North America.

The ferries along the coast of Norway are somewhat cheaper than a cruise, but still too expensive for most people on a budget.

The least scenic of the routes listed here is along the coast of China between Hong Kong and Shanghai. Although it's no cheaper than a train, it's an interesting and novel experience all the same.

The Washington State Ferries (http://www.wsdot.wa.gov/ferries), British

Columbia Ferries (http://www.bcferries.bc.ca), and Alaska Marine Highway [actually ferry] System (http://akmhs.com) all have extensive routes connecting offshore islands and mainland ports in the Pacific Northwest, British Columbia, and southeast Alaska. The longest through journey is on the Alaska Marine Highway, from Bellingham, Washington, through the Inside Passage to Skagway and Haines, the southernmost roadheads in Alaska. The 1,700-km (1,050-mile) trip takes four to five days if you don't stop over at any of the half-dozen intermediate ports. These public ferries carry automobiles as well as passengers, and they cost a fraction of the price—even for a private stateroom—of any of the cruise ships that follow the same spectacular route.

There are few passenger ships along most of the coast of Chile, the most obvious place in the world to expect to find them. The longest stretch with regular passenger ferry service is from Puerto Montt to Puerto Natales. That's just over 1000 km (600 miles), and a great 3–4 day journey, but still only a small fraction of the 5000 km (3000 mile) length of Chile.

## Lake and River Boats

River travel has declined less than ocean travel. It remains the dominant mode of inland transportation along most of the great rivers outside the First World. You can ride riverboats for long distances along the Nile, the Congo (Zaire) and some of its tributaries, sometimes the Niger, the Yangtze (pending completion of the Three Gorges Dam), the Yellow (Huang), the Irawaddy, the Paraná, throughout Amazonia, and from coastal ports into the interiors of Borneo and New Guinea.

Water transport is the obvious mode of travel in river deltas. There are excellent ferry services, for example, in the Pearl River Delta between Hong Kong, Macau, and Guangzhou (Canton), and the River Platte estuary between Argentina and Uruguay. Virtually everywhere in Bangladesh lies in the Ganges-Brahmaputra Delta, and there are many riverboats. There are trains in Bangladesh, but trips by train are apt to be interrupted by ferry crossings, washouts, or floods, so you might as well take a boat in the first place. Strangely, there are few long-distance passenger riverboats in most other South Asian countries. Most tourists drive through the Mekong Delta in Vietnam, but boats are available and give a better feel for the region.

There are ferries on all of the world's inland seas and great lakes. The one major exception is the Aral Sea, from whose tributaries so much water has been diverted for irrigation that it has shrunk to half its original size, leaving vast flats of blowing salt. There are a few in the sparsely populated northern parts of Canada. There are also public passenger ferries on Lake Titicaca, the lakes of the east African rift valley, and on the Great Lakes of North America. (The Great Lakes once had the world's largest car ferry fleet. One major ship still operates across Lake Michigan—see http://www.ssbadger.com—in addition to others to various Great Lakes islands.)

Third and Fourth World riverboats and lake steamers vary enormously. You may find yourself in a luxurious cabin on an aging colonial steamship, in a village of huts on top of a barge, or in an open canoe with an outboard motor. As with trains or buses, try to get a look at the vessel, or at least talk to people who've been on it, before you book your passage.

Water transport—more energy efficient and, perhaps more importantly, requiring less investment than roads—was favored by Second World economic planners and remains well developed throughout the former USSR. There are both slower large ships and smaller fast hydrofoils on the Volga, Dnieper, Amur, and Angara, among other rivers. There is a ferry across the Caspian Sea between Baku and Krasnovodsk. Long, narrow, enclosed hydrofoils with aircraft-style cabins and seating go the 650-km (400-mile) length of Lake Baikal in 12 hours. (Earplugs are recommended for the trip.) Many other countries use Soviet hydrofoils for their fast ferries.

First World river transport, where available, is generally more expensive than trains or buses. There are ferries on most rivers in Europe, although more of them are designed for sightseeing than for transportation. Except for a few Mississippi River cruises (at typical cruise prices) and a few short sightseeing rides, there are almost no river boat services in North America.

## Folding Kayaks

I debated whether to head this section "Portable Boats" or "Folding Kayaks." In the end, I decided it didn't matter, because folding (also known as "collapsible") kayaks are the only seaworthy portable boats. Sure, an inflatable raft is portable. But what can you do with it? A folding kayak, on the other hand, is the most seaworthy of all small boats. Its structure just happens to be such that you can take it anywhere—on the plane, on a train, on a bus, in a car, or maybe even on a bicycle.

Assembled, a folding kayak consists of a framework of wood, aluminum, fiberglass, or composite ribs and stringers (longerons), covered with a skin of rubberized fabric, vinyl, or plastic.

Disassembled, it consists of a big folded piece of heavy fabric and a bunch of rib and strut pieces and fittings. It can all all be portaged in one or two duffel bags that look like they might hold an old-fashioned canvas tent. It takes 10–45 minutes, depending on the model and your practice, to put one together or take it apart.

Folding kayaks have the same basic skin-and-bones structure, with lighter and stronger materials, as the original kayaks used for hunting, fishing, and transportation in the harshest conditions of the open Arctic. Folding kayaks have been sailed across the Atlantic, paddled around Cape Horn, and are regularly used by wilderness explorers, expeditions, and military commandos. Whitewater paddling races in the Olympics used to be exclusively for folding kayaks.

I say all this only to dispel the false image of fragility often created by the term "folding kayak." It's actually impossible for one to "fold" in the water, and unlike rigid kayaks they flex when stressed rather than cracking in half.

Lighweight single (one-person) folding sea kayaks weigh 14–18 kg (31–40 lb). Double (two-person) folding kayaks weigh 30–40 kg (66–88 lb). If you pack carefully, you can fit a single or half a double, and the rest of your gear, within the two pieces of luggage allowed on flights to and from North America. On flights subject to the 20-kg limit, the boat alone will use up your free baggage allotment. If you're bringing anything else at all, you'll have to pay for excess baggage.

Sale prices for new folding sea kayaks made in the United States or Western Europe start at about US$1,500 for a single and US$2,000 for a double. My partner and I got our first one used, for free, from a friend—to whom we will always be grateful—who hadn't used it in years. Even the more expensive makes and models are surprisingly cheap when you consider what they can do and how long they last. Ours is more than 30 years old and still going strong.

Soviet and Eastern European folding kayaks are cheaper. Most of those now being exported were originally designed for military use and, like other Second World products built to "milspec" quality-control standards, offer excellent value for the money compared with First World goods. If you don't already have a folding kayak, or are interested in getting another, and are thinking of paddling in the Second World, consider buying a local kayak, using it on your trip, and bringing it home when you return.

Imagine a boat that can be flown in with you by the smallest bush plane, or carried by pack animal, to the most remote lake or river. A boat that you can take anywhere there's a train, bus, or taxi (they'll fit in the trunk of most cars). A stable, seaworthy, capacious boat you can use for paddling, sailing, sightseeing, nature-and birdwatching (kayaks are wonderful in shallow wetlands), camping (a two-person folding kayak can carry as much gear as a full-sized canoe, easily enough for a week's camping trip), snorkeling, diving, and fishing. For pictures and descriptions of the cheapest and most popular USA-built models, see http://www.folbot.com.

Still, a folding kayak is a sizable investment, and transporting it isn't trivial. Carrying one, and your regular pack, on foot, is at the limit of most people's ability, and only possible for short distances. A kayak is too expensive to abandon, so you'll have to pay to ship it home separately if you are going on to places where you won't want to lug it around. Only a hard-core paddler, for whom paddling was the point of the journey, would want to take one around the world.

Folding kayaks are the original and optimal modern sea kayaks. But most people paddle them in flatter, safer waters: rivers, lakes, and protected bays and estuaries. Don't take one on the open ocean unless you are sure you know what you are doing.

Some sense of the possibilities opened up by a portable boat can be obtained from Paul Theroux's travelogue, *The Happy Isles of Oceania: Paddling the Pacific*, about a lengthy trip with a folding kayak. I don't like Theroux's attitude toward most of the places he writes about, and he doesn't say too much about his boat as such, but he uses it, matter-of-factly and to get to places and do things that would be impossible without it.

Folding kayaks are best known in Europe. In the United States, paddling organizations and publications are dominated by paddlers of rigid canoes and kayaks. Limited to transporting their boats on cartops or trailers, they pay little or no attention to paddling opportunities overseas, or to the information relevant only to folding kayakers, such as the proximity of train stations to suitable launch sites. General-purpose guidebooks, even for independent active sports and outdoor travelers, are written by people who've never heard of folding kayaks. The only general guidebooks in which I've seen them mentioned are David Stanley's *Moon Handbooks South Pacific* (Avalon Travel Pubishing) and *Eastern Europe on a Shoestring* (Lonely Planet).

I hope I've piqued your curiosity. Ralph Diaz' *Complete Folding Kayaker* will tell you everything you need to know if such a boat is right for you (see the Resource Guide). These technically elegant but simple boats have a worldwide appeal to technophiles, making Internet communication ideal for such a globally dispersed lot. The best place to find them is the Usenet newsgroups "rec.boats.paddle" and "rec.boats.paddle.touring," which is also the place to post queries about paddling possibilities in particular places.

# "The Plane Truth"

# AIR TRANSPORTATION

Air transportation, while not the largest part of the cost of most long trips, is nonetheless the largest part of the transportation budget and the largest single up-front expense for most independent travelers. As such, air tickets are the focus of many people's financial concerns, and many people focus solely on price when they are buying air tickets. Air transportation is about more than prices, though: finding the set of tickets that will be best for your trip is at least as important as getting the lowest price for them. Especially for around-the-world and other multistop itineraries, it's rarely obvious what will be the best or cheapest route, so buying airline tickets is very different from shopping for a known commodity. The most common serious mistake of air ticket purchasers is accepting cheap tickets that don't go to the places they are actually going, and then spending more money to get to their real destinations. A somewhat more expensive initial package of tickets could often get them to more of the places they actually want to visit, at a lower cost in the end.

This chapter will explain how to work with a travel agent (or as your own do-it-yourself travel agent, if you so choose) to plan your air travel itinerary and get the best available combination of the right tickets and the right price.

Air ticket prices, rules, and procedures are complicated and confusing. For reasons I'll explain later on, the airlines like it that way. It's hard to get good advice on fares, and harder to know who to believe. Most published advice about airfares is written either by people who work in the travel industry or by writers of destination guidebooks, neither of whom are usually a good source of consumer advice for air ticket purchases.

People in the travel industry have a financial interest in keeping their customers uninformed, so as to be able to get as much money out of them as possible. Almost everywhere I've worked as a travel agent, I've gotten complaints from bosses and coworkers: "Why do you spend so much time educating people rather than selling? Why do you want to educate potential customers anyway?" The airlines, in particular, are least likely to explain how their prices are structured. As I'll discuss, international airlines are actually forbidden, by mutual agreement, from admitting the existence of their main mode of discounting.

Guidebook writers are hired for their expert knowledge of destinations, not airfares. No matter how experienced they are as travelers or writers, they rarely have an inside knowledge of the air transportation industry, because that is almost impossible to acquire without working for an airline or discount travel agency. Forced to analyze the system from the outside, they engage in what amounts to reverse engineering: theorizing about what is inside a sealed black box by observing its behavior and what inputs produce what outputs. In fact, most published advice about air ticket discounting is speculation based on this sort of reverse engineering, not description of fact. On the whole, the sections on long-haul discounted airfares are the least accurate parts of most guidebooks for independent budget travelers. Some clever and plausible, but false, inferences have been widely reprinted and have become commonly accepted myths of budget travelers around the world.

Much of what you think you know about airfares may not be correct. You'll get the most out of this chapter if you put your preconceptions aside. I'll start by debunking some of the most widespread and misleading of the popular myths about airfares, with a particular eye to what mistakes people make on the

# KEY ADVICE ABOUT AIR TRANSPORTATION

- Don't assume you'll get lower prices on the Internet, or by going directly to the airlines. Not all ticket prices are available online. Because of the way international airfares are regulated, travel agents can sell tickets for less than the airlines themselves are allowed to sell the same tickets for. Because of the same regulations, airlines cannot directly acknowledge this discounting, and cannot give you any information about travel agents' actual discounted selling prices. There's little or no relationship between which airline has a lower official fare and which airline has a lower price from agents.

- Plan ahead. To get the best price on a complex multistop international flight itinerary, you need to buy your tickets at least a month in advance, preferably sooner. Start planning even earlier to leave time to work out your itinerary.

- Know where you want to go before you consult a travel agent. There is no standard route or fixed-price "go anywhere" ticket around the world. Before you can begin to get price estimates you need a list of specific desired destinations.

- Find a travel agency that specializes in tickets for independent world travelers. Around-the-world and multistop airline tickets are a small and esoteric specialty. Don't expect much help from airlines or all-purpose travel agencies.

- Choose a travel agent as you would choose any professional consultant. You're buying service and advice, not a commodity. Differences between good and bad agencies in quality of service—especially after you've paid for your tickets and hit the road—are far greater than differences in price.

basis of those myths. For those who want to understand the reasons for my advice, I'll next explain how airfares and ticket discounting really work in the section titled, "The System of Airfares." This section is rather technical because there's no way to explain discount airfares both simply and accurately. If you don't really care about the "whys" and just want to know how to go about getting the best tickets and price, move on to the final third of this chapter, "Arranging Your Air Transportation," which outlines how to choose and work with a travel agent, how to buy airline tickets, and things to be concerned with after you have your tickets.

## MYTHS ABOUT AIRLINE PRICES AND ROUTES

Myths about what routes are, and are not, permitted by affordable airfares lead many people to spend unnecessary time and energy trying to choose a route

---

- Buy your tickets from an agency that shops the global market in airline tickets. Buy your tickets far enough in advance for your agent to be able to import them for you from wherever in the world it's cheapest to have them issued.

- If your travel agent won't customize your route and tickets to suit your desires, find one who will. Buying tickets from a limited menu of "standard" options, or that don't include all the flights you will need, is likely to end up costing you more by the time you get to your real destination(s).

- Buy air tickets locally only as a last resort, if you can't get tickets on certain local airlines in advance or if you can't decide in advance what route you will want to follow. Expect to pay significantly more for the flexibility you gain by buying tickets as you go.

- Include as many of your flights as possible in the package of tickets you buy in advance. The more tickets you have to buy separately, at the last minute, or along the way as you are traveling, the higher your total ticket cost is likely to be.

- Don't postpone buying tickets just because you aren't sure of your travel dates. What you lock in when you buy your tickets are the price, airlines, route, and departure date. The dates of the rest of your flights can usually be changed for little or no charge as long as space is available.

- Insist on confirmed reservations for all flights before you pay for any tickets. So-called "open date" tickets have many drawbacks and no real advantages compared with tickets with confirmed but freely changeable dates.

For more information on the topics in this chapter, see the Resource Guide, in the back of the book, and the links on the Practical Nomad Web site at http://www.practicalnomad.com.

that conforms to "rules" that don't really apply to them, or to plan their trips in ways that result in needless inconvenience and/or expense. Because these myths are so widespread, I'll deal with them and their implications for destination planning here, even at the risk of getting ahead of myself.

Check out your transportation options before you make definite commitments: I've had calls from people who had already made arrangements to arrive in a city on a day when no flight arrived, t3rom one place to another more quickly than any scheduled service operated, or to follow itineraries for which they could not afford the tickets.

In summary, all of the major myths detailed below concern the degree to which it is possible or affordable to choose your own route. Each of these myths leads people not to plan their route in advance, either because they don't realize how many choices they have or because they don't realize the financial benefits of planning ahead rather than as they go. As a result, they fail to plan ahead, with the effect that they spend more than they need to, miss out on options to improve their trip, or find they can't afford things they could have afforded had they planned ahead.

Some people conclude, as an outgrowth of one or more of these myths, that airline fare rules dictate and limit the possibilities and affordability of travel routes, and thus their destinations. As a result, they try to plan their trips by choosing a *route* before they have really settled on *destinations*. Often, the result is that they plan a route that isn't what they really want, doesn't get them where they really want to go, isn't optimized for their needs and desires, or isn't affordable or feasible at all.

Before you even begin thinking about routes or fares, you should have at least a preliminary starting and ending point and a set of desired destinations. As a general principle, you should think about where and when you want to go before you start calling airlines or a travel agent. Once you have a tentative idea of what you might want, a good travel agent can assess whether it will be possible and what it might cost.

If you know where you are going by air, and if you will complete your trip within a year, it will be cheapest (with quite limited exceptions) to buy the tickets for that entire year of air travel as a single comprehensive package of air tickets, in advance, before you leave home. I advise strongly against buying tickets for flights you aren't confident you will want to take. But I'm a realist, and you should be too. If you want to choose your flight destinations as you go, you need to accept that your trip will be more costly than had you chosen the same destinations and bought tickets in advance.

## Myth I: "You Can Choose and Change Your Route as You Go"

Almost no reasonably priced ticket will let you choose your route as you go, or change it once your ticket is issued. Tickets can be issued with "open" dates but not with "open" places.

# BUYING DOMESTIC TICKETS EN ROUTE

Whenever you can, make reservations and buy tickets for domestic flights within other countries as part of a package with your international flights. Often they are cheaper that way, and that way you can lock in reservations and the price up front. Even most domestic flights within Third and Fourth World countries are operated by national airlines that participate in global electronic booking and ticketing systems. Always ask about any domestic or regional flights you are thinking of taking when you make your international reservations.

Occasionally, however, you have no choice but to wait until you get to another country before buying tickets for some domestic flights. China, Russia, and other republics of the former USSR are among the most commonly visited countries where many flights are operated by local airlines that aren't represented abroad.

If you can't make reservations or buy tickets from outside the country, you probably won't be able to get accurate schedule or fare information either. Don't count on any information about air service if you don't have a confirmed reservation or ticket. I've seen people get into real trouble by counting on the existence of a particular flight mentioned in a guidebook, especially if they count on it to operate on a particular day of the week.

Most people are more or less aware of this basic generalization. The problem is that there are exceptions, and people who know a little about the exceptions often think that the exceptions are much broader than they really are, largely because of misleading advertisements by the airlines. As a result, people who plan on using an "air pass" or an around-the-world ticket, in particular, frequently count on buying a general-purpose ticket and deciding later on, as they go, where to fly. In practice, almost all affordably priced tickets require you to choose your route (although not necessarily your dates) before you buy your tickets.

Certain air passes for travel within particular countries, and published around-the-world fares, do allow some changes of routes and destinations. These fares are marketed with sweeping claims about being able to "go anywhere we fly," and people mistakenly assume that these special fares have special prices that are cheaper than the alternatives.

### Why Plan Your Route in Advance?

Reroutable tickets, where they exist, are rarely the cheapest. Fewer routes qualify for air passes or published around-the-world airfares than people think. Except for Visit North America passes good in both the United States and

AIR TRANSPORTATION

Canada, there are few generally useful regional air passes. There is no real airline counterpart to the Eurailpass, nor is there any air pass good throughout Southeast Asia.

Around-the-world tickets purchased from an airline in the United States, starting and ending in the same place in the United States, via the Northern Hemisphere only, start at about US$3,000 for the simplest routes. But these tickets permit only a limited number of stops and routing choices. Alternatively, you might be able to get tickets to the same set of destinations for US$1,500 from a discount agency.

### Reroutable Tickets: Not as Flexible as They Seem

Airlines will tell you that you can change the route of an around-the-world ticket, within the allowable routes. But they don't tell you that from any given city reached on such a ticket there is usually only one city to which you can continue on an allowable route. It's rare enough that a given itinerary can be ticketed on any published around-the-world fare. It would be truly stellar good luck if a desired en-route change to such an itinerary were actually allowed on the same fare.

Similarly, an air pass on a particular airline is only good where that airline flies. You can't use a Thai Airways Discover Thailand air pass to get to Ko Samui, for example, because only Bangkok Airways flies there. It doesn't generally make sense to buy any ticket unless you have already decided where you are going, and if you do know where you are going, there are likely to be cheaper fixed- routing tickets for it.

If you want to get a reasonable price for your airline tickets, you need to decide, before you buy your tickets, all of the specific places you will fly during the time that those tickets are valid. You can save a significant amount of money if you make those decisions as far in advance as possible.

### Myth 2: "You Have to Follow Specific Routes"

There is no standard or usual around-the-world airline route, nor is there a standard ticket price. People who have heard about the routing restrictions of published around-the-world (RTW) fares often think that their choices are limited to these fares. They waste large amounts of time and energy in a misguided effort to shoehorn the itinerary they want into one that will qualify for such a fare. Or they assume that any destinations not on such a routing will have to be ticketed as separate side trips.

In reality, advertised around-the-world prices are almost never published fares that are limited to specific routes—advertised prices are usually just examples of combinations of consolidator tickets that can be modified and customized almost endlessly. Most actual around-the-world itineraries cannot be ticketed on any of the limited number of published around-the-world fares.

There is thus no point in restricting your consideration of possible destinations to ones that you think qualify for such fares or that you have seen advertised as examples of around-the-world prices.

As long as you don't limit yourself to published RTW fares, the key facts about packages of tickets that will get you around the world are as follows:

• You do not have to start and end your tickets in the same place.

• Your route does not have to be continuous.

• You do not have to travel in any particular or continuous direction or on any particular combination of airlines.

• You do not have to travel only on airlines that are part of the same marketing "alliance."

Nor are any of these things particularly likely to make your tickets more or less expensive. The majority of tickets sold by specialist around-the-world travel agents include backtracking, discontinuities, and combinations of airlines other than those that publish joint around-the-world fares.

## Myth 3: "Roundtrip Fares Are Always the Cheapest"

People who are traveling entirely within one country or region often overlook destination planning because they assume that roundtrip fares to a single destination and back to the starting point are much cheaper than any multistop or discontinuous tickets. This leads them to choose a single city to use as a "base," to which they buy a roundtrip ticket. They figure they don't need to decide until they get there which other cities they'll visit as side trips.

This approach is usually a mistake for an extended journey. Most destinations can more cheaply be reached as part of a through journey without backtracking, rather than as a side trip from a local or regional "hub". And roundtrip tickets are rarely cheaper than tickets into one city and out of another, as long as both are served by the same airline. So-called "open-jaw" tickets generally cost the average of the roundtrip fares for the two halves (outbound and return) of the journey.

An open-jaw ticket to fly into a city at one geographic extreme of the country or region, and out of the other, can save you from circling back to your arrival point to catch your return flight. But you can't realize those savings unless you have enough idea of where you are going to choose appropriate arrival and departure cities before you buy your tickets.

Every few days in the summer, for example, foreign visitors who bought roundtrip tickets to the East Coast of the United States show up in my office on the West Coast, wanting last-minute transcontinental one-way tickets to connect with their return flight to Europe. Even if they take a bus or train, their total cost ends up higher than if they had known they would travel to the West Coast and had gotten an open-jaw ticket in the first place, arriving somewhere in the east and returning from the west.

Airlines and travel agencies advertise roundtrip (or "half roundtrip") airfares without mentioning the possibility of open jaws at similar prices. If you ask about roundtrip fares, they'll only tell you about roundtrip fares. It sometimes takes extensive probing for me to find out that someone asking about roundtrip prices actually plans to visit many places and would be better off with an open-jaw ticket. Awareness of open-jaw ticketing is the single simple thing that could save the most travelers the most money and time.

## Myth 4: "Tickets Are Cheapest at the Last Minute"

Many people have heard they can get a cheaper ticket if they wait until the last minute, when "airlines sell off blocks of unsold seats cheaply to consolidators, who sell them for whatever they can get." This is not true.

Discounters don't pay the airlines up front to buy seats. So you are wasting your time if you try to bargain with travel agents on the assumption that they have already paid for a ticket and that they would rather get any money for it at all than have it go unsold. Neither a retail agent nor a wholesale consolidator pays a penny for a seat until a ticket has been sold to a specific person.

In the United States, last-minute fares or fares that will allow you to stand-by for any available seat have been set for business travelers and other desperate passengers who have to go, no matter what the price. The walk-up or stand-by fare has traditionally been the highest fare. Airlines have been quite willing to leave three seats empty that could have been filled had the walk-up fare been set at US$500, if that enabled them to extract US$2,500 from one last-minute business traveler. Not only does the airline get more money, but those who do travel are less crowded and happier.

The Internet has made it easier for airlines to offer discounted "Web fares" directly to the public at the last minute, if lots of seats remain unsold. But these are rarely as cheap as the prices offered further in advance, through consolidators, for those same low-season flights that the airline knows will be hard to fill.

The situation is somewhat different for land-inclusive tour packages. Many of a tour operator's costs are paid in advance. They may be willing to discount the land portion of a tour very deeply, at the last minute, if hotels have been pre-paid for rooms that will otherwise be empty. But inclusive tours are rarely the cheapest option for people willing to travel on their own, especially more adventurous, experiential, or long-term travelers.

## Myth 5: "Tickets Will Be Cheaper Locally"

Many people have heard (correctly) that tickets in some places are cheap, and conclude (mistakenly) that it will be cheaper to buy parts of their tickets en route than to buy them before they leave. In fact, those same tickets can probably also be obtained cheaply in advance, sometimes much more cheaply than if bought en route.

Deliberately not buying tickets to places you know you will go, and buying them separately en route, is almost always a mistake. Most of the people who buy air tickets en route could have gotten tickets to the same places, at a lower total cost, had they included them as part of the package of tickets they bought before they left.

An especially common, unnecessary, and costly mistake is to buy a ticket to one place for the sole purpose of buying a ticket there to some other place. Buying a ticket to Bangkok for a month is a mistake if your goal is to spend a month in Vietnam; likewise buying a ticket to London or Paris just to get to Africa. Through tickets from A to B and on to C are almost always cheaper than the combined cost of tickets from A to B and from B to C, even when B is a good place to get cheap tickets onward and even if you want to stop over and spend time in B on your way.

Flexibility, plans to use surface transportation, wanting the ability to make decisions on the spot, or wanting to travel for more than a year are good reasons not to buy air tickets in advance for particular portions of your trip. Saving money is not. Plan to pay a premium for the flexibility of buying tickets en route.

The shorter your trip, the more true this is, because if you are in a hurry you have to buy tickets at whatever price is available—if they are available at all. Unless you stay somewhere for several weeks or months, you'll have to buy tickets on short notice, when the cheapest tickets are gone.

Even if you have the time to wait around in London, Bangkok, or wherever for seats on the cheapest onward flight to become available, your expenses there are likely to offset whatever financial savings you expected on the air tickets.

If a separate ticket is appropriate for some part of your trip, a good agent can probably get it for you for less than you'd pay for it separately. Around-the-world agencies (agencies that specialize in long-haul and around-the-world travel) buy and sell tickets from each other—at preferred wholesale rates, from suppliers whose reliability and value they have had time to establish—in every major world city where you would be likely to consider buying a ticket en route.

Some people are misled by the air ticket prices in guidebooks. Like other prices in guidebooks, these costs are typically at least two years out of date. Even on routes without discounting (e.g., domestic fares within most countries), inflation alone is likely to make current fares 20–25 percent higher than those in the most up-to-date guidebooks.

When fewer people are traveling, as they were after 11 September 2001, airlines reduce capacity (supply), so as to be able to raise prices even with reduced demand. The long-term trend in airfares is likely to be upward.

On international routes, discount prices given as examples in guidebooks for budget travelers are typically the lowest advertised prices: i.e., the lowest conceivable prices for tickets purchased well in advance for the cheapest seats for low season travel on the cheapest airlines, exclusive of taxes, etc. Few people ever pay as little as the advertised prices—even the experienced travelers who write guidebooks and are familiar with the place and probably know some of the local language.

Some of the greatest cost savings in planning ahead are on domestic tickets within countries. First, domestic flights can often be included in through international fares at less additional cost than if ticketed separately, and often without liability for domestic ticket taxes. Second, special fares are available to foreign visitors for domestic flights within many countries, generally only on condition that tickets be issued prior to arrival in the country and in conjunction with international tickets. Once you arrive in such a country and find out the local fares, it's too late to take advantage of them.

In a number of large countries where internal airfares can be high, discounts or special fares for foreign visitors are available. These include the United States, Canada, Australia, Indonesia, and Brazil. Perhaps the greatest bargains are on travel within North America. Savvy American expatriates always buy tickets for their domestic travel at Visit USA or Visit North America fares before they come home from abroad. Foreign visitors are well advised to follow their example. Visit USA and Visit North America tickets are especially good value for multistop, discontinuous, and circle-trip air itineraries.

## THE SYSTEM OF AIRFARES

Like the rules of chess or of a computer programming language, airfares are an artificial and formal system, with an essentially arbitrary set of rules. Little about the system is natural, obvious, or intuitive. There are historical, political, and economic explanations for some aspects of it, but much of it could just as well have been set up differently. The system has its own jargon, in which some words are used to mean quite different things than they do in common usage. It's no surprise that most people find airfares confusing.

This is an inherently complex subject. I'll try to be as clear and straightforward as I can, but I'm describing a complex closed system that is protected by participants who have an interest in keeping you uninformed. There is little accurate public information about the airline industry, and most readers are likely to have, for understandable reasons, false preconceptions about it.

Experienced travelers, business travelers, and others who are reading this book mainly for inside information on airfares may find this the most useful part of the book. People who are mainly interested in general travel planning advice or who just want to know how to get the best and cheapest tickets, may want to skip this section entirely. If it all seems too complicated, by all means move on. But the reasons for some of the advice I give later will be more apparent if you understand how airfares and discounting work. If you find yourself asking, "Why does he say that?" about things in the later sections of this chapter, you may want to refer back to this part of the book.

## How Airfares Are Determined

Each country has its own rules for fares and flights entirely within its borders. For this reason, there are different rules, fare structures, systems of discounting, and optimal strategies for getting the best prices for domestic air tickets and for international tickets.

Domestic USA and international airfares aren't as dissimilar as they were a few years ago. Consolidator tickets (discounted tickets sold by travel agents for less than the published prices offered directly by the airlines), once limited to international routes, are now available for trips within the United States. And Web fares, originally offered only for domestic USA flights, are now widely available for international journeys. But domestic and international airfares are still subject to fundamentally different regulatory regimes, and the differences between international and domestic pricing remain important.

The United States has the world's largest domestic airline industry. Most air travel to, from, or within the United States is on routes entirely within the country, subject only to the domestic fare rules of the United States. Most information and advice about airfares published in the United States is based on domestic fare structures and is relevant and applicable to within the USA, within Canada, or between the USA and Canada.

Travel publications in the United States rarely identify whether they are talking about domestic USA or international fares, much less domestic fares within other countries. Given this, it's scarcely surprising that most American travelers make the same big mistake when buying international tickets, or tickets for flights within other countries. They assume that the same principles apply to these tickets as to tickets for domestic flights in the United States.

## Domestic Airfares

There is no international regulation of purely domestic airfares or airline operations. Each country can make its own rules, and nothing can be inferred from how things work in one country about how they work in any other. IATA member airlines (airlines belonging to the International Air Transport Association) that operate both international and domestic flights generally conform to international operational standards even on domestic flights, but they don't have to, and those operational standards don't govern their fares.

### Fares Within North America

For many years the USA government treated airlines like public utilities. The government regulated which routes each airline could fly, fixed their prices, and guaranteed them a profit. In 1978, domestic airfares and routes in the United States were deregulated. While the government continues to subsidize air travel and to license and certify airlines for operational competence and safety, airlines are now free to fly any routes, charge any fares, and make any profit they please. Airfares are now restricted only by the requirements of antitrust (antimonopoly) laws that prohibit the airlines from collaborating to fix prices—though they still do just that, with the government's help, on international routes. But that's for the next section.

The theory behind deregulation was supposedly that air service would improve if airlines were not required to prove that their operations were in the public interest, but instead were allowed to operate purely in their own profit interest. Whatever one thinks of this theory, deregulation has been a mixed blessing for travelers and airlines alike. Some airlines, most conspicuously American Airlines, have openly advocated a return to regulation. Presumably this is because American has faced more competition since deregulation, although it claims to have purer motives. Other airlines, such as Southwest Airlines and JetBlue, have expanded rapidly. Fares have increased and jet service has been reduced, in some cases eliminated entirely, in many smaller cities. Fares on the busiest and most competitive routes, especially the main transcontinental routes, have gone down. There are fewer nonstop flights and more hub-and- spoke operations, so a higher percentage of air travelers have to change planes. There are also new commuter airlines offering more turboprop and "commuter jet" connections between smaller cities (through hubs) and to places that never had direct service before. For better or worse, deregulation seems to be here to stay.

The present open-skies agreement between the United States and Canada has, in effect, created a single airline market. A special term, "transborder," is used by the airlines to distinguish flights between the United States and Canada from all other international flights. For pricing purposes, these transborder flights are treated like domestic flights, although the tax rules, the specific prices, and the numbers of competing airlines differ significantly between the United States and Canada.

Most of what I'll say here about USA and Canadian domestic fares applies equally to transborder fares between the two countries. Consider this the exception that proves the rule that domestic and international fare structures and discounting systems have nothing in common. Canadian domestic and transborder fares between the United States and Canada have, like domestic USA fares, been largely deregulated.

The airlines can set any fares they like within the United States and Canada, and can change fares as often as they like, without prior approval from the government or anyone else. They are also allowed to offer any prices they please on their own Web sites. If they want to lower the price, they lower the published fares, or offer a lower price directly to the public on their Web site. So getting the best price within North America means getting the best fare being offered directly by any of the airlines for the route and schedule you want to fly. This may seem tautologically true, but it isn't; for international tickets it isn't true at all, as you'll see in the following section on international airfares.

Finding the best fare is still a complex task. There are several million different fares in effect at any given time just between points within the United States. Each fare has between two and 10 pages of associated rules. Airfares have a bewildering variety of weird conditions. Travelers often ask their travel agents, "Doesn't the computer tell you what the best price is? These people and some computer programmers, may be surprised to learn that there is as yet no infallible computer algorithm for determining the lowest available published fare between two points in the United States on given dates, despite the best efforts of airlines using some of the world's largest commercial computer centers and most sophisticated artificial intelligence techniques. Human beings (i.e., travel agents, unless you want to do it yourself) still have to read rules to figure out which fares apply.

At first glance, fare rules seem to have no rhyme or reason. "Why does the price depend on whether I fly only on Tuesdays, at 2 A.M., or when the moon is full?" everyone asks. Try to look at the rules from the point of view of the people who make the rules—the airlines—and they will begin to make sense.

Airlines start with the highest fare that they conceivably hope to get anyone to pay, which they define as the full or normal fare. The "normal" coach or economy roundtrip fare from New York to Los Angeles and back, as the airlines define it, is thus more than US$2,000, or four to five times what most people would consider to be the norm. The full fare is unrestricted: fully refundable, freely changeable, available at any time, long in advance or at the last minute, on every seat of every plane on any airline. Anything cheaper than the full fare is considered a discounted fare, and has rules restricting its use.

The airlines' goal in discounting is to fill seats that would otherwise go empty, without diverting passengers who would be willing to pay higher prices. Fare rules have, in most cases, little or nothing to do with the airlines' costs and everything to do with airlines' perceptions of passengers' willingness to pay.

Airlines are neither irrational nor stupid. They spend huge amounts of money on market research and on sophisticated computer hardware and software for "yield management" (profit maximization). Looked at from the customer's perspective, or a cost perspective, fare rules seem bizarre and arbitrary. They are not. From the airlines' perspective, they are part of a highly developed, and largely successful, system for identifying exactly how much each passenger is willing to pay, and getting them to pay that full amount.

For example, it costs the airline the same amount to fly you from A to B and back, regardless of how long you stay in B. But most cheap fares—in many cases all but the most expensive fares—have both minimum and maximum stay requirements. Airlines have found that how long you want to stay is one of the best indicators of how much you are willing to pay, and set their fare rules accordingly.

The airlines' perception (probably a correct one) is that people who don't want to spend a weekend at their destination are business travelers who are able and willing to pay extra to come home sooner to spend the weekend at home with their friends or family. Airlines therefore use the requirement that you spend a Saturday night at your destination to be eligible for many cheap roundtrip fares as a way to identify people who are willing to pay more, and to make them do so. If you aren't willing to stay over a Saturday night to qualify for a lower fare, the airlines infer that you aren't really that price-sensitive, and they charge you more for the privilege of coming home sooner.

Similarly, the airlines' perception is that people who are staying only a week or two are vacationers, for whom travel is discretionary and who might not travel at all, or might go someplace else, unless they are offered a low price. Travelers who want to stay longer, on the other hand, are likely to be people with jobs or other strong ties to the place, and compelling reasons to go, who can amortize the cost of their tickets over a longer period, and who thus can be expected to be willing to pay more. So roundtrip fares for longer stays are higher, often much higher, than short-stay fares. The cheapest fares on USA domestic routes typically allow a maximum stay of 30 days, while the cheapest "tourist" roundtrip fares on international routes have maximum stays varying, depending on the route, from as short as seven days to as long as six months.

Because it's easier for potential customers to compare advertised fares than rules, most airlines closely track, and match, competitors' fares. Similar fares do not, however, necessarily have the same rules. An easy way for an airline to attract business at the expense of its competitors, without having to reduce its fares, is to make its rules slightly less restrictive. The airlines most likely to do this are ones that passengers would be less likely to choose if all else were equal.

If you are looking to find a way around some rule of a cheap fare that you can't comply with, check the rules of other airlines. Start with the least known or least popular airlines serving the route, especially those that don't have non-stop or direct service, and have only infrequent schedules, between the places. If there are many airlines in the market, there's a good chance that at least one of them has matched the others' fares but with a less restrictive set of rules.

You can try to sort through all the fares and rules yourself on the Internet, although almost no airline ticket Web site shows the complete fare and rule information you'd need to make an informed choice. Or you could call every airline, although the airline with the best fare may be one you've never heard of and wouldn't think to call. But you have little practical chance of actually finding the best fare and schedule without professional help from a travel agent. Would you call Kuwait Airways for prices from Amsterdam to Chicago, or Varig Brazilian Airways for prices from Los Angeles to Tokyo? Even if you did, these airlines wouldn't give you the tickets at the prices some travel agents offer on those airlines. It's travel agents' prices, not the airline-direct prices, that put these airlines among the price leaders in their respective markets.

If you want to teach yourself to be your own amateur travel agent on the Internet, be my guest. (You might also want to have a look at my other book in this series, *The Practical Nomad Guide to the Online Travel Marketplace*.)

Unless you have a natural aptitude for it, lots of time to spend studying, access to a skilled and experienced tutor, and place a low valuation on your time, arranging your own tickets is unlikely to save you money. But, as I said, be my guest.

If you go to a travel agent, expect to pay a fee for their consulting services, whether or not you buy anything from them. Travel agents in the United States are no longer paid commissions by most airlines (except for "commissions" on consolidator tickets, as discussed below). Travel agency commissions are being phased out in other countries as well. Even robotic Internet travel agencies charge service fees, or include the cost of their services in the prices they set. Only by buying directly from an airline—forgoing a travel agent's advice and consolidator ticket prices—can you avoid service fees.

Unless travelers are willing to pay a consulting fee, travel agents can no longer afford to take the time to give advice or search for the best deals. If travelers refuse to pay a fee, they have no one to turn to for airfare advice but the airlines themselves. This is a recipe for getting ripped off, or at least for paying more than would otherwise be necessary.

### Why Buying Directly from an Airline May Not Be the Best Deal

Airlines want consumers to think that if they sold all their tickets directly to travelers—either over the phone or via the Internet—and paid no commissions to agents, they would reduce their costs for distributing tickets. In reality, since they no longer pay commissions to most travel agents, it almost certainly costs an airline more to issue a ticket than to have a travel agent issue it for them. And that's as true on the Internet as offline. Most service providers would be delighted to outsource their distribution, at no cost, the way the airlines have.

The real reasons airlines want to get rid of travel agents—in spite of the money they save the airlines in ticketing and customer service costs—are to make it harder for new airlines to break into the industry and to make it easier to raise fares. Established airlines want to eliminate the role of the travel agent as an impartial consultant who might find a way to offer the passenger a cheaper fare on their flights, or who might (God forbid) recommend the competition .

The last thing Air Established wants is for a frequent flyer to call a travel agent who might tell them, "Did you know that Air Upstart is now offering a lower fare? You may not have heard of Air Upstart, but we've sold tickets on Air Upstart to several of our customers, and they said the service was good." Were it not for the travel agent, the travelers might never have heard of Air Upstart, or wouldn't have known what to think of them. They would simply have called Air Established, bought a more expensive ticket, and never known that they had an alternative. That's just what Air Established wants them to do.

Some people think that travel agents won't recommend the cheapest airlines because the agents will make less money. It doesn't really work that way. The service fees travel agents charge travelers for issuing tickets are generally the same amount per ticket, regardless of the fare. Travel agents compete with each other, and their competitive success depends on finding their customers the lowest fares that will suit their wants. Travel agents will only sell more expensive tickets if they can give customers good reasons not to buy cheaper tickets. This is part of the service they provide: who else will know how to decipher the fine print to tell you the hidden defect in the advertised special that really is too good to be true?

If you think this is all just a self-serving defense of my interests as a travel agent, think again: I'm urging you to seek the advice and assistance of a travel agent in buying tickets that cost an agent more to issue, in labor and overhead, than most travelers are willing to pay in service fees. Among themselves, travel agents talk constantly about how not to waste time on money-losing published-fare airline tickets, without alienating people who might later be in the market for tours, cruises, or other more profitable (for the agent) services. For the typical travel agency in the United States, airline tickets are now a loss leader. My interests as a travel agent would be served by telling you that you could do just as well, just as easily, by yourself on the Internet, or by calling the airlines directly, rather than asking a good travel agent for help. But it wouldn't be true.

What I will say, in my self-interest as a travel agent, is that in asking an agent to issue tickets at published fares you are asking them to provide you with consulting and ticketing services—the more so the more time they spend searching for the best fare for you. If you want a travel agent to work for you, and not for the airlines, you have to be prepared to pay them for their services in finding you the best fare. If you don't pay your travel agent a service fee, you can scarcely be surprised if they don't have your interests at heart.

### Domestic Fares in Other Countries

Few other countries have domestic fare structures as complex as those in the United States, although that is changing with the privatization and breakup of national airlines. In most countries there are only one or two domestic airlines, at least one of them owned or controlled by the government. Many countries have the simplest fare structure of all: a single flat one-way fare between each pair of cities, regardless of when you travel, when you buy your ticket, or whether you come back. People who come from such countries to the United States, or to another country with complex fares, are amazed and confused to find out that to get affordable prices in the United States they have to buy roundtrip tickets, for specific dates and times, in advance.

Even where there is only one price, rules for changing flight dates or times range from one extreme to the other. If you buy a domestic ticket in China, it is valid only for the specific flight and date for which it is issued. If you don't use it then, you can either throw the ticket away or keep it as a souvenir. Next door in Vietnam, dates and times of flights can be changed at no charge as long as space is available. Other countries fall in between. When buying domestic tickets locally, always read the fine print (if you can), or ask about cancellation and change policies if they are in a language you don't understand. Unless you are certain, and have it in writing, assume the worst.

Other countries have discounts (remember, the highest fare is considered the normal fare, and anything lower is considered discounted) for roundtrip travel, for travel at night, or for travel at other days or times when flights would otherwise be less popular and have more empty seats. Good guidebooks often give information on domestic fare structures, but they can't be relied on. General types of fares are less likely than specific prices to have changed since a guidebook was researched, but in my experience even good guidebooks are frequently wrong about fare structures. Inquire locally, and presume nothing.

Travelers often presume that domestic tickets can only, or most cheaply, be purchased within the country. This is not usually true. As I discussed near the beginning of this chapter, domestic tickets can be issued abroad for flights in more countries than most travelers imagine. And when it is possible to buy tickets abroad it is generally cheaper to do so than to buy them locally.

Sometimes tickets can only be

issued, or reservations can only be made, within the country. Sometimes the cheapest domestic airline is one that isn't represented abroad. But 95 percent of the domestic flights taken by adventurous around-the-world travelers can—and, when possible, should—be reserved and ticketed in advance. Unless you aren't sure in advance what flights you will take (and sometimes even then), or you can't get tickets in advance, it is more often than not a mistake to wait until you get to a country to buy tickets for domestic flights.

### Two Reasons to Buy Domestic Tickets Outside the Country, Even If the Prices Are Otherwise the Same

Tickets issued outside the country, in conjunction with international tickets, are usually exempt from sales tax, value added tax (VAT), or special air ticket taxes that apply to tickets bought locally. In some countries taxes can add as much as 17 percent to the price of domestic tickets purchased locally. Tickets for travel within the United States, for example, are exempt from the percentage tax if issued in conjunction with, and for flights connecting to, international travel.

Tickets on IATA member airlines issued outside the country of travel, even for purely domestic travel, are subject to IATA fare rules. This means that the only applicable restrictions are those specifically provided for in the published fare rules. If only one fare, with no special conditions, is published (as is the case on domestic routes in most countries), that fare by default is an unrestricted normal fare. So for the same price that you would pay locally for a nonrefundable, nonchangeable, use-it-or-throw-it-away ticket in India or China, you can get a fully refundable, freely changeable ticket on the same route if you buy it abroad.

### Domestic Flights Ticketed as Stopovers or Add-ons

Tickets for domestic flights do not necessarily have to be issued as separate tickets. Some of the greatest savings on domestic flights are when they can be issued as stopovers or add-ons to through international tickets.

Stopovers are fairly straightforward, although not everyone thinks to ask for them. On a ticket from Europe to Australia via the United States, for example, it may be possible to make stopovers in Washington and San Francisco, and to include the flight between Washington and San Francisco as part of the international ticket, at no additional fare or for much less than a separate ticket would cost.

Add-ons are less well-known or understood, but equally valuable. Most international flights operate only between capital cities or other big international gateway (port of entry) cities. But lots of people want to fly between airports not served by direct international flights. To attract their business, airlines provide discounts on domestic flights to the gateway cities where their flights originate and from the destination cities where they arrive.

If the same airline operates the connecting domestic and international flights, the add-on may be little or nothing (a so-called zero add-on between common-rated cities).

Competition forces some airlines to common-rate cities even when they have to pay another airline to carry passengers between them. Several Asian airlines fly to Los Angeles but not San Francisco, and to compete with airlines that fly from San Francisco most of them charge the same price for passengers starting from San Francisco as they do for passengers who board their flights directly in Los Angeles. They include the connecting flight on a USA airline between S.F. and L.A. at no extra charge.

Even non-zero add-ons are typically much less costly, and less restricted, than separate domestic fares. When a foreign airline contracts with a domestic airline to carry through passengers to and from its gateway(s), it is in a position to steer a large volume of business to the add-on carrier, with little or no marketing or sales effort on the part of the airline that gets the domestic business. So foreign airlines can, and do, negotiate extraordinarily low add-on prices per kilometer (per mile) of domestic flying.

Because the United States forbids foreign airlines to carry passengers entirely within the United States, most flights by foreign airlines make only one stop at a single USA gateway. Almost all foreign airlines serving the United States, whether they fly to East or West Coast gateways or both, have add-on agreements with one or another USA airline to carry people to and from their gateways. Roundtrip transcontinental USA add-ons are typically about US$300–400—as cheap as the cheapest transcontinental tickets on the busiest routes, and much less than the cheapest tickets between smaller cities.

From a point in the United States to a destination abroad, it's usually cheaper to get a through ticket, with an add-on than to get one domestic ticket to a USA gateway city and a separate international ticket from there. It's a particularly poor choice to use a "free" ticket obtained for frequent-flyer mileage to connect to an international flight, where all it will save you is what the add-on would have been. Price through tickets, with an add-on, before committing yourself to use frequent-flyer mileage credits to get to an international gateway from somewhere else in the United States or Canada.

The bottom line on domestic flights in any country: do yourself a favor and at least ask your travel agent, before you buy any of your international tickets, if domestic flights you plan to take can be included in your package of tickets.

## International Airfares

Remember what I said at the start of this section: international airfares and discounts operate in a  different way from discounted domestic fares. Try to shift your mental gears, put any preconceptions as well as the preceding section on domestic airfares aside temporarily, and read this section with an open mind.

### The Government and IATA Price-Fixing System

Almost all significant international airlines belong to an international price-fixing cartel called the International Air Transport Association (IATA). As a condition of membership, airlines that join IATA agree that they will sell tickets on international routes only in accordance with government and IATA rules and published price schedules (tariffs).

Published fares for tickets between any two countries are subject to bilateral agreements between the governments of those two countries. Many international airlines are owned by national governments. Even when they are nominally private, airlines are usually closely related to the national governments of the countries where they are based. Most governments in turn have an interest in protecting the profits of their national airline(s), and government-approved fares are therefore artificially high.

The requirement that fares be published and filed with governments is intended to allow government oversight of possible illegal practices and to ensure that, as "common carriers," they are treating all customers equally. But airlines don't want to make their prices public. Thus, even where bilateral

# AIRLINE ORGANIZATIONS

The International Air Transportation Association (IATA) —the international airline cartel—is sometimes confused with one or both of two other organizations, the Air Transportation Association (ATA) and the International Civil Aviation Organization (ICAO).

ATA is a trade association and lobbying group for the interests of airlines in the United States. USA antitrust law forbids ATA from price-fixing. ATA is mainly involved in lobbying the USA government to reduce taxes on air travel and increase the subsidies paid by the government. The subsidies to the airline industry are generated from general tax revenue, and thus are a subsidy paid to frequent flyers and the airlines by those who can rarely afford to fly. These in turn support air traffic control, airport construction, etc.

ICAO is a specialized agency affiliated with the United Nations. IATA and ICAO both have offices in Montreal, but their membership and functions are very different. IATA is an organization of airlines; ICAO is an intergovernmental organization. IATA is concerned primarily with fares, revenue accounting, and other financial issues. ICAO is primarily a technical organization; it sets standards for things like equipment and procedures for international air navigation or air traffic control.

agreements have been revised to permit airlines to set their own fares, most airlines still choose to publish fares substantially higher than their actual selling prices, in order to conceal their real price structure from their competitors.

IATA and government rules officially prohibit discounting below published fares. IATA member airlines may not sell tickets for less than the official fares in their approved tariff, on pain of expulsion from the price-fixing club and, in many countries, government sanctions.

No matter what they claim to the public, airlines like the government and IATA price-fixing system, and profit from it. Few airlines are willing to risk expulsion from the cartel, or running afoul of the law in countries that enforce the IATA rules. Except on the Internet, few airlines directly violate the IATA and government rules against discounting below published fares.

The Internet is a *very* strange exception, at least in the United States. Airlines that have complied with government and IATA rules for decades, and continue to comply offline, are openly selling tickets on the Internet at prices that have not been filed with, or approved by, governments or IATA. "Web fares" are based on the idea that airlines can ignore the law with impunity on the Internet.

(If that makes you nervous about what other laws the airlines are breaking on the Internet, it should. Obviously, consumers benefit from lower fares. But they don't benefit from a system that precludes government oversight of unfair or monopolistic practices, which is why the requirement to publish tariffs was retained when domestic fares were deregulated in the United States.)

Over the counter or on the phone, it's a waste of time to try to get an airline to sell you a ticket directly for less than the official fare. To get a ticket for less than the government-approved IATA fare, you have to buy it on the Internet (where only a limited range of discounted "Web fares" are offered) or through a travel agent.

### Commission Rebating by Travel Agents

Obviously, the government and IATA rules aren't the whole story. If tickets were sold only at published fares, the airlines would have too many empty seats. However, the goal of the airlines is to maximize revenue, not necessarily to fill every seat. If they can fill more seats while still getting passengers to pay the most they are willing to pay, they make more money. The problem for the airlines is to get as much money as they can for filling seats that would otherwise be empty, without destroying the system that keeps prices high for those for whom price is no object, and while diverting as few passengers as possible from official-price tickets to lower-revenue discounted tickets.

Travel agents are the essential element in the mechanism the airlines have adopted to deal with this revenue-maximization problem. Airlines can pay agents commissions, nominally as compensation for selling tickets. Government and IATA rules place no limit on the size of the commission an airline can pay a travel agent. Airlines no longer pay agents an across-the-board "base" commission, but they still pay "incentive," "override," or "bonus" commissions on certain tickets. These commissions are, theoretically, intended to increase the incentive for agents to sell tickets on those airlines and routes.

The easiest way for an agent to use a commission to increase sales is, of course, to give part of the commission back to the customer as a rebate or discount, making the effective price (after the rebate) less than the official fare. When you buy a ticket from an agent for less than the published fare, the ticket must still be issued at the official fare, as you'll see from the price printed on the ticket. (The only exception is if the ticket shows no price at all, or zero, or is labeled "free" or "bulk." If a ticket shows any face value, the face value has to be a published fare.) The difference between the fare printed on the ticket and the amount you paid is the amount of the agent's commission that has been rebated to you. The result is what is frequently called a "consolidator" ticket.

Government and IATA rules prohibit agents from using rebates of their commissions to reduce the prices paid by travelers for tickets. But agents are appointed by individual airlines, not directly by IATA, and IATA has no effective direct enforcement mechanism against agents. Nor have they any desire to create one, because the system of discounting through agents by commission rebates is as much the creation of IATA's members as are the rules that are supposed to prohibit it. Both actually serve the interests of its member airlines: to

# MEMBERS OF THE CLUB

Non-IATA airlines are not bound by IATA rules or fares. At times, non-IATA airlines have offered a cheaper alternative on certain routes. Unfortunately for passengers seeking cheap flights, most airlines find it more profitable to join the cartel than to try to compete with it, and there are presently almost no scheduled long-haul services by any non-IATA airline. Aeroflot, the last major hold-out, joined IATA in 1989. As IATA itself says, "Most of the major airlines of the world belong to IATA. Their membership is quite voluntary and most have chosen to be members because of the advantages this membership brings."

USA airlines have been particularly hypocritical about IATA, urging the USA government to impose trade sanctions against other countries for enforcing the IATA agreements governing their routes to and from those countries. But all USA-based airlines currently operating scheduled international services have chosen, voluntarily, to join IATA. Now they want to have their cake and eat it, too. As long as they choose to remain in IATA, their rhetoric about "free trade" and "freedom of the skies" must be dismissed as merely a lobbying ploy to get the government of the United States to intervene on behalf of their economic interests vis-à-vis those of foreign airlines with which their service would not otherwise be competitive.

make as much money as possible by getting each passenger to pay as much as they are willing to pay.

The letter of the law and the IATA rules are satisfied as long as the commission contract between the airline and the agent includes an agreement that no part of the agent's commission will be rebated to the customer or passenger. The airline has kept its hands clean with the government and IATA, even if both the airline and the agent know full well that the agent intends, and is expected, to offer discounts through commission rebating.

In some countries, including the United States, the contract clause against commission rebating or discounting is unenforceable under the laws of the country in which the contract is signed. In the United States, for example, the contract clause against commission rebating violates rules that prohibit distributors from fixing minimum retail selling prices. The entire IATA price-fixing scheme, for that matter, would violate USA antitrust law were it entered into and enforced in the United States, rather than by the international agreement under which IATA was incorporated in Canada.

No one likes having to sign contracts containing statements they don't mean, but the airlines, and the cartel that they have created and maintained, force agents to do this if they want to sell affordable tickets. In so doing, the airlines

AIR TRANSPORTATION

have cast an unwarranted taint of dishonesty on even the most honorable discount agents. In the United States, no one is deceived or defrauded by commission contracts, no matter what they say: neither the airline nor the agent intends or expects the other to abide by, or enforce, the clause against commission rebating. There is nothing illegitimate or underhanded about commission rebating in the United States.

Discounting through agents can be prevented only in countries where governments choose to enforce the treaty and IATA rules and the terms of agent-airline contracts against commission rebating. Nondiscount travel agencies, threatened by competition from commission rebaters, are wont to seek this sort of enforcement. In Japan, for example, distributors and manufacturers of all sorts of products are allowed to enforce minimum retail selling prices, and the government prevents travel agents from discounting. This is why tickets originating in Japan and other such countries are often cheaper if purchased and issued in the United States or some other country where discounting is allowed, rather than in the country where the flights begin.

All discounted sales of international air tickets for less than the prices in published tariffs (except, as noted above, for "Web fares" offered directly by airlines) occur through agents, through commission rebating, even where the rebating is not explicit. In some countries you actually have to pay the official fare and then get the discount back. In India, for example, international air tickets can only be purchased in hard currency, but the discount is rebated only in nonconvertible rupees. So there is no benefit to buying a discounted ticket in India unless you have enough time left in the country to spend those rupees before you leave. In most countries, including the United States and the UK, the norm is for the rebate to be included in the price estimated, advertised, or stated by an agent. You only find out what the official fare would have been if you look at your tickets after you get them. And not necessarily even then: some tickets—including both some highly restricted tickets and some almost totally unrestricted tickets—do not show any fare on their face.

### Airline Published Fares and Agent Selling Prices

Asking an airline how much they want you to pay for a ticket is like asking the IRS how much tax they want you to pay. Why should you expect airlines' telephone salespeople to tell you about their cheapest product rather than to try to sell you their most expensive one?

Fare tariffs and rules are published in hardcopy in a set of several telephone-book size volumes called the *Passenger Air Tariff*, and summarized in the *Official Airline Guide* (OAG). More complete and up-to-date air tariffs are published electronically through the computerized reservation systems (CRSs) used by airlines and travel agents, and accessible (but only in part) through the Web sites of CRSs and Internet travel agencies.

These tariffs of published fares and rules are *not* a useful resource for consumers interested in the lowest air ticket prices. For the best international prices, you have to go through an agent. Most experienced travelers agree that you are better off, in the long run, putting your effort into finding the right travel agent than into trying to find the right tickets and prices on your own.

That isn't to say that all travel agents are skilled at interpreting fare rules, advising on routes, or finding discounts. Given how little travel agents are paid, it's remarkable how many competent agents there are. In the United States, most travel agents are women, and the wage scales for travel agents are further reduced by its being regarded as "women's work."

In the United States and most other countries, there are no meaningful professional standards for people who call themselves travel agents. Whether there should be is a topic of hot debate within the profession. My own opinion is that travel agents have such different specializations, requiring such different skills and bodies of knowledge, that no single set of criteria could distinguish competent agents from incompetent. In my specialty, I consider myself an expert, but I'd flunk any travel agent qualification test that asked about the products most USA agents sell: cruises, package tours, Disneyland, all-inclusive resorts.

Different agents are best for different travelers. Few people from the United States travel abroad, compared to the numbers who travel within the United States, and most who do travel to a very limited number of places in Western Europe. Most USA agents have limited experience with international travel, and no experience with multistop or long-term travel or travel outside the First World. Thus, finding the right agent may take some effort.

Few travelers anywhere appreciate the diversity of skills required of travel agents, and if you've never worked with a good agent you may not know how much help they can be. But a good travel agent can offer prices you couldn't have gotten directly from the airlines and can advise you about routes and airlines you would never have thought of on your own.

Travel agencies have been leaders in computer use and networking for decades. The local travel agency in your town was probably the first local business to have a real-time connection to a global computer network, and travel agents were the first professionals all to have computers on their desks. The first local area network in most towns was at the travel agency office. Only sometime in the 1990s was the network of airline CRSs surpassed by the Internet, its only real rival, as the world's largest interconnected computer network.

Frequent travelers can be tempted by experiences with bad travel agents to conclude that travel agents know less than they about airline routes and fares, that agents have little to offer by way of deals or advice, and that they could do better for themselves by dealing directly with the airlines and cutting out the intermediary. Web sites that claim to give "direct" access to CRSs tempt travelers by promising to yield all the information travel agents have, and to enable trav-

# WHAT ABOUT THE INTERNET?

Consumers think of airline ticket Web sites as search engines for prices from all posssible sources, but they aren't. Airline Web sites, and the airline-owned Orbitz .com, show no consolidator prices at all. Aside from published and Web fares, major online travel agencies like Travelocity.com, Expedia.com, and Trip.com only list prices from their own consolidator contracts directly with the airlines—not those from the thousands of other consolidators around the world.

As I've explained, there's an entire global market of discounted "consolidator" prices for international tickets set by travel agents, not by airlines. For every published international fare, tickets can be available at hundreds of different, lower prices from different consolidators. These prices—the majority of international air ticket prices— are not shown in any computerized reservation system (CRS), are not available directly from the airline, and are not available from any Internet site that depends on airlines and/or CRSs as its source of fares.

Because each travel agent on the Internet has their own contracts with the airlines and their own network of suppliers, each ticket site has its own prices. AirTreks.com (where I work), includes fare components from multiple sources around the world in its online pricing of multistop tickets. But I know of

no Web site that searches the global consolidator market for prices of individual tickets.

Writing software to make consolidator ticket prices available on the Internet is a huge task. It's taken airlines decades and many billions of dollars to develop the current CRSs for published fares. Even the wealthiest Internet travel agencies will take many years to develop comparable systems.

Most Internet travel agencies only sell simple one-way and roundtrip tickets. Pricing around-the-world and other multistop international tickets is far beyond the current capabilities of their software. Most air tickets sold in the United States are for domestic travel, and even most international tickets are simple roundtrips. So most Internet travel agencies don't really care about the itineraries they can't price, and they aren't about to spend the money to develop the ability to deal with them.

For more about using the Internet to find simpler one-way and roundtrip tickets, as well as consumer advice for Internet travel purchasing, ideas for Internet travel research and planning, and tips for using the Internet while traveling, see my other book in this series, *The Practical Nomad Guide to the Online Travel Marketplace.*

elers to do anything a travel agent can do. But the CRS access provided by these gateways is actually indirect, through quite restrictive interfaces.

Even for published fares, the interpretation of airfare rules is as specialized a skill as the interpretation of legal statutes, requiring experience, knowledge of specialized terms of the art, and access to interpretive resources that travelers who aren't travel agents and haven't worked for airline rate desks aren't likely to have. Each of the millions of fares has pages of rules and restrictions.

Airlines have made determined efforts to automate the interpretation of fare rules, and airfare search software has long been a leading goal of artificial intelligence researchers. But no computer program can yet reliably determine the price applicable to a particular itinerary (specific set of flights), much less which alternatives might better suit a traveler's desires. No airline has been able to replace its rate desk with machines. Every airline maintains a staff of highly skilled human beings solely to interpret the rules of its own fares, and it's not uncommon even for rate desk employees to disagree with each other as to the fare that should be charged, according to the myriad rules, for a particular set of flights.

The problem is, of course, all the more complex when you are dealing with the fares not of one but of every possible airline. And the Internet gateways to CRSs don't even give access to all the software tools (helpful though fallible as they are) that travel agents who use the full- featured versions of the CRSs have for searching for, analyzing, and comparing fares and rules. (See the sidebar "What about the Internet?")

The more important limitation of the CRSs (Sabre, Galileo, Worldspan, Amadeus, etc.) is that they contain only official published fares. Most CRSs are owned by the airlines, and all of the CRSs depend on the participation of the airlines. The airlines do not, and by the very nature of the fare-setting system cannot, include in their databases any information whatsoever on agents' actual discounted selling prices. The rules, and the law, oblige airlines to pretend that they don't even know that agents offer discounts or sell tickets for less than published fares.

Actual selling prices are set by agents, not airlines. Agents' contracts with airlines determine what commissions are paid to them on which fares, and with what conditions. Agents' commissions in turn determine how far below the published fares they are able to set their selling prices. The real structure of discounted selling prices is determined by each airline's commission agreements with each of its agents, read in conjunction with its published fares and rules. None of this information is available anywhere on the Internet.

Commission agreements are, by nature, confidential contracts between agents and airlines, which both parties agree not to disclose to anyone else. All commission contracts contain confidentiality clauses. Most airlines offer high enough commissions to offer discounts only to selected agents. Airlines don't want other agents to find out how large are commissions they have agreed to pay to some agents, lest all their other agents ask for the same commissions. Agents likewise don't want competing agents to find out what deals they have been offered, lest they ask for and get them too. You will never see commission contracts or their terms published in CRSs, on the Internet, or anywhere else. They are compiled (and in some cases indexed by computer) only internally by individual discount agencies, and occasionally by consortia of discount agencies.

The discount airfare market is not a perfect or open market. Discount agents spend much of their efforts trying to find out which agents for which airlines in which places are being offered which commissions on which tickets on which airlines, with what rules, so that they can buy each ticket wherever and from whichever wholesale agent, or issue it under their own contract with the airline, as will be cheapest.

Airlines' local offices sometimes have a high degree of autonomy. An office in a particular obscure place may have decided to give a local agent a higher commission than any of that airline's offices in other places, enabling that agent to sell tickets more cheaply than any agent elsewhere. Differences in prices of tickets on the same route when bought in different places are usually mistakenly attributed to currency fluctuations. But the IATA system for calculating price equivalents in local currency is fairly effective in limiting the impact of all but the most rapid changes in exchange rates. Most variations of ticket price from place to place are due to differences in the commissions offered to agents in different places.

Demand for tickets between A and B (and willingness to pay, which is the airlines' measure of how much to charge) is generally highest in either A or B. It's harder to drum up customers for flights between A and B in other places. So there's often some other place C where some agent is given a higher commission on tickets between A and B than is any agent in A or B. For the airline, discounting in C has the advantage that it isn't likely to depress the market for tickets in A or B, where people are willing to pay more.

It is thus common for tickets for flights between two places to be cheapest in some third place. Not all airlines permit their agents to sell discounted tickets to customers in other countries—it's governed by the rules of their commission contracts—but many do. Most agents aren't set up to import tickets from other places and wouldn't know where to look or who to buy from in other places anyway. Those specialized discount agents who shop the global ticket market can offer much better prices on certain tickets than agents familiar only with prices from local sources.

Airlines' and agents' collections of information about the terms of their own and other airlines' and agents' commission agreements are their most important trade secrets. An agent's competitive edge in a particular market may depend on their knowledge of a particular supplier of especially cheap tickets on a certain airline and route. Industrial espionage and intelligence-gathering in the discount travel industry focuses on finding out who has what deals with whom, or which airline is offering what commissions to which agent where. Agents use all kinds of tricks to find new suppliers. Airlines use agents to find out what competing airlines are offering. Agents use customers to find out what competing agencies are offering. No one has complete information about ticket prices worldwide, but the traveling public has less information than any of the other players (airlines and agents).

The *price* at which a discounter sells a ticket should not be confused with the *fare* shown on the ticket. If you call the airline directly, and ask about a price that an agent or a friend told you about, the airline may well say, "We don't have a *fare* like that. If you want to get a *price* like that, you'll have to talk to one of our agents," which is technically true but sounds like double-talk if you don't know the code.

There is no necessary correlation between which airline publishes the lowest fare and which airline offers the lowest discounted selling price. Often an airline that sells most of its tickets through agents, at discounted prices, and few tickets at published fares, won't even bother to publish any but the highest fares. You can't count on such a negative correlation between fares and prices, but it is quite common for the airline that is actually cheapest to have the highest published fares.

### Is Commission Rebating Legal?

Commission rebating is perfectly safe. In a very technical sense it is illegal, but it's completely safe for travelers, and in all the ways that matter it might as well be legal.

Aviation treaties between the United States and many other countries provide that tickets between the United States and those countries will be sold only at prices approved by both governments. And there is a federal law (49 USC Sec. 41510, see also 14 CFR Sec. 221) that forbids the sale of airline tickets at any price that isn't published in a "tariff" filed with the government by the airline.

The official position of the government of the United States is that it wants to renegotiate all these treaties to eliminate the restrictions on "off-tariff" sales. But until that happens, these treaties require the United States to keep the law on the books—even though the government is publicly and openly opposed to it.

Obviously, the United States isn't about to do anything it doesn't have to do to enforce this law. But even that is a problem: the government can't just make a public statement that it is going to ignore the law. The closest it has come to that was a few years ago, when the U.S. Department of Justice announced a "proposed" official policy of nonenforcement of the law against off-tariff ticket sales. Because of the international treaty obligations of the United States, that "proposed" policy wasn't, and couldn't be, officially implemented. But in fact it was and is the real policy: no enforcement action will be brought against anyone by the USA government for off-tariff airline ticket sales unless there is evidence that someone is being defrauded.

I know this sounds bizarre, to say the least. But to reiterate, the upshot of all this is that travel agents can offer discounted tickets quite openly and *de facto* legally, and that travelers can buy them as safely as any other tickets.

As should be clear from the explanation above, all discounting of international tickets (i.e., sales by agents for less than published fares) involves the rebating of agent commissions to customers, in violation of IATA rules. As such, it could theoretically be grounds for civil action against the agent for breach of the terms of their contract with the airline. In practice, this is rare. An airline for which the agent is selling lots of tickets is unlikely to consider itself aggrieved by the agent's sales success. If the airline doesn't like what the agency is doing, or the prices at which it is selling tickets, it's easy enough for the airline to reduce the agency's commission or terminate its contract.

Airlines themselves created the consolidator ticket market, and perpetuate it by paying agents commissions that they know are being rebated to customers. Once an airline has set its commission levels, the airline gets the same amount of money regardless of whether the agent charges you the full fare (and keeps the commission) or rebates some or all of the commission to reduce the amount you pay. The airline neither knows nor cares how much you pay an agent for ticket. Airlines have no real reason to object to rebating, and no authority to do anything to the passenger even if they did.

The important thing for travelers to understand is that it is the agent, not the passenger, who is (arguably) breaking the rules by rebating their commission. Nothing in the IATA rules forbids customers from accepting commission rebates from agents.

Equally important, rebating of commission has no effect on the validity of the ticket. The agent may be liable for sanctions from the airline and/or IATA, but the ticket remains completely valid.

Some airline offices in countries that try to prevent agents from discounting will tell customers that discounted tickets (such as those issued in other countries) will not be honored. This is just a scare tactic to get people to buy full-fare tickets rather than importing discounted ones. Nothing in the IATA rules authorizes an airline to refuse to honor a ticket because of suspicion of commission rebating.

In practice, it's impossible to tell from a ticket itself whether the commission was rebated. If they show a price at all, all tickets, even discounted ones, show a face value that corresponds to some published fare. Once the ticket is issued, there's no way to prove how much anyone paid for it. Some foreign governments, and airline offices in some countries, don't like ticket discounting. But there's nothing they can do about it, if it happens in another country, even if it involves tickets for flights that originate in their country. If questioned by an airline, you are on the safest ground if you always say that you paid whatever price (if any) is shown on your ticket, or that you don't remember exactly how much you paid, and that you bought it in whatever place is shown on the ticket as the place of issue.

In theory, it's illegal in the United States for the passenger knowingly to accept a commission rebate. But this seems to be a sort of, "Don't ask," don't tell" rule: for tickets bought in the United States, the passenger is never told how much the agent paid the airline, or whether the retail price includes a commission rebate. It's hard to imagine a situation in any country in which any action could, much less would, be brought against a passenger for buying or using a consolidator price ("off-tariff") ticket.

As I've already explained, countries vary in the extent to which they permit enforcement of the IATA rules against rebating. In the United States, the prohi-

# BIG BUSINESS AND THE PEOPLE'S AIRLINE

Travelers often wonder why all major international airlines seem to be set up to cosset the rich luxuriously and expensively. How come a major international airline isn't committed to affordable, no-frills transportation for the masses? But there was, and to some degree still is, just such an airline: Aeroflot Russian International Airlines. Why is Aeroflot different?

In the First World, air travel is a luxury. Most Americans rarely or never fly. The standards of comfort, service, and amenities people expect of air travel are standards of luxury. Russia, much less the USSR, is a much bigger country and, despite a good rail system, one where national unity is far less possible without air travel. It was one of the outstanding successes of the USSR that air travel was made accessible and affordable to the masses. Certainly Aeroflot favors the privileged, the nomenklatura, the old and nouveau rich—but mostly it was in the business of providing basic, affordable, mass transportation.

Most other airlines started with only one class of service, deluxe, and only later added a "tourist class" section in the back of the plane. Even today, most airlines' profit margins are much higher in first and business class, to which they devote a disproportionate amount of the cabin space and of their spending on service, frills, and amenities. Aeroflot started with only one class of service, basic, and only later added smaller sections for the more privileged passengers. While Aeroflot now offers two or three classes of service on most international routes, they continue to put most of their emphasis on simply getting people from point A to point B and on service in the main cabin, where most of the passengers are. (First-or business-class tickets on Aeroflot are actually quite a bargain for travelers who just want a larger seat and more legroom.)

Aviation is big business. The Russian aviation industry poses a far larger potential threat to Boeing and Airbus than they want to admit. Ilyushin, Tupolev, and Yak jetliners don't have all the bells and whis-

bition on rebating, even if required by law and included in the agent's contract with the airline, has been held to be void and unenforceable under other laws against price-fixing. In the UK, the situation is a bit more gray, but no one I've talked to has ever heard of enforcement action being taken against a UK agent solely for commission rebating. In practice, no airline can compete in the cut-price London market without paying its agents high enough commissions to permit substantial rebates. European Union law has also been interpreted to protect both the right to buy and sell tickets at off-tariff prices and the right to import and export tickets across borders within the EU.

---

tles of the latest products from Seattle and Toulouse, but they cost only a fraction of the price. The latest wide-bodied long-range Ilyushin 96 (IL-96) airframe, for example, costs about a tenth of the price of a comparable First World airframe. Russian engines are less fuel efficient (fuel efficiency is a lower priority in Russia, an energy-rich country and the world's largest oil producer), and Russian electronic instrumentation is less sophisticated. But even completely equipped with Pratt & Whitney engines and Rockwell avionics from the United States, a new IL-96 costs less than half the price of any competing First World plane.

First World aircraft manufacturers, and the governments that back them, thus have a compelling multibillion-dollar-a-year interest in discrediting both Russian aircraft and airlines, in the hope of driving their competitors out of business or at least keeping potential customers from even considering them. Budget travelers, on the other hand, have a compelling interest in cheaper airplanes that make possible lower fares, and in an airline with a fundamentally different, no-frills philosophy that uses

cheaper, less luxurious planes to provide cheaper flights.

Since having been divested of most of its domestic operations in Russia and of its divisions in republics other than Russia (which became such "new" airlines as Uzbekistan Airlines and Air Ukraine, both of which now fly to the United States), Aeroflot is no longer, as it had been for many years, the world's largest airline. But because of the historic relations with the USSR, Aeroflot retains rights to fly more international routes than any other airline in the world. Aeroflot's main hub in Moscow, the easternmost major city in Europe, is well suited as a hub for intercontinental connections between Europe, Asia, and Africa.

Because it does things differently, Aeroflot often seems a strange airline, and in some respects it is. It doesn't know much about marketing, and it is often hard to deal with. But travelers who want to keep no-frills long-haul air transportation available as an alternative to expensive luxury owe it to themselves to at least consider Aeroflot (http://www.aeroflot.ru) and Russian aircraft where they are an option.

The number of countries that tolerate rebating is increasing slowly, but these countries are still a minority, and there are large regions of the world (including most of South America and Africa) where almost no country permits large-scale discounting. As a practical matter, you are unlikely to get more than a nominal discount in a country where the IATA rules are enforced. But my point is that you don't have to worry about it, because all liability rests with the agent, not the traveler. You aren't party to any agreement against discounting.

### Airlines and Discount Agencies

Airlines have a schizophrenic love-hate relationship with consolidator discount agencies. Airlines themselves created the system of discounting through commission rebating by agents, as a way to preserve the benefits of the IATA price-fixing scheme while still enabling them to offer prices that maximize their profits. Airlines hand-pick the agents to whom they offer special commission agreements, and the terms of those agreements are determined and subject to change by the airlines, not the agents. But airlines are reluctant to talk openly about consolidator prices, lest wider awareness of their availability and legitimacy undercut the willingness of most passengers to pay the official fares.

Airlines vary in their willingness to acknowledge the existence of their consolidators. Some airlines, hoping to talk you into paying the published fare, pretend not to know what you are talking about if you ask them about discounted prices. Others will refer you immediately to one of their agents even if you try to buy a ticket directly from them. These tend to be airlines that don't expect to be able to get people to pay their published fares and who, because they sell almost all their tickets through discounters, don't have enough staff to be able to handle direct sales to the public. But even these airlines that refer you to discounters won't discuss discount prices with you, only published fares.

Remember, airlines are only allowed to sell tickets at published fares; when they break this rule, they do so only on the Internet. If an airline is reluctant even to tell you its published fare, that's probably because it's so high, and bears so little relation to discounted selling prices, that it is afraid it would scare you away to another airline. Take it as a clue that if you contact the agent they send you to, the real selling price will be heavily discounted.

Some airlines deliberately foster the image of disreputability and unreliability of discount agents and consolidator tickets as part of their revenue-maximization (yield management) strategy. People who are truly price-sensitive, and couldn't afford to buy tickets at the official prices, will probably buy consolidator tickets even if they think of them as somehow tainted or of dubious legitimacy. The airlines are unlikely to lose these people's business. People who are afraid to buy tickets from discounters are usually people who are able and willing to pay more for the perceived greater security of getting tickets directly from the airlines, or from full-price agents.

Frequently, airlines' commission contracts with discount agencies restrict how the agencies can advertise. For example, they might be forbidden from mentioning the name of the airline or allowed to advertise or market only to a particular geographic or ethnic market. That doesn't mean, however, that you should pay for a ticket without knowing on what airline you are going to fly.

An agent should always tell you on what airline an advertised price is available; a price for tickets on a scheduled airline from an agent who refuses to name the airline before taking your money is presumptively a fraud. The only two exceptions are tickets for charter flights— no guarantees are usually made as to which airline will actually operate a charter flight—and the "opaque" or "white label" prices (as discussed below) offered exclusively through certain Internet travel agencies. In no other case should you buy tickets on a scheduled airline without knowing on what airline you hold reservations.

All airlines' commission contracts with agents I've ever seen are subject to change at the sole discretion of the airlines, with minimal or no notice. While some airlines maintain fairly stable long-term contracts, many airlines revise their commissions every few days in response to current load factors, advance booking levels, and competitive pressures. If an agent starts selling too many tickets at a discounted price, the airline will conclude that people are willing to pay more, and that it doesn't need to discount so heavily. The airline will therefore reduce the commission, forcing the agent to raise the selling price, or will terminate the contract and cease to offer any additional commission at all.

It's not common, but more than once I've seen airlines reduce ticket commissions overnight by more than US$500 per ticket. There are many "bait-and-switch" agents who quote low prices and then charge higher ones, but many price changes by agents are due to commission changes by airlines. Because agents are forbidden to disclose the terms of their agreements with the airlines, and wouldn't want to anyway, it's hard for travelers to know what's really going on. The result is that agents often take the rap when airlines raise prices, and that passengers find it harder to tell good agents from bad or to know whom to blame for price increases.

## Types of Fares and Tickets

"That's all well and good," some of you are probably saying by now, "But what kinds of ticket and airfare options does this leave us?" Within the framework described in the previous section, there's a complex structure of different types of published fares, consolidator tickets issued at published fares but sold for lower prices, unpublished "Web fares" offered on the Internet, and loopholes and ways around the system. Outside the IATA system, there are charter flights not governed by IATA pricing rules, subsidized tickets for courier travel, and an illegal black market in brokered frequent-flyer tickets.

See the "Types of Fares and Tickets" chart for a comparative summary of the advantages, disadvantages, and attributes of the different fares and tickets described in the following pages.

### Consolidator Tickets

Most advertised discount prices for international airline tickets are for what are called "consolidator" tickets. These are tickets on which, as discussed in the previous section, some of the travel agent's commission is rebated to the customer to reduce the effective selling price to less than the official fare.

Because a consolidator ticket is sold for less than the published fare, there is no such thing, strictly speaking, as a consolidator *fare*, only a consolidator selling *price*. This is how airlines or published-fare Internet sites can guarantee that they have "the lowest fare" even when they don't have the lowest price.

As discussed earlier, most airlines no longer pay a standard or "base" commission to travel agents as compensation for selling and issuing tickets. But those same airlines continue to pay "commissions" (expected and intended to be rebated to ticket purchasers) to consolidator agents, as a way of offering off-tariff discounts. Almost all airlines give at least some of their agents, somewhere, high enough commissions to enable them to offer discounts. Consolidator tickets are available on almost all airlines and routes, with two caveats:

First, you have to find the consolidator outlets. It's not surprising that the greatest discounts are often found through the most obscure and unlikely seeming agents in the last places you would think to look. That's perfectly consistent with the airlines' goal of discounting only through distribution channels that won't divert customers or depress prices in their primary markets. Retail travel agents who specialize in selling consolidator tickets are constantly tracking wholesale ticket prices and searching for new suppliers around the world. Their business success depends on it. Unless you get really lucky, you'll do better to go directly to a specialist who already knows where to find the best deal for your route than to beat the bushes on your own for every conceivable source of tickets.

Second, consolidator tickets are usually available only on flights on which the airlines expect that they would have empty seats if they didn't offer some tickets at less than the published fares. People who expect that discounts will always be available on all flights have missed the point of why airlines give discounts: to fill seats that would otherwise be empty.

For appearances' sake, the airlines generally offer a few reservations on each plane at consolidator prices even for travel at the busiest times (just as they usually offer a couple of seats on even the most popular flights for frequent flyer mileage redemption), but those few tickets may be sold within a few days of being offered, months before the flight. Some flights in peak season, especially flights around Christmas everywhere in the world and some other holidays in particular regions, routinely sell out months in advance. Some Christmas flights to Africa sell out by July at any price, much less consolidator prices.

"Yield management," the process by which airlines determine how many people to confirm on each flight, at any given time, in each booking class, is extraordinarily complex. I'll leave it as a topic for advanced classes in operations research. For our present purposes, it's an adequate approximation to conceptualize yield management as the allocation of the seats on each plane among "booking classes" that correspond to different fares. One (or more) of those booking classes is used for consolidator ticket bookings. Once the seats allocated to that class are reserved, no more consolidator tickets are available on that flight, even if seats allocated to higher-fare booking classes remain available.

Agents' commissions, which dictate their ability to discount through rebating, often aren't fixed until the airlines have enough of an idea of advance booking levels to know how much of a discount they need to offer to fill their planes. Some airlines fix commissions a year at a time, based on past experience of seasonal variations in load factors (percentage of seats filled). Other airlines set commissions one or two seasons (six weeks to six months) at a time, which is why you will sometimes be told that discount prices for your travel dates haven't been set yet. That doesn't necessarily mean that discounts will be offered later, especially for peak season travel. If flights are filling up on schedule, or are already fully booked, agents may never be offered any extra commission on them, and no discounts may ever be available on certain flights. An airline that generally gives agents a 30 percent commission may give only the standard 5 percent in peak season, leaving little or no margin for rebating.

Most flights aren't full, and consolidator tickets are usually available if you buy them at the right time. Airlines vary in the sophistication of their yield management algorithms. Some airlines don't segment their reservations by fare, so that you can buy a consolidator ticket even for the last seat left on the plane. In low season, when there are lots of empty seats, you are likely to have several choices of airlines at similar prices. In high season, you're more likely to find that fewer airlines have discounted seats available.

With those caveats about seasons and seats, consolidator tickets are available between more places than any other kind of discounted tickets, even on some lightly traveled routes between obscure places. Consolidator tickets are usually the only affordable choice for journeys other than short roundtrips, or for long stays. Unlike any other type of discounted ticket, consolidator tickets are available for long-stay roundtrips and for one-way, multistop, and discontinuous travel. If you are prepared to import tickets from a country where they can be issued and sold at a discount, consolidator tickets are available for travel originating in more places than any other kind of discounted tickets, even places where fares are high and no discounts are available locally.

### "Opaque" and "White Label" Consolidator Prices

Some consolidator travel agencies on the Internet have begun to sell tickets without telling customers on what airlines they will be flying. Your willingness to fly on whichever airline and route is cheapest is proof positive that you are price sensitive, not a business traveler who would otherwise buy a more expensive ticket in order to be able to select a particular airline. Airlines offer these agencies lower contract prices because they know that these prices will never be publicly advertised, or associated with the airline's name, or revealed to its competitors. These "white label" or "opaque" prices are, strictly speaking, a subset of consolidator tickets.

Thus far, these opaque or white-label prices have been offered only by travel agencies on the Internet. That could change, but probably won't. Online travel agencies specializing in these tickets include Hotwire.com, OneTravel.com, and Priceline.com. Other Internet travel agencies that mostly sell published-fare tickets, such as Travelocity.com and Expedia.com, have also begun offering a more limited selection of copycat opaque prices.

For flight within or from the United States, Hotwire.com has the largest selection of opaque prices. If price is truly the only object (it usually isn't), and you really don't care about the airline or route, or what time of day or night you fly, Hotwire.com is probably the first place to look for round-trip domestic flights in the United States.

OneTravel.com is less well known, but offers an interesting advantage: OneTravel.com shows the approximate time of day (a four to eight hour window) that the flights arrive and depart, and the number of stops and/or changes of plane, before you decide whether to buy. Most competitors don't give the exact number of stops or plane changes, and give a 24-hour window, so you don't know if you'll be on the first or last flight of the day.

Priceline.com is widely, but mistakenly, thought to be some sort of auction site. Actually, Priceline is an opaque or white label consolidator—with the huge disadvantage that they don't reveal their prices. Priceline says themselves, in fine print, that they aren't an auction. Priceline has fixed contract prices with airlines like any other consolidator. "Name your own price" is just a pricing mechanism. It ensures that you pay as much as you are willing, and no less. If you offer US$50 more than Priceline's contracted cost, or US$500 more, the airline, in most cases, gets the same amount. Priceline pockets the difference.

Individual offers to Priceline are not sent to the airlines, nor are they individually evaluated by the airlines. They are evaluated only by Priceline to see if you have offered enough more than Priceline's contracted cost to make your offer acceptable to Priceline. In most cases airlines don't even know how much you have paid, or how much Priceline has made on your tickets. (For more on the pitfalls of Priceline and its imitators, see *The Practical Nomad Guide to the Online Travel Marketplace*.)

These problems aside, the largest limitation to opaque or white-label prices is that they are offered exclusively for roundtrip travel on fixed, unchangeable dates, mainly within North America. They are worth considering for roundtrip domestic flights in the United States, but from what I've heard airline executives say, they aren't likely to become a useful option any time soon for longer stays, more flexible tickets, or one-way or multistop journeys. Airlines figure that people who want more complex itineraries or a longer stay at their destination will be willing to pay more for the privilege.

### Published Discount Fares

Airlines publish a variety of discounted fares in addition to the highest "regular" or "normal" fares. Advertised discount amounts or percentages are calculated from the highest possible fares; what you consider a normal price is probably described by the airlines as a 50–80 percent discount from the full "normal" fare.

I don't recommend published fare tickets in most cases where cheaper and/or less restricted consolidator tickets are available on the same routes, but it's useful to understand what they are and their hidden drawbacks.

The cheapest published fares offered directly by the airlines, published-fare Web sites, or offline travel agencies are almost invariably roundtrip fares; even when airlines advertise what looks like a one-way fare it usually turns out when you read the fine print to be a "half roundtrip" fare or "fare for one-way travel, based on roundtrip purchase." (I agree with you: these sorts of ads are misleading and should be prohibited. Some state law enforcement agencies also agree, but the federal government has "pre-empted" regulation of the airlines, so state and local authorities are powerless to stop these deceptive practices.)

There are too many types and names of fares (APEX, Super APEX, PEX, Superpex, Super Discovery, etc.), and too little standardization in how airlines use these and other names and assign fare basis codes, to make it useful to try to categorize or describe particular types of discounted published fares. Don't waste your time trying to figure out what the best fare for your itinerary will be called. The names are essentially arbitrary, and the same general principles apply to cheap published fares by any name or with any fare code.

During the occasional and short-lived "fare war," when some airline lowers fares dramatically and others are forced to match the special fare, published fares are sometimes lower than the cheapest consolidator tickets. But cheap published fares, especially during short-duration sales, are invariably among the most highly restricted of all tickets. The advantage to consolidator tickets is not that they are necessarily much cheaper than the cheapest published fares but that, because consolidator tickets are less restrictive, more travelers' desired itineraries qualify for them than qualify for the cheapest published fares.

The typical choice is between a completely nonrefundable, nonchangeable, use-it-on-the-ticketed-dates-or-throw-it-away roundtrip ticket at a published discount fare that must be reserved and purchased long in advance, permits no stopovers or discontinuities, and has extreme limits on minimum and maximum stay (typically a maximum of no more than 30 days); and a consolidator ticket that during a published fare sale or fare war may be slightly more expensive but that permits longer stays, date changes, stopovers, and discontinuities.

*continued on page 187*

# Types of Fares and Tickets

For more detailed explanations of each category see the appropriate text sections.

| Type of Fare or Ticket | Biggest Advantage | Biggest Drawback |
|---|---|---|
| Tickets You Have Earned as a Frequent Flyer | Free, if you didn't have to pay (or pay extra) for your tickets to earn the frequent flyer mileage | Your airline may not go where you want; tickets on airlines with frequent-flyer programs usually cost more, by more than the credits are worth. |
| Courier Travel | Where available, this is the cheapest option. | Not available on most routes |
| Charter Flights | Where available, this is usually the cheapest option. | Only available on limited routes, usually only at limited times of year |
| Airpasses and Foreign Visitor Fares | Sometimes cheaper than separate tickets (in much of the Americas, dramatically cheaper) and more flexible | Cost more than separate tickets in some countries. Sometimes available only if your international flights are on the airline of the destination country. |
| Web Fares and "Fare War" Sales | When and where available, these are usually the cheapest option. | Limited routes and unpredictable availability |
| Student Fares | Available for one-way and long-stay roundtrips | Limited routes; change fees; not always the cheapest; must be a student or college teacher |
| Consolidator Tickets | Greatest flexibility and widest range of routes of any discounted tickets | Available only from a small number of specialized agents in certain countries only, many of whom give only minimal service or advice |
| "Opaque" and "White Label" Consolidator Prices | No advance purchase; sometimes the cheapest option | Limited routes; instant purchase; no changes; possible early departure or late arrival |
| Group and Tour Fares | Often the cheapest airfare, if available, if you are taking a cruise or tour or booking a hotel or resort package | Limited routes and flexibility. If you don't want a package, it's only occasionally worth buying one just to qualify for the airfare. |
| Published Discount Fares | Most widely available discounted tickets | Most expensive discounted tickets |
| Published Routing-Based RTW Fares | Very few other legitimate discounted tickets are available in business or first class. | Extremely limited routes; actual routes often require many expensive side trips; coach fares overpriced |
| Published Mileage-Based RTW Fares | Very few other legitimate discounted tickets are available in business or first class. | Limited routes; actual routes often require expensive side trips; coach fares overpriced |
| Published Normal, Walk-Up, or Standby Fares | Most widely available type of tickets | Extremely expensive |
| Brokered Purchased Frequent-Flyer Tickets | Only discounted business- or first-class tickets available to most destinations | Illegal; costs can include fines and jail, plus additional fare, if you get caught. |

# Types of Fares and Tickets

| Price Range (for comparable routes) | Flights Typically Available: From | Flights Typically Available: To | Available for Flights Originating Outside Country Where Tickets Are Bought? |
|---|---|---|---|
| Free-Moderate | Only places served by certain airlines | Only places served by certain airlines | If the airline has local traffic rights on such a route |
| Almost Free-Low | Major international business centers only | Major international business centers only | Yes, but in practice it's very difficult to arrange. |
| Low | Major population centers | The busiest holiday and resort destinations only | Yes, but in practice it's very difficult to arrange. |
| Very Low-Moderate | Airports within certain countries served by particular airlines | Airports within the same countries served by the same airlines | Yes. Usually must be bought outside the country of travel, and not available locally. |
| Low-Moderate | Selected and unpredictable USA airports | Selected and unpredictable USA airports | Only when there's a fare war in that market |
| Low-Moderate | Most major cities | Most major cities | Sometimes |
| Low-Moderate | Anywhere | Anywhere | Yes |
| Low-Moderate | Most US Airports | Most US airports and some cities elsewhere served by USA airlines | No |
| Low-Moderate | Charters: big cities; scheduled airlines: most airports | Major resort, holiday, and package-tour destinations | Only through tour operators in the country where flights originate |
| Moderate-High | Most airports, often even minor ones | Most airports, often even minor ones | Yes |
| Coach: Moderate; business or first class: Low | Most airports, often even minor ones | Only certain destinations permitted by the routing rules | Yes |
| Coach: Low-Moderate; business or first class: Low | Most airports, often even minor ones | Only certain destinations permitted by the routing rules | Yes |
| High | Anywhere | Anywhere | Yes |
| Moderate-Extremely High | Only places served by certain airlines | Only places served by certain airlines | Usually No <br><br> (continues) |

# Types of Fares and Tickets
(continued)

| Type of Fare or Ticket | Likelihood of Availability: Low Season | Likelihood of Availability: High Season | Likelihood of Availability: Holidays |
|---|---|---|---|
| Tickets You Have Earned as a Frequent Flyer | Good | Poor; Fair if you book many months ahead | Bad-Nil |
| Courier Travel | Fair to any specific destination; Good if you don't care where you go | Poor-Bad, even if you plan far ahead | Nil |
| Charter Flights | Often not operated at all | Fair | Bad |
| Airpasses and Foreign Visitor Fares | Excellent | Good, if your schedule is fairly flexible or you book in advance | Bad-Fair |
| Web Fares and "Fare War" Sales | Good but erratic | Poor and erratic | Bad and erratic |
| Student Fares | Excellent | Fair | Bad |
| Consolidator Tickets | Excellent | Good; Very Good if you're not picky about airlines, routes, or exact dates | Poor; Fair if you book several months in advance |
| "Opaque" and "White Label" Consolidator Prices | Very Good | Fair and erratic | Poor-Bad and erratic |
| Group and Tour Fares | Excellent if tours are operating year-round; nil if not | Good, especially if you book several months in advance | Poor-Bad |
| Published Discount Fares | Excellent | Fair | Poor |
| Published Routing-Based RTW Fares | Excellent | Good if you're not in a hurry and your dates are flexible | Fair |
| Published Mileage-Based RTW Fares | Excellent | Good if you're not in a hurry and your dates are flexible | Fair |
| Published Normal, Walk-Up, or Standby Fares | Excellent | Excellent | Fair-Good |
| Brokered Purchased Frequent-Flyer Tickets | Excellent | Coach: Poor; business/first class: Fair | Bad-Nil |

# Types of Fares and Tickets

| Refundable if Entirely Unused? | Minimum Stay | Maximum Stay | Date Changes Permitted? |
|---|---|---|---|
| Yes, with penalties | Usually none | Varies (typically 30-90 days) | Usually for a fee, sometimes for free |
| No | 3-7 days | 7-21 days, rarely longer | No |
| No | Until the next charter flight back (3-7 days) | 30 days or more (or until the last charter flight back of the season) | Sometimes, for a fee |
| Yes, with penalties | Usually none | 14 days-1 year (usually 60 days in North America) | Yes, usually for free |
| No | 7-14 days | 14-30 days | No |
| Yes, with penalties | None | 1 year | Yes, for a fee |
| Usually, with penalties | None-7 days | Up to 1 year; no limit if you buy your tickets in stages | Yes, often for free |
| No | None-7 days | Usually 30 days | Usually no |
| Sometimes, with penalties | 2-10 days | 7-45 days (often may extend longer than the duration of the tour) | Sometimes not, sometimes for a fee |
| Sometimes, with penalties | 3-14 days | 7-90 days (up to 6 months or 1 year only on certain routes) | Usually for a fee, sometimes for free |
| Yes, sometimes with penalties | 14 days | 1 year | Yes (Free) |
| Yes, sometimes with penalties | 14 days | 1 year | Yes (Free) |
| Yes | None | 1 year | Yes (Free) |
| No | Usually none | Varies (typically 30-90 days) | Usually for a fee, sometimes for free (continues) |

# Types of Fares and Tickets
(continued)

| Type of Fare or Ticket | Open Jaws Permitted? | Stopovers Permitted? | Advance Purchase Required? |
|---|---|---|---|
| Tickets You Have Earned as a Frequent Flyer | Sometimes | Sometimes | None-14 days |
| Courier Travel | No | No | Highly variable (None-6 months) |
| Charter Flights | No | No | Highly variable (None-6 months) |
| Airpasses and Foreign Visitor Fares | Yes | Yes (usually limited in number, or charged for) | Before you leave your home country |
| Web Fares and "Fare War" Sales | Usually No | No | None-6 months |
| Student Fares | Yes | Sometimes | None, if space is available |
| Consolidator Tickets | Yes | Yes | None, if space is available |
| "Opaque" and "White Label" Consolidator Prices | No | No | None |
| Group and Tour Fares | Sometimes | Rarely | None-90 days |
| Published Discount Fares | Usually | Sometimes (often at substantially higher fare) | 7-21 days |
| Published Routing-Based RTW Fares | No, with very few specified exceptions | Yes, but only if possible within routing rules | None-21 days |
| Published Mileage-Based RTW Fares | Yes | Yes | 7-21 days |
| Published Normal, Walk-Up, or Standby Fares | Yes | Yes (sometimes at a higher fare) | None |
| Brokered Purchased Frequent-Flyer Tickets | Sometimes | Sometimes | None-14 days |

# Types of Fares and Tickets

| Allowable Time between Reservation and Payment | Available in Coach/Economy (Third Class)? | Available in Business/Club Class (Second Class)? | Available in First Class? | Available Roundtrip? | Available One-Way? |
|---|---|---|---|---|---|
| 1-3 days | Yes | Yes | Yes | Yes | No |
| Short but variable (no more than a few days) | Yes | No | No | Yes | No |
| Short but variable (no more than a few days) | Yes | Rarely | No | Yes | Rarely |
| Usually no limit, if tickets are bought before leaving home | Yes | No | No | Usually (but may only be allowed to transit or stop in each city once) | Yes |
| None-3 days | Yes | No | No | Yes | No |
| Typically 7 days | Yes | No | No | No (issued and priced as two one-way tickets) | Yes |
| Usually at least 7 days (unless reserved at the last minute) | Yes | Occasionally | Rarely | Yes | Yes |
| None (instant purchase required) | Yes | No | No | Yes | No |
| None-several months (but deposit required immediately) | Yes | Occasionally | Rarely | Yes | No |
| None-14 days (usually 3-7 days) | Yes | No | No | Yes | Rarely (except between North America and Asia) |
| Up to 14 days | Yes | Yes | Yes | No (must continue around the world) | No; must return to starting point |
| Up to 14 days | Yes | Yes | Yes | No (must continue around the world) | No; must return to starting point |
| No limit | Yes | Yes | Yes | Yes | Yes |
| Short but variable (no more than a few days) | Yes | Yes | Yes | Yes | No |

(continues)

# Types of Fares and Tickets
### (continued)

| Type of Fare or Ticket | Range of Routes Available | Best Suited For |
|---|---|---|
| Tickets You Have Earned as a Frequent Flyer | Poor | People who've earned mileage on business trips they didn't have to pay for |
| Courier Travel | Extremely Bad | Short low-season holidays from and to the biggest cities, especially if you don't particularly care where you go |
| Charter Flights | Bad | Short high-season holidays to the most popular destinations |
| Airpasses and Foreign Visitor Fares | Very Good in countries where available | People taking many flights (especially if in a short time) within a large country. Best in the US, Canada, Russia, Australia, Indonesia, Brazil, Argentina. |
| Web Fares and "Fare War" Sales | Fair (when there's a fare war) | Short-stay impulse travelers |
| Student Fares | Fair | Certain one-ways and long-stay roundtrips |
| Consolidator Tickets | Excellent | Complex, unusual, multistop, or discontinuous routes; one-way tickets; tickets originating in other countries; business or long-term travelers who need flexible dates |
| "Opaque" and "White Label" Consolidator Prices | Fair-Good within US; Bad elsewhere | Round-trip travel within the US when you don't meet advance purchase or minimum stay requirements for other tickets |
| Group and Tour Fares | Poor-Bad | People who would be reserving hotels, package tours, or cruises in advance anyway |
| Published Discount Fares | Good | Recommended only when nothing cheaper is available |
| Published Routing-Based RTW Fares | Bad-Poor | Business and first class, but only if the route suits your plans |
| Published Mileage-Based RTW Fares | Poor | Business and first class, but only if the route suits your plans |
| Published Normal, Walk-Up, or Standby Fares | Excellent | Not recommended if there's any other choice |
| Brokered Purchased Frequent-Flyer Tickets | Fair | Not recommended ever |

For all but the simplest trip for a brief visit to a single destination, the cost of backtracking or circling to other destinations from the single turnaround point of a roundtrip ticket is likely to more than offset the additional price of a ticket with stopovers, or an open jaw, that will take you to or from more than one destination. (Published one-way fares are invariably much higher than consolidator prices, and are rarely on sale.)

Particularly for one-way, long-term, or multistop travelers, or anyone seeking flexibility, the extreme restrictions on fare war tickets and other cheap published fares make them a last resort for tickets originating in places where no discounts are available locally, or for domestic flights on which there are no consolidator tickets. Often you can avoid the necessity to buy tickets like this at all by including countries where tickets are overpriced as stopovers on through tickets to onward points, and by buying domestic tickets at a discount in conjunction with, or as part of, international tickets.

An airline will only publish an especially low fare, much less initiate or join a fare war, when it has or expects to have an unusually large number of empty seats. In such circumstances, lots of seats are likely to be available for consolidator tickets as well. If there's time to meet the advance purchase requirements of the cheapest fare (typically at least two weeks) there's a good chance there's time to import a consolidator one-way ticket from someplace where it is cheaper than any published fare.

### Web Fares

The lowest prices offered directly by the airlines are "Web fares" offered exclusively on the Internet.

At first, Web fares were offered exclusively for weekend travel on routes within North America. The range of offerings has expanded gradually, but remains limited to roundtrip travel for short stays within limited ranges of fixed dates. And these deals are short-lived and deliberately unpredictable. If there's a Web fare available for your itinerary, great. But you can't count on one being offered when you want it. Like fare war tickets, they are extremely inflexible and of little, if any, value for longer stays or more complex or multistop itineraries.

Like published fares, Web fares are available directly from the airlines, and from many online travel agencies. But like consolidator prices, they aren't filed with IATA or the government or made available through CRSs or most offline travel agencies.

Ultimately, Web fares do not serve consumer interests. Airlines could easily elect to publish their "Web fares," include them in CRSs, and allow them to be sold by all travel agencies. For travel within the United States, remember, the airlines can publish any fares they like. All they would have to do is file their fares with the government (to ensure transparent pricing, and prevent possible collusion or anti-competitive practices), and agree as a "common carrier" to offer the same prices to all customers who meet the same conditions.

AIR TRANSPORTATION

But airlines don't want to publish their lowest fares; this would make them too widely available and would frustrate the airlines' goal of price discrimination (getting different people each to pay as much as they are willing). So what do they do instead? They offer unpublished fares, but only on the Internet, where they seem to have assumed that no rules apply. And they've gotten away with it, despite accusations by consumer advocates, CRSs, and offline travel agencies that the major high-fare airlines are using the non-transparency of Web fares to hide oligopolistic and strongarm pricing tactics against start-up and low-fare competitors. Refusing to file Web fares in published tariffs or make them available through CRSs does nothing to lower prices. It serves only to distort the market, frustrate government oversight of antitrust law, and reduce the availability of low fares.

If you're going to buy a ticket at a Web fare, buy it directly from the airline's own Web site. Participating airlines may also offer their Web fares on Web sites such as Orbitz.com (some of these airlines are also Orbitz.com's founders and owners), so these sites are useful tools for finding Web fares. But airlines often give bonuses, such as extra frequent flyer mileage credits, for buying tickets on their own Web sites rather than on sites like Orbitz.com. And some airlines—including major domestic USA discount airlines like Southwest Airlines and Jet-Blue, and many smaller international airlines— don't participate in Orbitz.com, so it's important to check their Web sites individually.

### Fares for Students and Teachers

Student fares are the best-known and most widely available of a class of published IATA-approved fares called "status" fares. By restricting eligibility for these fares to people who can prove they have a certain status indicative of limited willingness to pay—such as students or professors—airlines are able to offer these discounts with little risk that they will be used by people who would otherwise have paid higher fares.

Not all airlines offer student fares, and the rules and their prices vis-à-vis consolidator tickets vary. On most airlines, you must have a current, valid International Student Identity Card (ISIC) at the time of ticketing and when traveling on tickets at a student fare.

Being published fares, student fares should, in theory, be available directly from the airlines. In practice it's almost impossible to buy a student-fare ticket at an airline ticket counter or on an airline Web site. While they are published in the printed *Passenger Air Tariff* most student fares aren't programmed into the computerized databases of other published fares. Almost all student-fare tickets are sold by travel agencies, mainly by a few large agency chains specializing in the student market such as STA Travel (originally Student Travel Australia, but now operating in many countries including the United States, the UK, and Ireland) and Travel CUTS (owned by the Canadian Federation of Students, Canada's national student organization, but now with subsidiaries in the United States as well).

Student fares are distinct fares, with distinct rules. You can't combine two different kinds of discounts; there is no such thing as a student discount from any other fare. I know of no agency that will sell student-fare tickets for less than their face value.

Student fares are not necessarily the lowest fares, much less the tickets sold at the lowest prices. Consolidator tickets are often cheaper, and more flexible, than student-fare tickets. Student fares generally have change penalties (although small ones), unlike consolidator tickets that often permit date changes at no charge. Student tickets are available on fewer airlines than consolidator tickets, and more often on the airlines that are more expensive in the first place.

Because student travel agencies often deal only with student fares, and are often less familiar with the full range of other discounted tickets, it is not necessarily the case that a student will get the best price, particularly on an around-the-world ticket or multi-stop ticket, from a student travel specialist. Student fares are excellent values in some cases and relatively poor values in others. Before buying a student-fare ticket, I would always get an estimate on tickets to the same destination(s) from an agency whose expertise isn't limited to student fares.

Because they are intended for students studying abroad for a semester or a school year, student fares are generally available for longer stays (up to a year) than most other cheap roundtrips. This makes them the only cheap long-stay (more than three months) roundtrip tickets available on some, though by no means all, trans-Atlantic routes. Long- stay consolidator fares are much more widely available on trans-Pacific and other long-haul routes.

Many airlines have made teachers at post-secondary educational institutions eligible for the same fares as students, although rules on faculty eligibility for student fares vary from airline to airline. Like their students, professors may find student fares better or worse than consolidator tickets, depending on their itinerary.

No airline allows elementary or secondary school teachers to use student fares. The exclusion of teachers in lower grades is unfortunate and unfair (fairness being of course irrelevant in setting fares), because teachers often get paid less than college or university professors for higher-stress work, with few compensations except for the longest vacations of any major job category in the United States. A pity, because it's the academic calendar, and the opportunity it allows for travel, that attracts some people to teaching in the first place, or keeps them in it; certainly students would benefit if their teachers had more international travel experience.

### Fares for Package Tourists

IATA rules permit airlines to publish lower fares if they agree to sell tickets at these special fares only to people who have also bought package tours or other land services (hotel vouchers, etc.) that cost at least a certain percentage (usually 50 percent) of the cost of the tickets. These fares are called "inclusive tour" or IT fares. It seems a strange condition, but, as with all other discounted fares, the point is to ensure that the rules of these tickets preclude their use by the sorts of people who would be willing to pay higher fares.

Obviously, you have to be in a place where other fares are high, and other discounted tickets hard to find, for a package that includes the required minimum value of land services to cost less than other tickets would cost by themselves. In some countries, though, IT fares are so much lower than any other published fares that it is worth buying a package tour even if you don't plan to take the tour.

Some air-inclusive tour packages are designed and marketed with this in mind, with the full awareness and understanding of seller and buyer alike that most buyers of the package will throw the tour vouchers away and go off on their own once at the destination. If a proffered air-inclusive tour seems suspiciously cheap, or the seller of the tour seems surprised that you even ask about the accommodations or services to be provided, be alert to the possibility that it may be a tour of this sort.

The biggest problem with IT fares is that, to ensure they are used only by package tourists, they generally are available only on a roundtrip basis for fixed dates with quite a short maximum stay limit, usually 45 and sometimes only 21 or fewer days. Otherwise they work just fine, where they are available and suit your schedule.

### Group Fares

IATA rules also provide for group or GV fares, which, depending on the route and fare, require a minimum of 7–15 people traveling together on the exact same flights throughout their trip.

There's nothing wrong with GV fares if you are actually traveling in a group with a fixed and qualifying itinerary, although they aren't necessarily less than consolidator prices for tickets at other fares, and most groups don't use GV fares. But they are obviously not suitable for independent travelers, and like IT fares they are limited to roundtrips for short stays with fixed dates.

If you do have a qualifying group and itinerary, it's still worth going through an agent, rather than directly to the airline. Some agents are given special commissions, and give discounts through rebating, on group as well as individual fares. If a GV fare will be the best price for your group, a good agent will have every reason to tell you about it and to offer to sell you tickets at that price, or less.

Beyond a certain point, as the size of a group increases, airlines want more per person from groups than from individual passengers. An airline can sell a few seats cheaply to fill the plane, and still make money on the flight as a a whole if there are enough high-fare travelers. But if a group fills enough of the plane to displace those who would otherwise pay enough to cover the cost of the flight, the group has to pay its own way.

### Around-the-World and Multistop Tickets

Hearing there are special fares for trips around the world or around the Pacific Rim, or seeing advertised prices for such routes, is what starts many people thinking about the possibility of such a trip. But when it comes time to actually plan their itinerary, many people are misled and disempowered by published around-the-world (RTW) fares and advertisements. They conclude they have to stop in certain places, or follow a certain route, because, "all the [advertised] flights go that way." Or they ask, "Where can I stop on an around-the-world ticket?"

There are two fundamentally different ways that tickets can be issued for a trip around the world: either as a single ticket at an around-the-world fare published by an airline (or pair or alliance of airlines), or as a combination of discounted one-way tickets with stopovers. These two types of tickets have completely different rules.

Airlines offer very limited around-the-world ticket options. If you get an RTW ticket from the airlines, you have to start and end in the same country and are limited to a certain maximum distance (and sometimes a maximum number of stops) on the routes of a specific small group of "allied" airlines. On the more traditional of these RTW tickets, you must travel in a continuous east-west or west-east direction, without backtracking.

Very few people want to follow routes that satisfy these rules. Many long-term, multistop travelers don't happen to be going entirely around the world. In any event, most RTW travelers get a better price by buying a set of discounted tickets put together for them by a travel agent, based on their desired destinations. Most advertised RTW or other multistop ticket prices are actually prices for sets of tickets like this, and it's basically a waste of time to try to shoehorn the route you want to follow into one of the routes permitted by a published airline RTW fare.

With a customized set of discounted tickets, you don't have to start and end in the same place; your route does not have to be continuous, go in any particular direction, or be limited to any particular combination of airlines, number of stops, or maximum distance traveled; nor will you necessarily or usually save money by complying with any of those "rules." There is no standard or usual route or price. Prices vary greatly, depending primarily on the starting and ending points and specific set and sequence of stops you want, and to a lesser extent on the starting season and duration of your trip.

The first thing many people do when they start to plan a trip around the world is to try to work out a route that satisfies the rules of a published around-the-world fare. For budget travelers, this is a complete waste of time. Regardless of what sort of tickets or fare you use, you have to know what route you plan to follow before you can buy your tickets. Settle on a tentative set of destinations before you start to look for tickets or study fares.

### Published Around-the-World Fares

No one airline currently flies around the world. (The most recent airline to do so was Aeroflot, which discontinued service on part of its around-the-world route in early 2000.) Various partnerships of two or more airlines publish around-the world (RTW) fares.

Published RTW fares vary greatly by country of origin. So you can't assume anything from what a friend paid for a ticket, or was able to do, if that friend's flight started from another country—even if you want to travel on the same airlines. Trips originating in some other countries are substantially cheaper, and a better deal, than those starting in the United States, even if they're on the same airlines. (No, you can't buy an RTW ticket for a journey starting in one country, and use it for a journey starting in another. Flight coupons are valid only in the sequence issued, and I've heard from people who've gotten caught halfway through such a trip and had to pay thousands of dollars for new tickets.)

In order to keep them from being used by business travelers, most published RTW fares also require a minimum number of stops (most often three or four, of at least 24 hours each), a minimum trip duration (most often 14 days), and 21 days advance purchase.

Within these constraints, published RTW fares are of two distinct types: those restricted primarily by routing specifications and those restricted primarily by a limitation on total flown distance.

### Routing-based RTW Fares

The cheapest, but most restricted, published RTW fares are "routing-based" RTW fares offered by partnerships of two, three, or occasionally four airlines. Several hundred partnerships offer fares of this general type, each with its own peculiarities and prices. The same airline often has several routing-based RTW fares in conjunction with different partners. Many airlines have different sets of partners for RTW fares originating from different countries.

Regardless of the number of airlines involved, these fares are valid only for continuous travel on those airlines and those airlines only, beginning and ending in the same city, without breaks in the air itinerary to be traveled by land or sea, proceeding always in the same direction (east or west), without backtracking or transiting any city more than once.

Published routing-based third-class (coach or economy) fares around the world start at about US$2,500 for routes entirely within the Northern Hemisphere, beginning and ending in the United States. Fares including the Southern Hemisphere (Africa, South America, Australia, New Zealand, or the South Pacific) are at least US$1,000 higher.

All these prices are deceptively low, because ticketing most RTW trips at these fares would require multiple additional side trips, or sectors on other airlines, at additional fares. Most around-the-world itineraries require travel on more than just two or three airlines and at least some surface travel, neither of which is permitted by most of these fares. Similar routes can usually be ticketed more cheaply as a series of one-way consolidator tickets, as discussed in the following section.

Airlines will tell you, "Our around-the-world fare allows unlimited stops." But stops are allowed only where those airlines stop, and only within the permitted routes. The routing rules of published RTW fares are far more restrictive than they appear at first glance.

The routes of two airlines that offer a joint RTW fare may only fit together to circle the globe in two or three ways. Except for minor variations such as which domestic stops you make within the countries where the airlines are based, you can usually count on one hand the alternative routes permitted on any given routing-based RTW fare. Most of the cities shown on any given airline's international route map cannot actually be reached on any of that airline's and its various partners' routing-based RTW fares! They are dead-end spokes, not points on any through route.

Most airlines have hub-and-spoke route systems centered on the capital city or biggest airport(s) in their home country. Few airlines have extensive rights to carry people between other countries, except by way of their hub(s). Longer-range planes mean more and more nonstop flights from hub to spoke and back, with ever fewer intermediate stops in places along the way. If an airline serves many cities in a region, it probably serves most of them only from a hub that you are forbidden to pass through more than once without paying extra for separate side-trip tickets.

### Mileage-based Published RTW Fares

Mileage-based RTW fares are more expensive but usually more flexible than the routing-based RTW fares described above. Most fares of this type are offered by the brand-name airline marketing consortia ("alliances") such as the Star Alliance, Oneworld, and Skyteam. Starting and ending in the United States, these fares start at over US$3,500 for coach/economy (3rd class) travel.

Mileage-based RTW fares permit unlimited backtracking and retransiting of hub cities, as long as you confine yourself to the participating airlines, don't exceed a specified total allowance of miles or kilometers for the entire trip, and don't stop over in the same city more than once (you can usually change planes in the same city any number of times as long as you don't stop). Some have surcharges for stopovers or additional miles beyond the basic allotment (up to some maximum numbers of stopovers and miles).

These fares are an improvement over routing-based RTW fares, but not nearly as much of one as they might seem. You can often do more on one of these tickets, but you have to pay quite a bit more for it. And because you are still restricted to only a few airlines, you still have to follow their limited routes or buy additional tickets to bridge the gaps. Most cities are still reachable on such a fare only as side trips from one of the participating airlines' hubs.

If you want to go from South Africa to Senegal on a Star Alliance RTW fare, for example, you'll have to go by way of Frankfurt, thousands of miles out of the way, using up a huge portion of your mileage allotment. And you'll have a change of planes (no big deal) and perhaps an overnight layover (more of a nuisance and expense in an expensive country like Germany) to make connections. To continue on to anywhere from Senegal on this fare, you'll have to go back to Frankfurt again.

**Published RTW fares from Canada have sometimes been substantially lower than those from the USA. The price difference is sometimes enough to make it worth driving or taking a bus or train to Canada, in order to start your flight tickets form north of the border.**

The principal difference between a mileage-based RTW fare and a routing-based one is that on a mileage fare you can include a few side trips like this, although you can only make so many side trips without exceeding the mileage allotment. Because mileage fares are generally more expensive than routing fares, it's still unusual for one of them to be the cheapest way to get to any particular set of destinations.

For those who wish to fly in second class (business or club class) or in first class, however, published around-the-world fares are often the cheapest choice. Fewer discounts are available on business and first class one-way tickets than on coach tickets on most airlines and routes.

Published Northern Hemisphere around-the-world fares in business class generally start at about US$5,000 and US$7,000 in first class (from the United States, with the same caveat as above), but most actual itineraries require one or more side trips at additional cost.

Published RTW fares are fixed by the airlines, and are the same throughout the year. Airlines do not offer discounts or specials on these tickets, either directly to the public or through travel agents. The reason to go to a discount travel agent is not to get a discount on a published RTW fare but to see if there is a better and/or cheaper alternative to such a fare.

An agent who tries to tell you that you have to follow the routes or rules of published around-the-world fares probably isn't the sort of specialist from whom you should buy your tickets. If your routing happens to fit the route of a published around-the-world fare, and would be cheaper that way, a good agent will tell you so. In most cases it won't. Most routes actually flown around the world, much less most of those that travelers would like to follow, do not satisfy the rules of any airline's published RTW fare. Even those that do can often be more cheaply ticketed as a combination of consolidator tickets, as discussed below.

### Discounted Around-the-World and Multistop Tickets

Essentially all RTW and other multi-stop ticket prices advertised by travel agents are combinations of discounted (consolidator) one-way tickets strung together. Such a set of tickets permits you to use any number of airlines, to begin and end your trip in different cities, to travel some portions by land or sea, and to backtrack at will.

Depending on the route, prices for tickets like this start at about US$1,500 from the United States —less than half the price of the cheapest published RTW fares. At additional cost, you can go any place any airline flies, in any order. The shorter and more direct your path, the cheaper it is likely to be. But even small changes in an itinerary can greatly change the price, and there are few general principles behind these price differences (other than the general rule that the farther you fly the more it will probably cost).

Because one ticket with stopovers can cover several legs of your journey, and because good agents can offer a wide range of discounts on diverse routes, you can pay much less for these tickets from a skilled discount agency than you would pay if you bought separate tickets, even separate discounted tickets at the best possible prices, for each flight. Because consolidator prices are only available through travel agencies, you can't get tickets like this directly from an airline.

On the other hand, most agents rarely sell tickets for any sort of multistop, long-haul, long-term, or around-the-world travel. Because nondiscounted one-way fares on most routes are prohibitively expensive, constructing a set of tickets around the world at a competitive price requires access to a comprehensive network of discount contracts and wholesale suppliers of discounted tickets on one-way flights worldwide. Agents who don't sell tickets like this regularly have no reason and no way to negotiate discount contracts with airlines, or to keep track of prices from wholesalers, for one-way tickets between other countries. This is one type of travel where you have to go to a specialist to get any useful advice or a decent deal. See "Arranging Your Air Transportation" later in this chapter.

### Air Passes and Other Special Fares for Foreign Visitors

Air passes, special fares, or discounts are offered to foreign visitors for travel within many countries. These fares are sometimes substantially cheaper and usually substantially less restrictive than tickets available for purchase locally on the same routes.

Sometimes these are special published fares; sometimes they result from high commissions given to agents, and rebated, for domestic flights ticketed in conjunction with international flights on the same airline. This is one reason it is often advantageous to use a country's own national airline to fly to a country where you plan extensive domestic air travel. Some airlines give agents 50 percent commission, or more, on their domestic fares in conjunction with their international fares.

The common denominator is that, with few exceptions, tickets at these prices must be purchased outside the country, in conjunction with your international tickets. If you don't find out about them (or how expensive tickets are locally) until you arrive in the country, it's too late to do anything about it. This is one of the strongest reasons to plan even domestic air travel before you buy international tickets, and to include it in the wish list you give to the travel agent when you request a price estimate.

Even where prices are comparable to the cheapest local prices for fixed-date tickets, it's worth buying tickets ahead at a visitor fare to get tickets with freely changeable dates and no minimum stay or advance reservation requirements. On the other hand, some visitor fares (such as the 14-day Indian Airlines air pass and the 60-day Visit USA and Visit North America fares) have maximum stay limits too short for many long-term travelers, so be sure to check the maximum permissible stay before you buy such a ticket.

Not all visitor fares require you to reserve space on specific flights or even fix your routing, but it's advisable to do both, whenever possible, so as to be sure that the special fare is really a better deal than any alternative and that the flights and seats you want are available.

Special fares like these are available in the United States, Canada, Australia, New Zealand, India, Indonesia, Thailand, Russia, Argentina, Brazil, and many other countries. Air passes for each country have different rules. Some are confusing and many are little known to nonspecialist travel agents. Travel agents who specialize in a particular destination are most likely to know the ins and outs of air passes.

Because of the different rules governing domestic and international fares, there are relatively few multicountry air passes or special visitors' fares. Most so-called "regional" passes for multiple countries are valid only on one airline, to and from its hub. Getting between a series of other places in the defined region requires connecting back through the hub, and being charged for two flights, each time. Most "air passes" are not for unlimited flights but for a specified number of flights with an additional charge for each flight over the minimum number in the basic pass. With the extra flights, it ends up being as expensive, in most cases, as taking more direct flights would be.

### Subsidized Tickets for Couriers

Travel as a courier can be the cheapest way of all to travel. Sometimes couriers get their transportation provided for free. If you can get hired to travel as a courier on an itinerary that suits, courier travel is an unbeatable deal.

Obviously, there's a catch, or more budget travelers would fly this way. The catch is that most people's itineraries don't correspond to courier routes and schedules, and the few opportunities for courier travel on routes and schedules of greater interest to the general traveler are snatched up quickly, far in advance.

Courier travel works like this: in exchange for your agreement to accompany their cargo, a company that ships high-priority air freight (usually documents) subsidizes the price of your ticket. In effect, they hire you as a courier, but they don't pay you in cash. Rather, you pay them: they buy a ticket for you, and they charge you only part of what the ticket cost them. In return, they use your allotment of "free" checked baggage, and check additional cargo as your excess baggage.

The main reason for this arrangement is that baggage accompanying passengers is, so as not to delay travelers, given priority over unaccompanied cargo in customs inspection lines. In practice accompanied baggage is usually cleared within minutes or hours, while unaccompanied cargo can wait for days or weeks. In addition, airline rates for transporting excess baggage accompanying passengers (high though they may seem) are less than the rates for unaccompanied priority air cargo. By subsidizing a ticket for a courier to check their cargo as the courier's accompanied luggage, a shipping company gets their urgent shipments to the destination and through customs more quickly and cheaply than if they sent it without a courier.

As a courier, you are permitted only whatever luggage you can carry on, including a manifest of what has been checked in your name. You never see the checked cargo; you just get the manifest from the courier company's agent before you depart (usually you get your ticket at the same time). You deliver the manifest to an agent on arrival, usually along with your return ticket, which is given back to you with the return manifest when it's time for your flight home.

There is no such thing as a courier fare or courier ticket. Couriers travel on whatever tickets, at whatever fare, the courier or express shipping company buys for them. Usually they travel on cheap consolidator tickets, although courier companies are more concerned with schedules, routes, and cargo rates than with passenger ticket prices, so couriers often travel on some of the more expensive airlines. Couriers often mistakenly believe they are traveling on full-fare tickets because, like most consolidator tickets, theirs have a high face value and look, to the untrained eye, like full-fare tickets. This frequently leads couriers to think that their tickets have been more heavily subsidized than is actually the case. Whether couriers are eligible for frequent-flyer mileage and other such amenities depends on the rules of the particular consolidator agreement. The courier company doesn't care about such things and won't want to bother to research them for you in advance.

Because an agreement to travel as a courier is more in the nature of an employment contract, you have to deal directly with courier and express companies to arrange for work as a courier. (Couriers are technically freelance contractors of the courier companies; fortunately, the IRS doesn't yet require shipping companies to report the ticket subsidy as "income" for the courier's labor in accompanying the cargo.) Travel agents can't "sell courier tickets" or arrange courier travel.

Whatever their procedures for signing up couriers, the companies doing the hiring want their money's worth. Typically, this means you must travel roundtrip (because a roundtrip ticket for one courier costs less than two one-way tickets for different couriers) and come back soon. The more time you have at the destination, the more likely you are to wander off and fail to show up for the return flights, which can be disastrous for the courier company. A courier is often required to put up a substantial deposit (several hundred dollars) before the trip. If you don't show up for your scheduled flight home, you forfeit your deposit and will never again be hired as a courier. To simplify their scheduling, some companies want all their couriers to a destination to stay for the same amount of time. They might, for example, automatically assign each courier to the return flight seven or 14 days later.

One-way courier assignments are rare. Open-jaw or multistop courier assignments (except on a few routes with a mandatory one-night intermediate lay-over) are essentially unheard of. The most common lengths of stay for courier assignments are seven, 14, or 21 days. A few companies have begun to offer longer stays, particularly on trans-Pacific routes, because they have found that couriers allowed to stay longer are willing to pay a greater share of the price of their ticket, so the courier company can get away with paying less.

Longer assignments, peak-season assignments, and assignments to more touristic and less business-oriented destinations (when they exist) are likely to be highly coveted and to be awarded to experienced couriers. These are people who travel as couriers several times a year, are willing to go to unpopular and expensive places when a courier is needed on short notice (such as when a new freelancer flakes out and doesn't show up), and who have the right contacts for winning plum jobs.

Couriers are needed on routes where there is a large volume of high-value urgent cargo. Most of this cargo is business documents, and the main courier routes are trade routes between business and banking centers within the First World. There are very few couriers to anywhere in the Third World, and essentially none to the Fourth World. It's easiest to get a courier assignment, and your ticket will be most heavily subsidized, to places where local costs are high and during seasons when the destination is least attractive.

What does this mean? If a week in a cold, expensive place such as London or Tokyo in midwinter, for perhaps half the price of a low-season consolidator ticket, is attractive enough to be worth a moderate amount of extra effort to arrange, courier travel may be the way for you to go. Friends and lovers of expatriates, or anyone with a standing offer of a place to stay whenever they might get to some big business center, might also find it appropriate to their interests.

You may luck into something else that suits your fancy, or a company with more flexible options. But courier travel is of little or no use to most long-term, multistop, budget, or Third World travelers, simply because there are no courier assignments appropriate to their needs. Every day I get calls from would-be couriers who, unable to go where they want as couriers, have turned to other sources of discounts such as consolidator tickets.

If you can't get a courier assignment to where you want to go, you are unlikely to be able to piece together courier travel and onward transportation for a total price less than what discounted through tickets to your ultimate destination would have cost you in the first place. Even if you can get a free ticket as a courier to Tokyo, or a cheap one to Hong Kong or Singapore, for example, a ticket from Tokyo (or wherever) to your ultimate destination elsewhere in Asia may cost you more than you would have paid from home to your destination.

The best sources of information and advice on courier travel are subscription-based directories, newsletters, and Web sites listing which companies use freelance couriers on which routes, and giving advice on how to contact and get hired by them. Some of these call themselves "clubs," but they are really all just listing services.

Unfortunately, because many of their readers find they can't get where they want to go as couriers, these services are under pressure to offer advice on alternative ways of traveling cheaply. Most of their authors are experienced couriers, but only amateurs at airline and travel agency procedures. Like other outsiders who are obliged to guess at how the industry works, they sometimes guess wrong. Don't rely on courier travel experts for expertise about other sorts of tickets and fares.

### Charter Flights

Prices of transportation on chartered flights are not regulated by the IATA fare rules. At times, and on routes where charter flights are available, they are the cheapest way to go. But they are rarely available or suitable for long-term or multistop travel.

A charter works like this: a charter operator "charters" a plane by contracting with an airline to fly a planeload of people from one place to another, and contracts with passengers to provide them with transportation between those places. Charter prices are almost entirely unregulated: charter operators can charge whatever they think the market will bear.

The terminology is confusing: the charter operator doesn't actually "operate" the plane. Some charter flights are operated by airlines that specialize exclusively in charter flights, and some charter flights are operated by the same airlines that also operate regularly scheduled services. The "charter operator" is an intermediary between the passengers and the airline. Some charter operators sell tickets directly to the public, while others sell tickets through retail travel agents. Some sell tickets for air transportation only, some sell tickets only as part of an air-inclusive package, and some offer both options.

Charter-only airlines are subject to the same safety, airworthiness, maintenance, and certification requirements as scheduled airlines. The only difference in the planes used for charters is that some (not all) charter airlines use planes with single-class seating (no business or first class) and a shorter seat pitch (distance between seats from front to back) to maximize the number of passengers they can fit on a plane. Some charter airlines actually provide very good service, meals, etc., though most offer no-frills transportation.

Regular flights operate on the same schedule, with the same frequency, even when many seats are empty. Charter operators make money even with lower prices by filling every seat. Charter operators won't charter a plane somewhere unless they are confident of being able to fill it.

Most charters operate only to popular resort and tourist destinations in peak tourist season, when charter operators can count on regularly scheduled flights being full. Scheduled airlines can't readily add extra flights to accommodate peak or overflow demand. Most charter operators are either tour operators (who can count on filling charter flights with people on the tour they run) or wholesale consolidators (who charter planes on routes and schedules where they expect demand to exceed the supply of seats on scheduled flights).

Transportation on charter flights is generally sold only on a roundtrip basis for short stays between specific dates. A few of the largest charter operators sell tickets with options to return on flights from different places or on different dates, but few charter operators have extensive enough schedules to offer these choices. Charters are thus most likely to be a good choice if you are going from a big city to a single, popular destination for a known short period of time during a peak holiday season.

Trying to construct a more complex trip by combining charter flights with onward transportation on scheduled flights carries a serious risk of missed connections. A "ticket" on a charter flight may show a departure time or operating airline, but contracts for charter transportation invariably reserve the right to substitute airlines or means of transportation and to alter schedules by at least 24, often 48, and sometimes 72 hours. No compensation is due to passengers on account of such changes. All that a charter operator is contractually obligated to do is to arrange to have you transported, somehow or other, between the points specified within a few days, one way or the other, of the date contracted. Some charter operators reserve the right to cancel the charter if not enough people sign up. You'll get your money back if that happens, but it might be too late to find alternate tickets for a decent price.

Operating charter flights requires lots of working capital. Chartering a plane is a gamble: if not enough seats can be sold, the operator's costs to the airline, etc., for the flight may greatly exceed the amount paid by passengers. Airlines average these things out over many flights and routes, year-round, but charter operators are smaller and their business is by nature seasonal and focused on a more limited set of routes. An abrupt decline in tourism to a particular destination—such as from a widely publicized natural disaster or incident of political or criminal violence—can put a charter operator out of business. Bankruptcy of charter and tour operators is much more common than bankruptcy of airlines, and is the leading reason for travelers to be stranded abroad without transportation home. Operators specializing in a single destination are, of course, most vulnerable to any unexpected change in the volume of tourism to that place.

It's important to read the fine print of a charter contract carefully, and to understand clearly exactly what you can and can't expect. Do not purchase a ticket on a charter flight without buying trip cancellation and interruption insurance that covers you against bankruptcy of the charter operator. Do not buy your travel insurance from the charter operator: if it goes bankrupt without paying the airline that was supposed to transport you, it'll probably turn out not to have paid the insurance company either.

Prices of tickets on charter flights, even when the flights are operated by IATA member airlines, are not governed by the IATA pricing rules. So charters are the only cheap option available locally for travel out of some countries where IATA rules against discounting of scheduled flights are strictly enforced. However, you can usually avoid the necessity of buying charter tickets locally—and the attendant necessity of committing to dates in advance— by buying consolidator tickets out before you arrive in such a country, making it a stopover on a set of through tickets, or (if you live there) importing tickets from abroad.

### Collecting and Using Frequent-Flyer Miles

The cheapest tickets for all or (more often) part of some itineraries are eligible for credit in some frequent-flyer program or other. The number of miles the tickets will earn you depends on the specific itinerary. As a rule, though, tickets eligible for frequent-flyer mileage credit cost more than the mileage credits are worth. Either you have to pay more for tickets on an airline with a popular frequent-flyer program than for tickets on a cheaper airline, or only higher-priced tickets on a particular airline are eligible for frequent-flyer mileage credits. Frequent-flyer programs are, in effect, kickbacks to motivate business travelers to steer their business, and their employers' money, to more expensive airlines. It rarely makes sense for people like you, who are paying their own way, to buy tickets just to earn frequent flyer miles. All you're doing is paying more for your tickets in order to get part, but not all, of the price increase back as a kickback.

You don't get something for nothing. Airlines that provide "free" transportation pay for it by charging everyone more. This isn't the only reason USA airlines (the ones most committed to expensive frequent-flyer programs) aren't usually able to compete on price with non-USA carriers on international routes, but it is a significant factor. The extent to which frequent flyers are locked into particular airlines by mileage programs also enables the airlines with the biggest frequent-flyer programs to get away with lower standards of service.

Non-USA airlines that provide their passengers with mileage credits in the frequent-flyer programs of USA airlines have told me they pay three to five cents per passenger-mile to the USA airlines to buy those mileage credits; they feel they have to give them to attract business travelers who don't pay for their tickets but get to keep their frequent-flyer credits for personal use. One way or another, the airlines have to recover this cost in their prices. For most itineraries, the additional cost for tickets eligible for frequent-flyer mileage credit with major USA airlines is more than the likely value of the frequent-flyer mileage.

Don't count on frequent-flyer mileage unless you have specifically asked, and been told in writing on your itinerary, that specific flights will be eligible for a mileage credit in a particular frequent-flyer program. Different tickets, or tickets from different agents, even on the same airline, may differ in their eligibility for frequent-flyer mileage credit.

Rather than joining one airline's frequent-flyer reward program, and then always flying on that airline even when it's more expensive, I recommend signing up for every airline's frequent-flyer program, and buying tickets purely on price. If you fly regularly, you'll eventually accumulate enough credits in some program or other to earn rewards, without having had to spend extra money to accrue them. In addition, members of frequent-flyer programs are periodically sent coupons for discounts on flights. It's a way that airlines fill seats without having to announce publicly (by publishing a sale price and risking a fare war) that they are having trouble filling flights on certain routes or dates.

### Brokered Frequent-Flyer Tickets

There are few legitimate discounts on second-class (business or club class) or first-class tickets. Most front-cabin travelers' tickets are paid for by their employers, not out of their own pockets, so they choose airlines on service, not price. Airlines don't regard them as price-sensitive—probably rightly—and thus don't feel the need to offer discounts to attract their business. The airlines that offer legitimate discounts on business-or first-class tickets are, almost inevitably, those on which business-and first-class travelers don't want to fly.

The only way to get business-or first-class tickets on most airlines for less than full fare is in exchange for frequent-flyer mileage you or a friend has earned, or to use frequent-flyer mileage or other coupons to upgrade a coach ticket. Some people travel so much that they accumulate more frequent-flyer mileage credits than they can use and are willing to request "free" tickets or upgrades for other people in exchange for cash compensation, though this is in violation of airline rules.

Some black-market ticket brokers make their living by "selling" frequent-flyer tickets and upgrades. A would-be traveler pays the broker for a ticket, and the broker pays a frequent flyer to request a "free" ticket for the would-be traveler. Most advertisements for heavily discounted business-or first-class tickets, especially on USA and Western European airlines, are from these brokers.

These are not legitimately issued or traded tickets. Buying and selling frequent-flyer coupons or tickets is illegal and dangerous for buyers and sellers alike. Both the frequent flyer who requests the ticket and the traveler who uses it must sign statements that no money has changed hands; both are liable for the full fare and additional penalties if it did.

Selling frequent-flyer upgrade certificates, or most other upgrades, is equally illegal. If someone tries to sell you an upgrade certificate, or a coach ticket with an upgrade coupon attached, read the fine print on both sides of the coupon carefully. If it says, "void if sold," don't buy it. Trying to use a coupon you know is void because it was sold is punishable as fraud and/or theft of services.

It is extremely important to distinguish the legal, but against IATA rules, gray market in discounted tickets from the illegal black market in tickets issued in exchange for frequent-flyer mileage. Airlines themselves created the discount market and they endorse and perpetuate it by paying agents commissions that they know are being rebated to customers.

On the other hand, airlines do not want frequent-flyer tickets to be sold and do everything they can to stop it. If you buy a ticket from someone who obtains it for frequent-flyer mileage, the airline gets no money at all. Airlines go to great lengths to protect themselves against losing revenue this way. Airline employees get bounties for catching people traveling on brokered frequent-flyer tickets. If the airline finds out that a frequent-flyer ticket was sold, both buyer and seller (and intermediary broker, if there is one) are equally liable.

No matter what coupon brokers may tell you, there is no safe or legal way to buy someone else's frequent-flyer mileage or tickets. Buyers of frequent-flyer tickets are, in the eyes of the airlines and the law, committing a crime, construed in different jurisdictions as theft of transportation and/or fraud. If you are caught, you are subject to having the ticket confiscated as void, having both the ticket buyer and seller expelled from the airline's frequent-flyer program, losing any mileage credits in your accounts, and having to pay the full fare for any portion of the ticket that you have already used, in addition to any applicable criminal penalties.

## Restrictions on Tickets

Only the most expensive tickets at the full (highest) fare are unrestricted. Few people can afford to pay full fare for any flight, much less for each flight of a trip around the world. You can only get a reasonable price by buying what the airlines consider a special (restricted) fare, or by buying discounted tickets. All special-fare and discounted tickets, whether purchased through an agent or directly from the airline, have important restrictions and penalties.

### Which Tickets Are More Restrictive?

One of the most widespread myths about consolidator tickets is that they are highly restricted. This is, in some sense, true, although the restrictions don't necessarily matter to most budget travelers, as long as they know in advance what they are. What the airlines don't tell you is that it is even more true of the discounted tickets that the airlines sell directly to the public.

# FACTORS THAT MAY AFFECT THE PRICE OF YOUR TICKETS

Consider the following checklist before contacting your travel agent.

**Starting and Ending Cities:** A substantial proportion of long-haul tickets are one-way, or begun and completed in different places.

**Lists of Destinations:** Include all the places you intend to go, even if you think that they have to be ticketed as side trips or separate tickets, or that you will have to purchase tickets locally. Separate the must-see destinations from those that are optional.

**Surface Transportation:** Tell the agent if there are specific sections of your trip that you wish to travel by surface transportation (land or water), or would be willing to travel by surface means to save money.

**Ages of Travelers:** Infant, child, youth, or senior? You need to specify.

**Starting and Ending Dates:** If you aren't leaving for at least a month, it's usually sufficient to specify what month you intend to depart and what month, at the latest, you intend to complete your travel on these tickets. However, it is counterproductive to specify an exact departure date if you don't have to leave on exactly that day.

**Direction of Travel:** International fares are not the same in opposite directions. Finding the cheapest price and route each way is a separate problem.

**Openness to Modifications:** Are you interested in possible modifications of your proposed itinerary if they would save you money?

**Personal Schedule, Sequence, or Airline Requirements:** Most people are willing to make specific stops in whatever order is cheapest. If you aren't, tell your agent.

**Likelihood of Future Changes:** How likely is it that you will need to change your departure dates, stopover cities, or route after buying your tickets?

**Budget Limitations:** Given a budget, an agent can suggest whether meeting it is likely to require you to cut a few, many, or certain especially expensive destinations, or whether it will leave you money to add more destinations if you want.

**Class of Service:** Unless you say otherwise, agents will assume that you want prices for third-class (coach or economy) air travel.

**Excess Baggage:** How much luggage you will have can sometimes affect which tickets are the most cost effective.

If there is any one thing I say in this book that the airlines least want you to realize, it is this: *Discounted consolidator tickets on a particular airline and route purchased through a travel agent are, as a rule, significantly less restricted than tickets for the same flights purchased for a similar price directly from the airline.*

Why? The short answer follows from the nature of consolidator tickets, as discussed earlier in this chapter. Consolidator discounts are based on commission rebates. When you buy a consolidator ticket, you pay less (by the amount of the commission rebate) than its face value. If you buy two tickets for the same price, one from the airline and one through a consolidator, the consolidator ticket will show a higher face value, and will be governed by the rules of a correspondingly higher fare. Because the whole reason people pay higher fares is to avoid the restrictions on cheaper fares, the higher the fare the less restricted it is. So the higher-fare, higher-face-value consolidator ticket is less restricted than the lower-fare ticket that the airline sells for the same price.

Once you understand how consolidator tickets work, it's logical to expect that consolidator tickets would be less restricted, and this is indeed the case. Some of the advantages of consolidator tickets are those that are potentially most useful to the business travelers who avoid them for fear of their "restrictions," such as waivers of date change penalties or of requirements for advance purchase or minimum or maximum stay.

The details are actually a bit more complicated. The rules of discounted tickets purchased through an agent are a complex combination of the rules of the published fares at which tickets are issued and the rules of the commission agreement (which you, the buyer, don't and can't see). An agent may be offered different commissions on different types of fares, or on different routes, even on the same airline to the same destination. Determining what is or isn't allowed at a given selling price requires the agent to read and interpret, in combination, both the fare rules and the fine print in the commission agreement.

Once a ticket is issued, it is governed by the rules of the fare shown on the ticket, except as specifically endorsed (notated on its face) to the contrary. But endorsements can make the ticket either more or less restricted than it would otherwise be, and in either case may be in coded jargon. Without an understanding of the codes and access to the complete rules implicit in all fare codes, it's impossible to tell from the face of a ticket exactly what restrictions it has.

It's even harder, of course, with an electronic ticket. E-ticket receipts show only a fraction of the essential information on the ticket itself, and omit some things that can be critical to your rights. The only way to know what your e-ticket really says, or means, is to get a printout from the airline of the "passenger receipt" coupon, and then decode it the way you would a paper ticket.

Airlines' commission agreements with agents usually require some restrictive endorsements, but also allow some of the restrictions that apply to tickets purchased from the airline for the official fare to be waived. If they found it profitable to do so, the airlines could restrict consolidator tickets more than their cheapest published fares. But in practice, most airlines don't. For what it's worth, the most restricted consolidator tickets are on some of the USA-based airlines that are most opposed to discounting in the first place.

Airline employees can't always tell from the face of a ticket how much you actually paid for it. Sometimes they can: some airlines use codes that can't be altered without voiding the tickets to alert their agents to how much you paid. However, if you have a very high-value ticket, even if you bought it at a steep discount, you'll sometimes be treated like a full-fare passenger. Ordinary airport and in-flight service is about the same for all coach/economy passengers, regardless of how much they paid for their tickets. But passengers with full-fare tickets can be treated very differently when they want to make changes. With sufficiently high-value tickets you can often get away with making all sorts of changes, such as routing changes, that the airline is entitled to charge you for, and probably would charge you for, or prevent you from making at all, if it knew how little you paid. Never volunteer to an airline how much (or how little) you paid for a discounted ticket.

For the most part, the myth that consolidator tickets are highly restricted is sufficient to get business travelers to pay higher published fares. As long as the myth is widely enough believed, it serves its purpose for the airlines: insuring that people who are willing to pay more for a ticket they perceive as less restricted do in fact pay more. It's not necessary for it to be based on fact, or for the airlines actually to restrict consolidator tickets in ways that would make them less attractive to price-sensitive travelers who would choose not to fly at all rather than to pay a high published fare.

A common mistake is to call an airline to ask about its lowest published fare and its rules, then call agents for prices of discounted tickets on that airline, assuming that the agents' lowest prices will be subject to the same rules as the airline's lowest published discount fares. Any or all of the rules of discounted tickets may be more or less restrictive than those of any published fares. No assumption whatsoever about the rules of discounted tickets —such as permitted routes or stopovers, minimum or maximum stay limitations, or changes to date(s), destinations, or routes—can be made about discounted tickets on the basis of published fare rules. Different agents may have contracts with different terms.

The only way to find out any meaningful information about the rules of your ticket is to ask the specific agent from whom you intend to buy that ticket. Most discounted around-the-world and multistop tickets are less restrictive than most discounted tickets for travel within the United States. But you should ask before you buy tickets if you have any questions about the specific rules, restrictions, and cancellation or change penalties that will apply if you buy those particular tickets from that particular agent. If some particular rule or condition is really critical to your decision to buy a ticket, get the agent to put it in writing before you pay. Assume nothing.

Following is a list of some of the restrictions that can be placed on discounted tickets. I'll try to note which are likely to apply to which sorts of tickets, but in general any or all of these restrictions may apply to any discounted ticket, whether you buy it directly from the airline or from an agent.

### Validity Dates

The most important and widely misunderstood restriction applies to all one-way airline tickets at any price: no one-way ticket can be valid for departure more than one year from the date it is issued. Because most multistop and around-the-world tickets consist of several one-way tickets, this means that you must complete any travel for which you buy tickets in advance within one year of when you buy your tickets.

Many people have heard that open (undated) tickets, or tickets around the world, are valid for up to a year, but they don't realize that the clock begins to run on the year of validity the day the tickets are issued.

If you want to travel for longer, you'll have to buy tickets for only part of the trip at a time. This is rarely a real problem, because few people are actually sure of their plans more than a year in advance. But it's important to understand how the system works, especially if you find work, fall in love, or settle down somewhere along the way, but still want to get home without having to buy new tickets. Unused tickets can sometimes be submitted for refund after the expiration of their validity, but discounted tickets may have little or no refund value. Look at the date of issue imprinted near the upper right corner of each of your tickets. Each ticket is valid until, at the latest, one year after that date.

Roundtrip tickets can have a first departure date up to one year from the date of issue, and, in certain cases at certain fares, a return date up to one year after the date of first departure. If you are sure of your plans, ready to commit your money, and want to lock in a price long in advance of your departure—more than one year before your intended return—this is an advantage to roundtrip tickets.

Published around-the-world fares are considered roundtrip fares, and thus can be valid (if issued undated, i.e., left open-dated) for up to one year from the date of departure. Most around-the-world tickets, however, and most advertised prices around the world, are constructed as a combination of several one-way tickets, and thus can be valid up to one year from the date of issue.

Not all tickets, even if they are issued with open dates (i.e., are issued without reservations for any specific flights or dates) are valid for as much as a year. Roundtrip tickets may be valid for one, two, three, four, or six months, one year, or some other period. Most one-way tickets are valid either for a specific and fixed date, or for one year, but there are other possibilities as well. If you are unsure when or how long your tickets will be valid, ask before you buy.

The cheapest published fares generally permit only relatively short (but not too short) roundtrip stays. If you want one-way tickets or tickets for an especially short (less than a week) or long (more than three months) stay, consolidator tickets (and, if you qualify, student fares) are usually your only option at a reasonable cost.

## Date Changes

More and more tickets are valid only on the specific date for which they are issued. If you want to travel on a different date, you have to buy a whole new ticket, and you can throw the original one (and the money you paid for it) away. Some tickets can be changed, but only on payment of a fee. I've seen date change penalties ranging from US$25 to US$250 to 50 percent of the face value of the ticket, although there aren't necessarily any upper or lower limits. Some tickets—including those preferred by most long-term travelers—permit changes from one date or time to another at no charge, as long as the same airline has space available on a flight between the same cities as originally ticketed.

Date change rules are not always apparent, even to an expert, from the face of the tickets, and certainly not from an itinerary unless explicitly stated. In theory, under the IATA general rules of fare construction, dates are changeable at no charge unless stated otherwise somewhere in the rules, but in practice it is best to assume the reverse: tickets are valid only on specific dates, and cannot be changed, unless you are told otherwise. If there is any chance that you might want to change the dates of some or all of your flights, or if an agent tells you that date changes will be free, get it in writing, on your itinerary, before you pay for your tickets.

Watch out if your tickets are supposed to be changeable but they have an endorsement like, "CHANGE SUBJECT TO FEE," "CHG SUBJ FEE," or "CHG ONLY THRU AGT." Such an endorsement doesn't necessarily mean what it seems, but at minimum it probably does mean you will be charged for any changes unless they are made through the issuing agent. This can be quite inconvenient when you are abroad. If the price isn't much higher, try to get tickets that will permit you to make changes yourself directly with the airlines, without having to contact (or, worse, send the ticket back to) the issuing agent.

Most discounted tickets originating in the United States carry substantial penalties, not infrequently 100 percent of the fare, for changes of departure date from the United States. In most cases changes of departure date also require that the tickets be returned to the issuing agent, which can cause further delays and expenses. If you need to change your departure date from the United States after buying your tickets, you may have to pay for an entirely new ticket for the first leg of your journey. Roundtrip tickets are also much more likely than one-way tickets to have date change penalties, which are sometimes as much as 100 percent of the ticket's cost (i.e., they're entirely unchangeable).

Most other consolidator one-way tickets originating outside North America allow date changes at no charge, or for only a small fee. This is usually true whether the tickets are issued open or with confirmed reservations for specific dates. It is not necessary for tickets to be open for date changes to be free. (See "Making Reservations" under "Arranging Your Air Transportation" later in this chapter for more on open tickets and why to avoid them.)

Most around-the-world and multistop tickets are issued with a fixed date and penalties for changes to the date of the first flight, while the dates of all subsequent flights are changeable at no charge or for a fee. If the tickets can simply be "revalidated" with a sticker, the change fee is usually no more than US$50 per person per ticket. If the tickets have to be reissued, it's more often US$100–150. For a bit more money, you can often get tickets with even the first date changeable at no charge, or for a smaller fee.

In most cases changes can be made directly with the respective airlines. In some cases there are additional requirements, which an agent should tell you about. The most common of these is that any changes to the reservations for a certain flight must be made at least some period of time (most often seven days, but sometimes as much as 21 days) in advance.

One of the commonest explanations for differences in price estimates for long-term or multistop travel is that the cheaper estimate is for fixed-date tickets and the higher estimate is for freely changeable tickets, sometimes even on the same airlines. Most around-the-world and long-term travelers end up changing at least some of their flight dates. If you end up changing the dates of even one or two flights, date change penalties are likely to more than offset any up-front cost savings to fixed-date tickets, making them a false bargain. Even small date-change fees can add up if you reschedule each leg of a trip on multiple airlines, and have to pay a change fee to each airline.

The cheapest published fares almost always prohibit date changes. The ability to change dates, especially those of onward or return dates, for little or no charge is the single most significant advantage of consolidator tickets over tickets at comparable published or Web fares, and the one of most potential value to business and long-term leisure travelers alike.

### Advance Booking and Advance Purchase

Tickets for the cheapest fares generally must be purchased at least two to three weeks prior to departure on the first leg of the journey. Once you make reservations for such a fare, you usually have no more than 24–72 hours to buy your tickets, or your reservations will automatically be canceled.

In order to pressure travelers into impulse ticket purchases, the trend—especially on the Internet—is toward instant purchase fares that require "simultaneous reservations and ticketing." As this rule is implemented by airline software, it means that you can hold confirmed reservations for no more than about an hour before you have to decide either to buy the tickets or cancel the reservations.

Airlines want to get you to pay as far in advance as possible, because they get the use of your money, at no charge, between the time you pay and the time they have to spend money to transport you. The average time between ticketing and travel is critical to airlines' cash flows. If airlines offered lower prices at the last minute than in advance, potential passengers would be tempted to wait until the last minute, in the hope of a better price. In the meantime, they might decide not to go at all, or to choose a different airline. Airlines don't want people holding reservations who haven't paid. What if they don't ever pay, but don't cancel their reservations until it is too late to sell their seats to someone else? Cheap last-minute fares or long holds on unticketed reservations go against the airlines' long-term interests. Airlines have an interest in getting people to plan and pay far ahead, and their fares and discounts are structured accordingly.

It's widely known that many discount agents' agreements with the airlines include waivers of the normal advance purchase requirements for cheap fares. Some consolidator tickets are issued at fares so high that they don't require advance purchase, which has the same effect. When they get desperate, airlines offer cheap (but very highly restricted) Web fares at the last minute. Many people misunderstand what this means, and think that consolidator tickets are *always* available at the last minute.

Consolidator tickets can be issued at the last minute (provided there is time to get them to you) only if space allocated to those tickets is available at the last minute. In fact, consolidator tickets on many airlines are routinely sold out earlier than the advance purchase deadline. At the last minute, no discountable seats may be available, or you may have much less choice of airlines if you want a discount.

Of greater benefit to travelers who plan ahead is the ability of agents to extend the permissible time between confirmation and ticketing, giving you time to review your itinerary, consult traveling companions, and contact people you plan to meet before you have to commit your money. Obviously, time limits have to be short if you are leaving right away, and if you are departing within two weeks you may have to decide within a day or two of making reservations. Further in advance, agents can be much more flexible. Reservations for consolidator tickets can often be held for a week before ticketing, compared to at most three days for cheap published fares and no time at all (simultaneous reservation and purchase) for most Web fares. Airlines are cracking down, though, whether reservations are made through a travel agency or directly with the airline. Time limits for unticketed reservations are getting ever shorter, and even travel agents have trouble getting approval for extensions of ticketing deadlines.

### Transferring Tickets from One Person to Another

You cannot transfer any airline ticket from one person to another, or change names on reservations or tickets once they are made or issued. All airline tickets are "nontransferable." They can be used only by the person to whom they are issued. Passports or government issued identity documents are checked against names on tickets at check-in for all international flights, as well as on domestic flights in most countries, including the United States. You cannot give or sell an unused ticket to someone else to use.

You may read or hear about various scams used to travel on other people's tickets. They are all illegal, and risk both civil and criminal penalties for both the person whose ticket is used and the person who tries to use it. Don't try it. It's increasingly likely that both the ticket buyer and seller will both be caught and fined and the ticket confiscated. If you've already traveled when the scam is uncovered—tickets are sometimes, unexpectedly, checked and compared with passports on arrival—either or both of you could have to pay the full, nondiscounted fare for the transportation used. In the present climate of concern for terrorism and airline security, either or both of you could be arrested not merely for theft of transportation but on suspicion of terrorism or espionage if the ticket doesn't match the passenger's travel documents at all times.

### Cancellations and Refunds

Only full-fare tickets are entirely refundable if they aren't used. All discounted or special-fare tickets have cancellation penalties. Cancellation penalties can vary from US$25 to 100 percent of the fare or price paid (i.e., totally nonrefundable). It's generally cheaper to buy discounted tickets with cancellation penalties, and buy trip cancellation insurance, than to buy full fare tickets with no cancellation penalties. See the Safety and Health chapter and the section of the same name in the Resource Guide for more information on travel insurance.

Cancellation penalties and rules can be extremely complex. The refund value of a ticket can depend on which portion or portions, if any, have already been used; when the ticket is submitted for refund relative to the ticketed flight dates (the sooner the better); the rules of the fare shown on the ticket; the rules of the agent's contract with the airline; and the agent's cancellation policies.

If the agent bought the ticket from a wholesaler, both the wholesaler and the agent may impose cancellation penalties. If the ticket was issued in another country, the refund value can depend on the relative value of that country's currency and the currency in which your refund is paid at the time the refund is received. Each ticket that makes up a set of multistop tickets can have its own cancellation penalties, influenced by each of these factors.

It's impossible to say, in advance, exactly what the refund value of part of a set of tickets might be, unless you know exactly when and in what circumstances you might submit which portion(s) for refund. Any notice of cancellation penalties on a complex set of tickets is of necessity incomplete.

In some jurisdictions the law requires a full disclosure of cancellation penalties, but compliance would be impossible for even the best-intentioned travel agent or airline. (For what it's worth, travel agents generally do a better job of disclosing penalties than the airlines themselves.) A "full" disclosure would require dozens of pages of rules, conditions, and contingencies, couched in jargon incomprehensible to most travelers, and incorporating lengthier and less comprehensible general rules. I assume that the legislators who enacted these requirements had no idea what they really meant.

It's important to identify whether stated cancellation penalties are those of the airline, the agent, or both. "Cancellation penalty 25 percent of refund value of tickets" on an agent's itinerary means that the agent will keep 25 percent of any refund, after the airlines' penalties, as the agent's fee for processing the refund. Processing refunds is much more labor-intensive and costly for agents than issuing tickets, and this is quite a reasonable fee for an agent's services in processing a refund.

Because you actually paid less for a discounted ticket bought through an agent than its face value, you can't get the full face value back if you don't use it, even in the absence of any penalties. You can only submit such a ticket for refund through the agent who issued it, because only the agent knows how much of the commission was already rebated to you, and thus how much you really paid for it. The endorsement "REFUNDABLE ONLY THROUGH ISSUING AGENT," usually abbreviated "REF ISS AGT ONLY" or just "REF AGT ONLY," is used to prevent you from submitting the ticket for refund directly to the airline and getting more money back than you actually paid. This endorsement is the most common clue that a ticket was sold for less than face value.

Don't throw an unused ticket away just because it says "NONREFUNDABLE" or "NONREF." Such a ticket is not necessarily completely nonrefundable. These endorsements are sometimes used, like "REF AGT ONLY," merely to preclude your submitting the ticket to the airline for refund, or to indicate that it is not *fully* refundable. It may still have some, occasionally substantial, refund value, or be exchangeable for some amount of credit toward another ticket on that same airline. The only way to find out is to submit it for refund to the agent from whom you bought it.

Cancellation penalties are one of the more surprising advantages of consolidator tickets over cheap published fares. The cheapest published fares, including virtually all rock-bottom "fare war" tickets, are completely nonrefundable. Consolidator tickets generally have substantial cancellation penalties, and some are entirely nonrefundable, but most consolidator tickets have at least some refund value if entirely unused.

### Changing Airlines

Almost all tickets are, in airline jargon, "nonendorsable." This means that they are valid only on the specified airlines. If you want to change your flight or dates, you may change only to another flight on the same airline. Unless an agent specifically promises you otherwise, you should not expect to be able to use your tickets on any airlines other than those on which you are booked. Nonendorsable tickets usually say, "NONEND," "XX ONLY," "VALID XX ONLY," or "VLD XX ONLY," where XX is the two-letter code for the airline.

The exception is full-fare tickets, which may be the only ones available for certain flights. Full-fare tickets can be endorsed to any other airline with which the issuing airline has a joint ticketing agreement. Some tickets are partially endorsable: for example, a ticket on a non-USA airline may permit the use of any of several USA airlines between a city within the United States and the international gateway (point of connection to or from the international flight).

Some commentators point to the inability to change to another airline if your flight is canceled or delayed as a particular drawback of consolidator tickets. This makes no sense. Nonendorsable tickets can be, and often are, endorsed in such circumstances. And there is no real difference between the endorsability of consolidator tickets and tickets at discounted published fares. *All* discounted tickets are, in theory, nonendorsable. Unless you are traveling on business, or someone else is footing the bill, you probably can't afford full-fare endorsable tickets. The cheapest endorsable tickets on most routes are at least twice the price of discounted tickets, often much more. The cheapest endorsable tickets across the United States start at US$2,000, roundtrip. Unless you've traveled on business, or had to pay the full fare in an emergency, you've probably never seen an endorsable ticket.

In practice, the endorsement "NONEND" on a ticket means only that an airline isn't required to endorse the ticket to another airline. But airlines may endorse nonendorsable tickets if there is a good reason for doing so. That you have changed your mind, or don't like the schedule, or that the flight has been delayed is not a good reason. (In these cases, it's still worth asking the airline if it will endorse the ticket you already have before you break down and buy an entirely new ticket on another airline—airlines have been known to endorse ticket under these circumstances. Just realize that if your ticket says "NONEND", you are asking a favor, not claiming a right.)

That a flight has been canceled entirely might be good enough reason for the airline to endorse a nonendorsable ticket, though it depends on how many days it is until the next flight and whether it will be cheaper for the airline to pay another airline to fly you or to put you up until the next flight. (The airline isn't required to do either, but in most cases will do one or the other.) That the airline has discontinued service on the route entirely since you bought your ticket is almost always sufficient reason for it to endorse your nonendorsable ticket to another airline. In my experience, even airlines with poor reputations for customer service will do the right thing and endorse even very cheap, nonendorsable tickets in most cases when it is appropriate to do so.

### Changes of Destinations or Route
Many discounted tickets are nonreroutable ("NO RERTE"). This means that once the tickets are issued you cannot change the sequence of connection and stopover points specified on the tickets, even if the same airline also flies between the end points of your ticket by way of other places.

Tickets without stopovers are more likely to be reroutable, because if you aren't allowed to stop anywhere, the airline has less reason to care where you change planes. That's sometimes helpful if you want to change your travel date, and the only available seats on your desired new date are by way of an alternate transfer point. But a change to a different connection point, even without a stopover, is still considered rerouting, and is sometimes subject to fee or prohibited entirely.

In some cases additional stops on the same airline can be added or other changes made simply by paying a reissue fee and an additional stopover charge or the difference in fare. If you want to make a change, or discover that the airline has another route by way of a place in which you'd rather change planes or stop over, it's worth asking before you buy an entirely new ticket.

Changes of destinations are considered routing changes, and are likewise largely discretionary with the airlines. Some airlines allow destination changes to consolidator tickets for a reissue fee of US$50–150, as long as the price to the new destination would have been the same as to the original one. It never hurts to ask if you want to make changes, but you shouldn't buy tickets until you are sure of which places you want to fly to. You can't count on changing destinations without having to buy new tickets.

Both discounted published-fare tickets and consolidator tickets are, officially, equally nonreroutable. In practice, you are somewhat more likely to be allowed to change the routing of a consolidator ticket, especially if the airline office making the change doesn't realize how little you paid for the ticket. You can sometimes get away with all kinds of changes, within the routes of the same airline, on tickets with a sufficiently high face value.

### Stopovers

If you fly from A to B, spend some time in B, and then fly from B to C, B is considered a stopover. It is usually cheaper, when possible, to get a ticket from A to C, with a stopover in B, than to get one ticket from A to B and a second ticket from B to C. It's sometimes possible to combine a dozen or more flights in this way on a single through ticket with multiple stopovers, at an enormous savings over separate tickets for each flight.

If you want to fly from A to C, with a stopover in B, the obvious (although not necessarily the only) choice is an airline based in B. An airline based in B probably flies between A and B, and between B and C. Flying the airline of B between A and C probably requires a change of planes in B anyway, and some of the fares of the airline of B probably permit a stopover there. Distance permitting, the airlines of A and C probably fly nonstop between A and C, not stopping in B or anywhere else.

One of the ways an expert can use his or her skill in finding you the best tickets is to figure out where to break the tickets and start a new fare. Suppose you want to fly from A to B, B to C, and C to D. Is it cheaper to get one ticket A-B-C, and a second ticket C-D? Or is it cheaper to get one ticket A-B, and a second ticket B-C-D? Or is there some through fare that will permit the whole trip A-B-C-D on a single ticket? It's unlikely to be obvious to you, and only an expert is likely to find the right answer without a lot of tedious trial and error, if at all.

Stopover rules are not synonymous with flight routes. Flights sometimes make "technical" stops for refueling at places where they are not allowed to take on or discharge passengers. And airlines can forbid stopovers at other points or charge whatever they think the traffic will bear for them. So don't assume that because an airline's route involves a refueling stop in City X or requires a change of planes in City Y, all fares on that airline allow stopovers in X and/or Y, or that those stopovers will be free. Conversely, some airlines, especially in Asia, have interline agreements with other airlines that permit you to include a short flight on one airline on a through ticket on another airline, thus making possible stopovers that aren't on the routes of any one airline.

For example, many people assume that all or most tickets between Europe and the West Coast of the United States will permit a free stop in New York or elsewhere on the East Coast. But most flights between Europe and the West Coast follow nonstop polar routes. Even those airlines that offer service via connection points on the East Coast rarely permit stopovers of more than 24 hours.

As a legacy of the occupation of Japan after World War II, USA-based airlines have preferential rights to carry traffic between Japan and other countries. As Japan has become the world's most profitable airline market, attempts by airlines in the United States to expand their inter-Asia services from Japan have prompted increasingly strong opposition from Japanese airlines and the Japanese government. The United States has accused Japan of protectionism, even though the USA protects its domestic airline market—the world's largest and most profitable domestic market—by strictly forbidding Japanese or any other foreign airlines to carry local traffic within the United States.

USA airlines are under heavy pressure to increase the percentage of passengers on their inter-Asia flights from Japan who make connections directly from the United States, rather than originating in Japan, so as to prove that their Japan-Asia flights are intended to serve the USA market and not just (as it appears at present) to poach the lucrative Japan-originating market. As a result, most fares on USA airlines between the United States and mainland Asia require a change of planes in Japan but forbid stopovers there.

Most airlines consider stops of less than 24 hours as connections rather than stopovers, and don't charge for them. Depending on the schedules it's sometimes possible to circumvent the stopover rules by arranging as long a connection as is possible without exceeding 24 hours, if such a short stop will be of use or interest to you.

The cheapest published fares on most routes prohibit stopovers even at places where you have to change planes. One of the big advantages to consolidator tickets is that they usually permit stopovers at the airlines' hubs, sometimes elsewhere along the way as well, at least for a fee. All routes on Air France from the United States to Europe, Asia, and Africa, for example, require a change of planes in Paris. But only the most expensive Air France published fares permit stopovers in Paris, while almost all Air France consolidator fares permit stopovers in Paris at minimal additional charge.

### Discontinuous Routes

Tickets for discontinuous routes are not necessarily more expensive than tickets for continuous ones. It's possible to use a single through air ticket even if part of your trip between points in the middle will be made by surface transportation, or to get a roundtrip fare even if you fly into one place and back from another and/or return to someplace other than where you started from.

The airline term for any of these sorts of discontinuities is an "open jaw," shown on tickets by "SURFACE" (for "permitted surface transportation not included in airfare") and on itineraries and airline computer displays by "ARNK" (for "arrival to the point of origin of the next flight by means unknown," pronounced "a-runk"). If you plan an ARNK in your itinerary, make sure that the "means unknown" are actually possible: I've had customers propose sectors by surface transportation that would have required walking on water where there are no ferries, through minefields, across closed and fortified borders, and over roadless mountains.

There are four different kinds of open jaws, and different fares permit different ones. The four types are: open jaw at the origin, open jaw at the destination, double open jaw at origin and destination, and internal open jaw.

Many published roundtrip fares permit at least a single open jaw at either the origin or the destination. Only the cheapest published fares—most fare war tickets and many published international PEX and Superpex fares— prohibit all open jaws. Domestic roundtrip fares in many countries permit open jaws. In the United States, most year-round discounted fares permit open jaws, and most sale and Web fares don't. This is the biggest drawback to the cheapest published fares.

Most roundtrip consolidator tickets permit a single or double open jaw at the origin, destination, or both, as long as each surface segment (gap between the points of the open jaw) is between places in the same region (the same continent is usually sufficient). Sometimes the combined flights have to be on the same general route, sometimes not, depending on the airline and fare.

Most people conceptualize their plans in terms of continuous roundtrips, without considering whether open-jaw tickets would be preferable. For all but the shortest and simplest trips, they often would be. The simplest application of open-jaw routing is for people wanting to explore a moderate-sized region within which surface transportation is available and cheaper than air travel, but within which distances and/or costs are a disincentive to backtracking: the solution, get an open-jaw ticket arriving at one end of the region and returning from the other.

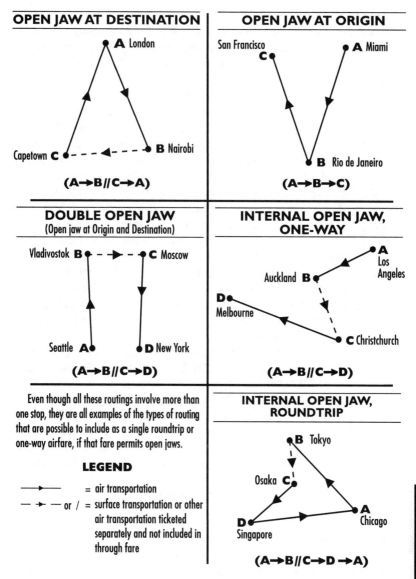

## OPEN JAW AT DESTINATION

A London
Capetown C – – – ◄ – – – B Nairobi

(A→B // C→A)

## OPEN JAW AT ORIGIN

San Francisco C
A Miami
B Rio de Janeiro

(A→B→C)

## DOUBLE OPEN JAW
(Open jaw at Origin and Destination)

Vladivostok B – – ► – – C Moscow
Seattle A
D New York

(A→B // C→D)

## INTERNAL OPEN JAW, ONE-WAY

A Los Angeles
Auckland B
D Melbourne
C Christchurch

(A→B // C→D)

Even though all these routings involve more than one stop, they are all examples of the types of routing that are possible to include as a single roundtrip or one-way airfare, if that fare permits open jaws.

### LEGEND

⟶ = air transportation

– ► — or / = surface transportation or other air transportation ticketed separately and not included in through fare

## INTERNAL OPEN JAW, ROUNDTRIP

B Tokyo
Osaka C
D Singapore
A Chicago

(A→B // C→D →A)

If open-jaw tickets would suit your needs, you'll probably have to ask to find out if they are available. Neither airlines nor discount agencies advertise open-jaw prices, even when they are available, simply because listing prices for all the possible combinations would take up too much space. Where they are available, open-jaw tickets are priced as the average of the roundtrip prices for the two different legs or, equivalently, the sum of the half-roundtrip prices.

### Amenities

When you buy an airline ticket, you are paying for transportation. If all you want is transportation, all that matters are the rules governing your use of a ticket for transportation: When can you go? Where? On what conditions? At what price?

The travelers on whose business the airlines make the most money, however, are business travelers who aren't paying for their own tickets, and for whose business it would therefore be futile to compete on price. Airlines throw in a variety of amenities to attract the business of the non-price-sensitive: frequent-flyer mileage credits, special meals, preferential and advance seating assignments, eligibility for upgrades if space is available in business or first class, etc.

All of these things are nice, if they don't cost anything. Don't let the sizzle distract you from the steak, though: the minute you indicate to the airlines, or an agent, that you are concerned with whether your tickets will come with these side dishes, you have told them that your priority is other than strictly price.

I've said it before, and I'll say it again: airlines set prices according to criteria intended to identify willingness to pay. If you care about frequent-flyer mileage, seat assignments, meals, upgrades, or the like, you are by definition not so price-sensitive. If you insist on these amenities, you are obviously willing to pay for them, and the airline knows that it can get away with charging you more for a ticket that qualifies for them.

Some airlines restrict consolidator tickets by making them ineligible for frequent-flyer mileage credit ("NO FF MILES" or "NO MILES"), special meals ("NO SPECIAL MEAL" or "NO SPML"), and/or advance seat assignments ("NO PRERESERVED SEATS" or "NO PRS") for which published-fare ticket holders are eligible. This is not because these amenities are expensive (except for frequent-flyer mileage credit) or because they can't afford to provide them on cheap tickets. These petty restrictions on amenities are primarily tools to identify those passengers who are willing to pay more, and to induce them to do so.

# ARRANGING YOUR AIR TRANSPORTATION

## Choosing a Travel Agent

The first step in arranging your air transportation is to find the right travel agent with whom to work. It should be clear by now that only through a travel agent's assistance can you get the lowest prices or tell which route and airlines will most cheaply connect your destinations. But there's a travel agency or two in every small town, and hundreds in major cities. The American Society of Travel Agents (ASTA), the USA trade association of travel agencies, has 24,000 members. With so many choices, how can you find which agent and agency will be best for you?

### Choose a Discount Agent

You may not think of yourself as being concerned primarily with discounts, but for complex multistop travel, you'll still be best served by a discounter. Published one-way fares are so much higher than discounted prices that constructing tickets around the world, or for any complex multistop itinerary, without discounts is likely to drive the price beyond the means of even the rich. Alternatively, if you're price conscious it's natural, but entirely fallacious, to assume that you'll get a better price if you go directly to the airlines and cut out the middleman. For those of you who skipped the previous technical sections on airfares, let me summarize: many discount prices are available only through specialized travel agents, and not available directly from the airlines.

You have to go to a discounter if you want discounts. Some agencies offering only published fares do no better at finding the lowest ones than amateurs can do themselves on the Internet, given enough time. This gives travelers the false impression that travel agents are unnecessary.

Good agencies, however, can be extremely helpful. Without a travel agent, travelers have no independent consultant to bring new competitors, new fares, and nonintuitive routes to their attention, and airlines can get away with charging more with less competition.

Most air tickets sold in the United States are domestic roundtrips, and most international tickets sold in the United States are the simplest roundtrips to Canada, Mexico, the Caribbean, and Western Europe. In the United States, international travel is a relatively small, specialty niche.

I would no more recommend buying an international ticket from an all-purpose travel agent than buying a package tour of Disneyland from an agent like myself, even if I asked the agent to try to find a consolidator (discounted) ticket. Agencies in the United States that call themselves generalists are in fact, by the nature of the USA travel market, specialists in domestic travel, cruises, tours and resorts. It wouldn't be appropriate for them to spend their time tracking down sources of tickets to Second, Third, and Fourth World destinations on airlines that don't fly to anywhere in the United States, for the same reasons that I don't spend any time inspecting cruise ships or resorts. You can usually tell an agency's real specialization from what they advertise.

If you ask ordinary travel agents to try to find you a discount on an international ticket, all they can do is call a few of the best-known wholesalers. When a customer insists on buying discounted tickets for an unusual destination or routing (especially around-the-world or multistop tickets) from a local agent, the agent will buy the tickets from a specialist discounter and mark them up to the customer. There is no advantage to dealing with a specialist through the intermediary of a local generalist: you can best take advantage of a specialist's skill by consulting them directly.

The situation is a bit better in some countries such as the UK or Australia where a higher percentage of travel is international, and where discounting is

# TRAVEL AGENCY PROFITS?

Profit margins for travel agencies are thin to nonexistent. Major airlines have eliminated any standard or "base" commission to travel agencies. Today, travel agencies make money only through service fees on published-fare tickets, or through their markup on discounted tickets, neither of which usually matches the 10 percent commission they used to get as standard. A US$50 service charge on a US$1000 published-fare ticket is equivalent to a 5 percent commission. Retail margins on discounted tickets, particularly in the most popular roundtrip markets, can be even less. Retail markups of US$20 over wholesale or net cost on US$1,000 consolidator tickets from the USA to India are common.

Airlines grossly exaggerate the commissions and profit margins of travel agencies. Because airlines are forbidden to admit publicly that they are aware of commission rebating, they include the amounts rebated to ticket buyers in all their figures for "commissions paid to travel agents." IATA rules make it impossible for anyone to compile accurate statistics on agency sales margins, after rebates, and airlines are happy to have an excuse to pretend that travel agencies are making much more money than they really are. Even travel industry trade journals, which should know better, publish these statistics on "commissions" without noting how meaningless they are unless adjusted, as they can't be, to account for commission rebating.

more widely known and accepted. Travel agents on the high streets of midsized provincial towns in England regularly sell both tickets on charter flights and consolidator tickets on scheduled airlines, although they still won't know what to do with inquiries about more complex routes. On the other hand, there are countries where discounting is unheard of and regarded as though it were illegal, immoral, or beneath contempt. If you don't know the country, it's hard to know what to expect. The first question to ask a travel agent is, "Do you sell discounted tickets to [wherever you are going]." If the answer is "No" you are wasting your time, and that of the agent. Thank the person, politely, and find another agent.

Finally, you should go to a discount agency in order to find an agent who will side with you, not the airlines. Travel agents have traditionally been agents of the airlines, not agents of travelers, with a legal obligation to advance the financial interests of the airlines against those of passengers. Some agents take this seriously, and consider it their duty to report you to the airline if they find out, for example, that you intend to use only half a roundtrip ticket when a one-way ticket would cost more than a roundtrip. If you come across an agent like this, take your business elsewhere.

Such agents are rare, though. Regardless of the law, most agents consider themselves as consultants to, and advocates for, passengers, not airlines. Airlines realize this, dislike it, but can't do much about it. Suing travel agents who search for and advise clients of the lowest rather than the highest fares, for breach of their responsibility as the airline's agents, would be a public relations disaster, even if such an action would be entirely within the airlines' legal rights.

You want an agent who considers it their job to get you the best deal, not to get the airlines the most money. The agents on your side are the ones willing to describe themselves as discounters and publicly promote the availability of tickets at prices below the airlines' published fares.

Airlines will not like some of the things I say in this book. I sincerely believe, however, that the interests of the airlines as well as of travelers are best served by making air travel accessible and affordable to as many people as possible, not by accentuating the exclusivity of air travel.

### Choose a Travel Consultant, Not a Ticket Broker

Don't get carried away looking for the ultimate in discounts. There are discounters and there are discounters. Even the most price-sensitive travelers, especially those who aren't intimately familiar with their destination, may find that it's worth paying a bit more for reliability, service, and a modicum of advice.

Shopping solely on price is a good way to ensure that the agency from which you eventually buy your tickets has cut its margin so thin that it can't afford to provide an acceptable standard of service. Labor costs are the largest expense for travel agencies, and the cheapest agencies can't afford to put experienced people on the phones or serving clients face to face. They discipline their employees to spend no more time with each customer than is essential to close the sale.

I can't pretend to impartiality on this issue, but my impression from working with thousands of around-the-world travelers is that their tendency is to overestimate the importance of price and underestimate the value of expertise.

Travel agents don't call themselves "travel consultants" for nothing. Most people planning a trip around the world need, and want, professional consulting and advice that they won't get from anyone but a specialized sort of travel agent. Most people simply don't know, and can't know in advance, what problems to anticipate or even what questions to ask. Travel agents who sell tickets as a commodity at the lowest possible prices, assembly line style, simply don't, and can't, provide that expanded service. And only an independent travel consultant—who isn't beholden to any one airline—is likely to be able to find which airline's routes will be best for you.

### Choose a Specialist

Choosing a discounter is, in a sense, just a special case of the larger principle of choosing an agency or agent with a specialization appropriate to your travel plans. It's difficult to separate choosing an agency from choosing an agent. Both are important. The agency needs to be soundly financed and accredited, and have contracts with the appropriate airlines. The agent needs to have expertise in your sort of travel, and in the kinds of travel services about which you want advice, whether they are cruises or long-haul airfares.

Some agencies specialize exclusively in travel of a particular type, or to a particular destination country or region. Other agencies have specialists in different areas.

Some agents opine that a competent travel agent can handle any kind of travel arrangements, anywhere in the world. However, travel and tourism is, by some accounts, the largest industry in the world. It is far too complex a topic for any one person to know everything about.

### Types of Discount Travel Agencies

There is no agreed-upon terminology for the various types of discount agencies. The most important differences for travelers are between wholesale and retail discounters, and between agencies whose deals are limited to particular markets and those that handle tickets to a wide range of international destinations. There is little if anything to be gained in price, and everything to be lost in advice and service, in buying from an agency that's primarily a ticket wholesaler, not a retail agency. Depending on your itinerary, I recommend buying your tickets either from a retail agent specializing in your specific destination or interest, or a specialist in around-the-world and multistop tickets.

# FINDING SOMEONE WHO SELLS DISCOUNT TICKETS

If you want a discounted ticket from point A to point B, the best way to start your inquiry to a travel agency is not, "Are you a consolidator?" They may say "No" because they are a retail agency and consider the term "consolidator" to apply only to wholesale-only agencies. Neither should you ask "Are you a bucket shop?" They may say "No" because they consider "bucket shop" to be a pejorative term connoting disreputability. Instead ask, "Do you have dis- counts on tickets from point A to point B?" or "Do you have discounts on multi- stop air tickets?"

Even better, ask, "What kind of travel do you specialize in?" See if the answer, unprompted, is cruises, package tours, "We do everything." If so, move on to another agency. If the answer is dis- counted tickets for independent travelers to Continent X, or customized tickets around the world, you may have found your agency.

Many people have heard that they should look for a consolidator or "bucket shop." I'll try to explain what I think these terms mean, but they are used inconsistently within the industry. Consolidators, bucket shops, and other sellers of discounted international tickets basically fall into three categories: wholesale consolidators, destination specialty agencies, and long-haul specialists who deal with many destinations and with multistop tickets.

### Wholesale Consolidators

Consolidators are agencies that have direct agreements with the airlines to get paid more than the standard commission, and thus are able to rebate some of that commission in the form of discounts to retail and/or wholesale customers.

In many cases, especially with larger airlines, consolidators are wholesalers who sell only through retail agencies, not directly to the public. Some people in the travel industry consider the term consolidator to refer exclusively to wholesalers, and would say that an agency isn't really a consolidator if it sells tickets directly to travelers.

Wholesale consolidators don't offer retail service. Buying from one may be fine if you want a straightforward roundtrip ticket, know what airline you want take, and exactly what dates you want to travel and when the flights operate. But of course many itineraries aren't like that, and most people need a retail agent's help to figure out what's the best ticket for them. Any retail travel agent can buy tickets from consolidators, and most agents who do significant international ticketing are familiar with a few big consolidators for major carriers.

Most publicly available lists of consolidators indiscriminately mix wholesale consolidators who also sell directly to the public with retail agencies, some of which don't have any direct contracts with the airlines. But it's a poor strategy to try to buy directly from a wholesaler.

Retail buyers of any product or service always like to think that they are getting wholesale prices. Buying directly from a consolidator that is primarily a wholesaler, you get the worst of both worlds: you get charged about the same amount as you would if you bought the ticket through a retailer, without getting the added-value service and advice that the retailer would give you for the markup. It's wholesalers who also sell retail who have created the false popular impression that agents who give discounts on airfares can't or won't provide consulting or other services.

An annoying number of people try to get wholesale prices by falsely claiming to be travel agents. It doesn't work, and only alienates retail and wholesale agents alike. If you aren't really a travel agent, you won't be able to pass for one. Don't try.

### Destination Specialty Agencies

Destination specialists include both tour operators (whose packages, except for some short-stay tours, are often quite expensive) and agencies selling tickets to the home country to immigrants and ethnic communities.

Frequently an agency operating tours to a particular country will have a discount agreement with the airline it uses for its tours (generally the national carrier of the destination) and will also sell wholesale tickets on that airline. One reason it does the wholesale business, even if the markup on wholesale tickets is very low, is to boost its volume of production (sales) with the airline, as many discount contracts are contingent on a specified sales volume and/or have year-end bonuses or additional commission rebates based on sales thresholds. The agency may be willing to sell tickets at retail as well; the problem in getting an air ticket from such an agency is that you're apt to get quite a hard sell for a tour, and no advice or encouragement for independent travel.

If you are ever in an immigrant or ethnic neighborhood, can't figure out where people are from, and don't want to ask directly, the easiest way to find out is to look in the window of the nearest travel agency to see what destinations are being advertised.

Other destination specialists sell tickets primarily to immigrants and their descendants traveling to visit friends and relations, or carry on business in the "old country." They sell few tours, because most of their customers are staying with local acquaintances. Ethnic specialty agencies often offer the cheapest roundtrip tickets, but have very limited offerings and are sometimes unaccustomed to dealing with people from outside their communities.

Some of these offices sell other products or provide other services in addition to functioning as travel agencies. Airline tickets may actually be a loss leader to attract customers for their other line(s) of business. It may be worth it to such a business to sell someone a ticket home at or slightly below cost, once or twice a year, if that gets them a loyal year-round customer for their barbershop, beauty salon, cafe, insurance brokerage, or whatever.

You can often find agencies like this through publications targeted at immigrants from the country you want to go to. Even in foreign-language ethnic publications the travel ads are generally recognizable, with at least the phone number, the destination cities, and the roundtrip prices in Latin letters and numbers. Even more than ads in the Sunday travel supplements of mainstream newspapers, a quick glance at the ethnic press will give you the best idea of the absolute lower limit of possible prices for tickets bought long in advance for travel in the most unpopular season on the worst airlines with the worst connections in the most undesirable or expensive stopover points.

The lowest advertised price is usually either a loss leader and/or a bait-and-switch gambit to attract callers. The lowest advertised prices for transoceanic tickets from the United States, for example, generally range from wholesale cost for the cheapest ticket to about US$20 below cost. It is unlikely that you will actually get a ticket for your itinerary at these prices. Most advertised prices are exclusive of taxes and perhaps other fees; even in the most expensive season the lowest advertised prices are usually for travel in low season, whenever that is.

But if you want the cheapest possible roundtrip from the United States to India, Ireland, Nigeria, or any other place from which there are large numbers of immigrants, you will find the lowest prices at a no-service "bucket shop" within the appropriate ethnic community. No general-purpose or general discount agency is likely to be able to beat the lowest prices of the agencies that sell nothing else but a massive volume of roundtrip tickets to a single destination. (I don't know how the term "bucket shop" originated, though I've heard lots of stories—all of them probably apocryphal. For a time, it seemed to be acquiring a wider meaning, but its usage seems to have reverted to describe only bare-bones ticket brokers.)

### Long-Haul, Multistop, and RTW Specialists

Long-haul and multistop agents subvert the airlines' conspiracy against discounting in all of the ways that I've been talking about in this chapter: rebating commissions on tickets they issue, buying tickets through wholesale consolidators on routes and airlines for which they don't have their own commission contracts, importing and exporting tickets, and so forth.

Long-haul agencies, and especially RTW and multistop agencies, specialize in knowing international airline route systems, fare rules, and the full range of consolidators (every airline has many consolidators); ticketing and fare construction techniques; and an arsenal of other tricks of the trade.

Long-haul and multistop agencies serve a limited and specialized subset of the air ticket market, and are mostly concentrated in a few world cities. The best places to find them include London, Bangkok, and San Francisco; some of the other places with many are Penang and Kuala Lumpur (Malaysia), Athens, and Sydney.

In the United States, most long-haul advertising is concentrated in the Sunday travel sections of the *San Francisco Chronicle*, *Miami Herald*, *The New York Times*, and *Los Angeles Times*. Most of the around-the-world agencies are actually located in San Francisco. In the UK, long-haul advertising is concentrated in the weekly entertainment calendar magazine *Time Out* and in newspapers for Australians and New Zealanders such as *TNT*. There are long-haul agencies all over London but especially in the West End and around Earl's Court. In Bangkok the most visible retail agencies are on Khao San Road in the Banglampoo district; agents there advertise mainly through touts and signboards on the sidewalks rather than in newspapers or magazines.

It can be worth looking far afield (with e-mail, your travel agency does not have to be physically near you) to deal with a good long-haul specialty agency. The overwhelming majority of travel agents don't even try to compete with bucket-shop fares. For that matter, most agents couldn't construct the sorts of routings the better long-haul and multistop agencies specialize in (especially customized around-the-world itineraries) at any price.

Around-the-world tickets are the epitome of the long-haul agent's art. Constructing an around-the-world fare requires both deciding at what points to break the tickets into segments and getting the best price for each segment (where each ticket may actually, with stopovers, cover several legs of the journey). It also requires advising travelers on destinations and routes, as most people aren't sure when they start planning an around-the-world trip exactly what stops they want to make, or in what order. Good around-the-world agents are rare, even in specialized agencies, but your average travel agent doesn't even know where to begin.

There are sometimes advantages in terms of consumer protections to dealing with an agency in your own country, but if there are no local discount specialists it may be worth buying tickets from an agency abroad (see "When Things Go Wrong" later in this chapter). You don't have to be in, or flying from or to, a city or country to deal with an agency there, if it can give you the best value for your money in price and service.

Many consolidators won't deal directly with the public, and wholesale ticket price tariffs are confidential. One of the most important skills for a long-haul agent is having a feel for the wholesale ticket market. It's one thing to ask your local agent to try to buy you a consolidator ticket. It's quite another for the agent to know who, and where, has the best price for what you want. Most bucket-shop tickets, if you inspect the validation, are not issued by the agencies you buy them from. If you already knew exactly where to buy your tickets, you could sometimes get a slightly better price directly. But the odds are that you couldn't and wouldn't find the best deal for yourself— the whole system is deliberately stacked against just that.

Around-the-world air ticketing is one of the smallest and most specialized of travel niches. There are probably no more than a hundred agencies and a thousand agents in the world who really specialize in these sorts of tickets. Look for someone who specifically advertises around-the-world and multistop tickets if that's what you want. Even most retail discounters only deal with basic one-way and roundtrip routings, not those with multiple stops and/or discontinuities.

Around-the-world ticketing is a global business. Local travel agents might buy from a domestic consolidator, but they probably have no idea that it is even possible to import your ticket from overseas, even if that would be much cheaper. Networks of multistop specialist agencies around the world regularly buy from and sell to each other and maintain databases of each other's prices. Costs of international money transfers, courier shipping, and international faxes and e-mail are less than the wide international variations in ticket prices.

Around-the-world specialty agencies pride themselves on being able to offer discounted tickets on the most complex routes and airlines. They invest heavily in negotiating the best possible contracts with appropriate airlines, locating and developing relationships with national and international networks of suppliers, and searching the worldwide discount ticket market to find new deals. Good around-the-world agencies will have discount contracts directly with many airlines. Where they don't have contracts directly with the airlines, they will buy tickets from a wide range of wholesale consolidators. When the airlines give larger discounts somewhere else, they will import those tickets from around the world.

### Telling Good Agencies and Agents from Bad

There is no simple or certain way to judge the qualifications or expertise of a travel agency or agent. Travel agency certification and appointment requires financing and technical competence in the mechanics of issuing tickets. In the United States, it requires no knowledge of destinations nor any evidence of competence to give travel advice. Travel agents talk about professional standards and credentials, but for the time being the travel agent community is too diverse for any likely agreement.

Different factors are appropriate to consider in choosing between travel agencies versus individual agents. What's important in an agency are adequate capitalization, sound finances, management integrity, and willingness to allow agents to spend time giving advice and not just selling. What's important in an agent are skills, appropriate specialized knowledge, an ability to relate to you and your trip, and a consulting, rather than sales, attitude. The same agency may have agents of varied expertise, with varied approaches to their work.

There is no one best agent for everyone. People are different, and travel differently. One of the most important and least-asked questions to ask a travel agent is, "How do you travel when you travel yourself?" An agent who wouldn't take the kind of trip you want, even if they had the time and money, is probably a poor choice to help you plan it. An agent's knowledge of your destination may be of little help if their knowledge is about the five-star hotels and you want to stay in local huts.

Look for an agent who views her-or himself as a consultant, advisor, and facilitator, rather than as a salesperson. Find someone who takes the time to ask questions, to listen to the answers, and to respond to your concerns. It's a very bad sign if an agent tells you a price without asking you any questions first, unless your trip is simple and your inquiry is unusually precise and complete. A good agent customizes each itinerary to best suit the wants and needs of the individual traveler; don't waste your time on an agency that sells around-the-world or multistop tickets from a limited menu or brochure. If one agency won't give you a price for what you want, go to another one that will.

As with other professional advisors and consultants, personal referrals from your acquaintances who've taken similar sorts of trips, and were happy with the service they received, are a good starting point in finding an agent. Part of being a good specialist is knowing the limits of your expertise. Agents often know which of their peers are reputable and which aren't. Good agents, if they are unable to help you, will admit ignorance and often will refer you to someone else who is reliable and more appropriate.

One thing not to rely on is favorable references provided by the agency itself. Except for complete frauds, even rip-off agencies have satisfied customers. The test is what they do when things go wrong. Most are pretty reliable, but you can't expect the best service at the lowest price. To the extent that two agencies have access to the same deals, and that the difference between their prices reflects differences in their labor costs, small variations in price have a disproportionate affect on the level of service they can afford to give.

Listings of specific travel agencies in guidebooks aren't much use either. I work for an agency that is written up in many guidebooks, so maybe I shouldn't say this, but most lists of agencies I see in guidebooks and references on cheap tickets intermingle reputable, disreputable, and long-out-of-business agencies. That's not the guidebook writers' fault: it's mostly that agencies come and go, or go bad, too often for any publication to keep up with the changes.

Don't even consider buying tickets from an agency that is not appointed by IATA. Agencies in the United States usually receive their IATA appointments through either or both the International Airline Travel Agents' Network (IATAN) and/or the Airline Reporting Corporation (ARC), whose logos are frequently displayed in their offices and on their literature. Subagents and non-IATA/IATAN/ARC agencies cannot issue any of their own tickets, but must purchase them all from other agencies, wholesalers, or the airlines. Since the basic qualifications for IATA, IATAN, and ARC appointments are proof of financial means and ticketing experience, non-IATA/IATAN/ARC agents are, by definition, inexperienced, under-financed, or both.

If you aren't sure of an agency's status, there's a simple test: ask to see some tickets they have issued. Don't write a check to a payee whose name doesn't match what's in the "issuing agency" box on any of their tickets. It's perfectly okay if many, even most, of their tickets, or all of your particular tickets, come from airlines or other agencies, but it's a red flag if the agent you're dealing with hasn't passed the tests or posted the bonds to be able to issue any tickets themselves.

In the UK, don't buy tickets from any agency that doesn't list an Air Travel Organiser's Licence (ATOL) number on its advertisements and receipts. (See the section "When Things Go Wrong," below, on consumer protection.) You can call the UK Civil Aviation Authority at +44-207-832-5620 or +44-207-832-6600 to find out if the ATOL number is valid, and to whom it belongs.

In the United States, look for a California Seller of Travel (CST) registration number in travel agency ads. Any agency with a national clientele has customers in California, regardless of where in the United States they are located. If they haven't bothered to register with the state, or display their required registration number, that's a bad sign.

Anywhere you encounter it, membership in the American Society of Travel Agents (ASTA) is a positive sign. But there's no reason to avoid nonmembers of ASTA; many good agencies in the United States don't choose to belong.

Except in certain other countries with their own licensing systems, most other memberships, accreditations, and endorsements are of little or no value to consumers in judging travel agencies. Some tourist boards and other trade associations issue certificates to specialists in destinations or types of travel, but there's little way for you to tell which are meaningful and which are handed out to every agent who requests a packet of literature about a destination, or attends a single marketing seminar. In any event, many of the best agents got their training through experience on the job and have no formal credentials.

Don't buy tickets from an agency that doesn't accept credit cards, if you can avoid it, whether or not you actually intend to pay by credit card. The fact that an agency doesn't accept credit cards is a strong indication that either it doesn't specialize in discounted tickets, and thus hasn't needed to establish a credit-card merchant account (airlines accept all major credit cards directly, on the agent's behalf, for full-fare tickets); or it has too little business experience, or too little capital or business credit, to qualify for a merchant account; or its merchant account has been revoked, which generally happens only if it has an excessive percentage of chargebacks (charges disputed by customers). If an agency accepts no credit cards, that's a red flag that its finances or business practices are suspect in the eyes of some people who should know: the bankers.

As for discount travel agency reliability, it varies. Caveat emptor. These agencies tend to be wheeler-dealers, and of necessity they cut their margins thin. Find out how long the agency has been around. Check it out with any professional or accrediting organizations to which it belongs. (See "When Things Go Wrong" later in this section for some suggestions.) Go to the office in person, if you can. If you don't completely trust the company to deliver, or the price is so good that you can't resist going through with a deal that seems too good to be true, pay by credit card so you can refuse the charge if you don't get your tickets. You'll probably have to pay 2–5 percent more for using a credit card, but it's simple, cheap, and effective insurance.

Before you pay for tickets, have the agent make confirmed reservations for as many of your flights as possible and give you a commitment that you'll have all or most of your tickets in hand within a month of payment.

Occasionally it won't be possible to confirm a flight or two in advance, especially for flights more than 10 months in the future. An airline may not have loaded its schedules and seat inventories into the computers yet, or may not respond to requests for confirmation. Tickets for one or two legs of your trip, even if you pay well in advance, may for legitimate reasons have to be picked up from the airlines or agents along the way.

But if an agency suggests that you will have more flexibility if you don't make reservations and just get your tickets open, or that you will be safer picking up your tickets along the way than carrying them with you, something is wrong. Most likely this means the agency won't issue your tickets until just before you start using each piece of your tickets. This is standard operating procedure for some large agencies of long standing, but I disapprove of it and think it's not in travelers' best interests. There's no excuse for holding other people's money at risk; in some jurisdictions, including California, it's illegal. I wouldn't buy tickets on these terms, but if you do pay for tickets to be issued much later, at least get a commitment from the agency guaranteeing that the agency, not you, will be responsible for changes in prices between when it takes your money and when it has your tickets issued (which it will probably be unwilling to give). If your credit card will only be charged as tickets are issued, what guarantee (if any) do you have that the total charges won't be more than you bargained for?

If you are leaving too soon (within a month) to get all your tickets before your departure, it's of the utmost importance to deal with an agency you trust completely. Different tickets from different agencies at different prices will take different amounts of time to deliver. It may be worth it to your peace of mind to pay somewhat more for tickets that can be issued more quickly, and in your hands before you leave, than for tickets that you'll have to pick up along the way.

If you have any doubts about an agency or agent, immediately before paying for your tickets check directly with the airlines to make sure that you are holding confirmed reservations. This is not always possible, as some of your flights may be on airlines that have no representation in the country in which you are buying your tickets. But where possible, it's a good idea. It's all too easy for bad agents to sell tickets to people who aren't really confirmed.

## When to Buy Your Airline Tickets

There is no simple answer to the question, "When should I buy my tickets?" One of the reasons to call a travel agent long in advance of a big trip—even a year before your departure—is to get their expert advice as to when to buy your tickets, along with a ballpark estimate of how much they might cost. For those with a choice of when to buy, factors to consider are the duration of your trip, the season in which you will be traveling, how long it will take to get your tickets, how far in advance the airlines set their discount rates, and, of course, how far ahead you are sure of your plans.

In general, the best time to buy tickets is usually between three and six months before your departure, perhaps somewhat longer in advance for travel during December or other peak seasons such as Lunar New Year in East Asia, Hajj in Saudi Arabia, or Passover in Israel.

### Reasons to Buy Tickets Further in Advance

Unlike discounted tickets purchased directly from the airlines, most consolidator tickets have no advance purchase requirements. I've sold tickets to people leaving the same day around the world. This does not mean that tickets will be just as cheap at the last minute. On the contrary, you will get the best price and have the most choices if you buy your tickets as far in advance as possible, unless there is a specific reason not to (see below).

If you buy tickets at the last minute, the cheapest seats on the cheapest airlines may already be sold, and you may have to pay much more for another airline or for a more expensive reservation category ("booking class"). Some countries also require confirmed reservations or tickets before they will issue you a visa.

Worst of all, you may find at the last minute that there are no flights on the route you planned, that your itinerary will be much more costly than your budget allows, or that all seats on a flight you counted on are sold out.

Getting the best price often requires having tickets issued in different countries. Sending payments to suppliers abroad and getting tickets back by air mail can easily take three weeks. If you want to have your tickets in hand at least a week before your departure, at the best possible price, you need to pay for them at least a month before your departure. Otherwise you may have to pay substantial rush charges, or pick tickets up overseas as you travel, an arrangement few people prefer and which can usually be avoided by advance planning.

Finding and verifying the best fare for an itinerary, deciding between alternatives, and finalizing reservations for specific flights often takes a couple of weeks from the first call to a travel agent to when a traveler is ready to pay for tickets. So you should contact a travel agent at least six weeks before your intended departure date if you don't want to be in a rush, longer if you want the best possible fare.

Published around-the-world fares typically require 21 days advance purchase, in order to keep them from being used by business travelers. Because the best deals for first-and business-class travel are often published fares, it is particularly difficult and expensive to arrange a first-or business-class multistop trip on short notice.

### Reasons to Wait to Buy Tickets Later

The only good reasons to delay buying tickets are to wait for airlines to set discount prices for your travel dates, to extend the validity dates of your tickets, or because you haven't yet made up your mind where you want to go or when you want to leave.

Airlines wait until they have a good idea how full their planes will be before they decide how deeply they need to discount their tickets to fill their planes. Most airlines set their consolidator prices only one or two seasons at a time, anywhere from one to six months in advance.

Some consolidators offer discounts on flights departing many months in the future. If the airline that is likely to be cheapest has already set its prices, an agent has every reason to tell you so to close the sale early. Sometimes you can get a really good deal by buying tickets up to a year in advance, but it is often better to wait until more airlines have set their discount rates. The best time to make reservations is usually just after most airlines have fixed their discount prices for your travel season.

However, waiting to buy your tickets in the hope that some airline will set lower rates is always a gamble. It is riskiest for high-season or holiday travel;

if no better deal materializes there may be no cheap seats left, or no seats at all, by the time you decide to buy your tickets. For example, international flights to virtually all places, regardless of whether you think of them as "Christmas destinations," are most heavily booked throughout December and into January. The cheapest December seats to many points in Africa are sold out in July or August.

If your trip will last more than one year from the date you buy your tickets, you will only be able to buy part of your tickets before your departure. If you tell a good agent your entire planned itinerary, and how far you are confident you will get within a year, they can advise which tickets it would be best to purchase in advance and where it will be best to buy the rest. (See "Buying Tickets En Route" later in this chapter.)

Because tickets are valid at most one year from the date of issue, and it can take a month of that year of validity for you to get the tickets, the practical limit to the duration of a trip, for which you purchase all your tickets at once, is about eleven months.

For shorter trips, it makes sense to wait to purchase your tickets until within one year of the last date you might want to return, so that you can buy your tickets all at once. If you plan to travel for more than nine or ten months, you may be better off buying your tickets in two or more stages, especially if you aren't certain how soon you'll want to return home. It's a real drag to cut your trip short solely because your tickets are about to expire. Far more people extend their trips longer than they had planned than come home earlier than they expected, so don't risk being forced to return sooner than you want to.

If you wait to buy your tickets, you risk that flights will fill up and/or prices will increase while you are waiting. Agents don't usually get advance notice of price increases, and unticketed reservations can be canceled without notice. Some agencies will offer to sell you vouchers for tickets to be issued in the future, subject to your agreement to pay any fare increase in the interim. If you accept such an arrangement, you have no protection if the airline increases its fare or discontinues service on the route before your tickets are issued. Don't sign a blank credit card authorization, or pay for vouchers without a written guarantee of the price for the actual tickets. Even if the agency guarantees the price, you have little recourse if anything happens to the agency between when you pay them and when they pay for your tickets.

If an agency issues portions of your tickets, one at a time, as you travel, they will be holding your money for months before they spend it. If an agency says there's no limit to the duration of your travels, it's a virtual certainty they are talking about taking payment now, issuing tickets later, and using your money in the meantime to solve their cash-flow problems. Don't let them do this. The only times to accept vouchers for tickets to be picked up overseas are when you are leaving on too short notice to get tickets in hand before your departure, or when the particular fare requires that tickets be prepaid for issuance directly by the airline at the point of departure (as has been the case for tickets originating in the Philippines and a few other countries).

The longer your trip, the more likely that your plans will change en route. Tickets bought in a single package are cheaper than tickets bought in several stages, but it's a false economy if you have to throw them away and buy other tickets when you later decide to go somewhere different. Buy tickets no further than you are certain of your desired route.

## Getting a Price Estimate

Once you have chosen a tentative set of destinations, the next step is to contact appropriately specialized discount travel agencies to get more precise estimates on how much air tickets will cost to include specific stops in a specific order on specific airlines.

Rating an around-the-world itinerary can take an hour or two of work, for which the agent is paid nothing if you end up getting the ticket elsewhere. Most agents will give only a very rough estimate of the fare unless you make clear, by given them a nonrefundable deposit, that you are really serious about getting your tickets from that agency, and aren't just shopping around. Deposits have been standard in the UK and other countries for years, and are gradually becoming the norm in the United States as well.

You may want to visit an agency in person, at some point, to check it out, but it's often easier to make initial inquiries by phone or e-mail. Don't be surprised that the price isn't in the computer and can't be given off the top of the agent's head. Inquiries from people who are leaving right away are likely to be worked on and answered soonest, and it may take a couple of days to get answers about prices for parts of your tickets from suppliers overseas in other time zones.

## Factors That May Affect the Price

Before you start contacting travel agencies, review the following list of factors that may affect the price of your tickets, and be sure your inquiry includes all the information they will need to give you an accurate estimate and to tell which airlines, routes, and tickets will be best for you. If you don't volunteer this information, and the agents don't ask, they'll have to base their estimate on some standard set of assumptions about what you want, which may not be correct.

### Starting and Ending Cities

The essential information most often omitted from requests for estimates is the most basic: where people want their tickets to start and end. Most people assume that their starting and ending cities are obvious, but they aren't. You may want tickets starting in the same city as the agency you are contacting for an estimate, but the agent doesn't know that. You may take it for granted that you want your tickets to include a flight back from what you specify as your final destination to where you started from, but not everyone does: a substantial proportion of long-haul tickets are one-way, or start and end in different places. Agents who specialize in around-the-world and multistop tickets are especially likely to get inquiries from all over and for flights from other places. I've gotten telephone calls from customers on every continent—including Antarctica—and it's not unusual for around-the-world agencies to get e-mail from Asia asking about prices of flights from Europe to the Americas, or to have customers in the United States buy tickets starting in Australia and ending in Africa.

### List of Destinations

Include all the places you intend to go, even if you think they have to be ticketed as side trips or separate tickets, or that you will only be able to purchase tickets locally for certain flights. You may be right, but if you don't tell an agent, and it is possible to include flights to those places more cheaply in some other way, you've deprived yourself of the possibility of a pleasant surprise. Give the agent a chance, and in the majority of cases they'll be able to include, at less cost as part of through tickets, at least some additional destinations you thought would have to be side trips. Don't exclude domestic flights in your own or any other country from your request for an estimate.

Don't include a place in your list of destinations just because you think you have to change planes there to get to where you really want. There's more than one way to get to almost anywhere, and the cheapest route and connection point may not be the most obvious one. By specifying a route or connection point, you may unwittingly rule out a cheaper one you didn't know about. To get the best advantage of the agent's expertise, list the places you really want to go, and let the agent figure out the best way to get you there.

Don't specify a particular airport (rather than a city or place name) unless your plans really require you to fly in or out of that airport rather than any other airport in the city or region. Doing this unnecessarily limits your agent's search. There may be more than one airport (even if you've only heard of one) and one you haven't heard of might be cheaper. If you say, "I want to fly to Heathrow," your agent will infer that you are unwilling to fly in or out of any of the other London-area airports (Gatwick, Stansted, Luton, or London City Airport) even if one of those would be much cheaper. Airline databases are organized by city names, not by island or region names. For example, databases list "Denpasar" (town name) rather than "Bali" (island name). So sometimes even a good agent may need to ask you the name of the city associated with the airport on a particular island or in a particular region. But if price is your most important consideration, let the agent suggest the cheapest airport in the area. You can always choose to pay more for a different airport if you don't like the agent's first, cheapest proposal.

If there are some places that are essential, and some that are less important, say so. One way to prioritize your goals is to flag each place on the list you give your travel agent as mandatory, optional, or incidental. An even better way is to divide your destinations into an A-list (mandatory), a B-list (highly desirable but inessential if the incremental cost is more than some threshold amount), and perhaps a C-list (worth stopping in if it doesn't add to the cost). Once you start working on your plans with a travel agent, you'll probably add some places to the C-list when your travel agent mentions them as free or minimal-cost additions, or as possible stopovers at required connection points.

If you are trying to decide whether specific options are worth it, be as precise as you can about your priorities. "I'd like to include Tokyo if it wouldn't add too much to the price," doesn't give an agent much to go on. What's too much? "Tokyo, if not more than US$500 additional" is more helpful.

### Surface Transportation

If there are specific sections of your trip that you want to travel by surface transportation (land or water), or would be willing to travel on the surface to save money, tell the agent. It's a good idea to identify which stretches you want to travel for the sake of the journey (a train trip across North America, Eurasia, or Australia, for example), and which you are planning to travel only in the hope of saving money. That way the agent won't waste time looking into flights for sections that you wouldn't want to fly, no matter what the price, but will know to tell you if surface travel in other places will cost as much as the additional cost of including flights. If you mention what means of surface travel you plan to use, an agent familiar with the region may be able to offer suggestions about its speed, cost, comfort, or feasibility. If you plan any major side trips by surface transportation, particularly to countries not included on your air route, it's a good idea to mention them as well, as those countries may turn out to have visa, onward ticket, or other entry requirements about which an agent can warn you.

### Starting and Ending Dates

If you aren't leaving for at least a month, it's usually sufficient to specify what month you intend to depart and what month, at the latest, you intend to complete your travel on these tickets. Sometimes you may need to specify when in the month you will depart (e.g., if that month is divided into several fare seasons), but it is counterproductive to specify an exact departure date if you don't have to leave on exactly that day.

If for some reason you need to leave on a specific date (not before and not after), you should say so explicitly, realizing that it may increase the price substantially. It can be a very expensive mistake to make schedule commitments before talking to an agent about air ticket prices and flight availability. If price is an object, find out the cheapest route and airlines and their schedules, make reservations, and only then make business appointments or commitments for tours or meetings with friends.

### Ages of Travelers

Airlines define children as those who are traveling before their 12th birthday and infants as those who are traveling before their 2nd birthday. Tell an agent before working out a price estimate or itinerary if you will be traveling with children and/or infants. The cheapest airlines and routes may be different for adults versus children and infants.

Do not assume that there is any standard discount for children, or that infants fly free on international flights, as they do on domestic flights within the United States.

**Child Discounts:** These vary widely. Full child fares are typically between 50 and 75 percent of full adult fares. But full fares are high, and discounted prices for adults are often lower than full child fares. Discounted adult fares are not necessarily combinable with any further discounts for children, so the cheapest ticket for a child may be at a discounted adult price. The cheapest ticket for a child can cost anywhere from 50 percent to 100 percent of the cost of the cheapest adult ticket on the same flights. Children not accompanied by an adult are carried only at the discretion of the airlines and, on most airlines, only on payment of an adult fare.

**Infant Discounts:** Infants must have paid tickets for all international flights on all airlines. Infant fares are typically 10 percent of full (not discounted) adult fares, and are subject to the same taxes as adult tickets. Some airlines, at their discretion, provide bassinets or other special accommodations (if space is available) for infants on long flights. But an infant ticket does not guarantee a bassinet or a separate seat; you must be prepared to hold an infant on your lap. Infant roundtrip tickets to distant international points, such as from the United States to Africa or South Asia and back, range up to US$200–300. Infant tickets around the world, on routes that would cost adults US$2,000-3,000 at discounted prices, might cost US$400-500.

**Youth and Senior Citizen Discounts:** Although some airlines offer special youth or student fares and discounts for senior citizens, these are only occasionally cheaper than the cheapest consolidator tickets. As with children's discounts, student and senior citizen discounts are rarely combinable with other discounts: being a student or a senior citizen won't entitle you to any reduction of the price of a consolidator ticket. Tell an agent if you and/or anyone else in your party qualifies for student fares or senior citizen discounts, but don't expect it to make any great difference to the total price of a set of multistop tickets.

### Direction of Travel

International fares are not the same in opposite directions. This sometimes comes as a surprise to travelers accustomed to domestic fares, which are usually the same between the same cities in either direction. Between countries, the fare from B to A can be twice the fare from A to B, or vice versa. It's quite common for an airline to offer discounts in one direction on a particular flight, and no discounts at all the other way. Rules and conditions for flights in opposite directions can be different as well.

So the prices of tickets around the world, or on any international route, in opposite directions, are entirely independent of each other. Rarely are the same set of airlines and connecting points cheapest to the same destinations in opposite directions. Finding the cheapest price and route each way is a separate problem.

Most around-the-world travelers, in order to be in certain regions in certain seasons or for other reasons, have a preferred overall direction of travel (although as noted earlier your route need not go in a continuous direction). If you truly don't care, or are open to reversing your general direction for a much better fare, say so. A good agent can usually tell fairly quickly if one direction or the other is likely to be dramatically cheaper, without the need to work out precise estimates for both.

### Personal Schedule, Sequence, or Airline Requirements

If you have to make stops in a certain sequence, have already made specific schedule commitments—a tour, a cruise, business appointments, whatever—or need to be on specific airlines or flights, tell the agent.

Most people are willing to make specific stops in whatever order is cheapest. If you aren't, tell your agent; that way time won't be wasted trying to save you money by rearranging your list of destinations.

The dates and even the months of all flights between the first and the last are usually irrelevant to the price, unless it is essential for you to leave, or arrive in, certain places on exact dates. Because the cheapest flights may not operate on the particular days you need to travel, you may have to pay considerably more to travel on some days than others.

The less time you want to spend in each city, the less likely it is that the cheapest flights will operate on the days you want. This is the main reason why tickets for quick trips around the world, especially by businesspeople who want to spend only a couple of days in each city, usually end up costing more than tickets for much lengthier leisure trips. If you can, make your air travel reservations for such a trip before making your business appointments. Just tell the agent what you need: "I need one business day in Jakarta, three in Hong Kong, and two in Sydney, in whatever sequence would be cheapest."

In most cases, travel funded by the USA government must be on USA-based airlines wherever possible. Large parts of the world, including almost the entire continent of Africa and most of Asia between the Middle East and the Pacific coast, aren't served by any USA airline, and the rules in such cases are a bit arcane. If you are constrained by these or other rules to travel on certain airlines, it's essential for an agent to know to give you a meaningful price.

Finally, if you are meeting or traveling with someone else who already has tickets this can actually simplify the agent's task, but it can greatly increase your cost. You can't count on finding seats on the same flights as your traveling companion for the same price they paid, or at any price; if you want to travel together it's important to make your reservations as soon as possible. If one of you is getting your ticket paid for by someone else, and one will have to pay, try to work out both prices before either of you buys your ticket. If you start shopping for the second ticket only after the first one has been purchased, you may find out that it's on the airline that offers the smallest discounts or on a flight that has no more seats available.

### Budget Limitations

Don't be coy about your budget. Given an approximate budget for air tickets, an agent can suggest whether meeting it is likely to require you to cut a few, many, or certain especially expensive destinations, or whether it will leave you money to add more destinations if you want. You may save an agent hours of research into prices and save yourself a few days' wait for an estimate that would be completely beyond your means.

### Class of Service

Unless you say otherwise, agents will assume that you want prices for third-class (coach or economy) travel.

Upgrading from coach to first or second (business or club) class is neither simple nor inexpensive. Discounts on first-and business-class tickets are generally smaller than coach discounts, and many airlines offer no discounts at all in first or business class. So first-and business-class passengers are even more likely than coach passengers to have to be willing to accept less-preferred airlines and routes in return for discounts. But the people who travel in business and first class tend to be the least flexible about airlines and routes, for the same reasons that they are flying in the front cabin in the first place.

The airlines and routes that are cheapest in coach may be completely different from those that are cheapest in first or business class. Discounted business-class tickets typically cost at least twice as much as discounted coach tickets to the same set of cities, and usually even more than that. (My rule of thumb is that discounted business-class tickets typically cost about US$100 per flying hour more than discounted coach tickets.) If you wouldn't be willing to pay at least twice as much for business class as for coach, or even more for first class, don't waste an agent's time researching the best first-or business-class prices.

Travelers accustomed to fully refundable, easily rerouted full-fare first-and business-class tickets should also keep in mind that discounted tickets in any class will be more difficult (if not impossible) to reroute or refund. Buying discounted tickets with cancellation and change penalties is likely to prove a false economy for business travelers who often cancel trips at the last minute or change their destinations en route.

### Likelihood of Future Changes

How likely is it that you will need to change your departure dates, stopover cities, or route after buying your tickets? It may be worth paying more for tickets that are more flexible with respect to any of these things, especially date changes, or buying tickets for only the part of your journey for which you are sure of your destinations and route.

Tickets with flexible dates for most or all flights are available for not too much more than fixed-date tickets on many routes. Tickets on which destinations can be changed are much harder to find at a discount. If an agent says that it will be no problem to completely reroute your trip, or change destinations, probe carefully to find out if that means tickets aren't going to be issued for each of your flights until just before your departure, allowing the agent to sit on your money, at your risk, in the interim.

### Excess Baggage

How much luggage you have can affect which tickets are best. Breaking the fares and ticketing differently can determine whether each passenger is entitled to free carriage of two pieces of luggage of 32 kg (70 lb) each or only a total of 20 kg (44 lb). If you need to bring two full suitcases, the excess baggage charges may be more than the difference in price between the tickets.

From time to time, one or another airline offers to carry extra baggage, at no extra charge, for passengers on certain routes, on certain tickets, or who buy tickets through certain agents. These promotions come and go, but excess baggage charges are steep and it's worth asking if you will have a lot of luggage.

Lastly, travelers with especially valuable, fragile, or important items in their luggage (none of which are ever recommended, of course) may prefer to pay more for more direct routes or ones with fewer plane changes, to minimize the possibility of loss, damage, or delay of their luggage.

### Openness to Modifications

Are you interested in possible modifications of your proposed itinerary if they would save you money? Rigid is a dirty word in USA culture, so everyone is "flexible." Be realistic: how flexible are your plans? Would you be willing to fly from New York rather than Boston, to stop in Amsterdam rather than Paris, or to take a train from Bombay to Delhi if each of those choices would save you US$50? US$500?

If you could save considerable money by some slight change in your itinerary, a good agent should point that out when asked. If you are indifferent between several choices, you can say so: "leaving from wherever on the West Coast would be cheapest," "returning from wherever in Western Europe would be cheapest," "stopping in either Bangkok, Kuala Lumpur, or Singapore."

If you ask for the cheapest price, a good agent will suggest whatever direction of travel and sequence of stops would be cheapest. This is not always a consistent course from east to west or west to east, nor is it always the most obvious or direct route. Flights simply don't exist on many frequently requested routes. Most around-the-world itineraries require at least some connections in places that weren't in travelers' initial lists of requested destinations.

### When Do You Plan to Buy Your Tickets?

If you specify a departure date within 3–6 months, you'll probably get a fairly precise estimate of what your tickets will cost if reservations can be made and confirmed and you are willing to pay within a week to a month.

If you ask for estimates for tickets to be bought more than a month or two in the future, either because you aren't yet ready to buy or because it isn't yet within a year of your intended completion of travel, you may only be able to get a rough estimate of what your tickets will cost, and what routing and airlines are likely to be cheapest.

In the early stages of planning and budgeting, many people find that getting a rough preliminary price estimate can help them figure out what set of stopovers is likely to be both feasible and affordable. A good agent can also troubleshoot your proposed itinerary and give advance warning of potential problems as well as advice on how to avoid them: "You aren't allowed to enter or leave Myanmar except by air," or "You aren't allowed into Indonesia or Australia unless you already have a ticket out of the country."

In certain cases, if you are sure of what itinerary you want, airlines may accept reservations even further in advance than the discount rates have been determined and hold the space for you until prices are set. This generally makes sense only if you are waiting for prices for flights that are likely to become heavily booked in the meantime, especially during holiday periods, and/or you are certain that you will want to be on specific flights. If this is the case, tell your agent.

An agent can't and won't spend many hours figuring out exact current prices, all of which could change tomorrow, if you don't plan to buy your tickets until months later. What you can get is a rough estimate, usually to the nearest US$500. The simpler your itinerary and the sooner your proposed departure, the more precise the estimate.

## Interpreting Price Estimates

A price estimate for airline tickets should specify the airlines, the set and sequence of stops, any special rules or restrictions, which (if any) of the dates can be changed after ticketing, and at what (if any) cost.

It's a bad sign if you ask for flexible tickets and an agent starts by giving you a price for tickets with substantial date-change fees, unless it's for a good reason, such as that flexible tickets would cost US$500 more. Whatever the reason, any change fees beyond US$50 or so per flight should be called to your attention.

Be aware that a price estimate for tickets is only an estimate, not a firm quote, no matter what language is used. Fares and ticket prices are not and cannot be guaranteed until tickets are paid for in full and issued. This holds true even if you make reservations directly with an airline for tickets at a published fare, receive a written or printed itinerary, and are told that your reservations will be held until a specified time. A reservation guarantee means the airline won't cancel your reservations, not that it won't change or discontinue the fare.

Airline discount contracts with agents permit the airlines to change prices and terms at any time without prior notice. All estimated prices are subject to the availability of space, unless that agent has already made confirmed reservations for you. A common mistake is to compare estimates for prices on unnamed airlines, or on airlines or fares on which no space is available, with estimates for prices for which space is actually available. An estimated price for tickets on an unnamed airline or airlines means almost nothing. Don't presume that space is actually available until you have a confirmed itinerary in writing.

An agent has to base an estimate on certain assumptions. Unless customers tell me otherwise, I generally assume that they want the cheapest available coach tickets on any IATA airline, that they will be able to fix their departure date before purchasing tickets, that they need to be able to change the dates of all subsequent flights at minimal charge, that they will use all their tickets within one year of the date they pay for them (not the date of departure), and that they would be willing to accept nonrefundable tickets valid only on certain airlines. I estimate a price accordingly.

If the price the agent quotes you has other restrictions, she or he should tell you. For example, it is sometimes much cheaper to fix the date of your last as well as your first flight, to use a restricted (minimum stay/maximum stay/date change penalty) ticket for a particular flight, to use tickets that permit travel only during certain seasons or are valid only for six months rather than a full year, or to use tickets that can be changed but only for a fee.

Agents shouldn't suggest airlines or flights that they wouldn't take themselves. But if you don't like an agent's suggestions or would prefer a different routing or set of airlines and connection points, make your wants known.

The cheapest prices are usually for midweek departures (Monday through Thursday, or Sunday through Thursday, depending on the airline). You can expect to pay US$20–50 more to leave on a weekend (Friday through Sunday). But in some cases it makes no difference. Ask on which departure days an estimate applies. If you ask for the lowest possible price, most discount agencies will include a discount for payment by cash or check in the estimate they give you. Ask if they accept credit or charge cards, and how much more the tickets will cost without the cash discount.

A good estimate will probably give a variety of options, such as different cities in which you could arrive, depart, or stopover for the same or a similar price. If you are interested, an agent should be able to tell you which additional stopovers an estimated price would allow at little or no additional cost, which other potentially interesting stopovers could be added at significant (but potentially worthwhile) additional cost, which stopovers could be eliminated for substantial cost savings, and/or which alternative stopover points could be substituted at the same price (e.g., "any one city in Europe served by Gulf Air"). You should also be able to get an estimate of how substantial your savings might be if your stops or dates were rearranged (e.g., "The price would be US$200 less if you left before the end of May rather than in early June").

## Finalizing Your Route

Depending on the degree of certainty in your plans when you first call, it can take several successive revisions— first of cities and routes and then of dates and flight times—to arrive at your final itinerary. You may want to do research about possible stopovers or alternate destinations you hadn't considered, or reconsider how important certain places or a certain sequence of stops are. This is one of the best reasons to start getting ticket price estimates well in advance, before you've locked yourself into any commitments.

Feel free to ask about alternatives ("About how much more would it cost to add a stop somewhere in Africa, and where would be cheapest?" "About how much, if anything, would we save if we skipped this stop?" "Is there somewhere else in that region that would be much cheaper?" "Would we save anything if we took a train from Q to R?"). But keep in mind that changing even one stopover point can require completely different airlines and fares and an hour of research. Telling agents more about your plans and the purpose of your trip enables them to make appropriate suggestions for the itinerary with which you'll be happiest.

If you don't like an agent's proposal, say what's wrong. It's your trip, and the agent should want you to go away—and come back—happy. If you call a discount agency, they will probably start with the cheapest airlines and routes to your destinations. But that's no reason for you not to insist on more direct flights or different airlines, if they are available and you feel they are worth it. If an agent won't give you what you want, find one who will.

Keep in mind, though, that a good agent has probably started by finding the cheapest available airlines and routing, which is probably what you asked for. So the answers to all questions of the form, "Could I do something else instead?" are likely to begin, "Yes, but it will cost more." A skilled specialist can give you the best price in significant part by finding the cheapest set of airlines and sequence of stops. You can ask for prices on specific airlines if you need them, but you should know that specifying particular airlines and flights you want to take, or rearranging the stops in other than the cheapest sequence, can easily double or triple the price of your tickets.

## Making Reservations

Once you have agreed on an estimated price for a specific route and set of airlines, chosen between any stopover alternatives, and decided on your preferred dates for each flight, the next step is to try to make reservations.

### Deposits

Some agents will ask for a deposit before they will make reservations for you. Such a deposit is usually not refundable unless the agent is unable to confirm reservations for you for the estimated price. If you change your mind after making a deposit, and decide not to travel or to get your tickets from another agent, the deposit goes to pay for the agency's consulting services. Typical deposits, if required, might range from US$50 per person for a simple one-way or roundtrip consolidator ticket to US$500 per person for tickets around the world.

A booking deposit is a service charge for the agency's time and advice. Any deposit that isn't applied to your tickets goes to the agency, not the airline; scheduled airlines do not accept partial payments or deposits for individual tickets. A deposit does not guarantee the fare. A ticket cannot be issued and the fare cannot be guaranteed until the airline is paid in full. (Fares aren't guaranteed even after tickets are issued, but airlines almost never assert their right to collect additional money for fare changes between ticketing and travel.)

It is largely a matter of local custom whether agents require deposits for individual bookings on scheduled airlines. In the UK, most agents require deposits before they will make reservations for any discounted tickets, even simple roundtrips. In almost all countries, deposits are required before agents will work on pricing or booking around-the-world or multistop international itineraries.

In the United States, it used to be rare for agents to ask for deposits. Since 1995, elimination of base commissions paid to travel agents in the United States has forced agents to reassess their business practices. Most now require deposits before investing a lot of time in complex itineraries, or charge hourly consulting fees. It's not unreasonable: most professionals require a retainer before they'll provide anything more than a brief initial consultation, and a travel agent may have to do a couple of hours' work just to give you an initial price estimate. Some agencies still don't charge deposits, but they can't afford to give much free advice and often offer bare-bones service, if any, once you've paid for your tickets. You get what you pay for.

Deposits for groups work differently than general booking deposits. Reserving a block of space for a group almost always requires a deposit to protect both the agent and the airline against having the space go empty if the group doesn't materialize. In such a case most of the group deposit goes to the airline, not the agent, and the airline may be willing to give a contractual guarantee of a price in exchange for an initial deposit of 10–25 percent of the total price and a commitment to a date for full payment. Charter operators also sometimes guarantee prices in exchange for partial payment, on condition that the final balance be paid by a specified date.

Except for a deposit to an agent, making confirmed reservations does not place you under any obligation whatsoever. You owe nothing to the airlines if you cancel or change your reservations prior to paying for tickets. An agent who charges you for changes to reservations, prior to full payment, is simply charging you for the time to make the changes.

### Names on Tickets

You must specify each passenger's first and last name, gender, and age (if a child or infant) at the time you first make your reservations. Last names and first initials are not sufficient; some airlines will issue tickets that way but others require full first names. Airlines are quite aware that the only reason to put only a first initial on a ticket is to facilitate having a family member use the ticket if you can't, which violates their rules against transferring tickets. Middle names are not needed and aren't always even accepted. Names in reservations and on tickets should match those on passports at the time of travel.

A ticket cannot be issued in a name different from the name in which space was first reserved, and an increasing number of airlines forbid any changes to names on reservations. Any attempt to change the name on a reservation that has already been made may cause the airline to cancel the reservation entirely. No changes may ever be made to any names once tickets are issued. If space has been reserved in the wrong name, you may be able to make new reservations in the correct name—but only if space is still available.

Misspelled names on reservations and tickets, while unfortunate, are common, do not usually cause any problems, and are usually better left alone once reservations have been made. However, passengers traveling on tickets with a different surname (such as a married or maiden name) or substantially different given or taken name (such as a nickname) from the names on their passport may experience considerable inconvenience or delay en route. It is important to give full, correct passport names when you make your reservations.

Because the price of your tickets may depend greatly on whether space is available in particular booking classes on particular airlines on your travel dates, it is helpful to give an agent the legal names of all those who will be traveling when you first ask for an estimate, particularly if you want to leave soon or have very specific date requirements for certain flights. If an agent has your names and there are only a few seats left, the space can be held for you for the best fare. Otherwise you risk having the last seats reserved by someone else while the agent is waiting to get the names of the travelers.

### Confirmed Dates vs. Open Dates

I strongly recommend that you make confirmed reservations for each flight before you pay for any of your tickets. That way you can be sure that the tickets you are buying will permit you to fly on an acceptable schedule on which space is available. It's more work for an agent to make reservations than just to issue open tickets, but it's almost always in your interest to have confirmed reservations whenever possible.

"Reservation" and "confirmation" are not synonymous. If you are on a waiting list, you have a waitlisted reservation, but it's not a confirmed reservation. "Open" tickets are tickets issued with no reservations at all.

Open tickets have a deceptive allure of freedom. If you have an open ticket, it's tempting to think that you can fly whenever you want. But that's not what an open ticket means. An open ticket allows you to fly only when the specified airline has a flight between the specified places on which space is available. If you insist on buying open-dated, unconfirmed, or waitlisted tickets, you assume all risk that space will not be available. You are not entitled to a refund or to any waiver of refund penalties if you can't use such a ticket because there are no seats available.

Saying that a ticket is open means only that you have no reservations, not that it is a one-year ticket or can be used at any time. If you pay only a low season fare, an open ticket may be usable only during low season, not high season. If you buy a roundtrip ticket with an open return, the return flight coupon is valid only on dates that satisfy the requirements of the fare for minimum and maximum stay. Suppose the fare permits a maximum stay of three months, and you decide

In early 2003 the Transportation Security Administration proposed a requirement for all travelers on flights to, from, or within the USA to provide additional information before they can make any airline reservations: home address, home phone number, and data of birth. This information would be passed on to the government and used to decide who the TSA would search more intrusively or refuse to allow to travel on common carriers (airlines trains, ferries, and busses). It's part of the TSA's highly controversial "Computer Assisted Passenger Pre-Screening" system, version 2. Like its less invasive predecessor, CAPPS-I, in use since 1998, CAPPS-II appears more likely to be useful for government surveillance and monitoring of travelers and compilation of government dossiers of travel records than for terrorism prevention. See the *Practical Nomad* Web site for more on the status of CAPPS-II and other privacy and civil liberties issues for travelers.

you want to use your open return ticket to come back after two and a half months. If no seats are available for the next two weeks, and you can't use your ticket before its validity expires, that's your tough luck. Because your ticket is already partially used, the remaining portion is likely to have no refund value.

The further in advance you make reservations, the more advance notice you will have of the airline's schedule, and the better chance you will have of getting space on a flight closer to the date you want to travel.

When you want to use open tickets, you may find that all flights are full for some time (perhaps because of a local holiday, festival, season, or special event of which you were unaware) and thus that you have to wait for some time for space on an onward flight, particularly if such a flight operates only once or twice a week. Even some daily flights can be fully booked a month or two ahead at busy times of the year.

Some countries require not merely onward tickets but confirmed onward *reservations* as a condition of admission. If you arrive in a place with open tickets and no onward reservations, you may be denied entry to the country unless you can confirm onward reservations on the spot. Having an open ticket may heighten the suspicions of immigration inspectors that you intend to stay longer than is permitted, or to seek paid employment without a work permit.

It's easier to change the dates of confirmed reservations than to make reservations to use open tickets. Once you buy an open ticket, the airline has your money whether you ever fly or not. If flights are full, the airline can keep your money, and never have to provide any services. Unless you pay full fare for a freely refundable ticket, you aren't entitled to your money back if you can't use an open ticket because no seats are available when you want to fly.

Some airlines would rather confirm someone who hasn't yet paid for a ticket, and will pay only if they are confirmed, than confirm someone who already has an open ticket. A few airlines are notorious for telling people with open tickets that no seats will be available for months—even when their planes have lots of empty seats—and making them pay large sums to upgrade their tickets, or buy entirely new tickets at higher fares, unless they want to wait forever. If you have a confirmed reservation and want to change it, the airline knows it will have to provide the transportation you've paid for, one day or another, and has no reason not to allow you to make a change if space is available.

### When to Buy Open Tickets

Except when people insist on them, I issue open tickets without confirmed reservations only when circumstances make it impossible to obtain confirmation in advance, such as for flights further in the future than the range of the airline's reservation system (usually 10–11 months into the future), or when the airline will only give confirmation locally at the point of departure, or on some especially remote routes flown by airlines that don't have offices in the United States or don't participate in computerized reservation systems. These are circumstances to buy open tickets by necessity, not by choice.

If a travel agent is reluctant to reserve specific flights for you, take it as a warning that the airline's schedule is such that if you found out the actual schedule you wouldn't want those tickets (e.g., the only flights involve a three-day layover in a dangerous, expensive hellhole), and/or that space is not likely to be available on the dates you are likely to want to fly, and/or that the agency has cut its profit margin so thin that it can't afford to take the few minutes to make your reservations (which is a pretty good indication that it'll be even less willing to take time to help you if you have problems once it has your money).

Some travelers buy open tickets because they are afraid that if they buy tickets with reservations for specific dates, they might get stuck with fixed-date tickets by an agent who promises them changeable tickets. If you mistrust an agent that much, buy your tickets elsewhere. Pay a little more to someone you trust to provide the promised tickets and to make confirmed reservations.

### Schedules, Times, and Flight Duration

If you make reservations in advance, you'll be forewarned as to the frequency, times, duration, and likely ease or difficulty of changing your flights. Many people overestimate the frequency of international flights and underestimate the amount of time they will spend in transit in the course of a trip around the world.

they will spend in transit in the course of a trip around the world.

If you are going directly from one side of the planet to the other, you may be obliged to spend a night or two en route, even on the fastest and most expensive flights. Flying time alone for some through flights is more than 24 hours. Even the most direct routes between many cities take two to three days of total travel time. If you are accustomed to 30–60 minute connections between domestic flights in the United States, don't be surprised to find that 4–18 hour connections between international flights are common. Outside the First World, with certain exceptions, flying anywhere can be expected to be an all-day pro-

# THE BEST OF BOTH WORLDS

Some people think that only open tickets permit date changes. This is not true. Any ticket that can be issued with an open date can also be issued, at exactly the same price, with confirmed reservations for any date on which space is available. The option will remain to change those reservations, at no charge, at any time, any number of times, to any other flight between those airports on that airline on which space is available. You would also be permitted to standby for last-minute cancellations and take any available seat on any similar flight. There is no limit to how many times you can change your reservations, and no charge for changes no matter how many times you make them. There is no advantage to an open ticket over a confirmed but freely changeable ticket. None. Ever.

I would not buy an open ticket if I had a choice. I would never buy a ticket from anyone who tried to sell me an open ticket, or claimed that open tickets were in any way preferable to confirmed but changeable tickets, or hesitated to make reservations for me on specific flights.

By having both confirmed reservations and freely changeable tickets, you have the best of both worlds. If you want to spend more or less time than you planned in a place, you are free to do so. But if all the other flights are full, you still have a set of reservations to fall back on. It's routine for travelers holding open tickets to have to wait a couple of weeks for space to be available on the flight they want, sometimes much longer.

ject no matter how short the flight: you go to the airport first thing in the morning and hope that by the end of the day you have gotten to your destination. In many countries, any flight that operates at any time on the scheduled day is considered on time!

***Only the More Popular Transcontinental and Transoceanic International Flights Operate as Often as Daily.*** Many flights, and on some significant routes the only flights, operate as infrequently as once a week. For example, as of this writing there is only one flight a week between the world's two most populous countries, India and China (flights to and from Hong Kong excepted). If there is daily service on a route, it is likely to be at the same time each day. "What day(s) of the week does that airline fly between those cities?" is usually a more appropriate question than, "What times are their flights on such-and-such a day?"

Most people, especially independent travelers without advance hotel reservations, find morning arrivals more convenient than evening arrivals. Similarly, most people prefer late-night departures to late-night arrivals. If there is more than one flight on the day you want, most thoughtful agents will book you on a morning flight or an overnight flight that arrives in the morning, unless you tell them in advance that you prefer otherwise.

If a competent agent has booked you on a flight that arrives at 2 A.M., it's probably because there is no alternative for the same price. Many factors other than passenger convenience influence airline schedules, such as optimum use of expensive airplanes and competition between airlines for gates and landing, takeoff, and customs slots at preferred times. The cheapest airlines sometimes get the worst time slots.

Flights between Northern and Southern countries are usually scheduled to optimize connections for passengers from the North who generate most of the revenue, resulting in less than optimal arrival and departure times in Southern cities. Indira Gandhi International Airport in New Delhi, for example, is busiest between 2400 and 0300 (midnight and 3 A.M.), and half-deserted at midday.

***All Times Shown in Airline Timetables and on Itineraries Are in the Official Local Time.*** Some countries enforce the use of an official time at variance with local custom. Timetables in the USSR all used to be on Moscow time, and usage of local time in Asian Russia is still somewhat inconsistent, so be sure to check if schedules are in local or Moscow time. China continues to decree the use of Beijing time for all official purposes, including tickets and printed timetables, throughout its possessions, which would otherwise span four time zones.

In East Turkestan, where the sun may rise at 0300 (3 A.M.) and set at 1500 (3 P.M.) Beijing time, local people use several inconsistent varieties of unofficial "Xinjiang time." There are similar situations in Tibet. "What time is it?" in these areas is a highly politicized question, and the answer may depend on your informant's ethnicity (Han Chinese, Uighur, Tibetan, or whatever) and political allegiance as well as the proximity of the secret police. It can be hard to get a straight answer; some Han Chinese, especially people in state enterprises (such as tourist offices and state-owned hotels) are reluctant to admit the existence of local time. But you should always verify which type of time (Beijing time or some other time) is meant.

***Standard Itineraries Don't Show Flight Duration.*** They are hard to figure out without being certain of the time differences between departure and arrival cities. Ask your travel agent to give you a separate printout of actual flight durations and times and the locations of intermediate stops on multistop flights (some CRSs permit this), or have the agent go over them with you.

***Itineraries Will Show Whether or Not Flights Are Nonstop, but Don't Necessarily Show Whether You Have to Change Planes.*** Under current law in the United States and most other countries, airlines are permitted to give a single flight number to two or more connecting flights, and to advertise the set of flights thus designated as a direct or through flight, despite the change(s) of planes. One of the two connecting flights may even be operated by a different airline.

The airlines' own telephone reservation agents are the worst offenders in not telling you that you will have to change planes. "Oh, yes, we fly from A to B" from an airline agent may well mean that they fly from A to their hub at C, and from C to B, with a change of planes and a 24-hour layover, at your own expense, in C. Even if they say, "We have a flight from A to B," that flight may well involve what is euphemistically referred to as a change of equipment at C. Most people would describe this as a set of connecting flights by way of C, and certainly not as a direct or through flight. If you aren't sure, ask specifically whether a through or direct flight is on the same plane.

Why do the airlines do this? Airlines that don't really have direct flights between two places, but who want make the connecting flights by way of their hubs or gateways appear more attractive, give connecting flights through flight numbers to compete with airlines that really do have direct (same-plane) service. It's cheaper to add labels than to add flights. By having flights from San Francisco, Los Angeles, and Chicago to New York, and from New York to London, and by giving the New York-London flight four flight numbers (one number from New York to London, and one through flight number including each of the connecting flights from San Francisco, Los Angeles, and Chicago), an airline can pretend to offer direct service from each of the four cities while actually paying for only one trans-Atlantic flight.

This fits the textbook definition of fraud. Airlines label connecting flights as direct or through flights for the sole purpose of misleading people and hiding the implications of the change of planes. The worst case is a flight with a change of equipment at the point of arrival to a country, such as a flight from Europe to the West Coast of the United States with a change of equipment at an airport in the East or Midwest. You have to get off the plane, claim your luggage, go through customs and immigration, check your luggage back in, and then get on another plane to complete the flight. Such flights should not be called direct.

Travel agents didn't come up with this scheme and can't do much about it. Agents have no control over how airlines number their flights. Airlines won't always permit travel agents to book connecting flights as two separate flight numbers. In the United States, the consumer fraud divisions of several states have sought to stop the labeling of connecting flights as direct, but regulation of the airline industry has been preempted by the federal government, which has as yet taken no action on this.

I encourage travelers to complain to the airlines, and to the federal government, whenever you find yourself on "direct" flights that aren't. The same goes for other airline scams like advertisements for "half roundtrip" or "one-way based on roundtrip" (huh?) prices, or advertised prices at which no seats are really available. These practices wouldn't be allowed in any other industry, and much of the blame rests with government regulators who have chosen to look the other way as systematic fraud has become standard operating procedure in airline marketing.

***Tickets and Itineraries Won't Necessarily Show the Name of the Airline That Actually Operates the Flight.*** A large and increasing number of "codeshare" flights are labeled with one or more flight numbers of airlines other than the one that operates the flight. Airlines claim code sharing and alliances enable them to offer better services like through ticketing, baggage transfers, and frequent flyer mileage credits between alliance partners. But that's a lie. None of those services requires alliances or code sharing. The international standards that the airlines themselves established decades ago through IATA permit all IATA member airlines, not just alliance partners, to publish through fares and establish interline ticketing and baggage transfer agreements. Any IATA-appointed travel agency can sell tickets on any IATA airline, including tickets at a single through fare for a multi-airline journey. And even alliance members often give frequent flyer mileage credit for travel on non-alliance airlines, without code sharing.

Code sharing is unnecessary for, indeed irrelevant to, any legitimate purpose or actual service. Code sharing doesn't enable an airline to fly to any more places. It just enables the airline to mislead travelers into thinking that they fly to places they don't. As with direct flights that require a change of planes, I call that fraud.

You check in for most codeshare flights at the counter or gate of the operating airline, not the airline whose name appears on your tickets. Codeshare flight numbers aren't always posted at airports, or are only posted in the proper terminal (which you can't find without knowing which airline operates the flight). Ask what airline to check in with, at which terminal, when you call to reconfirm each flight, especially if you think it might be a codeshare or the flight number is four digits long.

### Waiting Lists

If it isn't possible to confirm reservations for the price you want on the flights you want, an agent may put you on a waiting list for one or more flights or give you an itinerary showing that certain flights are on request or not yet confirmed.

Requested or waitlisted flights may be confirmed in five minutes, or the day of the flight, or any time in between, or never. If only a few reservations on each flight are allocated to the cheapest tickets, you may be waitlisted for a flight on which only a few people are confirmed, and which is likely to end up flying half empty. That you are on a waiting list does not mean that a flight is full or sold out.

Airlines won't tell you, and won't usually tell travel agents, exactly how many people are on the waiting list, or how far overbooked a flight is. The more closely agents work with particular airlines, and the more tickets they sell on a particular route, the better their ability to get you confirmed and the better their sense of your chances of confirmation.

Confirmation of requested or waitlisted flights is never a sure thing. If you are on a waiting list for more than two weeks, make confirmed reservations—as a backup to the waitlisted reservations—on another flight, another date, another airline, or with another agent, even if they are more expensive. If you can't be confirmed, it doesn't matter how low the price would be if you were confirmed. The only prices that ultimately matter are those for which reservations can be confirmed.

A common problem is to be given a low price estimate, get on a waiting list, wait for weeks or months without confirmation in hope of a really cheap ticket if you are confirmed, and end up not getting confirmed for that ticket and having to buy a much more expensive ticket at the last minute. Some bad agents deliberately quote prices on flights they know they have little or no chance of confirming, in order to get you hooked into a form of bait-and-switch in which they will end up selling you a much costlier ticket later on.

If a travel agent has placed you on a waiting list, you may be able to improve your chances of getting confirmed by calling the airline yourself to ask them to confirm you from the waiting list. But you should only do so after the travel agent has put you on the list, and only if they are having trouble getting you confirmed. Do not be surprised, and do not argue, if the airline mentions that the reservation was made by an agency other than the one you dealt with. It may have been necessary or required for your agent to make the booking through a wholesaler either as a condition of the fare or to use "block" space held by another agent or wholesaler on an otherwise sold-out flight.

If you are confirmed on less-preferred but acceptable flights or dates, you can get on the waiting list for your preferred alternatives at the same time. As long as your tickets permit date or flight changes, you can stay on the waiting list up until the time of the flight, even after you have your tickets. Just keep checking with the airline at intervals. If and when the waitlist clears, you have to choose between the original and the newly confirmed flights.

### Don't Make Your Own Reservations

Contrary to some ill-advised recommendations, you should not make reservations directly with the airline, over the phone or over the Internet, and then try to shop around for the best price at which to have them ticketed. Doing this reduces your chances of getting the best price, or of getting confirmed on the flights you want, and may result in all your reservations being entirely canceled without prior warning.

There are many booking classes, and there is no way you can tell in which class to make reservations for the cheapest fare. The cheapest published fare may be booked in one class, the cheapest discounted fare in another. Different discounters may have different contracts requiring bookings in different classes.

Even some airlines that have only one coach booking class require reservations for special fares to be made only by agents directly with the airline, through designated agents, or in special booking classes that are not listed in the OAG, most CRSs, or publicly accessible Web sites, and whose existence the airlines won't disclose to retail callers.

Travel agents can more easily prioritize you on the waiting list if they make the reservations for you. Most airlines have at least two, usually three, levels of waiting lists. Names on the regular waiting list—the only one on which you can place yourself directly—are considered for confirmation only after all names on the priority list—on which travel agents can place you—and the highest priority list, on which you can be placed only by special request by the airline itself.

Waitlist clearance requests are more likely to be acted on if they come from the travel agent rather than the passenger. It doesn't hurt to call the airline yourself as well, once an agent has gotten you on the waiting list, but it's usually more effective to let the agent try first.

If travel agents make reservations for you, they may be able to use block space held by them, by the airline, or by a consolidator for all or part of your itinerary. This may be difficult or impossible if you have already made reservations for all or part of your itinerary, because many airlines prohibit or restrict the combining of flights from different reservations.

Finally, some airlines refuse even to consider for confirmation passengers holding more than one reservation; some airlines will automatically cancel all reservations, whether or not confirmed, of anyone found to be holding multiple bookings. You and your travel agent(s) may be given no warning before both sets of your duplicate reservations are canceled.

It is thus imperative that, if you have for some reason already made reservations with the airline or with another travel agent, you advise an agent of this immediately. If you don't, the agent may make another booking for you, and both your reservations may be canceled. If space is still available, the agent will probably take down the names and flight details, make new reservations for you, and have you call the airline to cancel the reservations you made directly.

Computerized reservation systems limit the ability of agents to retrieve reservations made directly with the airlines. For this reason, if you did not make the reservations through your chosen agent, it is often more difficult to assist you with special meals, seat assignments, boarding passes, or schedule changes. In short, it only creates work and inconveniences both you and the agent not to make your reservations through the agent from whom you will buy your tickets.

### If You Can't Be Confirmed

Price estimates for tickets made before you have reservations are best-case estimates of what the price will be if you can be confirmed in the appropriate booking classes on flights on the specified airline(s) and route. An estimate is no guarantee that space will be available for the price. Agents should give realistic estimates of probable availability, but they are sometimes overly optimistic, or just guess wrong.

If you can't be confirmed for the estimated price, you will have to choose either to pay more than estimated for tickets on the same route, or revise your route or choices of airlines. An agent will probably give you a new proposed itinerary, based on whatever is closest to the original estimate in schedule, route, and price. You are under no obligation to accept it, and there are probably other possibilities. If these choices involve other stopover possibilities, you may want or need to do further destination research before you decide. In the worst case, you may have to go back and forth several times with the agent, at successively higher prices, before you find an acceptable price and routing for which you can actually be confirmed.

It's annoying to have to revise your plans just when you thought you had made your decisions and were ready to make your reservations. Just don't blame it on the agent— the most tempting target just because they, not the airline, are the one you are dealing with directly—unless you suspect them of deliberately misleading you about the likely prospects for confirmation. If you suspect this, go elsewhere for your tickets. This happens often with many bad agencies; indeed, it's their standard modus operandi and the classic form of travel agency bait-and-switch. (The ongoing dilemma of legitimate agencies is whether to advertise or estimate prices they know aren't likely to be available, or whether to state prices that will appear excessive compared to bait-and-switch ads.) But don't jump to conclusions. Travel agents don't control seat allocations and only get what the airlines give them to sell. Predicting when which booking classes will be available on which airlines can be an exercise in crystal-ball gazing. You have to rely on your own judgment of the agent's and agency's integrity.

## Paying for Tickets

When your reservations are confirmed the agent will give you an itinerary showing the flights, dates, times, airlines, price, and deadline for payment. Reservations for around-the-world or other multistop itineraries can be held for anywhere up to a week before payment is required. Airlines keep shortening these time limits, but you should have at least a few days week to review and consider the itinerary before you have to pay. In no case, even if you are in a rush, should you authorize payment before you have seen a complete written itinerary.

If full payment is not received by the deadline, the agent or the airline may cancel your reservations, although they can be rebooked if the space and the fare are still available.

You can't expect an agency to release tickets until a personal or company check has cleared, which can take 5–10 business days for out-of-state checks within the United States. For tickets needed on short notice you may have to pay by credit or charge card, cashier's check (bank check), traveler's check, money order, or cash. If you don't pay by personal or company check, you won't have your canceled check as a receipt, so be sure to get a receipt and itinerary when you pay.

If you pay for discounted tickets by credit or charge card, you'll probably have to pay 2–5 percent more than if you pay by cash or check. This may seem strange, because the airlines charge the same amount no matter how you pay, but it is a consequence of the nature of discount tickets.

When you buy tickets at a published fare, the actual charge to your card is made by the airline, which receives the full amount and eventually pays part of it to the agency as its commission. Because the airlines have extremely large volumes of business, they are able to negotiate very low fees, as a percentage of their charges, from the credit and charge card companies and banks. The fees they pay are close enough to their costs of processing check payments, and collecting on bad checks, that they choose to absorb any slight difference in total costs.

As a corollary to the IATA and government prohibitions on selling tickets for less than published fares, an airline cannot charge your card less than the face value of the ticket. In order for you to be charged less than the official fare, the charge must be made by the agency through its own merchant account, not by the airline. Banks regard travel agencies as prone to disputes and chargebacks by customers that are costly for them to investigate, and that may lead to losses that the banks have to absorb. In some countries it's almost impossible for a travel agency to get a credit-card merchant account. As smaller businesses, travel agencies have to pay much higher percentage fees for processing of charges than do the airlines, even when they can get their own merchant accounts. If a travel agency charges US$100 to your card, they only get US$95–98; the bank with which they have their merchant account keeps the other 2–5 percent as what it calls its "discount." The agency doesn't get the money instantly, either; it takes 2–5 business days.

Profit margins on discounted tickets aren't enough to permit agencies to absorb the bank's credit and charge card discounts. In order to offer the option of credit-card payment, they have to charge what amounts to a surcharge.

Here's where the real problem comes in: credit-card companies don't want consumers to realize that paying by credit card costs more money, even if it does. Court challenges have compelled them, most reluctantly, to permit merchants to give discounts for cash or check payment, but have thus far upheld their right to prohibit surcharges for payment by credit card. What's the difference? Semantic. Travel agencies, like gas stations and other narrow-margin merchants, are required to use confusing and evasive-sounding language about cash discounts, rather than credit-card surcharges. It isn't their idea, and they don't like it. If you don't like it either, complain to the credit-card companies and urge them to allow credit-card surcharges to be honestly and plainly labeled as such.

For your own protection, never authorize credit-card charges by phone, especially for as large and complex a purchase as a set of tickets around the

# E-TICKETS AND TICKETLESS TRAVEL

While airlines are trying to promote "e-tickets" and ticketless travel as a "convenience" to passengers, e-tickets were actually developed solely to serve the interests of the airlines, not those of passengers.

Most users of e-tickets don't realize their drawbacks, and wouldn't choose them if they did. Here are some of the advantages of paper tickets, especially for international travel and travel anywhere outside the First World:

• Flights still operate when reservation computers are down, but only holders of paper tickets are transported, because e-tickets can't be verified offline. E-ticket holders get left behind.

The idea of accepting an e-ticket for travel outside the First World, and relying on the computer links to be working and to be able to retrieve the e-ticket when one shows up to check in, is laughable to anyone familiar with the reliability (not) of real-time international communications to and from much of the world. Some flights are scheduled to operate only once a week, and it could be worth quite a lot not to get left behind and stuck somewhere for an extra week at your own expense.

• For international travel, tickets are required by many countries (including, for most foreign visitors, the United States) as proof of onward or return transporta-

tion for immigration purposes. A traveler arriving in a country on one airline, and leaving on an e-ticket on another, is currently unable to provide any proof of onward transportation at check-in, and can be refused passage if the onward e-ticket can't be verified—if, for example, an inter-network link is down when they check in.

Airlines are developing interline links, and connections to immigration authorities, for just this purpose. The prototype "Electronic Travel Authorization" (ETA) system, including links to airline ticketing databases, was implemented in 1997 in Australia. Although the Australian government and the cooperating airlines assure travelers that they do not need paper proof of their tickets or ETAs, I've had several clients who found the ETA links down at their point of departure when they checked in for flights to Australia. They would have been refused passage had I not insisted, against government and airline advice, on providing them with paper copies of their ETAs.

• E-tickets are especially disadvantageous in the event of a strike or operational problem affecting an airline. Normally, major airlines honor each others' tickets (even, in the interest of converting passengers' loyalties, inexpensive "nonendorsable" tickets that they are not required to honor) during strikes and the like. But they can't access, verify, or honor other airlines' e-tickets. As e-ticket usage has increased, each impending airline strike has prompted an increasingly overwhelming run on airlines and travel agents of passengers trying to get their e-tickets printed in order to be able to get them accepted by other airlines during a strike.

• Changes to e-tickets can be made only through the airline. Holders of "open-dated" or freely changeable tickets can make new reservations through any travel agency or even another airline, an especially useful option when traveling internationally in areas where a particular airline may be hard to reach or may have no local office at all. Even if tickets have penalties for changes, travelers with paper tickets can make new reservations through a different travel agency or even through another airline, and pay the change fee when the tickets are reissued at check-in.

• Airlines can't always associate paper tickets with specific reservations. If you buy a paper roundtrip ticket, and travel only one way, the airline generally has no way to know that you didn't use your ticket for the second half of the roundtrip. If you use only part of an e-ticket, the airline does know. They are legally entitled to bill you, after the fact, for the difference between the (lower) roundtrip fare you paid, and the (higher) one-way fare for your actual trip. You are legally and contractually obligated to pay up, or face charges for attempted fraud or theft of services. (I know it sounds unfair, but that's the law, and the contract you agree to when you buy a ticket.)

The best parallel with e-tickets may be ATMs, which were originally promoted (against substantial consumer resistance) as a "convenience" to bank customers. Once they were established, it became clear that the purpose of ATMs was to cut banks' labor costs, not to serve customers. Now profitable bank customers get (and many have proven to prefer) first-class service from human tellers. Less wealthy customers get second-class robotic service from ATMs, or have to pay transaction fees each time they deal with a human teller.

Once they discover the hidden drawbacks of e-tickets, many travelers will be willing to pay extra for more flexible and reliable paper tickets. Something that used to be free—a paper ticket—will become an added-cost option offered only to high-fare travelers, very frequent flyers, or those willing to pay explicit paper-ticket surcharges.

Ask for paper tickets whenever they don't cost extra, and consider paying the extra fee for paper tickets on flights outside the First World. If you can't get a paper ticket, or chose not to pay extra for it, get a printout from the airline, on ticket/boarding pass stock, of the "passenger receipt" coupon of your e-ticket.

world. If you want to pay by credit card, mail or fax the agency a written authorization attached to a copy of your itinerary, so you have it in writing both how much you agreed to pay and what tickets you are supposed to receive. If you are authorizing a charge over the Internet, print the complete itinerary, terms and conditions, and charge authorization before you push the "buy" button.

The agent may be able to issue some of your tickets as soon as your payment has cleared. Others may have to be issued by the airlines or by wholesalers around the world. Paper tickets are being phased out, and some of your tickets may have to be issued as electronic tickets. You should get a printed confirmation with a reference number for each e-ticket; if possible, get a printout from the airline, on ticket stock, of the "passenger receipt" coupon. (If you have a choice, avoid e-tickets. See the sidebar, "E-Tickets and Ticketless Travel.") Don't expect to get tickets on the spot, even if you pay cash, unless you've been specifically told, in advance, that this will be possible. Typically it takes up to about three weeks to get all the components of a set of around-the-world tickets. If you pay a month in advance, this gives you a safety margin of about a week for unexpected delays in ticket issuance or shipping.

It shouldn't take more than month to get your tickets from a reliable, honest agent, barring unusual complications. The most justifiable reason for delay, especially with complex tickets or one where any portion comes from overseas, is that one of the prices has changed and a different source or fare construction has to be found. Customers find this hard to understand, but it isn't always possible to call or fax an overseas or even a domestic supplier to verify every price each time an estimate is given to a potential customer. Even if it is verified at the time of the estimate, or at the time of the customer's payment to the agency, it could change by the time the agent's payment reaches the supplier, by air courier, 2–3 business days later. Even if the supplier still rebates the same commission percentage, the airline could change the published fare from which the rebate is given.

Like it or not, fares and prices change constantly, and no estimate is or can be guaranteed until the tickets are actually issued. Good agencies will absorb small price fluctuations in the interest of keeping customers' business and good will, but sometimes a price change greatly exceeds what can be covered from the agency's markup. You'll be offered a choice of paying more to cover the price increase, or getting your money back.

Once the agent has your tickets, you should either pick them up in person or have them sent to you by messenger, Express Mail, FedEx, or the like. Don't trust airline tickets to regular mail.

Proofread your tickets, one flight coupon at a time. Mistakes are made by agents, airlines, in transmission of messages between computers, and in misunderstandings of what you, the customer wanted. Minor discrepancies in flight times on tickets are nothing to worry about—times on tickets are only advisory, and over the course of a long trip are prone to change some, anyway—but differences in names, flight numbers, dates, airlines, or cities should be brought to the agent's attention immediately. Time is of the essence if some errors are to be corrected without further expense. If you don't understand anything on your tickets, ask the agent to explain it.

You should also double-check your tickets after you check in for each flight, before you leave the counter. Make sure the correct flight coupon, and only the correct flight coupon, has been taken. It's surprisingly common for a harried ticket agent to tear out the wrong coupon, or for two coupons to stick together and get pulled for one flight. Once you leave the counter, such a mistake can be almost impossible to correct without buying new tickets.

Amazingly, airlines claim the right to increase fares even after tickets are issued, but I've only heard of two that ever do, and then only if tickets are issued "open," i.e., without confirmed reservations for specific dates. I assume that they are trying to prevent regular business travelers from beating fare increases by stocking up on undated tickets for future travel just before scheduled fare increases. Once you have confirmed reservations and tickets in hand, but not before, you can consider your price to be for all intents and purposes fixed.

In consideration of other travelers, you should tell any agent or airline with whom you have made reservations if you decide not to use them, so that they can release the space to someone else who wants it. Don't assume that they will be canceled automatically; they probably will be eventually, but it's only courteous to cancel the reservations as soon as you decide.

## Reconfirming Reservations

As soon as you have your tickets you should call the airlines to reconfirm your reservations, that is, to tell the airlines that you will definitely be using your reservations. They might tell you that you have to reconfirm again closer to the flight date, but it's never too soon. Reconfirm early and often until each flight.

You must reconfirm your reservations for each flight at least 72 hours before that flight departs. If the airline has not heard from you by then, they are entitled to (and you should assume that they will) cancel all your reservations for all the flights in your itinerary and give your seats to someone else. Your tickets will usually remain valid, but you will have to start over from scratch in making new reservations.

The most common misunderstanding of reconfirmation is to think that you are supposed to reconfirm within 72 hours of the scheduled departure time, and thus deliberately to wait to try to reconfirm until after your reservations have already been canceled for failure to reconfirm. You should call more than 72 hours ahead, not less than 72 hours.

If your tickets are issued less than 72 hours before your departure, you should call the airlines as soon as you get your tickets. In such cases the agent should reconfirm your reservations as soon as tickets are issued or received, but all airlines prefer (and some require) that you reconfirm directly, not merely through your travel agent.

If you will be connecting directly from one airline to another, particularly if the first airline has an office in the United States and the second does not, the first airline may be able to reconfirm your reservations on the second airline as well. Whenever possible, though, it is best to call each airline separately.

Agents in some countries will offer to reconfirm your reservations for you, for a fee. This is a waste of money. Airlines never charge for reconfirming reservations. If airline employees ask you for money to make or reconfirm reservations, they are asking for a bribe. A few bad airlines are notorious for grossly overbooking their flights and then only reconfirming passengers who pay hefty bribes.

Most airlines operating in the United States and Canada have toll-free 800, 866, 877, or 888 numbers for reconfirmation. These numbers are all listed with directory assistance at 800-555-1212; you can also get airline numbers from your travel agent. Some smaller airlines, airlines that have offices in North America but no direct flights, and airlines represented only by general sales agents do not have toll-free numbers. If the airline doesn't have a listing with toll-free directory assistance, get the airline's reconfirmation number from your travel agent when you get your tickets. Most airline offices in the United States without toll-free numbers are in either New York, Los Angeles, or Miami, but there are so many area codes in those cities that you might have to try directory assistance for a dozen area codes to get the number you need.

It's a good idea to reconfirm all of your flights before your first departure, if the airlines have offices or representatives where you are, just to be sure that you really have reservations. Doing so does not, however, obviate the necessity to reconfirm your next onward reservations at each point where you stop over, at least 72 hours before continuing your journey. Suppose you fly from A to B, spend a week in B, and then fly on to C. At some time after arriving in B, and at least 72 hours before your flight from B to C, you must contact the airline on which you plan to fly from B to C to reconfirm your intention of using your reservations on that flight.

It is usually easiest to reconfirm your departure from a city if you do so at the airport when you first arrive, thus avoiding any problems using the local telephone system or communicating in the local language. It's sometimes a bit of a nuisance—you may have to go around from the arrival area to the departure area to find a ticket counter where you can reconfirm your onward flight, just when you are eager to get out and about in the new place—but I find it's usually worth the effort to reconfirm on arrival.

You can reconfirm your reservations either in person at the airline's counter at the airport or a city ticket office, or by phoning the airline's local phone number. Local telephone numbers for reconfirmation of reservations in each city an airline serves are usually listed on ticket jackets and are always available at airline ticket counters and city offices. Have your tickets handy when you go or call to reconfirm your reservations, because the airline may need to verify your ticket numbers, booking class, or other information on your tickets.

It can be difficult or impossible to reconfirm your onward reservations while in remote areas. If you will be trekking in Nepal, for example, and will return to Kathmandu just in time for your onward flight, you will need to reconfirm your reservations before you leave on your trek.

If you are staying more than a few days, it's a good idea to check again to see if the time or date of your flight has been changed, and to verify when you must check in. Airlines try to notify passengers of schedule changes—that's why they always ask for a local phone number when you reconfirm. But budget travelers often don't know where they are staying and don't have a reliable fixed phone number.

Some airlines will not reconfirm you unless you give them a local phone number. If you have to, make one up, or give them the number of some big hotel (whether or not you are staying there) or the American Express office. The risk of not being notified of a last-minute schedule change is preferable to the near-certainty of having your reservations canceled if you don't reconfirm. Remember that if the airline doesn't have a way to notify you of last-minute changes, it's your responsibility to keep checking with them regularly, up until the day and time of the flight, for possible changes.

It's important to reconfirm your reservations, even if the airline says it isn't required. Eliminating the reconfirmation requirement is a labor-saving measure for the airline, not a service to passengers who need to know, as far in advance as possible, if their reservation has been lost or their flight has been rescheduled. And no matter what the airline tells you, they still might cancel your reservations if you don't reconfirm them. If the flight is overbooked, those who haven't reconfirmed will usually be the first to have their reservations cancelled.

Airlines do not guarantee their schedules. If you are booked on a dozen flights over a period of six months, you can expect that the schedules for two or three of them will change in that six months. Schedules for international flights are rarely changed more than a few hours at a time, but you cannot rule out the possibility that the weekly Tuesday morning flight on which you were booked could have become the weekly Friday night flight by the time you fly.

Dates, times, and flight numbers may all change. Each time you reconfirm, verify the flight number, date, and departure time and those of any flights to which you will be connecting without an intermediate stopover of more than 72 hours. Don't just ask, "Am I still confirmed," or you may be told, "Yes," without being told on what flight or when you are confirmed. Especially with a flight that might be a codeshare, or when departing from an airport with more than one terminal, verify with which airline and at which terminal you should check in, and how long before the flight you need to check in. Most airlines require you to check in two hours before international flights, but more time is required for special security checks on certain routes.

Reconfirming your reservations does not prevent you from later changing them if you decide to move on sooner or later than you had planned. If you change your reservations, however, you must be sure to reconfirm your new reservations. If you have reservations and decide not to use them (usually because you have decided to take an earlier or later flight), especially if you change your mind when you have already reconfirmed, please be considerate enough of others to call and cancel your reservations. Everyone on the waiting lists for that flight will thank you. No-shows (people who make reservations but don't show up for flights) force airlines either to overbook or to fly with empty seats. Overbooking inconveniences travelers when the airlines, forced to guess, guess wrong about how many people won't show up. Empty seats force airlines to raise prices to everyone to cover their costs. Don't be a no-show. You can cancel your existing reservations even if you don't yet know when you will want to travel, and make new reservations later (subject to the availability of space).

If you already have your tickets ands change from one flight to another, you can reconfirm your new reservations at the same time as you make them. Reservations for flights leaving within 72 hours should be reconfirmed at the same time as they are made.

Finally, when you reconfirm your reservations it is a good idea to ask each airline for its "record locator" for your reservation. This is a string of 4–6 letters and/or numbers that identifies your reservation with that airline; you will have a different record locator for your reservations with each airline. Having your record locator will help the airline find your reservation more quickly if you need to make changes.

### Special Service Requests

For security reasons (so the airlines and airports say) boarding passes for many international flights, even on the best airlines, can only be issued when you check in at the airport. You can usually request specific seating when you make or reconfirm your reservations, but on no airline are seat assignments guaranteed, even if you are issued boarding passes in advance. Airlines always reserve the right to substitute equipment—a larger or smaller plane, a different model, or one with the seats arranged differently—at any time, regardless of what is shown in timetables or on itineraries.

Even airlines that reserve most seats in advance generally assign certain seats only at check-in. Many travelers prefer the "bulkhead seats" in the front row of each section of the cabin, which have extra leg room. But these are often assigned only at the gate, and priority for them is given to passengers with special needs for extra space (e.g., with a broken leg in a cast or an infant in a bassinet).

Some people prefer aisle seats, so they can get up to walk around, fidget, stretch, or use the toilet without having to disturb their seatmates. Others prefer window seats so they can spread out, settle in, and work or sleep uninterrupted. Some find being near the window enhances their fear of flying, and prefer to be in the middle section of a twin-aisle widebody. Others, like me, think they aren't getting their money's worth if they are missing out on the unique perspective of the view from the air. ("I believe that anyone who flies in an airplane and doesn't spend most of his time looking out the window wastes his money," writes Marc Reisner in the introduction to *Cadillac Desert*.) It's a good thing our desires differ: if we all preferred windows, or all preferred the aisle, fewer of us could be satisfied with our seat assignments.

Frankly, I've never understood the fuss some people make about airplane seating preferences. Unless you are business traveler on a short trip to a distant place, your time in planes is a small fraction of your time on the road. No car or bus seats, and in most places only first-class train seats, are as comfortable as third-class seating on most airlines. I've spent 18 hours in the worst seat on a Boeing 747 (the one next to the emergency door where the normal knee and leg space is occupied by the rigid housing for the inflatable escape slide/life raft that protrudes into the cabin from the inside of the door). I'd have chosen another seat if I could (I was traveling on a discounted travel-agent ticket that didn't allow me to pre-reserve a seat) but even the worst seat on the plane isn't that bad.

If you want special meals, you should request them when you reconfirm your reservations, as many airlines will not honor special meal requests made less than 48 or 24 hours before departure. Special meal options vary by airline. Some airlines, for example, have as many as four choices of vegetarian meals (Chinese, Hindu, Western, and ovolacto) while others have none.

If you will require special seating, assistance, or services for any reason, you should let the airline know your needs as early as possible, the more so the more unusual or difficult to accommodate your needs are. It's best to make any requests yourself, directly to the airlines, as not all interfaces between airlines' and agents' computer systems can be relied on to correctly transmit special service requests, or responses to them. Airlines automatically tell people whose requests aren't on record, "Your travel agent didn't request this properly." Usually, in my experience, the travel agent did request it, but the message wasn't received or acted on properly. If special services are important to you, it's worth calling the airline directly to make them, and to make sure they are understood.

### Frequent-Flyer Mileage Credit

If you want to receive credit in a frequent-flyer program for certain flights, you should give the airline your frequent-flyer number when you reconfirm your reservations and when you check in for each flight, and save your boarding passes and the "passenger receipt" coupons of your tickets until you receive credit for the flights on your frequent-flyer mileage statement.

If your mileage is not credited on your next statement, you can still get credit by sending your boarding passes and receipts directly to the frequent-flyer program for manual processing. This is especially important in order to receive credit in one airline's frequent-flyer program for flights on another airline, because such mileage is less likely to be credited automatically.

## Canceling and Changing Reservations En Route

Once you're on the road, it's generally easiest to make changes to your reservations directly with the local offices of the airlines. You can phone them (provided the phones work, and you've figured out how to use them), go to their ticket offices in person, or go to their ticket counters at airports they serve. Few airlines allow changes (especially to consolidator tickets) through their Web sites, and almost none have publicly available customer-service e-mail addresses. Airlines often have offices or general sales agents in cities and countries they don't actually fly to.

Alternatively, you can look for a general sales agent (GSA). A GSA is a confusing sort of entity, subject to IATA rules different than those for airlines themselves or regular travel agents. A GSA is not owned by the airline, but acts and looks to passengers more like an airline office than a travel agent. In computerized places, GSAs usually have terminals linked to the airlines' internal reservation systems, and can reconfirm flights, make changes to reservations, and do most other things you'd expect an airline office to do, including those that regular travel agents usually can't.

Most GSAs, like airlines, sell tickets to the public only at published fares. Others act like wholesale consolidators, selling discounted tickets to retail travel agents but not to the public. And a few sell discounted tickets directly to the public. To confuse matters, some regular agents falsely style themselves general sales agents just to inflate their images. But regardless of whether they sell tickets, or from whom you bought your ticket, an agency listed in the airline's timetable or on ticket jackets as a GSA should be able to make and change reservations and reconfirm flights on that airline.

Have your tickets with you when you go or call to cancel or make changes, because the airline may need your ticket number or other information from your tickets. If you already have reservations, give the airline your reservation record locator. If you don't have the record locator, give them your name and the flight number and date on which you have reservations.

Don't make new reservations for different flights without canceling the original ones. If you do, both sets of reservations may be canceled automatically as duplicates, even if they are for flights on different dates or at different times.

If you make changes in person, the airline will usually put a sticker on your ticket showing each new flight on which you are booked. If you are making changes in person, whether at an airline office or travel agency, always ask if revalidation stickers are available. These stickers aren't essential, but it can sometimes be helpful later to have proof you have confirmed reservations on the new flight. Another option is to ask for a printout showing that your new reservations are confirmed (status code "HK" or "KK" for "confirmed", or "RR" for "reconfirmed").

Revalidation stickers are rarely used anymore on USA domestic flights, except when they are part of through international tickets. USA airlines are phasing out the use of revalidation stickers on their international routes as well. With some of them, your ticket will continue to show the old flight, but will be valid for the new flight as long as your reservations are properly confirmed and reconfirmed. With the worst USA airlines, however, revalidation stickers cannot be used and all changes—even the simplest flight or date changes—require that tickets be reissued for a fee.

If the airline is unable to confirm space for you on a flight you want, you have three choices. You can ask to be put on a waiting list and check back at intervals to see if you are confirmed; it's best also to confirm space on an alternate flight in case the waitlist doesn't clear. Or you can go to the airport and stand by for space freed by last-minute cancellations. Or lastly, contact your travel agent for assistance in confirming the flight you want.

If you have an open ticket, and the airline is uncooperative in making reservations for you, this last alternative may be your only viable option. Airline employees have been known to demand bribes to confirm space for passengers with open tickets, in which case the agent from whom you bought your tickets may be able to help.

Changes made to your reservations after your departure, whether by you or the airline, or bookings made for "open" tickets, will not necessarily show up in the agent's computer. So you'll need to tell the agent your names and the exact flight(s) on which you want to be booked.

Depending on where you are, it may be difficult for the agent to reply. If you don't get an answer, that doesn't mean that the agent hasn't made or confirmed reservations for you. Check with the airline a few days later to see if you have reservations on the flight(s) you want. If your original reservation is still not confirmed, have the airline check to see if it has new reservations for the same flight(s) on a separate record with a different record locator number.

If you decide that you won't take a flight on which you are booked, it is extremely important to cancel your reservations for that flight, whether or not you are ready to make new reservations on another date or at another time.

You don't need to cancel the rest of your reservations, just the flight(s) that you know you won't be on. But if you don't cancel your reservations, and fail to show up for the flight, the airline is entitled to cancel your reservations for all the rest of your flights, and to tell any other airlines on which you are booked to do likewise.

In order to encourage people to tell the airline if they don't plan to use their reservations, many airlines penalize no-shows. If you don't show up for a flight, and don't cancel your reservations, you often forfeit any possibility of a subsequent refund.

If you had a ticket that permitted free date changes, it remains valid for a flight at a later time or date. But having once no-showed, you can expect to get the lowest priority and the least sympathy from the airline in trying to get a seat on a later flight. If you decide not to use the ticket at all, it may no longer have any refund value. If you cancel your reservations prior to your scheduled flight, however, you retain the option to use your ticket later or to submit it for whatever refund value it had in the first place.

When you have a confirmed but freely changeable ticket and cancel your reservations, your ticket becomes, in effect, "open." You can make new reservations whenever you wish, within the validity time of the ticket—indicated either by a "not valid after" entry on the flight coupon or, in its absence, one year after the date of issue of the ticket.

If you cancel your reservations for a particular flight and are considering not using that ticket at all and submitting it for refund, it's advisable to do so in person at an airline office or ticket counter. Get written confirmation of the cancellation in the form of either a revalidation sticker on the flight coupon showing that the ticket is now "open," or with a new flight date if you have new reservations on another flight; a validated notation on the ticket; or a validated printout of the airline PNR (passenger name record) showing the flight as canceled. Save the cancellation confirmation, and submit it with your ticket if you do end up submitting the ticket for refund.

If you won't be using your reservations for a specific flight, but are sure you will use your ticket eventually, and aren't concerned with its refund value, or if it is already totally nonrefundable (as is more often than not the case if it is already partially used), there is no need to bother with this, and you can cancel or change your reservations, or make new ones, over the phone or through a travel agent.

## Buying Tickets En Route

Most people who travel around the world end up buying some air tickets along the way, either because they add side trips, left some gaps in their itinerary, or decide to travel by air where they had planned to travel by land or water. The more time you spend on your trip, the more likely this is; if your trip lasts more than a year, you're sure to have to buy your tickets in stages.

If you will be buying tickets in stages (some before you depart and more along the way), make sure your initial set of tickets satisfies the following criteria:

- The tickets must end in a country you will reach within a year of buying them. (Otherwise some of them will expire unused and be wasted.)

- They must end in a country you can get into without an onward ticket.

- They should end in a location where you can buy an onward ticket for a reasonable price (or from which you can make your way by land or sea, without an onward ticket, to somewhere you can do so).

- They should end in an area where you will be staying long enough to arrange onward tickets.

Once they know your entire plan, a good agent can advise you where is likely to be the best place to break your tickets, which ones you should buy before you leave, and where to buy the rest en route.

You may be able to get a good deal on tickets, even while you are overseas, from an agent in the United States, your home country, or somewhere else entirely. This is especially likely to be true if you find yourself needing a ticket in a country where there are no local discounters. I have clients in Japan, China, South America, and several countries in Africa, for example, who find that many tickets, especially one-way tickets, originating in these places are cheaper bought in San Francisco than bought locally.

Many people are scared to buy tickets from abroad. Airline offices in some countries—especially Japan and some of the more expensive Western European countries— will often tell people that tickets issued outside the country for flights originating within the country will not be valid. They are lying. Ignore them.

I've issued thousands of tickets, quite legally, originating in other countries. Since most multistop and around-the-world routings require more than one ticket, strung together, the majority of tickets I and other around-the-world specialist agents sell actually originate in countries other than those in which they are purchased or issued. I've never heard of anyone having any trouble using tickets solely because of where they were issued.

One of the fundamental purposes of the IATA standards and rules for airline ticketing is to permit any office or appointed agent of an IATA member airline, anywhere in the world, to sell tickets on that airline originating and terminating anywhere in the world. The country of sale is not necessarily the country of origin for the flight. The entire IATA currency-equivalence scheme exists solely for situations where tickets are sold in one country for flights that originate in a different country. There are boxes on every ticket, and international designators in every international fare calculation, that would never be needed if tickets could be sold only in the country of origin of the flight.

IATA rules require all IATA member airlines to honor tickets validated in accordance with those rules anywhere in the world. For an airline to refuse to honor valid tickets, solely on the basis of where they were issued, would be a grave violation of IATA rules for which the airline could be expelled from the cartel. No airline that I know of actually refuses to honor such tickets, no matter how much it tries to intimidate passengers into paying more for locally issued tickets.

United States law makes it especially difficult for airlines to prevent USA travel agents from matching local fares on flights within other countries. USA law requires any airline doing business in the United States (i.e., any airline with an agent in the United States, even if it doesn't fly to the USA) to offer for sale in the USA all fares offered by the airline anywhere in the world.

To offer a fare for sale in some other country, but not in the United States, is construed by the USA as a trade sanction against the United States for which the United States is entitled to retaliate. So an airline rule requiring that tickets at a certain fare be issued only in the country of origin, and not in the United States, could subject the airline publishing and enforcing such a restricted fare to an embargo on operations or sales in the United States.

Because no airline wants to be excluded from the large and lucrative market in the United States, no airline actually enforces a rule against using tickets imported from the United States. Most even acknowledge this exception in the fine print of their otherwise-restricted fares: a common fare rule is, "May be issued only in the country of origin, or in the United States and its possessions." They can (and sometimes do) try to keep USA agents from finding out what prices are issued locally, but they can't stop USA agents who find out what the local fares are from selling and issuing tickets at those "local" fares.

For this reason, claims that domestic fares within a country are cheaper if tickets are purchased within the country are almost always false if the tickets are issued in the United States, even when they may be true for tickets issued in other countries.

The willingness of discount agents to export tickets varies from country to country. Some airline offices in some countries include conditions in their contracts with agents forbidding those agents from exporting tickets to customers abroad. Other contracts give smaller commissions, and thus permit smaller discounts, when tickets are sold to customers not residing in the country of purchase. Some airlines give their agents commissions that are independent of where their customers live.

Within the European Union, attempts to restrict the importing, exporting, use, or transborder advertising of discounted tickets have come under successful legal attack by agents and passengers alike. All European test cases to date have held that EU rules providing for a common market, and guaranteeing buyers and sellers from any EU country equal treatment without regard to nationality, are violated by any rule attempting to restrict transborder sales or marketing of discounted tickets within the EU. So under EU law, you're entitled to purchase tickets in the UK or Greece, for travel originating in another EU country, in perfect confidence that the airlines must honor your tickets as long as they are otherwise valid.

In general, agents in the UK are nonetheless still among the least willing of any discounters to export tickets, with a large proportion flatly refusing to sell any tickets not originating in the UK, for fear that if they do so the airlines will discontinue the deals on which they depend. Airline offices in the United States less often place such restrictions on their discount agents. More international tickets are exported from the United States, for flights originating elsewhere, than from any other country.

By far the best place to find agents willing to sell tickets originating anywhere, and send them to you wherever you are, is on the Internet. Around-the-world agents, as a group, have been a conspicuous presence among the first travel agents on the Internet. Any retail agent with a major business in exporting and importing tickets to a worldwide clientele is accessible by e-mail.

That doesn't mean that buying around-the-world or multistop airline ticket can be a completely automated process, or that you have to make a choice between buying tickets from Internet robots or from a human travel agent. The best of the around-the-world and multistop specialty agents offer Internet tools to help you plan your trip, estimate prices, and evaluate preliminary alternatives; personal e-mail, telephone, or in-person consultation to help you optimize your itinerary and answer your questions; and availability of customer service by e-mail or fax throughout your trip in case you have problems with your tickets.

As of 2003, only one agency in the world, AirTreks.com (where I work), provides price estimates on its Web site for customizable multistop itineraries. Other RTW agencies just have sample routes and prices on their Web sites. That means you'll have to e-mail, fax, or call them with your specific itinerary, then wait up to 2–3 days for an estimate. Not necessarily such a big deal if you're planning your trip well in advance, but the delay can make it harder to explore the cost implications of alternate routes and destinations.

Of course, if you do plan on buying tickets from agents in your home country, or anywhere else, while abroad, it's worth checking before you leave to make sure they will be willing to do this and to find out how best to work with them from wherever you'll be. Work out how you'll be able to communicate with them, and how you'll be able to arrange payment.

## Lost or Stolen Tickets

Treat your airline tickets like cash. It can be difficult, time-consuming, and expensive, when it is possible at all, to replace them if they are lost or stolen. You may have to pay in full on the spot for replacement tickets, and the airlines are not obligated to refund the price of the original tickets until they have expired unused, which may not be for a year. If you're traveling on an electronic ticket, original receipts may be essential to get past security checkpoints, as proof of onward passage for immigration purposes, or if the airline loses the record of your reservations or e-tickets, as can happen.

Travel agents cannot replace lost or stolen tickets. All claims for replacement or refund of lost or stolen tickets must be made directly to the airline on which the original ticket was validated. Before any claim can be considered, the airline will need you to provide, or will need to obtain from the issuing agent, the details of the missing tickets.

You have the best chance of obtaining timely replacement—rather than long-delayed refund—of lost or stolen tickets if you can present photocopies of each missing ticket to the airline with your request for its replacement.

If you don't have copies of your tickets, the airline cannot replace or refund them without first verifying the issuing agency or office, date and place of issue, ticket numbers, routing, fare basis, validity dates, and how much you paid for the tickets.

Even in the best of circumstances, time differences may mean that you have to wait two days for the airline office where you present your refund claim to send a message to your agent in the United States, and get an answer back, usually by way of that airline's USA office. If weekends and holidays intervene, you could have to wait a week.

If the airline agrees to replace or refund your missing tickets, it will require you to pay a service charge, typically US$50-100 per ticket. It will also require you to sign a sworn declaration that you did not sell, give away, or gamble away your original tickets and that you will reimburse the airline for the value of the tickets if they have been, or are later, used for travel by someone else.

Carry your airline tickets in a money belt inside your clothes. In two separate safe places, in your most secure pieces of luggage, carry sets of photocopies of each of your tickets along with any other important documents.

If you're traveling with a companion, it's a good idea for each of you to carry a second complete set of the other's document copies, in case one of you has both your money belt and your luggage stolen. To be really safe, leave yet another set with someone back home whom you can contact to fax copies to you in an emergency.

Airlines are not responsible if you lose your tickets, or if they are stolen. Airlines are not required to replace lost or stolen tickets. Some airlines categorically refuse to replace lost or stolen tickets under any circumstances. If you lose a ticket on such an airline, or have it stolen, you will have to pay in full for a replacement ticket, at the prevailing price (which may be much more than you originally paid). Airlines like this include Southwest Airlines (a domestic airline in the United States), Kenya Airways, and Indian Airlines (the main domestic and regional airline in India, not to be confused with the long-haul international airline Air India).

## Cancellations and Refunds

If you cancel all or part of your trip after you buy your tickets, you will have to submit the unused tickets for eventual refund, less penalties. Refunds can take up to a year, and partially used tickets are usually completely nonrefundable.

If you change your route or set and sequence of stops, you may have to buy new tickets and send the unused ones back for refund, less penalties. If you buy new tickets, you will have pay for them in full. Even if the old tickets are wholly or partially refundable, you will not get a refund for them until later. If tickets are reissued or exchanged for new tickets, however, the value of the old tickets can sometimes be applied directly to the value of the new tickets (less penalties, plus a reissue fee of US$25–150, and any difference in between the fare for the old and new routing or destinations).

For this reason, it's best to exhaust your efforts to exchange your existing tickets for tickets closer to what you want, to have them reissued, or at least to find out how much those options will cost before you buy any new tickets. Once you have bought new tickets, it's too late to apply any of the value of the old tickets to the new ones. One of the most costly mistakes is to buy new or replacement tickets on the assumption that the old ones will be fully, freely, and/or immediately refundable.

It is essential that you cancel your reservations, prior to the scheduled flight(s), if you wish to obtain a refund for tickets for those flights. If you don't show up for a flight for which you hold confirmed reservations, the airline is not obligated to give you any refund. Many airlines won't. If you cancel your reservations in person at an airline office, ask for written confirmation of the cancellation. If you cancel your reservations by phone, write down the name and title of the person at the airline who canceled them for you, the date, the place, and the telephone number at which you reached them. Some airlines will not give refunds without proof that reservations were canceled.

Some people think that if they cancel their reservations, or don't travel, they have "canceled their tickets" and will automatically receive a refund or credit. It's not so simple as that, or so fast. Technically speaking, you cannot cancel tickets. You need to cancel your reservations to protect your right to a refund, but that's not sufficient; you still need to submit the physical tickets before the airline or agent can process them for refund. No ticket, no refund. Nondiscounted tickets can be submitted for refund directly to the airline, but discounted tickets must be submitted for refund through the agent who sold them to you, because only that agent knows how much commission was rebated and how much you actually paid.

If you have an "electronic ticket," or were going to travel on a ticketless airline, refunds can be even more problematic. With physical tickets, you have an (unused) paper ticket to prove that you didn't travel. With an e-ticket, it can be much harder to prove that you didn't actually travel. Airlines don't send refund checks or issue credits for unused e-tickets automatically. You have to go through the same process as for a refund of a physical ticket, with the additional burden of proving that you didn't travel.

If you don't use an e-ticket, try to get your ticket coupons printed out (to submit with your refund request) when you cancel your reservations. If that isn't possible, ask for a printout of your e-ticket receipt and a written confirmation on airline letterhead or itinerary paper that you cancelled your reservations, signed and dated by an airline employee with their title and employee number. Problems with e-ticket refunds are surprisingly common.

Each ticket, whether for one or several flights, must be processed separately. Old-style tickets are written or printed on little booklets of thin carbon paper that bind together up to four flights on one ticket. Some tickets are still issued that way, and some are still handwritten. But most paper tickets now use the "ATB" ("automated ticket and boarding pass") format, in which each flight coupon is a separate computer-printed card. With ATB tickets, it can be hard for those not skilled at reading tickets to tell which flights are part of the same ticket.

You need to submit all unused flight coupons and the associated passenger receipt coupon(s). Once you return a ticket to the agent, the agent returns it to the airline with a refund claim form. If the agent bought the ticket from a wholesaler, they have to go through the wholesaler, who submits it to the airline in turn. Eventually, if the airline approves the refund claim, it calculates how much is due, after penalties, and notifies whoever issued the ticket (the wholesaler or retail agent) of a credit. The wholesaler then pays the agent, who can then pay you; both the wholesaler and the agent deduct their own penalties, fees, or service charges from the refund as they pass it along.

When a ticket is refunded, the airline recalls any commission that was paid to an agent on that ticket. As a condition of issuing tickets, an agency must agree to allow the airline to take this money, or any other money the airlines claim from it (for example, if the airline believes that the agency should have charged a higher fare for a ticket), directly out of the agency bank account, without prior notice. Front-line agents take the brunt of travelers' complaints about fares, refunds, and penalties, but agencies are really at the airlines' mercy and can only do what the airlines permit.

If you are submitting a ticket to an agent for a refund, you should expect the agency to charge you a cancellation fee. When a ticket is sold, and then submitted for refund, an agency has to do the same work it would have to do if you actually traveled, plus the work of processing the refund. Unless it deducts some sort of fee or service charge from the refund, it ends up having done all the work of selling and refunding the ticket for free. Anything the agency was paid by way of commission is snatched back by the airline. Even if it deducts the original commission from the airline's refund before paying what's left to you, it has still been paid nothing for its services in processing the refund, which is invariably more time-consuming and labor-intensive than issuing the tickets was in the first place.

Airline cancellation penalties vary widely. A typical set of tickets around the world consists of 3–10 separate tickets, each of which has its own cancellation rules and penalties of anywhere from about US$50 to 100 percent. Typically, the eventual refund for an entirely unused set of around-the-world tickets is somewhere between 50 percent and 75 percent of the total price originally paid and takes 3–9 months. It is not always possible to know in advance the exact amount of the refund, since refunds for tickets priced in foreign currency can be affected by currency fluctuations.

If you have to cancel your trip for medical reasons, try to get a letter to that effect from a doctor. Depending on the airline and fare, some or all of the normal refund penalties may be waived for medical reasons. Many people mistakenly assume that all airlines and agents always waive all cancellation penalties in cases of cancellation for medical emergencies, but this is not correct. Even legitimate and documented medical reasons may not be cause for waiver of penalties, depending on the rules of the airline, fare, ticket, and agent. Some airlines only waive penalties if you or a traveling companion dies, and some not even then.

One reason the airlines are increasingly reluctant to give medical exemptions from cancellation penalties is that they have been widely abused by passengers with fraudulent or forged medical excuses. It's tempting to ask (or even pay) a friendly doctor to write a letter for you when hundreds of dollars in penalties are at stake. But some airlines spot-check medical refund documentation, so if you submit a fraudulent or forged note from a doctor both you and the doctor risk criminal prosecution for attempting to defraud the airline. This sort of fraud only makes the airlines more suspicious and slows down legitimate refund claims. If an airline won't waive penalties for your legitimate medical claim, the people you should blame are all the people who've ripped off the airlines in the past with bogus medical excuses.

Most international airlines that still make any special allowance for medically required cancellations now require an original letter (not a photocopy or fax) in English or the national language of the airline's home country, signed and dated by a doctor, on the doctor's printed letterhead; or a certified copy of a death certificate. It's hard to tell in advance whether a doctor's note will make a difference to your refund, and it's difficult to obtain one after the fact, so it's always best to get one at the time you get sick or injured if there's any chance that it might require you to cancel or change your flights.

The most common causes for cancellation are accidents, illnesses, family emergencies, and other circumstances covered by trip cancellation and interruption insurance. This sort of insurance is advisable, as the cost is generally far less than the difference between discounted tickets with cancellation penalties and fully refundable full-fare tickets. (For more information, see "Travel Insurance" in the Safety and Health chapter.)

## When Things Go Wrong

There's a whole closet of fears of what can happen after you give your money to a travel agent for airline tickets. What happens if the agency goes bankrupt or never gives you your tickets? What if the airline cancels the flight, discontinues service on the route entirely, or goes out of business? How can you reduce these risks, and what can you do if you have problems or complaints?

### Problems with Airlines

Most complaints about airlines relate to secondary aspects of service, not to the basic question of whether they provide transportation from point A to point B as contracted. The real questions are what to do if the airline on which you have a ticket no longer flies from point A to point B, having discontinued service on the route, or has gone out of business and no longer flies at all?

## Discontinued Routes

What happens if you buy a ticket to fly from A to B on Airline C, but by the time you want to use that ticket Airline C no longer flies from A to B?

This isn't common, but it's not rare either, especially if you are traveling for a long time. Airlines are constantly adding new routes and dropping or changing old ones. It's not surprising that flights that are being heavily discounted because the airline has trouble filling them are sometimes those that end up being discontinued entirely. Most of the time, the airline itself is still in business, and it's only a particular route that is dropped from its schedule. As long as the airline is still flying, it wants to keep its customers' goodwill, and it will usually do much more than it legally has to.

If the airline still serves A and B, it will invariably accommodate you on whatever route or connections it still flies between the ticketed points, even if your ticket was issued as nonreroutable or valid only on direct flights that no longer exist. You may end up flying a few days earlier or later than you had expected, or taking longer to get where you are going, but these sorts of things aren't usually a problem for long-term travelers. Sometimes you get a stopover you hadn't paid for, or a night in a hotel at the airline's expense in some city where you have to make connections. If you do, make the most of it. Airlines aren't required to put you up, even if you have to spend the night, but you can always ask.

If the airline no longer flies to A and/or B at all, it has two choices: it can endorse your ticket to another airline or it can give you a refund. Try to get it to endorse your ticket to any other airline that will get you to your destination, or an acceptable alternate destination. (Sometimes when a route is discontinued, it's because circumstances in the destination are such that you'd no longer want to go there.) If you were already flying on the cheapest airline, on a discounted ticket, a refund of what you paid for that portion of your ticket is almost certain not to be enough to buy a ticket on any other airline.

The decisive factor in whether you are provided with a refund or alternative transportation is usually whether you had confirmed reservations for a specific date. Your only right in either case is to a refund, and your only sure protection is trip cancellation and interruption insurance. In practice, if you have specific reservations you will usually be provided with alternative transportation, while if you have only an open ticket you will get only a refund.

Airlines look at it like this: if you hadn't made any reservations, you had no expectations of flying on any particular date. Once it has given you a full refund you are in exactly the same situation as if you had never bought a ticket on their airline in the first place, and you have no cause for complaint. If you have reservations for a specific date, on the other hand, it will usually make some arrangement to get you there around that date.

## Airline Bankruptcies

Airline bankruptcy is a risk no matter which airline you have tickets on. Fears that smaller, more obscure, or non-USA international airlines are more likely to go out of business are not well-founded. You are in less danger of airline bankruptcy on the small, underfinanced national airline of a Third or Fourth World country, which for reasons of national prestige will be bailed out by its country's government if it loses money, as it probably does, than on a larger airline based in the United States where the government subsidizes the airline industry as a whole but takes a minimal role in protecting individual airlines.

Most countries have a national airline whose continued operation is considered to be in the national interest, even if it has nominally been privatized. The United States is virtually unique in having no government-owned airlines and no one airline linked to its national image. The United States also has had far more airline bankruptcies than any other country, of airlines large (Pan Am) and small (USAfrica Airways), and the USA government has a proven record of letting airlines go out of business even when that will strand passengers.

A government-owned national airline is unlikely to be allowed to go out of business unless the government of the country is bankrupt. But increasingly, national airlines have been at least nominally privatized. In the past, many more travelers were affected by failures of private USA airlines than by failures of foreign national airlines. Today, the problem of airline bankruptcies is no longer confined solely to the free-market United States. Privatizing the national airline, and then allowing it to go bankrupt, can be a form of de facto repudiation of government debt. That's an attractive option for many governments.

A travel agent that sells you a ticket valid at the time it is issued is not responsible if the airline later goes bankrupt. In this circumstance, the only place for you to seek a refund is directly from the airline, through its trustees in bankruptcy. Because secured creditors take precedence, and because struggling airlines by definition have highly leveraged and precarious cash-flow positions, there isn't usually much, if anything, left for ticket holders when the remaining assets of a bankrupt airline are liquidated.

Other airlines have no obligation to honor tickets from a bankrupt airline. Why should they? If they do, they write off the costs of transporting holders of worthless tickets on a bankrupt former competitor as a marketing cost, in the hope of winning the loyalty and future business of frequent travelers on the route. More often airlines will offer a special concessionary fare, just high enough to cover their costs, to holders of tickets on the failed airline. But you can't count on such generosity.

The only way to protect yourself against losing your money if an airline goes out of business between when you buy your tickets and when you travel is to buy travel insurance that covers "supplier default." See the section on "Travel Insurance," in the Safety and Health chapter.

### Problems with Travel Agents, Tour Operators, and Charter Operators

While travel agents that issue tickets on IATA airlines must meet certain accreditation standards, IATA doesn't really regulate relations between travel agents and their customers.

Until you get your tickets from an agency, the matter is one of local law. Agencies must post bonds to help ensure that the airlines will get paid if the agency goes bankrupt, but tickets already issued by an agency remain valid even if the agency's bond is insufficient to pay off the airlines, as it often is if an agency goes out of business. The standard bond for agencies in the United States is US$20,000, far less than many agencies' weekly payments to the airlines.

Once you get your tickets on a scheduled IATA airline, you are protected, even if the agency you bought the tickets from goes out of business the day after you buy the tickets, and whether or not the agency has paid the airline. Once you receive valid airline tickets, most issues are between you and the airline, and are governed by airline or IATA conditions of carriage.

Your rights in a dispute with a travel agency, charter operator, or tour operator are limited to those available under the laws of the jurisdiction in which the other party to the dispute operates or is chartered, or where the transaction occurred. Local rules vary. If you plan to buy tickets or a tour in another country, either check out that country's laws or assume that the rule is caveat emptor.

### The UK Air Travel Organiser's Licence System

The world's best system of consumer protection for air travelers is in the UK. There, all sellers of airline tickets or tours that include airfare, except in cases where a ticket on a scheduled airline is supplied immediately in exchange for payment, must have an Air Travel Organiser's Licence (ATOL), which is issued by the Civil Aviation Authority (CAA). ATOL holders must include their ATOL number in advertisements and brochures, and on confirmation invoices and receipts. "If it hasn't got an ATOL, don't book it at all," is the advice of the CAA for UK buyers of air tickets or any package that includes air transportation.

To obtain an ATOL, an applicant must provide the CAA with audited accounts including profit and loss statements for the previous three years (or a current balance sheet for a new business) as well as financial projections for the year including a cash-flow forecast and budget of income and expenses. A major reason few ATOL holders fail is that in the UK underfinanced companies or individuals don't get licenses to sell air travel in the first place.

ATOL applicants must also post a bond with the CAA to cover the cost of providing for their customers if they go out of business. The size of the bond is proportionate to the size and nature of the business and must be reviewed and renewed each year. If an ATOL holder fails, or is financially unable to provide the contracted tickets, air transportation, or other tour services, the CAA uses the licensee's bond money to provide those services, or refunds, to all those who have paid. If the bond is too small, any shortfall is made up from an Air Travel Trust administered by the CAA. The trust was financed for its first two years by a nominal tax on tickets and tours, but since 1978 has earned enough interest on its investments to be entirely self-supporting.

The record of the CAA in administering this system is impressive. Claimants against failed ATOL holders do not have to sue or advance money out of their own pockets; the CAA steps in directly to arrange transportation home or pay refunds. In 1995, the first year in which the current ATOL rules were in effect, 11,417 people were flown home by the CAA when tour or charter operators failed while they were abroad. Refunds were paid to another 124,641 people who had not yet commenced their travels. Repatriation costs and refunds totaled UK£16 million (US$25 million).

The ATOL system was prompted by concerns about the reliability of travel agencies, tour operators, and charter operators, not scheduled airlines. An ATOL number can be based on an airline's guarantee that the agency is appointed by the airline, and that the airline will guarantee the validity of tickets sold or issued by the agency. If the ATOL agency goes out of business after taking your payment, the airline is still required to give you a ticket, whether or not the agency paid the airline. Once you have your ticket on a scheduled airline, however, the seller's ATOL number does not protect you against failure of the airline. Thus, even in the UK you need to take out supplier default insurance to be protected against bankruptcies of scheduled airlines.

The ATOL scheme protects travelers at minimal cost while being welcomed by legitimate travel agents and tour and charter operators as enhancing their credibility and putting their underfinanced and dishonest competitors out of business. Its exemplary success, which has improved rather than detracted from the position of the UK as one of the world centers of airline ticket discounting, puts the lie to any claim that effective consumer protection regulations cannot coexist with an open and vigorously competitive market. I commend it to the attention and careful study of would-be regulators, and of consumers, in other countries, especially as the model for any future national system of protection for travel consumers in the United States.

### The California Seller of Travel Law

In the United States, the only special provisions for sales of travel are matters of state law, not federal law. Mainly in response to concerns about fraudulent sales of package tours and failures of charter operators, rather than tickets on scheduled airlines, several states have enacted licensing requirements for sellers of travel.

The most important of these is the California Seller of Travel (CST) law, which took effect in 1996. Despite significant problems, the CST law is being held up (as California laws often are) as a model for other states. For that reason, and because California is one of the world's centers of discount airline ticket sales, it warrants a closer look at what, if any, protection it provides.

The CST law was obviously inspired by the ATOL law, but differs from it in critical ways:

First, it applies only to sales by California businesses to customers in California; it provides no protection to interstate sales. These would be exclusively the province of federal law, if there were any on this issue, which there isn't. It's laughable to suggest that the sale of travel is not at least a national, if not a global, business.

Second, while the CST law requires sellers of travel to register, it requires no evidence that they have adequate working capital or realistic budgets. Anyone, or any business, can register as a CST; registration is purely clerical. The contrast in this regard between the questions asked on the ATOL application and CST registration forms is striking.

Third, the Travel Consumer Restitution Corporation (TCRC) set up under the CST law does not itself do anything to arrange transportation or any other travel services in the event of bankruptcy or default of a CST registrant. The TCRC will only reimburse travelers, after the fact and after they prove their claims against a registered seller of travel, for costs of alternative arrangements, which they will first have to make and pay for out of their pockets.

Fourth, because most CST registrants need post no bond, and because the restitution fund is financed only by an assessment on registrants limited by the law to US$200 per registrant per year, with a target balance of only US$1.6 million, there is no guarantee that enough money will be available to pay the claims that could arise if a large tour or charter operator or agency goes under. (As I've noted, about US$25 million a year is spent on repatriation and refunds in the UK, which has only about twice the population of California.)

Fifth, despite having weaker provisions, the CST law has not won the acceptance or support from the industry that the ATOL prototype has.

The bottom line is that the CST law provides even California travel consumers, buying from registered California sellers of travel, little real protection, and provides a poor model to anyone considering similar legislation.

### USA Consumer Protection for Credit-Card Purchases

By far the strongest consumer protection provisions in the United States are those applicable to credit-or charge-card purchases. The single best way for buyers in the United States to protect themselves against an agent taking their money but not producing tickets is to buy tickets from an agency in the USA and pay with a credit or charge card.

You aren't required to pay credit-card charges for goods or services you didn't receive. If you haven't received your tickets, you can contest the charge when your bill arrives. The matter is referred to the chargeback departments of the bank that issued your card and the bank with which the agency has its merchant account, both of which function as arbiters. The burden is on the agency or merchant to prove that you authorized the charge and that you got what you paid for. If it can't come up with proof (a written and signed charge authorization and copies of tickets), it's an open-and-shut case, and the charge will be removed from your bill without your ever having to pay.

Once you dispute the charge, your bank takes over as your advocate with the merchant's bank: you don't have to do the work of making demands on the merchant or trying to collect. If the agency or other merchant is out of business, or the bank can't get its money back, that's not your problem. It's the bank that advances money to the merchant, and the bank that is required to absorb any uncollectible losses from disputed charges.

If you pay by cash or check, the agency has your money. If it doesn't deliver, you may have to sue, and the burden is on you to prove that you didn't get your tickets. If the agency goes out of business before you can get a legal judgment, and collect on it, you're out of luck.

These provisions only apply to purchases made in the United States with credit or charge cards issued by USA banks. In practice, disputes with foreign merchants by holders of USA-issued cards are referred to the same chargeback departments, who try to follow the same procedures as they would with a USA merchant. If the merchant can't document authorization for the charge, or delivery of the goods or services, and the card-issuing bank can't get the money back from the merchant's bank or the merchant, it isn't required to remove the charge from your bill or take the loss. Usually, however, it will, in the interest of keeping your account and to avoid being accused of being complicit in any fraud or illegal activity by the merchant.

How aggressively the chargeback department will pursue your dispute with a merchant, and how willing it will be to remove a disputed charge from your bill, depends to significant degree on the status of your account and how much the card-issuing bank wants your business. In my experience, American Express is significantly more likely to side with the customer than are Visa or MasterCard issuing banks. A bank where you also have other accounts may go further to keep your business than one with which you only have a credit card.

There are usually separate customer service and chargeback departments for holders of higher-fee premium (gold or platinum) credit and charge cards. In disputes with merchants, banks are more likely to give the benefit of the doubt to premium cardholders than to holders of standard cards. This is the best reason I know of to pay the extra fee for a "silver," "gold," or "platinum" card.

Don't go overboard with chargebacks. They are appropriate mainly in cases where a merchant doesn't deliver at all, or is out of business; they are not an appropriate way to deal with disputes over terms and conditions. Don't charge back an entire amount if only part of it is in dispute. Treat a chargeback as only half a step short of a lawsuit: a next-to-last resort before turning to the courts. Merchants justifiably don't like people who initiate legal action without first trying to resolve their disputes informally. Once you initiate a chargeback, you have defined the relationship with the merchant as adversarial, and can expect few concessions. If a dispute is a matter of judgment, interpretation, or misunderstanding, rather than of simple nondelivery, your best bet is to try to negotiate a settlement directly with the merchant before contesting the bill and initiating a chargeback.

Unjustified chargebacks against travel agents usually involve people who change their minds between authorizing a charge for tickets or other travel arrangements and receiving their tickets or vouchers or leaving on their trips. They think that because they had not yet received the tickets, or never used the tickets, they shouldn't have to pay for them. It doesn't work like that. From the moment you authorize a charge for tickets or travel arrangements, you are morally and legally bound to pay the bill. The agent relies on your authorization to start sending payments to airlines or other suppliers as soon as your charge is approved. If you dispute the charge, you are stiffing the agent unfairly. If you change your plans, you must pay the bill, bring any tickets or vouchers you have received back to the agent, and wait—perhaps several months—for any refund, less any cancellation penalties.

### Consumer Protection in Other Countries

Some countries license or regulate travel agencies, but in others there is no special system of licensing or regulation of air ticket sellers, and sales of air tickets are subject only to whatever general rules apply to any retail sales. Absent any special provision to the contrary, your only legal recourse if you don't get what you pay for is the legal system in the jurisdiction of the sale. If you buy tickets in a foreign country, that's probably no use: you aren't likely to be sticking around long enough to sue anyone. All you can do is to try to choose a reliable agent in the first place. (See the section earlier in this chapter on "Choosing a Travel Agent.")

If you pay by credit card, you may have some recourse through your card-issuing bank, but your rights vary from country to country, and in many countries it's almost impossible to find an agency that accepts credit or charge cards in payment for discounted tickets. You can take out travel insurance to cover losses from supplier bankruptcy or default, but that, too, is hard or impossible to find in many countries. Read the fine print closely: most travel insurance policies will not cover purchases made directly from suppliers or agents in other countries. These are strong reasons to buy tickets through an agency in your home country, against which you can have recourse under your local procedures or through travel insurance.

### Where to Complain

Complain first to the people who caused the problem. If it's a complaint about service by an airline, complain to the airline. If you don't like a hotel, complain to the hotel management. Agencies don't own the airlines and are limited in their ability to control airlines' behavior or obtain redress for grievances against them, especially as to the quality of service.

If you have a financial dispute, complain to whomever you gave your money to. Your money may have been passed on to someone else—it's not uncommon for there to be a chain of three or four intermediaries between a retail agency and the airline or supplier of travel services, especially if the supplier is in a different country—but it should be possible to forward your complaint and claim down the same chain.

Good businesses want to hear from dissatisfied customers, and would rather have a chance to make things right, or at least explain their side of the story, than have you denounce them for something that might not have been their fault, or for which they would have been willing to compensate you. Be realistic and fair—asking for your entire payment back because of a minor problem with your trip will only reduce your chances of a mutually agreeable settlement—but do specify exactly what you want done, or how much you want to be paid.

Many businesses in the United States belong to Better Business Bureaus. Complaining to the Better Business Bureau (BBB) is usually a waste of time. The BBB is not a consumer organization but a business organization. Like most self-regulation schemes, its main purpose is to enable businesses to claim that the government doesn't need to protect consumers because merchants are policing themselves. It is designed by businesses to protect their images, not to be an advocate against them. The BBB has no enforcement power whatsoever. It can cancel a merchant's membership if the merchant doesn't answer your complaint at all, but as long as the business sends any response a complaint is simply logged and forgotten as unresolved. The BBB is, in my opinion, a sham; many businesses know it is and refuse to waste their money on membership. Membership in a BBB is no measure of legitimacy.

Although it is also an industry self-policing organization, the American Society of Travel Agents (ASTA) has a much better track record of pursuing consumer complaints. ASTA requires its members to adhere to certain standards of ethics and business practices, including responding to complaints, and can expel members who are found not to. In the United States, I would hesitate to do business with an agency that is not a member of ASTA, and I would not do business with one whose membership has been revoked or withdrawn. An agency that doesn't renew its ASTA membership probably does so to forestall an expected expulsion, or because it can't afford the dues; either is an extremely bad sign.

ASTA's Consumer Affairs Department (see "Consumer Protection" in the Resource Guide) provides an informal mediation service to assist in resolving disputes with members and a complaint reference service that will give you a profile of past complaints to ASTA, if any, about travel companies. You can check with the department for an agency's complaint record and membership status, or for information on how to pursue a complaint against a member.

Remember that all agencies, especially large, long-established ones with lots of customers, are likely to have had at least some complaints. The red flags are many complaints, recent complaints, a high proportion of unresolved complaints, revocation of ASTA membership, or use of the ASTA logo despite not being an ASTA member.

ASTA functions as an industry networking group, so many tour operators and non-USA travel agencies with USA clients or clients visiting the United States are members. There's a fair chance that any local agent in another country belongs to ASTA. ASTA will get involved in mediating disputes with any member, even ones involving local transactions with members in countries outside the United States.

### Consumer Protection on the Internet

For the most part, Internet ticket purchases are subject to the same consumer protection rules as in-person, telephone, or mail-order purchases. Your most important protection, on the Internet as anywhere else, comes from the rules for credit-card payments and disputes. The most important things to do to protect yourself are to pay by credit card, to read all the rules before you pay, and to print out your final confirmed itinerary, price, and all the rules and conditions before you click, "Buy."

Most disputes over ticket purchases involve people who don't read, don't understand, or don't pay attention to the rules for cancellations, refunds, or changes to their tickets. Because they don't intend to cancel or change their plans, they don't notice or don't remember the cancellation or change penalties, or perhaps that the tickets can't be changed or refunded at all. Later, they complain about the penalties: they say, quite truthfully, that they don't remember being told that the tickets weren't refundable, reroutable, changeable, or whatever.

I know nobody reads the fine print, especially when it's so easy just to click on "I agree." But if you don't read the rules, you have no cause for later complaint if you don't like them. On the Internet, the only way you can later prove what you agreed to, what you were supposed to be charged, or what the rules of your ticket were supposed to be, is to print them all out before you buy and save them until your trip is complete.

While the basics of consumer protection are the same online as anywhere else, the Internet poses a variety of special issues of its own: security, privacy invasion, and so forth. These are important, but beyond the scope of this book. Privacy, security, and consumer protection questions peculiar to the Internet, as well as advice on using the Internet for travel planning and purchasing and while on the road, are dealt with at length in my companion volume in this series, *The Practical Nomad Guide to the Online Travel Marketplace*.

# "*Papers,*
*Please*"

# TRAVEL DOCUMENTS

Travel documents—passports, visas, and other government permits—are an unavoidable necessity of international travel, required for crossing international borders or for travel within particular parts of a country. Most around-the-world or multicountry travelers need visas in addition to a passport for at least some of the countries they visit. The more you travel, the less you will like passports and visas, but the best way to avoid problems with travel documents is not to leave them to the last minute.

To a government, a "travel document" is what you use as proof of your identity and nationality when crossing an international border. Usually this is a passport, although certain kinds of special documents are issued to stateless people (i.e., people who do not have citizenship in any recognized country) for purposes of international travel. Most countries are reluctant to admit people who are or may become stateless. Stateless people (mainly refugees) have great difficulty traveling, and you should let your travel agent know as early as possible if you or someone traveling with you is stateless (e.g., traveling with a refugee re-entry permit or any travel document other than a passport). In common usage, the term "travel documents" also applies to visas and other entry and travel permits.

This chapter follows the chapters on transportation because most people don't get visas until after they've arranged their long-haul air transportation. Sometimes there are good reasons to wait as long as possible (as long as you leave ample time for delays and surprises) before actually having your visas issued—such as maximizing the period of their validity. Some visas can't be issued until you have made onward airline reservations, or even have tickets in hand. But I strongly urge you not to make definite plans or buy tickets without first carefully investigating the documentary requirements for the trip you want to take. I've known people to invest months of effort, commit themselves to a vacation schedule, and buy expensive nonrefundable tickets, only to find out the rules have changed since the "current" guidebook they relied on was researched and, they cannot get the visas or permits their plans require.

## PASSPORTS

If you are considering any international travel, one of your first steps should be to obtain a valid passport. If you already have a passport make sure it is still valid and will remain valid until at least six months, preferably a year, after you return to your home country. There are exceptions to the rule—USA citizens can travel to and from Canada and Mexico without passports, for example — but in general anyone wishing to cross any international border, anywhere in

# KEY ADVICE ABOUT
# TRAVEL DOCUMENTS

- Get a passport before you try to travel anywhere across any national border, even just to Mexico or Canada.

- Verify the current visa and entry requirements of each country you want to visit directly with each country's embassy or consulate.

- Remember that travel is not a right. Maybe it should be, but it isn't. Other countries don't have to let you in if they don't want to. Ask for permission politely and respectfully.

- Approach visa applications and border crossings as learning experiences and opportunities, not confrontations or ordeals.

- Play by the rules. When you are dealing with foreign governments, you are not in control. Trying to claim special privileges (especially as a citizen of the United States) or to assert your nonexistent authority will only reduce the chances that you'll be allowed to go where you want.

- Respect foreign laws, even if you don't like them. Violations of other countries' customs and immigration rules are no joke. They are real crimes with nasty names like "smuggling," "theft," "fraud," "subversion," and "espionage," and penalties to match.

- If you're a USA citizen and you want to be treated better by foreign governments, lobby our own government to treat foreign visitors and would-be visitors to the United States better.

- Never judge a country by its border guards, customs and immigrations inspectors, or police. Would you want foreign visitors to judge the United States by the conduct and attitudes the immigration, customs, or border patrol officers of the Department of Homeland Security?

For more information on the topics in this chapter, see the Resource Guide in the back of the book, and the links on the Practical Nomad Web site at http://www.practicalnomad.com.

the world, must present a valid passport issued by the government of the country of citizenship.

Passports are strongly recommended for all international travel, even in cases where they aren't strictly required. A surprising number of USA citizens, for example, have difficulties crossing the USA-Canada or USA-Mexico borders that could have been avoided had they carried valid passports. Getting a passport is easier than trying to travel without one. If you don't have, or can't get, a passport, or if you insist on traveling without one, you'll need some other official identity document with your photo on it for any air travel, including domestic air travel within the United States and most other countries.

The United States doesn't have a national ID card, and domestic air travelers within the United States used to be able to travel without identity papers. This made it relatively easy to travel on other people's tickets and thus buy and sell partially used tickets. However, in 1995, in response to a bomb scare, several major USA airports and airlines implemented what were intended to be temporary checks of all passengers' ID documents. The airlines suddenly realized how much potential revenue was being lost by people traveling on other people's nontransferable tickets, and the ID checks were made nationwide and permanent. (It's still not clear whether it's the USA government or the airlines that have actually imposed the ID requirement.) As of 2003, although legal challenges to the ID requirement are pending, it is no longer possible to fly with someone else's ticket.

It's now impossible to check in for any flight, even a domestic flight in the USA, without showing a government-issued ID with your photo on it. If you show up without a government photo ID, or if you show up for an international flight without a passport, you will be refused boarding. If you don't have a driver's license, and don't want to get a passport, most USA state governments will issue a state photo ID for non-drivers that's accepted for domestic USA flights. But a passport costs only a little more than a state ID, and opens the door to the entire world. Do yourself a favor: get a passport.

Almost all other countries also require air travelers to carry and show photo ID. On domestic flights locals must show national ID and foreigners must show passports. In countries where prices for locals and foreigners differ, this also ensures that foreigners have paid the foreigners' price. It is sometimes possible—although illegal—for foreigners who can pass for locals to travel on local-price train tickets. However, it is almost impossible for foreigners to travel on local-price air tickets without forged local identity papers to match their tickets.

I recommend you start working on getting a passport at least 4–6 months before you plan to leave. Most people don't need that long to get the travel documents they need before they leave, so don't panic if you're leaving in a couple of months or weeks and don't yet have a passport. But if you're interested enough in international travel to read this book, and don't have a passport, do yourself a favor and start the process now. You cannot begin to apply for visas until after you receive your passport; you may need to send your passport back and forth to several embassies or consulates to obtain visas; and some visas take several weeks each to issue. It may also take much longer than you think to track down and order an original of your birth or naturalization certificate—a prerequisite to getting a passport.

The "Passports" section of the Resource Guide gives information on passport issuance offices and application procedures for citizens of some of the principal English-speaking First World countries: the United States, Canada, the UK, Ireland, Australia, and Aotearoa/New Zealand. This information, like all third-party information about government rules, should not be taken as definitive. Rules change. Verify current requirements, fees, office locations, etc., with the relevant authorities before making definite plans, submitting a passport application, or going out of your way to visit a passport office.

## USA Passports

Given the lengths some people from other countries will go to acquire a USA passport, it may be surprising that fewer than 20 percent of USA citizens have a passport, the smallest percentage of any First World country. (The percentage has gone up sharply in recent years, but that's more as a result of immigrants and long-term permanent residents getting USA citizenship than of native-born USA citizens getting passports.)

USA passports are the most valuable and widely useful travel documents in the world, getting you into more countries, more easily, than any other. If you hold a USA passport, you are one of the world's travel elite. Consider yourself privileged, and take advantage of the opportunities it gives you.

In addition to the information below on USA passports and applications, I encourage you to consult the excellent Passport Services Web site maintained by the U.S. Department of State at http://travel.state.gov/passport_services.html. It includes current forms, fee schedules, and instructions and a searchable database of places where passport applications are accepted.

**REAL LIFE**

Not long ago, I got a late-night phone call for advice from an acquaintance who planned to get on an international flight the next day, and had discovered he didn't have a valid passport. Why? He hadn't bothered to check his passport, and hadn't noticed that it had expired. Fortunately, he was in San Francisco, where there's a passport office. He got an appointment at the passport office downtown for 12:30 P.M., showed up with his bags packed, and made his 6 P.M. flight (4 P.M. check in) with his new passport. That's not something you want to put yourself through if you can avoid it.

### Applying for a USA Passport

USA passports are issued by the Department of State. If you are a citizen and resident of the United States, it is easiest to apply for or renew a USA passport at a USA Post Office. Postal workers will check your application and documents and forward the application to the Department of State with their certification that they have verified your citizenship and identity. The State Department will send your passport back by mail. Many local Post Offices accept passport applications. If yours doesn't, someone there can tell you the nearest office that does. You can also apply in person at one of the Department of State Passport Agency offices, although the State Department strongly discourages applications at its offices and subjects them all to a an extra fee for expedited service (US$60 per person, as of 2003).

If you are renewing a passport, you can do so by mail. But even then you should bring the envelope to the post office unsealed, and have the postal worker verify you've completed all the paperwork in the accepted manner before you send it in. If you are outside the United States, you can apply for a new passport, such as for a child born abroad of USA parents, or renew your existing passport—preferably well before it expires—at any embassy, consulate, or diplomatic office of the United States.

The application form for a USA passport asks when and where you are considering travel, which needlessly deters some people from applying until their travel plans are certain. The only reason for the question is to prioritize rush applications by departure date. Of those who pay for rush service, those who are leaving soonest, or who are going to places for which they will need time to get visas, will get their applications processed first. You can say you are going anywhere legal anytime within the next 10 years. What you say doesn't matter: you will not be held to it or penalized if you don't go, and it will not be recorded in your passport.

Passports can be issued the same day if necessary, but only at one of a handful of State Department passport offices in major cities (see the list in the Resource Guide), and only with payment of a substantial additional fee for in-person service. Rush applications are processed in order of urgency. Most people requesting same-day service are told to come pick up their passports a few days later, unless they are leaving that very day.

If you really need a passport right away, be prepared to spend several hours, all day if necessary, waiting in line to submit your application and receive your passport. But it is possible to get a passport and get on a plane the same day. People going abroad unexpectedly on short notice —most often for business or for family emergencies—do it every day.

Passport application forms and instructions are available at State Department passport agency offices, from post offices, from some travel agents, or on the Internet. Whether applying at a post office or State Department passport office, be sure to bring all of the following:

- two recent passport photos (Get plenty of extra photos while you are at it, for visa and other permit applications.)

- your original birth certificate (not a photocopy)

- your driver's license or state photo ID card

- your previous passport, if any, whether or not it is still valid

- the passport fee in cash, personal check, traveler's checks, or money order (US$85 new passport fee, plus US$60 rush charge applied to all applications at passport offices)

- if you require your passport the same day, your tickets or itinerary on travel agency forms or letterhead showing that you are scheduled to depart the United States within two weeks

Most State Department passport offices are open by appointment only. You must call ahead to be assigned a specific time to show up with your application. Call or check the State Department Web site before you go to verify whether any of these requirements, especially the fees, have changed. If your documents aren't in order at the appointed hour, you'll be sent away and won't be able to come back until you've made a new appointment.

If you don't have both a birth certificate and a state photo ID card or driver's license, or if you weren't born in the United States, check with the Passport Agency in advance for other acceptable forms of proof of citizenship and identity.

Unless you request otherwise, you'll get a standard 24-page passport with four pages of fine print and 20 pages for visas. That's plenty for most trips around the world, unless they involve a lot of country-hopping. If you expect to fill up more pages than that over the next 10 years, you can get a 48-page passport at no additional charge, if you ask when you first apply. Make sure your request for a 48-page passport is prominently indicated on the application form itself, especially if you applied by mail. Requests made on a separate cover letter are apt to be separated from the forms during automated processing, and disregarded, as happened the last time I renewed my passport. It's no big deal if you do run out of pages in your passport later. You can get extra visa pages glued or sewn into your USA passport at no charge at any USA passport office or USA embassy or consulate; most people can't even tell they aren't part of the original passport.

The State Department says that normal passport application processing and delivery by mail within the United States takes 3–4 weeks. It's best to allow considerably longer, at least 6–8 weeks. For an extra fee you can speed up the process by having your passport returned by Express Mail, which is fast, secure, and traceable. Registered Mail is secure but slower than regular mail; Priority

Mail is no faster than regular mail and is equally untraceable. As with any valuable item, don't send your passport by regular mail.

Though standard USA passports are valid for 10 years from the date of issue or renewal, you shouldn't wait until your passport has expired to renew it. Because many countries will not admit you unless your passport is valid at least six months beyond your intended date of departure from (not arrival in) the country, I recommend renewing your passport a year before it expires. If you've packed your passport away, aren't sure where it is, haven't looked at it in a while, or don't know exactly when it expires (USA passports used to be issued for shorter terms), get it out and check it now.

If you need any further impetus to get your passport (and visas) well in advance, consider what happened when the USA government suspended operations in November of 1995 as a result of budget disagreements between President Clinton and the Congressional majority. Issuing passports and visas was deemed "inessential," and USA passport offices, embassies, and consulates were closed well into 1996. Tens of thousands of people who had planned to go home or bring their relatives to visit over the holidays were unable to do so because they had not yet gotten their USA passports or their visitors' visas to the United States when the government shut down. Visas are solely the responsibility of the traveler, not the airlines, and those who had bought non-refundable tickets but not travel insurance were out the cost of their tickets as well. You never know what will happen. Get a passport now, while you are thinking about it.

If you are citizen of a country other than the United States— even if you are a permanent resident and have a USA green card or re-entry permit—your passport must be issued or renewed by the government of the country of which you are a citizen. USA passport offices do not provide services to holders of non-USA passports. If your non-USA passport has expired, or is about to, you will have to contact the embassy or consulate of that country to renew or extend your passport.

### Problem Countries

Restrictions are imposed by the USA government on USA citizens and their use of USA passports for travel to an ever-changing list of countries. As of 2003 these countries included Cuba, Libya, and Iraq. USA citizens who visit these countries cannot legally be denied re-entry to the United States (international law guarantees the right of return to one's home country) but can expect harassment, possible prosecution, and/or passport revocation if their passport has been stamped in any of these countries. I've known USA citizens who've traveled in Libya and Iraq, and thousands travel in Cuba, but it's important to be aware of the possible consequences before taking such a trip.

**North Korea:** The Democratic People's Republic of Korea (DPRK)—more commonly known as North Korea—is no longer on this list. The United States legalized travel by USA citizens to North Korea in early 1995, and USA passports are valid for travel to North Korea. Unfortunately, North Korea stopped issuing visas to USA tourists only a few months later.

**Iran:** There's still an embargo on importing Iranian goods into the United States, but travel by USA citizens to Iran, and spending for tourist purposes in Iran, are now legal. It may come as a surprise to some readers, but visitors from the United States to Iran since the late 1990's report a warm welcome from most people they meet in Iran.

**Cuba:** Of the problem countries, Cuba is the closest and most visited by USA citizens. Tourist travel directly from the United States to Cuba is not permitted by the USA government, and USA travel agents are forbidden to arrange flights or tours to Cuba for tourists. The only legal travel by USA citizens is for purposes other than tourism, such as for certain cultural exchange programs with special licenses from the Office of Foreign Assets Control of the U.S. Department of the Treasury (http://www.ustreas.gov/offices/enforcement/ofac) which administers USA trade embargoes. Only travelers on these licensed programs, or meeting other very limited exceptions to the embargo regulations—and not tourists—are allowed on the few direct charter flights between the United States and Cuba. All other travelers, including all tourists, must go illegally by way of a third country. It's quite easy, and relatively low-risk if you are careful. But it is illegal.

Most travelers from the United States to Cuba go by way of Canada or Mexico, although connections are also possible through various other countries in the Caribbean and Central America. Flights from Canada or Mexico to Cuba, and any desired advance hotel or tour bookings in Cuba, must be arranged through an agent in Mexico, Canada, or elsewhere, not through a USA agent. If you don't speak Spanish and have only limited time, it is probably least complicated to arrange an excursion from the United States to Cuba on a package-tour basis through Canada. You can reserve flights from Canada to Cuba in advance through a Canadian agency, with or without a package tour, and arrange flights from the United States to Canada to connect straight through to your flight to Cuba. Going via Mexico (there are flights from Mérida, Cancún, and Mexico City) may be slightly cheaper on an air-only basis, although it's harder to arrange in advance and you'll probably need to spend at least a few days in Mexico arranging onward travel to Cuba.

Don't try to check your bags through between the United States and Cuba in either direction. When returning to the United States, claim them in Canada or Mexico and remove any Cuban tags. Allow sufficient transit time to clear Canadian or Mexican arrival and departure customs. The greatest risk is that the forms for re-entry to the United States ask you to list *all* countries you've visited since leaving the USA You either have to lie (itself a crime) and say only "Canada" or "Mexico," or risk lengthy questioning, search, and possible sanctions by including Cuba on your customs declaration.

Make sure you don't have any Cuban markings in your passport or on your luggage, and don't attempt to bring any detectable Cuban goods back into the United States.

The USA government would certainly frown on your trip to Cuba, and might consider it a crime. On the other hand, there are strong arguments that the USA embargo of Cuba is illegal. For decades, USA citizens have been engaging in campaigns of civil disobedience, openly defying the USA embargo and asserting the freedom to travel to Cuba. Many others have traveled quietly to Cuba, for any of the reasons they might travel anywhere else. Only a handful of the most conspicuous and outspoken USA travelers to Cuba have been fined or prose-cuted. Although only a few USA citizens have been sanctioned, you shouldn't risk consequences that you wouldn't be willing to face.

For referrals to agents in Canada or Mexico for travel to Cuba, check local newspapers or Web sites in places outside the United States, where tours to Cuba are legal, and are widely and openly advertised. Or contact any of the offices of Cubatur, the Cuban national tourism promotion office, listed below. Canada is a cheaper call from the United States and easier to contact by phone, and the staff of the Toronto office speaks excellent English. They might not mail information to the United States (although they sometimes do if you imply that you aren't a USA citizen), and they probably won't send a reply fax to the United States. However, if you telephone them they have no way of knowing that you are calling from the United States, or are a USA citizen, unless you tell them. Obviously, Cubatur doesn't accept or agree with the USA government's attempts to interfere with travel to Cuba by USA citizens. But the USA govern-ment can make lots of trouble even for their offices in Canada and Mexico. Don't go out of your way to tell them you're a USA citizen or make things harder for them than they are already. The USA has no basis to complain if they answer questions or send literature to people they think are foreign citizens residing in the United States.

- Cubatur Toronto: +1-416-362-0700
- Cubatur Montréal: +1-514-875-8004
- Cubatur Mexico City: +52-5-574-9454
- http://www.cubatravel.cu

## Hostile Countries

Passports can present special problems if you want to visit countries hostile to each other. Some countries will not let you in if your passport shows you have previously visited certain other countries. This is most likely to be a problem if you want to visit Islamic countries after visiting Israel. Syria and the United Arab Emirates, among other countries, will not admit anyone whose passport shows evidence of a visit to Israel. This isn't true of all Muslim-majority countries, of course: exceptions include Egypt, Jordan, and Turkey, all of which now have diplomatic relations and open borders with Israel. A variety of tactics can sometimes, but not always, get around these rules and situations.

### Loose-leaf Visas and Entry/Exit Stamps

In some cases it is possible to avoid having the visa or entry and exit stamps of a pariah country appear in your passport (by "pariah" I mean a country that is disapproved of internationally; I don't mean that I agree with these judgments). Many communist and formerly communist countries, including Russia, follow the former Soviet practice of issuing visas as separate documents, which was intended to prevent the United States or other capitalist governments from blacklisting or discriminating against visitors to the Second World. Unless you need to keep the record of your visa out of your passport (for purposes of admission to a subsequent country), having as many of your visas in your passport as possible gives you the fewest vital documents to lose.

Israeli and (for USA citizens) Cuban authorities are usually willing to put entry and exit stamps on a separate paper if you make it a point to ask them, politely but clearly, each time you present your passport. Be sure you make this request, and that the border officials understand it, before you hand over your passport. You must be very careful to avoid any indication of your visit to the pariah country in your passport. If you get an entry stamp on a separate paper, keep that paper with your passport throughout your stay (you may have great trouble leaving the country without it), but remove it as soon as you leave and before showing your passport to officials of any other countries.

### Duplicate Passports

It is sometimes possible to obtain two passports from the same country, with the second passport valid only for travel to a specified country. In the United States, these passports were most often issued for travel to South Africa or Israel, because almost every other country in Africa barred entry to anyone with South African visas or passport stamps, and most Islamic countries barred entry to those with indications of having been in Israel. But it's now possible to travel in most of Africa with South African visa stamps, and in more and more places with Israeli ones. Most of the few countries that still ban those who have been to Israel, such as Saudi Arabia, are largely closed to tourists anyway, and will search you thoroughly for a duplicate passport for Israel or a loose paper with Israeli entry and exit stamps if a discontinuity in the entry and exit points in your passport (e.g., exit by land from Egypt, followed a few weeks later by entry by land to Jordan) leads them to suspect that you've been in Israel. I can think of few circumstances in which a duplicate passport would now be useful to a USA citizen and tourist, although the U.S. State Department will still consider applications for them on a case-by-case basis if you believe you need one. Check with your country's Foreign Ministry or with your country's consulate or embassy if you are abroad. If you are a USA citizen, check with one of the State Department's passport agency offices.

## Dual Citizenship

"Dual citizens" or "multiple citizens" are entitled to citizenship of more than one country. Some of these people have more than one passport from different countries. Dual or multiple citizenship is usually acquired by unusual circumstances of birth. My mother, for example, was born of USA-citizen parents on the territory of what was then the British colony of India and had become, by her 21st birthday, Pakistan. When she turned 21 she kept exclusive USA citizenship, but had she realized her options she could have chosen multiple citizenship with the UK and (by the terms of partition) either India or Pakistan. In a world of increased global mobility and intermarriage, voluntary and economically compelled migration, and involuntary displacement of peoples across national borders, multiple citizenship is more common than might be imagined.

The advantage of dual citizenship is that it can get you into more countries: if you have trouble getting a visa for a country with one of your passports, there's a chance that a different country's passport will get you in, let you stay longer, and/or generate fewer hassles. You must figure this out before you apply for a visa or try to enter the country, and you have to use the same passport to enter, travel throughout, and leave that country. Even friendly countries won't like it if you apply for a visa first with one passport and then with another, or show one passport on arrival and a different one on departure; in the worst case, you could be held on suspicion of espionage or smuggling or prosecuted for immigration fraud.

If you use one passport to visit a country that is seriously hostile to a third country from which you also hold a passport (e.g., you use a USA passport to travel to Saudi Arabia while also holding an Israeli passport) you'll at least need to hide your other passport throughout your stay. But it's safer not to bring it with you at all. Discovery of your dual citizenship, while in a hostile country, is likely to mean, at a minimum, immediate expulsion as persona non grata and a permanent ban on re-entry.

Immigrants usually lose their former citizenship (if any) when they become citizens of their adopted country. But most immigrants prefer not to give up their original citizenship, and more and more countries (including the USA) are changing their laws to allow dual and multiple citizenship.

The problem with dual citizenship for travelers is that it may be involuntary: a substantial minority of countries refuse to recognize voluntary renunciation of citizenship. If you were born outside the country of your parents' and your citizenship, there is a good chance you are considered a citizen of another country, whether or not you realize it or have ever had a passport from that government. If you return to the country of your birth or former citizenship, you run the risk that it will still consider you a citizen, even if you and your adopted country no longer do. This can lead to your not being allowed to leave without obtaining a new passport and exit permit from the country whose citizenship you have renounced or never knew you had. You may be subjected to such requirements of local law as taxes (including back income or excise taxes for the period when you were out of the country), military conscription, family law (your marriage, divorce, or adoption may not be recognized even if it is valid in the country of your other citizenship), and defamation or national-security law (i.e., you can be held to answer, as a local citizen, under local law, for critical or "antinational" statements or actions even if made while in another country on another passport).

These are particularly common problems because escaping conscription, war taxes or other taxes, arranged or child marriages or inequities of family law, and differences of opinion with the national government or national-security apparatus are all common reasons for people to have emigrated in the first place. Check local rules carefully before you visit any country with a conceivable claim on your citizenship. For USA citizens, special pitfalls affecting dual citizens and immigrants from other countries are usually covered in Consular Information Sheets. A foreign government, even that of a country in which you hold dual citizenship, can offer only very limited assistance if you are prosecuted as a local citizen.

## Passports and Documents for Families

It's sometimes possible to include dependents (minor children and, in some countries, a wife or wives) on the same passport with parent(s), guardian(s), or husband. Don't do this unless you have to. Whenever possible, each person should have a separate passport. It's especially tempting to include an infant on its mother's passport, just to have one fewer document to carry or worry about losing. But what if there's an emergency and one has to return home while the other has to stay; e.g., if one is hospitalized and can't travel, while the other must be rushed to another country for surgery or treatment? Without a separate passport, the dependent can't travel alone, no matter what happens. It's possible to get a separate USA passport for even a day-old infant, and that's the trend in other countries as well.

Involuntary and illegal international transportation and trafficking in children, international flight with children in custody disputes, transborder adoption brokering, recruitment of child prostitutes, and out-and-out child slavery—all of these problems are gaining global recognition. As with sex tourism and trafficking in women, not much is really being done—too much money is at stake for that—but to make a show of addressing these problems, some countries have imposed special documentary requirements on minors crossing their borders.

A minor child accompanied by both parents is likely to get little special scrutiny if all three (child and both accompanying parents) have the same family name. If the parents have different family names, bring a copy of the child's birth certificate. If either parent's, or the child's, name on the birth certificate doesn't match the name on the passport, bring documentation of the name change.

If only one parent or guardian will be traveling with the child, bring proof of parentage, adoption, or guardianship as well as notarized permissions from all parents or guardians not accompanying the child. If someone other than a parent or guardian is the child's companion, it is essential to get notarized permissions from both parents or any guardian(s) for the child to travel with the appointed companion.

This didn't used to be required, and it may seem excessive, but it's not. I hear regularly from grandparents and other travelers with children who are turned back at borders or refused boarding on international flights because they don't have notarized proof of permission, from both parents, to travel internationally with the children.

A power of attorney authorizing the traveling companion to make health care and emergency treatment decisions for the minor child is also a good idea for any but the shortest trip, lest vital time be lost trying to contact the parents or guardians from a remote or inaccessible place.

Unaccompanied minors may need, and should be prepared to present, proof of permission to travel from both parents or guardian(s). Airlines also have their own special requirements, varying by airline, for transporting unaccompanied minors, if they are willing to do so at all. Most airlines charge unaccompanied minors an adult fare to compensate for the additional cost of looking out for them.

## Lost or Stolen Passports

If your passport is lost or stolen, report it to the local police at the first opportunity. Get a copy of the police report, or at least all possible details about it (name and title of the officer to whom reported, where, when, file number, etc.) and a letter from the police confirming that you have reported the loss or theft of your passport. Take the police report to your country's nearest consulate or embassy. It will expedite matters greatly if you have a photocopy of the missing passport.

If you renew your passport, or get a new one for some other reason, save the old one even though it's no longer valid. An expired passport is perhaps the single most useful document with which to start—even better than your birth certificate, because it has a photo—if your personal documents are lost, stolen, or destroyed and you need to replace them all from scratch. I'd normally leave it in a safe deposit box (in case my house burns down) or with a contact back home while I'm traveling abroad. But some people bring an expired passport with them (especially if they've been traveling long enough to have accumulated more than one), packed separately from their current passport, as backup identification.

The United States has an embassy (or another office that fills its role and can issue replacement passports) in virtually every country to which it is legal for USA citizens to travel. Citizens of other countries, however, may find themselves without a passport in a country where their country does not maintain an embassy. This can be an extremely difficult situation: you may not be permitted to leave without being able to show proof of when you entered, or you may be fined on the presumption that you lost your passport to hide the fact that you overstayed your visa.

You shouldn't agree to leave without a passport until you are certain that the country to which you are departing will let you in. If it doesn't, you could be trapped in no-man's-land at the border, or the airport, in limbo without a passport and unable to go anywhere. If you are stateless, you either have to make special arrangements, confirmed in writing, that you will be allowed to proceed to some country where you have verified that your passport can be replaced, or that you have to get permission to return directly home. This is quite a drag if you're halfway around the world, in the middle of your trip. In a real emergency go to the embassy or consulate of whichever locally represented government has the closest and friendliest relationship with your country's government. At the very least they will probably help you contact your country's government to find out how you should proceed.

USA and other First World embassies overseas can be extremely suspicious of budget travelers seeking replacement of lost or stolen passports. Too many travelers who have run short of money overseas have found that passports are the most valuable and salable remaining possessions. (USA passports are the most valuable of all passports on the black market.) Expect to be questioned closely about how your passport was lost or stolen, to pay a stiff fee for its replacement, to have to execute a sworn declaration that you didn't sell it, and to have the whole replacement process drag on for several weeks. It might take only a few days, but it's likely to be that fast only if you're a middle-aged white businessman in a white shirt, dark suit, and tie.

Replacement passports issued outside the country of your citizenship are often valid for a shorter time than passports issued in your home country, although in the case of USA passports, replacements can be issued as valid for a full 10 years. Replacement passports are technically just as good as any other but are sometimes viewed with suspicion by immigration officials in subsequent countries who wonder if you destroyed your old passport to get rid of something that would have precluded entry to their country, such as a visa or entry stamp from an enemy country, or a notation that you had previously been deported, forbidden to return, or declared persona non grata. So if you get a "temporary" replacement passport issued abroad, I'd recommend renewing it (thus getting a new standard passport), as soon as it's convenient after you get back to the United States or your home country.

Once you've replaced your passport, you'll have to replace any visas that were in it, starting with your visa (and/or entry stamp or permit) to the country you are in at the time. It's harder to get visas replaced than it is to get them in the first place, and it generally involves considerable delay. It's a judgment call that you have to make before you approach each embassy or consulate of a country: you may have an easier time if you simply say you want a visa than if you say you had one but lost it or had it stolen. But if the country's record-keeping is sufficiently systematic to indicate you already had a visa, and you didn't say that, suspicions may be aroused and you may not get a new visa at all.

I'm getting ahead of myself. Before you can replace a visa, you have to get one. Just what is a visa, anyway?

## VISAS AND OTHER PERMITS

Many people are intimidated by visas. Visa rules are arbitrary and sometimes strict, and by the time you realize you've made a mistake it can be too late to do anything about it. If you plan ahead, however, visa rules will rarely prevent you from going where you want.

Visas are legal documents issued by governments, so dealing with them inevitably requires a certain familiarity with, and tolerance for, bureaucracy, legalism, and jargon. I'll try to explain as simply as possible—without sacrificing critical details—what visas are, how to find out if you need them, how to get them, and what else you need to know about entry requirements and crossing international borders.

### What's a Visa?

A visa is an authorization (usually a stamp in your passport, but sometimes a separate document or a record in an electronic database) issued by the government of the country you wish to visit, as one of the preconditions of admission to the country. However, a visa is not a guarantee of admission to any country. On arrival, you may also have to show sufficient funds to support yourself, an onward or return ticket, and/or whatever else the particular country requires. Other typical requirements are discussed later in this chapter.

USA citizens can visit many countries without visas and can obtain visas to some other countries on arrival. Citizens of some other First World countries have a pretty easy time as well. But you should check the current visa requirements of each and every country you will visit or pass through before you finalize your

**REAL LIFE**

One stateless refugee from Iran, Mr. Mehran Karimi Nasseri, lived in the transit lounge at Charles de Gaulle Airport in Paris for 11 years, from 1988 to 1999! By the time he was allowed to enter the European Union, psychologists feared that he had become so "institutionalized" to life in the airport that he would be unable to function in the world outside.

plans or purchase tickets. You may need to get a separate visa for each country; you may even find that it is not possible to stay as long as you had hoped or to go to some countries at all.

## Why Do I Need a Visa?

International law gives each country complete discretion to prohibit, restrict, or impose whatever conditions it pleases on most visits by citizens of other countries. International law recognizes a right to return to one's home, but no general right to travel or tourism. Some countries entirely prohibit tourism. Others impose all sorts of restrictions, conditions, and bureaucratic procedures to be followed by would-be visitors. Some countries have predictable biases regarding who they admit; others are inexplicably arbitrary. Count on nothing. Consular officials don't have to give you a visa, give you any reason why they won't, or answer to anyone except their home government. Treat them with the utmost respect and courtesy, no matter how well or badly you may feel they are treating you.

**REAL LIFE**

In 1993, an entire tour group from Malaysia was arrested on arrival in Boston by immigration officials who couldn't believe that they were really tourists on a US$6,000 per person around-the-world package tour, rather than illegal immigrants. (Yes, that was a very cheap price: it was a very fast tour, emphasizing opportunities for shopping.)

In the case of the United States, immigration inspectors are required to refuse entry to anyone they suspect of planning to work in or immigrate to the USA, even if that person has a valid tourist visa. Yet many visitors to the USA find that ordinary Americans are remarkably friendly to individual foreign tourists. And as a USA citizen, I've been warmly welcomed in countries where the first question asked of me was, "Why is the USA government so hostile to our country?" Don't judge any country by its government or its border guards, no matter how strong the temptation. Get a visa, if need be; go there; and experience it for yourself.

The underlying principle of most entry requirements is reciprocity. If Country L is willing to admit citizens of Country M without visas, Country M will usually do the same for citizens of Country L. If another country has made it especially difficult for citizens of your country to get permission to visit, it's probably in retaliation for the special difficulties its citizens face in visiting your country. If you want visa rules relaxed, start by lobbying your own country's government to relax its rules for foreign visitors.

If you're a USA citizen, in particular, try to keep visa hassles in perspective: I know of no country in the world whose consular, immigration, and customs authorities consistently treat would-be foreign visitors worse than does the United States. And no country has a more rigid "onward ticket" requirement for entry than the United States, has more complicated and confusing visa forms, or is less tolerant of people who don't speak, read, or write the one official language. All applicants for tourist visas to the United States are required to appear in person at a USA consulate or embassy for an interview-cum-interrogation. The majority of USA tourist visa applicants from some countries are turned down.

Under the Visa Waiver Program, citizens of certain First World countries are allowed to visit the United States without visas provided they have a return ticket and meet various other criteria. All other visitors to the United States need visas. Check with any USA embassy or consulate, or the U.S. State Department's Web site for foreign visitors to the United States at http://travel.state.gov/visa_services.html, to find out whether citizens of your country are currently included in the Visa Waiver Program and the current requirements for visa-free entry to the United States.

Fortunately for USA citizens, the allure of tourist dollars is such that few other countries treat USA citizens who want to visit half as badly as the United States treats foreign would-be tourists. (As of 2003, only two significant countries, Turkey and Brazil, were charging USA citizens the same US$100 for a tourist visa that their citizens have to pay for tourist visas to the United States.) USA citizens are the world's greatest beneficiaries of nonreciprocal visa-free entry requirements and fees.

All visa requirements are subject to change at any time without warning or notice. Don't rely on guidebooks or word-of-mouth from people who have visited a country in the past. Check the current visa requirements with your travel agent or directly with the consulates or embassies of each country you plan to visit. Don't rely on embassy or consulate Web sites: many aren't kept up to date, and it's much safer to phone or, if possible, visit a consulate or embassy in person. The more countries you plan to visit, the earlier you need to get started. List every country you will pass through, no matter how briefly. Go over the list with your travel agent, or contact each country's embassy or consulate. Find out each country's requirements, and get answers to such questions as:

- Do I need a visa?

- How long will I be allowed to stay?

- Will I need an onward or return ticket?

- Are there other restrictions on entry or travel that I should know about?

For each country that requires a visa, get a copy of the application form, all instructions, and the address and phone number of the nearest embassy or consulate that issues visas. Find out if visas for the country are stamped in passports, issued as separate documents, or issued electronically.

If you have a passport from a First World country and are planning a trip through many countries, typically most will let you in for a short visit without a visa, and the remainder will give you visas pretty much for the asking, provided you follow the proper procedures. You may find that a few places you want to go won't let you in at all, or will do so only if you comply with requirements that would be impractical or cost more than you would be willing to pay. A critical few will probably have entry requirements (such as stay limits or requirements for onward tickets or entry and exit only at certain points) that, while not prohibitive, will compel you to adjust your route, schedule, or means of transport. For this reason, even if you don't actually get your visas until you have your tickets, you should verify the entry requirements of every country you plan to visit before you schedule or pay for any tickets or tours.

## Where Do I Get a Visa?

Permission to enter any country's territory must be obtained from that country's government, or the representatives of that country's government abroad. In most countries the division of the national government that deals with the admission of foreigners is the Foreign Ministry or Ministry of Foreign Affairs; in the United States the relevant branch is the Department of State. In either case its offices outside its own territory are called embassies or consulates, which together compose a nation's diplomatic or foreign service staffed by its diplomatic corps.

An embassy is a country's primary diplomatic office in another country, usually located in the other country's capital. All embassies issue visas. (Between Commonwealth countries, all of which nominally recognize the British monarchy as their common sovereign, what would otherwise be an embassy is called a "high commisison", headed by a "high commissioner" rather than an ambassador.) A consulate general is a subsidiary office in another city, but one that usually performs almost all of the functions of an embassy, including issuing visas. A consulate is a lower-ranking office and may not issue visas; you may have to apply to a consulate general or embassy for a visa. An honorary consulate is the lowest level of diplomatic representation. An honorary consul is usually a part-time diplomat (an honorary consulate usually shares its office with the honorary consul's business or professional office) and does not ordinarily issue visas, although some do.

It's not always obvious to first-time international travelers, or to those who simply haven't needed a visa before, that your own country's government has no role whatsoever and can offer no assistance (unless you are a government official), in obtaining permission for you to visit other countries. If you are a USA citizen, don't waste time asking the U.S. State Department or a USA embassy or consulate whether you need a visa to some other country, or appealing to them for assistance if some other country turns you away. They have no authority over such matters and will not be able to help you. Because of the frequency with which it is asked such questions, the U.S. State Department has compiled a summary of other countries' entry requirements for USA citizens. It is useful but not authoritative, has no official weight, is often out of date, and should not be relied on. Specialized references for travel agents and airlines are updated more often, although they are still only informational.

### Who's in Charge?
The first step in figuring out whether you need a visa is figuring out what country exercises sovereignty or actual control over the place you want to go. If you know what country you wish to tour, it's relatively easy. But if the region you want to visit is colonized, occupied, or divided, you have to figure out who's in control of the particular part you want to visit.

Some divided regions are often mistakenly thought to be unified, independent countries. Borneo and New Guinea, for example, are islands, not countries, though many people interested in visiting them assume that such large places must be sovereign. Borneo includes all of one country (Brunei) and parts of two others (the Malaysian states of Sarawak and Sabah and the four Indonesian states of West, East, South, and Central Kalimantan). New Guinea is divided about in half between Papua New Guinea (often called PNG, which also includes New Britain and some smaller islands) and the Indonesian province of Papua (West Papua). Completely different rules apply to visitors to each part of these islands, as well as different ways of getting there and away.

Visas for possessions of the United States such as Puerto Rico, Guam, American Samoa, or the USA Virgin Islands must be obtained from USA embassies or consulates.

Visas for France's overseas territories such as French Polynesia and Kanaky (New Caledonia), and overseas departments such as French Guyana, Reunion, Guadeloupe, and Martinique, must be obtained from the embassies or consulates of France.

Visas for Northern Ireland, Bermuda, various Caribbean islands of the British West Indies and British Virgin Islands, the Falkland (Malvinas) Islands, and Gibraltar must be obtained from the embassies or consulates of the United Kingdom of Great Britain and Northern Ireland.

Visas for East Turkestan and Tibet must be obtained from China; visas for the Cook Islands (capital Rarotonga) from Aotearoa/New Zealand; and visas for Kashmir from either Pakistan or India, depending on which side of the Indo-Pak cease-fire line you want to visit. The Kashmir Valley has been annexed by India but is presently unsuitable for tourism because of fighting between Kashmiri nationalists and the Indian Army. The Karakoram Highway to and from China goes through areas administered by Pakistan pending a plebiscite throughout Kashmir—to which plebiscite India has renounced its commitment. Ladakh and Jammu are considered part of Jammu and Kashmir State and are controlled by India.

Visas for Western Sahara—if you can get them, which is quite unlikely, but which would be important to the possibility of trans-Sahara travel—would have to be obtained from the embassies or consulates of Morocco, which has occupied the entire country.

Visas for the different regions of Kurdistan must be obtained from the embassies or consulates of Turkey, Syria, Iran, or Iraq, none of which admit that such a place as Kurdistan exists, or want anyone to visit who might think or learn otherwise.

As of this writing, visas for even the self-ruled areas of Palestine must be obtained from Israel. This is quite likely to change, with the Palestinian authorities eventually obtaining some autonomous power to authorize visits. Check the most current rules before you head for this area.

Some sovereign micro-states find it too expensive to maintain their own foreign service, and contract with some other country (usually the former colonial power) to represent them and handle their diplomatic affairs abroad. For some it was actually a condition of independence and internal autonomy that they allow their former rulers to continue to handle their foreign relations.

Monaco, for example, is independent but is represented abroad, and allows entry and exit to be controlled, by France. Instances of this elsewhere are declining but still surprisingly numerous, particularly in the Caribbean (represented by various European countries) and the Pacific basin (represented in different cases by the United States, France, Australia, and Aotearoa/New Zealand, depending on which sphere of influence different island groups are or were in).

### Unrecognized or Unrepresented Countries

Certain countries present particular problems in finding embassies or consulates, for any of several reasons. Some countries either don't recognize each other (usually because of hostility) or don't maintain representation in each other's countries, usually because they can't afford to maintain embassies in low-priority countries with which they have little trade or exchange of people. In such cases you will probably need to obtain visas in some intermediate country along the way, as is discussed in "Getting Visas Outside Your Home Country," later on in this chapter.

Occasionally two countries that have broken off diplomatic relations but that still have important issues to negotiate will have their interests represented by intermediary countries. It works like this: the USA Interests Section of the Embassy of Switzerland in Cuba is technically a part of the Embassy of Switzerland but serves to represent the interests of the USA government in dealings with the government of Cuba. In actuality this is often a shell game: the USA Interests Section is likely staffed by nationals of the United States, not Switzerland (although they carry Swiss diplomatic credentials) and is located not in the same building as the Embassy of Switzerland but in a separate building, formerly the USA Embassy, which now flies the flag of Switzerland. Where one exists, an interests section may be able to issue visas, but more likely can only provide information or advice. The staff of an interests section is generally preoccupied with diplomatic business (espionage, for example) other than tourism and can offer only limited assistance to travelers.

Sometimes countries maintain representative offices other than embassies or consulates in each others' countries, at a level short of full diplomatic recognition. For example, a Vietnam liaison office opened in Washington, DC, in early 1995, several years before the United States and Vietnam exchanged ambassadors or established full diplomatic relations.

As a condition of the agreement to situate the headquarters of the United Nations (UN) in the United States, the USA is required to allow UN members, even those not recognized by the USA, to maintain missions to the UN. So the governments of Cuba, Iran, Iraq, and North Korea, which have no embassies in the United States, have offices at the UN in New York. However, these offices are allowed to remain only on condition that they confine themselves to representing their countries to and at the UN. Under pain of expulsion from the United States, they cannot issue visas, provide tourist information about their countries, or otherwise function as embassies. Don't even ask them to do such things.

Direct flights between two countries require bilateral agreements that can only be negotiated and agreed to if the countries maintain diplomatic relations. So if you are flying directly from Country A to Country B, you can more or less count on finding an embassy of B in A, and vice versa, or at least tolerance between the two governments. If you are traveling indirectly (stopping or changing planes in some other country in between) or by other means than air, check carefully in advance to be sure there is an embassy where you will need one.

### Diplomatic Pariahs

Countries considered international pariahs, for one reason or another, may be denied recognition or the exchange of ambassadors as a sign of other countries' disapproval of their existence, governments, or policies. At various times, Israel and South Africa have been major victims of such policies. Until the 1990's, both had embassies in most First World countries but few Second, Third, or Fourth World countries.

If a country doesn't recognize a government, it generally doesn't recognize passports issued by that government as valid travel documents. So Israeli and South African passports weren't valid for travel in most of the world, and citizens of those countries were only able to travel widely if they held second passports from other countries.

The situation with respect to both countries has changed markedly since the 1995 elections in South Africa and the creation of areas of limited Palestinian autonomy. Almost all countries now recognize South Africa and admit its passport holders. In addition, South Africa has opened new embassies in all the larger African capitals and many other countries. South Africans may now travel almost everywhere. Israel is still unrepresented, and Israelis are barred from travel, in many countries, including most OIC (Organization of the Islamic Conference) countries in Africa and Asia, but not nearly so many as before. Israelis (and foreigners) may now cross back and forth between Israel, Egypt, and Jordan.

Since 1994, Israelis may travel to India and Thailand, although not to most other South and Southeast Asian countries.

### Divided Countries

Some divided countries with claims on each other's territory don't recognize each other and/or break off relations with any country that recognizes the enemy.

The governments of North Korea (the Democratic People's Republic of Korea, or DPRK) and South Korea (the Republic of Korea, or ROK) each claim to aspire to the reunification of Korea—on their own terms. North Korea's two neighbors, China and Russia, and a few other socialist countries recognize both the DPRK and the ROK. Almost all other countries, including some of the non-Russian ex-Soviet states, recognize only the ROK. It is almost impossible to arrange travel to the DPRK except as a side trip from China or Russia, or to get any information about travel to the DPRK except from the Korea International Travel Company (KITC) offices in China or Russia.

China (the People's Republic of China, or PRC) claims that Taiwan Province is an integral part of its territory. Actually, Taiwan is an offshore island with a distinct people and culture that was only ruled by China for a small fraction of its long recorded history. For many years the Kuomintang Party (KMT), which ruled Taiwan after it fled the revolution in China, considered the Republic of China (ROC) to be the legitimate government of all China, including the mainland.

For now, most countries, including the United States, recognize only the PRC. Money talks, though, and the lure of Taiwanese trade and investment has enabled Taiwan to maintain functional relations, trade ministries, and visa-granting offices—embassies or consulates in everything but name and diplomatic status—even in countries that formally recognize China's claim to sovereignty over Taiwan. In the United States, visas to Taiwan are issued by a network of offices of the Coordinating Council for North American Affairs of the Republic of China on Taiwan, or CCNAA. Similar offices, with a plethora of euphemistic names, represent Taiwan in many other countries. A full list is available from any of these offices, the Taiwan Visitors Bureau, or any of the Taiwanese airlines.

Neither the PRC nor the ROC cares whether you have visited the other or have the other's visa stamps in your passport. Taiwanese are actually major investors in, and traders with, the PRC, largely by way of Hong Kong.

## Bad Neighbors

Many neighboring countries have border disputes and poor relations. Often they accuse each other of supporting "separatist" or otherwise dissident groups or movements in each others' territories, or have conflicts over transborder migration (the USA-Mexico conflicts over this are by no means unique). In such cases relations may be strained; even where borders are open, obtaining visas in a neighboring country may be harder than in some neutral country farther from the dispute.

A notable example is India and Pakistan, between which relations are as hostile as those between the United States and the USSR at the height of the Cold War. It's actually quite easy, interesting, and worthwhile for foreigners to cross back and forth between India and Pakistan. Officials and ordinary people in both countries welcome visitors from the other side. There are usually direct flights, inexpensive ones at that, between Delhi and Lahore, and sometimes between other cities. But very few locals are allowed across the Indo-Pak border. I once had lunch with a professor at one of the leading universities in the region whose life's work was the study of regional political relations, yet who had never been permitted to visit the other side.

The two countries, barely on speaking terms with each other, allow only minimal diplomatic staff in each others' countries. Periodically they aggravate the problem by expelling each others' representatives or closing consulates for spying under cover of diplomatic immunity. As a result, there are always too few visa officers, sometimes none at all, which means long waits.

If you want to visit India and Pakistan, try to get visas for both in other countries somewhere—anywhere— outside South Asia.

## Sources for Visa Information

While the government of the country you wish to visit is the ultimate arbiter of its visa requirements, it is best to review visa requirements and application procedures first with a good travel agent. You can spoil your chances of getting a visa at all if you don't know what to tell the embassy about your profession, purposes for visiting, etc. Some countries, for example, will give visas to visitors such as students, researchers, journalists, or businesspeople with professional reasons for their visits, but not to tourists. Other countries give visas to tourists but not to researchers, journalists, or people wanting to do business. It may be essential to emphasize certain things on your application for a visa to country A, and essential not to mention the same things at all when dealing with the officials of country B. A travel agent familiar with the country you wish to visit can advise you what to say and not to say (within the bounds of honesty) to maximize the chances that your requests for visas will be approved.

It can be difficult to get clear information from some consulates and embassies. Visa services may, if you ask nicely, give you a visa application form for a particular country, but they make money by submitting visa applications for you, not by giving advice on how to apply for visas on your own. Visa requirements can be imposed, removed, or changed overnight, and visa information in guidebooks or any printed reference can be out of date. Travel agencies that specialize in international travel keep files of visa applications for the more commonly visited countries that require visas. If you have trouble getting them, the agent may be able to get them for you. If you have trouble understanding the forms or instructions, a travel agent familiar with consular lingo may be able to interpret them for you. Travel agents who can't or won't give you basic advice on visa requirements either don't specialize in international travel or have cut their profit margin too thin to allow them to take the time to give good service. Travel agents can't be expected to know all the visa rules of every country or to process your visa applications for you for free. But they should be able to tell you which countries require visas, give you addresses and phone numbers of consulates, and warn you of onward ticket and other special requirements (such as needing a local sponsor or proof of prepaid accommodations or tours).

Do not rely on guidebooks as authorities on visa requirements. Good guidebooks do have helpful information on unusual rules or country peculiarities, but rules change all the time. And it is imperative to verify anything in a guidebook with a consulate, embassy, or good travel agent. If a guidebook says that citizens of your country can get visas for Country P from an embassy in City Q, but the embassy of Country P in your country says this is not possible, it's much more likely because the rules have changed than because the embassy doesn't know its own rules. It would be a serious, albeit common, mistake to set off for Q, counting on getting a visa there, unless you want to go to Q regardless of whether you can get into P.

## Visa-Free Entry and Visas on Arrival

Many countries admit USA citizens without visas, or issue visas on arrival for tourist visits of limited duration. If the embassy or consulate tells you citizens of your country don't need visas for stays of your intended duration, you can probably take what they say at face value, although you still need to find out what items—photos? cash? onward tickets?—you will need at the border to be admitted.

Entry without a visa almost always requires an onward ticket and/or proof of sufficient funds to buy one and to pay one's expenses for as long as one is authorized to stay. If you want to leave a country by land or water, or to buy your onward ticket in that country, it is more likely that you will need to get a visa. Visa-free entry permits and visas on arrival sometimes authorize travel only to certain parts of a country. If you want to travel to remote, politically sensitive, or specially protected regions, you are more likely to need a visa and even a special permit in addition to a visa.

Many people misunderstand "You *can* get a visa on arrival," or "You *can* extend your visa once you are there," as meaning, "You *should* wait to obtain your visa upon your arrival," and don't get visas in advance unless they have to. I advise exactly the reverse. It's almost always easier to get into a country if you have a visa in advance, even if visas aren't strictly required. Getting a visa in advance will save time and complications at the border, and will make you less vulnerable to demands for bribes or to changes in visa rules. It's easiest if you apply for a visa in the country where you are a citizen. If your application for a visa on arrival is, for any reason, denied, you have little recourse other than to turn back. If you apply in advance and are at first turned down, you may have time to correct the deficiency in your application and try again. But there is little reason to get a visa if you are certain that your stay will be short enough that you won't need one. Your travel agent should be able to tell you which countries will admit you without a visa, for how long, and with what restrictions.

## Visa Services and Travel Agents

It is generally better for you to obtain your own visas, rather than to have a travel agent or visa service obtain them for you, unless you don't have time to do it yourself. Travel agents and visa services generally charge about US$50 per visa over and above the fees charged by the consulate or embassy. For this fee, they will obtain the application forms and instructions, advise you on how to fill out the forms, and take or send your application and passport to the embassy or consulate and back again.

Your visa application is no more or less likely to be approved if it arrives through a travel agent or visa service than if it comes directly from you. Visa services and travel agents don't pay bribes and have no special influence on consular officials. If you call a visa service and ask them "Can you get me a visa for Country Q," they'll say, "Sure. No problem." What this means is if you satisfy all of the requirements for admission to Country Q, the visa service can get you the forms, show you how to fill them out, and send them to the embassy. If the embassy of Q has already told you a visa application can only be approved if accompanied by an invitation from a citizen of Q in good standing on a form endorsed by the Ministry of Foreign Affairs of Q, applying through a visa service will not obviate or change that requirement. Visa services have little control over the processing of your application once a consulate or embassy has your documents. Visa services can guarantee neither results nor processing time.

The biggest advantage of visa services is that all the good ones in the United States, regardless of where they are based, have representatives in Washington, DC, who can "walk" your visa applications from one embassy to another in rapid succession. This saves you the two days it would take by Express Mail or Federal Express to get your passport back from each embassy, verify the visa was issued correctly, and send your passport on to the next embassy. If you ask an embassy to send your passport directly to another embassy, you have no way to know which embassy is responsible if it is lost. You can't and shouldn't trust an embassy to return your passport to anyone but yourself, your travel agent, a very trusted friend, or a visa service. If you need many visas in a hurry, you may have no choice but to use a visa service, but this is an expensive option that can usually be avoided by planning ahead.

The only countries for which you may need special help from a travel agent are those few that require special "visa support" such as an invitation or proof of a prepaid tour (notably Russia and most formerly Soviet countries) or for those that don't issue visas in your country.

## How to Apply for Visas

The essential thing to keep in mind is that in asking for a visa you are asking for a favor, not claiming a right.

Most of today's sovereign countries were colonies when I was born in early 1960. Eighteen new countries became independent in that year alone. In Northern countries, especially those that were (or still are) imperial powers, we take sovereignty for granted—even in the United States, whose great contribution to global political thought has been its revolutionary defense of the right to wage armed anti-imperialist guerrilla warfare against the occupation forces of a foreign ruler, as articulated in a declaration of independence that is used as a model for the manifestos of many a modern national liberation movement. Formerly colonized Southern countries that have more recently won their independence, frequently at great cost, cannot be expected to be so sanguine about their sovereignty.

The right to determine who comes and goes is an essential signifier of sovereignty. To imply to embassy or consular officials that you have a right to visit their country—as you do if you ask, "How do I get a visa?" rather than, "May I please get a visa?" or "What can I do to maximize the chances that you will choose to give me a visa and let me into your country?"—is to imply that they aren't really sovereign, and that foreigners, like the former colonialists, are exempt from the obligation to comply with their local laws. In such a situation they are likely to feel that self-respect, and their duty as diplomats to uphold the national honor and preserve the perquisites of the national government, compel them to assert their sovereignty by denying your request. You may think this sounds far-fetched, but I've seen it happen. Diplomacy is often carried out by symbolism, and these are the terms in which diplomats are trained to think.

On the other hand, if you approach consular officials with genuine humility and deference, as someone who likes their country and wishes to be allowed the privilege of sharing its pleasures and learning more about it by visiting, they are usually happy to oblige. Attitude and sincerity are everything.

Most consulates give application instructions either on the visa forms or on a sheet accompanying them. Failure to follow the instructions can cause your application to be summarily rejected and the fees forfeited. You do not necessarily, or even usually, get your money back if you are refused a visa. Most consulates are reasonably accommodating and helpful, but some are minefields of bureaucracy. If the instructions aren't spelled out in the materials from the consulate, call the consulate and verify each of the items in the sections below, before you take or send in your application.

In 1998, Australia became the first country to issue "electronic travel authorizations" (ETAs) instead of stamping visas in passports. Other countries are likely to follow suit once the bugs are out of the system. The ETA application process is completely different than that described below: you apply for an ETA to Australia through your travel agent or the airline on which you will be flying to Australia, or (for an additional fee), through the Australian government's ETA Web site.

A link between the Australian government computers and the CRSs used by airlines and travel agents permits the government to verify that you have an onward flight reserved before they issue the ETA, and permits the airline to verify that you have an ETA before they let you on their plane to Australia. Insist on getting a printout of your ETA from the travel agent or airline that obtains it for you. You'll need it if the CRS, the government's computer, or the link between them is down when you are checking in for your flight to Australia. The Australian government says printouts aren't necessary, but I've had several clients who would have been refused boarding if I hadn't given them printouts of their ETAs.

### Bring Your Passport
When applying for a visa, unless told otherwise, assume you must send or bring your actual passport (not a photocopy), valid until at least six months after your proposed date of departure from the last country you intend to visit. If only a copy of your passport is required, that means the visa will be issued as a separate document, not stamped or pasted into the passport. In such cases the copy need only be of the page(s) with your name, date of birth, photograph, passport number, place of issue, and dates of issue and expiration of the passport; in recently issued USA passports these are all on one page.

Before you start getting visas for a trip, make sure you have enough blank pages for all the visas, entry stamps, and exit stamps for the entire trip. If your USA passport is already full of visas and stamps, you can have extra blank visa pages sewn in by the passport office at no charge. Citizens of some other countries may need to replace or renew their passports when the visa pages are filled. Allow two full pages for each country you plan to visit: one full page for each visa plus another page per country for entry, exit, and customs stamps. You probably won't need that many pages, but it can help you avoid the hassle of applying for (and paying for) a new visa because it was in a passport that filled up and had to be replaced.

The longer the trip, the more pages you will need for re-entry permits, visas, visa extensions, or additional entry and exit stamps for multiple or extended visits or additional countries you hadn't included in your original plans. If it looks like you might run out of passport pages before you get home, check with one of your country's embassies or consulates at the next possible opportunity—especially if your country has few consulates or embassies in the region—to see about having pages added or getting your passport renewed.

## Application Forms

Most countries allow you to submit photocopies of their forms; however, each must be signed with an original signature in ink. A few countries accept applications only on their original forms. A faxed or photocopied signature on the form(s) is never acceptable. If you will be applying for someone else (e.g., if one of you is going to a consulate or embassy to get visas for several traveling companions), get the forms and have your traveling companion(s) sign them in advance. If you aren't sure how to fill out some parts of the form, have them sign several blank or partially completed forms (three or four copies will generally suffice) so that you will be able to submit the applications once you find out what to put in the remaining blanks. You will not be able to apply for a visa for someone else (e.g., someone out of town or in another country) without an original signature on one or more application forms.

Standard questions on visa forms include the following:

- current name

- name at birth (if different) or any other names ever used

- names of parents

- marital status

- name of spouse

- date and place of birth

- current citizenship/nationality ("Citizenship" and "nationality" are often distinct terms and can have peculiar local meanings: "nationality" is often used to distinguish first-and second-class citizens under local law; foreigners can usually get away with giving the name of the country that issued the passport in response to both questions; e.g., I always put "USA" in both places on forms, and have never had a problem)

- citizenship/nationality at birth (same issues as above)

- passport number (You'll memorize this before long, because it's required on hotel registration forms in most countries.)

- date and place of issue of passport (You'll memorize this too)

- home and/or business addresses (If only one is required, use whichever sounds more respectable.)

- occupation (This is sometimes a tricky question: certain occupations, varying from country to country, may be disfavored or suspect; "journalist" and "missionary" are usually bad; "student" can be good or bad; "teacher" is usually much better than "student.")

- name and address of employer (Long-term travelers don't generally have a bona-fide current employer, but "unemployed" or "traveler" are unacceptable answers and "self-employed" is often suspect. Officials rarely if ever check, so if you quit your job to travel you can probably get away with giving your previous employer; if freelance, give your "doing business as" name [e.g., "John Doe Consulting"], or a current or recent client; if you are or recently were a student, list the school as employer.)

- religion (If you are even nominally religious, you should be honest but no more specific than necessary; e.g., write "Christian" rather than "Protestant" or any specific sect or denomination.  Individual Jews are generally welcomed in even the most Islamic and anti-Zionist countries as long as they aren't Israeli citizens and don't have Israeli stamps in their passports. Citizens of Islamic countries, whether or not they are personally Muslim, are subject to harassment throughout the Christian and Jewish First World no matter what their personal beliefs, so they might as well be honest on the forms. Atheists—regarded as infidels everywhere outside the Second World, and widely persecuted—may wish to consider remaining closeted and allow themselves to be taken for Christian, as I often do; Pagans, Wiccans, and adherents of "new religions" are likely to be misunderstood and/or regarded as heretics or would-be proselytizers, and may wish to do likewise. Missionaries—generally disfavored as agents of cultural imperialism—and religious pilgrims—sometimes given the best treatment, sometimes the worst, depending on the relationship between the government and the religion in question—should check with their religious authorities for possible special procedures before they apply.)

- whether you have previously visited the country to which you are applying

- dates of any (or the most recent) prior visit(s)

- whether you have ever previously had a visa application rejected, been denied entry, or been deported or declared persona non grata in this country (Occasionally they ask if you've been kicked out of any country, on the theory that if somebody else didn't want you, they probably don't want you either.)

- names(s) of any relatives or friends you intend to visit (It's best to leave this blank unless local sponsorship is required, to avoid possible hassles for you or local contacts.)

- purpose of visit ("Tourism" is generally acceptable and sufficient.)

- desired duration of visit (Err on the high side.)

• desired number of entries (Err on the high side. If possible, ask for "multiple-entry" rather than a fixed number of entries.)

• intended date of arrival (Most visas don't specify an exact date, so this isn't usually critical; check in advance if you have any doubt.)

• intended place(s) of entry and exit (Find out in advance if you will be held to these; usually you won't but sometimes you will, although they can often be changed later, for a price.)

• place(s) you intend to visit (Again, find out in advance if these will actually be entered on your visa; they usually won't.)

• "sponsor" or "person or organization to be visited" (If you see this question, get professional advice from a travel agent or visa service before you submit the application.)

Every country has a few other unique questions of its own. I continue to be amazed at the variety of things governments consider relevant to their decisions of whom to admit.

### Photographs

Most countries require two or three photos of each visa applicant. Visa and passport photos are of standard size worldwide, although local identity cards in some countries use photos of other sizes. Most countries accept black-and-white photos, which are sometimes cheaper. Image quality isn't critical. Technically they're not quite the official size that most countries specify, but some people get by with 35mm contact prints. Color inkjet or laser prints are usually unacceptable, unless they are so high quality as to be mistaken for photographic prints. Visa photos are almost always cheaper in quantity, so always order a few extra as on any extended trip you are likely to need photos for visas and other special travel permits obtained en route. All kinds of documents require visa photos, often multiple photos, from visas themselves to visa extensions, trekking permits, permits for special areas, liquor permits (for tourists in Islamic countries), scuba diving certifications, and public transit passes.

Be very careful of how you look in your visa photos, as it may determine where you are allowed to go. Because you aren't likely to look your best while traveling, a good strategy is to bring a black-and-white negative you are happy with and get prints made cheaply in some country where they are cheap, 10 or 20 at a time. Most countries specify that visa photos must have been taken within six months or a year, but unless your appearance has changed or the photos are dated this requirement is difficult to enforce. Unless told otherwise, sign each photo on the back in ink and staple them to a top corner of the visa form(s) to keep them from being separated from your application.

## Length of Stay and Number of Visits

Before you apply for a visa, you need to decide approximately how soon you will be entering the country in question, how long you want to stay, and whether you will enter the country more than once. Keep in mind that every time you so much as leave the transit area of an airport in a country—even to spend a single night en route between other countries—you will have to go through customs and immigration. If you take a side trip from one country to another country and back to the first, you will need a double-entry visa (or a second visa) to re-enter the first country. Review your planned itinerary carefully, counting every entry and how long you will be in each country, to determine what visas you will need. It's surprisingly easy to overlook an extra entry "in transit" or a small side trip to a neighboring country. Be sure that the visas you want are actually available for the countries you wish to visit (some countries simply don't give multiple-entry or long-stay visas) before you commit yourself to an itinerary that will require them.

If you aren't sure whether you will need a longer-than-minimum stay or multiple-entry visa, and the cost isn't absolutely prohibitive, get a visa for the longest stay and largest number of entries you might conceivably want. Contrary to what some people will tell you, it is almost always easier to get a long-stay multiple-entry visa in advance, preferably before you leave your home country, than to get separate visas for each entry or to extend your visa once you've entered on a short-stay or single-entry visa.

> For trekkers in Nepal, unlike visitors to most countries, there is no advantage to getting a visa in advance. Even with a visa in advance, you still need to get a trekking permit after you arrive in the country and arrange your trek.

Permits to enter without a visa, or visas issued at the border, are often issued with the condition that they cannot be extended or renewed. Visa extensions and renewals are a time-consuming hassle at best, aren't always possible (they are especially difficult for visitors to the United States), generally entail substantial fees (and sometimes bribes), and should be a last resort where long-stay visas can't be obtained in advance at any price, or where your plans change drastically en route.

In many countries applicants for visa extensions or renewals are presumed to be seeking illegal employment. If you are even considering the possibility of under-the-table employment or long-term residence, get the longest-duration multiple-entry tourist visa possible, preferably before you leave your home country, even if the price seems unpleasantly high. If you actually find a job, especially if as a tourist you are allowed only a few months entry at a time, and have to leave the country and come back in at regular intervals, you'll be glad you got a multiple-entry visa. You'll avoid getting quizzed each time as to why you keep coming and going and if you are really touring.

Overstaying a visa is a serious offense. You have broken the law, you want to leave, but both the government of the country you are in and the individual officials with whom you are dealing have you at their mercy. You can usually get out by paying a fine, but the fines are set high enough to be a significant deterrent and source of revenue for the government. Fines of US$20–50 per person per day that you overstay your visa are common, although much higher fines are possible. Demonstrate that you have that much money by paying the fine, and the border guards are likely to want a comparable amount in bribes for themselves as well. Overstaying a visa to the United States will get you entered into the computerized database of undesirables and prevented from coming back to the USA for an especially long time.

It's essential to understand clearly just what the validity dates of your visa mean, so that you don't get visas too far in advance, for too short a stay, or for the wrong dates. The most common reason to have to get visas along the way is that you are traveling for a long enough time that visas issued before your departure would expire before you got through some country. Every country does it a little differently, but most visas follow one of the following three patterns. Regardless of which system is used, you will probably be asked your intended arrival and departure dates on the visa forms. You should figure out which system is used before you fill out the forms.

**Fixed Dates:** The most restrictive countries (including as of this writing Russia, most former Soviet republics, Saudi Arabia, and Vietnam) issue visas for a specific range of dates. They may have an overall stay limit (for Vietnam, it's 30 days) or they may be limited only by the range of dates for which you have booked a tour, prepaid accommodations, or been invited by your local sponsor. Unless you need every day of the maximum visa duration, give an arrival date a few days earlier than you intend and a departure date a few days, even a week, after you intend. When arranging an invitation or sponsorship, try to get one that covers at least a week on either side of your intended stay.

You can be admitted to the country later than the arrival date on your visa, and you can leave earlier than the specified departure date, but you cannot arrive any earlier or leave any later. If you show up at a land border early, you will be turned away. If you manage to get an airline to carry you, and arrive by air the day before your visa comes into effect, you will be detained in limbo at the airport until your visa becomes valid and you can proceed through immigration. (This happened to one of my clients whose flight to Russia was early, arriving before midnight instead of after.)

Changing the dates on a fixed-date visa, once it is issued, generally requires paying a new visa fee. If the original visa required proof of reservations or sponsorship, changing the dates will require similar proof for the desired new dates. The positive aspect of fixed-date visas is that there is generally no limit to how far in advance they can be issued, as long as you know the exact dates you intend to visit.

**Validity from Date of Issue:** Some visas are valid for a specified period beginning from the date of issue of the visa. China is the major example: standard visas to the PRC are valid 90 days from the date of issue, and can't be extended. This means that you must not merely have arrived but have left China within 90 days after you get your visa. If you want to maximize the length of your stay in China, you need to get your visa as close as possible to the date you arrive in China. Many people get visas for the rest of China in Hong Kong for this reason. However, Chinese visas are no cheaper or easier to get in Hong Kong. It's not necessary to go through Hong Kong to get to many other places in China. Going from Europe or North America to Beijing or elsewhere in northern China via Hong Kong is particularly indirect. If you are going directly to China, it makes more sense to get your visa for China in your home country just before you leave. At the moment, China is eager to attract USA and other foreign visitors to improve its image, and San Francisco is the easiest place in the world to get a Chinese visa. In Hong Kong, you'll usually have to prepay for at least a minimal tour or reserve a hotel for the first couple of nights to get a visa. In the United States, no such documentation is required. Check with the consulate or embassy of the PRC for current rules.

**Validity from Dates of Issue and Arrival:** Most visas have two distinct ranges of validity dates: an overall validity period, beginning from the date of issue of the visa, and a stay limitation, beginning from the date of arrival. A typical visa might read, "Valid for one entry, within six months from [date of issue], duration of visit not to exceed 60 days." Or, "Valid for multiple entries, within five years of [date of issue], duration of each visit to be determined at the point of arrival."

The language is sometimes ambiguous. In the first example above, must you be out of the country within six months of getting the visa? Or might you enter the country five and a half months after getting the visa, and not leave until 60 days later, seven and a half months after getting your visa? Different countries use the same language and mean different things. Remember, they are the ones who decide what their rules mean and enforce them. What you think your visa "ought" to mean is quite irrelevant. If you have any doubt, ask. If there's a language problem communicating with the consular officials, draw them a picture: a map of their country, stick figures of you entering and leaving, and calendars showing the dates you plan to come and go.

### Fees

Visa fees and acceptable forms of payment vary widely. Almost all embassies and consulates accept certified or cashier's checks and postal money orders. Some also accept cash (exact change only); some accept personal checks. Some accept neither, some accept both. Most will accept traveler's checks, but only if you have checks for the exact amount due. I know of no embassy or consulate that accepts any credit or charge card. In other countries, especially those with currencies that aren't freely convertible, some consulates and embassies will only accept payment in USA dollars or other "hard" currency, not in local currency.

### Processing Time

Some consulates take three weeks to process routine visas and charge as much as US$100 extra per visa for same-day service, if they are willing to provide it at all. Others routinely issue visas on the spot while you wait, at no additional charge. Consulates and embassies observe the holidays both of their home countries and of their host countries. Many accept visa applications only during a few hours of the day, and/or require that applications be submitted by a certain time (typically in the morning) if visas are to be picked up the same day (typically late in the afternoon). Call before going to any consulate or embassy to verify it will be open at that time on that day.

### Proof of Onward or Return Passage

In order to avoid having to bear the cost of deporting foreigners who run out of money, many countries (including the United States) require that tourists present proof that they have tickets out of the country before they are allowed into the country. Sometimes this proof is required before a visa will be issued, sometimes not until you arrive at the airport or the border. You may not even be allowed to board a flight bound for such a country without showing an onward ticket to the airline on which you will fly into the country; many countries (including the United States) have shifted the burden of enforcing onward-ticket and other immigration rules onto the airlines.

For each passenger an airline transports to the USA who is denied entry to the USA for any reason, the airline must pay an administrative fine to the USA government of US$3,000. The airline is also responsible for the costs of deportation (i.e., the airline must transport the person back or pay another airline to do so) and for the costs of detainment pending deportation if the person contests deportation. A good-faith effort to verify that passengers have proper documents for admission to the United States is not sufficient grounds for waiver or reduction of the fine or responsibility for costs. Millions of dollars in fines are levied every year. With this kind of money at stake, airlines can't afford to take risks. Unless they are certain that you will be admitted, they will deny you boarding. It doesn't matter that had you gotten to the country you might have been able to persuade the immigration officer that you had enough money to pay for a ticket out, or would be leaving by a route for which tickets could only be purchased in-country.

Many people are tempted not to take onward-ticket requirements seriously because they heard from someone who got in without showing an onward ticket. But often the source entered by land or water, not by air. Or the source entered by air and didn't realize that the airline clerk at check-in looked at the next coupon—the ticket out—as well as the ticket in, and that the immigration officer didn't need to ask for or look at onward or return tickets because the airline had already done it.

Airlines have no discretion to waive onward-ticket requirements. They have no reason to anyway: if you have to buy an onward or return ticket on the spot, before you can board your flight, the airline with whom you are trying to check in is the one from which you will most likely buy it. Your plea to an airline to transport you to a country with an onward ticket requirement will fall on deaf ears.

If you do somehow get to such a country without an onward or return ticket, you will have to buy a full-fare ticket out of the country, on the spot, before you will be allowed to clear arrival customs and immigration. If you arrive at a land border where there is no ticket office, you will be turned back.

Some countries will accept a letter from a travel agent certifying that you have paid for your tickets, even if you have not yet received them, as sufficient proof of onward or return transportation for a visa. They will still check your actual tickets on arrival; don't think that you are home free when you get a visa. Others will accept proof of sufficient funds to pay your way out, usually shown by a current bank statement or, on arrival, by a sufficient quantity of cash or traveler's checks, in lieu of an actual ticket out. Some countries enforce their "ticket out" requirements more strictly than others, but don't count on being able to break the rules. You are slightly more likely to be admitted without an onward ticket if you arrive by land or water, rather than by air. A roundtrip bus, train, or ferry ticket, even if nonrefundable, is also apt to be less expensive than an air ticket out.

Fellow travelers will try to tell you lots of tricks for avoiding onward-ticket requirements. Put them out of your mind. Governments call these scams "immigration fraud," and they consider them serious crimes. The way to deal with onward-ticket requirements is to comply with them by having an onward ticket before you board a bus, train, plane, or ferry bound for a country with such a requirement.

If you can't get the ticket you actually plan to use in advance (most often because tickets for surface transportation are only available locally, or perhaps because you intend to walk, bicycle, or hitchhike), get another ticket that will satisfy the immigration requirements and that you can refund later. The easiest ticket to refund in another country is an airline ticket purchased with a credit card directly from a major airline with offices in many countries. A fully refundable paper ticket purchased directly from the airline is the most expensive kind: you may have to tie up hundreds of dollars, and a refund may still take months. But given time, you can get your money back. Tickets purchased from a travel agency may only be refundable through that agency—no good once you are in another country; and tickets purchased by cash or check may be refundable only in the local currency of the country of purchase—no good if it's not freely convertible.

### Proof of Sufficient Funds

Occasionally you'll be required to provide proof that you have enough money to support yourself during your stay. If you're a First Worlder planning to spend as much in a month in a Southern country as the average annual income of its citizens, it may seem absurd that its government is worried that you might become a burden on its economy, or take jobs away from locals who are paid US$1 a day or less. It's not as far-fetched or unreasonable as you may think. For one thing, far too many thoughtless people from rich countries actually do run out of money, impose themselves on the hospitality of their hosts, and expect someone else to bail them out and/or pay their way home. Poor countries can't afford to subsidize rich but imprudent travelers who take their First World privilege so much for granted that they expect not to have to suffer the consequences if they run out of money; their attitude is deeply offensive to locals and is reminiscent of the arrogance, assumption of privilege, and appropriation of local resources of the former colonial masters. Let me put it more bluntly: if you expect local people to take care of you if you run out of money, you have the attitude of an imperialist and can expect to be treated like one.

In addition, there is an element of reciprocity in many immigration requirements. Southerners who seek to visit the North, no matter how rich they are and how secure their jobs at home, are invariably suspected of intending to immigrate permanently, to work illegally (taking jobs away from locals, even if the only jobs open to undocumented immigrants are ones most locals don't want or wouldn't take for the low pay), and/or to impose themselves on the local welfare system. Southerners seeking to spend even one night in Western Europe in transit between, say, Africa and the Americas are often required to have proof of fully prepaid hotel reservations and onward tickets before they can get the required transit visa. One of the few ways Southern governments have to educate Northerners about how they treat would-be visitors is to give them a small taste of these rules when they visit the South.

Proof of sufficient funds is sometimes an alternative to proof of onward tickets, and where possible is usually preferable, enabling you to get your visa before you actually have your tickets and giving you more flexibility in your onward route. For visa applications, sufficient funds are usually demonstrated by a bank statement. On arrival, as discussed later on under "Border Formalities," you'll need hard cash or traveler's checks.

### Invitations, Sponsorship, and Tour Requirements

An invitation to a particular country or proof you have reserved or paid for tours or accommodations are uncommon requirements, but are by no means unheard of. In most cases it is possible to arrange for an invitation or for prepaid tours or accommodations, but the cost may be beyond your budget. This is especially likely to be true for countries such as Bhutan where all tourist services must be reserved through a single (monopolistic and overpriced) government tourist agency, or where the government allows only a limited quota of tourists and auctions the visa allotments to the highest-bidding tour operators. You may decide not to go to these countries at all, or to spend much less time in them than you had hoped. This is one of the most important reasons to advise your travel agent of every country you plan to visit (whether or not it is included in your air itinerary) and to check all visa requirements well before you buy your tickets or commit yourself to travel in particular places.

Countries such as these are among the few places where guidebooks (at least those for independent travelers) can really be helpful in getting visas. Guides for independent travelers often give advice on loopholes in sponsorship requirements, which are the cheapest tours and accommodations that satisfy prepayment requirements, and leads for finding sponsorships or invitations for sale. Just be sure to verify anything in a guidebook with a travel agent experienced with the country or with the country's embassy or consulate.

Travel agents and tour companies can sometimes arrange invitations or sponsorship without your having to actually book a tour, or for a longer period of time than that of a tour. Some companies sell invitations. Booking a two-day tour or a couple of nights in a sufficiently expensive hotel, in some cases, will suffice to get you an invitation for a week or two. Just because a country doesn't give visas to "tourists" doesn't mean tourists can't get visas. In several countries the norm is for hotels or tour companies to invite their guests and clients for "business" visits, their business being, I suppose, spending money on travel. Most tourists in the United Arab Emirates and some other Gulf states are sponsored by the hotels where they stay. Most independent travelers in Russia have business visas obtained in this way; even guests of the hostels in Moscow and St. Petersburg are considered business, not tourist, visitors.

### Immunization, Health, or Medical Certificates

Very few immunizations are required by governments anymore for purely tourist visits. Health, not the law, is the main factor in deciding which immunizations you need. A sizable number of countries, however, require some sort of certification of acceptable health from applicants for long-stay visas, especially those seeking residency or employment visas.

The most problematic of medical requirements is that visa applicants present proof of a recent negative AIDS test. Only a few countries require AIDS tests of all foreign visitors. But many countries require testing of all long-term visitors and bar even short-term visitors who volunteer that they are HIV-positive. You should ask the consulate or embassy of any place you plan to spend a long time or seek work or residency whether it requires AIDS testing.

### Spending or Moneychanging Requirements

Another way of keeping out the riffraff and boosting the contribution tourists make to the national economy is to require that tourists change a certain amount of money into local currency upon arrival. As of 2003, countries with such requirements include Iran and Myanmar/Burma. Sometimes this is a flat amount per person; more often it is a per diem amount for each day one's visa or entry permit is to be valid. Either way, the exchange is likely to be at an artificially low rate, and one is forbidden to exchange the local currency back into any other currency.

About all you can do is to change the excess local currency on the black market, but it may be worth so little (because of the rate at which you were forced to buy it) that it's not worth the risk of getting caught (or entrapped) by black marketeers. When you have to change money, don't count on getting any of it back. This sort of requirement is almost never mentioned on visa forms. If you don't ask, and it wasn't in effect when your guidebook was researched, you won't find out about it until you get to the border, or have already gotten off the plane. If you don't have US$20–50 per day (typical amounts required), or don't want to spend that much, you'll be stuck. So make it a point to ask when you apply for a visa if there are any currency-exchange requirements upon entry.

### Entry Points, Exit Points, and Routes

Mere existence of a land border between two countries is no guarantee of the existence of a border crossing. There are no permitted crossing points, for example, anywhere on the land borders between India and China, or India and Myanmar/Burma. Moreover, many border crossings are open to locals but not to foreigners or tourists. Tourist visas to many countries frequently require entry and/or exit only by air, sometimes only at a single airport. Do not assume just because there is a border, or even because a map shows a road or railroad across it or a customs and immigration post at it, that you as a foreign tourist will necessarily be able to cross the border at that point. Sometimes you must specify your intended points of entry and exit on your visa application. Sometimes you can change them later, sometimes not.

### Internal Travel Restrictions or Permits

Parts of some countries are entirely closed to tourists. In most cases, permits for visits to restricted areas, if they are obtainable at all, can be obtained only after you arrive in the country. Issuance and denial of these permits is highly arbitrary and often at the discretion of local officials. As of 2003, commonly visited Asian countries with restricted areas that are entirely off-limits to tourists, or that require special permits, are China (Tibet and parts of East Turkestan), India (parts of Kashmir and the northeast), Pakistan (parts of Kashmir, the Northwest Frontier Province, and the Northern Areas), Indonesia (parts of Papua, Borneo, and Timor), Malaysia (parts of Borneo), and Nepal (most trekking areas).

A visa or entry permit is generally valid throughout the country, but there are a few exceptions. Military reservations, war zones, and areas near borders with hostile neighbors are usually off-limits to all civilians. "Politically sensitive" or "minority" areas of the country are often closed to tourists, even those with visas to visit the country at large. These terms are usually euphemisms for areas where the authority, jurisdiction, or legitimacy of the central government is not accepted by the local population, and/or where dissent is being repressed. Frequently the "protection" of minority, indigenous, or tribal peoples is used by central governments with less-than-benign motives as an excuse to prevent contact with foreigners.

In a few countries, your visa lists, and is only valid in, specific cities, districts, or provinces. Countries such as this tend to be countries requiring prearranged tours or sponsorship, and the city list on such a visa is limited to those cities specified both on your invitation and your visa application. This makes it essential to discover any such requirements before you request an invitation, much less apply for a visa. If an invitation is required, check whether is must specify a list of places to be visited, or if your visa will be valid only for those places.

***Getting Internal Travel Permits:*** There is no standardization in where or how to get permits for restricted areas once you are in a country. Sometimes you have to get them in the national capital, even if the region you want to visit is thousands of kilometers away. Sometimes you have to get them in the provincial or district capital or in the nearest village. Access to restricted areas is usually controlled by police, soldiers, or some sort of ministry of internal affairs. By and large, these are not the friendliest people to deal with. At best you are at the mercy of their discretion, and they know it. At worst, they are supposed to turn you down, and you can only go where you want by persuading them to break the rules (and perhaps risk their jobs and careers). They will test your humility, patience, and knowledge of how to adapt and get things done in the local culture.

Guidebooks often have useful information on where and how to apply for permits to restricted areas. They can be helpful ("The office is behind an unmarked door on the left, opposite the first alley in from the square . . ."), but offices move, rules change, and even a new guidebook may already be out of date. Try to check with other travelers who have recently gotten the permit you want before trying to get one yourself, or before setting off for some place where you hope to be able get one. It may help to do some other business in the area first to learn how to conduct yourself properly. Plan your approach carefully, and be on your best behavior. Remember, they are in charge. You have no legal right to travel anywhere. Demands will get you nowhere. Have a good reason to offer for your request: idle curiosity is not likely to suffice, nor is simply "tourism." Your best chances lie in establishing a genuine human rapport with the permit-issuers, on their terms. Offering bribes, unless they are requested as "fees," is more likely to harm than help.

If restrictions are attached to a permit, don't jeopardize the chances for future travelers to get permits by breaking the rules of yours. If a special permit is required, you can take it for granted you'll be the object of special scrutiny while in the restricted area. Some permits require you to hire an approved guide or military escort or to travel in a certain manner. Our permit to visit the Khyber Pass, between Afghanistan and Pakistan, required us to hire a private car at our own expense, but which came with our personal soldier to ride shotgun, gratis. We were the only ones to receive permits on a day when a long line of other tourists, who hadn't observed the local dress code or proprieties, were being turned down. On the drive, there wasn't any real danger, and the soldier had only a carbine while the tribesmen, who materialized from the rocky surroundings when the car overheated, all had Kalashnikov assault rifles. But his presence was a signal to people in the tribal areas around the pass that we were under the protection of the central government, and his bayonet came in handy to unjam the sticky hood latch. We were advised when we got the permit to tip both soldier and driver at the end of the day, which we did, happily.

### Sending Visa Applications

The only safe ways to send a passport or to have it returned are by personal or messenger delivery, Express Mail, FedEx, or similar traceable delivery services. It is not safe to send your passport by regular or certified USA Mail. Certified USA Mail is not expedited and can neither be insured nor be traced if lost. Registered USA Mail is handled separately and must be signed for by each postal employee who handles it; it's is extremely secure but extremely slow. Registered mail between the California and Washington, DC, can take three weeks or more each way.

If you can, apply in person. Get a receipt for your passport when you drop it off, and bring the receipt with you when you pick up your visa. If you can't apply in person, I recommend sending your visa application by Express Mail or FedEx and enclosing a prepaid Express Mail or FedEx return envelope and completed airbill. You can put an Express Mail stamp on the return envelope or have the return FedEx shipping charged to your credit card. Keep a record of both the shipping and return airbill numbers so you can have the shipment traced if the embassy or consulate doesn't receive your passport, or if you don't receive it when you expected.

Call the embassy or consulate the day it should have received your application (the next business day if you sent it by overnight express) to confirm receipt and to verify what day to expect it back. If someone says it wasn't received, have it traced. If it was delivered, tracing will give you the name of the person at the consulate who signed for it, and you can call back and ask for the person by name. If you don't receive your visa and passport the day you expected, call again to confirm they were sent back to you. If the embassy or consulate says they were sent, have the return airbill number traced. If, after tracing, the embassy or consulate and the Postal Service or FedEx disagree as to whether your passport was received or sent back, trust the Postal Service or FedEx. Most embassies and consulates are reliable, but passports can still get lost. Don't let your passport out of your hands if you are leaving so soon that you won't have time to replace it if it is lost. Finally, proofread each visa carefully as soon as you receive it, as mistakes (including misreading applicants' handwriting on the visa forms) are surprisingly common. If the visa isn't in a language you can read, try to find someone who can read and check it for you.

All this may sound intimidating, but it shouldn't be. I have yet to see a foreign visa application as confusing as a USA tax return, and most are much simpler. Most USA travelers have never had a visa application turned down, or been turned back at a border. Plan ahead, fill out the forms, follow the rules, be patient, and soon you'll be on your way.

## Visas for Citizens of Different Countries

Any or all of the visa rules may be different for citizens of different countries. Always inform your travel agent and any visa services, embassies, or consulates you speak with of your citizenship, or they are likely to give you the wrong information about visa requirements, fees, and rules. In general, they will assume you are a citizen of whatever country you are in, but you can't count on that any more than you can count on them to guess correctly what passport you hold if you don't tell them.

Make sure you know what passport each of your intended traveling companions is holding. Longtime USA or Western European residents often have been unable or have not wished to change their citizenship. People you assume hold USA passports may well be permanent resident aliens who remain citizens of and travel on passports from their homelands. You may have to adjust your plans to accommodate the restrictions placed on your traveling companions.

Rumors, reports from other travelers, or even printed advisories about visa and entry requirements are worse than useless unless they specify the citizenship of those to whom they apply. (It's especially unfortunate, given the global reach of the Internet, how often Internet inquiries or postings about visa requirements fail to mention travelers' nationalities.) Your friend, or your friend's friend, who had no trouble getting a visa to such-and-such a place, may not have had the same passport as you. One of the most common reasons for visa problems is relying on advice from people who turn out to be citizens of a country that is subject to different rules of admission.

In general, citizens of First World countries are able to visit many countries without visas and get tourist visas to all but a few of the rest without undue difficulty. Citizens of Southern countries—Central and South Americans, Asians except Japanese, and especially Africans —need visas to almost everywhere, and are likely to require prepaid accommodations to visit most Northern countries. You may be a doctor, banker, engineer, USA resident and green-card holder, or the spouse of a USA citizen, but if you're from the global South, most Northern visa officers are still likely to assume by your passport (and perhaps your skin color) that you are just another would-be illegal immigrant. That was true even before 11 September 2001. Since then, Southerners visiting the North are likely to be treated as suspected terrorists as well, especially in the USA. Citizens of Second World countries are increasingly treated like Southerners as well when they try to visit the First World.

Note particularly that your residency in a country or your relationship to a citizen of that country is relevant only to your entry into that country and no other. Given the difficulty of obtaining a USA green card (permanent residency certificate and work permit) many card holders think their travel difficulties to other countries are over. Not so at all. A USA green card, in conjunction with your passport, will help you return to the United States. It is of no value whatsoever in seeking to enter or leave any other country, and exempts you from none of the visa or other requirements normally applicable to people who hold whatever passport you hold.

## Stateless People

If you are a "stateless person"—that is, you are not a citizen of any country, which probably means you have no passport at all—it should be the first thing you tell your travel agent. You will find it extremely difficult to cross any international boundaries and are likely to be harassed by immigration officials everywhere. Even if you have a visa for your destination, it will be exceedingly difficult to pass through anywhere else on the way there. In addition, you may need transit visas in advance, even for places where you want to change planes without leaving the airport.

This might seem a minor matter. Why would stateless people want to travel, anyway? The problem is that stateless people are especially likely to want to travel across national boundaries. Some countries, such as Saudi Arabia, Kuwait, and the United Arab Emirates, practice forms of apartheid under which only descendants of certain ethnic and/or racial groups are eligible for citizenship even if they are born in the country. A large proportion of those classified as foreigners in such countries are actually the native-born children of guest workers, who have never lived or qualified for citizenship anywhere outside the country of their birth and are therefore stateless. Larger numbers of stateless people, however, are refugees and forcibly displaced people. Refugees get little choice in where they go. Frequently they have lived and made friends in several countries, and their relatives often end up in different countries. These stateless people are often very eager to visit their friends and family members around the world, and/or to revisit their homeland. Practically speaking, this is close to impossible unless or until they acquire citizenship somewhere. Most stateless people who live legally in the United States are refugees with re-entry permits issued by the USA Re-entry permits are accepted in lieu of passports for entry to the United States, but they are not passports. No other country is required to honor them or admit their bearers, and most don't.

No country wants to give refugees or foreigners greater privileges than its own citizens, so no one is likely to create or recognize a "refugee passport." No solution seems possible, short of an anarchist system in which sovereignty, citizenship, and passports are all eliminated. Pretty unlikely.

## Getting Visas Outside Your Home Country

If you will be traveling only for a few months, you may be able to get all the visas you'll need before leaving your home country. Do so if you can. You won't save money or time by getting your visas outside your home country. Visa fees are generally set by nationality, so you will have to pay the same amount for a visa to a given country no matter where in the world you apply. Better to spend a little time and a few dollars on postage and phone calls in your home country, where you know how things are done and foreign consular staff speak your language, than to spend days of your vacation trying to find consulates and figure out procedures in a foreign city where the instructions may all be printed for local citizens in their national language, where no one may speak your language, and where you may have to leave your passport at each consulate or embassy for several days. Embassy and consular officials are selected for their language ability in the (or a) local language; in another country, you have no right to expect them to speak or print forms in your language and have no cause to complain if you can't speak or read the language of whatever country you are in. Document checks are routine in most of the world: are you prepared to explain to the police who stop you, in a language they will understand, that you have no identity papers this week because you left your passport with your visa application at the embassy of Country X? Hotels in most countries check passports when you check in, so you may not even be able to change hotels, much less leave the city, while you wait for your visa. The only visas to get abroad are those you *can't* get before you leave home.

Visas for a few countries can only be issued by the embassy in the country of which you are a citizen. USA citizens are only supposed to be able to obtain visas for these countries from their embassies in the United States, although exceptions are sometimes possible if you have enough money and/or patience. (If you are turned down for a visa in the United States, it can't hurt to try wherever else you have a chance. Just don't count on having better luck anywhere else). It's easy to get the wrong idea about this from reading guidebooks. Guidebooks to a country usually list neighboring countries in which you can get visas, and what they cost according to current information when the book was researched. This is useful information to those who arrive in the region without the necessary visas, and only then decide that they want to visit the country. But don't think that because you *can* get a visa in the next country, or because visas were cheaper when the book was researched, it will be easier or cheaper to get visas in a neighboring country than in your home country. Getting visas in neighboring countries—like doing anything else at the last minute—should be treated as a last resort.

The embassy where you apply may also have to check with officials in its home country, and perhaps with the embassy in your home country, to see if there is any reason not to give you a visa. (Every country, including the United States, maintains a blacklist of people who have been declared personae non grata.) If the communications infrastructure in the country where you apply is poor, getting approval from the home office often takes days and sometimes weeks, especially because the home office may have little motivation to spend money on telexes, and may have to get several requests before they reply at all.

The country for which this is most often a problem for USA citizens is India. The lists of USA citizens who have offended the government of India are maintained by the embassy and consulates of India in the United States. If a USA citizen applies for a visa to India anywhere outside the United States, they have to wait—often for weeks—for approval from the Indian consulate in the part of the United States where they live before their visa to India can be issued. In the United States, on the other hand, USA citizens can get visas to India issued the same day.

The longer your trip, the more likely it is you will have to get some visas along the way. But plan carefully. For each country for which you will need to get a visa en route, find out where that country has a diplomatic office that issues visas, and be sure you will be staying in that area long enough to get a visa. Give yourself a generous time allowance for delays.

If you plan on getting a visa for Country Q in City R, call the embassy of Country Q in your home country, well before you buy your tickets (much less leave your home country) to verify that Country Q still has an office in City R that will issue visas to citizens of your nationality.

# BORDER FORMALITIES

At first, borders may seem intimidating and strange. After you've been traveling for a while, they will seem mostly bureaucratic and boring, and it will take an effort to continue to see them as an exciting first glimpse of a country and its ways. For those who haven't experienced this already, here are a few tips, with the caveat that procedures often change, and every country does things just a little bit differently.

## Airport and Airline Security

If you are crossing an international border by air—as you probably will much of the time—you'll have to deal with airport and airline security inspections even before you get to the government border inspections.

Americans are sometimes worried about whether foreign airlines and airports have adequate security, and the USA government feeds these fears by its periodic complaints about foreign airport security. In recent years, for example, USA airports have been required to display notices cautioning passengers that airports in Lagos and Manila "do not meet USA security standards." These warnings strike most foreign observers as absurd, because the United States has long been notorious for having some of the world's most lax airport security standards. I don't mean to suggest that they be changed: terrorism is rare because few people are terrorists, and police states tend to be more violent, not less. But I do want to reassure Americans who haven't traveled abroad before, and who are afraid that passengers won't be adequately searched, that they and their fellow passengers will be at least as carefully scrutinized elsewhere as they ever are in the United States.

Some airport and airline procedures in the United States have changed since 11 September 2001. It's arguable whether these changes are actually related to safety or security, and it's equally arguable whether safety or security changes were really needed. Many of the changes appear to be intended to reassure travelers, and make us feel less afraid, rather than to make us safer. (See the sidebar, "Travel Safety and Civil Liberties: Fear vs. Danger.")

Whatever the reasons for the changes, their effect has been to bring the United States into closer conformity with the preexisting international airline and airport security norms, and to reduce the discrepancy between domestic and international check-in, inspection, and screening procedures.

It used to be that travelers who were used to domestic USA flight procedures had to learn a whole new set of rules for international flights, and vice versa. Now, there's much less difference between procedures in the United States and in the rest of world. No one who's gotten accustomed to the procedures for domestic flights in the United States (check-in two hours before departure, repeated searches and demands for identity documents, soldiers with guns, etc.) should be greatly surprised by anything that happens on a typical international flight or in an airport in the rest of the world.

### Military Presence

Airports are considered to be of great military importance. Many airports routinely handle both civilian and military flights. The success or failure of coups, revolts, and invasions has hinged on military control of airports. Consequently airport guards are typically the highest-ranking class of national police, soldiers, or both.

In the United States, National Guardsmen in camouflage clothing with M-16's have appeared in airports only since 11 September 2001. Elsewhere in the United States, police are rarely seen outside ghetto areas carrying more than pistols, and soldiers rarely function as police. In most other countries, the nuances of the distinction, if any, between soldiers and police are likely to be invisible to foreigners without military training. It is perfectly normal, and no indication of any special reason for alarm, to see military fortifications encircling an airport, or to have your papers checked by soldiers in full battle dress carrying rifles or machine guns. This isn't a response to the events of 11 September 2001: soldiers in airports have been standard operating procedure at airports around the world for years. I don't mean to condone governmental paranoia, and I certainly don't want to encourage complacency in the face of the militarization of civil society. But if you haven't seen this before, you do need to get used to a more naked assertion of the violence that underlies governmental power, so that you are prepared and don't misinterpret or overreact to its manifestations at airports and elsewhere.

### Luggage

When you check in for your flight, international or domestic, your identification papers will be checked, and your luggage, including both checked and carry-on items, is subject to inspection. Airlines are entitled to require you to open your luggage for inspection for prohibited items. If you don't want to open your bags, you shouldn't bring them on the plane. I've had my bags opened by airport security more often than by customs.

# TRAVEL SAFETY AND CIVIL LIBERTIES: FEAR VS. DANGER

Fear has profoundly affected travel since 11 September 2001. It's understandable that travelers are afraid. But what are we afraid of? And how should we deal with our fears?

Fear is nothing to be ashamed of. Fear is instinctive, whether it be fear of flying, fear of terrorism, or fear of the unknown. Fear serves a purpose in the human animal: it warns us of danger. And our most irrational fears ("phobias") are, almost by definition, those least subject to conscious control.

Because fear is perceived as a sign of danger, our instinct is to assume that whatever is scary is dangerous, and that the degree of danger we're in is proportional to the fear we feel.

Most people are aware that the correlation between fear and danger isn't perfect. But as I discuss in the chapter on safety and health, there's a far greater difference between fear and real danger than most travelers imagine. Before you go to a place you haven't been before read a good guidebook to find out about the dangers you don't know to be afraid of, and to learn what are the scary-seeming things that are really harmless and nothing you need to worry about.

Serious problems tend to arise, however, when we attack the sources of our fears while mistaking them for sources of danger.

We're afraid of flying, for example, so we avoid flying, even though the alternative, surface travel, is actually much more dangerous. Similarly, we avoid the

Carry-on luggage is more likely to be opened than checked baggage. Many items that are permitted in checked baggage, notably knives, batteries, and electronic equipment, are often prohibited in carry-on luggage. The theory is that these items are harmless in the cargo hold but, if carried on, might be used as, or used to conceal, a weapon for hijacking. I've been required to check even the smallest Swiss Army knife and the batteries from a camera, even before 11 September 2001. If removing the batteries from your camera requires opening the camera and exposing the film, make sure you remove any film from the camera before each flight. If you have things that might conceivably be usable as weapons, or that would be difficult to unpack, unwrap, or open up for inspection, put them in checked rather than carry-on luggage. Each country and airline makes its own judgments about what to permit on its flights, so it's useless to argue, "But some other airline or country let me carry this on."

If an electronic item (e.g., a Walkman, camera, or laptop computer) can't be opened for inspection without damaging it, the usual test is to require you to turn it on and demonstrate it at the security checkpoint. If it doesn't operate, it might be a case hollowed out to hold a weapon, and it won't be allowed

---

unknown, the "foreign," because it raises our instinctive fear of the unknown—not because "strange" places are actually more dangerous than our daily lives at home.

Looked at in terms of danger, it's hard to understand the decision made by so many Americans in the aftermath of the attacks of 11 September 2001. Many people from the United States chose to confine their travel to the United States—the place where the attacks took place—rather than going to safer places abroad. But looked at in terms of instinctive fear of the unknown, it makes perfect sense: when you're afraid, you avoid the scary—and anything strange is scary.

Similarly, "profiling" of airline passengers was in effect on September 11, but proved a failure in terms of safety. But because the profile matches the profile of most people's fears, selectively searching those who fit the profile is highly effective in allaying those fears (except, of course, if we're in the class of people, mainly those of South Asian or Arab ancestry, being selected for special scrutiny) even if it doesn't make us any safer.

Many people understand, intellectually if not emotionally, that making travel safer won't necessarily make it less scary. What's less obvious, but at least equally important, is that making travel less scary won't necessarily make it any safer. The greatest danger for travelers in the present situation is the potential for attacking people and things who pose no real danger. In doing so, we'll attack our own freedom and security, ultimately making ourselves less safe. The consequence would be the sacrifice of our freedom to our fears, without gaining any safety or security. That would be tragic for travelers and civil liberties alike.

through. This is no joke: if your laptop computer's batteries are dead when you get to security, and you've already checked your power cord or adapter, you risk having your expensive appliance confiscated and destroyed. If it isn't working, the batteries are low, or you have the least doubt whether it will function on demand at security checkpoints, put it in your checked luggage.

You can expect to be questioned closely about each checked item. "What's in this luggage? Did you pack it yourself? When did you pack it? Has it been continuously in your sight since you packed it? Did anyone give you anything to carry for them or to put in your luggage?" The point of these questions is to ensure nothing gets onto the plane unless it is accompanied by a passenger. For the same reason, some airlines bring the luggage carts out on the runway alongside the plane and make each passenger identify their luggage again just before boarding the plane. If a bag hasn't been personally identified by a passenger who has been seen to board the plane, it will be turned over to the bomb squad for destruction. Unattended baggage in waiting areas is similarly presumed to be dangerous, and is removed and destroyed. In some countries with ongoing civil wars waged in part by bombings in public places, such as the UK and Israel, it can be difficult to persuade a stranger to watch your bag while you go to the toilet.

All baggage, checked or carry-on, will be x-rayed at some point, whether in your sight or not. (See the section on "Cameras and Film" in the "Packing Suggestions" section of the Baggage chapter for advice on X-ray protection for film.) X-rays and magnetometers (metal detectors) can damage magnetic media (e.g., computer floppy disks and hard disks) as well as photographic film. Whenever

## REAL LIFE

Flying from Paris to New York I once got a lesson in the importance airlines attach to unaccompanied baggage when I was delayed at immigration after checking my bag. As I became convinced that I would miss my flight, two security guards came running up, calling out, "Mr. Abouk? Mr. Abouk?" I recognized this as a semblance of my name, Hasbrouck. They pulled me out of line, whisked me through passport control, and hustled me off to the gate at a run. My traveling companion, already on board, was startled to see me arrive as though under arrest, with a guard on either arm! The door was immediately closed and the plane left, a few minutes late. I was lucky they found it easier to delay the flight and find me than to search for my luggage and remove it before the flight could depart.

Airlines have reason for these concerns. In 1985, an Air India flight from Toronto was blown up over the Atlantic Ocean, killing all 329 people on board. The bomb was in the luggage of a terrorist who checked it through from a connecting flight from Vancouver but who never boarded the Air India plane. Today, all baggage is matched with passengers, and unaccompanied bags removed and destroyed, even on domestic flights in the United States— not just on international flights or flights within other countries.

possible, don't bring your only copies of data with you on a plane on magnetic media. If you have important electronic data (e.g. digital photos), consider emailing them and/or burning them onto CDs, which are optical devices immune to X-ray or magnetometer damage.

## Airport Taxes

To get out of most countries you have to pay some sort of "departure tax," "airport fee," or "security fee," typically in the range of US$5–10 but occasionally as much as US$50. Some countries arrange to have these taxes and fees collected by the airlines at the time of ticketing or check-in, while others collect them directly from travelers at the point of departure. Some departure taxes apply only to air travelers, while others apply equally to those departing by other means. Be prepared for possible departure taxes when buying international train, bus, or ferry tickets; at stations and docks; and at land border crossing points. Usually you pay more on departure than on arrival, but the United States charges more to get into the country (as of 2003 a total of US$28.30 in arrival tax and three separate "user fees" for the "services" of customs, immigration, and agricultural inspectors) than to get out (US$13.20 departure tax).

The amount of the departure tax is usually only a minor nuisance, but it can be a larger problem if you don't have the appropriate currency to pay it or if you go past the payment point without paying. One of the first things you should do when you get to the airport is figure out how much the departure tax is and where and in what currency you need to pay it. Sometimes the tax must be paid in local currency, sometimes in foreign "hard" currency. Find out which before you exchange your local currency, as there may be no more moneychangers beyond the point where you have to pay the tax. If you don't see any signs indicating where to pay the tax, ask fellow travelers. Local businesspeople have probably been through this particular airport before and are most likely to know its procedures.

Two common systems are to collect the tax at a counter or kiosk near the international departure check-in area, or to have it collected by airline staff at the check-in counter. If you try to check in and your tickets are in order, but the airline clerk indicates that something is missing, it probably means you need to go back and pay the tax. If you get a tax sticker or stamp on or in your ticket, boarding pass, or passport, or a chit or receipt for the tax, hold onto it until you are out of the country. You never know at what point(s) it will be checked again, maybe even as you are walking across the runway to your plane.

## Immigration

Customs and immigration are often spoken of together. They are actually distinct functions, usually performed by different officials. Immigration is concerned with the passage of people across international borders, customs with the passage of luggage, cargo, money, and goods. The norm is to go through immigration or passport control first, then customs, both on arrival and on departure, although occasionally both functions are performed by the same person or at the same desk.

Immigration officers can ask you anything they feel is relevant to their determination of whether to let you in, and if so for how long. You have no other choice but to answer their questions: international law construes your attempting to cross a border as consenting to as thorough and intrusive an interrogation and search as that country deems necessary.

### Maintain a Good Attitude

I don't mean to imply that you'll get the third degree. Most immigration inspectors are underpaid and bored, but nonetheless courteous and friendly. If they ask you personal questions, they are probably genuinely curious, just trying to make conversation, or practicing their language skills. Your best bet is to approach them with the attitude of a guest: "I'm interested in your country, and I'm grateful to you for being so hospitable as to allow me to visit." Begin to learn how local people do things. Start practicing your greetings in the local language. This may be difficult when a guard has an Uzi or Kalashnikov machine gun pointed at you, but that's just standard operating procedure at many borders and throughout many countries. It bears repeating that though a visa may be necessary, it is never a sufficient condition for entry. Flourishing your visa as though it gives you the right of entry or deprives the immigration officers or border guards of discretion to turn you away will only alienate them and invite them to reject you. If your visa says, "Good for one visit, for up to 60 days," the immigration inspector at the border has discretion to admit you for 60 days, two weeks, 24 hours, or not at all. The way to maximize your chances of a longer stay is (surprise!) to treat the officials as human beings, be "nice," and above all don't be demanding.

### Bribes

Do not offer bribes. If a bribe is really essential it will be described as a "fee," "fine," or "tax," and should be paid as such. You'll do yourself far more damage by offering a bribe when it isn't called for than by waiting for the rare official to make it explicit by demanding a "fee." Bribes are much less common than most guidebooks would have you believe. I've only had to bribe a border guard once (I knew it was a bribe because, in a receipt and red-tape-crazed country, I got no receipt), and I know people who've traveled around the world two or three times and never paid a bribe.

### Immigration Requirements

Immigration inspectors may check that you have onward or return tickets, or sufficient funds to pay for onward transportation and to support yourself for the duration of your permitted stay. You can expect both to be checked again on arrival even if you had to show them earlier to get a visa.

Practically speaking, long-term travelers, even those on a budget, should have a sufficient reserve for emergencies, in cash or traveler's checks, to satisfy most countries' requirements. At most borders you should be prepared to show at least US$500 in the South, US$1,000 in the North, in hard-currency cash or traveler's checks. Up to US$2,000 can improve your chances anywhere. You can probably get in with less, but you risk being limited to a shorter stay.

Credit cards (American Express is more widely recognized and useful for this purpose than any other card) are sometimes helpful and may be considered sufficient proof of adequate financial means. You can't count on it, though. Proof of the means to buy an onward ticket may be accepted in lieu of the ticket itself, especially if you enter the country by land or water rather than by air. If you don't have an onward ticket, find out in advance how much one costs, and be prepared to show that much money. Credit cards are more likely to be accepted as evidence of your ability to pay for a ticket out than as evidence of the ability to support yourself in the country. This is entirely justified, since in many countries airline tickets are almost the only things you can pay for with credit cards. ATM cards are next to useless for this purpose, since there's no way for the border inspectors to verify your bank balance.

### Paperwork

It's perfectly normal for visitors, even those who already have visas, to have to complete a variety of paperwork on arrival. Airlines frequently give out some or all of the forms for entry to the plane's destination for you to complete during the flight. Take advantage of the opportunity to do so, and to consult

with fellow passengers and/or the flight attendants if you aren't sure how. The form for entry to the United States by non-USA citizens is by far the most complicated I've seen. Most airlines seem to agree, and the in-flight magazines of international airlines serving the United States usually contain lengthy multilingual explanations of what to put in the many inscrutable, English-only boxes.

A common system is to give you a form on arrival that must be completed and turned in on departure. This may be one or more of the copies of your visa application, entry application, or visa; a stub or portion of your entry permit; or an "entry/exit form," "immigration permit," "tourist card," or some other document. You may have to produce this form each time you register at a hotel; have it stamped or notated by the hotel each night; or have it stamped by the police in each city you pass through or stay in.

If the border officials hand back any official documents with your passport, including copies of any of the documents you gave them, check before you move on to see if you will need them when you leave. If you aren't sure, or don't understand the answer (most likely because of a language problem) assume that you will.

You can take it for granted that anything clipped or stapled into your passport on arrival, or an obviously two-part or half-completed form, is some sort of entry/exit document that you will be required to show to get out of the country. Guard it as carefully as your passport. If you lose it, you will be presumed to have thrown it away to hide having exceeded your authorized stay or because you entered illegally, and will at a minimum be fined. If you have a chance, especially if you are going to be spending a long time in the country or traveling extensively to remote areas within it, make a few photocopies of your entry/exit form(s), and secrete them with the copies of your passport.

## Customs

Many people find customs and its terminology and procedures even more intimidating than immigration. It's really just bureaucracy: most travelers have nothing to declare and have no serious problems with customs.

### Customs Declarations

The first steps when going through customs are to fill out a customs declaration form, sometimes also a currency declaration, and to decide whether you have anything or nothing to "declare." To "declare" something means exactly what it implies: to tell the government of the country into which you are bringing it that you have it. Declarable items are not necessarily illegal.

Governments have all sorts of reasons for making you declare certain kinds of things. They may restrict the quantities of an item that can be imported, or subject them to "duty" (see the following) in order to protect, and thus promote, local production of similar items. They may want to know about certain categories of goods that might contain forbidden materials (most often this applies to books, other printed materials, recordings, objets d'art, antiques, archaeological artifacts, and high-value portable electronics), so as to subject them or the people carrying them to special scrutiny. They may just want to keep records of the import and export of certain goods. Whatever the case may be, they don't have to give you a reason.

Traditionally, you stepped up to a counter where you were asked, "Do you have anything to declare?" and you answered either "No" or "Yes, I have such-and-such quantities of such-and-such items." Nowadays declarations are usually made in writing on a form completed and signed on arrival (or distributed on the airplane and completed in flight) or by choosing to go through a "red channel" or "green channel" at the exit from the immigration hall. Going through the green channel (usually indicated by a green traffic light, a green sign, or "Nothing to Declare") is the equivalent of saying, "I have nothing to declare." Going through the red channel (red traffic light, red sign, or "Items to Declare") means, "I might have something to declare."

No matter how many times you've been through the process, read the customs declaration form before you sign it. Different countries require you to declare different things; requirements change, and they are often stated in peculiar (or peculiarly translated, if translated at all) terminology. Occasionally you'll run across border officials who make a habit of entrapping travelers in some obscure declaration requirement (failing to declare, say, how much photographic film or how many audio tapes they have, or whether they have a mobile phone) and shaking them down for fines or bribes in exchange for allowing them to proceed. The best way to avoid such problems is to make sure that your declaration is scrupulously complete.

If you aren't sure which exit to use, use the red channel. If you aren't sure whether to declare something, then go through the red channel line and ask. When you get to the front, before you hand in your declaration, say, "I have [quantity] of [type of item]. Should I declare it?" If you don't understand the answer, or still aren't sure, list the item(s) on your declaration.

### Duties and Taxes

Duties and taxes on imports and exports cause much unnecessary confusion. Unless you are a professional importer or exporter, you don't need to worry about them any more than you worry about paying sales or value-added tax on the things you buy at home. For the curious, here's a summary of the terminology and rules.

A duty or tariff (as in the "General Agreement on Tariffs and Trade," or GATT) is a tax a country imposes on imported goods of a certain type. Almost anything you can think of is subject to a duty somewhere. A duty is usually assessed either per quantity (so much per liter of distilled alcohol or per meter of silk cloth, for example) or as a percentage of the value of the imported goods (200 percent of the assessed valuation of imported automobiles, for example). In general, the baggage and possessions of a traveler are considered to be "imports" subject to the usual duties of the country into which they are brought.

Two standard exceptions to the duty rules combine to create the phenomenon of the "duty-free" shop. First, most countries exempt certain quantities of particular goods from the usual duties if they are brought in by travelers for their personal use. Second, most countries do not charge a duty or impose local sales taxes on goods that are exported or imported solely for re-export to another country. Goods sold by duty-free shops are free of local taxes and duties on condition that the goods are only for export and cannot be used or consumed in the country of purchase. To enforce this requirement, duty-free shops are usually located beyond the immigration checkpoints in the departure or transit areas of airports. The world's largest are in Dubai, where the transit terminal resembles a shopping mall with everything from jewelry stores to luxury-car showrooms.

As long as your purchases from the duty-free shop are within the amounts exempt from duty in the country of your destination, they are taxed in neither country. Naturally, this exemption is most useful if they are (1) small (so that you can easily carry them with you), (2) heavily taxed, and (3) expensive (to make the savings worthwhile). The merchandise for sale in duty-free shops is just what one would expect: small, expensive items subject to high "luxury" and "sin" taxes, especially the most expensive brands of hard liquor, perfumes, tobacco products, watches, and designer jewelry. If you regularly buy these items, and if you are on the last leg of your trip home (so that you don't have to schlep them around through a bunch of other places), it makes sense to buy them at a duty-free shop. If you're not in the habit of buying products like these, and somewhat lower prices aren't enough to make you take a sudden interest in them, or if you've got a lot of other stops before you get home, don't waste your time in duty-free shops. Anything not subject to special taxes will be cheaper at ordinary shops and markets elsewhere than it will be in the airport. This tends to be particularly true of local folk arts, handicrafts, clothing, souvenirs, and the like.

Some people, and some books, will advise you to try to make a little money by buying the maximum amount of whiskey and cigarettes you can bring into the next country duty-free, and then trying to sell it on the black market on arrival. This is always illegal, often dangerous, and rarely even profitable. It's axiomatic that black-market prices and potential profits are highest where prohibitions are most strictly enforced. Where there's money in it, there's danger. Where it's no problem (actually, carrying around a bottle of expensive whiskey without breaking it is apt to be a problem in itself), there's no money it. Some countries look on alcohol the way others look on cocaine, and vice versa. Even in a country where it's legal to bring in whiskey for your own use but not for sale, merely having it may identify you as decadent and disrespectful of local mores to the border guards who are deciding whether to admit you, turn you away, or shake you down.

The only time I buy anything in a duty-free shop is if I'm stuck with local currency that I can't exchange and that isn't worth anything outside the country. Better to spend it on overpriced souvenirs than to throw it away, although sometimes the money is sufficiently interesting-looking to make a better souvenir than the overpriced trinkets one could buy with it in a duty-free shop.

### Registering Declared Items

Some items must not only be declared (e.g., "two still cameras and 20 rolls of film") but must be itemized by make, model, and serial number on your entry/exit papers or in your passport itself on the page with your visa or entry stamp to the country. When this is required, it means that the items in question are heavily duties and/or taxed. Many countries deem importing foreign-made luxury goods—cameras, VCRs, automobiles, etc.—to be a less appropriate use of scarce foreign exchange reserves than importing of capital goods (machine tools, manufacturing machinery, textbooks) that will increase the country's production capacity. Luxury consumer goods are often subject to higher duties and taxes than any other class of imports.

Tourists and short-term business visitors—whose money the country wants, and whom it doesn't want to alienate unduly—tend to carry just such goods, such as still and video cameras, Walkman stereos, and laptop computers. The usual solution is to exempt certain quantities of common impedimenta of tourism from the normal duties, provided that visitors bring them solely for their own use while in the country and (most importantly) agree to take them away again when they leave. The quantity limits, which vary by country (typically one or two still cameras, one video camera/recorder, one audio player and/or recorder, one portable computer, and some numbers of rolls of film and recording tapes or computer disks) are imposed with the assumption that anyone bringing in larger quantities of goods intends to sell or give them away in the country.

Some people think that having their camera's serial number noted in their passport on entry is for their protection or will make it easier to take it out of the country. It's not and it won't. Items like these are recorded in your passport for the sole purpose of making it harder for you to leave the country without them, so that you won't evade duties and taxes by bringing them in as a tourist, duty-free and tax-free, and give them away (to a friend or relative) or sell them while in the country. Customs officials are after people who try to finance their trip by bringing in heavily duties or taxed items like laptop computers and selling them on the black market.

I wouldn't try to smuggle these things; declare them if they are listed on the forms. However, I would never go out of my way to declare them on arrival where it wasn't required or ask that they be noted in my passport. If some item is noted in your passport and is lost or stolen (these kinds of items are, of course, the most theft-prone), you will have great difficulty leaving without paying the duties and taxes required to import the item. Duties can be as much as five times the value of luxury goods like these, so the cost may be prohibitive.

It is imperative to report such a loss or theft to the police immediately. At a minimum, you will need proof that you have reported the loss or theft and that the police have been unable to find or recover the item. Getting this proof can take days. Because the police know you can't leave without the documentation only they can provide, they are likely to take the opportunity to ask for bribes for expediting the process. But if you offer a bribe without prompting, they can make your situation worse by arresting you for attempted bribery or demand a larger bribe not to do so. All in all, it can be a big hassle.

On the other hand, registering an item with the USA Customs service can be useful. If you plan on taking something with you on your trip that you bought in the United States, that was made in another country, and that's expensive enough to be subject to duty if you are bringing it into the United States for the first time, you can register it with the USA Customs Service before your departure. They will give you a certificate to show on your return to prove that you bought it in the United States before your trip, and thus that it isn't subject to duty when you "re-import" it to the USA with you when you come home. The United States has relatively few import duties, so this is unlikely to be an issue. If it is, the USA Customs Service offices at which you can register foreign-made items before your trip are listed at http://www.customs.ustreas.gov/top/offctext.htm.

### Art, Artifacts, and Antiquities

One reason people travel is to see monuments and artifacts of the history and culture of the places they visit. Too often, they find that the finest examples of local artistic, cultural, and even architectural traditions were long ago looted by imperialist collectors and archaeologists. Even the finest murals from inner rooms of rock-cut tombs and temples were sawed out in sections, hauled away, and re-assembled as the prized exhibits of museums in London, Paris, New York, Boston, and Chicago, leaving gaping holes in the walls of the sanctuaries for those who visit these sites today.

To stem the ongoing theft of what they have left of their cultural heritage, and to preserve the attractions of their country for citizens and future visitors alike, most formerly colonized countries have special restrictions on the export of artworks, antiquities, and archaeological artifacts. Typically, these things are defined as national treasures, and their export is categorically prohibited. Exactly what constitutes an antique or an artifact isn't always clearly defined, but common sense is usually a sufficient guide. Here's a rule of thumb: If you can afford it without having to think about the price, it's probably a legal fake. Real antiques cost real money. Good modern reproductions of museum pieces, or modern works in classical styles, can be harder to get out of the country than obviously fake "antiques" or works in modern styles or media. This is unfortunate, because it reduces the export market that might support continued work in traditional artistic styles. High-quality modern art in a classical medium or style is really one of the best souvenirs, if you can afford it. But bringing it out of the country is likely to require at least a purchase receipt, the more official-looking the better. In some countries, you'll need certification from a government agency or appointed specialist (art historian or curator) that the work is not an antique or national treasure.

In creating a demand for these antiques, buyers and collectors are also to blame for creating a financial opportunity for impoverished local people who can earn the equivalent of a year's wages in a day by working in the jungle digging up burial mounds instead of plowing fields. The damage will only stop when those who can afford to buy these treasures choose not to.

Don't buy antiques or archaeological artifacts. Don't buy anything else from people who sell these things, and tell them why. Encourage other travelers to boycott them. If someone shows you a piece of pre-Columbian pottery, don't say, "What a find!" Say, "Doesn't that belong in a museum, where everyone could see it?" If each visitor takes away a tangible piece of the past, nothing of the past will be left for the future.

Buying or smuggling forbidden antiquities or artifacts is considered not merely theft but theft from the collective cultural heritage of a people. You aren't just stealing: you are stealing from a nation; in many countries all antiquities, in whomever's possession, are officially deemed the property of the state. Even if the objects you buy or take have no ritual or religious value (which they often do), you aren't just taking souvenirs: you are stealing icons of the identity of a people. You are stealing the national soul and will be treated accordingly. You can expect little sympathy from your own country's government if you are caught and fined or imprisoned for trafficking antiquities or archeological artifacts.

## Smuggling

Forbidden items, quantities of items that should have been declared and weren't, and quantities of items in excess of those declared are all considered contraband. Carrying contraband across borders is smuggling. Failure to declare an item that should have been declared is considered smuggling even if the item could have been declared without penalty, as is going through the "green" channel when you have anything, even something legal, that should have been declared. This is a crime, often a fairly serious one.

You will probably only have to make a declaration of goods, and perhaps pay duty, if you have accumulated souvenirs or gifts worth more than the duty-free allowance. Luggage weight limits, and the impracticality of carrying large quantities of stuff very far, make this most likely on the last leg of your trip, when you may have bought a bunch of gifts for friends back home and several bottles (only one of which is duty-free) of foreign liquor that you can't get at home.

Don't bother to try to smuggle this sort of stuff in. To have to "pay duty" isn't a fate worse than death, and it's not worth risking serious fines to avoid the modest duties on a moderate excess of gifts and souvenirs or a few extra bottles of alcohol. If it's worth bothering to carry it home, it's worth paying the duty on it. The best souvenirs and gifts are things that aren't available at home at any price, not things bought solely because they are slightly cheaper than they would be at home.

If they are caught, some people think they can get away with saying they "forgot" to declare something, and they will at worst have to pay the duty. At worst, you will have to pay the duty and pay a fine and go to jail. If you declare it in the first place, all you have to do is pay the duty.

Because foreign tourists are less likely to be suspected of smuggling than locals at some borders, smugglers often try to hire them as freelance couriers for all sorts of contraband. Professional smuggling for profit is too risky for amateurs. Leave it to the pros. Smugglers (or their agents) hang out in places frequented by travelers, especially places frequented by budget backpackers. If your money is running out, the fast and easy-seeming money may be tempting. Don't do it.

Smuggling wouldn't pay well if it weren't dangerous. The contraband may be a commodity that seems innocuous to you, or that you've never heard of, but no one would be smuggling it if there weren't serious sanctions against it, or such high duties on it, or such scarcity of it that people were willing to kill for it. If someone wants you to smuggle something, and won't tell you or show you what it is, assume the worst: that its possession is a capital offense.

Foreigners and tourists aren't above the law. Foreign tourists have been executed for possession of drugs in Singapore and Malaysia, and foreigners caught smuggling alcoholic beverages into Saudi Arabia can be beheaded. It doesn't happen often: knowledge of the possible penalties scares most people away. Capital punishment doesn't deter crimes of passion such as murder, but it does deter purely economic crimes, such as smuggling, by all but the most economically desperate people.

Foreigners convicted of smuggling or other crimes, whether in the United States or any other country, are not deported immediately. They must "serve" their sentence in a local prison, and pay off any fine, before being deported.

If you choose to carry contraband, you have a moral obligation to tell everyone traveling with you. If you are in a taxi or minibus, and carrying drugs, there's a good chance that everyone in the vehicle will at least be arrested, and quite possibly imprisoned for some time, if you are caught. The local driver may be more severely punished than you or any of the other foreign travelers, especially if you've hidden the contraband anywhere in the vehicle other than on your person. You have no right to risk other people's lives or liberty without their knowledge or consent.

### Searches

You are subject to as complete a search as the border authorities choose to conduct. If nobody who went through the green channel was searched, nobody would declare anything or go through the red channel, and the system wouldn't work. Spot checks and searches are made at random and on the basis of hunches, profiles, watch lists, and informers' tips. Don't be surprised if, from time to time, you are approached after you've gone through the green channel, just as you are about to leave, and are asked to "step over here" or "into this room" for further questioning and/or search.

They can ask you anything they want, whether or not you deem it relevant to your entry to the country. You don't have to answer, but they don't have to let you in. Honesty is, I think, the best policy for most travelers. They can open your luggage and examine everything inside it. They'll usually give you a chance to open it for them, but they'll cut or break it open if you won't. They can pat you down, feel all over you, or strip you naked and examine your body cavities. Women entering most countries are entitled to insist that body searches be conducted in private by female officers, but at remote border crossings this may not be honored, or might entail waiting for several days, in detention, for a female officer to arrive. People entering the United States who are suspected of having swallowed condoms or balloons full of drugs can be, and are, confined in a "dry cell" without a toilet for several days, and made to defecate in a bucket until the entire contents of their intestines have been excreted and examined for drugs.

The people who search your belongings aren't required to repack your bags or put things back where they found them. You can ask them, politely, and they may give you minimal help, maybe let you use some of their tools, if you obviously won't be able to proceed without it and are holding up the line. But they are entitled to dismantle your suitcases or vehicle looking for drugs, if they feel like it, and then stand around laughing at you and at your most intimate possessions while you try to put them back together and repack them. You can't count on any compensation for damage done in the course of a search, even if no contraband is found.

### Money

Currency declarations are a special kind of customs declaration. Sometimes they are made on the same form as the rest of your customs declaration, sometimes on a separate form. As with other immigration and customs forms, you should retain your currency declaration (if it is given back to you) on the assumption that you will have to turn it back in when you leave the country. Know how much money you have, in which currencies and forms (cash or traveler's checks), before you get to customs. You don't want to attract attention by digging it all out of your luggage and counting it in plain view.

Some countries don't care how much money you bring in or out, or in what form. The United States allows the import and export of any amount of any currency except currencies of blacklisted countries like Cuba, and only requires you to declare amounts over US$10,000 in cash or "negotiable instruments" such as traveler's checks.

Other countries have a range of currency declaration requirements and restrictions. Typically, First World countries care mainly that you have enough money to pay your way during your stay. If the local currency is "hard" or freely convertible on the open market, they don't much care whether you have your money in dollars, pounds, Euros, yen, or whatever, as long as you have enough—but not so much as to look suspicious.

Some poorer countries make you exchange a certain amount of money on arrival, either a fixed amount per visitor or a per diem for the duration of your intended stay. In such cases, you'll either have to change your money into non-convertible currency (with which you can't do anything except spend it in the country) or at an artificially low exchange rate (which makes it more akin to a head tax on tourists). These requirements are annoying but straightforward, and there is nothing you can do about them. Don't waste your time trying to argue: insisting that you can't afford to change that much money will only convince them not to admit you to their country.

Second World countries all used to have controlled currencies that were worthless anywhere else. This has changed. Full convertibility of currencies like the Russian ruble, much less other Second World currencies, is still some ways off. But the huge discrepancies between "official" and "market" exchange rates have been greatly reduced and private moneychanging legalized in most places. Currency declarations are still required, but where there's no big black market, not much attention is paid to them. (See "Cashing Checks and Changing Money" in the Bottom Line chapter.)

These days the strictest currency controls are found in certain Third and Fourth World countries, often ones suffering from hyperinflation and excessive national debt, where the official exchange rate (at least for tourists) is grossly disproportionate to the exchange value of the local currency on the black market. Currency controls are used to prevent visitors from cutting costs by buying local currency at the more favorable black-market rate. By forbidding you from importing local currency, or limiting the amount you can bring in to a nominal amount, they prevent you from buying it cheaply on the black market outside the country. And by keeping track of how much foreign currency you bring in and out, they try to stop you from changing money on the black market within the country.

This latter is a difficult task requiring constant vigilance. It works like this: when you arrive, you declare how much money you have. Whenever you exchange money legally, you get an official receipt. When you leave, you turn in your arrival declaration and all your receipts, and declare how much money you have left. If the sum of all the receipts and your remaining foreign currency adds up to less than the amount you declared on arrival, you are assumed to have exchanged the difference illegally on the black market. Unfortunately, the same result can be produced by miscounting your money on arrival, or by losing any one of your receipts during your stay. Be extremely careful not to lose your exchange receipts unless you are absolutely sure that you won't need them when you leave.

Visitors can get around the system by hiding and not declaring on arrival the money they intend to exchange on the black market. This leaves customs officers little choice, if they are actually to enforce the law, but to conduct aggressive searches and interrogations of arriving visitors to ferret out hidden money. These searches can be humiliating, but consider how little space it takes to hide a US$100 bill or one of the new €500 notes (500 Euros are worth about US$500), and how thorough a search it would take to find one hidden in someone's underwear.

As with other kinds of smuggling, the only places where there are real savings in black-market moneychanging are those where it carries at least some risk. Don't change money on the black market until you've been in the country long enough to be reasonably sure that it's both worthwhile and safe. Expatriate foreign residents are probably the best sources of information about where, how, and at what price to change your money. Be discreet and polite in asking anyone—expats, locals, or fellow travelers—about black marketeering. Everyone may be doing it, but it's still a crime.

## Health Inspections

There are two possible types of health inspections and immunization requirements at international borders: those because of conditions within the country you are entering (extremely rare), and those related to conditions in a country you are leaving, or which you have recently visited (a possibility in cases of yellow fever, SARS, or other unusual disease outbreaks).

Most people expect health requirements on entry to be related to health hazards in the country in which you are arriving, but that's not the way it works. Rules at borders are designed to protect the country against external threats, in health as in other matters. If yellow fever is already endemic, a country doesn't care if people who arrive are immunized against it. But if you arrive from a country with an endemic contagious disease like yellow fever, or an outbreak of SARS or Ebola fever, countries where those diseases *aren't* prevalent will want to be sure that you have been tested or immunized before they let you in, or may quarantine you until they can tell if you are infected. So health requirements on entry are mainly about what diseases are uncommon where you are arriving, but common where you have previously been.

The key to sorting this out is the sequence of countries you will visit, and the amount of time you will spend in each. That's what a competent travel health professional will need to know before they can provide you with immunization recommendations or warnings about possible quarantines. In general, health inspectors at borders are interested in where you have been for the 30 days before arriving in that country.

The primary reason for immunizations is health, not government requirements, as is discussed in more detail in the Safety and Health chapter. You should, however, have your International Certificates of Vaccination (yellow book) handy at borders, because it may be ritualistically examined even where no immunizations are required.

Countries that require AIDS tests for entry generally require them before they will even issue visas, so you are unlikely to be confronted with a border AIDS-testing requirement. Many countries don't require tests but do ask if you have AIDS or any other communicable disease. Obviously, if you say you are HIV-positive, they won't let you in. If you say you are HIV-negative, they are extremely unlikely to check your word.

## Agricultural Inspections

Some countries, particularly geographically isolated ones such as island nations, have special inspections or "disinfecting" procedures in an attempt to prevent visitors from bringing in exotic (nonnative) strains of plant or animal diseases, parasites, blights, pests, or vermin.

Sometimes an inspector walks through the cabin of the plane, before passengers disembark, spraying pesticide or disinfectant in the air and over the passengers. It's ineffectual and annoying, but there is nothing much you can do about it except to send a letter later to the country's government or embassy recording your displeasure and desire that the spraying be discontinued.

Spraying aside, agricultural inspections should be taken seriously. A foreign disease or blight, to which local strains of crops or livestock are not resistant, or a pest that has no local predators, can devastate agriculture. There are many historical examples of ruinous results from inadvertent import of vermin, pests, and diseases.

It's easy for even dead animal or vegetable material to harbor microscopic eggs or seeds. Once introduced, pests can be impossible to eliminate. If you bring in an agricultural pest—lurking in some harmless-looking fruit or flowers you can't resist bringing home—people whose crops are ruined will curse you for generations to come.

The United States, Australia, and Aotearoa/New Zealand have particularly stringent agricultural inspections. In general, you are forbidden to bring meat or fresh fruits, vegetables, or plants into these countries. Canned or preserved foods may be allowed, but you can't always count on it. All agricultural products must, and should, be declared.

California, the center of fruit and vegetable growing in the United States, has its own agricultural inspection stations at borders with other USA states as well as at airports and international borders. Driving into California from another state, you have to stop at a checkpoint and declare your fruits and vegetables. Any agricultural products suspected of harboring pests or blights are subject to confiscation and destruction, without compensation.

## Dress for Success

When dealing with border guards, customs and immigration officers, and the officials who decide whether or not to issue special travel permits, it's most important to conform to local norms of dress, appearance, and behavior.

That doesn't mean you should try to pass for a local. Unsuccessful attempts to "go native" are often resented and interpreted as condescending. It's all too easy to misunderstand the symbolic meaning of an article of apparel or ornamentation, and inadvertently wear something you've seen beautiful local people wearing on the streets that actually identifies you as, say, a prostitute. It's safer to appear to be what I (and the officials with whom you are dealing) hope you are: a friendly, respectful foreigner. If you are obviously a foreigner, especially one visibly of a different race or ethnicity, the question to ask is "How would this official consider it respectful for a foreigner like me to dress and behave?"

I'm not saying you have to respect the bureaucrats, or pretend you do if you don't, but neither do you have to go out of your way to tell them what you do think. You may think they are thugs working for a government that rounds up the local people at gunpoint to put them in slave labor camps. However, you won't get to talk to those local people at all if you voice those opinions to the permit-granting or -denying officials.

In your own country, you know the nuances of expressions of disrespect or disagreement, and what you risk by showing them. In a foreign culture, you risk making a much more hostile or personal statement than you intended by voicing criticisms or flouting local norms. Besides, like many officials, they may have their own personal criticisms of the government and its policies.

Never present yourself at a government office in shorts, T-shirts, or jeans; in clothes that aren't clean; or without having recently bathed and groomed yourself. Why take the chance, even in Australia, where certain styles of shorts are considered respectable attire for men in many settings, or in the United States and Canada where jeans are acceptable almost everywhere? At land border crossings in the bush it may be difficult, but you'd still be amazed at the extent to which local travelers in such a place manage to spruce themselves up on arrival. After all, an intercity bus ride may be the trip of their lifetime.

I know some people who carry an entirely separate outfit just for border crossings. But if you feel that you need a whole new wardrobe to look acceptable at the border, maybe you should think again about whether your day-to-day attire is giving more offense, or closing more doors, than you have realized or want.

**REAL LIFE**

In appearance, I fit the profile of a hippie. My hair comes below my shoulders, it's usually in a ponytail, and I have a full beard 15 cm (six inches) long. In the tropics I wear sandals, even to business meetings. Nonetheless I routinely get into places where most tourists aren't allowed, and I've never been turned down for a visa or official permit. I've never been treated like a hippie, been searched for drugs, or had my bag opened (except once when it broke open on the baggage conveyor). Even in notoriously anti-hippie Singapore they didn't cut my beard or hair but only asked me, with friendly curiosity, if such a long beard itched!

## Attitude and Behavior

Some visitors tend to focus exclusively on dress and external appearance to improve their success rate with local bureaucrats. These things are important, but less so than attitude and behavior.

In most places I'm taken for an expatriate foreign resident rather than a tourist. Part of making a good impression is certainly dress: my customary traveling clothes are long pants (not jeans) and long-sleeved shirts with collars, and I carry a tie to put on at borders and official offices. But the biggest factors, I think, are attitude and behavior. My delight at getting to another country is always genuine, and I anticipate with pleasure my first opportunity—border formalities—to experience its ways. I approach each encounter with officialdom as an adventure and a learning opportunity. Try to cultivate these attitudes, even if they aren't easy or instinctive.

Behavioral norms vary greatly from place to place. While waiting in line, watch how local people in front of you act (do you sit? stand? bow? shake hands?). If a particular permit or bit of official business is especially critical to your plans, don't apply for it on your first day in the country. Go to some other offices, do some other business, and get a feel for local ways. If you've merely omitted one step or document, you may be able to come back once it's completed, but once an application has been denied, you don't usually get a second chance.

Above all else, accept that you are not in control. You may not like it, but you cannot do anything about it. Many people, particularly from privileged Northern backgrounds, who are accustomed to getting their way, are deeply threatened by having to place themselves at someone else's mercy. People from the United States and Australia, with our ideologies of self-sufficiency as the measure of self-worth, can be among those most uncomfortable in situations of dependence on others' judgments and decisions. Even those without conscious racism may find that subconscious racism enhances their discomfort if they are in the hands of people of another race whom their culture has taught them to fear. This is especially true at borders and in police and guarded government offices where those

**Try to keep your cool and be polite whatever happens with officials. Don't raise your voice, and don't make any sudden movements or threatening gestures. Train yourself to relax and slow down when you are tempted to panic.**

people of the race they associate with danger are, in the normal conduct of their jobs, pointing guns at them.

These people tend to react in exactly the worst way due to their (correct) perception of a loss of control. Because this threatens their sense of self they try to take control of the situation, which is bound to come across to local officials as an assertion of superior status. This is most counterproductive of all when those making this assertion are from a country with an imperialist history (the United States, UK, France, Russia, Japan, etc.) or from a race with a history of illegitimately claiming superiority over the race of the official. This pushes all the wrong buttons of the postcolonial psyche.

The usual result is an escalation by both parties of their claims to being in charge. "No, you listen to me," "I have a right . . .," "You must . . .," "I need . . .," "Who do you think you are?" In such a war of status, authority, and obligation, the traveler will always lose. Better to accept from the start what you will eventually be compelled to accept anyway: they are in charge. That you perceive you need something does not imply that someone else perceives an obligation to give it to you. Do you feel obligated to give your money to every beggar? Poor people know better than the rich how little anyone really needs.

Situations of dependence, inferior status, and lack of privilege may be, for Northerners, among the most important learning experiences of world travel. Most people never have the degree of privilege that Northerners take for granted. To come to terms with what it is like to be in such situations is to come to terms with what life is like for most people in the world. Some people confront this shortly after they are inducted into the military, or when jail or prison doors close behind them, and they realize that they have to take what's coming whether they like it or not. Some people experience it, even in the North, by being on the bottom of the hierarchies of class, wealth, age, race, ethnicity, or gender-based privilege. Some people experience lack of privilege for the first time when they travel abroad.

Remember, your self-worth comes from self-respect, not from anyone else's judgment of you. There is no shame in doing things under duress, or being judged falsely. Don't let it get you down or make you panic or lose your temper. One of the central lessons of the Gandhian analysis of power is that submission need not mean disempowerment. The most effective way to resist the impositions of illegitimate authority is simply to retain your pride while doing what you have to do.

I won't pretend it's always fun, but awareness and anticipation of these situational dynamics can help you keep your reactions under control and avoid making bad situations worse.

**REAL LIFE**

I was scared the first time a soldier pointed his gun at me while I was trying to ask that my photographic film not be put through the X-ray machine. I kept my hands in the air and kept talking. I was on the verge of giving up —better to lose my photographs than my life— when a higher-ranking officer noticed what was happening, recognized my lead-lined film bag, and told the soldier to lower his gun and hand-inspect it. These days, it's probably not even worth asking to have film hand-inspected: *everything* gets x-rayed.

# "Sound Body
## and Mind"

# SAFETY AND HEALTH

## TRAVEL SAFETY AND HEALTH RISKS

Most people think of the risks of travel in terms of exotic illnesses, flight safety, and terrorism. Typically, travelers' concerns for a safe trip manifest themselves in three questions: "Is this a safe airline?," "What shots are required for this country?," and "Is there a government advisory about terrorism in this country?"

Statistically speaking, however, these questions say more about travelers' fears than about the actual dangers of travel. Travel by land or water is far more dangerous than travel by air; serious injury—most often from road accidents—is much more likely than serious illness; most violent crime against travelers is economic, with no obvious political content and no relation to terrorism; hygiene and behavior have more effect on travel health than do inoculations; and government advisories are a poorer indication of the risk of violence than daily newspapers.

The real hazards aren't what most people are afraid of, and just listing the factors that make for a safe trip fails to address some of the things most travelers fear. This chapter is therefore, of necessity, as much about fear and its causes as about actual travel risks, safety, or health.

I realize, of course, that fear is not a rational phenomenon. Nothing I could say, and no amount of evidence I could produce, would allay some people's fear of flying or fear of terrorism. But choosing an airline they think of as safer is unlikely to allay their fears either. Driving rather than flying will only increase the risk of injury or death. And you're in no greater danger of terrorism while traveling than you are if you stay home.

Be honest with yourself about your fears. If you know you'll be too frightened to have a good time, or a productive trip, it doesn't really matter whether your fears are well founded. You may want to try to change your fears, or learn to deal with them differently. But that may not be quick or easy, or possible at all. If you can't overcome your fear, you should change your plans, and do something less scary that you can enjoy.

# KEY ADVICE ABOUT
# SAFETY AND HEALTH

- Don't be afraid to travel.

- Take trains, where possible, rather than buses, cars, or trucks; outside the First World, don't travel by road at night. If there is no train and the roads seem unsafe, consider flying.

- Bring a water purifier. Don't drink the water outside the First World without first boiling, treating, or purifying it.

- See a doctor or health professional at least a month before any trip outside the First World, and follow his or her advice about immunizations and other preparations. Get a prescription for sterile disposable hypodermic needles, and bring them with you.

- Don't have unsafe sex, or at least have safer sex.

- Read the local newspapers and pay attention to what's happening around you. Talk to local people, not just other travelers.

- Buy trip cancellation and interruption insurance to cover the cost of cutting your trip short and coming straight home in an emergency.

- Verify that your medical insurance covers you when you are abroad. If it doesn't, consider changing insurers or getting supplemental travel health insurance. Find out in advance what forms or documentation you'll need to submit with an insurance claim for medical expenses abroad.

**For more information on the topics in this chapter, see the Resource Guide in the back of the book, and the links on the Practical Nomad Web site at http://www.practicalnomad.com.**

If you *want* to travel, and fear is getting in the way, knowing that your fears are unsupported by risk statistics is unlikely to make you unafraid. But that knowledge and understanding may free you to deal with, and overcome, your fear as a phenomenon in itself.

I am neither a health professional nor a psychologist, and this chapter is not intended as a replacement for professional health advice. Rather, it is intended as an overview of common concerns about travel safety and health and an introduction to some risks you may not have thought about. This chapter is intended to supplement the Moon Handbook, *Staying Healthy in Asia, Africa, and Latin America*, by Dirk G. Schroeder, which I recommend that you read before your trip and carry with you.

# Transportation Safety

### Surface Transportation

Road travel and, to the extent that you use it, water travel outside the First World are likely to be the most dangerous parts of your trip. Road accidents are the principal cause of injury and death to travelers abroad. "An estimated quarter of a million people worldwide die in automobile accidents each year," according to the Worldwatch Institute. The United States accounts for only about 10 percent of that number, despite the fact that a much larger proportion of the world's cars are driven in the United States, over greater distances.

For example, both the USA military and the Peace Corps consistently report that the most frequent causes of death and injury for their personnel abroad are motor vehicle accidents. Military personnel are most often hurt or killed in cars and trucks. Peace Corps workers, with less money, are more likely to be hurt or killed on the more cheaply obtained two-wheelers: motorcycles, scooters, and mopeds.

Motor vehicles are the leading cause of accidental death even in the United States, where we have some of the world's best roads and safest and slowest highway drivers. Road travel is significantly more dangerous in most other First World countries than in the United States or Canada, largely because of higher speeds. Americans are often surprised and frightened to find that Europeans routinely drive and pass other vehicles at 110 km/h (70 mph) on narrow two-lane roads between hedgerows with blind corners and no shoulder (verge in British usage). Europeans are much more shocked to find that the maximum permitted speed in North America, even on a straight, flat, limited-access multi-lane divided highway (dual carriageway)—the fabled American open road—is 120 km/hour (75 mph), and that most American drivers don't go much faster than the speed limit.

A passing note to those tempted to speed or break other traffic laws: don't. Traffic violations that would entail minor fines in your home country may land you in jail in another, because traffic police often don't trust that a foreigner given a ticket will pay it, or that a foreigner cited and released will show up later in court.

Bus and car crashes are frighteningly common in the Second, Third, and Fourth Worlds, where roads and vehicles alike are in much poorer condition than in the First World. Even in places with very few motor vehicles, they are always running into each other, and/or off the roads. The Worldwatch Institute reports that "developing" countries have fatality rates per vehicle mile up to 20 times higher than industrialized countries. One newspaper editor in the United States told me that she got in the habit of using stories of Third-World road crashes for filler at the bottom of columns, just because they were so common on the wire-service feed. On any given day, she could count on finding a current story about a lot of people getting killed in a crash. "Didn't a bus just run off the road somewhere?" became shorthand in the newsroom for, "I need a paragraph to complete this page."

Trains are everywhere significantly safer than any road vehicle. I haven't been able to find comprehensive world statistics on train and bus safety, but in the United States the automobile accident rate per passenger-kilometer (or passenger-mile) is almost ten times that of Amtrak trains.

Boats, especially smaller ferries across open ocean or flooded rivers, are at least as dangerous, per passenger-kilometer, as are cars and buses. Ships and ferries are a smaller factor in overall travel safety only because most people take them only for short distances, where there is no alternative. Most ferries and ships that sink or capsize either were overloaded or were traveling in flood or storm conditions for which they were unfit or unprepared. Use common sense. Take a critical look at the ship or boat, and the conditions, before you board. If you are chartering a boat, try to get a sense of the captain's competence. Don't take it for granted that ships or their captains are licensed, regulated, or inspected by the government, or that any of these things proves they are safe.

It may not reassure you about safety in the air, but as nearly as I can determine, you are more likely to be killed driving to or from the airport (even on the safest roads) than on any given flight, even on the least safe airline. If you want to play it safe, fly. If you don't fly, take a train if there is one. Locals, and even many guidebooks, often recommend buses as faster, more frequent, and more direct than trains. Rarely do they mention how much safer trains are than buses, which only becomes more true the poorer the country.

Road accidents are the most common reason for long-term travelers to cut their trips short and come home early. So far as I know, none of my clients has ever been in a plane crash; a couple of times a year, I hear of one who's been seriously hurt in a road crash. And this in spite of the fact that most of my clients travel five or 10 times as far by air as they do by land.

Given that most of the danger of travel is in surface transportation, and that most independent travelers choose to travel mainly by bus or train, flying more and choosing trains rather than buses may be the two simple choices you can make that will most increase your chances of surviving your trip.

I don't necessarily recommend that you fly whenever possible. Traveling around the world involves, of necessity, taking some risks. And there are many other factors than safety to consider. If the price is the same and I have the time, I almost always take a train: I see more, meet more diverse people, and eat better food. Trains are generally more comfortable and, in much of the world, more reliable. Given the need for early check-in and the likelihood of delays and cancellations of flights, trains are often as fast as planes for distance up to at least 1,000 km (600 miles): an all-day journey whether by air or rail. Changes in airline and airport procedures that increase the total time required for a trip by air have substantially increased the distance over which trains are competitive with planes.

### Air Travel Safety

I can only repeat what I've said already: air travel is safe. Air travel safety is, or should be, a nonissue, except to the extent that it influences you to fly rather than to use other means of transportation.

There are differences between the safety of different airlines. But all airlines are so safe compared to surface travel, that the choice between the most and least dangerous airline in the world will have a negligible effect on your chances of surviving your trip. Your time in the air is the safest part of your trip, and the part you should worry about least. Relax and enjoy it. Anywhere in the world, how you get to the airport has more effect on your safety than which air-

# THE POLITICAL ECONOMICS OF AIRLINE SAFETY

Aeroflot, the leading Second World airline, does some things differently than First World airlines. The United States and the USSR, the world's two greatest technological rivals (especially in aerospace) pursued parallel but often quite different technological paths, each with its own technical standards, norms, and expectations about how things are done. One of the most interesting things about visiting the former USSR is seeing the areas— small and large—where Soviet engineers found different but equally valid solutions to similar technical problems. Separate doesn't mean equal, but neither does different mean inferior.

Many foreigners, accustomed to pristine cabins and restaurant-quality food, confuse "service" with safety. They assume that if an airline doesn't wash or paint the interiors of its aircraft cabins as often as other airlines, it doesn't overhaul the engines as often either. They have it backwards: with limited resources, it's better to spend them on safety-related mechan-

ical and aeronautic essentials than on food, cleanliness, or terminal esthetics.

As long as Aeroflot didn't belong to IATA and didn't publish statistics on its safety record, there was at least some excuse for the persistence of the myth that Aeroflot is unsafe (even if the myth's primary cause was anti-communist, anti-Soviet bigotry). But Aeroflot's IATA membership and its publication of more detailed and better safety statistics than many of the world's international airlines should by now have dispelled that myth. Aeroflot's international safety record looks even better now that Aeroflot Russian International Airlines has divested itself almost entirely of domestic flight operations within Russia.

Other than its budget philosophy (see the sidebar "Big Business and the People's Airline" in the Air Transportation chapter), Aeroflot's big advantage is that its expenses for aircraft construction and maintenance, pilot training, and fuel, not to mention labor, are all in local curline you fly on. On scheduled jet flights, it makes no sense to worry, on grounds of safety, about which airline or type of airplane you take, where you sit, or other similar issues.

Perhaps the least rational thing to do about airline safety is to choose to travel by land or water instead of flying. Certainly the stupidest advice I've ever seen in a government travel advisory was the U.S. State Department's recommendation that USA government employees in Russia travel by land rather than by air. It's difficult to believe that the people who issued this advisory had ever been on a Russian road. Aeroflot is far from the world's most dangerous airline, and even the worst of the other Russian domestic airlines are so much safer than Russian

rency—even on international routes where most revenue is in hard currency. This gives Aeroflot an enormous edge over airlines everywhere in the world except North America and Western Europe (the only other regions that build their own large passenger jets). And, given the current undervaluation of the ruble, Aeroflot may have an edge over North America and Western Europe, too. Most countries have to buy their planes, spare parts, and pilot training from the United States, Western Europe, or Russia. The poorer ones—those least able to afford it—also have to pay for maintenance services that they aren't equipped to provide in their own countries. Russia is able to afford (in rubles) standards of equipment maintenance and staff training that most Second, Third, and Fourth World airlines can't hope to match if they have to send their planes back to factories abroad if they want them inspected or overhauled.

The most unsafe international airlines, according to statistics I've seen, are mostly in Africa. That's an indictment not of Africa, but of the impoverishment and marginalization of Africa by the international financial system. Worse still, I sus-

pect, are domestic airlines in poor countries, which are often wholly or largely unregulated and report few if any statistics. The worst are probably those in countries that have devalued currencies, that have few tourists or wealthy foreign travelers (who can afford to demand a higher standard of safety), but that are large enough in area and population, and where surface transportation is bad enough, to create sizable domestic airline markets despite their poverty. Domestic flights in, for example, Nigeria or Congo (formerly Zaire), come immediately to mind.

In 1992 I traveled entirely around the world on Aeroflot (one of only two airlines at that time on which that could be done), flying more than 30,000 km (20,000 miles) on international, domestic, and inter-republican flights within and between four of the former Soviet republics. The service on international flights was good, and I never doubted that I was safer flying than I would have been driving. I would definitely choose Aeroflot again, all else including price being equal, over some airlines based in the United States.

roads or rails that safety is one of the strongest reasons to fly, not drive, when in Russia, as anywhere else.

### Fear of Flying

If air travel safety is (or should be) a nonissue, fear of flying is, unfortunately, an all-too-real issue for many people. I can offer only limited advice, but I'll try to offer a few observations on the fears that many of my clients and fellow travelers have described, in the hope that this will help some of you come to terms with your fear of flying.

The first step in dealing with fear of flying is recognizing that the issue is your fear, not actual safety. Fear is real, as is the pain and anxiety it causes, and you may feel you need to do certain things when you fly, such as choosing certain airlines or airplanes, in order to feel comfortable before or during the flight. But in the long run, pandering to your fear will not eliminate it. Only confronting your fear itself will enable you to understand, overcome, or cure yourself of it.

Most people in First World jet-age societies realize that people who are too afraid ever to get on an airplane have a problem, and that their problem lies in their fear and not in airplanes. Many people who have only a mild or moderate fear of flying may be experiencing a rational response to a societal myth (albeit a false myth) more than a consciously irrational phobia.

Unfortunately, the news media—supposed guardians of truth—reinforce the myth that flying is unusually dangerous, and that the alternatives are less so. If 10 or 100 people are killed in an airplane crash, anywhere in the world, it is front-page world news. For that matter, even one death in an air crash, or an unscheduled landing in which no one is hurt, is often major news in the United States. There is never a front-page headline, much less one every day, to remind us that 100 people died on roads in the United States and 1,000 on roads around the world yesterday, and the day before, and the day before that.

Whatever the reasons, it seems clear that our society manifests not so much an individual as a collective social phobia about flight. Perhaps it is a mechanism to mask our even more extreme collective social denial of the risks of the road. Too much would have to change in the infrastructure of our society, or we'd have to go about our daily affairs in too much fear, if we were to acknowledge how dangerous are the cars that we depend on.

For some people, simply learning how little factual basis there is for fear of flying may be sufficient to reduce or eliminate their fear. For people who want assistance, particularly those with extreme fear (especially those who are unable to bring themselves to fly at all), several airlines and other organizations (see references in the Resource Guide) offer classes in overcoming fear of flying. These are usually one-or two-day courses that include counseling, group discussions, exercises in relaxation and preparation, flight simulations, and finally a short graduation flight on a chartered plane so that course participants don't have to worry about being embarrassed by their fear in front of experienced and

# SHOULD WE TRAVEL?

**Should we still travel around the world, after what happened on 11 September 2001?** Yes, absolutely. Now more than ever. The sad events of September 11 carry, I think, a clear message that isolationism is impossible in an interconnected and interdependent world. Now more than ever, we need international awareness and understanding. We need to recognize our common humanity—and the suffering that unites us—with people everywhere of all races and cultures. And we need to understand the ways in which, for better or worse, our decisions affect others (and vice versa) around the world. What greater victory could we hand the terrorists than to allow them to deprive us of our humanity, and to drive us to emulate them in isolating ourselves from world opinion?

**But is it safe to travel? And to travel overseas?** Yes, absolutely. Now more than ever. The September 11th attacks have, I presume, disabused us of any notion that staying home can keep us out of harm's way. Bad things can happen anywhere. And travel abroad is no more risky than travel in the USA—in fact, statistically speaking, it's often safer. Not that this means people from other countries should stay away from the United States! We have our share of crazies, as does every country, but you'll find that the USA is still a wonderful place to visit, and on the whole most Americans remain (knock wood) very welcoming to for-

eigners. Most of the risks of travel, as I'm constantly reminding other travelers (and reminding myself) are the commonplace risks of our everyday lives at home: car accidents, slips and falls, etc. Most of travel safety at home or abroad is simple common sense, like not forgetting to watch where we're putting our feet when we're distracted by looking at the sights and scenery.

**Is it safe to fly?** Yes, absolutely. Now more than ever. Per mile, air travel is a hundred to a thousand times safer than any alternative means of transportation. That safety will only be improved in the wake of the events of September 11. Your time in the air is unquestionably the safest part of your trip. One of the saddest consequences of the September 11th hijackings will be if they scare large numbers of people into driving rather than flying. The inevitable result would be an increase in the tens of thousands of people killed on the roads in the United States each year. Fear of flying is real. It's common. And it's understandable. But fear is a very different issue from safety. If you're afraid, deal with your fear, even if that isn't easy. But don't assume that airplanes are dangerous just because they are, for you, scary. At the end of the day, our safety and security depend most of all on understanding between people around the world—understanding that is the result, above all else, of the direct personal contact, experience, and learning that result from international travel.

unafraid people. The groups that run these claim a high success rate, and I've heard several accounts of people who were able to fly for the first time after completing such a class.

### Healthy Flying

The health effects of flying come primarily from the cabin atmosphere. What else is there to affect your health when all you really do on a plane is sit in an armchair for a few hours? Three aspects of the air in the cabin are significant: pressure, humidity, and smoke.

**Low Air Pressure:** Virtually all airplanes used by scheduled passenger airlines have pressurized cabins, including most turboprops. The only exceptions are some of the smallest, piston-engine planes (air taxis, bush planes, or flight-seeing planes) that carry fewer than 10 passengers and fly at such low altitudes that no pressurization is needed.

Aircraft cabins are not, however, maintained at sea level pressure. At cruising altitude, cabin pressure is typically equivalent to the normal air pressure at an altitude of about 2,500 meters (8,200 feet) above sea level. A lower pressure would place the passengers in danger of altitude sickness; a higher pressure would place more stress than necessary on the cabin walls and fuselage, which have to contain the pressure.

People who have difficulty breathing at sea level have progressively more difficulty at higher altitudes. When people are advised by a doctor not to fly, it's usually because of the lower air pressure. Such people are usually also advised to avoid spending time on the ground at high altitudes.

**Low Humidity:** At cruising altitude, aircraft cabin air is drier than the air in the driest desert. It would be possible to humidify the cabin air, but if this were done, pressure fluctuations would cause condensation, which could short out electrical equipment. Few airline passengers realize that they are in the driest environment they will ever experience. Nor do they deal with it appropriately. It's easy to get dehydrated in any desert, and far easier if you don't realize that you're in a desert. In air as dry as that on an airplane, it's almost impossible to avoid some degree of dehydration.

Most of the discomfort experienced by airplane passengers is actually unrecognized dehydration. If you get headaches or feel light-headed during or after long flights, for example, it's probably because you are dehydrated. The low air pressure, which requires you to breathe a larger volume of air (which carries away more moisture) to get the same amount of oxygen, accentuates the dehydrating effect of the low humidity. Some travelers who don't like using airplane toilets make things worse for themselves by deliberately reducing their fluid intake so they won't have to urinate in flight. Not having to urinate regularly is a sure sign of dehydration.

The only way to avoid dehydration is to drink lots of fluids before, during, and after each flight, especially a long flight. It's almost impossible to drink enough to keep yourself properly hydrated on a long flight. Worse, many of the drinks you are offered in flight are apt to be alcoholic or caffeinated, both of which make you urinate more and enhance dehydration.

I drink as much water as I can (a liter or quart or more) just before boarding any long flight. I bring at least a liter water bottle on any flight, and drink a total of two or three liters or quarts of fluids on a transoceanic flight. If that sounds excessive, consider how much you would drink during a comparable amount of time sitting in the shade in the desert, and then allow for the fact that the air on an airplane is much drier.

This still isn't enough to avoid arriving moderately dehydrated. I keep drinking as much as I can for several hours after I arrive. To rehumidify my throat and nasal passages, I try to get out into humid air, and/or take a shower or steam bath, as soon as possible after a flight.

**Smoke:** Everything about an airplane accentuates the ill effects of smoke. An aircraft cabin is, of course, a closed environment, and on many types of planes the air is recirculated repeatedly. Regardless of where smokers are seated, everyone on the plane is exposed to smoke. The low air pressure makes you breathe a larger volume of air (and smoke) than you would to get the same amount of oxygen at sea level. And the low humidity dries out your nose and throat, greatly reducing your body's ability to filter out smoke and dust before they reach your lungs.

Airlines would prefer that no one smoke on planes. Smoking increases maintenance and cleaning costs, and smoke particles are extremely dangerous to electronic equipment. Cabin air on flights on which smoking is permitted does not meet some standards for long-term occupational exposure, and flight attendants in the United States won a substantial monetary settlement in 1997 from a group of airlines for damages caused by chronic exposure to smoky cabin air.

The stated goal of the airline trade association, ATA (the Air Transport Association), is a total worldwide ban on smoking on airplanes. Only fear of losing market share to competing airlines that might still permit smoking keeps most airlines from immediately banning smoking on board. The airlines would like nothing better than for governments to impose bans on smoking that would affect them all equally. Several airlines have requested exemption from USA antitrust law to permit them to collaborate on a joint ban on smoking.

In 1995, I took my first smoke-free transoceanic flights across both the Atlantic (10 hours) and the Pacific (12 hours). I was amazed at how much of the discomfort I associated with such long flights turned out to be due to breathing secondhand smoke.

Whether you smoke or not, and whether you like it or not, you can expect smoking to be permitted on fewer and fewer flights. Flights on which smoking is permitted are clearly the exceptions. They do still exist in many places and on many airlines, however, and enforcement is sometimes lax. So you can't count on always finding smoke-free flights.

The transition to smoke-free skies is going surprisingly smoothly, and with surprisingly little anger from smokers. Interestingly, a number of people who smoke prefer smoke-free flights. Six months after one airline banned smoking on all its flights, I talked to a check-in agent who said that only about one passenger on each full Boeing 747 (out of more than 300) complained when told smoking wouldn't be allowed.

## Jet Lag

"Jet lag" is the disruption of the body's normal daily rhythms that results from traveling across time zones more rapidly than your body can adjust, and trying to function on a cycle out of sync with your body's internal clock. Jet lag has nothing per se to do with flight or jets, although only airplanes cross time zones quickly enough to produce its symptoms.

If you travel from one time zone to another, your body takes time to re-adjust. In the extreme case, if you fly across the pole of the Earth to a place on the opposite side of the planet, so that it is noon at your destination when it is midnight at your departure point, it's normal for it to take one to two weeks for your body to fully adjust to the new time zone. There aren't many flights this close to either pole, though I was once on one with a 12-hour time difference. Lesser time changes will require less adjustment time. Until your body synchronizes itself with the time zone where you have arrived, your natural cycles will make you sleepy in the daytime and awake and alert at night, according to the patterns in the place you left.

There is no way to prevent or eliminate jet lag. The body's clock is autonomous and self-regulating, not under any conscious control. "Scientists are working on it," as they say, but don't appear close to finding a rapid way to reset the body's internal clock. Jet lag pills, diets, and miracle cures are either pure quackery or at most tools that can somewhat reduce, not eliminate, the time it takes your body to adjust to rapid changes of time zone. Some people naturally take more time to adjust to time changes than others, but with sufficiently large and rapid time changes everyone experiences some degree of jet lag.

The only things that have been proven to reduce the time it takes to adjust to a new time zone are exposure to as much sunlight as possible on arrival (artificial light is not bright enough to make a difference) and shifting your daily cycle before departure (by waking up and going to sleep earlier or later) in the direction you wish your body to adapt for your destination. This latter works only if you are free to keep strange hours for several days before you leave, and if you plan carefully and have a good understanding of your body's cycles.

If jet lag is unavoidable, why should you worry about it? Developing an awareness of jet lag and your body's rhythms can help you better cope with and be prepared for its effects. For several days after you take a long east-west or west-east flight, keep track of what time your body thinks it is, based on what time it is in the place you left, and your body's normal rate of adjustment, and take that into account in your activities. Awareness of your biological rhythms is the key to coping: anticipating, recognizing, and allowing for jet lag.

Don't try to drive when your body thinks it is the middle of the night, is least alert, and wants to sleep. Don't waste your time lying awake when your body thinks it is midmorning and is keeping you fully alert. If you think about your body's cycles in advance, you can plan accordingly so you don't schedule an important business meeting on your first day in a new time zone at a time when you can predict that your body will be trying to put your mind to sleep. Instead, schedule a late night out, when your body will think it is daytime and wouldn't let you sleep anyway.

I carry a clock and a watch that shows the time in two time zones, and I keep conscious track of what time my body thinks it is. With practice, you can often feel the physical and mental manifestations of your daily cycles. Body temperature, for example, varies daily by more than a degree C (two degrees F). When I feel myself unusually cold and want an extra sweater on my first day in a new time zone, I know that it is because my body, in the night phase of its cycle, is reducing my temperature, and I am reminded to make allowances for the fact that my mind is probably at its nighttime low ebb of alertness and function. Similarly, when I wake up hot in the middle of the night, I know that my body, thinking it is morning, is warming me to wake me up, and that it is probably pointless to keep trying to sleep or stay in bed. I might as well get up and make what I can of the night. I actually find dawn walks in new cities, usually prompted by jet lag, to be a particularly educational and enjoyable way to get a feel for places. I have vivid, pleasant memories of the first mornings after most of my long westbound flights.

## Travel Illnesses

### *Traveler's Diarrhea*

The most common travel ailment is traveler's diarrhea. You're likely to get diarrhea from time to time no matter how careful you are. It's unpleasant but temporary and rarely life-threatening.

The best way to reduce your risk of diarrhea is to boil or treat (with iodine or a filter that includes iodine) the water you drink, and not to eat uncooked, unpeeled fruits or vegetables.

The major danger of diarrhea is dehydration; if you keep drinking adequate amounts of fluids, diarrhea often goes away on its own, without the need for drugs. Drugs should be a last, not a first, resort.

If it's possible, stop and rest until you recover; it's not worth trying to travel or keep up a schedule with diarrhea. The likelihood that you will get diarrhea and be unable to travel for a few days every few months in the South is one of the reasons not to plan a fixed itinerary that doesn't leave you free to spend a few extra days wherever you might get sick.

### Sexually Transmitted Diseases

The most common serious diseases of travelers, and those for which travelers most often need professional medical treatment, are AIDS and other sexually transmitted diseases (STDs).

This should come as no surprise. Travel is romantic— that's part of its attraction and joy. There's always been a special genre of romance and fantasy about travel and travelers. Some people travel in search of love and/or sex, and some find either or both unexpectedly. When someone calls me from halfway around the world to try to change the route of the rest of a trip, the most common reason for the change is having fallen in love with another traveler with a different itinerary.

Some travelers are celibate or monogamously coupled, but lots of travelers aren't, and they may have sex with other travelers and/or with local people they meet along the way. Travelers have always been, and remain, among the major transmission vectors of all communicable diseases, but especially of sexually transmitted diseases.

It's tempting to wish that your vacation travels could be a vacation from concerns about safe sex. But that would be a serious mistake. Rates of HIV infection among sex workers in Bangkok, or among the general population in some African countries, are higher than they are among sexually active gay men in San Francisco, or intravenous drug users in New York City. Other STDs are equally prevalent, or more so. Increasingly many strains are resistant to antibiotics, and some—like herpes—are incurable.

It's also common, largely as a result of unconscious race and class bias, to assume falsely that sex with fellow travelers, especially those from backgrounds like yours, is automatically safer than sex with prostitutes or other local people.

A very high percentage of sexually active travelers get one or another (or several) STD at some point in their travels and a sizable percentage of your fellow travelers are carrying one or more STD. Avoid unsafe sexual practices, and be as safe as you can, no matter who your partners are. Be prepared for the possibility of sex even if you don't expect it; people have been known to change their minds.

Unfortunately, some of the places where the risk of STDs is highest are places where prostitution and sex tourism are pillars of the economy, and where little is being done to promote safer sex or awareness of STDs, lest fear of AIDS or other STDs detract from the profits of the sex industry. You won't be reminded of AIDS or other STDs, or of the dangers of unsafe sex, in the places where it matters most; try to remember this at appropriate moments as you travel.

Condoms and other aids to safer sex are among the health and hygiene supplies you should bring with you. Condoms and other contraceptives aren't always available, and they are often of unreliable quality. Bring plenty: if you end up with extras, you'll have no difficulty giving them away. Sexual lubricants are also hard or impossible to find in many places: one person I know was asked to bring sexual lubricant to some people abroad, as one of a handful of the most-coveted things from the United States that they couldn't get locally.

Venereal disease clinics are a fixture of travelers' ghettoes around the world. Long-term or follow-up treatment (which you are especially likely to need if you get infected with a disease strain that is resistant to common antibiotics) can pose more of problem.

In regions with strong sexual taboos, considerate treatment of sexual or reproductive health issues may not be forthcoming even from medical professionals, especially for women and gay men. This applies not just in parts (although by no means all) of the Third and Fourth Worlds but equally in some parts of the United States, where some major tourist attractions are more than 400 km (250 miles) from any medical facility willing to perform an abortion, and sexually active unmarried people are shunned as sinners.

### Exotic and Tropical Diseases

Horror movies notwithstanding, rare and exotic diseases are just that: rare. The common tropical diseases are the ones you will find described in standard health guidebooks and health advisories; the more serious common ones are those for which the greatest efforts have been made to develop vaccinations and treatments. New contagious diseases, such as SARS in 2003, or the intermittent outbreaks of diseases like Ebola fever, are by their nature unpredictable, impossible to plan for—and infrequent.

There is a certain "Heart of Darkness" fear of the unknown behind travelers' fears that strange (to them) places may harbor strange plagues. Without meaning to belittle the risks of diseases, I think most travelers worry about them more than is warranted.

You should, of course, get any immunizations or other shots recommended for the places you are going, take any recommended prophylactic drugs against common diseases (principally malaria) for which there are no vaccines, and take appropriate preventive measures (such as long clothing and insect repellent) against local parasites and vectors of disease. Beyond that, worrying will get you nowhere.

### Other Medical Issues

Travelers actually have more problems abroad from conditions that predated their travels, and from illnesses and injuries that they would have been just as likely to have at home, as from illnesses peculiar to travel to the places they are visiting.

The travelers who most often require medical evacuation, for example, are elderly passengers who have heart attacks on cruise ships (which, presumably, they would have been just as likely to have at home), followed in frequency by divers, climbers, and other travelers engaging in activities that are intrinsically dangerous anywhere in the world.

Get a thorough general physical examination, and a dental examination and cleaning, before any long trip abroad, especially if you'll be in very poor, remote, and/or dangerous places. More than one of my clients has learned from a predeparture check-up of an illness or condition that precluded taking the planned trip. If there are medical procedures or dental work that might need to be done while traveling, but that could be taken care of before you leave, elect to have them done at home, before your trip. You don't want to have to have medical or dental treatment abroad if you don't have to.

If you wear glasses or contact lenses, get an eye exam as well. Make sure you have both a written copy of your current optical prescription and a spare pair of glasses in the sturdiest, most crush-proof case you can find.

I recommend strongly against contact lenses for travel outside the First World, particularly in dry, smoky, polluted, or dusty areas. Contact lens supplies are heavy and bulky to carry and hard to find or expensive in many areas. Sterile conditions are hard to obtain, and eye infections are a serious risk. If you insist on wearing contact lenses, it's essential to carry medication for eye infections and to know how to use it. Eye infections can cause permanent vision damage unless treated immediately.

Travelers who have worn contact lenses for years, grown accustomed to them, and prefer them to eyeglasses may be tempted to disregard this advice. Lots of travelers set out with contact lenses. Most of them soon switch to glasses. I'm not sure I've met anyone who has kept on wearing contact lenses after more than a month or two of continuous travel outside the First World.

If you have any pre-existing illnesses or medical conditions that might require treatment, bring an ample supply of any appropriate medications and supplies. Know what to do if your condition flares up, and carry documentation of your condition so a traveling companion or health worker will know what to do if you are unable to tell them.

If you do get sick, medical care almost anywhere else in the world is cheaper than it is in the United States, sometimes even free. Visiting foreigners are covered under reciprocal agreements between many countries' national health plans. Most physicians in Third and Fourth World cities were trained in the First World and speak at least some English, although if you get really sick or badly injured, you'll probably want to come home for treatment by your regular health care provider.

**REAL LIFE**

When one of my clients has to cancel or cut short a trip because of illness, it's almost always an illness unrelated to travel.

### Disabilities and Physical Limitations

People with pre-existing physical conditions that affect their ability to travel, such as blindness, paraplegia, or mobility limitations tend to write off the possibility of travel outside the First (and maybe Second) World. Guidebooks for travelers with disabilities focus on First World destinations where the most money has been invested in the technological infrastructure for travel by people with disabilities, such as wheelchair ramps, lift-equipped buses and taxis, and Braille signage.

Outside the First World, guidebooks for disabled travelers, slow walkers, etc. focus on a small number of specialized operators of group tours for people with disabilities. (See the Resource Guide for some sources of information on accessible travel.) The possibility of independent Third World travel is scarcely ever mentioned.

Depending on your condition, the Third World may not be as inaccessible as you think. While it is certainly true that there are few, if any, special facilities for disabled people, that doesn't mean that there aren't other ways to provide for your needs. Care and assistance for disabled people are among many areas where labor-intensive low-tech methods are used in the South to solve problems that we in the North are accustomed to seeing addressed through capital-intensive higher-tech means. These are often just-as-effective, if different, solutions to these problems. Where labor is cheap, they may be more appropriate.

People with disabilities will probably have to give up, temporarily, much of their self-sufficiency if they want to travel in the South. But if you are prepared to pay people to help you, you may find that you can get to far more places, and do far more, than you had imagined. Where there are no wheelchair ramps, you can hire people to carry you. Where there are no Braille signs, you can hire a personal guide and interpreter of the sights. Hiring a full-time personal attendant or two to carry you on and off trains and help you around may be no more expensive, in a Southern country, than hiring a self-drive car or van with hand controls would be in a Northern one.

In the South, where labor is cheap, it's perfectly normal to have personal servants, and in hiring attendants, guides, porters, or escorts you are only doing what a local person with your disability, and as much money as you have, would do. The greatest difficulty may simply be finding reliable people to hire, or lining them up in advance.

For those with disabilities who find this concept intriguing, and are excited at the possibility of finding ways to travel in places they thought would be off-limits or unmanageable, John Hockenberry's *Moving Violations*, the memoirs of an international diplomatic and war correspondent who uses a wheelchair, provides some excellent examples and food for thought.

## Violence and Crime

Many people are worried about crime, terrorism, war, and political violence. These worries are understandable, but largely unfounded. Whatever we once thought, we've all learned that the United States is not exempt from terrorism. Most victims of terrorism, in the United States and around the world, are people in their own homes, workplaces, and communities, not travelers.

Despite the widespread hostility toward various policies of the USA government, individual American tourists are in serious danger of terrorism or political violence in very few places. (See the sidebar, "Should We Travel?")

Americans tend to identify very strongly with the USA government, and thus to identify foreign peoples with "their" governments. Not so in most other countries. Most of the world's people don't live in democracies and don't expect governments or their policies to be indicative of the desires of the people. Some of the places I've been most warmly welcomed were ones where the USA government was widely hated. Many experienced travelers report similar experiences of being invited into homes where the first question asked was, "Why is the USA government doing X, Y, or Z to our country? Why does your government hate us?" People in the most "anti-American" places are, on the whole, remarkably friendly to American people.

You are unlikely to end up in a war zone inadvertently if you pay the least attention to local current events. It's certainly a good reason to read the local newspaper(s) whenever you get a chance—not the internationally distributed *USA Today* or the *International Herald Tribune*, which will tell you about events in the United States but much less about what's going on where you are.

Past wars pose more serious and less obvious dangers for tourists than current wars. Large areas of the world, including several entire countries, should be avoided due to land mines. Most heavily mined countries were poor even before the wars that generated the minefields and have little money even to mark known minefields. Local people in these areas take it for granted that everyone knows not to wander around anywhere they don't have to, or pick up or touch anything on or in the ground.

Modern warfare does not confine land mines to well-defined minefields. There are perhaps 100 million unexploded mines scattered in dozens of countries around the world, and 5–10 million more mines are produced each year. These mines, some from as long ago as World War II, kill thousands of civilians a year in areas no longer at war.

Any list of war zones would be rapidly out of date. But the pace of mine clearing is so inherently slow that travel to the countries presently heavily mined will remain dangerous for decades or centuries. So I don't expect to be able to recommend to tourists in my lifetime the most heavily mined countries, Afghanistan and Cambodia. Likewise, travel to Angola, El Salvador, Eritrea, Ethiopia, Iran, Iraq, Kuwait, Mozambique, Nicaragua, Somalia, Sudan, rural Vietnam, and much of the former Yugoslavia will (barring miraculous improvements in de-mining technology) remain unsafe for our lifetimes except for travel in the main cities and along the busiest—and thus highest priority for de-mining—highways and rail lines.

Many of these countries have never been of major tourist interest. But the lure of Angkor Wat still draws many tourists to Cambodia in spite of the better-publicized hazards of guerrilla attacks on tourists. I'm not out to scare people unduly. I want to encourage travel wherever it's possible. But anyone who is tempted to go to Cambodia should know that field research by Physicians for Human Rights estimates that "In Cambodia . . .one out of every 236 people has lost at least one limb to an exploding mine." Do you really want to risk being next?

If you don't want even more of the world to be rendered off-limits by land mines, I encourage you to support the International Campaign to Ban Landmines (http://www.icbl.org). The ICBL was little-known when I mentioned it in the first edition of this book, but gained prominence when it won the 1997 Nobel Peace Prize. An international treaty banning landmines came into effect in 1999, but as of 2003 the United States remained the most important country not to have ratified it, and the world's major advocate of continued manufacture and deployment of land mines.

Terrorism aside, few countries have as much violent crime as the United States, and in few countries are criminals as apt to be armed, especially with guns, as they are in the United States. At the same time, foreigners afraid of USA crime may be reassured to hear that most lifelong USA residents have never been the victim of a violent crime. Travelers anywhere in the world are far more likely to have their belongings stolen than to be violently attacked.

Violence against women and children is a problem throughout the world. But most of this violence is within families, not against travelers or other strangers. American women traveling abroad, whether in Europe or in the South, in groups or couples or alone, generally report much higher levels of sexual harassment than in the United States, but a lower level of perceived danger of sexual assault or violence. Most of the danger of sexual assault or rape, from the anecdotal evidence I've heard, is the danger of date rape by fellow travelers in guest houses and hostels, not of rape by locals. (See the Resource Guide for sources of advice and mutual support for women travelers.)

Americans and other travelers from countries where significant sectors of society are coming to disapprove of excessive family violence may find it hard to get used to seeing women and children "put in their places" in public or private by elders and male family members. If you complain, realize that you risk having the violence redirected at yourself. Some visitors to the United States, on the other hand, may find it equally hard to accept that some strangers in the United States will feel entitled to criticize them if they hit their wives or children, while others will even call the police to try to have them arrested.

# HEALTH PREPARATIONS

## Immunizations

### What Shots Do You Need?

Current official USA government inoculation and antimalarial requirements and recommendations for all countries are available from the Centers for Disease Control and Prevention on the Internet at http://www.cdc.gov/travel.

In addition to country listings of vaccination requirements, the CDC produces advisories intended for both health professionals and lay readers on the health hazards of each world region and what to do about them. Included are preventive and treatment strategies for particular diseases, such as malaria, and information about current disease outbreaks, epidemics, and emerging diseases and health hazards. Few other countries have the resources to produce such a comprehensive and continuously updated collection of travel health advice. CDC advisories are much less politically biased than U.S State Department travel advisories and are a useful resource for English-literate travelers from other countries as much as for those from the United States. A few countries do require vaccinations that would not otherwise be recommended, while most of the CDC recommended inoculations are not required by any government.

Some immunizations require a series of injections several weeks apart, and you shouldn't get too many shots at once. You generally need to start taking antimalarial drugs two weeks before you expect to arrive in a malarial area. So you should start getting immunizations and prescriptions at least a month, better six weeks, before your departure. Most people expect injections, but some immunizations are actually oral vaccines.

In order to know what vaccinations and prescriptions to recommend, a doctor or clinic will need a complete list, in sequence, of all the countries you plan to visit. The sequence is important because some countries require immunizations against certain diseases only if you have previously visited certain other countries where those diseases are found.

If you don't have one already, get a passport-sized yellow International Certificates of Vaccination booklet when you get your first immunizations. (Most travel doctors and immunization clinic provide them.) Make sure each immunization is entered in your yellow booklet with the doctor's signature, date, and stamp. Keep your yellow booklet with your passport; it can be essential when crossing borders and impossible to replace if lost. If you lose it and can't prove that you have had the required immunizations, you may have to be immunized on the spot at a border, by whom and with whatever equipment happens to be available, whether it is sterile, unsterile, or reused.

### Where Should You Get Your Shots?

If you're going on a long or arduous trip, the first place to go should be your regular doctor, health maintenance organization (HMO), or health service. You should get a general health check-up before an extended trip, and you might as well get your immunizations, antimalarial prescriptions, etc., at the same time and place. Some HMOs and public health services have in-house travel clinics or travel health specialists on staff.

If you don't have a regular health care provider, your doctor is unfamiliar with travel health issues, or you are certain you are in good general health and are only taking a short trip, there are specialized travel clinics in some major international gateway cities. Some are downtown, to serve business travelers; others are located in or near seaports or airports. Travel clinics generally keep the usual vaccines in stock and provide prescriptions for antimalarials and/or syringes or other prescription travel health supplies at no additional charge with immunizations. You may have to go to a travel clinic for some of the less-common immunizations, as some vaccines are expensive and have such short shelf lives that most doctors don't keep them in stock.

Some travel clinics are strictly immunization centers, offering minimal advice or other services. The most efficient have drop-in hours when no appointments are needed for standard services, and charge only per immunization. These are usually the cheapest and easiest places to go if that's all you need. Others, especially those that are part of teaching hospitals, offer more comprehensive travel health counseling and advice. They tend to require advance appointments and to charge much more, including per-visit fees in addition to fees for immunizations. But their personnel are willing to spend more time answering your questions or explaining recommendations for special cases.

## Health and Hygiene Supplies

*Staying Healthy in Asia, Africa, and Latin America* has detailed health, hygiene, and first-aid packing lists for travel to more and less remote areas.

*Staying Healthy* is the first thing you should buy for your travel first-aid and medical kit. Read it before you leave, and bring it with you. Long before I began to write this series for Avalon Travel Publishing and before *Staying Healthy* was published by Avalon Travel, I carried a copy on each of my trips abroad and I recommended it to all of my clients. I'll give only a few additional packing notes.

Toilet paper (even American-style toilet paper) is available most places there are foreign tourists, even in places where most local people don't use it. I try to pack several rolls anyway: if I start out with half a dozen rolls of toilet paper in my luggage, I know I'll have room for the books I'll acquire along the way. You may tend to accumulate souvenirs or other things to bring home, rather than books —my traveling companion accumulates silks and other fine textiles—but the principle is the same.

Condoms, other contraceptives, and sexual lubricants, are all unobtainable outside the largest cities in many regions, and uncommon and expensive (or of poor quality) even there. Bring enough to last a long while, and stock up when you can. Women should consider bringing medication for vaginal yeast infections. Yeast infections are common side effects of travel stress and antibiotics, and the medication can be hard to find.

Tampons are hard to find and expensive in much of the world. If you have a strong preference for a particular type, you may have to carry enough for many months at a time. Sanitary napkins are more widely available, though again of erratic quality. Some women travelers switch to menstrual pads or sponges that can be washed and re-used, such as are used by most women in the world. Some find they prefer them, and never switch back, even after they return home to the First World. However, when traveling in areas with questionable water quality make sure to use only potable water for washing the pads or sponges.

If you can get a prescription for them, bring a few sealed disposable sterile needles and syringes. These are available over the counter in most of the world, but not necessarily just when you need them. If you need an injection (such as of antibiotics for severe infection), supply your own needle and syringe. This is actually the normal practice for those who can afford new needles in many countries.

Needles and syringes are routinely reused, often without sterilization or cleaning with bleach, in much of the world. Dirty used needles are sometimes repackaged and resold as new and sterile in some countries. Injections and blood transfusions in many countries carry a serious risk of AIDS or other blood-borne diseases.

Many people are afraid to carry needles and syringes, lest they be suspected of being drug addicts. If it came to that, I'd rather come under suspicion of drug use than get HIV/AIDS from a contaminated needle. In practice, I've never had a problem carrying needles and syringes in my medical kit, and I've never heard of anyone else having a problem either, unless they were also carrying illegal drugs.

A discussion of this topic on the Internet (in the "rec.travel.misc" Usenet newsgroup) prompted people to write in from all over the world, all reporting that they had carried syringes across all sorts of borders without incident or difficulty, even when their packs had been searched, their medical kits opened, and the needles scrutinized. The only place I worry about it at all any more is coming back into the United States, where I make sure I have the prescription with my needles. And of course I never carry illegal drugs across borders. If the substance you think you need isn't available on the other side of the border, that's a sure sign the risks of possession or smuggling are too high.

## TRAVEL INSURANCE

"Travel insurance" is a confusing term, as it is used to refer to insurance against many different types of risks: travel medical insurance, medical evacuation (medevac) insurance, trip cancellation and interruption insurance, supplier default insurance, baggage insurance, etc. Many "travel insurance" policies offer a confusing bundle of coverage and options; read the fine print to be sure you understand what you are paying for and what is (and isn't) covered.

Some travel agents and tour companies provide information on travel insurance, but you should never buy travel insurance directly from a travel agent or tour company. Your payment should be made directly to the insurance company or an independent insurance agent. If you pay travel agents or tour companies for insurance, and they go bankrupt, you are likely to find that they had failed to pass on your insurance premium to the insurance company and that you are not insured.

Some tour companies allow you to pay an additional fee, up front, in exchange for a waiver of their usual penalties if you have to cancel your trip. In effect, this means that you are paying a higher price for a less-restricted ticket or package. This is not really insurance, though it's quite legitimate. It may or may not be a good deal, depending on the relative sizes of the waiver fee and cancellation penalties, but you should at least look at the numbers and consider it.

Some regular insurance agents handle travel insurance, especially long-term comprehensive travel medical insurance. If you're traveling for six months or more, or if you plan to travel regularly throughout the year, it may be cheaper to include travel coverage with your regular health coverage than to buy a separate policy targeted at travelers. Check with your regular insurance agent to see what they can offer.

You can also get travel insurance from specialists in the field. These include travel insurance companies, direct providers of medevac and travel emergency services, and independent travel insurance brokers and agencies that can help you compare the offerings of different insurers. Some companies are listed in the Resource Guide to help you get started on your research.

I recommend trip cancellation and interruption insurance and, if available, supplier default insurance for all long-term travelers. Travel medical insurance and medical evacuation insurance are appropriate for some but not all travelers, depending on your situation, overall health, and what (if any) other insurance you have.

### Comprehensive Travel Medical Insurance

Comprehensive travel medical insurance is for people who don't have any other medical insurance, even at home. Since most people who can afford it have health care coverage in their home country, often through their employer, comprehensive travel medical insurance is mainly of interest to long-term travelers who've left their jobs and lost their insurance coverage at home, or to those living and working outside their country of citizenship or permanent residence. The best policies for long-term travelers are often those marketed to expatriates, rather than to travelers. Check publications and Web sites targeted at expats and international students and volunteers for advice and recommendations on this sort of insurance.

Since comprehensive health insurance covers most medical expenses while you are traveling, even routine care, premiums are high: US$5 a day or more, which many long-term budget travelers consider to be prohibitively costly. Travel health insurance won't usually (except in the case of special plans for foreign visitors to the United States) pay overseas bills directly; it will only reimburse you after the fact. It is generally secondary insurance; that is, it will only reimburse whatever your primary insurance (if you have any) won't pay. If you already have health insurance, it may already provide better coverage than you realize for expenses for emergency treatment abroad. Such medical care as is available in many places is often inexpensive or free anyway. And if you get really sick or badly injured, you'll probably want to come home rather than having major surgery or long-term treatment abroad.

For all these reasons you may not want this sort of insurance unless you don't have any other health insurance, are in especially poor health (in which case I'm not sure I'd recommend a trip around the world), are especially cautious, or are taking a relatively short trip to an expensive place.

A common strategy is to keep up your regular health plan at home while you are traveling, assuming the risk that you will have to pay out of your own pocket for any health expenses not covered by your insurance, and to buy trip cancellation and interruption insurance (see below) to cover the cost of getting home if you should become badly hurt or seriously ill.

### Emergency Travel Medical Insurance

Emergency travel medical insurance is for people who have medical coverage at home, but whose health plan at home doesn't cover them while they are traveling. Emergency travel medical insurance only covers emergency services abroad; once you get home, you're on your own (or presumably, back under your regular home coverage) for any necessary follow-up treatment or continuing care. Most health insurance plans and health maintenance organizations in the United States include their own provisions for emergency care while abroad, at least for trips of less than 30 days. Check with your current insurer or HMO before you waste money on an emergency travel medical plan that might duplicate your existing coverage.

Supplemental or emergency medical insurance is essential for all foreign visitors to the United States. Because the United States has no national health program, it also has no reciprocal agreements to provide care for visitors whose health care at home is provided by their countries' national health systems. Health care in the United States, for those without insurance, is almost entirely on a cash basis. Only the most limited emergency medical services are available to those without insurance or the means to pay. Medical treatment in the United States is several times more expensive than in most other First World countries, and many USA doctors and medical facilities will not provide services, except in life-or-death situations, without advance payment or proof of insurance. A single day in a hospital as a result of a car crash in the USA could easily cost US$10,000, possibly more.

Don't even think of visiting the United States without a supplemental medical insurance policy, preferably from a company with its own USA office that can make payments directly to USA health care providers, rather than requiring you to pay and reimbursing you later. Most travel agents specializing in travel to the United States can provide information on insurance plans of this sort.

Carry proof of insurance at all times while in the United States. Most insurance companies will issue you an insurance card with a contact number that a doctor or hospital can call, before providing medical services, to verify that you are insured and that payment will be made. Keep this card in your money belt with your other essential documents.

### Medical Evacuation Insurance

Medical evacuation (medevac) insurance covers the cost of an air ambulance and related services if you are so badly injured, or become so ill, that you can't come home (or get to a suitable medical facility) on a scheduled commercial passenger flight.

Emergency medical evacuation by chartered air ambulance can be prohibitively expensive. Cost aside, arranging for an air ambulance, attending physician and nurse, customs and immigration clearance for the onboard equipment, life-support facilities at each refueling stop, etc., is more than most people could or would know how to do on their own. But medical evacuations are less common than people think. Even very badly injured travelers usually can come home on regular flights after no more than a couple of weeks of emergency treatment and stabilization abroad.

Most places with airports have scheduled service that can get one to a city with a sophisticated modern hospital more quickly than an air ambulance could arrive. The kinds of risky sports and activities that are most likely to lead to the need for evacuation, such as scuba diving, mountain climbing, and motor sports, are often specifically excluded from insurance coverage as uninsurable risks.

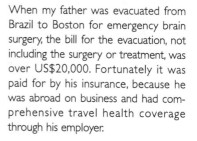

**REAL LIFE**

When my father was evacuated from Brazil to Boston for emergency brain surgery, the bill for the evacuation, not including the surgery or treatment, was over US$20,000. Fortunately it was paid for by his insurance, because he was abroad on business and had comprehensive travel health coverage through his employer.

Medical evacuation insurance is most appropriate if you will be taking an especially dangerous trip (but not one involving an activity excluded in the fine print of the policy) or one through regions inaccessible by, or with especially infrequent, commercial air service. If you aren't insured and can't afford an air ambulance you may have to wait longer to recover, and endure considerably greater discomfort or pain, to fly home on a scheduled airline. If you can afford it, it's probably a good idea in any case, and if you ever need it you certainly won't regret the expense of insurance. But if you can't afford it, I probably wouldn't let that alone stand in the way of your trip.

### Trip Cancellation and Interruption Insurance

Trip cancellation and interruption insurance covers the cancellation or refund penalties and the cost of getting home if you have to cancel your trip, or cut it short, for specified reasons. The covered reasons vary (read the fine print), but typically include injury or illness to you, a traveling companion, or a member of your immediate family. Itinerary changes due to the outbreak of war or a terrorist incident in an intended destination may or may not be included, or may be covered only at additional charge.

Trip cancellation and interruption insurance is available even to people who don't buy any other form of travel insurance, and is much cheaper, especially for long-term travelers, than travel medical insurance. The cost is a fixed percentage of the cost of your air tickets (typically 4–8 percent), regardless of the length of your trip.

Although most tickets around the world will allow you to change the dates of each flight at no charge, they will not permit you to change the airlines or sequence of connections. So getting home on the original routing, even if space is available on the next flight on each leg of the trip, could easily take you two or three weeks. The alternative, of course, is full-fare, fully reroutable and refundable tickets. But the cost of trip cancellation and interruption insurance is a tiny fraction of the difference in cost between fully refundable, reroutable tickets and discounted nonrefundable, nonreroutable tickets. It's cheaper to get tickets with penalties and get trip cancellation and interruption insurance than to get fully refundable tickets.

Trip cancellation and interruption insurance won't cover you if you simply change your mind, or if the reasons for a business trip change. Some but not all plans cover you if you are denied a visa or denied entry. Most won't cover you for pre-existing medical conditions. Other than these, the reasons for canceling or cutting short a trip that they do cover are the most frequent reasons for people with nonrefundable tickets to have to change their plans.

Family emergencies are an especially common reason to need trip cancellation and interruption insurance. Most people are uncomfortable with acknowledging that a parent or other immediate family member is in sufficiently poor health that cutting short a trip in case of hospitalization or death might be necessary. But this is actually a common reason to come home early, and if you bought insurance at least your choice of whether to come home if someone gets sick or dies won't have to be influenced by concerns of cost.

Road accidents—which can leave you in no condition to continue your trip and in need of lengthy rehabilitation and follow-up treatment that you would prefer to undergo at home—are the other common reason for trip cancellation and interruption insurance.

Because the likelihood of a claim is directly related to the length of your trip, but the premium is the same whether you will be leaving tomorrow and home in a week or leaving in six months and home in a year, the longer your trip and the further in advance you buy your tickets the better the buy this sort of insurance is likely to be. I highly recommend trip cancellation and interruption insurance for all long-term travelers.

### Supplier Default Insurance

Supplier default insurance covers any money you lose because of the bankruptcy of an airline, cruise line, tour operator, or other provider of travel services. Most trip cancellation and interruption policies used to include supplier default coverage, but supplier default coverage has been drastically cut back since 11 September 2001. Some travel insurance companies no longer offer it at all, while others pick and choose which travel suppliers they will insure. Read the fine print. (For more advice on airline bankruptcies, see the Air Transportation chapter.)

# "When in Doubt,
### *Leave It Out.*"

# BAGGAGE

## AIRLINE BAGGAGE LIMITS

On most international flights, airline rules limit you to a total of 20 kg (44 lb) of luggage per person total. Carry-on baggage is limited to five kg (11 lb) and is included in the overall limit of 20 kg, even if it weighs less than five kg. Even if all you have is only a single bag small enough to fit under the seat and weighing less than 20 kg, the airline is not obligated to let you carry it on. The airline can require you to check any bag weighing more than five kg.

Not all airlines strictly enforce luggage limitations. But it's possible to get a strict check-in clerk on any given airline and flight, so you can't count on checking or carrying on more than the rules allow. To see if you're within your free baggage allowance, do as the airline will do: put everything you aren't actually wearing on a scale together, including your purse, shoulder bag, camera, and anything else you plan to carry on or check.

Many Americans with extensive travel experience find this hard to believe. They say, "I travel overseas and back all the time, and I've never been limited to 44 pounds." They infer from this, erroneously, that they will never actually be limited to 20 kg, even on an around-the-world trip. What they don't realize is that different rules apply on flights to, from, and within North America than on flights everywhere else in the world.

### Two Pieces or 20 Kilograms?

The international baggage standard is the "weight" limit: 20 kg per coach passenger, 30 kg for business class, 40 kg for first class. Passengers traveling on flights to, from, or within North America, or on tickets issued at through fares to or from North America, are the exception: under the "piece" limit, they are entitled to two pieces of checked luggage per person. Size and weight limits under the piece system vary by airline, but 60 or 70 lb (27 or 32 kg) per piece is usual. Whether the piece rule or the weight rule applies depends on the fare as well as the flight.

Passengers traveling on through fares to or from North America are governed by the piece limit on the entire portion of the journey included on a through fare. For example, on a trip from the United States to India, a passenger tick-

# KEY ADVICE ABOUT BAGGAGE

- When in doubt, leave it out.

- Keep your luggage within the standard international airline baggage limit: 20 kg (44 lb) total per person including all carry-on items.

- Always get to the airport prepared to check your luggage. Never count on being allowed to carry it on, regardless of its size or weight.

- Don't cut corners on key items of your gear like your pack and water purifier. For prolonged hard traveling, the best quality you can afford is worth the price.

- Carry your passport, tickets, and other vital documents in a money belt or otherwise hidden inside your clothes. Carry backup photocopies of everything in your money belt, and leave another set behind with a trusted friend.

- Don't worry too much about what you forget, lose, or break. You can find almost anything you really need along the way, or find some local substitute to serve the same purpose.

- Don't feel dependent on any of your things. They might get lost, stolen, or broken. Be prepared to improvise.

- Don't count on care packages. Mailing things home is usually slow but more or less affordable and reliable, but having things sent to you while you are traveling is often difficult and/or expensive.

For more information on the topics in this chapter, see the Resource Guide in the back of the book, and the links on the Practical Nomad Web site at http://www.practicalnomad.com.

BAGGAGE

eted on a through fare is entitled to two pieces (not just 20 kg), even on the Europe-India or East Asia-India leg on which local passengers are being allowed only 20 kg.

But if these onward connecting flights are ticketed at a separate fare (even if it is written on the same ticket), they are subject to the weight rule, just like local passengers on these flights.

This is particularly significant if you want to take more than 20 kg of luggage between North America and points to which there aren't direct flights, mainly in Africa and South Asia. It is often possible to get slightly cheaper tickets between the Americas and Africa or South Asia by breaking the fare (and, frequently, by switching airlines) at an intermediate point in Europe or East Asia (such as London or Bangkok). But an often-unanticipated consequence of doing so is that the baggage limit is reduced to 20 kg on the portion of the journey away from North America. Consequently, the excess baggage charges for the two pieces allowed on a through fare can easily exceed the apparent up-front savings of breaking the fare at an intermediate point.

If you'll be flying on different airlines for portions of your journey, and want to be allowed more than 20 kg, always make sure either that you will receive a through fare ticket or that your tickets will be endorsed to permit baggage on the piece rule. It's especially difficult to know for sure what your tickets say about baggage limits if you have electronic rather than paper tickets. You have to ask; if it's important, get it in writing. Some people deliberately travel between Australia and Europe via the United States, rather than via Asia, in order to be allowed more luggage.

Usually it's impossible to ticket around-the-world itineraries entirely on fares

---

# CHECK IT OR CARRY IT ON?

Travelers can be divided into those who always try to carry everything on, and those who try to avoid carrying on any more than essentials. I suspect I'm in the minority in the latter category, but here are some of my reasons:

• When changing planes, I'd rather have the airline be responsible for transferring luggage and guarding it during the transfer and layover. That way I don't have to watch it, carry it into the airport toilet or restaurant, etc. (This is most important if I have a long enough layover to want to go into the city or outside the airport, or if the change involves a change of terminals and/or airports.)

• I've been in many places where I had to check bags anyway. Because you have to be prepared at the check-in point for the possibility that you may have to check your main pack (and thus have to have your essentials separated out so that you can carry them on if necessarily), why not just check the things you are already prepared to check? If you expect always to carry everything on, you may be unprepared and ill-equipped if you have to check some things, or you may rashly check everything and be really SOL if your bag is lost or delayed.

• You may have to check your bag because the plane is full and the overhead bins are full; or because the type of plane has no, or less than usual, space for carry-on bags; or because you have something in your bag that is not allowed to be carried on, for "security" reasons; or because your bag weighs more than five kg (the carry-on limit in some places); or simply because the airline feels like it (they can make you check anything). As more items are prohibited from carry-on luggage, the

from or to North America. So at least part of an around-the-world journey, and in most cases all but the flights to, from, and within North America, will be subject to the 20-kg baggage limit.

## Domestic Baggage Limits

There is no standardization of baggage limits on domestic flights within different countries. Some countries allow an amount corresponding to either the international weight or piece rule. But not all. You must verify baggage limits for flights entirely within any country with the airlines on which you will fly.

If you can't do so any earlier (e.g., because the airline in question doesn't have an office in your country), check the baggage limits when you reconfirm any domestic flight. You can generally count on being allowed at least 20 kg on any flights operated by jet aircraft, even on domestic flights. Limits are generally set lower only when space or payload capacity on the plane is less. The smaller

less likely it is that you'll be able to carry everything on, and the more it makes sense to plan to check as much as possible.

• It is often faster, sometimes substantially so, to check your bag and then breeze through the security inspection to the gate than to wait for your entire pack to be searched as carry-on at the checkpoint. Security searches of carry-on baggage, even in the United States, are becoming more time consuming and thorough, and it's a toss-up whether fragile items are more likely to be damaged by baggage handlers, if well packed, than by hurried cops or soldiers trying to pry unfamiliar objects open to see if they contain bombs when they are searching carry-on. You can leave the airport more quickly if you don't check your bags, if all goes well, but you can often arrive at the airport later if you plan to check your bags. I more often find myself arriving at the departure airport late and in a hurry than needing the

maximum time advantage in leaving the airport at my destination.

• Even if I have time for my bag or pack to be searched as a carry-on, I may not wish to call attention to every little item in my luggage. I often carry legal items that I would just as soon not have waved about, passed from hand to hand, be asked to explain, or have brought to the attention of the governments of the countries to or from which I am traveling or in which I change planes. Yes, all luggage is subject to search by customs and border guards, but in practice departing checked airline luggage is much less likely to be opened than is carry-on luggage. For example, I've often seen guards pulling condoms, tampons, etc. out of carry-on baggage, waving them about, and demanding that the people carrying them explain what they are (through a language barrier). Not my cup of tea. I'd rather leave such things in the bag I check.

the plane, the smaller the luggage limits. If the plane on a domestic flight has a capacity of fewer than about 20 passengers, there is a good chance luggage will be limited to 15 kg (33 lb) or even 10 kg (22 lb) per passenger. If limits like these apply, count on them being strictly enforced, with all carry-on items included in the weighing.

If there isn't room on the plane, the airline is entitled to send your free baggage separately (usually on the next flight, whenever that may be). Don't argue if it wants to do this. Better to do without your luggage for a week, if that's how long it is until the next flight, than to overload and endanger the whole plane and everyone on it. Travelers commonly encounter small planes and small baggage limits like these on flights to short mountain airstrips in Nepal, to small islands anywhere, to remote jungle clearings in Indonesia and Papua New Guinea, and to safari camps in Africa.

Baggage limits on flights within the United States used to be exceptionally loosely enforced. Airlines would routinely waive excess baggage charges. However, increasing recognition of cargo and excess baggage as a profit center has reduced USA airlines' willingness to waive excess baggage charges. In addition, the integration of baggage record-keeping with passenger reservations (through systems in which baggage tags are printed directly by, and logged in, the computerized reservation system), mandated by governments in the United States and abroad as a security measure, has largely eliminated the discretion of counter and gate agents to check excess bags without charging for them.

## Excess Baggage

Excess baggage is very expensive. The standard charge for excess baggage is one percent of the full first-class fare per excess kilogram (even if you are traveling on a discounted coach-class ticket), payable separately for each flight. If you must take excess baggage on some portion of your trip, shop around: particularly on flights to and from North America, some airlines charge a flat rate per piece (typically US$100–125) that is substantially lower than the per-kilogram charge.

Airlines are not required to accept excess baggage at all. On some small planes that service remote areas such as African safari camps, they simply don't have room for it and won't carry it at any price. Nor will excess baggage necessarily be put on the same flight with you, even if paid for as accompanied baggage.

Unaccompanied baggage is considered air freight and charged at cargo rates. Air cargo rates are higher per kilogram per kilometer (or per pound per mile) than most coach rates for passenger transportation, and airlines have higher profit margins on cargo than on passenger operations. Shipping excess baggage separately by air will be substantially more expensive in almost all cases than paying excess baggage charges. It is also much easier to get goods through customs as accompanied luggage—even in excess, dutiable amounts—than as unaccompanied freight. Barring special problems, you can walk all your accompanied luggage through customs as soon as you arrive. If you ship something separately it can take weeks to clear customs, or cost substantial "expediting fees" or bribes to get it sooner.

These differences in the price, speed, and ease of customs clearance of accompanied baggage vis-à-vis air freight are the reason express shipping companies subsidize air tickets for couriers to accompany their most urgent consignments. The amount the courier company contributes toward the cost of the courier's ticket is offset by the savings on shipping charges and customs clearance time.

## Oversize Items

Unlike weight limits, size limits vary from airline to airline. It is irrelevant to Airline J whether Airline K accepted something or charged extra for it on some other flight. If you have or expect to have anything larger than an ordinary suitcase, call each and every airline on which you plan to travel, in advance, to find out whether it will accept it and, if so, how much it will charge.

Rules for oversize baggage (e.g., surfboards, bicycles, and skis) vary greatly from airline to airline. Most airlines have set fees for specific items of this sort. Check with each airline on which you are booked for its fees (some carry surfboards for free, some charge US$150 per board per flight) and regulations. Does it require bicycles to be dismantled and/or boxed? Does it provide the boxes, or must you have your own? Does it require oversize baggage to be checked in early? How early? If you will be changing planes, find out if you will be charged additionally for each flight, or only once for the entire through journey.

## Animals and Plants

Transporting pet animals is even more complicated and expensive. Tickets for pet transportation are generally closer in price to tickets for people than to the charges for an amount of excess baggage similar in size and weight to that of the pet. If you want to bring a pet, tell your travel agent as early as possible. Check with the airline(s) and any country to or through which you'll be taking an animal to verify their procedures for cages, check-in and pick-up times, vaccinations, quarantine, etc.

Many countries require arriving animals, or those of certain species or categories, to be quarantined (isolated) under observation for a period of time in order to tell if they have any diseases not found in the country. This is to ensure that arriving animals won't bring in exotic diseases or parasites to which local animal populations, especially commercial livestock, are not resistant. You will have to pay the cost of keeping your pet in quarantine for this time. Find out in advance how long your pet will have to be quarantined, and how much it will cost.

No doubt some readers are wondering why anyone would take a pet with them around the world. Some people buy tickets around the world when they

Twice in my travels my luggage has missed a connection and ended up in the wrong city. In each case, my bag was delivered to the place I was staying, undamaged, three or four days later. When it happened on a domestic flight in the United States, when I checked in for my next flight with the same airline, I was reimbursed against receipts for up to US$100 in clothes, toiletries, maps, and film bought while my luggage was missing. When it happened on an international trip to the Third World, with an Asian airline very conscious of lost face, both my traveling companion and I were upgraded to business class by way of apology for having misplaced our luggage.

are relocating overseas for most of a year and want to visit other places on the way there and/or the way back. Sometimes they want to bring their pets with them for the year abroad, particularly if they have children. I don't think the cost and hassle is likely to be worth it, but some people do.

Imports of living plants are subject to even more stringent controls. Inadvertently imported weeds that interfere with agriculture, plants that crowd out indigenous species, and plants harboring blights, pests, or diseases have caused immense damage to agriculture and natural ecosystems alike in many countries. The decision to introduce a new plant species into a bio-region where it isn't already found is not one to be made lightly, nor one to be made by amateurs.

Once a new plant or pest is introduced it can be impossible to eradicate (many pests and blights have stages in which they are invisible). Moral: Do not take live animals, plants or seeds—including fresh fruits and vegetables or uncooked meat—across international borders, no matter how innocuous (and attractive) they may seem.

## Lost Luggage

If your luggage doesn't arrive on your flight, file a report and description with the airline for tracing. Most "lost" luggage either got left behind or put on the wrong plane. The airline will usually notify you and deliver your luggage to you once it finds it. Airlines won't volunteer to pay to replace things in delayed luggage, but if you ask, can present receipts, and don't appear to be trying to inflate your expenses or take advantage of the airlines, they're usually willing to reimburse reasonable expenses.

Attach labels, with at least your name, securely to both the outside and the inside of each piece of your luggage. If your luggage is mangled in a conveyor, outside tags are likely to be torn off. Keep enough clothes and other essentials in your carry-on luggage to tide you over for a few days if your checked luggage is misplaced or delayed.

BAGGAGE

# CHOOSING YOUR LUGGAGE

Many factors go into your choice of luggage: sturdiness, security, comfort, capacity, personal preference. Whatever you do, choose carefully and don't scrimp. Living out of a suitcase for months, you'll become acutely aware of its every shortcoming. It's worth spending twice as much to get exactly what you want.

## Types of Primary Luggage

Most long-term travelers settle on a single soft-sided "travel pack" made out of the heaviest possible nylon fabric, with either a shoulder strap, back and waist straps, or both. For independent travel outside the First World, leave your Rollaboard behind. Wheels are great on hard, smooth surfaces, but dead weight on your back everywhere else. You can get luggage with both wheels and backpack straps, but in most of the world streets and sidewalks (if there are sidewalks) are too rough for wheeled luggage to be useful.

### Proper Fit

The fit of a pack is very personal, depending on your height, build, and posture. Don't buy your pack by mail order, over the Internet, or anywhere you can't try it on. Test a pack on your back with weight in it, adjusted to the best fit possible, for as long as your patience and that of the store will permit. Good travel gear stores such as REI have sandbags or other weights handy and expect you to wander around the store with a pack on your back. It may take half an hour before you can tell whether it will be comfortable after months of constant use.

### Good Workmanship

Whatever sort of bag you choose, check the design, construction, materials, and workmanship closely. Look for a bag without entangling external straps but with sturdily attached rings or loops by which to tie or lock it to luggage racks and bus roofs. Look for double-stitched seams sealed with waterproofing and bound against fraying, and the largest, best possible quality zippers and fittings. Most soft luggage fails first in the zippers, seams, or points of stress where straps are attached. Long-term independent Third or Fourth World travel is the torture test of luggage. It's possible to get a bag with a lifetime guarantee of the zippers and stitching. It may be worth it (it certainly has been for me), but you are unlikely to be able to have warranty repairs made until you get home.

### Mending

I use heavy-gauge nylon thread for mending, but fine fishing line and dental floss have both been recommended to me for use in sewing up torn bags. If you can, seal the seam and stitching after any mending. On a long trip, I carry a small tube of sealant and some patching fabric.

### Waterproofing

Waterproof all the stitching in your bag with "seam sealant" from a camping-supply store before you use it, even if it's brand-new and supposedly water-proof. While you're at it, seal the seams in your waterproof raincoat, jacket, or poncho. When your bus is caught in a downpour with your bag on the roof, or your bag is thrown in a mud puddle, you'll be glad you waterproofed it.

### Straps

If you want a backpack with straps, either get a "travel pack" with removable straps, or one that has a zippered panel to cover the straps, or bring a sturdy bag large enough to entirely enclose the pack. The straps of ordinary backpacks are prone to snag in airport baggage conveyors, causing the bags to be torn apart. Some airlines won't accept ordinary backpacks as checked luggage, or refuse to accept any liability if they are damaged. Some people mistakenly think that the point of convertible travel packs is to "look like a suitcase," and thus appear more respectable. But outside the First World, a travel pack is a symbol of (foreign) wealth. The real point of the cover over the straps on a convertible pack is to enable you to check it as airline luggage without having to sign a liability waiver.

### Bag Covers

Whichever type of luggage you choose, a cover bag adds weight but protects your luggage against water, dust, mud, and scrapes and renders it much more nondescript. It's especially useful protection when you have to tie your bag on top of a bus. If you can't find a ready-made cover bag, consider having one custom-sewn. Travelers in many parts of the world routinely encase their luggage in cloth bags (usually sewn-on muslin, canvas, or burlap sacking), and doing likewise is the best way to keep yours from standing out as that of a (potentially rich) foreigner.

### Appearance

Cover bag or not, choose luggage that's generally nondescript in appearance, not something in flamboyant colors that scream "high-tech and expensive" and will cause it to be singled out by every potential thief. Use some form of cheap but distinctive marking (diagonal strips of colored tape or marker on the sides, for example, or distinctive bits of ribbon or straps) to enable you quickly to distinguish it from other similar bags when you're trying to spot it on baggage carousel, or verify at a glance that it's still on the roof of the bus after a meal stop.

### Locks

Make certain it will be possible to lock each and every external compartment on your bag. Get a small combination lock (you don't really want to carry around and keep track of keys, do you?) for each compartment, and don't forget to lock your day pack. Make sure the lock for the main compartment is large enough to use as the lock on your hotel room door. The size commonly used for gym lockers should be just right. Many hotels, including all but the most expensive Third and Fourth World hotels, don't provide locks, or don't provide secure ones. Instead, they have hasps on the doors; guests are expected to provide their own padlocks. A combination lock is especially useful for this purpose if you will be sharing rooms with your traveling companion. If there won't be any other way to secure the bag to luggage racks, consider bringing a short (perhaps 12- to 18-inch, 30–45 cm) length of chain to use with your main lock for this purpose, especially while sleeping in open-compartment railroad cars.

## Secondary Bags

Resist any temptation to carry multiple small bags rather than one large one. At times it will be all you can manage to keep a safe eye and hold on to one bag while jostling through a crowd or onto a bus. If you bring a small day pack as well as a larger pack, make sure you can stow it entirely inside your main pack. A zip-off day pack that attaches to the outside of a backpack is all too easily unzipped by thieves when it's behind your back and out of your sight, even while you are walking. Despite their drawbacks, it can be hard to find a travel pack without a zip-off day pack, but I recommend it.

In early 2003, the Transportation Security Administration started asking air travelers in the USA to leave their bags unlocked. If you lock your bags, the TSA might break the locks to search your bags. But many airlines' "conditions of carriage" still require that bags be locked, and provide that the airlines aren't liable for damage to checked luggage unless it is locked. There's a clear contradiction between the demands of the TSA and of airline contracts. It's likely to take the courts years to decide who is responsible for damage done to locks and luggage by the TSA, or for items missing from bags broken open by the TSA. Internationally, at least, I still recommend that you always lock your bags. If they arrive damaged, file a claim with the airline to whom you consigned your bags, and let them sort it out with the TSA.

If you're stuck with a bag with a zip- off day pack, at least make sure its construction is such that you can lock the day pack securely onto the pack so it can't be unzipped or cut free, and that you do always remember to lock the day pack onto the main bag.

## Theft

Fanny packs, belt pouches, shoulder bags, and knapsacks are all vulnerable to slashers. You defeat the security value of a sturdy main pack if you carry your valuables in a thinner bag. Make sure that even the thinnest parts of the fabric and straps are thick enough to resist a good-sized knife, and that the straps can't readily be opened or released from behind. Even a belt pouch worn in front of your body is easy to snatch if the strap can first be cut or opened in back.

## Day Pack Contents

Identify exactly what you will need for a day's sightseeing or exploring (sunglasses, water bottle, guidebook, map, camera, spare film, rain jacket or sweater, etc.) and how it will fit in your secondary bag. Even if you don't do a full-blown travel test with your primary bag, at least try out your secondary bag (most likely a shoulder bag, belt pack, or day pack) for a few days to make sure it's comfortable and holds what you want without tempting you to carry around too much. You'll be carrying it almost all the time, so make sure it's just right.

If you check your main pack on a flight, bring whatever essentials you would need for the next week, and couldn't easily buy, in whatever you carry on. Airlines rarely lose luggage, but even good airlines misplace a bag or two on each flight. Sooner or later, you'll arrive somewhere without your checked luggage. Your bag will almost always turn up, usually in a few days, but if it's sent on the next weekly flight you might have to do without it for that week. Be prepared.

## Carrying Valuables

Carry your passport, tickets, address list, contact numbers and addresses for reporting your credit cards lost or stolen (remember, toll-free numbers won't be accessible outside North America), and other critical documents in a money belt or some other sort of pouch hidden entirely inside your clothes.

Never carry anything valuable in a belt or pouch outside your clothes: an external belt pouch is the obvious place for your valuables and will be the first thing any thief demands if you are robbed. Don't trust a money pouch around your neck, even inside your clothes: if the strap is strong enough not to break if snatched, it's strong enough to strangle you if snatched. It's especially dangerous to reinforce a fragile-looking cloth neck strap with wire strong enough to become a garrote. Your life is worth more than your money.

### Photocopy Your Documents

Before you leave, and after you've completely packed, empty your money belt onto a photocopy machine and make three or four copies of everything in it except the cash. Everything. If it's important enough to be worth carrying in your money belt, you'll want the copies if your money belt is lost or stolen. Don't forget to include copies of any essential data that you keep in electronic form, such as the contacts stored in your cell phone (mobile phone) or PDA. If you can find it, use waterproof paper for the copies. (Some map and travel stores sell waterproof paper for use in making waterproof printouts from digital map databases. Look for it near the map CD's or the print-on-demand topographic map kiosk.) If you are writing things like your contact list to carry in your money belt, use pencil or waterproof, non-bleeding ink. Test it. Anything in your money belt will be subjected to prolonged damp, sweaty, heat.

### Pack Duplicate Documents

Pack a set or two of copies of your documents in your luggage, separately from your money belt, in a waterproof pouch or zip-lock bag. (I bury one copy in my main pack and another in my day pack or shoulder bag.) Leave a set with a trusted contact whose phone number you have memorized and who could fax copies to you in an emergency. Ticket or passport numbers and issue and validity dates are helpful, but the numbers alone are no substitute for photocopies or faxes if you need lost or stolen documents replaced. If you are traveling with a trusted companion, exchange copies of each others' documents.

**REAL LIFE**

One of my most versatile traveling garments is a vest I designed for myself with four zippered pockets in the lining large enough for my airline tickets, passport, and other valuables. It's especially good for airports: tailored like the vest of a suit and worn with a tie, it makes me look much more respectable and businesslike to customs and immigration inspectors, at a small fraction of the weight and bulk in my luggage of a suit jacket. Because it fits closely, it would be almost impossible for a pickpocket to get into the inside zippered pockets while I'm wearing it. It also enables me to keep my passport and tickets secure but accessible for the inevitable succession of inspections and checkpoints, without my having to get in and out of my money belt in public. I've had several vests like this over the years: when one gets worn, or my shape changes as I age, I have a new one made the next time I'm someplace tailoring is cheap. The most recent one cost less than US$10.

### Money

Carry the current day's supply of local currency separately from your passport, main supply of USA dollars or other hard currency cash, or other essential documents, so you don't expose the real valuables every time you buy something. Put enough official-seeming but inessential stuff in your wallet that a thief who takes it will believe he's gotten everything. If you are going to need something from your money belt, get it out in advance, while you are someplace private. *Never* go into your money belt in public, or give any indication that you have one.

### Pockets

Never carry anything of any value in a rear pants pocket or outer shirt or coat pocket. Any outside pocket can be picked. For a price, you can get travel garments that come with hidden or interior pockets. Or, if you have clothes made or altered, you can have secure (preferably zippered) hidden pockets put in wherever you find convenient. This sort of tailoring can be very cheap in the South, so I wouldn't spend too much extra money getting special travel clothes before your departure. If you want pockets to hold a particular type of object, such as an airline ticket jacket, leave a sample with the tailor as a guide for the size and shape of pocket to make.

**A trick to protect against pickpockets or simply losing things out of your pockets (such as when sleeping on a jolting train) is to sew strips of heavy-duty Velcro inside the openings of your pockets. You can get sew-on Velcro tape by the yard at some camping-supply and sewing-notions stores. Bring extra to alter the pockets of clothes acquired on your journey. Leave a gap in the Velcro at one edge of the pocket just large enough to get one finger in to pull the Velcro open. It sounds odd and takes some getting used to, but pulling open the Velcro requires a hard enough pull and makes enough of a tearing noise to get your attention and scare off a pickpocket. Try it!**

## PACKING SUGGESTIONS

### Weight

Whatever luggage you bring, make sure it weighs under 20 kg (44 lb) and has space and weight to spare (for the things you'll inevitably acquire along the way) when packed with everything you want to bring. You'll sometimes have to walk considerable distances, and some of your sightseeing will probably be done with your pack on your back.

The more experienced the traveler, the less she or he tends to bring. Airline rules impose an upper limit on how much luggage you can bring without paying prohibitive excess baggage charges (see the beginning of this chapter), but you probably shouldn't bring even that much unless you are comfortable carrying it all on a lengthy walk.

After a shakedown period, most long-term travelers find their luggage weighs between 10 and 15 kg (22 and 33 lb), depending on personal style and the climate. Hot, dry climates require the least amount of clothing and the most room for extra water. Cold weather requires heavier clothing; humid weather requires more frequent changes of clothing. In more remote areas you may have to do more walking, encouraging you to lighten your load, but you may also need to carry things you don't need in cities such as a sleeping bag or tent and perhaps a heavier first-aid kit.

I won't presume to tell you what to bring, and this isn't a comprehensive packing checklist. Rather, the following sections will give some limited advice on specific items about which travelers, especially novice travelers, often have questions.

A commonly recommended test of your luggage and packing is to pack your bag (including full water bottles and a stock of food for a day-long bus or train trip) and take a day's sightseeing excursion around your hometown by foot and bus.

## Sleeping Bag or Sleep Sack

One of the most difficult decisions can be whether to bring a sleeping bag. They are big, heavy, expensive, and hard to sell for a good price or to send home from overseas. You can get a heavy bag anywhere, but good lightweight ones are much cheaper in the United States than in some other parts of the world.

Bringing a sleeping bag is a matter of personal preference. I've carried a lightweight down sleeping bag even to generally hot places and haven't regretted it. Sometimes the only clean hotel or the only available space on a train is overly air-conditioned. Sometimes bed linen is filthy or nonexistent. Sometimes it's simply cold at night, even in midsummer in hot climates, especially in the desert and at high altitudes where the temperature can drop by 25 degrees C (45 degrees F) at night.

A lighter alternative to a sleeping bag is a "sleep sack": basically a pair of thin sheets (or one larger sheet folded in half) sewn together along three sides and open at the top, like an uninsulated sleeping bag. Guests at many hostels are required to provide either a sleeping bag or a sleep sack, and inexpensive ready-made sleep sacks are available from Hostelling International-USA and many other hostel associations. A sleep sack provides cleanliness but no real warmth. A sleep sack rolls up much smaller than a sleeping bag but isn't much lighter than the lightest bag. It comes down to your priorities of weight versus warmth.

## Camping and Trekking Gear

If you will be camping or trekking for only a small part of your trip, it's probably easier to rent or buy tents, boots, parkas, etc. locally than to lug them through lots of places where they aren't needed. Don't count on beating the weight limits on luggage by wearing your boots or parka onto the plane, unless you're prepared to wear them on every flight throughout your trip.

### Tents

Camping is the cheapest form of accommodation in much of the United States, Canada, and Australia, but you can't get to most campsites without a car. And if you have a car, you needn't be concerned with how heavy your tent is. Big, heavy, old tents suitable for car camping but too heavy for backpackers are very cheap. You might as well buy one locally if you want it for a camping road trip in one of these countries if it is the only place you'll use it, rather than pay a lot of money for a lightweight backpacker's tent and haul it around the world. Accommodations are sufficiently cheap in most Third and Fourth World cities and towns that few travelers want a tent unless they are really backpacking in the wilderness. Even small towns in remote areas have some sort of hotel.

One place you might want a tent is Africa, especially for extended or overland travel away from big cities. The safari tradition and style of travel has created a better infrastructure of developed campsites in East and Southern Africa than in most of the Third World, and there are places in Fourth World Africa where there are no hotels, or no cheap ones. A tent is particularly useful if a bus or truck stops for the night, or gets stuck for a week, in the middle of nowhere.

### Camping Stoves

Try not to bring a camping stove, even if you plan on backpacking. Airlines are legitimately concerned that stoves or fuel containers could leak, burst, catch fire, or explode. Don't try to sneak a stove or fuel bottle onto a plane. For safety's sake, be honest about what's in your luggage; if the airline won't accept it, leave it behind. Pressurized butane, propane cartridges, or gasoline are obviously explosive and unacceptable. You could bring a stove that uses fuel cartridges and try to buy cartridges on arrival. But you have to accept the risk that you might not find them and might have brought the stove for naught. You could bring a gasoline (petrol) stove with a totally empty and clean fuel tank, and buy fuel locally. But you might have to leave the fuel tank or the whole stove behind if you can't clean out all trace of flammable residue before you go home or go on. Airline staff can and will check camp stoves carefully, and refuse to accept them as luggage if there's any smell of fuel or any evidence that they've ever been used. At some airports frequented by campers, "Do you have any camping equipment?" is a standard question at check-in.

Your best chance of getting on the plane with a stove is with one that burns what is called, in USA usage, "kerosene." (The same liquid fuel—the primary constituent of the fuel for jet airplanes—is called "paraffin" in British usage. Paraffin in USA usage means a petroleum-derived wax used for candles, not a liquid fuel. You can't predict which term will be used where in the world, and lots of confusion ensues.) Unlike gasoline, which is highly volatile and explosive, kerosene is merely flammable. It's also more widely available than gasoline, especially in lightly populated areas. You are unlikely to be allowed to check a can of kerosene or a kerosene stove with a full tank on a plane, but you have some chance of checking a kerosene stove with an empty tank. Kerosene stoves are more expensive and harder to use than gasoline or propane stoves, but reliable lightweight backpacking ones are available.

## Clothes

In my opinion, clothes are one of the least important things to worry about when packing, especially because most will wear out in a few months of hard traveling. Before long, most of your clothes will be ones you've acquired along the way.

### Sizes

If you are an unusual, hard-to-fit size or shape, you'll have to choose carefully so that what you bring will see you back home (unless you are going someplace where clothes can cheaply be made to measure, in which case bring some particularly well-fitting items for a tailor to use as patterns). Europeans and Americans of average size may find that they are unusually large by the standards of most countries, and that most clothes made for locals are too small (although your weight may vary widely while you're traveling).

### Locally Bought Clothes

If you find some specific items are essential to your comfort—a particular sort of lightweight long underwear or a particular style of bra—by all means bring some. (Proper fit is more important with underwear than outerwear, high-quality underwear has a higher warmth to weight ratio than any outerwear, and high-tech underwear can be hard to find in many places.) But with a few other exceptions the best clothes to wear are locally bought clothes. I have yet to find a place where whatever sort of clothing was locally appropriate wasn't locally available. If you don't bring enough of the right clothes, or need different clothes for different places, you can get them where you need them. If it's hot, buy lightweight clothes in local styles. If it's cold, buy a locally knit sweater or two. You'll be comfortable, you'll fit in better with the locals, and you'll come home with wearable souvenirs.

The one obvious exception is if you're going to a cold, expensive

**REAL LIFE**

Teva sandals (waterproof, with tire-like tread and nylon webbing straps with Velcro closures) are comfortable, secure, and double as shower shoes (essential!). Unlike most sandals, they are comfortable for hiking, scrambling on rocks, and carrying a heavy pack. They've rapidly becoming the standard travelers' shoes in warm climates.

Badly made imitation Teva knock-offs can be had in Bangkok for as little as US$5 a pair. I have no financial interest in Teva, but I think it's worth paying full price for real Teva sandals, both for better workmanship and to fairly reward the inventor and patent holder for a simple but clever and successful idea. The experience of one couple who talked to me after traveling around the world for six months illustrates my point: she had taken my advice and, before they left, got a new pair of Teva sandals that lasted through the trip; he didn't and regretted it—he went through three pairs of knock-offs in a month.

**BAGGAGE**

place, such as Japan or Switzerland in winter, in which case it would be best to get your warm clothes someplace cheaper. I recall buying an extra Kashmiri sweater and European-style long pants and shirt in the heat of New Delhi in November in preparation for my next stop, Paris.

### Shoes

Bring good shoes. Comfortable, durable shoes are a distinctively First World luxury. American athletic shoes are status symbols throughout the Second, Third, and Fourth Worlds, and with good reason. Most Fourth World people wear no shoes at all. Most Third World people wear simple rubber or plastic flip-flop sandals. And most Second World people wear shoddy, uncomfortable shoes that are often held up as the epitome of ill-made communist consumer goods. When available locally, good shoes are expensive. If you don't want to wear cheap sandals, choose your traveling shoes with care.

I know one experienced, very self-sufficient traveler who arranges to have a new pair of his favorite walking shoes sent to him every six months or so, wherever he is. I bring a pair of lightweight walking shoes and a pair of good sandals or dress shoes, depending on the climate.

## Water Purification

Many parts of the world lack sewage treatment systems, and you should assume that tap water anywhere is undrinkable unless and until you can assure yourself otherwise. For the most part, only people from the USA ever expect to be able to drink tap water.

### Bottled Water

Bottled water is not always available—no matter what anyone may tell you—and is often expensive (in many cases only foreign tourists can afford not to drink local water, no matter how polluted or contaminated everyone knows it is). Rely on bottled water, and you'll eventually get dehydrated, or get desperate and drink tap water (and get sick).

### Water Bottles

Bring leak-proof water bottles to hold at least two liters (two quarts). You can always find some sort of water bottles locally, but not necessarily leak-proof ones. Nalgene bottles are the best, worth tracking down before you leave, and scarce and pricey on the secondhand market in Second, Third, and Fourth World travelers' centers. (One of the few ways that the Second World is decidedly Southern is the poor quality of public water treatment systems. Do not drink untreated water in the former USSR any more than you would in India or China.)

Fill your water bottles, turn them upside-down, shake them vigorously, and leave them standing upside-down overnight to see if they leak before you put them in your pack for the first time. Fill new plastic bottles with a strong baking soda solution and let them soak overnight to help get rid of the smell and taste of plastic. Avoid putting full water bottles in your airplane luggage, as pressure variations may cause them to leak.

### Iodine or Purifier?

You should also bring either iodine water purification tablets (light and cheap, but give water a bad taste, and are not recommended for long-term use due to the possible adverse health affects of iodine accumulation in your body) or a backpacker's water filtration system (heavier, cumbersome, and expensive, but doesn't flavor or taint the water with chemicals). The cost of a purifier (US$75–100) may seem steep, but it's a small part of what you could easily spend on bottled water if you're traveling for months. Purifiers are designed for varying degrees of treatment, which is why some medical authorities are reluctant to endorse them. Purifiers that use either a second-stage ultra-filter or a trace of iodine (much less than if iodine were used alone) to kill viruses are the most effective, and are more convenient than either boiling or iodine tablets.

## Cameras and Photographs

Whether to bring a camera is one of the things to think about most carefully. If you do bring a camera, you will be stuck with it—on your person, always—for the duration of your trip. Having photographs of your trip can be nice when you get home, and for many people photography is itself a major reason to travel. But having a camera sets up a barrier between you and everyone you meet. Having traveled both with and without a camera, I'd generally recommend against bringing one. If you're unsure, consider sightseeing for a day around an unfamiliar town and trying to meet and talk to people, once with and once without a camera around your neck all day.

If you bring a camera, bring the lightest, simplest, cheapest, most reliable camera that will serve your needs. Consider resistance to dust, humidity, and physical shock, as well as power requirements. If your camera requires anything other than standard AA or AAA batteries, bring spares. If the batteries are rechargeable, make sure you have suitable power adapters for the recharger (see "Electrical Power Adapters" below for information about batteries, chargers, and power supplies).

### Digital or Film?

Digital cameras have many advantages over film cameras for long-term travelers. They are smaller and lighter than film cameras of comparable quality. Because they have fewer moving parts (no film transport mechanism), and because the imaging system can be entirely sealed against dust and dirt (no need for an opening for the film to pass through), they are much less prone to breakage and mechanical damage. Perhaps most important for long-term travelers, you can keep your digital photos on memory chips, or burn them onto CD's, that weigh less, take up less space, and are less fragile than film (exposed or unexposed), slides, or negatives.

The advantages of film cameras are higher resolution than all but the most expensive professional digital cameras (although this may change by the time you read this), lower initial cost (usually made up for in the long run by the cost of film and developing), and lower power consumption (none at all for a manual film camera without a flash). Even with motorized film advance and rewind, automatic electronic focus and exposure controls, and occasional use of the flash, I can shoot two dozen 36-exposure rolls with my 35mm film camera on a single battery. I have to recharge the battery in my digital camera at least five times that often, more if I'm viewing photos on the camera's screen. If I'm using the camera's screen a lot as a viewfinder, instead of the optical viewfinder, I have to recharge the digital camera battery almost every day.

With a film camera, getting prints or slides is a straightforward process, as is sorting and filing them. Getting prints from digital photos, or getting them onto a computer for viewing, is a bit more complex. But it's getting easier all the time; if you found it easy to set up and configure your own computer, or to start using e-mail for the first time, you shouldn't have too much trouble setting up a system to handle your digital photos. But if you don't have a computer, or if you needed to ask for someone else's help to set up your computer, you may want to think twice about buying a digital camera without a more technically knowledgeable friend as an advisor.

If you already have a film camera you're happy with, and you don't want to have to deal with chargers, power adapters, or computers, there's no need to switch. But if you're buying a camera for your big trip, already have a computer, and aren't intimidated by learning to use new hardware and software, I'd recommend a digital camera.

Advertisements and hype aside, what should you look for if you are buying a digital camera for international travel, or planning to take one with you on a trip abroad?

### Types of Memory

Digital cameras use a bewildering variety of similar, but incompatible, removable memory chips: compact flash (CF) cards, memory sticks, multimedia cards (MMC), smart media cards, and secure digital (SD) cards. All of these work basically the same way, but they are different sizes and shapes and have different connectors. Which is best? All else being equal, the one that's cheapest per image, easiest to find, and most likely to be compatible with whatever computer you find in a cybercafé or at a friend's home or office. As of 2003, this was compact flash (CF) memory. CF cards are the de facto standard for the majority of digital cameras as well as a large variety of other portable electronic devices such as palmtop computers and PDA's. In a pinch, you stand a better chance of being able to borrow a CF card from someone else until you can download your photos, or of buying one locally (even at kiosks or small local shops in tourist destinations) than any other kind of memory chip. And far more cybercafés have CF card readers (sparing you the need to install any special drivers for your camera's cable connection) than have readers for other types of cards.

As an alternative to solid-state memory cards, you can get micro-miniature disk drives that fit into a CF card slot. I don't recommend them. Microdrives have tiny moving parts, and are extremely fragile. As with any computer hard disk, they eventually "crash" and fail catastrophically, without warning. Friends of mine have lost large photo collections when their microdrives crashed. Memory cards, on the other hand, have no moving parts are almost impossible to break. Microdrives are slightly cheaper and larger capacity than the largest CF cards, but the differences are small, and not worth the lower reliability.

### Buying More Memory

As with film, bring as much digital storage media (cards, disks, or whatever) as you can afford. The more memory you have, the more pictures you can take before you have to transfer your photos to a computer and burn them onto CD's. It's worth shopping around for memory cards: some camera shops charge five times as much for the same cards as Internet or storefront discounters. Prices on the road will be higher still. Generic memory cards are produced in the same chip factories as the brand-name ones, and seem to work just as well. Check with local electronics discount stores, or Internet price comparison Web sites like Pricewatch.com. Memory cards are expensive, and small enough to be easily lost or stolen. Beyond a certain size you may be better off with more smaller cards, so you don't lose so many photos if something happens to one of your memory cards.

### Batteries and Chargers

Digital cameras use much more power than most film cameras. A few digital cameras use standard AA or AAA batteries, which are preferable because in a pinch you can find them everywhere. But single-use batteries are expensive and produce extremely toxic waste, so even with such a camera you might want to get a couple of sets of rechargeable batteries and a compact battery charger.

Most digital cameras use proprietary batteries that are expensive, hard to replace while you are traveling, and can only be recharged either in the camera or in a special charger. A separate charger with a spare battery is much better than a charger built into the camera: you can leave one battery in your hotel room charging while you are using the other in the camera. And only the charger and battery, not the entire camera, is at risk of being stolen while it's charging.

Finding a safe place to leave a camera or other electronic device plugged in and charging can be a particular problem for travelers staying in hostels or other dormitory accommodations. Proprietary batteries and chargers are less likely to be stolen, since they are unlikely to fit anyone else's devices.

### AC Adapters and Power Supplies

As with any electronic device for travel, look for a dual-voltage "auto-switching" or "universal" charger or AC adapter for your digital camera that handles 100–240 volts, 50–60 Hz. (Standard 110–120 volt devices made for use in the United States won't work, and may catch fire or explode, if plugged into 220–240 volt power outlets in most of the rest of the world.) Shop around: most cameras (and other devices) distributed in the United States with cheaper single-voltage AC adapters and chargers are also available in versions with dual voltage power supplies, often for the same price. You'll also need a set of half a dozen plug adapters, but remember that these don't convert the voltage or frequency. Plug adapters should only be used with dual voltage devices, or ones that you are sure are made to operate on the voltage and frequency of the local power supply.

If you're going to be trekking or traveling "off the grid," you can get solar battery chargers for AA or AAA batteries. But solar chargers are only available for standard batteries, not for proprietary camera batteries. If you think you'll need to rely on a solar charger, get a camera that uses standard AA or AAA batteries.

### Viewing Digital Photos While on the Road

You may want to look at the photos you've taken before you get home, to decide which ones to save and which to delete, or just to see how well they've turned out. Almost all digital cameras let you review the photos you've taken on a viewfinder screen the size of a postage stamp. If you want a larger view, you'll need to either carry a laptop computer with you (not recommended for most travelers, as discussed below), go to a cybercafé (with an appropriate cable and either your camera itself or a separate reader for whatever type of memory card it uses), or connect your computer to a television.

Not all cameras are capable of displaying photos on a TV, and not all TV's have the proper input connector. But even in relatively cheap hotels, some TV's do, and it's often more convenient to review your photos in your hotel room than at a cybercafé where you are paying by the hour. Video cables are camera specific: if your camera comes with a video output cable, bring it with you on any extended trip.

### Transferring Photos to a Computer

You can delete photos you don't want, to make room for more, directly on your digital camera. To do anything else with your pictures—edit them, crop them, e-mail them, or upload them to a Web site—you first need to get them onto a computer. Different cameras have different kinds of connections, but in general you can either connect the camera directly to the computer with a camera-specific cable, connect a memory card reader to the computer, or use the cybercafé memory card reader, if they have one for your type of memory card (CF card, memory stick, or whatever). Connecting the camera is likely to require installing special drivers on the computer, which means carrying a software CD with the drivers and getting permission to install them. Cybercafés are surprisingly accommodating—more so than they probably ought to be— to customers who want to install drivers for their digital cameras or memory card readers. Separate card readers are small, cheap (less than US$20) and are more likely to work without installing any special drivers, so if you have room it's worth getting one to take with you, especially if you can find one that works without the need to install special drivers. Some laptop and palmtop computers have memory card slots (usually for CF cards). For laptops without memory card slots, you can get adapters to use a memory card in a PCMCIA (PC-card) slot for less than US$10.

It's one thing to use a digital camera with your own computer, once you've gotten it all set up. It's another thing to use it on a strange computer in a cybercafé. Before you leave home, take your travel kit to a friend's computer or a cybercafé and test your ability to get your photos off your camera and onto a CD. Otherwise you're likely to discover too late that you didn't bring an essential connector or the CD with the necessary drivers for the camera.

### Editing Photos

Most digital cameras come with image editing software you can install on your PC. On the road, you'll also find basic (and sometimes advanced) image editing software at most cybercafés. Especially if all you want to do is select, organize, and crop your photos, and you don't use a specific high-end image editing program, it's probably counterproductive to bring a laptop computer with you solely or primarily to deal with your digital photos. You can probably do it better in a cybercafé, without the expense, risk of theft, and fragility of a laptop with a hard disk. (See below for more on choosing and using laptop and palmtops computers for travel.)

### Emailing Photos and Putting Them on the Web

Don't do this unless you have to. From time to time, you'll find a cybercafé with a high-speed Internet connection. But that's rare. Sending photos over a dial-up connection, even if you have your own laptop with you, is likely be very slow. Most of my clients who set out intending to maintain a Web site of photos while they travel around the world abandon their plans as soon as they hit their first Third World country, and discover how much time it takes. You may want to e-mail an occasional choice photo to friends or family, or post it to a Web site. But wait until you get home, or until you get lucky with a cheap cybercafé with a very fast connection, before you try to e- mail or post a whole gallery of photos.

## Storing Photos and Getting Them Home

If you don't have enough memory cards to last through your trip, the best way to save your photos and get them home safely is to burn them onto CDs. You could bring a laptop with a built-in or external CD burner with you, but that's not necessary: most cybercafés will burn a CD for you for US$5 or so, once you've transferred your photos to their computer. CD's are fairly durable, and they are immune to airport X-rays and metal detectors. But they can get dropped, broken, or scratched, so I'd burn at least 2 (preferably 3) CD's of any photos I wouldn't want to lose. If you are traveling with a companion, you can each carry a set, and you can mail another set home. Digital photos can, in theory, be e-mailed home. But the slow connections to the Internet available from many parts of the world could make this prohibitively time-consuming.

## Protecting Film

If you bring a film camera, wrap your film in reflective foil to protect it from heat and sun (a section of an ultrathin "space blanket" works well for this purpose) and a lead-lined bag to protect it from airport X-rays.

Most checked and carry-on baggage may be x-rayed. You can ask for hand inspection of photographic film or magnetic media (computer disks, audio- and videotapes, and cassettes), but more and more airport guards will insist on putting it through the metal detectors and/or X-ray machines. Don't be fooled by claims that the X-ray levels are "film safe." That's what they say at all airports, no matter how untrue it is. X-ray machine damage is cumulative: the more times you have to out your film through the X-ray machine, the more likely it is for fogging to be visible.

If you want to carry your camera on, you may have to open it and/or remove the batteries at the airport security checkpoint. (Some airlines categorically forbid batteries in carry-on luggage, and will confiscate any they find.) Opening some cameras risks exposing the film. To be on the safe side, take the film and batteries out of your camera before each flight, and put the batteries in your checked luggage. Once you've developed the film, the slides or negatives are unaffected by X-rays, so it's safest to have any important photos developed before your next flight.

## Bring Plenty of Film

Remember to bring ample film; it's cheaper in the United States than most other places, and of reliable quality. Unexposed film has a fairly long shelf life, and you can never be sure of the quality of film bought while traveling. If you can, bring enough film to last through your trip. I've never heard anyone complain about having too much film left over, while lots of people run out or have to barter with other travelers for more film.

## Film Processing

Integrated automatic color slide and negative processing and printing machines are now found in tourist spots throughout the world, and you can get film developed fairly reliably almost anywhere. Prints are heavy and bulky compared to slides or negatives, so you'll probably want to wait until you get home to have your photos printed.

## Audio and Video Devices

Audio and video devices are problematic to travel with. They attract thieves like magnets; they weigh you down; they require coddling against the dust, smoke, and hard knocks of prolonged traveling; and they are difficult to get repaired if they break down outside the First World. They are much greater power hogs than still cameras. "Disposable" batteries are a major source of toxic waste, while rechargeable batteries require you to stay in places with reliable electrical supplies and leash yourself to them while recharging your electrical equipment.

### Video Cameras

Digital video camera/recorders keep getting smaller and smaller, but they are still too valuable to leave anywhere, including a hotel room. ("Leave your valuables in the hotel safe," some guidebooks say. But only expensive hotels—rarely hostels, guest houses, or budget accommodations—have safes.) A video camera, like anything else, will seem much heavier after you've had it on your body for a few weeks or months. Some video camcorders are no larger than still cameras, but they are much more complex and fragile, and go through batteries (not to mention videotape) much more quickly than still cameras.

### Audio Players

Many travelers like portable stereos for listening to music in waiting rooms and on long bus and train rides. I prefer conversation to music, and I don't think people who isolate themselves in their headphones even realize they are missing out on conversations with other travelers. I know, though, that it's partly just a matter of taste, and that some people get more impatient than others at delays or long trips, or feel lost outside their accustomed musical environment.

Personal stereos are security blankets for a lot of travelers. Put on a familiar piece of music, close your eyes, and you can escape from strange, perhaps threatening or overwhelming stimuli into a comfortingly familiar inner world. The danger is that you'll become so dependent on your Walkman as a psychological crutch against culture shock that you won't know what to do if it's stolen or breaks down. The barriers it helps maintain will keep you from getting past your fear to the point where you can fully experience your surroundings.

If you bring a portable stereo player, bring a cheap one you won't miss if it is stolen or breaks. Judging from the anecdotes I've heard, they are the items most often stolen from travelers by other travelers, even though most travelers carry cameras worth more than their stereos. Be especially watchful of your Walkman, CD, MP3, or minidisc player inside dormitories, hostels, and guest houses.

Tape, CD, and minidisc players have moving parts that are very vulnerable to dust and grit. (Of these three, for what it's worth, minidisc players are smallest, sturdiest, and have the longest battery life; most can record as well as play.) Solid-state MP3 players or radios with no moving parts are much more likely to survive prolonged traveling. CD players in particular eat lots of batteries. Third World batteries are often expensive and of extremely poor quality. They won't last as long, and they are more likely to leak or corrode and ruin your equipment. If you expect to use a personal stereo a lot, consider taking along a couple of sets of rechargeable batteries, a recharger, and a set of power adapters. If you are getting several devices, such as a digital camera and a personal stereo, try to get ones that can share the same batteries and charger—most likely AA, since that the only battery type commonly used for both.

### Radios

Radio broadcasting frequencies and modes vary widely from place to place. Local broadcasts in different countries are on completely different bands. If you want a radio solely to listen to local broadcasts in a single country, buy it there. Only two types of radio are worth bringing with you: a short-wave radio (for long-range broadcasts from home, or for use in countries where there is no local broadcasting in a language you understand); or a multiband radio including short-wave bands (for local broadcasts in a variety of countries). In some places the only radio broadcasting is on short-wave bands. Compact (Walkman-sized) high-quality short-wave and multiband radios designed for travelers are available but expensive. The top-of-the-line Sony ICF SW100 is an amazingly full-featured little gem but lists for almost US$500. Bottom-end pocket shortwave receivers start at about US$100—not worth the price for most people. Such an expensive radio is something to keep quiet, to keep well hidden, and to listen to in the privacy of your hotel room. Fortunately, radios like this are unusual enough that most people mistake them for much cheaper AM/FM radios or cassette players.

Personally, I'd be more apt to get a short-wave radio at home and listen to English-language broadcasts from the place or region I'm going to before I leave (a surprising number of countries broadcast in English) than carry around an expensive radio just to listen to BBC or Voice of America (VOA) news. After all, I hear the voices of America all the time. I go to other countries to hear their voices, and most of the time I'd rather get my news from their perspective by reading their English-language (or local-language, if I know it) press.

On the other hand, I might invest in such a radio if I were traveling for a long time through an especially unsettled region where news travels slowly and little is published in English, or what is published is heavily censored or not to be believed. In places like this, in times of coup or confusion, even the locals, those who can, listen to the BBC or VOA, or watch CNN to find out what is happening in their own country. Many expatriate First World residents in the Second, Third, and Fourth Worlds have short-wave radios in their homes for emergency use. Local English-language publications often list BBC and/or VOA frequencies and schedules, both for their news value and because local people learning English often use BBC or VOA broadcasts to improve their oral comprehension and accents.

## Laptop Computers

Staying connected on the road no longer has to mean carrying a heavy, fragile, and expensive laptop computer. The proliferation of cybercafés has made it largely unnecessary to bring your own computer to get on the Internet, even from out-of-the-way places.

You might think that the more remote the location, the more necessary it would be to have your own computer. But that would be wrong. The more remote the location,

These days when people ask me, "What's the best type of computer to carry with me on a long trip?" My first answer is usually, "None!"

especially in the Third World, the greater the advantages to paying a small fee to someone else to find an Internet service provider and reliable power supply and to get a phone and network connection to work. The places where cybercafés are easiest to find and make the most sense are places where it takes a cybercafé professional to solve the local connectivity problems. I get e-mail every day, for example, from clients at cybercafés in Kathmandu and on Kuta Beach in Bali. I wouldn't want to have to make a dial-up connection from my own computer in either of those places.

There are still reasons to carry a computer: if you need to be able to connect securely and privately; you need to use specific programs or access data that won't be available or accessible from a cybercafé; or you want to be able to use your computer in places other than cybercafés (planes, trains, hotel rooms, etc.).

All cybercafés and public Internet terminals are inherently insecure. All of them. Always. No matter how secure the Web site, your browser, or your e-mail encryption. On a public terminal, you can never be sure that your keystrokes and display aren't being remotely monitored and/or recorded across the local network—before they can be encrypted (encoded) or secured for sending across the Internet. With your own laptop, you can (if you are careful) make sure that everything sensitive is encrypted before it leaves your machine. But for me, it's not worth carrying a laptop just to get a secure Internet connection. There are alternatives to online banking and I don't carry company secrets. When I want to write, I can go to a cybercafé, or use a pen.

Wanting to stay in touch by e-mail, browse the Web, or edit digital photos is not enough reason to carry a computer around the world. I wrote the book on the Internet for travelers (*The Practical Nomad Guide to the Online Travel Marketplace*, the companion volume in this series, which includes a great deal more advice and information about accessing and using the Internet while traveling, either from public terminals or your own laptop), but even as I use the Internet more and more on the road, I bring my computer with me less and less.

If had to bring a computer, what sort would I recommend? Anything I say about prices or specifications will undoubtedly be obsolete before you read this, so it's probably pointless to make specific recommendations. But I will say that, after having used their laptops for some time, many of my friends with larger, heavier, and more powerful computers have become jealous of my much smaller and lighter machines, even though they lack some feature of heavier models. If I had to buy a new computer today, for limited but essential use on an extended nonbusiness trip outside the First World, I'd buy a Psion, HP Jornada, or Sharp Zaurus palmtop model with a keyboard but without a hard disk.

If you are buying a computer with travel in mind, get the smallest, lightest computer that will serve your purposes. As technology evolves, you can do more and more with a tiny handheld computer with a touch-typing keyboard, modem, Web browser, and e-mail program. Which features do you actually need? How will you actually use it? How much time will you spend carrying it around? Before you buy a full-size laptop, find a rigid object of similar size and weight, then carry it around all day, treating it as though it were worth several thousand dollars and could never be left unattended. Before each trip, especially a lengthy trip other than for business, or outside the First World, think, "Do I really need to bring my computer?"

As a portable Internet access device, a full-size laptop is overweight, overpriced, and overkill. Unfortunately, there's been relatively little effort put into development of good handheld Internet terminals. Most laptop computers have been designed primarily as stand-alone portable PCs, not Internet devices. The best handheld e-mail and Web terminals have been from Psion, a company few people in the United States have ever heard of. Don't be discouraged if most laptop salespeople start out by showing you things that are way too big to lug around all the time. There are smaller alternatives, if you are prepared to seek them out from companies like Dynamism.com (see the Resource Guide).

Because most laptop computers are bought or leased by businesses that trade them in regularly for newer models, there's a glut of high-end second-hand "off-lease" and trade-in laptops a year or two old. A laptop you take traveling won't look new for long, anyway—so why not consider a used computer for US$1000 less than a new one? If you just want a basic Internet, typing, and digital photo editing terminal, you can find one used for US$200–400.

Avoid carrying a computer in a fancy case or one with a computer company name or logo that might as well say, "Steal me." Use a nondescript case, preferably one with no labels or logos, that doesn't look like a computer case at all. (The same goes for cameras and other devices, but laptop computer cases are the most easily recognized because of their greater size.) One of the overlooked advantages of computers smaller than standard laptops is that they are less conspicuous. Most people think that the case for a large subnotebook is an odd-shaped purse, not a computer, and I have one smaller palmtop with a Web browser and e-mail client that fits in my pants pocket.

If you bring a computer with you, have a backup plan in case it is lost, stolen, or broken, or the hard disk crashes and all your data is lost. Laptop computers aren't designed to withstand many of the bumps and shocks they get in routine First World use, much less world travel. A fall of six inches or a foot will often crash a laptop's hard disk or break the screen. (With no hard disk drive and no moving parts except the keyboard, simpler handheld computers are much more rugged. Psion palmtop computers, for example, are rated to survive a one meter (three foot) drop onto a hard floor undamaged.) And there's always the possibility that your computer could be stolen, as every year several hundred thousand laptops are in the United States alone. You can get insurance to cover the monetary loss, but money won't help much if you've lost irreplaceable data.

## Electrical Power Adapters

Using electrical or electronic equipment with foreign power supplies can be more difficult than most people think.

There are two standard voltages (110–120 volts and 220–240 volts), two standard AC frequencies (50 and 60 Hz), and about 10 different types of wall outlets and corresponding plugs in use in different parts of the world. The United States uses 110–120 volts, 60 Hz AC, and two types of partially compatible plugs and outlets (two-prong nongrounded and three-prong grounded). Not all countries have a single national standard; I've found three different kinds of plugs and two different voltages and frequencies in different parts of the same country. In rare instances you may even encounter DC or other voltages.

There is no easy, simple, or cheap device that will enable you to use electronic devices with power systems other than those for which they were designed. Voltage and frequency converters are relatively heavy and expensive. Plug adapters are deceptively cheap and simple: using an adapter to plug something into the wrong voltage can ruin the equipment or cause it to overheat, catch fire, or explode. The danger is greatest if you inadvertently plug 110–120 volt devices (such as those made for use in the United States) into 220–240 volt power supplies (such as those throughout most of Europe). Japan uses 100 volts (half the country at 50 Hz and half at 60 Hz), which is just enough of an undervoltage to damage much equipment made for the United States.

Most electrical and electronic equipment will not work on the wrong voltage. Most manufacturers produce different models for different countries (for most types of equipment only two basic models are required, for 100–120 and 220–240 volts) rather than trying to build a single universal or dual-power model. If you want to use something in a particular place, you have to find out what kind of power (voltage and frequency) is used there and buy a model designed for it. Only after you are sure that it has the proper type of power supply should you get a plug adapter, if necessary, to plug it in.

Many digital cameras, portable stereos, laptop computers, and mobile phones (cell phones)—the electronic devices most often carried by travelers—are available with multiple-voltage power supplies capable of operating from all standard power types with only plug adapters and no need for external voltage or frequency converters. The key words to look for or ask about are an "auto-switching" or "universal" power supply, rated to accept an input range of at least 110–240 volts, 50–60 Hz. The one on my computer is rated 90–264 volts, giving it a decent tolerance for brownouts and surges. There's rarely any difference in price between the same product with a single-voltage power supply or with a "universal" adapter.

The same device may be distributed with different AC adapters, depending on where it's sold. Product specifications don't always distinguish whether the AC adapter is available in two alternate models, one for 100–120 volts and one for 220–240 volts, or whether there is a single model capable of operating on either voltage. Sometimes the only way to tell for sure is to open the box and read the label on the adapter before you buy.

Third World electrical systems pose additional problems, even if you have the proper plug adapters and equipment with a universal power supply. Power supplies in much of the world are intermittent. That a country or city has a central electrical power supply does not imply that power is available 24 hours a day, every day. Power may be supplied only for certain hours each day, or at unpredictable hours if the generators or their fuel supply are unreliable. Power lines may go down or short out, and distribution problems may make power outages common even where there's no problem with generation. In some places there is no city power, and hotels or other buildings have electricity only while they run their own generators, which they don't usually do around the clock.

If generating capacity is inadequate to meet city or countrywide demand, the most common load-management strategy is that of "rolling blackouts," when power is deliberately shut off to some areas to keep the overloaded system from shutting down entirely. (Californians experienced these, briefly, in the summer of 2001.) Depending on the extent of the capacity shortfall, your hotel's neighborhood may have power for 20 hours a day or two. Sometimes there is a predictable daily or weekly schedule or rotation, sometimes not. This is a problem if you are using equipment that can be damaged by a power failure while it is plugged in and in use, especially a computer. If the power is unreliable, it's safer to use your computer on the batteries, unplugged, and shut it down while it's plugged in to recharge.

Most battery chargers and rechargeable devices are such that if the power supply from the wall plug ("mains" in British usage) fails while the charger is plugged in, the batteries will gradually discharge through the charger until they are completely dead. So you can't count on waking up or coming back to a recharged set of batteries if you leave them plugged in to charge overnight or while you go out for the day. Some equipment could lose data or settings this way. Try to find equipment designed so the batteries can be removed from the equipment while charging.

## Odds and Ends

One small item you might not think to bring is a pocket compass. I use mine constantly, mainly to orient myself when using city maps. You get off the bus or come out of the subway and know from your map that you want to walk north. Or you get on the bus, knowing you want to go north but are unsure if this bus will go the right way. The sun isn't visible, and you don't speak the language. Which way is north? Especially if you're good at reading maps, you'll find a compass—even the tiniest one—more useful than you could ever imagine.

As a general-purpose tool, I recommend a Leatherman tool or similar multi-tool—it's expensive, but worth it. The pliers in a Leatherman tool make it useful in many more situations and for many more tasks than a Swiss Army knife. Remember to put it on your checked baggage for each flight, however—if you try to carry any knife onto a plane, it will be confiscated and destroyed.

If you don't have one already, I'd get a small waterproof LED flashlight or head-lamp. LED's last for at least ten times as long on a set of batteries as standard incandescent lights. That's long enough that you don't have to worry about conserving batteries, or finding your flashlight batteries dead just when you need them.

Snapshots of your home, neighborhood, family, friends, and workplace, or postcards of your home city or region, are handy when people ask about your life and where you are from. You might even want to bring extras so you can give them to people who befriend you or help you out.

Consider having some business cards ("name cards") printed up with your permanent contact information. They'll save you copying your address out over and over to exchange with people you meet. When you're dealing with businesses or bureaucrats, having "business" cards (even ones that don't mention a business or title) can often enhance your perceived status and legitimacy. You can buy pages of blank card stock preformatted for business cards from any office supply store, and print yourself up a few cards on your computer. Or you can get a few hundred in a standard design for US$30 or so from any print shop. If you run out, you can get more printed abroad for even less.

A number of common household items can be hard to find when you want them, and are apt to come in handy:

• Ziplock plastic bags for separating things in your pack, and for keeping them dry when your pack gets soaked (no pack is really waterproof)

• a few large tyvek envelopes—sturdier and lighter than manila folders for keeping papers, folded maps, etc. clean, dry, and sorted

- a flat rubber universal sink stopper (so you can wash out your clothes in sinks that don't have stoppers)

- safety pins (They double as clothespins that can't blow off the line.)

- a small roll each of Scotch tape and of duct tape

- a few rubber bands and paper clip

- ten meters (yards) of the strongest lightweight waterproof braided cord you can find—"parachute cord" or something thinner (to use as a clothesline, tying together gear, and a thousand other odd jobs)

- a meter (yard) or two of picture wire (very strong and versatile for diverse jury-rigging and mending tasks)

- a couple of self-adhesive nylon patches for tears or punctures in packs, raincoats, etc.

- velcro strips to have sewn into the pockets of clothes you buy or have made (Ten cm or 4 inches is enough for a typical pockets.)

- a rigid cardboard or plastic tube just long enough to fit in your pack (Without a tube, it's almost impossible to get prints, maps, posters, or artwork home undamaged.)

## SENDING THINGS FROM HOME

Don't count on being able to send things or have them sent to you while you are traveling abroad. If you forget something, run out of something, or discover you need or want something you hadn't thought of before you left, you'll probably have to find it locally or do without. If there are things you'll want for only part of your trip, it's generally much easier to bring those things with you and send them home when you're done with them, rather than to schedule the part of the trip using those things at the end.

International package shipping, whether by post or through private shipping companies, is either very slow or very expensive. American Express offices will accept only mail—letters and small packets of papers or documents— for American Express clients. American Express offices will not accept or hold parcels, packages, deliveries from any sort of private delivery service (FedEx, DHL, etc.), or anything that has to be signed for. General delivery or "poste restante" (postal services for sending mail or packages to be held for pickup at a specified post office) are generally adequate for noncritical letters (which could as easily have been sent as e-mail), but insufficiently reliable for urgent or valuable shipments.

Any international shipment is potentially subject to customs duty (see the chapter on travel documents). Small, valuable items—the sort of thing you might be tempted to have shipped to you—are often subject to duty. A friend accidentally left their camera with an acquaintance they visited in another country. She could have had it shipped, but the duty to bring it into the country where she was would have exceeded the value of the camera.

If you need something to continue your trip, you need to know when it will be available for pick-up. (If you send things home from abroad, on the other hand, you usually aren't too concerned with how long it takes them to arrive or clear customs.) Shipping times are unpredictable, and mail sent for general delivery will only be held for a limited time before being returned, destroyed, or sold as unclaimed. Postal parcels can take weeks or months to clear customs. So even if you know your own schedule precisely in advance (which you may not) there is no way to send a parcel, especially by the cheapest means (surface or boat mail) with any assurance that it will be available for pick-up at the time you will be in the place where you are sending it.

Some travelers try to save weight by shipping heavy items they will need for only part of their trip to somewhere they can pick them up along the way. This makes sense only if you have a reliable contact who lives there to whom you can ship them and who can hold them until your arrival. That works if you have lots of lead time for delays in shipping and customs, and if the items are heavy or important, but not truly essential. A certain percentage of mail does get lost even within or between First World countries, and international parcel insurance is expensive.

People are commonly tempted to ship ahead trekking, camping, and sports equipment (a reasonable idea if you have a reliable local contact to whom to ship them); warm clothing for cold climates (ditto, if you are going first to the tropics or to places where it is summer, and then to an expensive cold country);

guidebooks (rarely worthwhile, as most guidebooks can be bought along the way); and maps (a judgment call, as they are often unavailable locally but are usually both lightweight and important enough to carry with you).

Resupplying prescription drugs, if you run out and can't find them locally, is the most difficult thing. Try to bring enough to last through your trip if at all possible. Shipping and courier companies are extremely wary of being used by shippers of illegal drugs, making it extremely difficult to get them to accept shipments of any drugs, even legally prescribed pharmaceuticals.

## SENDING THINGS HOME

It's possible to send things home from most major cities. Most parcels will, eventually, reach their destinations. But the process of mailing is, in many cases, neither simple nor quick, and unless you pay a small fortune your things may take months to arrive by surface mail. Don't plan on mailing things home if you can help it. If you must, send the things you would least mind losing, even if they are expensive, and do not send things with great sentimental value. If you have to mail a package home, budget a full day for the process. If it doesn't take that long, consider yourself lucky.

Try to find a post office that regularly deals with foreigners. Sometimes there's a special office for international mailings. Wrap everything you want to send carefully and tightly. Pad fragile items well, and make sure they don't have room to shift. Don't seal your parcel before going to the post office, as it may need to be inspected first. In some areas of the world, you may find that parcels have to be sewn up in cloth, in which case there will probably be someone providing this service just outside the post office.

Local mailing procedures vary, but you should always be sure that all stamps on your letters and parcels are canceled in your sight. If they aren't, the stamps may be stolen and resold or reused, leaving your mail with insufficient postage. International parcel post rates vary too widely for any useful generalizations. Because postal rates are based on the official, often artificial, exchange rate, mailing can be either insanely cheap or insanely expensive, depending on the relationship between the real and official value of the local currency.

For information on sending and receiving letters as a means of communications, see the section in the following chapter in the following chapter on "Postal Mail" under "Communication."

# "Life
### on the Road"

# PRACTICALITIES

## TRAVELING COMPANIONS

Your choice of with whom to travel is really inseparable from, and should be made simultaneously with, your choice of where to go. You may want to change your destinations to accommodate the wishes of a desired companion, or you may want to choose a different companion or set out by yourself if you find that your would-be partner wants to go to different places than you. Few choices will affect the nature and quality of your travel experience more than your choice of traveling companion(s), or your choice to travel alone.

My impression is that too few people think carefully enough about their choice of traveling companions. Whatever the reason, it's certainly the case that more people are dissatisfied, after the fact, with their choices of companions (including, for some, the choice to travel alone) than are dissatisfied with their choices of destination.

Before you commit yourself to a long or complicated trip together, try to take a short "shakedown" trip, at least a weekend getaway, to get a feel for each other and how you will travel together. It'll be well worth the expense if it spares you a disastrous long trip with someone incompatible.

Make sure you agree not just on where you want to go but on what you want to do there, and why. One of the most common mistakes in travel planning is to get together with a group of people who want to go to "the same place," and not to realize until you get off the plane that one of you wants to spend time in the brothels, one on the beach, one in the shops, one in the temples, one in the museums, one in the cafes, one in the villages, and one in the mountains. That may be possible, but if you are going to split up immediately on arrival there isn't much point in going out of your way to travel together in the first place.

Make a list of where you want to go, what you want to see or do there, and what your goals and priorities are for the trip. Do this separately, without consulting each other, and then compare your lists.

Because reasons for going places or seeing things vary so much, and because it's often the small details of daily traveling life that cause the most friction, it's especially important not just to list destinations or sights of interest. Get together with everyone with whom you are considering traveling, and have each one of you describe to the others, in as much detail as possible, what they envision a typical day or two on the road would be like: what you will do, where you stay, where you will eat, how you will get around, how you will make decisions, etc. As you listen to your prospective traveling companion(s), try to actually visualize the trip described, and to compare it with your own vision of the trip you expect to take.

These predeparture exercises are no less necessary if you plan to travel with a spouse or lover. Travel can place severe stress on a relationship, in ways different than love, marriage, or living together. Don't take for granted that someone you love and/or can live with happily is someone with whom you'll want to travel, or that someone you fall in love with on the road, and with whom you love traveling, is someone you'll love to settle down with or live with at home. Conversely, people who set out in couples should leave themselves open to the possibility that they might split up along the way, and that even if they do, they might want to be together once again when they get back home. Travel can bring out behavioral traits and aspects of people's personalities that aren't visible, or don't cause problems, at other times. Don't take for granted that you know your lover's tastes in travel if you haven't traveled together before.

I've made long international trips both alone and with a partner. I know that the issues that cause the most problems in our relationship, and to which we

## KEY ADVICE ABOUT LIFE ON THE ROAD

- Choose your traveling companion(s) at least as carefully as your destinations. Consider how you want to travel, not just where, in choosing your companion(s).

- Travel responsibly and sustainably. Consider the impact of where and how you travel on both the physical and cultural ecology of the places you visit.

- Travel in as local a way as you can. You'll spend less, learn more, and do less ecological damage.

- Don't worry. Things will work out. Most pre-trip nightmares don't materialize. The necessities of travel are the necessities of daily life; everywhere in the world, you'll find that people have ways of dealing with them.

- Expect more severe culture shock when you return home then while you are traveling. "Home" may not have changed, but you will have, and your home will seem different to your changed self.

For more information on the topics in this chapter, see the Resource Guide in the back of the book, and the links on the Practical Nomad Web site at http://www.practicalnomad.com.

have to pay the most attention when we are traveling, are, at least on the surface, quite different from those that dominate our disputes at home.

There are a variety of travel matchmaking services: travel clubs, "traveling companion wanted" ads in travel magazines, and Internet travel newsgroups (especially the Usenet newsgroup "rec.travel.budget.backpack"), bulletin boards, and chat rooms. These may be helpful ways to make initial contact with potential traveling companions, if you want them and can't find them any other way, but I wouldn't commit to an extended trip without meeting all my companions face-to-face. As when answering any personal advertisements, make sure any sexual hopes or expectations are made explicit in advance.

Regardless of who your traveling companion is, don't think you have to spend all your time together as a single unit. Many travelers spend more of their time with their travel partner than they would ever otherwise spend with anyone, including a spouse or lover. You might even want to plan to take breaks from each other's company, whether for an hour, a day, or a week at a time. Some travel experiences are only available to solo travelers. It's a recipe for resentment for neither of you to feel able to cope on your own, and even worse if only one of you feels dependent on the other. Be alert to particular disparities in power and dependence if one of you is better at communicating with local people (either because of better knowledge of a language or better skill at nonverbal communication), is much more familiar with the place, or is much more experienced at travel.

Women are much more likely than men to take on a traveling companion, primarily because they don't feel confident that they will be able or comfortable enough to travel alone. At the risk of presuming to give advice to women about a problem men don't usually share, allow me to suggest that mere fear of solo travel may be the worst reason to take on a traveling companion, unless you can find someone with whom you have a great deal more in common than your fear. *A Journey of One's Own: Uncommon Advice for the Independent Woman Traveler*, by Thalia Zepatos (see the Resource Guide), has more thoughts for women on the choice of whether to travel alone or with a partner.

That you both want to visit the same place or region says little about whether you have common interests, goals, desires, or travel styles. If the main thing you have in common is your fear of traveling alone, you aren't likely to get along well on the road. You'll tend to reinforce each other's fears, not empower each other to embrace and experience local cultures and ways. Interacting, out of fear of the unknown, mainly with each other, you'll rapidly get as tired of each

**REAL LIFE**

Sometimes I travel for adventure, excitement, education, and immersion in the place I'm going and its sensory stimuli. Sometimes I travel for vacation, rest, relaxation, contemplation, and an escape from sensory stimuli. One of the worst trips I've ever had—with some of my best friends—was when I wanted the latter, and my companions wanted the former.

other, lovers or not, as people can in any marriage of convenience, unless you are lucky enough to discover that you have many shared interests other than wanting to travel and not wanting to do so alone.

Many such traveling partnerships break up mid-trip, often in ways that leave resentment on both sides. Typically, one or the other partner grows out of the fear faster than the other. The one who is ready to travel more adventurously and get off the beaten track, or is no longer afraid of solo travel and wants to go off alone, resents being held back by the other. And the other one resents being pushed to change, or feels "abandoned," or accuses the partner of "betraying" their agreement to support each other, the raison d'être of their partnership.

If at first, or in particular places, you aren't comfortable traveling alone, rest assured that there will be other travelers who feel likewise, and with whom you can join up. It's common for pairs, trios, or larger impromptu groups to come together for anything from a day's sightseeing excursion to a month's trek or overland journey through a country or region. Some travelers who leave home and return alone spend most of their days in the company of other travelers, whether for safety or conversation or to save on hotel costs. Even people who prefer to travel alone often team up to share chartered vehicles in places where public transportation is expensive, impractical, or doesn't go where they want, such as for a camping trip across the United States or Australia or for drives through African wildlife preserves.

You have to try hard to find a place where there are so few travelers that ad hoc companionship isn't available to those who want it. I generally avoid travelers' ghettoes and hangouts, but they are excellent places to find partners for onward travel or excursions. Hostels, guest houses, and cafes everywhere have bulletin boards for "companion(s) wanted" and "rides to share" notices. When you both are already on the road, it's a lot easier to figure out whether you and a prospective fellow traveler have similar styles and will get along than if you try to choose a travel partner before your departure.

## TOURS AND GUIDES

Escorted tours around the world are few, especially compared to the incredible diversity of itineraries followed by independent travelers. Tours are usually very expensive relative to independent travel, and limited in time, relative to the duration of most independent trips around the world. The longer the duration of your trip, the more the greater cost of travel by tour becomes a factor. And there are also significant ecological and other reasons to prefer independent travel even if you could afford a tour. Most around-the-world and other long-term travelers, both perforce and by choice, end up traveling unescorted, independently (i.e., not with an organized group), and arranging their own accommodations and other travel services as they go.

## Ecotourism and the Ecology of Independent Travel

Ecotourism and "responsible travel" are growing trends, reflecting rising public awareness of the ill effects and irresponsibility of much tourism, and a desire on the part of increasing numbers of travelers genuinely to immerse themselves in the places they visit.

But what is "ecotourism?" How should a concern for the environment influence the way you travel? And is it really more "green" or "responsible" to take an ecotour than to travel on your own?

All travel, and especially long-haul air travel, has adverse ecological consequences. Unlike trains, which if electrified can get power from a variety of renewable sources, airplanes all fly on fossil fuel ("jet fuel" is kerosene). The present window of opportunity for transoceanic air travel—affordable to large numbers of people—is likely to be, in historical terms, a brief one before the world runs out of oil. There is no such thing as "sustainable" or "low-impact" air travel.

More of the effects of travel on the physical environment are related to transportation, such as petroleum extraction, refining, distribution, and burning, or the cutting of trees and paving of land for roads, than anything about what you do when you get where you are going. It makes no sense to label a trip as "ecotourism" if it involves flying 20,000 km (12,500 miles) from one continent to another and back for only a few weeks.

If what you are seeking is an environment relatively uncrowded and undamaged by people, a more ecological choice for North Americans may be to stay closer to home. As the most geographically (if not culturally) diverse country on Earth (only China can compare), the United States has become a major ecotourism destination for travelers from overseas, especially from crowded parts of Europe and East Asia that lack American-sized open spaces, parks, wildlife preserves, and wilderness areas.

Given that getting there by air is an unavoidable ecological cost of long-distance travel, ecological responsibility in travel means both minimizing the avoidable environmental costs and trying to make a positive contribution in some other way to offset them. That's what ecotourism is supposed to be about.

There are serious problems, though, in realizing those goals in any prearranged tour, largely stemming from the high costs of these tours. Tour operators in the First World spend more on marketing, support, and other costs in their country (where wages, after all, are at First World levels) than on tour services in destination countries in the Third or Fourth World. This is another way of saying that tourist services purchased locally in a Third World destination country would typically cost no more than half what they would cost as part of a tour prearranged through a First World operator. Tour travel itself, moreover, is skewed toward more expensive, usually meaning higher-impact, travel.

Few people would knowingly pay twice as much to arrange a tour through an operator in their own country if they believed themselves capable of arranging it locally, or doing it themselves independently. So tour operators have a vested interest in promoting fear, disempowerment, and ignorance on the part of would-be travelers, and in keeping people from learning how to travel on their own, as part of persuading them that they can't or wouldn't want to travel on their own and that it's worth paying the price to book a tour in advance.

To compound the problem, most self-styled ecotourism publications are financed primarily by advertising from tour operators, and thus can ill afford to criticize or to provide information that would reduce the market for the products of the industry on whom their existence depends.

There is an obvious contradiction between persuading people that they need a tour operator as an intermediary between themselves and the local people and environment, and persuading people to immerse themselves in and learn about the local environment by interacting with local people.

Prearranged tours add foreign agents, middlemen, and communications and money-transfer costs to the costs of services provided in the destination country, thus greatly inflating the price of travel. And those agents and middlemen all have an incentive to push tourists to more expensive tours to maximize their commissions. Because travel on a tour basis is more expensive, people on tours are, on average, richer people (or at least people traveling more expensively) than independent travelers. And there's the rub, or at least part of it.

Wealth is power. The more expensively tourists are traveling, the more power they wield to have the local environment altered to suit their needs and desires. And, quite frankly, richer people are more accustomed than poorer people to having their desires accommodated regardless of the consequences for others. They frequently have higher expectations of Western norms of luxury and service, and are less culturally diverse than a more economically diverse range of tourists would be. The result is these tourists create greater material and cultural pressures to reshape the local environment in a Western mold than would an equal number of tourists traveling more cheaply.

The poorest tourists simply don't have the economic clout to transform their destinations. They have to learn the local culture and language, even perhaps studying them before they arrive, to survive and get around. They stay in the places local people stay, eat the local food, and use the local mass transportation. Having more time than money, and being more dependent on local goodwill, they are compelled to be both more patient and more tolerant. They can't afford to change things much, and they leave them pretty much as they found them.

People traveling more expensively are also likely to have less time, and, being more rushed, are both more able and more willing to make ecological (and other) compromises to fulfill their travel agendas in their limited time: flying rather than taking trains, driving rather than walking, and in general supporting infrastructure changes to make the "marquee attractions" more "accessible." They also have less time to develop an awareness of what this sort of development, and the effect of their own visit, leaves behind.

Anthropologist and travel scholar Klaus Westerhausen makes all these points strongly in his study of the most independent, lowest-budget, longest-term travelers, and the changes in the places they visit, *Beyond the Beach: An Ethnography of Modern Travellers in Asia* (see the Resource Guide).

People traveling on their own who can't afford to charter private transportation are less likely to get into the most environmentally sensitive areas, because these are likely to be without regular public transport. There is a strong argument, in fact, for city tourism as having less impact on either the physical or the cultural environment than the tours to less densely populated (or even unpopulated) areas that are more often thought of, and promoted, as ecotours.

Even the more sensitive travelers on prearranged tours are limited in their opportunities either to become aware of the ecological implications of their visits or to adapt their styles of travel to minimize those effects. Distributing the costs of prearrangement over many people makes group travel more affordable than individualized prearranged travel, so travelers who prearrange their itineraries are more likely to be in groups than ones or twos. Participants in escorted groups inevitably do much of their socializing within their groups, making them less aware of the local culture and their own effects on it than independent travelers immersed in and interacting constantly with the culture. Tour groups are further insulated from such interaction and awareness by their escort, who inevitably has a vested financial interest in making them feel good about their experience.

Equally important is the fact that even those who want to adapt can't, because everything on the tour has been committed to before the tour began. Unfortunately, what the traveler has committed to is more the image of the tour than the experience of the tour, because the tourist has to buy and pay for the tour before experiencing it. No matter how wonderful the tour is, it won't sell if it doesn't promise (in advance) what people think (in advance) they want, or think will be appropriate. What they find they want, or decide would be appropriate, when they get there matters much less.

Even some tour operators admit, in confidence, to arranging trips in a way that they themselves would never choose, but that "the customers want." If prepaid tourists discover on arrival that what they thought they wanted, and have already bought, is culturally or ecologically inappropriate, they are stuck. Travelers who make their arrangements locally are more likely to notice, and at least have a chance to consider before committing themselves, the implications of the style of travel they are contemplating.

I don't want to seem too critical. I strongly support ecotourism. I do want to encourage travelers to acknowledge responsibility for their effects on the physical and cultural ecology of the places they visit, and to use the lessons they learn from travel to live more responsibly when they return home.

Ecotourism operators run the gamut from politically committed, money-losing environmental organizations to utterly unprincipled hucksters looking for new marketing angles to sell the same old tours in new packaging. But nothing about ecotourism or responsible travel, or their values, requires a tour, and even the best tours have several strikes against them, as I've tried to explain.

Independent travelers, of course, run the gamut too. It's all too easy to fall into a rut of going from one place listed in a guidebook for foreigners, or recommended by other foreigners, to another; to stay and eat only in places catering to, and patronized exclusively by, other foreigners like you; to spend most of your time in ghettoes of foreigners; to socialize mostly with other foreigners; and to interact with local people only as service providers. Some people argue that, to the extent that they succeed in getting "off the beaten path" or into newly touristed areas, independent backpackers are the vanguard of cultural imperialism and the destructive effects of mass tourism.

But I would argue strongly against letting yourself be talked into an "ecotour" as necessarily being a "more ecological" or "more responsible" way to travel than traveling on your own. (For both sides of this debate, see the "Backpackers" and "Guidebooks" special issues of Tourism Concerns's journal, *Tourism In Focus*, listed in the Resource Guide.) To me, the key thing is that if you make your own arrangements, you have to take personal responsibility for the ecological implications (physical and cultural) of the way you travel. Traveling independently means not having a tour operator to rely on for ecological awareness or decision-making. It's past time, however—at least in my opinion—for independent travel to be recognized as offering more diverse possibilities for ecotourism, and greater opportunity for responsible tourism, than any tour.

## Local Tours and Guides

If you can't or don't want to do something on your own, it's often better to arrange for a tour, guide, or helper locally than to try to book one in advance from abroad.

Some people are afraid to wait until they arrive to book a tour, lest it be too difficult to arrange on the spot. Rest assured that it is just the opposite: unless money is truly no object, it is usually easier to arrange a tour locally. You will have more choices; it will be much easier to get firsthand references, check out the tour operator, and make an informed choice; and the prices, even for tours with operators with agents abroad, are typically only half what the same tours would cost if booked from abroad. Typically only a fraction of the higher-priced local operators have agents abroad or Web sites.

The main exceptions are things that are rationed in some way, or which only a limited number of people can do, and for which the quota is likely to be filled, or all the permits taken, by the time you arrive at the destination or the jumping-off point. Permits for raft trips through the Grand Canyon, for example, are allocated months in advance, based on a waiting list several years long. But there are fewer exceptions like this than most travelers fear.

Locally operated tours run the gamut from half-day or full-day guided sightseeing trips around a city by bus or van to two-week package excursions by air to neighboring countries. You can hire a guide, translator, porter, or car and driver by the hour, day, week, or month—whatever you want and can afford.

The best way to learn about and choose between local tour operators and guides is personal investigation and firsthand references from fellow travelers. Visit the office (if it's a big enough operation to have one). Look at the vehicles. Talk to the people yourself. Whether you are hiring a freelance guide or booking a two-week package tour from a large local company, talk to at least one, preferably two, different fellow travelers who have used its services before. When you are on the spot, there's no need to settle for anything less than such direct and detailed information.

It's not hard to find references and recommendations of the good guides and companies, and warnings about the bad. The pros and cons of guides, porters, and local tour companies are a standard topic of conversation in every travelers' hangout. Mention that you are considering a tour operated by Company C to D, or are negotiating with head Sherpa E to arrange a trek, and you are apt to be inundated with advice about their pros and cons. As with recommendations further afield, remember that not everyone likes the same thing, or the same sort of tour. Some companies are unequivocally bad, but few are unequivocally good for all tastes. Listen to what everyone has to say, but choose what you think will be right for you, even if it's not what everyone else is doing, or would want to do.

Where tourists have come from different countries and speak different languages, English is the most common "link" language for tour narration, even if it's no one's first language. City tours may be available in other languages as well, but in big cities they are always available in English. The same is largely true for at least the more common longer tours.

You can sometimes trade your services as a language tutor and practice conversationalist for the services of a guide and translator. Don't agree to this unless you are willing to keep your end of the bargain. If you want your guide to do their best, do the best job of teaching that you can in return.

## Overland Expeditions

Almost the only affordable *long-term* tours are a variety of so-called "overland expeditions," primarily in Africa and Eurasia. These trips are distinguished by their distinctive mode of transportation and accommodations: short-wheelbase high-clearance trucks (or occasionally vans or buses) outfitted with seats that convert to sleeping berths for 10–30 passengers.

Depending on the operator, weather, and terrain, you either sleep in bunks installed in the truck or in small tents you set up each night. Occasionally you may stay in a hotel in a town. Meals are usually prepared and eaten collectively in a camp kitchen from ingredients bought in local markets, supplemented with a limited supply of food provided by the expedition outfitter.

The quoted prices for expedition tours are very cheap considering their duration but are rarely all-inclusive. Typically, the tour price paid to the operator in advance covers only a seat/berth in the truck, any furnished gear (you may have to bring your own tent and/or sleeping bag, or pay extra to rent one), and the salaries of the driver/guides (usually two or three per truck). Contributions to a shared fund ("kitty") for food and other joint costs along the way, as well as all restaurant meals, hotel stays, fees or tips to local guides, museum and park entrance fees (especially high at some African wildlife preserves), and personal expenses, are additional.

Typical routes for expedition tours are between Europe and West Africa (via the Sahara), East Africa and Southern Africa, and Europe and South Asia (via Kurdistan, Iran, and Pakistan). Typical trip are anywhere from three to 12 weeks in duration, sometimes longer if you combine several sequential trips.

Imagine spending all day, every day for weeks, riding in a truck with a group of people you didn't choose as companions and who start out as strangers, and camping every night with the same group of people. Sometimes the group coalesces and most of the people get along with each other. Sometimes not.

When you stop, you all get out of the truck together. You do get some time for individual sightseeing, if you so choose, in cities. But most days you are on the road, in or near the truck, all day. Most of your opportunities to see local things and talk to local people are constrained and shaped, for the worse, by the simultaneous presence of your 10 or 20 traveling companions, all trying to join the conversation or take pictures of the same sight.

I can't recommend overland expeditions as "tours" because of the limited opportunities they give their passengers to actually experience and interact with the people and places they drive through, because the group dynamics are so unpredictable (notwithstanding the best efforts of the driver/guides), and because such a high proportion of people who set out on these trips don't complete them. I should note, however, that most of those who drop out continue traveling on their own, and that some of them feel that the overland expedition experience helped empower them to travel on their own in places they wouldn't otherwise have felt comfortable starting out alone.

Because of the high drop-out rate, expedition trucks frequently have spaces available on an ad hoc basis for people who meet them along their way and are willing to pay a prorated price (often quite negotiable) to join them for part of a trip. You can't count on finding an expedition operator with spare seats on a specific route at a specific time. But if you happen to meet one, joining on temporarily may be the best away across a stretch where there's no public transit, such as the Sahara, and for a limited stint the price may be excellent value for the transportation alone.

## ACCOMMODATIONS

Even experienced travelers planning their first independent trip to a new part of the world sometimes fear that they won't find a place to stay. There are a variety of ways, most of them easier than you might think, to have a bed waiting for you, or find one as you arrive. Experienced travelers rarely worry about finding a place to sleep, not because they've learned any special room-finding skills but because they've learned that's it's not really that hard to find rooms on arrival.

I should note, however, that choices of accommodations ("Is this place really worth US$5 a night more than the other?" "Should we agree to take this room for this price, or keep looking for a better or cheaper hotel?") figure prominently in the rankings of things about which traveling companions argue. This is definitely one of the things to talk through with prospective companions before you agree to travel together.

## Hostels

Hostelling International is the world's largest accommodation provider. Most "youth" hostels accept reservations. Almost none have age limits. Procedures vary. Check with the local affiliate of Hostelling International for details. (See "Accommodations" in the Resource Guide for worldwide HI contacts.)

HI operates its own computerized reservation system for hostels in international gateway cities. Most other hostels accept reservations by mail, and increasingly many take reservations over the Internet. Book early. Hosteling organizations have trouble affording large enough facilities in popular cities.

Hostels are few outside the First World. But hostels offer the cheapest reservations in major cities in the United States, Canada, Western Europe, Japan, Australia, and New Zealand.

As long as they don't claim to be affiliated with Hostelling International, anyplace that wants to can call itself a hostel. Standards and services of private and unaffiliated hostels vary. Overall, in my experience, private hostels tend to have a younger, more party-oriented clientele. Guests at HI hostels tend to be quieter, with less alcohol and more of a mix of ages. The Resource Guide lists several directories of private hostels.

## Home Exchanges

You go on vacation from Point A to Point B. You leave your home empty in A, and rent a place to stay in B. Meanwhile, there's probably somebody else traveling from B to A, leaving their home vacant in B and renting a place to stay in A. Wouldn't it be nice if you could connect with each other, and arrange to each stay in each other's home? In a nutshell, that's a home exchange.

When it works, a home exchange is almost miraculous: You each get the use of an entire, fully furnished and equipped, home—probably much larger and more comfortable than any vacation home you could afford—and *neither of you pays a penny!* Nothing else comes close for value in long-term vacation (or other travel) accommodations.

Why doesn't everybody do this? The catch has always been the difficulty of identifying someone compatible and trustworthy, with the mirror image of your itinerary, wanting to travel between the same places, on the same dates, in opposite directions. That, however, is exactly the sort of matching task for which the Internet is perfect.

Arranging a home exchange is usually a three-step process. First, you sign up with a home exchange matching service, and complete a profile of your home, when you want to travel, and where you want to go. Then, the service posts your listing in their search directory of available homes for exchange, and gives you access to other members' listings. When you find a potential match, you can contact them by e-mail to get to know each other, see if you think an exchange will work, and negotiate the details.

You can take as much time, and ask as many questions as you like, before you decide whether you're willing to let someone live in your home while you're not there. Of course, you'll be living in their house at the same time, so you both probably have the same concern for having your homes be well cared for. Mutual trust and advance planning are essential.

How easy it will be to arrange an exchange for your home depends largely on the attractiveness and location of your home. Most, although not all, home exchanges are within the First World, especially within and between the United States, Canada, and Western Europe. Home exchanges are most attractive for families and longer stays. If you own a home, and if you want to settle down somewhere abroad for a month or two, a home exchange may be the way to afford it.

### Hospitality Exchanges

Hospitality exchanges are similar to home exchanges, except that they involve hosting people in your home while you are there, and staying with other people in their homes, rather than exchanging the use of your home for theirs.

As with home exchanges, hospitality exchanges are generally based on directories of members of a matching service. Also as with home exchange networks, most hospitality exchanges now operate on the Internet. You sign up as being willing to consider requests for hospitality by visitors. When a fellow member of the service wants to visit the place where you live, they can contact you and ask if you're willing to put them up on certain dates. You can always say no, without any obligation to give a reason, although of course the system works on mutual generosity and willingness to play host as often as you play guest. When you want to go somewhere, you can contact fellow members in that location to see if one of them might be willing to put you up.

Hospitality exchanges are not a substitute for other sorts of travel accommodations, and visits are generally limited to a few days. Guests are often expected to help with household tasks, although the norms of the relationship vary from one hospitality exchange service to another. Hospitality exchanges are mainly a way to meet people in a different place, and get experience of what their lives are like, rather than a way to cut the cost of travel. Many hospitality exchange networks are organized around "affinity groups" of people who share certain values or interests. It's not for everyone, but at its best a stay in a local person's home can be the highlight of your trip.

### Homestays

Whether or not you've arranged it in advance, try to stay with local people whenever you get a chance: friends, relatives, friends of friends, people you meet along the way, people whose "guest houses" or "hostels" are no more than spare rooms in their houses. You'll often be more crowded and less comfortable than in a hotel—one of the greatest luxuries of life in the United States, relative to even other wealthy countries, is how much living space most of us have —but you'll learn more and have more fun. Family homestays (the most informal sort of "bed and breakfast") are currently the standard form of budget accommodation in much of the Second World, where budget hotels are only gradually appearing.

Some people, especially women, worry about whether to accept offers of hospitality, especially from strangers. Use the same caution you would in the United States. Many things that would be considered sexual harassment in the United States are considered flattery elsewhere, but violation of a woman's honor is a much more serious offense in many other countries than in the United States. I've heard more anecdotal stories of sexual harassment and date rape between foreigners at backpackers' guest houses than between foreign travelers and local hosts.

Sooner or later some of the people you've stayed with —perhaps those you least expect—will make their way to your country, and your home, expecting you to put them up. Do so. Graciously.

If you're uncomfortable with this idea, don't let people you meet take you into their homes. It's unfair and improper, to say the least, to accept offers of hospitality you wouldn't be willing to reciprocate. If they offer you the best room in their house, realize that they would probably expect you to do likewise.

### Hotel Reservations

It's possible to reserve a hotel room in advance in most large cities, even most Third World capitals, but often only at the most expensive hotels. Sometimes there is no middle ground. The only hotels set up to handle advance reservations from overseas may be the Intercontinentals and their ilk. In many cities there are few if any midrange hotels between, say, US$20 and US$150 a night; in some the spread is even wider: there are local-style hotels at local prices and five-star international hotels at five-star prices.

A common request to a travel agent is, "Can you reserve a midrange hotel— say, US$50 a night—for my first night in City X?" In many cases, it's not possible, and I would not recommend it even when it is.

Cheap hotels don't participate in computerized reservation systems. Few midrange hotels listed in Moon Handbooks or similar guides to regions outside the First World, or that I would recommend, can be reserved by travel agents by computer.

The cheaper the hotel, the less likely it is to pay a commission, the less likely it is to cover the cost of faxes or phone calls, and thus the more likely that a travel agent will have to charge you a fee for faxing or telexing to make reservations you could as easily make for yourself.

Cheap hotels are cheap in part because they haven't invested in computer links or a telex. You may be able to make reservations directly with them by phoning or faxing, but unless you have a reference from a reliable fellow traveler you'll have to commit yourself to a place sight unseen, which is generally an unnecessary risk. Question people who recommend a hotel as to how recently they stayed there, what it was like, and their tastes in travel.

The cheapest hotels that can be booked from abroad are often an otherwise poor value, because they rely on one-time, transient business, not the loyalty of repeat guests, and their competitive advantage is the very fact that they can be booked from abroad, not anything to do with their facilities or service.

Hotels that you reserve directly on the Internet are even more of a risk, since you don't have a local travel agent through whom to seek recourse if there's a problem. Frequently the hotels popular on the Internet are those that have invested in their Web site rather than their service.

### Guidebooks

Good guidebooks will give you an idea of the sort of accommodations—guest houses, hostels, homestays, etc.— that you are likely to find in a particular place, and perhaps even in what neighborhood of the city you are likely to find the cheap ones concentrated. Look for books written by people who travel the way you do, on your sort of budget.

It's easy to choose your lodgings entirely from those listed in a guidebook, but it's neither necessary nor recommended. Places listed in books are guaranteed a steady stream of customers, books in hand. If a guidebook lists two places in a neighborhood, odds are that there's a third across the street or around the corner that's not in the book and that has to, and does, try harder to provide better service. I find the general information on types of lodging and ways of doing things in particular countries more useful than specific places to stay. Types and styles of accommodations vary greatly from country to country, and it helps a lot to know what to look for, and in what part of town. My own preference is to try to stay at places that aren't in guidebooks and have few foreign guests.

"Current" editions of guidebooks are typically based on research at least two years old. Check the date of any guidebook, and allow for changes and inflate your price expectations accordingly.

### Local Recommendations

Talk to people on the plane, train, etc., especially people who are from the place you are going to. Most people are proud of their home and happy to talk about it to foreigners. If you already have specific lodging in mind, ask a local if they've heard of it, or of the address. They may never have heard of the hotel, but they may be able to warn you off if it has a bad local reputation or is in an undesirable or unsafe neighborhood.

Even if you don't get specific hotel recommendations, you're likely to get good advice about local transportation and sightseeing. I always ask, "Where should I go that most tourists don't go?" If you hit it off with locals and they are going your way, they may offer you a ride, or even invite you to stay in their home.

### Touts

People who worry that they will be unable to find anywhere to stay probably have yet to encounter "touts," people who are paid to find customers for shops, services, and especially hotels. They may be on the staff of a hotel, or more often the hotel simply puts out the word that anyone bringing a customer in the door gets a certain cut of the first night's rent. Touts are essentially a labor-intensive form of advertising. More appropriate technology for most of the world, I'd say, than a computerized reservation system.

In a poor country, the hotel's cut is enough to motivate large numbers of otherwise unemployed or underemployed people, often children or teenagers (who are also likely to be the ones studying English or other foreign languages at school) to hang out at airports, bus and train stations, and ferry docks propositioning likely looking people (i.e., any foreigner, especially with a backpack). Many taxi drivers also work as touts.

You don't pay the tout's cut directly; it will automatically (and inescapably) be included in the price the hotel quotes you if you come in with a tout. It's not uncommon to be followed by more than one tout, even if you've picked out or been referred to a hotel already, and then to have them both argue with the hotelier about which one brought you in and should get paid.

A tout may not take you to the best or cheapest hotel, but you don't have to accept the first place, or any place, you are taken to. And if you just want to get to sleep, you can always take a room for just one night and look for somewhere better, at your leisure and without your luggage, the next morning. You'll find it easier to find places, and get better prices, in the morning without your luggage. The later it is, and the more burdened you appear to be, the more desperate and willing to pay you will be assumed to be.

Anywhere you need one, you'll find a tout (or one will find you). Touts only get paid if they succeed. You can count on them to find you the last vacant room in the city. Most of the time you'll only find touts a nuisance. I'll always remember the sight of police beating a crowd of touts back with sticks to make way for our bus to get into the station in one tourist town. But when it's late, you have no reservations, and you just need to find somewhere to sleep, let the touts help you. Their cut is a small price to pay for expert assistance.

### Wait Until Morning

If you arrive too late at night, you may be better off spending what's left of the night in the airport. A few hours in a waiting room until it gets light and the city wakes up may be better (safer, especially) than searching for a room at 3 A.M.

At more than one airport, I've found that the staff have assumed that anyone arriving late would stay the night. They led me straight to a quiet, dark lounge or courtyard full of other foreigners dozing on couches, chairs, and the floor. Waiting rooms and trains are among the places that even noncampers find a sleeping bag handy.

It's rare not to find a hotel (more often many of them) within walking distance of any major train station. But if you don't, or don't want to go out until dawn, there are hotel rooms inside or adjacent to some train stations, and a smaller number of airports, that are rented by the hour to arriving, departing, and transit passengers. In South Asia, where they have an especially long tradition, they are called "retiring rooms," and that's what you should ask for.

### Styles of Accommodations

You typically have two main choices in a Third World country, particularly one on a "standard" backpacker tourist route, or with a well-developed infrastructure for independent budget travel. On one hand, there are dormitory or hostel-like "guest houses" catering almost exclusively to, and providing many special services for, foreigners. Services at such places may include ride sharing and notice boards, equipment rental, local sightseeing recommendations and tours, and directions to the next major stop on the standard tourist route in each direction. On the other hand, there are more expensive low-to mid-range local hotels, usually catering to the middle-class local travelers.

Most foreign backpackers stay in the foreign backpacker hostels and guest houses. Because these are usually the only places that rent beds in dorms, rather than private rooms, they are usually significantly cheaper than the cheapest local hotels that are clean and comfortable enough to be acceptable to most foreigners. And they are usually the most obvious and easiest places to find, the ones most guidebooks and fellow travelers will recommend, and the ones most touts will take you to first if you look like the sort of person who stays at them.

I'd like to encourage you, if you can afford it, to spend the extra money to stay at local hotels, or at least to try them from time to time. The advantages, to my mind, are many. In a local hotel, you get to spend time with locals and learn about their lives, something that won't happen in a guest house for foreigners. Local travelers can be one of the best sources of advice, tips, and recommendations that other foreigners don't know about and you won't find in guidebooks.

The staff is less likely to be tired of answering the same ignorant questions from every foreigner and more likely to be willing to help you. If foreigners don't often stay at a hotel, or eat at a restaurant or street stall, the proprietor is likely to feel that your patronage enhances the status of the establishment and to make an extra effort to please you.

It's all too easy to get stuck on a standard tourist route, seeing, staying, and eating with the same fellow travelers in guest houses and cafes in town after town, night after night. Hanging out mainly with other foreigners, as is to a degree inevitable if they are the people you stay with, slows down the process of cultural assimilation and can blind you to the local culture and values.

If you get in the habit of only staying in places where you see other foreign faces, you become less likely to consider going off the beaten track to a place where you know, or suspect, that you won't find such a hostelry because there aren't enough foreign visitors to support one, and local travelers prefer private rooms. But visits to places with fewer foreign visitors are, as a rule, much more rewarding than time in tourist centers.

Wherever you stay, never agree to pay for a room without inspecting it carefully. Americans, who are used to standardized chains that can be counted on by brand name alone to provide a predictable set of features and level of comfort and cleanliness, are known worldwide for their willingness to rent rooms sight unseen. Feel free to ask for a better or a cheaper room, or a cheaper price for the one you've been shown. You're not rude to haggle with a hotelier; rather, you're a sucker not to.

Sooner or later, you'll end up in a bad hotel. Whatever happens, remember that, "You can take anything . . .for a little while," as my friend Kay Burns quotes her friend Mary O'Shaughnessy. Even if you've reserved a room, you're only committed for one night. All hotels raise their rates for those who arrive late, tired, and desperate. You can stay one night and look for somewhere better or cheaper in the morning, at your leisure and without your luggage.

### A Few Words about Toilets

Some people are afraid of foreign toilets and look down on unfamiliar designs of toilet as primitive and unsanitary. This is really a cultural issue more than anything else, but because it often becomes an issue in the choice of hotel rooms I'll discuss it here.

There are two basic types of toilet in the world, for those who have toilets—at least a billion people, possibly two, have no toilets and use the fields, woods, or roads. Europeans (white people) sit on toilets that are essentially chairs with holes in the seats. Everyone else squats over holes at floor or ground level. A well-made non-European toilet slopes down slightly toward the hole to drain spills and has raised blocks or footpads 2–5 cm (1–2 inches) high, a little larger than foot-size, on either side of the hole to keep your feet clean and dry. Europeans wipe themselves with sheets of soft paper after using the toilet. Other people wash themselves with water after using the toilet, usually using their left hand to wash with.

There is nothing more or less modern, per se, about the European or "Western" sitting toilet versus the Asian and African or "Eastern" squatting toilet. Either type may be clean or dirty, may be dry or water-flushed, and constructed of porcelain, metal, wood, or other materials. There is no reason to think that people should or would want to learn to use sitting instead of squatting toilets, or that those who squat are primitive. Many people accustomed to squat toilets find the thought of putting their bodies directly on a toilet seat that hasn't been washed since someone else sat on it, or of wiping themselves with a piece of paper instead of washing properly with water, to be appallingly backward and unhygienic.

Some of the best hotels in West Coast North American cities offer rooms with squat toilets (clean, porcelain, water-flushed) for those of their guests (mainly Asian business travelers) who insist on properly sanitary modern conveniences and who are unwilling to put up with such a disgusting item as a sitting toilet, which many see as epitomizing Americans' and Europeans' general personal filthiness.

There is a strong anatomical argument that squatting is a more natural position in which the body functions better and more comfortably. A large number of "Westerners" find that they prefer "non-Western" toilets.

Where toilets aren't clean, the argument in favor of Asian ones over European ones is compelling. Far better to squat over a dirty hole than to sit on a dirty seat. In most of the world, sitting toilets are rare. Local people can't imagine that one could be expected to sit directly on the seats, so when confronted with a European toilet they squat on the rim of the bowl, or on the seat, leaving them filthy. (Don't be surprised to see footprints or shoe marks on the seat of a Western toilet.) A squat toilet is more likely than a sit-up toilet to flush properly even if the drain is partially blocked and the water pressure low.

Where you have a choice of a hotel room with a Western toilet and one with an Eastern toilet, the room with the Western toilet will typically be more expensive, and the toilet dirtier. Most of the time preference will not be an issue, however: when you need to go, you'll use whatever is available by way of a toilet, or the local equivalent thereof. If squatting doesn't come naturally to you, or is hard, practice your deep-knee bends before you leave.

# GUIDEBOOKS FOR INDEPENDENT TRAVELERS

Guidebooks vary greatly in their intended purposes and audiences. Look for ones written by people who travel the way you do, on your sort of budget, with your sorts of interests. Don't be surprised if you don't find many: most guidebooks are written for people with less time, more money, more limited interests, and more fixed advance plans than most long-term budget travelers.

The more difficult a place is for independent travelers, the less likely most guidebooks are to say anything about practicalities. The reason is that, if a place is difficult to travel in independently, most people who go there will go in escorted groups. Most guidebooks are, for maximum sales potential, written for the largest possible audience.

If most people who visit a place are in escorted groups, there will be little market for a guidebook that emphasizes how to go it alone. Instead, guidebooks to such regions tend to focus on the meaning and interpretation of the sights included on the standard tour itineraries, or perhaps on how to choose a package tour. Such books may make interesting reading before or after your trip—"practical" guidebooks often give short shrift to social, cultural, political, ethnic, religious, and artistic background and interpretation—but if they don't answer your basic "how-to" questions they probably don't warrant space in your luggage. Lines like, "You will probably be taken to see the…" and "You will probably stay at the…Hotel," or simply the absence of any information about how one gets to the places described, should alert you that a particular guidebook is not intended to meet the needs of independent travelers, and independent travel in the region it covers may not be easy or common.

The bottom line is that independent budget travelers are, especially in the United States, a very small niche market served by only a small number of highly specialized guidebook publishers. There are a few independent guidebooks to particular places. But most English-language guides to independent budget travel are part of one or another series of guidebooks from the name brands of the field, such as Avalon Travel Publishing's Moon Handbooks and Rick Steves' guides, Lonely Planet's Travel Survival Kits and On a Shoestring guides, Footprint Handbooks, Rough Guides, the Let's Go series, and so forth. (See the Resource Guide for reviews of the major guidebook series.)

None of these series covers the entire world, but together they come close, with substantial overlap (and competition) between them. Each has a standard format, but the volumes in each series vary greatly depending on the knowledge, skills, and perspectives of the individual authors. I've found good and bad titles in each of the series I've used. Some of the same authors have written guidebooks about different places for more than one of these series. But don't buy any book just because it's part of a series. Try to talk to people who've used the current (or at least a recent) edition of that particular volume. Keep an open mind. The best guides for some places aren't part of any series. Some are self-published by their authors, as the first titles from both Moon Handbooks and Lonely Planet once were.

Moon Handbooks and Lonely Planet have some books printed in Asia, and they are almost as widely available in major cities in Asia as they are in Western Europe, Australia (where Lonely Planet is headquartered), or the United States. You can often find used copies, especially of prior editions, very cheaply. Depending on the place, and if you aren't relying on them for specific hotel recommendations or prices, old editions are often sufficient for many purposes.

So, depending on your route, there's usually no reason to start out with guidebooks for other than your first few destinations. You can usually buy or trade for the rest along the way, although I'd recommend checking them out of the library and at least skimming the relevant volumes before your departure.

Don't take any guidebook as gospel. Each person experiences the same place differently, even if it hasn't changed—which, after all, is one of the main reasons to want to see things for yourself in the first place. You may be older or younger, richer or poorer, more or less adventurous, or simply interested in different things than the author of any given book. Leave yourself room to form your own impressions as you travel.

Some destination guidebooks are updated (albeit sometimes cursorily) every year. You can usually identify these by a prominent identification of the issue year or designation of the annual edition on the cover. Such a guidebook can be expected to have been updated in the year preceding the issue date, i.e., the 2001 edition should give information accurate as of 2000. This means that old issues are actually a year older than most people figure them to be.

Most Moon Handbooks, Lonely Planet, and competing guidebooks to areas outside the First World are updated every two to three years. They should, but rarely do, have a prominent identification of the press date or the range of time during which the research and writing was done. Check any guidebook carefully for a line such as, "Prices given in this book are those that were in effect as of [date]," or "Research for this book was conducted during the period from [date] to [date]" Typically, you have to look closely at the copyright, publication, and edition notices to figure out when a guidebook was written and revised. Remember that a new printing does not necessarily mean any change to the text. Figure that research for a new book or edition was probably done one to two years before its publication date. Adjust your expectations of prices for inflation, exchange-rate changes, and the inevitable price increases at those establishments listed in guidebooks.

Updated does not mean researched or written. Hotels may be visited, or they may simply be telephoned to verify that they still exist and to get their new prices. Most general and descriptive copy—the sorts of things you read to decide where to go, as opposed to where exactly to stay once you get there—stay the same from one edition to the next.

The thicker and weightier the book, the harder it is for an updater to check every detail for each new edition. A provincial town may be added to a guidebook because a writer happened to visit it on one research trip. If it's days off the usual travel routes, and not especially recommended or interesting, it may not be visited again for two or three editions. It's quite possible to find that the isolated beach was ruined by an oil spill, or the cheap hotel was demolished to make room for a soot-belching factory, five years before the current edition of your guidebook was printed.

Some publishers and authors keep descriptions of war zones and otherwise off-limits areas as they were when it was last possible for foreigners to visit them, even when these descriptions are long out of date. Such information is better than nothing, but only if its nature is clearly identified, which it isn't always.

Locally produced guidebooks, unlike local language texts, are rarely of much practical use to independent budget travelers (although they may be of considerable educational value for what they reveal of how local people see foreigners). Local writers, even when they try to write for foreigners, tend to have too little perspective to realize which aspects of their ways of doing things will need explaining, or how to explain them in terms that will be familiar to audiences in the United States or Europe.

Those people in most Second, Third, and Fourth World countries who write well enough in English and who are sufficiently conversant with USA or European ways to be capable of writing a practical guide for foreign visitors are precisely those who have the sorts of skills and privileges that enable them to leave their homeland to make more money elsewhere. The dearth of good locally published guidebooks is a symptom of the "brain drain."

Locally produced cultural and artistic guidebooks are often more helpful, particularly in regions whose art and culture are little noticed in the United States. Where they can be found in English, I find newspapers, magazines, popular novels, and even textbooks intended for local audiences to be, on the whole, better guides to the local culture, issues, mindset, and worldview than anything written for, much less by, foreigners.

## MAPS

Finding maps locally is hit or miss, with little rhyme or reason to how useful or easy to find they will be. I recommend bringing with you whatever maps you think are essential, particularly large-scale maps of countries and regions and any specialized maps you'll need for trekking or the like. I bring the best maps I can find, and I've never regretted it.

Within cities, you can probably get by on the maps included in a Moon Handbook or Lonely Planet guidebook, with some help, especially on transit routes, from whatever city map you can find locally. Government and transit maps are usually better than so-called "Tourist Maps." The former can be superb, (e.g., in China, parts of India, and, when you can find them, in the former USSR). The latter tend to have pictures of tourist attractions rather than any useful detail. Good maps of larger regions are usually harder to find locally than good city maps.

Maps of most of the world are substantially harder to find in the USA than are guidebooks to the same places. If you can't find the maps you want locally, check the "Logistics" section of the resource guide for listings of map stores in the United States and the UK with comprehensive catalogs and worldwide mail-order services.

# GOING OUT OF THE WAY TO HELP

We were studying our map in Urumchi, East Turkestan, trying to figure out the way back to our hotel, when a smiling Chinese soldier (in a uniform accessorized with a pearly necklace and a lace-frilled blouse) came up to us, obviously offering to help. She spoke no English, and we no Chinese. She gestured to the map. We pointed to our hotel on the map. She led us to the bus stop, waited with us for the proper bus, led us on, bought us tickets, rode with us, led us off the bus at the proper stop, and marched us up to the entrance of the department store next to our hotel!

It took us a moment to realize that she must have thought we were pointing at the store on the map. A finger is an imprecise pointer, and it was a very precise Chinese map. Now she was waiting for us to let her know what we wanted to buy. She may have been part of a foreign army of occupation, but she had gone out of her way to "Serve the Peo-

© Edward Hasbrouck

ple" by helping us, and we couldn't just walk off to our hotel. She would think us ungrateful and probably never help a lost tourist again. We hastily thought of something we could buy (fabric and thread to sew up a package we were about to send home), communicated it to her (with pantomime of sewing). She led us to the sewing notions counter, bowed, turned, and went away beaming at her good deed. Having preserved her face, we continued on to our hotel.

## COMMUNICATION

### Languages

Most people traveling around the world, or to any large number of places, don't stay in one region long enough to learn very much of any language they didn't already know. You can probably get around most big cities with only English. You'll probably need at least some French in West and Central Africa, some Spanish in Central and South America, and some Russian anywhere in the former USSR.

But even a few words of another language will not only make life much easier but open a remarkable number of doors that you would otherwise never even have known existed. Even the slightest knowledge of the local language (or even of another foreign language) can be surprisingly useful and sometimes essential. And you're far more likely to inadvertently patronize or offend those with whom you have no common language.

### Doesn't Everyone Speak English?

It's a common axiom that, "These days, everyone speaks English," and there's a certain truth to it. No language is as widely studied as English, and no one monolingual in any other language would have nearly as easy a time traveling around the world as a monolingual English speaker.

But most people in the world—even in places where English is the official "national" language—don't speak English. India, for example, is commonly, and correctly, cited as a country where it's easy to get around with only English. But only a few percent of Indians speak English. Fewer are actually fluent, though there are still more English speakers and a larger English-language publishing industry in India than in, say, Canada. South Asian English is as distinct and as "legitimate" a dialect of English as is, say, Kiwi or Australian.

W"hat do you call a person who speaks three languages?"

"Trilingual."

"What do you call a person who speaks two languages?"

"Bilingual."

"What do you call a person who speaks only one language?"

"American."

English is not an easy language to learn as a second language. It has an unusually large vocabulary in common usage, unusually many irregularities, words and pronunciations borrowed and derived from an unusually wide range of other source languages, and almost no standards of spelling whatsoever. We who are native speakers are lucky. Be considerate of those who aren't. Use plain, simple language and common, unambiguous words. Don't use slang, unobvious idioms, or (except in a technical context) jargon. For an excellent primer on how to make yourself understood, in English, by nonnative speakers, see Chapter 5, "How to Make Your English More Understandable," in *Merriam-Webster's Guide to International Business Communications*. (See the Resource Guide.)

### Separated by a Common Language

Americans should know that, despite the increasing use of American English as the standard language of international business (and an increasing effort by students of English as a foreign language to learn American pronunciation and slang), British English is the international standard of written and spoken English, and that which you are most likely to encounter anywhere outside the Americas. If an English word or phrase ("W.C.," "paraffin lamp," "torch") seems strange to American eyes or ears, first try to interpret it as British ("toilet," "kerosene lamp," "flashlight"). Try to avoid using expressions whose meaning depends on whether they are interpreted as British or American (or are specific to any other English dialect, for that matter).

## Make an Effort

Even if you don't learn more than a few words, it's worth making whatever effort you can to learn the rudiments of any language widely spoken anywhere that you'll be for more than a few weeks. Don't be afraid to fail, to mispronounce, or to mangle the language. You are certain to be better received even if you try and fail to communicate in a locally used language, than if you make no attempt at all to communicate in any language other than English. Perhaps surprisingly, even your crudest efforts will be especially appreciated by those who are most proud of their language.

The key elements in learning a new language, communicating with limited common language, and communicating nonverbally are a lack of inhibitions and a willingness to try, to make mistakes, and at times to fail completely. You have to accept that you will sometimes make a fool of yourself or come across as a churl, even when you get your message across. People who restrict themselves to saying what they are confident they can say properly in a new language say much less and learn languages more slowly.

In a pinch, try any and every language you know. You'll be surprised how often you'll find someone who knows the same foreign language as you, in a place you would never have expected and where it's no one's native language. A common language need not be anyone's first language and often isn't.

## Language Learning Materials

It's difficult to find classes or textbooks in the United States for some of the languages that are most useful for world travel, such as Mandarin Chinese, Hindi, Urdu, Arabic, Russian, Portuguese, or Swahili. Fortunately for English speakers, textbooks, dictionaries, and phrasebooks for students of English are produced in virtually every country and language of the world.

These materials are intended for people who already know the local language(s) and are trying to learn English, not vice versa, and are often of poor quality. But they are usually cheap, readily available, and far better than no dictionary or phrasebook at all. The choices of words, phrases, and expressions for translation can also be a good introduction to the concepts that are considered important in the local culture.

In some multilingual countries and regions where English is used as a link language, one can even find textbooks for locals intended to teach local and regional languages through the medium of English. This is especially true in India, where no one language is spoken by a majority of the people and English is the second language of most university-educated people. Rather than separate texts for learning, say, Hindi, for speakers of Tamil or Telugu, one is likely to find "Learn Hindi Through English" texts for use by people from throughout the country.

If you can't read or pronounce the local language, you can still point to the group of characters alongside the English word or phrase you want to communicate in a phrasebook or bilingual dictionary. Someone who can't speak or read any English can reply by looking up an answer in the other half of the book (assuming it's a bidirectional dictionary or phrase book—some aren't), then pointing at the English alongside it. In a country like China with widespread literacy, you can carry on a surprisingly complex, if slow, exchange this way.

### Nonverbal Communication

Sign language, gestures, and onomatopoetic sounds have limited utility in the *total* absence of common spoken or written language. They can, however, enormously extend the communicative value of even a few words of a common language. Play "Charades" with your traveling companions before you leave, or in waiting rooms or on boring journeys, to improve your ability to get across essential travel concepts ("Where is the toilet?" and the like) nonverbally. Several companies (see the Resource Guide) make laminated pocket cards with "vocabularies" of simple pictograms to illustrate common travel concepts (train station, toilet, doctor, etc.). These can be surprisingly useful as aids to nonverbal communication.

Some things need no words: anyone walking into a hotel with a pack is presumed to want a room; anyone walking into a restaurant is presumed to want a meal; anyone walking into a depot is presumed to want to buy a ticket or board a bus or train to somewhere; anyone studying a map is presumed to be trying to get to the place pointed to on the map; and nothing more need be said for most people to make an effort to help you.

### Language Etiquette

Be considerate of the effort people are making to understand and assist you. If you don't speak a word of their language, it's your fault, not theirs, if they understand your language imperfectly. If you walk into a restaurant, can't read the menu, and are brought a meal, you are obligated to pay for it (and to make at least a show of eating it) even if you find it inedible. Never mind that it wasn't what you thought you were signing that you wanted and that you think it overpriced. They are more likely to have tried to accommodate a distinguished guest by serving you a local delicacy (albeit perhaps one that is an "acquired taste") rather than to have intended to turn your stomach or overcharge you.

It's sometimes rude to accept a pro forma ritual offer of hospitality, but in general it's safer to take offers of assistance at face value and to assume that to refuse them will be taken as a sign of hostility. Saying "No" can make the one offering lose face and should be done as tactfully as possible.

# Alphabet Table

## Hebrew

| | | |
|---|---|---|
| א | aleph | ' |
| ב | beth | b, bh |
| ג | gimel | g, gh |
| ד | daleth | d, dh |
| ה | he | h |
| ו | waw | w |
| ז | zayin | z |
| ח | heth | ḥ |
| ט | teth | ṭ |
| י | yodh | y |
| כ ך | kaph | k, kh |
| ל | lamedh | l |
| מ ם | mem | m |
| נ ן | nun | n |
| ס | samekh | s |
| ע | ayin | ' |
| פ ף | pe | p, ph |
| צ ץ | sadhe | s |
| ק | qoph | q |
| ר | resh | r |
| שׂ | sin | ś |
| שׁ | shin | sh |
| ת | taw | t, th |

## Greek

| | | |
|---|---|---|
| Α α | alpha | a |
| Β β | beta | b |
| Γ γ | gamma | g, n |
| Δ δ | delta | d |
| Ε ε | epsilon | a |
| Ζ ζ | zeta | z |
| Η η | eta | ē |
| Θ θ | theta | th |
| Ι ι | iota | i |
| Κ κ | kappa | k |
| Λ λ | lambda | l |
| Μ μ | mu | m |
| Ν ν | nu | n |
| Ξ ξ | xi | x |
| Ο ο | omicron | o |
| Π π | pi | p |
| Ρ ρ | rho | r, rh |
| Σ σ | sigma | s |
| Τ τ | tau | t |
| Υ υ | upsilon | y, u |
| Φ φ | phi | ph |
| Χ χ | chi | ch |
| Ψ ψ | psi | ps |
| Ω ω | omega | ō |

## Cyrillic

| | | |
|---|---|---|
| А а | | a |
| Б б | | b |
| В в | | v |
| Г г | | g |
| Д д | | d |
| Е е | | e |
| Ж ж | | zh |
| З з | | z |
| И и, Й й | | i, ĭ |
| К к | | k |
| Л л | | l |
| М м | | m |
| Н н | | n |
| О о | | o |
| П п | | p |
| Р р | | r |
| С с | | s |
| Т т | | t |
| У у | | u |
| Ф ф | | f |
| Х х | | kh |
| Ц ц | | ts |
| Ч ч | | ch |
| Ш ш | | sh |
| Щ щ | | shch |
| Ъ ъ | hard sign, silent | |
| Ы ы | | y |
| Ь ь | soft sign, silent | |
| Э э | | e |
| Ю ю | | yu |
| Я я | | ya |

The letters in the right-hand columns are approximate English phonetic equivalents of the foreign letters in the left column. The alternate forms of various letters are dependent upon where the letter falls in a given word.

## Alphabets

If you'll be spending much time in a place with a different alphabet, it's worth learning the letters of the local alphabet to sound out signs, place-names, etc., written in Cyrillic, Greek, or whatever, even if you don't learn to read or speak the language (refer to the "Alphabet Table" on the following page). Aside from the virtue of being able to use a map in the local language, once you can sound them out, many common words in Russian and Greek are obviously recognizable cognates of their English equivalents. At first glance, this may look like a formidable task, but it actually takes only a few days for most people to be able to recognize Greek or Cyrillic. Hindi or Hebrew is harder; most difficult are scripts like Arabic (and related scripts used for Persian, Urdu, etc.), in which the ligatures make it harder for novices to distinguish the individual letters and there are fewer cognates with English.

## Units of Measurement

Every country except the United States (and some colonies and "possessions" of the United States) uses the metric system of units. Americans who want to travel abroad must learn to deal with metric units. You can get tables of equivalents and calculators with conversion programs, but in the long run it's better to learn to think and make mental estimates of quantities directly in metric units, without having to convert them to USA units. That way it's more likely that it will be intuitively obvious in what units signs or prices are posted, and you'll be more likely to recognize if you're being short-weighed or otherwise cheated.

Outside the United States, all signage can be presumed to be in metric units. Which metric unit may not be posted, or may be in a language you don't understand, but if you can think in metric you should be able to tell from the approximate magnitude whether, for example, the distance on a road sign is in meters or kilometers, or a price is per gram or kilogram. It seems to be particularly difficult to learn to think in a different temperature scale, and Americans abroad may need to remind themselves repeatedly that temperatures everywhere else are given in degrees Celsius (also called Centigrade), not Fahrenheit.

Nonstandard units are sometimes used, particularly for foodstuffs and other commodities in local markets. Good guidebooks will sometimes tip you off to this. Prices in such cases are usually negotiable, anyway, and if you are in doubt you can usually get the quantity you are haggling over measured out for inspection before you agree on a price. Sometimes not, and every practiced traveler has been known to buy more than they could possibly use of something, and on some other occasion to get only a tenth of what they expected for the price, as a result of confusion of units. Take it in stride; consider it part of the price of your education in local customs.

People in other countries, especially those who have visited the United States and had to deal with USA units, sometimes remember to do visitors the favor of reminding them that they are using metric units. Foreigners in the United States can expect no such consideration. Most native-born USA citizens have never traveled abroad, are barely aware that the internationally standard metric system exists, or regard the metric system as an exotic foreign curiosity. They certainly won't call your attention to the fact that they are using nonstandard units, because in their minds they are using the only standard units they know. In the United States, "How much is that in kilos?," "How far is that in kilometers?," or "How hot or cold is that in Celsius?" will get you either blank looks or completely wrong guesses.

Visitors to the United States may chafe at having to learn an absurdly complex set of units that they will need to know nowhere else, but there is no real alternative. See the "USA-Metric Conversion" chart at the back of the book for a guide to the meaning of USA units of measure in standard (metric) terms.

Don't trust people who try to do conversions for you, because they frequently get them wrong. ("Let's see: is a pound about 450 grams, or is it 4.5 kilos?") USA units are far too confusing for most people who didn't grow up with them to keep straight. Ask people to state quantities and measurements in units to which *they* are accustomed, and either learn to think in those units yourself or do your own conversions.

In the United States, quantities of many foods used in cooking are specified by volume. This is true even of dry solid foods that are sold by weight, not by volume! Only people on controlled diets weigh their food in the United States, and kitchen scales are known as "diet scales." In the rest of the world, cooks measure most such foods by weight, and every kitchen has a cooking scale (metric, of course). It's quite difficult to figure out volumetric equivalents for weights of foods. So if you bring a cookbook back to the United States from abroad, it will have instructions like, "start with 200 g of flour." You'll need to bring back a (metric) kitchen scale as well, or search hard to find a metric "diet scale," to use a foreign cookbook in the United States.

## Times and Dates

### Time

Everywhere except the United States, all tick-  ets, timetables, public notices, and signage are in 24-hour time. There is no ambiguity. If your ticket reads "0600," you are scheduled to leave at 6 A.M. If it reads "1800" you are scheduled to leave at 6 P.M. If you see "10:00–16:00," "1000–1600," or simply "10–16" as the only numbers in the middle of a sign in a language you don't understand in front of a museum, it's a safe bet that it's open from 10 A.M.-4 P.M.

In the United States, 24-hour time is used only in the military and is popularly referred to as "military time." Official notices, posted hours of opening and closing, and even transportation tickets, schedules, and timetables are invariably in 12-hour time. Sometimes "A.M." (ante meridiem) or "P.M." (post meridiem) are spelled out, but in common usage they are often left implicit. Only by knowing the context, and the cultural norms, can you tell if "Open 8–3" means 20:00–03:00 (as it might for a nightclub) or 08:00–15:00 (as it might for a shop). For a restaurant, it might mean either, depending on the clientele.

On tickets and in timetables "A.M." is sometimes shortened to "a" and "P.M." to "p." Often a less obvious, more ambiguous code is used, such as printing "A.M." times in medium-weight roman type and "P.M." times in italic or boldface type, or vice versa, or printing one or the other in parentheses or in a different color. There is no standard. In the United States, it is imperative always to ask whether times are A.M. or P.M. In USA usage, "7 o'clock" is just as likely to mean 7 P.M. (19:00) as 7 A.M. Many visitors miss planes, trains, buses, and appointments, or show up 12 hours early for them, by erroneously assuming that hours less than 12 are before noon (A.M.), or by confusing or failing to recognize the codes used in a particular timetable for "A.M." and "P.M."

### Calendars and Dates

The Christian calendar is used for schedules and most business purposes everywhere in the world, even in non-Christian regions where a different calendar is used for religious purposes. Aside from knowing when holidays will be, it's rarely necessary to know what year, month, or day it is in any but the Christian calendar. The largest exception is the month of Ramadan, during which observant Muslims fast from dawn to dusk. Exceptions are made for travelers, but travel anywhere in the Islamic world is different—and usually more difficult—during Ramadan.

In the United States, the month is usually given first, followed by the date: "August 2nd," "August 2nd, 2005," or "8/2/05." In most of the rest of the world, and invariably in international usage, the date precedes the month: "2 August," "2 August 2005," "2/8/05," or "2-VIII-05." To further complicate matters, many foreigners convert their dates to the USA format when communicating with people in or from the United States. So there is no way to be sure whether "11/6/04" means November 6, 2004 (the most likely meaning in the USA) or 11 June 2004 (the likely, but not certain, meaning in the rest of the world). Because of the inherent ambiguity of such usage, months should never be written or abbreviated in numbers. Always write out, or abbreviate, the name of the month in letters.

Because all international airline tickets are written in English, any travel agent or airline employee must know how to recognize the date format used on tickets, in which the name of the month in English is truncated after the first three letters: "02AUG05," "06NOV04," "11JUN04." This is a good form to use when, for example, you are sending a fax to request a reservation at a hotel where you aren't sure whether, or how well, anyone speaks English, or when writing down a reservation request to give to a booking clerk at a train station with whom you have no common language. Two-digit years remain in post-Y2K use on airline tickets, as in the preceding examples, and in some other places, but for the sake of clarity it's always better to use four-digit years (e.g. "2010" rather than "10").

Most printed representations of the Christian calendar in any language follow a common format, with each week as a horizontal row, starting with Sundays as the left-hand column and the days of the month arranged from left to right and then top to bottom. The exception is in the former USSR and some other places (formerly) in the Soviet "bloc" or sphere of influence. On Russian calendars, each week is a vertical column, starting with Mondays as the top row, and the days are ordered first from top to bottom and then left to right. The difference sounds simple, but it's harder to get used to than you might think.

Weekly schedules are largely determined by the dominant religion. In Christian countries most offices and some shops are closed on Sundays, sometimes also on Saturdays. In Islamic countries most offices and shops, depending on the orthodoxy of the country and the proprietor, are closed on Fridays, sometimes also on Thursday afternoons. Orthodox Jews in all countries close their businesses from sunset Friday to sunset Saturday. Some businesses in Israel are required to close during those hours; Israel's national airline, El Al, grounds its entire fleet of aircraft during those hours, considerably complicating its scheduling and raising its costs. The hegemony of Christianity is such that most countries that are neither Christian, Muslim, nor Jewish not only use the Christian calendar but, for those who get a day of rest, some version of the Christian workweek.

Daily business, office, shop, and restaurant hours vary more from establishment to establishment than from country to country. Government offices may have standard hours nationwide, and it can be helpful to know whether most people take a nap after lunch or eat dinner especially early or late by the norm of your native country. But you can't assume too much about any particular business's hours of operation just because a guidebook tells you that "Most businesses are open 09:00–17:00." If you are planning to be in a city for only a few days and will need to deal with a particular business or office, call ahead to verify its days and hours, even if you have a guidebook that lists the hours of the specific office, as these things do change from time to time.

## Numbers

Except for nonmetric units of measurement, only one number system (the base 10 place-value system) is in common use everywhere, and there is a tendency to think of numbers as universal and invariant. Forms of written and other symbolic representations of numbers, however, vary more widely than most people, even most travelers, realize. In different places numbers may be communicated by calculator displays, at least two distinct sets of finger signs, two important forms of written numerals, and three major types of abacus.

### Finger Signs

Whole numbers up to 10 are often indicated with the fingers. This is the normal way of indicating how many items you want to buy if you don't speak a common language. (For larger numbers or negotiating prices, which usually involves numbers of more than one digit, you'll need something more sophisticated.)

Europeans and Americans raise a number of fingers, on one or both hands, corresponding to the number they want to indicate. Many gestures with upraised fingers are obscene in one place or another, and pointing at people is often thought of as rude and/or insulting. Be alert to how people react, and stop using a gesture immediately if it appears to give offense. Consult a local person if some gesture keeps being misunderstood or taken unkindly.

There are standard one-handed Chinese signs corresponding to each digit up through 10. These are so taken for granted in China (representing up to a sixth of the world's population, after all) that it is hard for many Chinese people to believe that foreigners don't understand them. It is as difficult for many people in China to recognize that a foreigner holding up fingers on both hands might mean "seven" as it is for most foreigners to recognize that a Chinese gesture with the fingers of one hand might mean "seven." Pointing or beckoning with raised fingers is especially rude in China, and it is best to avoid indicating numbers with your fingers unless you have learned the one-handed Chinese signs.

Russians use yet a third system: they count by curling fingers into their palm, rather than by extending fingers. If some fingers are curled in, and some extended, it's the number of curled fingers that is being indicated. It's a small conceptual shift, but surprisingly difficult to adjust to.

### Electronic Calculators

Electronic calculators have become affordable and ubiquitous even in the Third World, and moneychangers and businesses that cater to foreigners around the world have calculators on which to show prices to customers who can't speak the language or read the price tags. All calculators use "European" numerals, as discussed below. The problem with relying on calculators is that if you have to be shown a price on a calculator you will be known not to be able to read the price tags and will generally be charged more for your ignorance. To merchants, "calculator dependent" means "dupe." The ability to use any other means of communicating numbers will enable you to negotiate better prices.

### Written Numerals

Numbers spelled out in words, or included with text, are written in as many forms of letters, numerals, characters, and scripts as are written languages. Only two forms of numerals, however, are in general use in signage, pricing, accounting, and the like.

# NUMBERS TABLE

| Printed European | Handwritten European | Arabic |
|---|---|---|
| 0 or Ø | *0* or *ø* | • |
| I | *1* or *1* | ١ |
| 2 | *2* | ٢ |
| 3 | *3* | ٣ |
| 4 | *4* | ٤ |
| 5 | *5* | *ο* or ٥ |
| 6 | *6* | ٦ |
| 7 | *7* or *7̶* | ٧ |
| 8 | *8* | ٨ |
| 9 | *9* | ٩ |

Nomenclature poses a problem. I choose to call these two sets of digits, as represented in the adjacent chart, "European" and "Arabic" numerals, respectively, while recognizing that neither of these labels is standard. There are no standard labels.

What I refer to as "European" numerals are used in most of the world, including all of the Americas, Europe except Turkey (if you consider Turkey to be part of Europe, which is a matter of dispute), Oceania, and most of East Asia. These are often referred to as "Arabic" numerals, because these evolved from Indian numerals by way of Arabian numerals, and to distinguish them from "Roman" numerals. But Roman numerals are obsolete, and today the principal alternative to European numerals is a set of numerals used in Arabic. So calling the numerals used in modern European languages "Arabic" would only confuse matters.

What I refer to as "Arabic" numerals are used in some (not all) countries that do (or, like Turkey, did) write their languages, such as Persian and Urdu, in Arabic script. One scholar labels these "Eastern Arabic" numerals, while noting that Arabs refer to them as "Indian" numerals because they are closer to the original Indian forms than the alternative European forms that evolved from them.

India is the principal country in which both systems of numerals are widely used: Arabic numerals by Muslims and Urdu-speakers; European numerals by Hindi-speakers and most others. The use of Arabic numerals is almost universal in Pakistan, where the national language is Urdu, except among the most Westernized.

Several of the Arabic digits are prone to be mistaken for different European digits. The Arabic five looks like a European zero, and the Arabic six like a European seven or one (as discussed below). If you'll be spending much time any place where Arabic script is in common use, take a little time to learn the Arabic numerals so you can read posted prices and check the addition on bills.

Numbers are written the same way with either type of numerals, in base 10, place-value notation, from left to right or right to left, with the least significant (smallest) digit farthest to the right. Numbers in either system are aligned vertically and added in columns.

Three of the European digits have variant forms, two of which sometimes cause confusion.

Zero is sometimes crossed, especially on computer printouts, or when it is necessary to distinguish the numeral zero from the letter O. Some people don't know what to make of a crossed zero, but no one is likely to mistake it for any other digit.

Seven and one cause problems. Europeans cross their sevens and write their ones with a bold upstroke, or exaggerated serif, to the left of the top of the main stroke. Americans don't cross their sevens and often write their ones as a single, unadorned vertical line. Americans often mistake a European one for an uncrossed seven; Europeans often mistake an American one for an upper-case letter I, or can't make anything of it at all. It's safest to cross your sevens and write your ones with a minimal but visible upstroke.

In American and British usage, a comma is used to separate each group of three digits (e.g., millions from thousands) when writing numbers larger than 1,000, and a period ("decimal point") is used to separate digits greater than one from those less than one. In Continental European usage, these are reversed: a comma is used in place of a "decimal point" and a period is used as a thousands separator. What is written in the United States as "12,345.67" would be written in France as "12.345,67."

Outside of Europe and North America, it's difficult to predict which of these styles of writing and punctuating numbers will be used. As with most such things, it depends largely on colonial history and spheres of influence. Be alert to the possibility that either style may be in use.

In South Asia, large numbers are expressed, even in English usage, in "lakhs" (hundreds of thousands) and "crore" (tens of millions), rather than in millions and billions. Commas are accordingly used to separate lakhs and crore, rather than millions and billions. What would be written elsewhere as "100,700,000" and read as "one hundred million, seven hundred thousand" would be written in South Asia as "10,07,00,000" and read as "ten crore, seven lakhs." When no units are specified, quantities expressed in lakhs and crore can be presumed to refer either to rupees (the national units of currency in India, Pakistan, Sri Lanka, and Nepal, each with a somewhat different value) or to numbers of people. The population of India, for example, is about 100 crore.

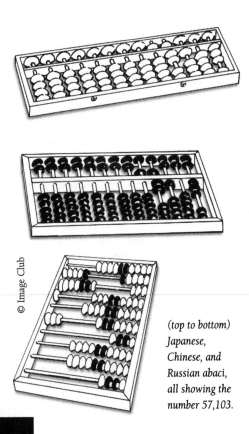

© Image Club

(top to bottom) Japanese, Chinese, and Russian abaci, all showing the number 57,103.

## The Abacus

For addition and subtraction, an abacus in the hands of a skilled user is faster than any electronic calculator. The abacus remains in widespread use, especially in small shops, in China, Japan, and the former USSR and by people from these regions in other places.

It's not hard to learn how to use an abacus, and it's easier still to learn just enough to read numbers displayed on an abacus. If you can read an abacus, you can tell how much other customers are paying even when their money changes hands too quickly for you to count it. An abacus is an ideal tool for negotiating prices, because you don't have to re-enter an entire number but need only slide back and forth those of the beads that correspond to the difference between the asked and offered amounts, moving fewer and fewer beads as you approach agreement. And because, despite its ease, few foreigners learn how to read an abacus, someone who is abacus-literate will be presumed to be have some knowledge about local prices and will probably be offered a price closer to the local norm in the first place.

The Chinese and Japanese styles of abacus are fundamentally the same and are read exactly the same way. Each consists of a frame holding a row of vertical rods (most often of bamboo) divided by a horizontal bar toward the top of each rod. On each rod are sliding beads, usually of wood. The beads on each rod are used to represent one digit. The number of rods, and thus the maximum number of digits that can be represented, varies from abacus to abacus. As in writing, the least significant (smallest) digit is by convention represented on the right-hand rod, with progressively larger digits (tens, hundreds, etc.) on successive rods to the left.

PRACTICALITIES

On a Japanese abacus (*soroban*) there are four beads on each rod below the separator bar and one bead above it. On a Chinese abacus, there are five beads on each rod below the bar and two above it. The significant beads are those that are slid against the separator bar. Each upper bead that is moved down to the bar counts five, and each lower bead that is moved up to the bar counts one. So the digit eight is represented by sliding one bead down from the top and three up from the bottom.

The extra beads on the Chinese abacus enable one to represent numbers as high as fifteen in a single column, which is useful in borrowing and carrying between columns, at intermediate stages of calculations, without having to do so in your head.

The Russian abacus (*stchety* or *schoty,* literally "counter,") is oriented at right angles to the Chinese or Japanese, with the beads on horizontal rods or more often wires, usually arched upward slightly from the frame so that the beads have to be lifted over the crest of the bow to move them from one side to the other.

There is no separator bar, and there are 10 beads on each wire. Each bead that is moved to the left side of the frame counts one. The beads are usually colored in black and white, with the two center beads on each wire the opposite color from the four outer beads on either side (4–2–4), but that is just to facilitate telling, at a glance, how many beads have been moved from one side to the other. The black and white beads count the same.

The least significant (smallest) digit on a Russian abacus is represented on the lowest wire, with successively larger digits above it. Toward the bottom of the frame is a wire with only four beads (colored 1–2–1). This is not considered a digit. It acts like a comma or decimal point and is most often used in shops to separate kilos (above) from grams (below). Historically it was also used to separate rubles from kopecks, but kopecks are now worth so little as to no longer be a useful unit of currency.

### Orders of Magnitude

No matter how numbers are communicated, be aware that the units and the position of the decimal point are rarely explicit. In the United States, the same price may be written as "$10.00," "10.00," "$10," "10-," or simply "10." On a display of fabric, this would be understood to be a price per yard (of whatever width); on coffee, per pound (or perhaps per half-pound, in a specialty shop); on beer, for six bottles, 12, or 24, depending on the packaging. Only someone familiar with the cultural norms of the country could tell which is implied, and even then would sometimes have to read the fine print on the price tags or ask.

If, through inflation, the fundamental unit of currency has become so small that little can be purchased for less than hundreds or thousands of currency units—as a rule of thumb, any time currency is denominated in units worth less than one USA cent (1¢, or US$0.01)—you can count on one or more zeros being dropped from prices in common usage. The trick is in figuring out whether a marked price of "1" means 10, 100, 1,000, or 1,000,000 currency units, something you can only learn by asking and by watching what others pay.

If you are shown a price and aren't sure how many zeroes to add or where to put the decimal point, offer the smallest amount you think it could possibly mean. If you are wrong, they'll let you know, and no real harm is done even if they act insulted. Of course, if you offer 10 or 100 times too much (not as absurd as it sounds in a new place where prices may be much less than those to which you are accustomed), they will simply nod and accept the windfall, leaving you poorer and no wiser.

### Currency Units

This problem is complicated by the fact that abbreviations for currency units are not standard and are often omitted in common usage. To make matters worse, many countries have currencies with the same name, and prices for foreigners are often stated in foreign currencies. With dozens of different "dollars" in use in different parts of the world, but the USA dollar the most universally recognized currency, it can sometimes be very hard to tell if a quoted price is in USA dollars or local dollars (which may be worth only a fraction of a USA dollar).

An unambiguous set of internationally recognized two-letter country codes and three-letter currency codes has been adopted by the International Standards Organization (ISO) and should be used whenever possible. The ISO code for each country's currency consists of the two-letter code for the country followed by a third letter, usually the first letter of the name of the unit of local currency. So, for example, the United States of America is "US," and the local currency is in dollars, thus the ISO abbreviation for US dollars becomes USD. Similarly, the United Kingdom is abbreviated as "GB," and the currency is the British pound, abbreviated as "P," which yields the currency code of "GBP." Some are less obvious than others, and people who make up what they think to be the ISO code for a currency often get it wrong.

The two-letter ISO country codes are recognized by most travel agents and airline staff and are becoming more widely known as a result of their adoption as geographic suffixes to Internet domain names everywhere except in the United States. (If someone's e-mail address is janedoe@something.com.au, her host computer is in Australia; marysmith@something.edu.ca is an address in Canada.) Oddly, the ISO country codes are not used or recognized in postal addressing. The three-letter ISO currency codes are in common use in some places and recognized by virtually all banks and moneychangers. It's becoming increasingly common for banks and moneychangers to post exchange rates in ISO codes rather than abbreviations or symbols like "$" or "£," a trend I applaud.

Much of Western Europe now uses the same unit of currency, the Euro. But during the transition period, it's still sometimes ambiguous whether prices in the "Euro zone" are in national currency or in Euros. Ask if there's the least doubt, to avoid nasty surprises. If there's a language problem, write down the symbol or abbreviation for the local currency and for the Euro (€), point to the price, and have them point to one of the currency labels. The ISO code for the European Union is "EU" (the main EU central government Web site is at http://europa.eu.int), the ISO currency code for the Euro is "EUR," and the abbreviation for Euro is the symbol "€," placed before the number. The largest Euro note, for example, is EUR500 or €500. there are coints for Euro cents (€0.01) and for amounts up to €2. Euro notes are the same throughout the region. Euro coins issued in different countries have different images on the back side, but you can use any Euro coins or notes anywhere throughout the Euro zone.

# KEEPING IN TOUCH

It's nice to get messages from home, and from time to time it's essential for travelers to contact people back home, or vice versa: to take care of business, deal with the unexpected, pass on important news. Communicating on the road is getting easier all the time, but it still has its pitfalls.

## E-mail

E-mail is the primary means of communication for international travelers. It's cheap, fast, allows both parties to ignore time differences, and available wherever there are power and phone lines. It's not very reliable, and you never know for sure that a message has arrived unless you get a reply, but it's so cheap that you can afford to re-send a message several times, or to different addresses, until it gets through.

The discussion that follows is only an introduction to the most important issues in using the Internet while traveling. For much more on this and related topics, see the chapter on "Using the Internet While Traveling" in my companion volume in this series, *The Practical Nomad Guide to the Online Travel Marketplace*.

### Cybercafés and Public-Access Terminals

Today, cybercafés and public-access Internet terminals are everywhere and anywhere. Drop me in a city of half a million people or more, anywhere in the world, and within a day I'll find a way to send you e-mail.

Cybercafés aren't just for travelers. In much of the world, cybercafés are the standard mode of Internet access and most people's introduction to Internet use. Why not? Most of the world's people can't afford a "personal" computer. And even for those with their own computers, Internet access from a cybercafé can be less expensive than over a dial-up connection from home, where local phone calls may be metered.

# PLACES TO LOOK FOR INTERNET ACCESS

Where do you find a public Internet-access terminal? Here are some places to start:

- cybercafés
- hostels
- libraries
- telephone calling shops
- computer gaming centers
- airports
- hotels
- business service centers
- computer stores
- photocopy shops
- convention and trade show centers and venues
- colleges and universities
- friends and hosts
- expatriates

Typical prices for Internet usage range from US$1/hour in the Third World to US$5–10/hour in the First World. Where the rates are higher, the minimum time increment usually is too, so even at the most expensive places you can get online for 10 minutes to check your e-mail for no more than US$1–2.

### Finding Cybercafés

The Resource Guide includes links to some online directories of cybercafés. Don't worry too much if none are listed in the place you are going: it's usually much easier to find them once you arrive. Many public Internet access sites describe themselves primarily as Internet phone call centers or network computer game parlors. Likewise those with few regular foreign customers, or that get all their business by word of mouth, may not think to list themselves in English-language international cybercafé directories. The word "Internet" seems to be the same in every language, or at least to be recognized: a foreigner saying "Internet?" and looking lost will usually be pointed in the right direction pretty quickly.

### Alternative Connection Sources

Can't find a cybercafé? Look for a youth hostel or backpacker guesthouse, even if that's not where you want to stay. Hostelers and backpackers are a core market for cybercafés. More and more hostels have added in-house cybercafés, or Internet terminals in their lounges, to serve their guests and make a little extra money. Even if a hostel doesn't have its own cybercafé or public Internet terminal, if there's a cybercafé in town, the hostel proprietor is bound to know where it is (and probably has that information posted on the hostel bulletin board).

Public Internet access terminals have different roles in different places, especially where most local people don't have their own computers or don't have high-speed Internet connections. I've been in places where most local use of cybercafés is for phone calls over the Internet, and cybercafés advertise themselves primarily as long-distance and international call shops. In many other countries, cybercafés are mostly centers for multi-player network games, and are located and advertised as gaming parlors. (Not the quietest or calmest places to work on your journal or correspondence!)

Hotels that cater to foreign business travelers often have "business centers": miniature all-purpose service bureaus that provide faxing, photocopying, printing, Internet access, and sometimes other services such as rush business card production, secretarial services, and/or foreign language translation.

In the most poorly connected country, the hotel where the international businesspeople and journalists stay may be the only place with a reliable Internet connection, even if it relies on a satellite dish on the roof (to bypass the dysfunctional local phone system) and costs US$5 a minute.

In a pinch, it never hurts to ask around on a college or university campus: "Hi! I'm visiting from out of town and haven't been able to find a cybercafé anywhere around here. Do you perhaps know of somewhere I might get on the Internet to check my e-mail?" If you come across as a nice person, not pushy or demanding and not a stuffed shirt in a suit, there's a good chance that someone will take pity on you and let you use their account.

Other places to find publicly accessible Internet terminals include libraries, convention and trade show centers, airports, colleges and universities, and any of your local friends or hosts.

**PRACTICALITIES**

In an emergency, ask expats or local computer users, very politely, if they know anyone who could send an e-mail message for you. Be concise. Per-minute access costs and per-message or per-byte charges for both sending and receiving e-mail are apt to be many times higher for them than you may be accustomed to in, for example, the United States.

### Learn Various Systems

You can't predict what hardware or software you'll find available in a cybercafé. Be prepared for a Windows PC or a Macintosh, Netscape or Microsoft Internet Explorer, or maybe even something different. I've used public terminals with Linux boxes, Unix thin clients, and the Opera or Lynx browsers. If you get a chance, try all of these out at a cybercafé or on a friend's computer. Familiarize yourself with the basic menus, so you'll be able to recognize and navigate them on a computer with the operating system, labels, and menus in another language. (That's not as much of a problem as it sounds like it might be: English is the lingua franca of computing worldwide, so the technical guru at any cybercafé usually knows enough English to guide you through essential tasks.) The more different systems and programs you're familiar with, the better your chances of being able to do what you need on to do on a strange computer. Unless you have your own laptop computer, you'll probably have to use a Web interface to your e-mail, so try it out before you leave to make sure it meets your needs.

### Preparation and Practice

However you plan to connect, the keys to making successful use of the Internet while traveling are preparation and practice. Try doing whatever it is you'll want to do on the road from a cybercafé or public Internet terminal in your hometown. Try to check your e-mail or send a digital photo from a friend's computer you haven't used before, with a different browser and operating system than you are used to. Or take your portable computer to a friend's house, or a pay phone, and try to connect.

Maybe everything will work right the first time. If so, you're lucky. More likely, you'll find that there's some missing piece of hardware or, more likely still, some software compatibility or configuration glitch that limits what you can do or prevents you from accomplishing some task you'd counted on. In that case, you're even luckier that you found the problem before leaving home, while you still have a chance to solve it before your trip. Problems discovered only after you're on the road often can't be solved until you get back home again.

When you're home and checking your e-mail every day, you're unlikely to fill up your e-mail box. But when you are traveling, you may only check your mail once a week or less. Try to get an e-mail account with as large a size limit as possible. Before you leave, try forwarding all your e-mail to the account you'll be using while traveling, and letting it accumulate for a week or two to see if you exceed your quota. It's common for mail to travelers to be returned with a "mailbox is full" message, or to be deleted without notice to the sender.

### Backups and Precautions

Don't count on uninterrupted Internet access to vital data like your address book, itinerary, or financial data. Back them up, and bring backups with you. The server or connection might temporarily be down when you need it; your ISP, e-mail provider, or other service provider might go out of business or increase its fees; or you might need it when you're in the odd place with no cybercafé.

You can probably fit your contact list and address book, favorite Internet sites (bookmarks, favorites, or hot list), any documents you might want to consult, and scanned images of the documents in your money belt on a single CD you can use in any computer. Bring a couple of copies, carefully packed. CDs are fairly sturdy, but can get scratched or broken if they are dropped or stepped on.

While you are at it, make copies— perhaps on the same CDs—of your paper address book, the data on your electronic organizer or PDA, and the phone numbers stored on your mobile phone. Any of these can be difficult or impossible to reconstruct if you lose them while traveling.

You'll undoubtedly add addresses of people you meet along the way, so be sure to make regular backups of your updated info, and/or e-mail copies of your updated info to your home address or a friend periodically. You can eventually replace a passport, but the truly heartbreaking loss for most travelers whose luggage goes missing is the loss of their address book and the contact information for the people they've met on their trip.

E-mail attachments and binary encoding often aren't received usably. If you send digital photos or critical data by e-mail, don't delete the originals until you get confirmation that the e-mail has been received and that the photos or data are viewable. If you keep a journal you want to preserve, send copies of each entry to a couple of different e-mail addresses, and don't delete the original from the floppy disk you carry with you until you have confirmed that someone has received it and backed it up.

Never store any of your passwords or log-ins on disk, unless the file is heavily encrypted with a strong password, and don't allow them to be stored as

PRACTICALITIES

cookies on the system you are using. It's too easy to forget to delete the cookie file when you are finished using the terminal in the cybercafé, or to leave your disk behind in a cybercafé. If you have too many passwords to memorize, write them down and keep them in your money belt.

## Postal Mail

You can send mail from almost anywhere. Regular mail can be slow, and sometimes gets stolen, but most of it will eventually arrive. Just don't rely on it for anything urgent, essential, or valuable. (The following section gives general advice on postal procedures and letters as a means of communication. For more on the pitfalls of sending and receiving parcels as a way to lighten your luggage, see the preceding chapter.)

### Addressing and Stamping Envelopes

Even in places where the local language is written in a different alphabet, you can address outgoing international mail in the Roman alphabet. For maximum comprehensibility, write the delivery address in plain block capital (upper-case) letters. Take your mail directly to a post office (international mail is sometimes handled at a separate office or counter) and insist on seeing all the stamps canceled in your sight. Uncanceled stamps are liable to be removed and resold, leaving your mail undeliverable for want of proper postage. (See the final section in the "Baggage" chapter for more information on postal services.)

### Delivery Times

International air mail generally takes from less than a week to a month (in the worst case) to arrive. International surface mail can take many months, and the cost savings on letters or post cards is rarely worth it. Nowhere is the sobriquet "snail mail" so appropriate as with intercontinental surface mail.

### Receiving Mail

You can receive mail, at pre-arranged mail drops, in three ways. You can have mail sent to local people who you know you will be visiting (the best choice, if you are sure they are there and that you will see them). You can have mail sent to American Express offices (if you have an AmEx card). You can also receive mail by "general delivery" (often known by its French name, "poste restante") at major post offices.

The main problem with getting mail either care of AmEx or general delivery is that they only hold envelopes for a limited amount of time, after which they are either thrown away (more common) or returned to sender. So you have to have told people, in advance, not only where you will be but when you will be there to check your mail, you have to keep your schedule, and your correspondents have to time the sending of mail to you so that it arrives before you do, but not so far in advance that is has been returned before you arrive and check for it. Of course, it doesn't work at all if you need to get a message in a hurry, or if you don't know in advance where you're going next.

AmEx no longer publishes a printed directory of its offices and the list of AmEx office and agents on their Web site doesn't identify which ones accept mail for AmEx cardholders (not all do). So the only way to find out where your friends or family can send you mail is to call AmEx, or go to an AmEx office in person, and make them check for you. But it's worth it if you want or need to get postal mail. AmEx is substantially more reliable, and vastly easier to deal with, than general delivery in most places outside the First World, although there are exceptions.

Formats for addressing mail for general delivery vary somewhat from country to country. The general idea is that you send a letter addressed something like this:

DOE, Jane General Delivery (Poste Restante) Main Post Office (GPO) Street Address City, Postal Code COUNTRY

The letter is held at the "general delivery" department of the specified post office—in effect a sort of "will call" department—for a certain amount of time during which, if Jane comes in and asks for her mail, she will be given it. Not all post offices handle general delivery. Sometimes all general delivery mail to a city is sent to one office, which is just as well. The worse case is when you have to specify at which post office a letter is to be held. If none is specified (as, for example, if you don't know that there is more than one) your letter can be waiting at one office while your correspondent checks for mail at a different office across town, and is told they have none. All in all, general delivery should be a last resort, or a way to receive notes and greetings that won't be missed if they aren't received, and require no reply.

## Telephones

National telephone systems and calling procedures vary greatly. You might be able to dial international numbers directly from a public pay phone or phone booth on the street, or you might have to go to the international calling office in the central telephone building to make an international call. In some countries, you go to the post office to make long-distance or international phone calls. In other countries, private telephone centers (often found combined with cyber-cafés) are cheaper and/or easier to deal with than government telephone offices or phone booths. Prepaid or stored-value international phonecards may be a great deal or a rip-off. Cellular phone (mobile phone) calls may be much cheaper, or much more expensive, than you are accustomed to at home, and paid for in different ways.

Good guidebooks to a country should explain how to use the phones, where to find public phones, and which calling and payment system is cheapest. (But phone systems are changing fast, so be prepared for things to be different than when the guidebook was researched.) If you think you'll be making local calls, and aren't sure what the system is, ask someone on the plane before you arrive, or in the airport, where you are likely to find English speakers.

## Costs and Payment

Phoning home is usually expensive. International phone calls from public telephone offices in some countries can cost US$3–5 per minute; satellite phones in the most remote areas can charge US$10 per minute; hotels routinely mark up telephone charges by 100 percent or more.

Around the world, the proliferation of mobile phones ("cellular phones" in the United States) is making the public pay phone obsolete. Coin-operated phones are an especially endangered species—most pay phones now accept only credit cards or calling-card numbers (in the United States and Canada) or stored-value telephone debit cards (in the rest of the world). If you don't have a mobile phone, and plan to use public phones, it's generally a good idea to get a telephone card as soon as possible after you arrive in any country where you'll be for a while. Depending on the country, they're sold from vending machines, at post and telecommunications offices, and/or in convenience stores, newsstands, tobacconists, and the like. Prices typically start at US$2 to US$5. Sometimes you throw telephone cards away when you've used up the stored value, but more often you can "recharge" a card, at the same places you buy them, for less than the price of a new card.

## Telephone Strategies

Phoning home is a hit or miss affair, especially if you're trying to reach a business (or someone you don't want to wake up) from a different time zone. It's usually possible to call home and leave a message, but much harder to get a reply. It may not be possible for people to call you back unless you are staying at an expensive hotel, or have a working mobile phone (see the section below).

A common strategy if you get an answering machine (as is, of course likely) is to leave a message saying, "I need you to do X, or to answer question Y. I'll call you back at time Z the day after tomorrow to find out your answer." This rarely works. For one thing, there is often ambiguity or confusion on the part of one party or the other as to what time or date (remember the International Date Line), in what time zone, is meant. (It's less confusing to say "It is now time T on date U, local time, here in place V. I will call you back W hours from now.") In the second place, the person you are calling may be out of town for a few days, may not get the message, or may not be able to make themselves available at the time you have said that you will call back. In the third place, given the vagaries of telephone systems, and often the long wait for an outgoing international line, you can never be sure that you will be able to call, and get through, at any precise time.

### Calls to International Hotels

In an emergency, if it is essential for someone to be able to call you back, consider checking into an expensive hotel. High-priced "international" hotels have 24-hour switchboards and backup power generators. The kinds of places where international journalists and businesspeople stay place a very high priority on keeping their phones working; in Second and Fourth World countries, many have international satellite telephone links that bypass the domestic phone network entirely.

### Voicemail

In theory, you could get a voicemail box at home and call in to check it from wherever you are, but the cost (not to mention the time waiting in lines at public telephone offices) of doing so wouldn't be worth it for most people traveling outside the First World, and probably not for most people traveling abroad at all. Remember that "toll-free" access numbers only work from within the same country (or sometimes between the United States and Canada), not further abroad.

### Tone Dialing

You can't count on finding touch-tone phones in some of the more remote parts of the world, so if you need to access any services that require touch tone dialing (such as pagers, voicemail systems, and the like) you'll need to bring a pocket tone generator with you. These are small boxes the size of a pager, with a speaker you hold up to the phone and a keypad you push to play tones into the phone. They also come in handy if you travel a lot domestically, or within the First World, and want to be able to check your voicemail from dial pay phones. Some electronic organizers and PDAs include built-in tone generators. Otherwise, you can get a simple tone dialer from Radio Shack or other such stores for US$20 or less.

Voice-response systems often require you to enter names, passwords, or other information on a touch-tone keypad using number equivalents for the letters (ABC=1, DEF=2, etc.). Phone keypads in other countries may have no letters, or may have them in another alphabet. (The same goes for ATM and credit/debit card keypads, which can be a problem if you remember your PIN by an alphabetic mnemonic.) If you don't have the telephone keypad and the mapping of letters to numbers memorized, bring a copy with you.

### Wireless Phones

Travelers in much of the world have grown accustomed to taking their mobile phones (cell phones) with them wherever they go, even internationally. You can too.

(An important note on terminology: What Americans call a "cellular phone," "cell phone," or "cell" is called a "mobile phone" or "mobile" everywhere else. This isn't an issue of American versus British usage. On this one, it's the United States and Canada versus the rest of the world. The American terms, especially the one-word shorthand "cell," are completely unknown, and likely to be misunderstood.)

You may have heard that American cell phones can't be used abroad, but that's only half true. Most cell phones in the United States and Canada operate on incompatible, nonstandard systems, and won't work anywhere else. But service on the global standard GSM system—in operation essentially everywhere in the inhabited world except Korea and Japan, where they are working on it—is available in the United States and Canada, with coverage extending to the majority of the population. The frequencies used for GSM services in North America aren't used in many other places, but GSM phones are available that cover multiple bands, so the same phone can be used both in North America and elsewhere in the world.

Seamless international mobile phone roaming is great —but it can be expensive. I can use my dual-band GSM phone in most of the world, but it costs me US$5 a minute in roaming fees to make or receive calls when I'm abroad.

Once you've got a suitable dual-or tri-band GSM phone, though, there's a better way: One of the advantages of the GSM system is that the phone number and account details are on a removable, interchangeable, thumbnail-sized smart card ("SIM card," or simply "SIM"), separate from the phone handset. Swap your SIM card for a new one—a matter of less than a minute—and you've got a new, local phone number in a new country.

Some mobile phone companies "lock" their handsets so they can only be used with their own SIM's, but some GSM operators in the United states recognize that international roaming is a selling point for their phones, and will give you the unlocking code for the asking, after you've had your phone for a couple of months, as long as you've paid your bills on time. Or you can buy an unlocked phone from someone other than your phone service provider—the whole point of the GSM standard is that the phones are interchangeable, unless

PRACTICALITIES

they are locked. Most phones that are sold outside the United States are bundled with service plans and locked, or expensive, so it's better to get an unlocked phone before you go.

The key point is to make sure that you have a phone that is GSM, unlocked, and works on the frequency band(s) in use in the countries where you will be traveling.

GSM World (http://www.gsmworld.com), the GSM trade association, has a directory by country of GSM operators and which bands they use. If you aren't sure where you might want to use the phone, get one that works on as many frequency bands as possible. If you have specific countries in mind, see which frequencies have service in those countries before you buy a phone.

The minimum "world phone" is dual-band, 900 MHz/1900 MHz. 1900 MHz is used for most GSM service in the USA, Canada, and some countries in Latin America. 900 Mhz is the band with the best coverage in the rest of the world. Tri-band phones are usually 900 MHz/1800MHz/1900 MHz. 1800 MHz is widely used outside North America, including in some places with no service at 900 MHz or 1900 MHz. A tri-band phone can be used almost everywhere in the world where there is digital mobile phone coverage. The fourth and newest GSM band, called 850 MHz or 800 MHz (both these terms are used to refer to the same range of frequencies), is being used first in the USA. It's unclear if it will be used anywhere else, or if it will create a demand for quad-band phones. As with any electronic equipment, try to find a phone with a dual-voltage or "universal" AC adapter/charger.

Compared to the cost of calling from your hotel, or even from phone booths, prepaid SIM's for a GSM phone can be cheap enough to pay for the phone in a week or two of travel, tops—less if you're traveling on business, and using the phone a lot. Regardless of whether you use the phone for outgoing calls or not, you've got a fixed local number where people can call you back, at no further cost to you, even if you're moving from city to city, in airports and train stations, or staying in hostels and budget hotels without phones in the rooms. (The system in the United States, where you have to pay to receive calls on your cell phone, is quite unusual internationally. Most prepaid SIM cards allow unlimited incoming calls at no charge.)

If you travel overseas even occasionally, and are signing a new wireless phone contract, do yourself a favor and get GSM service—if there is coverage in your area— and a dual-or tri-band phone. Get an unlocked phone, or one the company will agree to unlock, and get it unlocked as soon as possible. Even if you don't have cell phone service, or if you are going traveling for a long time, and giving up your service, you can still bring an unlocked multi-band GSM phone—sans SIM—with you to use with locally-purchased prepaid SIM's.

Most prepaid SIM's only work in one country. If you are going to be in many different countries for too little time to get a separate SIM for each, there, there are a few special SIM cards for travelers that can be used worldwide. The per-minute calling rates are much higher than for single-country SIM's, and they don't have free incoming calls, but it can be useful to have one as a backup. Specialty companies like Telestial.com sell both single-country and global roaming SIM's, or you can buy single-country prepaid SIM's once you arrive.

## Faxes

Not everyone has e-mail, and faxes are the next best means of international communications. (Many small and local hotels, for example, have fax machines but don't yet accept reservations requests by e-mail.) You can say more, for less money, with less chance of being misunderstood, in a one-page fax than in a three-minute phone call. You can find a fax service bureau in any city in the world.

### Fail-safe Fax?

Fax transmission protocols aren't fail-safe, and don't include redundancy or (in most cases) error checking. Do not rely on a "transmission confirmation" printed out by a fax machine as proof of whether or not it was received. It is surprisingly common to get both "false positive" confirmations of faxes that weren't received and "false negative" error messages when faxes actually were received in good order. There just isn't any certain way to tell whether or not a fax was received.

### Line Noise

Line noise can cause faxes not to be sent or received at all, or to be cut off in mid-page or mid-transmission. The worse the phone lines are, the more important it is to keep a fax short to maximize the chances that it will get through between interruptions in the phone connection, or bursts of noise. If a fax does come through over a noisy line, the noise will manifest itself as random black pixels, as though the page had been more or less heavily airbrushed or spattered with small specks of ink. Use white paper, black ink, and large bold block letters to maximize the chances of legibility when faxing to or from places with bad phone lines.

### Power

As with voice telephone calls, it's easier to send faxes home than to receive faxes from home while on the road. Don't count on getting a reply fax at a public telephone office or fax service bureau. You can only send or receive faxes when the telephone system and the electrical power are working at the same time. If both telephones and power are subject to frequent outages, the windows of opportunity for faxing may be quite limited. You can send faxes out, from such a place, during those windows. But someone trying to reply, and who has no way to know when the power and phones are on at the receiving end (or whether the real problem is something else, such as that they have been given the wrong number), may have poor odds of getting through. If they have to try many times, the odds increase that they will get a false confirmation, and think their reply has gone through, before it actually has. If business hours don't correspond, and the power or the fax machine are shut off at night, it may be impossible for them to reply unless they do so in the middle of the night at their end.

## International Telephone and Fax Numbers

Perhaps the most common reason for people not to succeed in calling or faxing you back is that they are dialing the wrong numbers. People who don't make many international calls are often intimidated by strange-looking phone or fax numbers, and have no idea how to interpret them. And the same number is likely to be written in many ways. If you get a message from someone abroad, saying, "Call me back" or "Fax me back at this number," the likelihood is that you don't need to dial some of the digits they have given you, but do need to dial some that they didn't give you.

It doesn't have to be like this. The number of digits in phone numbers varies, but they are actually more standardized than are the ways that they are written. And there is an unambiguous international format in which any phone number can be completely specified.

### *Plus Format*

The essential elements of a phone number are a country code, a city or area code (if there is one), and a local number. To write a number in international format, start with a plus sign (+), followed by the country code, followed by the city or area code, followed by the local number. My phone number, for example, is +1-415-824-0214 in this so-called "plus" format.

If you are within the same country and city or area code, you typically dial only the local number. In this instance, if you are calling from within area code 415, you would dial simply 824-0214. (From many offices or hotels with multiple lines or extensions, you would precede this with the code to get to get an initial connection to an outside line, typically 9 in the United States.)

If you are in the same country, but in a different city or area code, you dial the long-distance access code, followed by the city or area code, followed by the local number. In the United States and Canada, the long-distance access code is "1." So if you are in Chicago, you could call me by dialing 1-415-824-0214. So far, so good.

If you are in a different country, you dial the international access code, followed by the country code, followed by the city or area code, followed by the local number. In other words, you dial the international access code, plus exactly the numbers that follow the "plus" sign when the number is written in the "plus" format. The plus sign itself, like any hyphens or parentheses, is simply punctuation, and is not dialed.

The "plus" format has been adopted by all major wireless phone manufacturers as the standard for global roaming. If you enter phone numbers into your mobile phone (cell phone) in "plus" format, your calls will be completed correctly wherever you are able to roam—without you having to know, or enter, what country you are in or the outbound international access code.

### International Access Codes

Note that the international access code varies from country to country, the most common code being "00." From the United States and Canada it is, as already noted, "011." The international access code needed for all outbound international calls from a country is something completely different from the country code needed for all inbound international calls to a country. Many people confuse these, and if you ask someone for one, you are as likely as not to be told the other. Many people assume that the international access code is the same from all countries. There's no reason for it not to be, but it isn't.

If you have the number, correctly written, in the plus format, all you need to know to call it from anywhere in the world is the international access code wherever you are. You don't need to ask, "Which of these numbers do I need to dial, or not to dial?" All you need to ask is, "What is the international access code to make a call from here?"

In the UK, for example, the international access code is "00." So to call me from London you would dial 00+1-415-824-0214.

It is an unfortunate coincidence, causing vast amounts of confusion, that the long-distance access code within the United States and Canada is "1," and that the country code for calls to these places from other countries is also "1." The "1" in these two cases serves completely different purposes. Within most other countries, the long-distance access code is something other than "1" (most often "0," though there is no rule or standard). And, of course, every other country (except those included in country code "1") has a different country code.

In domestic usage, many people omit their country code. In a counterproductive effort to be helpful, people are wont to precede their phone number with their international access code (useful only when dialing out of their country, not into it), or their long-distance access code (useful only when dialing within the country, not internationally). The outbound international access code or the domestic long-distance access code are no more part of the number, proper, and should no more be included when writing it, even if you need to dial them, than is the 9 or other number you may need to dial to get an outside line from the phone on your desk.

People in the United States who write all international numbers with "011" (the international access code for calls from the USA) at the start are doing no one in any other country code a favor. The same number in New Delhi that I reach from the USA by dialing 011-91-11-123-4567 would be reached from London by dialing 00-91-11-123-4567 and from Australia by dialing 0011-91-123-4567. The clearest way for people everywhere to write this number is +91-11-123-4567.

## Converting Numbers to Plus Format

Converting a number you are given by someone abroad to the "plus" format typically involves removing some extraneous leading digits (international or long-distance access codes) and adding the country code (and sometimes city or area code), if it wasn't specified. A good pocket guide to city and country codes is invaluable in figuring out how to interpret numbers given to you in non-standard formats other than the "plus" format. There are several on the Internet, but you aren't likely to be on the Internet when you need them. See if you can get a printed one from your long-distance telephone company.

For example, the city code for Central London is 207. A business in Central London with the local number 123-4567 might print its number on its letterhead or fax header as "020-7123-4567" or "(020) 7123-4567," which is how you would dial it from elsewhere (outside the 207 area) in the UK. The country code for the UK is 44, so in the "plus" format this would be written as +44-207-123-4567 or +44-20-7123-4567. In the United States, the international access code is "011." So to call this number from the USA, I would dial 011+44-207-123-4567.

## Area/City Codes

Phone numbers and prefixes are constantly changing. In London, for example, city codes were changed in 1995 and again in 2000. The "207" area is what used to be "171" and before that "71." Not all books, and references have yet been updated. The business with the number in the preceding example might well still be using old letterhead showing its number as "0171-123-4567," or perhaps even "071-123-4567."

In the United States, a great many new area codes (city codes) have been added in recent years, and more codes are added each year, to accommodate demand for more phone lines, pagers, mobile phones, fax lines, and modem lines. If you are trying to call a number in the United States, and get a different party or are told that no such number exists, it may be that it is in an region that has been assigned a new area code. Call the operator (outside country code 1, have your operator call an operator in the USA) to check whether there is a new area code for that city or town.

If you are given a number beginning with a zero, the leading zero is probably the long-distance access code used within the country and should not be used when calling from outside the country. The only major exception I know of, where a city code actually begins with a zero, is Moscow, Russia (city code 095).

## Country Codes

Most country codes identify a single county. The major exception is country code 1, which includes the United States, Canada, and various "possessions" of the United States. The codes for regions within countries are called "area codes" in country code 1, and "city codes" in the rest of the world. Some countries do not use city codes, usually because they don't have enough phones to need them. When calling such countries, follow the country code directly with the local number. Country codes, city codes, and local numbers vary in length, as does the punctuation (such as parentheses or hyphens), if any, within and between parts of numbers. Fortunately, if you have a number correctly written in the "plus" format, and are calling from another country, you don't need to worry about which part of the number is the country code, which the city code, and which the local number. Just dial the international access code, plus all the numbers after the plus sign, in the order they are written. The punctuation (commas, hyphens, or periods), is optional and arbitrary, is never dialed, and can be ignored.

### Toll-free Numbers

Many businesses have special numbers that can be called at no charge to the caller, even from outside the local area. These are most popular in the United States and Canada, where all numbers in country code 1 with area code (city code) 800, 866, 877, and 888 are reserved for these so-called "toll-free" numbers. Various sorts of "freephone" schemes, with various formats, are used in other countries. They aren't really free, of course; this just means that calls to these numbers are paid for by the recipients rather than the callers.

Unless the holder of the number has agreed to pay for incoming international calls, you cannot call a "toll-free" number from another country. Some 800, 866, 877, and 888 numbers can be called only from the United States, some only from Canada, some from either country. Most businesses in the USA don't think the business they would get from customers abroad would justify the cost of accepting the charges for phone calls from all over the world. Because they won't agree to accept the charges, virtually no 800, 866, 877, or 888 numbers can be reached from anywhere outside country code 1. Most freephone numbers in other countries are likewise valid only within those countries.

The problem this causes for would-be visitors to the United States and Canada is that toll-free numbers are often the only phone numbers advertised or listed in literature from businesses in the travel industry such as airlines, railroads, bus lines, car rental companies, and hotel chains. If you are trying to reach such a business from abroad, and have only a toll-free number that doesn't work from where you are, try having an operator in your country call an operator in a major city where the company is likely to have a local office (such as a city or airport ticket counter for an airline) to get a local number. If a local office can't help you, they will probably be able to forward your call internally to the "toll-free" line you couldn't call directly. Or you can call a friend in the United States or Canada with a multiline phone, or office switchboard, then have them call out to the toll-free number, and conference the two lines together. International callback services that route calls between other countries via the United States can also be used to reach 800, 866, 877, and 888 numbers from abroad.

*Merriam-Webster's Guide to International Business Communication*, (see the Resource Guide), contains a clear and concise chapter of advice on "How to Get Phone Calls and Faxes Through," as well as a great deal of useful information on telephone number and postal address formats for selected countries. Unfortunately, it focuses mainly on the First World (thus ignoring problems like those discussed above of power reliability and phone line access) but travelers anywhere will find the general introductory chapters worth reading to give themselves a sense of what sorts of variations they can expect, and for general communications procedures, even if none of the country chapters pertain to specific places they are going.

# CULTURE SHOCK

"Culture shock" is the inability to adapt to, or feel comfortable with or in, the cultural setting in which you find yourself. The term "culture shock" is unfortunate, as it implies a sudden and jarring experience and suggests that culture shock will hit you hardest at the start of your trip or when you first arrive in a different culture. Very few people actually experience a rapid onset of disorientation on their first sight, sound, smell, touch, or encirclement by strange people in a strange place. At first, most people find it exciting and fun. Only as time goes on does the constant sensory overload become overwhelming. This results from not being assimilated enough to automatically filter out those stimuli to which one need not pay attention, and thus having to pay attention to everything.

Having taken, and enjoyed, short trips to exotic and diverse places is little indication of how much you will be affected by, or how well you will cope with, culture shock on a long trip. Culture shock is a long-term phenomenon, and by the time you realize that you are suffering from it, it has probably been sneaking up on you for weeks. After 4–6 months of travel, when culture shock typically reaches its peak, it is also apt to be mixed with a fair amount of simple homesickness, from which it is not always easily distinguished.

For any but the most manic, it's impossible to sustain the level of alertness and awareness of one's self and one's surroundings that is required to keep adapting to new cultures for more than a few weeks or a month at a time. The hardest work of travel is the work of cultural adaptation and learning. Plan to take periodic breaks or "vacations within your vacation," or to settle down periodically in places where you can stay long enough to acclimate to the area and relax your hyperalertness and hyper-self-consciousness.

## Avoiding Culture Shock Through Preparation

Preparing for travel in a way that minimizes the likelihood of an unpleasant degree of culture shock is not primarily a matter of learning specific facts about the culture(s), people(s), customs, or mores of your destination(s). Paradoxically, learning more facts about "the way it is" can serve to give you more fixed expectations that make it hard for you to cope when you encounter—as you inevitably will, no matter how much you know—things that are unfamiliar, unexpected, and confusing. People who set out without a clue, and who know and accept that they haven't a clue, sometimes do much better, because they realize from the start that they have much to learn to get anywhere. It's important to cultivate enough patience and trust to be able to go along with things, up to a point, without being too bothered by the fact that you haven't yet figured out what's going on, or what it means.

I am not an advocate of ignorance: most travelers spend too little time studying the places they are going, before they leave, to maximize the educational value they could get out of their trips. That's okay; I also realize that education isn't everyone's primary purpose. But it's important to understand that the kind of learning that will help you avoid culture shock is the kind of learning that enhances your humility, your open-mindedness, your awareness of the extent of your ignorance, and your desire to learn more. You won't avoid culture shock with the kind of learning that enhances your sense of "being in command of the situation" or convinces you that you know all you need to know about where you are going.

Some of the people who experience the most extreme culture shock are academic experts, with the utmost book-learning of a place, who fail to allow for their ignorance of its reality. People who have been in a place in the past, and whose expectations don't allow sufficiently for the extent to which it has changed, can also be shocked, culturally and otherwise. This includes immigrants returning home after even as few as a couple of years abroad. A common theme in the writings of Southerners who go North to boarding school or university is the culture shock of their first return from school to their homeland and their village.

Culture shock is, fundamentally, a symptom of unsuccessful or incomplete cultural adaptation, assimilation, and acceptance. Preparation for avoiding cultural shock is thus primarily attitudinal: learning how to adapt to, assimilate into, and accept cultural diversity. A diverse, multicultural outlook and awareness is the best immunization against culture shock. Recognize that people elsewhere do things differently. Don't presume that different means inferior, or ascribe unfamiliar attitudes or actions to barbarism or backwardness. Instead, start with the assumption that there is a reason for a behavior that is functional in its context, and try to figure out what that is.

### Cultural Adaptation

Several manuals for foreign living listed in the Resource Guide (intended variously for foreign students, businesspeople, missionaries, and volunteers) contain exercises and activities you can do before you leave. These activities help you to prepare yourself by improving your attitudes and developing your skills.

The kinds of exercises and lessons used by trainers in cross-cultural communication, cultural adaptation, and cultural awareness are familiar to far more people today than they were a decade or two ago. As First World countries such as the United States, Canada, Australia, and, to a lesser extent, the UK, have begun to acknowledge their multicultural, if not multinational, character, large numbers of students, especially in public (government) schools, have begun to receive at least a rudimentary consciousness-raising in cultural sensitivity and awareness of diversity. CNN has given people a more diverse (albeit distorted by editorial selection and voice-over interpretations) range of images than were previously available, making written descriptions of other worlds seem more real.

> **REAL LIFE**
>
> Sixty percent of USA college students polled in 2002 believe "developing a better understanding of the values and history of other cultures and nations that dislike us" is a better approach to preventing terrorism than "investing in strong military and defense capabilities at home and abroad."

### Make It a Learning Experience

Whoever you are and whatever you do, you are less likely to get frustrated by the differences between local ways and those to which you are accustomed to at home if you treat "doing things" as a learning experience rather than as ancillary to the "real" travel goals of sightseeing or whatever. If you regard buying a ticket (or whatever bit of business) as no more than an unavoidable necessity, and the ticket-seller as no more than an obstacle on the way to the thing you have set out to see that day, you close yourself off to the chance that you might be able to learn from the transaction or the accompanying conversation. Approach these encounters as part of the travel experience, not as things getting in the way of it, and you'll stand a better chance of finding the educational silver lining in the bureaucratic clouds.

### Nontourist Opportunities

Some experienced travelers, myself included, seek out opportunities to do things from which they can learn about everyday nontourist life. I go into schools of English and volunteer myself as a guest native speaker for conversation practice; I go into local department stores away from tourist districts even when I have nothing to buy, to see what is on the shelves; I enjoy it when I can find excuses to go into business and government offices in different countries to see what the offices look like, how people are dressed, and how business is done.

An often-rewarding exercise is to seek out someone in your trade, career, or profession, the office of a relevant trade union or professional association, or any group with whom you have something in common. People are remarkably receptive to being approached on this basis: "Hello! I work as a . . .in America. I see that you are a . . . .May I look at your (shop, office, etc.)? What is it like to be a... here?" At the least, you'll get a tour of the workplace. If you hit it off, you might be invited home (if home and workplace are different—many people can't afford separate living and working spaces) for a family meal, the sort of thing that can be the highlight of a trip.

## Poverty and Beggars

Travelers from the North on their first visit to the South often expect to be shocked by their encounters with poverty and begging. It's an extremely difficult issue, and there's certainly an argument that people who are, in global terms, rich, should be troubled by the economic differences between themselves and most of the people in the places they visit. Why are we so much wealthier than they are? Is it fair? Is it inevitable? Can we do anything about it? Should we? Must we? Beggars confront us with these questions in the most direct and personal terms, and sometimes in so many words: "You are rich. I am poor. A dollar means little to you, and much to me."

However you respond, there is no reason to let these issues deter you from travel. Travel doesn't cause the problems, or create the moral issues; travel just makes them harder to ignore. Beggars and poverty are as real when they are 10,000 km away and out of sight as they are when a beggar is standing in front of you on the street, wizened arm and empty hand extended. A permanent change in consciousness often brought about by world travel is an enduring awareness of the reality of poverty, suffering, and inequity.

At one time, people from the United States were relatively unlikely to see people sleeping in the streets or begging unless they traveled abroad in the South. Now, homelessness and begging are no longer novelties for people who've spent time in any big USA city, especially any of those where, due to temperate climate, homeless people are less likely to freeze to death.

Today, people from other First World countries, or even poorer countries that nonetheless have stronger socioeconomic safety nets, often have their first contact with homelessness and begging during foreign travel. Often, that first contact comes—unexpectedly—in the United States. Many visitors are unprepared to see so much conspicuous poverty and suffering in such a rich country as the United States.

Tourists tend to notice homeless people more than the locals, who have come to take them for granted. I've seen many a foreigner, but never once a local, photographing or filming beggars and street-sleepers. Foreigners, less inured to begging, are also more likely than locals to give to beggars, leading beggars to congregate in districts frequented by foreign tourists. This is true in the United States, and it's true around the world. As a traveler, you will be asked for all sorts of gifts and favors, from money to sponsorship for immigration to the USA.

It's up to you to decide how you want to respond. Travel, and learning more about the world, can only give you a better basis for making judgments and choices about your actions and role in an interconnected world.

## Sexual and Gender Mores

Some of the cultural norms that vary most from culture to culture are those related to sexual and gender relationships and behavioral expectations. There are many societies in which it is considered offensive, and either an invitation to rape or a sign of prostitution or perversion, for a woman to expose any skin except her face, hands, and feet in public; for a woman to go out without a male relative as an escort; for an unmarried couple to appear together in public, much less share a room in a hotel; or for even a married couple to engage in such public displays of affection as holding hands, much less hugging or kissing.

Local people may not be able to afford to refuse money from rich foreigners who do such things, even while they talk behind the foreigners' backs about their bad manners or perversion. You can't assume that because "everyone" (i.e., all the foreigners, or those who adopt their manners to wait on them) does something, it is okay or doesn't offend the locals. I've been in many places—especially, but not limited to, romantic or beach resorts in Third World countries—where virtually all the foreign tourists dress or act in ways that the locals consider grossly offensive, but where the locals put on fake smiles and pretend not to mind because the foreigners are the source of most local money.

### Issues for Gays and Lesbians

Lesbians and gay men are rarely able to be entirely out of the closet, even in relatively tolerant countries such as the United States. Most gays and lesbians have some experience of having to hide the nature of their personal relationships, represent their relationships with companions as being of a different nature than is actually the case, or refrain from public displays of affection lest they offend other people around them. Constant awareness of how other people might judge and react—perhaps with violence—to expressions of sexuality or displays of affection is a matter of survival for gays and lesbians everywhere.

Pairs of men or women often travel together as platonic friends (in the case of women, often for protection against sexual harassment), rather than love. In some cultures it's common for two women, or two men, to walk hand in hand together, or embrace each other when meeting or parting, and nothing sexual is inferred from such behavior. Except when asking for a double bed rather than two single beds, it's rarely necessary for lesbian and gay couples to call attention to their sexual orientation, and most of their problems traveling are the same ones they have with homophobes at home.

## Issues for Straight People

For straight people, travel in other cultural regions is often their first encounter with these issues. If you are accustomed to being able to walk hand in hand or share a hotel room with someone of the opposite gender; to speak publicly of sex; to wear shorts, short (i.e., shorter than ankle length) skirts, short-sleeved shirts, or shirts with low necklines; or to travel alone as a woman you will find that there are places where you either have to make adjustments to suit local mores (such as by pretending to be married to your traveling companion, or pretending to have a husband or male relative "back at the hotel"), or offend some people. I won't tell you to pander to other people's prejudices, if you have decided that they are illegitimate, but I do suggest that you give careful consideration, in advance, to actions that will alienate you from the people from and about whom you are trying to learn.

## Relative Values

Before you dismiss other cultures' sexual and gender values as "backward" or inferior, let me remind you that some of the attitudes and practices most degrading, repressive, and exploitative of women and children are engaged in by First Worlders at the expense of Third World people. It's hard for me to see how it is fundamentally worse to keep women in purdah, or to mutilate the genitals of women at puberty, than it is for sex tourists to create the demand for prostitutes that leads to the kidnapping of women and children into sex slavery in the brothels of Bangkok or Manila; to pay starving parents to sell their babies for international adoption (some adoption agents are, in essence, modern-day slavers); or to give so many Second, Third, and Fourth World women no economic hope but to sell themselves into mail-order marriage with a First Worlder— usually through a First World facilitator or intermediary who profits from promoting the image of Asian or Russian women as more submissive than Americans or Western Europeans.

The international traffic in women and children has become such a serious problem that several countries have taken legal steps to try to reduce it, largely without success. We may not approve of these activities, but we share responsibility for them if we know about them but do nothing to stop them. I figure we have at least as much responsibility to clean up our own society's act (the "demand side" of these activities and abuses) as to complain about other societies on the "supply side." I do my own small part by refusing to knowingly deal with sex tourists or traffickers in women or children.

## Immigrants Returning "Home"

### USA Immigration Policies

Virtually no Asians or Africans were allowed to immigrate to the United States between 1917 and 1965. Asians were categorically barred from immigration, on explicitly racial grounds, from 1917 to 1952. The immigration quotas by national origin, for Africans and Asians alike, remained vanishingly small until the first of several reforms starting in 1965 loosened the restrictions. There ensued a continuing small (relative to continued immigration of white people from Europe to the United States) but significant wave of immigrants of a new type. Continuation of the quotas, combined with competitive educational, professional, credential, and job-skill preferences within the quota from each country, meant that legal immigration from Asia and Africa remained largely confined to doctors, engineers, academics, and other holders of advanced degrees, many of whom came to the United States first as foreign students.

### Brain Drain

Some of the results of these criteria may surprise you, although they shouldn't. Indian-Americans have the highest average educational levels and incomes of any national-origin group in the United States. African-born Americans have the highest average educational levels and incomes of any group by continent of birth, including native-born North Americans.

There were similar increases in immigration from the South, also primarily by the most highly educated technical specialists, to various other First World countries during the same period. While Southerners also went to the Second World for education and training, often on scholarships, they were more likely than those who went to the First World to be sent home on completion of their schooling. The overall phenomenon came to be called the "brain drain," as Southern countries protested that their best and brightest young professionals were being lured away by the former colonial powers just in their post-independence hour of greatest need for skilled personnel.

### The Second Generation

As the children of the brain drain—second-and third-generation Asian-Americans, African-Americans, Asian-Canadians, and African-Europeans, for example—come of age, many of them are seeking an understanding of their parents' cultures and homelands, through study and travel. In 1978, the students in my introductory class in South Asian civilization at the University of Chicago were almost all white. Most were would-be "orientalists" and "classicists"; my interest in contemporary South Asia was considered strange. Today, the majority of students in similar classes at USA universities are second-generation South Asian-American children of immigrants. At the University of California at Berkeley, where the tenured faculty of the Center for South Asian Studies was entirely white, a new endowed chair (faculty position) has been funded by the South Asian-American community. Similar changes have been occurring in other "Area Studies" programs that, in the United States used to be dominated by a mix of racist "classicists" and CIA contractors.

Second-and third-generation immigrants, or first-generation immigrants who left the land of their birth as infants, face special problems of cultural adjustment and understanding in "returning" to their parents' or grandparents' homelands. They may have higher expectations for themselves, and more of an emotional investment in whether they fit into the culture and society, or how they react to it. They may have to confront the realization that they aren't totally at home, or accepted as part of the dominant or normative culture, in the place their family is "from" any more than in the place they grew up. If they are returning to a place where they look like the locals, and perhaps speak the language, they may be held to a higher standard or cultural conformity, while travelers whose race and/or speech makes them stand out as foreigners, on the other hand, are usually tolerated in violating many local norms, on the generous assumption that as ignorant foreigners they don't know any better.

## Coming Home

The common assumption is that it will be most difficult to deal with the first "foreign" place you visit, and that it is easiest to work your way gradually through places more like home to those that are more different. Few people expect coming home to be difficult at all, or expect a problem in coming more or less straight home from the most exotic and remote place on their itinerary. "After that, I'll be ready to come home," they think.

It's partly a matter of taste. Some people jump in, head first, all at once. Some prefer to wade in slowly, one step at a time, so that they have the reassurance of knowing they can decide to back out before they get in over their heads.

But the reality is that, for a variety of reasons, coming home can be the most culturally difficult leg of your journey, and that giving yourself a chance to readjust gradually may be at least as important at the end of your trip as at the beginning.

I often talk with my clients in the first days, weeks, or months after they have returned from lengthy trips. Almost without exception they report significant symptoms of culture shock. No matter where they went, the majority say that

PRACTICALITIES

adjusting to being back in the United States was more difficult, psychologically, than dealing with anything that happened along the way.

There isn't a magic cure for this "reentry shock," although there are suggestions in some of the books in the Resource Guide. I recommend both a gradual return, as just described, and allowing yourself time to adjust to being back before you have to resume your "normal" routine. Plan on wanting time to reflect and absorb the lessons of the trip. You'll recover from the jet lag in a week, but you may not get over the changes that a trip has brought about in yourself for months or years, if ever. Don't rule out the possibility that your life may be completely transformed by a trip around the world.

# "How Much
### Will It Cost?"

## THE BOTTOM LINE

### YOUR TRAVEL BUDGET

Most people underestimate how much their trip will cost. It's both more common and more problematic to budget too little, or not to budget at all, than to budget too much. Be realistic, and give yourself a margin for error proportional to your unfamiliarity with the nitty-gritty of travel in places you are going, the uncertainty in your plans, the flexibility that you want to leave yourself, and the degree to which you can afford to exceed your budget.

Take all prices from guidebooks, friends, and acquaintances with a grain of salt. Many budget travelers make a sport of how cheaply they can travel—or, more often, of how cheaply they can claim to travel. Those who talk most loudly and often about prices are usually those who are most boastful about their thrift.

Guidebook writers are usually honest, but the figures they give are still misleading. Guidebook writers are experienced travelers, familiar with the country and how to travel in it, and speaking at least some of a local language. As soon as they write a place up in a guidebook, the place has a guaranteed stream of business from readers of that guidebook, so it can (and usually will) raise its prices. You can't realistically hope, and shouldn't expect, to travel as cheaply as the guidebook author.

Before using any prices in a guidebook, check to see what exchange rate was in effect at the time the book was compiled. (If the book doesn't say, throw it away.) Convert prices to your currency at that rate, even if the local currency in which the book gives prices is worth much less in your currency today.

As a rule, the more rapidly a country's currency is declining in value against First World currencies such as the USA dollar, the higher inflation is likely to be and the more likely prices are to be fixed in hard currency or its equivalent. In many countries tourists are required to pay for certain services either in hard currency or in local currency, which must be purchased at an artificially high "official" or "tourist" exchange rate. This is often true of air tickets, but also of hotels and train tickets.

Hard-currency price equivalents are more stable over time in most countries than local-currency prices, and a better guide to what your costs will be. You can sometimes get windfall bargains in the brief period between the devaluation of a currency and the adjustment of prices, but such opportunities are fleeting.

# KEY ADVICE ABOUT MONEY MATTERS

- Budget conservatively. Most people under-budget. It's better to have money left over than to run out.

- Include everything in your budget. Often overlooked or under-budgeted major expense categories include immunizations and health supplies, luggage and gear, land transportation such as Eurail passes, and additional air tickets purchased en route.

- Don't try to set a single per-diem expense figure for every country. Break your trip down by how long you plan to spend in each region or country, and budget separately for each. Don't rely on one of my sample budgets. Make your own budget.

- Expect to spend significantly more than the prices in guidebooks. Guidebooks are written by expert travelers. If you need to consult a guidebook to predict your expenses, budget at or above the high end of any range it gives. Inflation and the effect of being listed in a guidebook will have increased prices from those in even current editions of guidebooks.

- Compare the cost of travel to other things you spend money on. The average (including business travelers) total budget for someone going overseas from the United States for six months in 1998 was US$7,092 including airfare, all prearrangements, and all expenses en route. Long-term, independent world travel is extraordinarily affordable, and an extraordinarily good value.

- Bring a mix of cash, traveler's checks, and plastic. Don't rely exclusively on any one way of getting money. Don't use Internet banking unless you bring your own computer.

- Arrange with a friend or relative to manage your essential financial affairs while you are out of the country. A trusted contact at home is crucial when the unexpected happens.

For more information on the topics in this chapter, see the Resource Guide in the back of the book, and the links on the Practical Nomad Web site at http://www.practicalnomad.com.

Even hard-currency price equivalents are subject to world inflation. When I travel, I figure that a typical current edition of a guidebook is based on research done two years ago, and that inflation in most of the world is at least 10 percent a year. I plan on spending 20–25 percent more than the prices in "current" books.

In places where there are no hotels comparable to those in the United States or elsewhere in the First World, it's difficult to predict how much you will need or want to spend. Most people find their personal comfort level fairly quickly, but it's hard to anticipate such things as whether you'll want air-conditioning in the tropics (where the cheapest air-conditioned rooms can cost twice as much as otherwise-nicer ones with ceiling fans), or how often you'll feel the need for running water, hot water, or a private toilet and/or bath.

Around-the-world travelers have a wide range of incomes and budgets. You'd be surprised how often you see Banglampoo backpackers in beads and tie-dye climbing into cabs from Khao San Road to Bangkok airport with garment bags full of custom-tailored suits they've had made to wear at their office jobs back home.

Given these factors, I can't give a single answer to the question, "How much will it cost?" Instead, I'll try to give an outline of items to include, and some wide ranges of possible costs for you to use in projecting your personal budget.

## Advance Expenses

Most people spend more before their departure—not including their airline tickets—than they ever imagined. You may find this figure shocking, but first-time international travelers equipping and preparing themselves to set off for a couple of months or more outside the First World can expect to spend, and should budget, at least US$500 per person (some people spend US$1000) on equipment, supplies, and expenses other than tickets. Where does all this money go?

### Travel Documents

A new USA passport costs US$85, US$60 more for rush service. Two or three visas (averaging US$20 each—some cost up to US$100), roundtrip Express Mail or FedEx for sending visa applications to any consulates or embassies you can't get to in person, and half a dozen photos for passport and visas typically bring the total cost of travel documents to US$200 or more for a multicountry trip if you don't already have a passport. If you will need visas for certain countries but can't or don't choose to get them before you leave, at least check with the embassies for the current visa fees and include them in your budget, because you'll have to pay them sooner or later, wherever you get your visas.

### Immunizations and Health Supplies

Even at a clinic that charges only per inoculation, a course of recommended immunizations for tropical Third World travel and filling the prescriptions for antibiotics and assorted other medical supplies will cost you US$100 or more. Adding the cost of stocking a reasonable first-aid kit (including adequate supplies of any medication you regularly need) is likely to bring the cost of health and hygiene preparations closer to at least US$200 (a bit less if you are sharing some of these supplies with a traveling companion; more if you are traveling alone). The prices of even nonprescription first-aid supplies and toiletries add up remarkably quickly.

Up the ante further if you haven't had a recent general physical examination (a must before a multimonth Third World trip), wear glasses or contacts (get your eyeglass prescription checked and get prescription sunglasses and a spare pair of regular glasses), if you regularly use any expensive or prescription medications, or if you feel it necessary to use specific types of toiletries or cosmetics that you can't count on finding along the way.

I strongly recommend a water filter for long-term travel. They start at about US$50, but most of those worth bothering to carry cost US$75–150. For more than about six person-months, you'll probably need to bring a spare filter cartridge (US$25–75).

### Luggage

A good travel bag generally costs US$200–300. You can find one for US$150, but the small savings aren't worth it for the differences in quality, features, and durability. Most other sorts of luggage you may already have won't work nearly as well. It may seem like a lot, but a really good travel bag will be hard to find along the way if you set out with one that proves inadequate or uncomfortable. If you're going to be living out of it for the duration of your trip, it's worth paying the price to get durable, well-fitting luggage exactly suiting your needs.

### Shoes and Clothing

As I explained earlier in the packing section, I don't recommend major advance investments in clothing. But I would recommend a suit of lightweight silk or synthetic long underwear, if you don't have some already (US$40–50), and new shoes or sandals, unless yours have very little wear (say one very durable pair of shoes and one of sandals, at US$75 each, for a total of US$150). Buy new shoes just far enough before your departure to get them well broken in and be sure that they'll be comfortable; don't try to break them in on the road.

### Guidebooks and Maps

You need to budget for guidebooks and maps whether you buy them in advance or as you go. Moon Handbooks or comparable guidebooks are typically US$15–20 each for large countries or regions. Good maps of countries or regions the size of large USA states or Western European countries run US$10–20, potentially much more if you need specialized or detailed maps such as for trekking or bicycling, or are traveling to places where maps are hard to find.

Traveling at a typical pace, budget a minimum of US$25 a month on guidebooks and maps, twice that or more if you are traveling through more places more quickly, a bit less if you're the sort who never looks at a map—though you may regret it and will never know what you miss.

### Other Advance Expenses

Other big-ticket items to budget for if you will be bringing them are a lightweight sleeping bag or sleep sack and any photographic equipment and supplies you plan to bring. If you bring a camera, bring as much film or digital memory as you can afford and find space for; it's likely to be more expensive to buy more along the way. Don't forget to include in your budget how much you'll have to pay to get your film developed, or for cybercafé time and services (CD burning) to deal with your digital photos.

## Long-Distance Transportation

As I've already tried to explain, the cost of air tickets depends entirely on the specifics of your itinerary. What's easy to overlook is that your transportation costs don't end with the air tickets you buy before you leave.

You can currently fly around the world for as little as US$1,500 on certain routings. But, as I said in the "Air Transportation" chapter, scrimping on the initial price of tickets is, for most people, a false economy. If you are definitely going to some other places along the way, and will have to fly there, it will almost always be cheaper in the long run to include those flights in your initial package of air tickets, rather than to buy them later as separate side trips.

Similarly, some of the money you save on air tickets by leaving gaps in your air itinerary to be traveled by land or water must be budgeted for the cost of using land travel. Third World trains are an excellent value, as are trains in the USA for those budget travelers with plenty of time, but the costs are nontrivial.

It's easy to be misled by the seeming affordability of third-class train tickets and local bus rides in guidebooks. A high proportion of travelers from the First World, even budget backpackers, find themselves choosing first class on Third World trains and taking so-called "luxury" buses for any but the shortest journeys, finding the greater comfort well worth the extra cost.

So you may save US$150 or so by not including flights between Bangkok and Singapore, or between Delhi and Bombay, but you'll need to set aside about US$50–100 of that for first-class train tickets between either of these pairs of cities. Both these train trips are worthwhile for the experience, and for the places you can see and stop off in along the way, but the bottom-line savings are minimal if you are interested neither in the train journeys for their own sake nor in visiting any of the places along the way.

Include in your budget your best estimate of the cost of traversing any gaps in your air itinerary, or of any intended side trips by land or water. If you have any doubt about the level of comfort you will require, budget for the highest available category of land transportation ("foreigners' class"). Don't commit yourself to traveling in, say, "hard seat" class on a Chinese train unless you know you can take it.

Long-haul land or water transportation in the Fourth World, where it is possible at all, is usually very cheap, very slow, and very uncomfortable. Train travel in the Second World is, at present, often as cheap as in the Third World and almost as comfortable as in the First World.

Land and water transportation in the First World, on the other hand, is apt to be a major expense. Rail or bus passes can be good values, especially compared to the cost of air tickets within Western Europe or other wealthy regions, as a quick look at the following list shows. However, they can still be a significant part of your total transportation costs.

- A one-month second-class youth (under age 26) Eurailpass costs US$664.

- A 21-day "ordinary-class" (second-class) Japan Rail Pass costs ¥57,700 (currently US$490).

- A 10,000 km (6,200 miles) Aussie Kilometre Pass for Greyhound Australia bus travel within a six-month period costs A$1195 (currently US$700).

- A 30-day North American Rail Pass valid throughout the United States and Canada costs US$674 in peak season (Jun 1 - Oct 15), US$475 off-peak (Oct 15 - May 31).

Even if you don't make any definite commitments to a specific route, it's best to plan your route through such expensive regions in advance, both so as to estimate what it will cost and to know whether individual point-to-point tickets, a pass, or even some flights (especially if they can be included with your through tickets) will be best for your specific destinations.

Planning how you will close the gaps in your air itinerary will also give you a chance to assess the distances you plan to cover and the time it will take. When you start looking at train and ferry schedules, what seemed like "places" on the map resolve themselves into large regions, continents, and subcontinents.

Indonesia, for example, extends farther than the lower 48 states of the United States. Within the two months' maximum that tourists are allowed to stay, it's difficult to get from one end of the archipelago to the other without flying. Bangkok, Thailand, is relatively close to Bali, Indonesia, in comparison with the whole of Asia. But "close" in this case is 2,400 air kilometers (1,500 miles), or a minimum of a week of travel time by buses, trains, ships, and ferries.

Unless you plan ahead, you can wind up like the foreigners on their first visit to the United States who get off a plane in New York City, rent a car, and only then ask "How far to the Grand Canyon?" You can get anywhere in the continental United States by car, just like the guidebooks say, but it takes time and might cost you a lot.

To give you a sense of relative scale, it takes 3–4 days and nights by train to cross either Europe, Australia, or for that matter North America. It's 5–6 days and nights across China, 7 across Russia. Even from north to south (the shorter direction across China), Hong Kong is 1,900 km (1,200 miles) from Beijing. Africa is 8,000 km (5,000 miles) north-south and 6,500 km (4,000 miles) east-west; it's almost 1,400 km (900 miles) from one end of South Africa to the other. Even in smaller Third World countries two-day train and bus journeys are not uncommon, and at the slow pace of the Fourth World, they are routine.

# USA TAX LOOPHOLE FOR UNPAID SABBATICALS AND LEAVES OF ABSENCE

For some taxpayers in the United States, the tax benefits of taking an unpaid sabbatical or leave of absence, or simply having less income for a year, may offset or even exceed the income lost. Some people could actually end up with more money, in the long run, by making less money, or no money at all, for a year!

This is one of the consequences (unintended, so far as I can tell, and thus far almost totally unnoticed) of the 1997 and 1998 changes in tax law establishing so-called "Roth Individual Retirement Accounts" (Roth IRAs).

To make a very long story short, contributions to a Roth IRA aren't tax-deductible, unlike contributions to a regular IRA. But once you put money into a Roth IRA (as long as you don't withdraw it before you are 60) neither the money in the Roth IRA nor any accumulated interest or appreciation are ever taxed again. No federal income tax, no capital gains tax, no tax on withdrawals, no state or local income taxes, nothing.

Withdrawals from a regular IRA, on the other hand, are considered taxable income regardless of your age.

If your income for a given year is less than US$100,000 (for an individual or a married couple filing jointly), you can convert an existing regular or traditional IRA of any size to a Roth IRA by paying tax on the converted amount as regular income in the year it is converted.

In many cases, putting the same amount into a Roth IRA, and allowing the earnings to compound tax-free, can result in a much larger after-tax nest egg than putting it into a regular IRA. So can converting an existing IRA into a Roth IRA. The big drawback is that Roth IRA conversions or contributions are taxed, and that you can't convert your IRA if your income for the year is too high.

So there can be major benefits to converting your IRA to a Roth IRA in a year when your income is as low as possible, so that you are in a lower tax bracket and the tax on the conversion is less.

A six-month to two-year trip around the world routinely includes US$500–1,000 worth of First World land travel (typically bus or train travel in the United States, Canada, Australia, and/or Western Europe), US$500 of long-distance train tickets outside the First World, and US$100–500 for air tickets bought along the way (such as for side trips, places where for unanticipated reasons buses proved slower or more uncomfortable than expected, or places where there turns out to be no alternative to flying).

There is no "typical" trip, so don't stick these numbers in your budget blindly: try to estimate your likely costs. It's especially important to get prices in

---

(Remember, the tax savings on the conversion will be multiplied many times, because all earnings on the additional amount will accrue tax-free until you withdraw the money after age 60.) For those fortunate enough to be making more than the conversion limit (not uncommon for a two-income married couple filing jointly), there can be even greater benefits to a sabbatical or leave that brings your income below the threshold for a year, thus creating a one-time opportunity to convert your existing IRA to a Roth IRA. And knowing that you'll be able to convert it to a Roth IRA may influence how much you want to contribute to your regular IRA in the years before your sabbatical or break in employment.

To summarize: If you are taxed in the United States and are considering taking a sabbatical or leave of absence that might significantly reduce your income for a tax year (now or in the future), you should investigate the possible financial benefits of:

• converting some or all of your regular or "traditional" (non-Roth) IRA to a Roth IRA during the year when your income is lower

• putting money, or putting additional money, into your traditional IRA (or opening a new traditional IRA if you don't have one), in anticipation of converting some or all of it to a Roth IRA during the year when your income is lower

I'm not an attorney, accountant, or tax adviser. Financial decision-making, especially retirement and long-term tax and investment planning, can be extraordinarily complex. Your decisions will depend on what assumptions you make about imponderables such as future inflation, earnings, and tax rates.

You can take the best advantage of these potential benefits if you start considering them several years before the year in which your income will be lower. It's probably just as well that sabbaticals are so rare—if they were more common, Congress probably wouldn't have created this accidental tax break for sabbatical-takers. But you can't expect financial advisers to think about these issues unless you prompt them, and the implications of unpaid sabbaticals aren't incorporated in any standard IRA or other financial planning software or modeling tools.

advance, and to include them in your budget, for any likely side trips by air or other air tickets to be bought en route. It's not uncommon for people who rely on obsolete guidebooks to budget US$200 for a side trip that will cost US$1,000, and that they end up being unable to afford.

## Daily Living Expenses

Perhaps the most obvious and also the most difficult task in estimating how much your trip will cost is estimating your daily living expenses: lodging, food, local transportation, and incidentals. How can you tell how much you'll spend in a country or region you've never been to before, or if you've never traveled abroad independently, or for as lengthy a period of time? The single budgetary question I'm asked most often is, "How much can I expect to spend per day on a trip around the world?"

There is no easy answer, but here is some general advice and a few rules of thumb:

First, don't try to estimate an overall per diem average to cover travel in different countries or regions. Break down your trip according to how long you plan to spend in each place. Budget separately for each country, or at least for each region of similar price levels and styles of travel. There is no average that will make sense in both the United States and Mexico, Singapore and Indonesia, or Western and Eastern Europe. At a minimum, estimate how much of your trip will be in each of the First, Second, Third, and Fourth Worlds, and draw up a separate budget for the time in each of those worlds.

Second, budget at the high end of the range of your uncertainty. Any of your sources are more likely to give you estimates that are lower than what you actually spend than higher. No matter how recently your sources were there, prices are likely to have increased. And in cultures that take pride in thrift, most people exaggerate how little they spent. People who were on tours or stayed in Intercontinental-type hotels should be ignored as sources of budget advice for independent travelers. Inexperienced travelers are likely to make occasional costly mistakes or be overcharged. Most long-term travelers splurge occasionally on a dose of luxury, such as a night in a fancy hotel. Budget for all of these things. It's much better to have money left over than to run out.

### Accommodations

Costs of places to sleep are the most difficult costs to predict, in part because travelers' choices can vary so much, even in the same city. If there is nothing available between a noisy, windowless US$5 cubicle with a sagging, vermin-infested mattress, a filthy toilet and cold shower down the hall, in a hotel that rents most of its rooms by the hour to prostitutes and their clients, and a US$150 air-conditioned room with a telephone, television, and private bath with running hot water at the Intercontinental or Intourist Hotel, which will you choose?

The example is extreme, but the situation is not unknown. More routinely, in the Third World, you'll face choices such as how much it's worth to you to have air-conditioning versus ceiling fans, a private room versus a bed in a dormitory, a private toilet and shower versus shared ones, or a Western-style (sitting) toilet versus an Asian (squatting) one.

Any one of these choices could double the price of your bed or room; together, this set of choices could make a 10-fold difference in your costs, as could the general level of cleanliness and sanitation you feel is worth paying for.

One tends to learn from travel in the poorer parts of the world that many of our perceived material needs, no matter how strongly desired, are far from essential. Most First World people are capable of making do, often quite happily, with less. One of the main determinants of one's travel costs is the extent to which one can adapt one's desires to what is locally available and affordable. A realistic self-assessment on this score should be your first step in deciding whether your spending will be at the high or low end range of travel costs in the regions you will travel.

### Food

Food is the greatest bargain of travel in the Third and Fourth Worlds and the great bugaboo of travel in the First World. While you can find beds in youth hostels in Western Europe for little more than the price of similar ones in China, many travelers find that eating in Western Europe and Japan is the most unavoidably expensive part of an around-the-world trip. Restaurant meals are labor-intensive, and it's labor that determines expense in the high-wage First World countries.

Cooking for yourself is difficult to arrange and frowned on, even forbidden, by most hotels. You can manage on bread and cheese in Western Europe, but you'll get tired of it after a while, and you'll have a hard time finding a place where you can cook yourself a hot meal (what the British advertise as self-catering). You have a good chance of finding hostels or motels with cooking facilities in the USA, Canada, Australia, and New Zealand. It's no coincidence that these are countries where travel by car is especially common, because a car makes it easier to carry one's own food and even cooking utensils.

Many people and guidebooks will advise you not to eat food from street vendors, or that the only safe food is that in hotel restaurants. These guidebooks probably aren't for you. Following this advice for months on end would be intolerably boring and excruciatingly expensive, and not possible in much of the Third and Fourth Worlds outside the biggest cities with their international hotel chains. Prices of food, like everything else, at five-star hotels in poor countries are generally higher than at similar hotels in the United States.

Most around-the-world travelers end up avoiding pricey hotel food, except where breakfast is included in the room rates, or an occasional splurge at a good hotel buffet.

You'll probably eat most of your meals at small local restaurants and street stalls. You'll probably get sick occasionally. So what? The alternative is to pay 10 times more for all your food—and to miss the best and most interesting local cuisine.

### Local Transportation and Sundries

Cost of local transportation, museum admissions, and other sundries are mostly negligible except in the First World, where they can cost as much as hostel accommodations.

Sightseeing by public mass transit in New York, Paris, London, or Tokyo, it's not hard to spend US$10 or more per person per day on subway and bus fares. Local transportation will cost much more if you ever take taxis in First World cities, as most travelers do at least occasionally, either because there is no bus going their way or because they can't find the bus stop or figure out the bus routes.

Museum admissions in the First World are typically US$5–20. (Museums in the United States are typically cheap compared to those in Western Europe.) Seeing the highlights of several museums in one day can be a pricey proposition. Admissions to theme parks such as Disneyland can be more than US$50 per person per day, not including food or drink. The only Third or Fourth World admission fees approaching this cost are the entrance fees to African wildlife preserves (which offset the income lost to agriculture by preventing farming in the parks and funding efforts to suppress poaching), the fees for some World Heritage Sites, or the fees collected for permits to climb some mountains—usually scaled according to the altitude of the peak.

## Clothing

As mentioned in the baggage section, I have yet to find a place where locally appropriate clothes weren't also those that were most readily available locally. Plan on buying most of your clothes as you travel, and budget accordingly.

Third World clothes are cheap, but—given that most of the clothes available for sale in the First World are made with Third World labor—we are already accustomed to paying little more than Third World prices for clothes. What you can get more cheaply in poor countries is custom-made clothing. In some countries, ready-made clothes convey higher status ("She's so rich she doesn't sew her own dresses; she buys them at a store."), and made-to-measure clothing is actually cheaper than ready-to-wear.

You'll need to get new clothes as you pass from one climate to another, sometimes when you pass from one cultural region to another, and when your clothes wear out. Even the sturdiest fabrics and construction wear rapidly when they are hand-washed by hand-pounding on rocks (standard operating procedure for the South Asian *dhobi* and other Third World launderers and laundresses), and the poor-quality dyes that are often used in poor countries can fade relatively quickly in the tropical sun.

## Gifts to Your Hosts and People You Meet

If you plan to stay with friends or their family, you'll probably be expected to act as a courier and perhaps to bring substantial gifts. In many countries remittances from those working outside the country are the largest source of foreign exchange, and those who return (or send emissaries) from abroad are expected to send back everything from appliances to food for those left behind.

Try to sound out your contacts in your own country, before you leave, as to what is expected or appropriate. In some countries it may be a terribly insulting faux pas to offer money to defray the costs of putting you up. If your hosts are among the local elite, even in a Third or Fourth World country, they may even be so much richer than you that nothing you could contribute would even make a difference.

In most countries, however, it would be more insulting not to offer to pay your hosts. This is most likely to be the case in the former USSR and elsewhere in the Second World. If you're in doubt, you can always offer nonmonetary gifts.

You'll have to make your own judgments, in accordance with the local mores, of what to do if your hosts decline your gifts but seem to you to be genuinely in need. Norms of hospitality in much of the world are very strong. Don't be surprised if you are offered the only milk, meat, sugar, or eggs in the house, or if the whole family sleeps on the ground outside so that you can have the only bed. Just remember that you would be expected to do likewise, should the opportunity ever arise.

Try to give gifts of real practical value. Avoid the cultural imperialism of bringing high-tech consumer goods, baubles, cosmetics, tobacco, or alcohol for gifts or barter.

## Souvenirs

The sky's the limit. Just don't get carried away and forget that you have to get them home. Knickknacks tend to seem less worth buying after you've carried them on your back for a few months.

If you plan to spend serious money on specific souvenirs—a carpet in Peshawar, Pakistan, say—price similar items before you leave home. You may be surprised to find that, in a global economy built on cheap bulk shipping, the price difference at the source is so little that it does not offset the nuisance of dragging things home.

I prefer souvenirs that aren't available at all at home. Despite the fact that books in English, especially nonfiction, are published in even the most obscure corners of the world, almost none of them are distributed in the United States. Even books from major centers of English-language scholarship, like India, are extremely hard to find in the United States. So I always come home with as many books as I can manage. Reading the thoughts of the people in places I've visited is, for me, a way to extend my intellectual journey long after my physical return.

# SAMPLE BUDGETS

I hesitate to give sample budgets at all, for fear that too many readers will look only at the trip durations and the bottom lines, adopting them wholesale. I also fear some readers will reject any realistic high-side budget for first-time travelers as excessively upscale.

These budgets are intended for relative novice travelers: more experienced travelers already know their spending rates in a particular type of country. Many people travel significantly more cheaply than these budgets, but I strongly discourage you from counting on it unless and until you have enough travel experience to be certain that you'll want to and be comfortable doing so. Per diem costs tend to be less for long-term travelers, both because the longer they spend in a place the more they learn about the local style of bargaining and ways to do things cheaply, and because they can amortize fixed costs over a longer time period.

In that spirit, here are a few estimated sample budgets. I include them to give you an idea of what a budget might look like, not to be relied on in estimating how much you will spend. Remember that all prices given in this book are likely to increase with inflation.

None of these sample budgets include the inherent expenses of traveling, such as maintaining the rent or the mortgage on a house, apartment, or storage locker in your home country; paying your health or other insurance; or payments on student loans, car loans, credit cards, or other debts. These are expenses you would have whether traveling or not, but it's obviously essential to include them in financial planning for your trip. The more you can cut back on these expenses, such as subletting your house or apartment, the more money you'll have available to spend on the direct costs of travel. Obviously, these budgets don't include the value of your time, or lost income, which are actually the largest costs of long-term travel.

Nor do these examples include any allowance for tours or guides. The occasional guide for the day, day-long sightseeing tour of a city, or excursion by hired car can probably be accommodated within these budgets. But if somewhere you plan to take a multiday guided tour, adjust your budget accordingly. A few days rafting a wilderness river; a weeklong camping safari in East African wildlife preserves; a guided climb of Mt. Kilimanjaro; a 10-day trek in the Himalayas; a weeklong excursion by jeep from Kathmandu, Nepal, into Tibet; or the minimum tour required to get a visa to country that will only give visas to those on tours—any of these could set you back US$500, quite possibly twice that, even on a budget tour.

I don't generally like tours, but there are some things, including all of those I've just listed, that you simply can't do on your own. A high percentage of even budget travelers decide to splurge when they are in a place where they have a once-in-a-lifetime opportunity. Some expensive things really are worth it. If you know you plan to safari, trek, or tour, add it to your budget. Even if you don't, try to leave yourself an allowance for occasional unexpected opportunities for guided adventures and for unexpected restrictions forcing you to do things on a tour basis that you had hoped to accomplish more cheaply on your own.

Note that these examples don't include any projection for earnings along the way. Unless you have a firm job commitment in advance, or unless you have very unusual skills or credentials that you have verified are in extraordinary demand in some specific place, don't count on traveling for any longer than you can afford with the money you have in hand when you leave. If you want to, you may be able to find work along the way. But pick-up jobs are unlikely to pay more than enough to live on.

It's easiest to find work in the First World, but the kinds of jobs that are available to travelers are generally menial jobs that pay menial wages—washing dishes, waiting on tables, picking fruit—not jobs on which you can save money toward further travels.

In the South, in a country where the average wage is a dollar a day, there are apt to be very few jobs that pay enough to support a First Worlder at even a backpacker's standard of living. In most Southern countries, you'll be competing for those elite jobs with a host of unemployed or underemployed local university graduates who are apt to have far more impressive credentials and more advanced training than you.

It's possible for native speakers of English with university degrees and/or credentials in teaching English as a foreign language to support themselves as English teachers, at a backpacker's living standard, in many countries. But it's hard work that not everyone is capable of or enjoys, and in those few countries where it pays enough to allow you to save money, employers are quite selective about who they hire. Don't count on it unless you have a definite job lined up in advance.

Finally, all of these examples include a substantial allowance for contingencies. If you're lucky, you won't need it, but you can't count on being lucky. Give yourself plenty of margin for error.

Toward the high end, here's how one backpacker's budget might look for a three-month solo trip, including 10 weeks in good local hotels in the Third World (e.g., Asia excluding Japan, Taiwan, or Singapore) and three weeks in budget hotels in the First World (e.g., Western Europe or Japan). I would consider this a budget for ample comfort (reasonably clean private rooms, first-class trains and buses) but not an American standard of luxury.

| | |
|---|---|
| Advance expenses | US$700 |
| Air tickets | US$2,200 |
| Long-distance bus and train tickets Third World (first class) | US$500 |
| Eurailpass | US$600 |

Accommodations
  Third World @ US$25/day . . . . . . . . . . .US$1,750
  First World @ US$60/day  . . . . . . . . . .US$1,200

Food
  Third World @ US$8/day . . . . . . . . . . . . US$560
  First World @ US$30/day . . . . . . . . . . . .US$600

Local transport and sundries
  Third World @ US$2/day . . . . . . . . . . . . US$140
  First World @ US$10/day . . . . . . . . . . . .US$200

Clothing . . . . . . . . . . . . . . . . . . . . . . . . .US$150

Books and maps . . . . . . . . . . . . . . . . . . . US$100

Gifts to local hosts . . . . . . . . . . . . . . . . . US$100

Souvenirs to bring home  . . . . . . . . . . . . . US$200

Contingency fund for emergencies . . . . . . .US$1,000

**Total**  . . . . . . . . . . . . . . . . . . . . . . . . **US$10,000**

For someone trying to stretch money out over a longer time, here's how another person's budget might look for a year-long trip, sharing rooms with a companion, with one month camping and/or staying in hostel dormitories in the First World (e.g., Australia), one month staying with families who take in paying guests in the Second World (Eastern and Central Europe), six months in budget guest houses in the Third World (e.g., Asia), and four months in the Fourth World (e.g., in Africa). This is a budget for patient, physically fit travelers willing to accept significant discomfort at times, to adapt to local ways of doing things, and to abandon any expectation of doing things the same way they would at home in the USA or Western Europe.

Advance expenses  . . . . . . . . . . . . . . . . . . .US$700

Air tickets . . . . . . . . . . . . . . . . . . . . . . . . US$3,500

Long-distance bus and train tickets
  Fourth World  . . . . . . . . . . . . . . . . . . . . US$200
  Third World (second-class trains) . . . . . . .US$500
  Second World . . . . . . . . . . . . . . . . . . . . US$200
  First World (mostly buses) . . . . . . . . . . . .US$400

Accommodations
  Fourth World @ US$4/day . . . . . . . . . . . .US$480
  Third World @ US$8/day . . . . . . . . . . . US$1,440
  Second World @ US$12/day . . . . . . . . . . .US$360
  First World @ US$20/day . . . . . . . . . . . . .US$600

Food
    Fourth World @ US$3/day  . . . . . . . . . . . . .US$360
    Third World @ US$6/day . . . . . . . . . . . . .US$1,080
    Second World @ US$10/day  . . . . . . . . . .US$300
    First World @ US$20/day  . . . . . . . . . . . .US$600

Local transport and sundries
    Third and Fourth Worlds @ US$2/day  . . .US$600
    Second World @ US$6/day  . . . . . . . . . . . .US$180
    First World @ US$10/day  . . . . . . . . . . . . .US$300

Clothing  . . . . . . . . . . . . . . . . . . . . . . . . . . . . .US$400

Books and maps  . . . . . . . . . . . . . . . . . . . . . US$200

Gifts to local hosts  . . . . . . . . . . . . . . . . . . . . US$300

Souvenirs to bring home  . . . . . . . . . . . . . . . US$300

Contingency fund for emergencies  . . . . . . .US$2,000

**Total**  . . . . . . . . . . . . . . . . . . . . . . . . . . **US$15,000**

Some people are surprised that the bottom lines on these budgets are as large as they are. These budgets are, however, all-inclusive. Ask people how much they spent on a trip, and most of them will overlook some of these costs.

What sort of trip might be possible for much less money? Here's a budget for a frugal traveler spending three months exclusively in the Third and Fourth Worlds, flying to several places on one continent, staying exclusively in dormitory-style guest houses or hostels or sharing a room with a companion in the cheapest local hotels, getting around by rented bicycle or local bus (never taxi), and traveling most long distances within the region by second-class train. This budget should make clear that the largest factor in the cost of your trip is in which world(s) you travel.

Advance expenses  . . . . . . . . . . . . . . . . . . . . US$500

Air tickets  . . . . . . . . . . . . . . . . . . . . . . . . . . US$1,800

Long-distance bus and
    train tickets (second class) . . . . . . . . . . . . .US$300

Accommodations @ US$5/day  . . . . . . . . . . US$450

Food @ US$4/day  . . . . . . . . . . . . . . . . . . . . US$360

Local transport and sundries @ US$1/day . . . .US$90

Clothing  . . . . . . . . . . . . . . . . . . . . . . . . . . . . .US$100

Books and maps . . . . . . . . . . . . . . . . . . . . . . US$100

Gifts to local hosts  . . . . . . . . . . . . . . . . . . . US$100

Souvenirs to bring home  . . . . . . . . . . . . . . US$200

Contingency fund for emergencies  . . . . . . .US$1,000

**Total**  . . . . . . . . . . . . . . . . . . . . . . . . . . **US$5,000**

One of the drawbacks of traveling on a low-end budget such as this is that dormitory-style accommodations are usually found only in towns and cities with substantial numbers of tourists. Unless you are willing to put up with exceptionally "rustic" accommodations, getting off the beaten track often requires staying in local hotels that, while excellent value for the price, are significantly more expensive than dorm beds in hostels in travelers' ghettoes. This budget also leaves little room for occasional short airplane flights or rides by chartered car or taxi to places that can't be reached by train or bus. A little bit more money can buy you a great deal more freedom to go where you want.

These are merely three examples, none of which may correspond to your style of travel or level of comfort, or the division of your time between more and less expensive places. They are intended to give you an idea of the kinds of things to include in your budget, not to be relied on for the bottom line.

You are likely to spend less than these budgets rather than more. In 1989, I traveled around the world for four months, sharing rooms with a companion, for a total of today's equivalent of US$4,000 per person including airfare and a Eurailpass. (We were entirely in the Third World except for two weeks in Western Europe, where we stayed with friends and relatives.) But inflation marches on, I'm cautious when it comes to making recommendations about money, and most people would rather come home with money left over than run out halfway around the world. All else being equal, I would organize the overall direction of my trip with the most expensive places at the end, so that my stay there could be cut short if my budget was running low.

Once again, the most important thing is to break down your trip according to the amounts of time you plan to spend in more and less expensive countries, as I've done here, and to estimate per diem expenses separately for each. Whether you spend two weeks or a month in Western Europe before continuing to South and Southeast Asia for the balance of a trip can make a US$1,000 difference to your total budget. Plan accordingly.

## HOW TO BRING MONEY

Financial systems are varied and unpredictable. ATM withdrawals are generally the easiest and cheapest way to get money while traveling, but you can't count on them being available. Bring both travelers checks and cash for times and places ATMs aren't available, aren't working, or have excessive fees.

## ATM Cards

Where you can find an ATM in working order that accepts your card, ATM cards are generally the cheapest way to get money while traveling. Because ATMs dispense money in local currency, an ATM withdrawal transfers money to you from your bank account back home, and converts it to local currency, in a single transaction.

You can leave most of the money you'll need for a long trip safely in your bank (or in a money-management, investment, or brokerage account with check-writing privileges) at home, even earning interest. If you don't want to leave that much in a checking account, you can probably arrange overdraft protection to automatically transfer money from your savings account to your checking account as needed to cover your checks.

Many ATMs have multilingual user interfaces. If there's nothing on the screen in a language you understand, look for the word "English," or the stars and stripes (USA) or Union Jack (UK), as the symbol for "click here for instructions in English." The major ATM networks all have directories of locations of linked ATMs on their Web sites. (See the Resource Guide.) You aren't likely to be online when you are looking for an ATM, but these directories can help give you an idea of how easy it will be to find ATMs linked to your bank in the places you are going. Are they only in the capital city, or are they in smaller places as well?

Check your bank's rules for foreign-currency ATM withdrawals carefully before you leave. Some banks impose per-transaction surcharges for foreign currency withdrawals, some don't. Some charge 3 percent above the interbank (wholesale) exchange rate, some charge only 1.5 percent (see the discussion of exchange rates in the next section).

Charges and withdrawal limits can be imposed both by your bank and by the one that owns the ATM where you withdraw the money. Some banks will reimburse fees charged by other banks to use their ATMs. If you're withdrawing money often, this can be a significant benefit.

All else being equal, it's generally cheaper to make one larger withdrawal than several smaller ones, since there are almost always per-transaction fees from one or both of the banks involved (the card issuer and the ATM owner). Get as much money at a time as you are allowed, you are comfortable carrying in cash, and you are confident you will use before having to exchange it for another currency (you lose a percentage on every currency conversion).

If you plan to use your card overseas, or at any ATMs other than those of your own bank, change your PIN (access code) to one no more than four digits long. Some ATMs only transmit the first four digits of the PIN. If your PIN is longer you won't be able to withdraw money. In the worst case, the machine could seize your card on suspicion of fraud—a huge hassle if you're halfway around the world.

ATM and debit cards have different, worse, rules for unauthorized or fraudulent usage then do credit cards. Make sure you know exactly what your maximum loss is if your card and/or PIN are stolen. For cards issued in the United States, your loss is usually limited to US$50, but only if you report any loss, theft, or suspicion of fraud to your card issuer within 48 hours. Check each of your statements carefully and immediately when you receive them. (The need to get your statements even while you're traveling, and to be able to review them immediately, is one of the largest drawbacks to carrying an ATM or debit card on a long trip.) Report any discrepancy or suspicious charge immediately, by phone and by follow-up letter by express mail. If you don't report an unauthorized charge in time, you could lose the entire contents of your account, and/or your entire credit limit.

ATM cards can't be relied on to the exclusion of other ways of accessing your money. I've seen many a traveler stranded for lack of money because they counted on being able to use a card that didn't happen to be accepted locally, or was accepted only by a bank or ATM that was closed, out of service, or out of cash. Have a backup.

## Debit Cards

Cash withdrawals on some debit cards carrying credit card logos (e.g. VISA or MasterCard) are treated as ATM withdrawals. On other similar-looking cards from different issuers, cash withdrawals are treated as "cash advances" and subject to a minimum one month's interest, which can add another 1.5 percent to your costs. Check with the bank that issued your card, before you go, to see whether your debit card is really an ATM card (good) or a credit card (bad), for purposes of cash withdrawals.

## Credit and Charge Cards

It's easy to imagine, in this era of electronic commerce, that you could set off on a trip around the world with only plastic to pay for it all. Bank card companies are fond of telling us in how many places, "worldwide," their cards are accepted. But outside the First World, credit and charge cards are of limited use for independent or budget travelers, except for large luxury splurges or emergency expenses like a hospital bill or a ticket home.

Contrary to credit-card companies' propaganda, credit cards are not widely accepted for purchases outside the First World, and almost never at any but the most expensive establishments. In a Third World country, if you have only a credit card to pay for a hotel or a meal, you are likely to be able to eat and sleep only at the most expensive hotel in town. You can get cash advances with credit cards, but those are more expensive than ATM withdrawals.

Most credit-card issuers charge per-transaction fees for foreign currency purchases. These fees are a small percentage of a large purchase, but can add up quickly if you use a credit-card for a large number of small purchases.

You can never predict which type of card will be accepted in a given place. It's a tradeoff: If you carry more types of cards (assuming you have them) you have a slightly better chance of being able to get cash advances, or charge things on your cards, in more places. But you have more cards to carry, more cards to lose, and more financial risk if your cards are lost or stolen, especially if they are stolen in a remote or inaccessible place where it's a long time before you are able to report them stolen.

## Lost or Stolen Cards

Whatever card(s) you carry, keep copies of the cards and instructions for reporting lost or stolen cards with the copies of your other vital documents, separate from the cards themselves. If your card and/or PIN are lost or stolen, report it immediately, both by phone and by follow-up letter by express mail. (Email isn't usually sufficient to protect your legal rights.)

Remember that you can't call a USA or Canadian 800, 866, 877, or 888 number, or most other national "freephone" numbers, from other countries. If the card itself only gives a "toll-free" number for reporting lost or stolen cards, check your most recent statement or call the card issuer, before you leave, to get a number that you can call from overseas.

Stolen credit cards make their way rapidly into the hands of large-scale professional criminal gangs that will run up thousands of dollars of charges within days or even hours. The sooner you report a loss or theft or your card and/or PIN, the lower your liability for unauthorized use.

Replacements for some types of cards, such as American Express cards, can be obtained while you are traveling, through bank offices overseas. Other cards may not be replaceable until you get home, which is one more reason to have a backup means of access to your funds back home, and an emergency supply of cash and travelers checks.

## Cash

Unfortunately, there is really no way to avoid carrying a significant amount of cash. USA dollars are the world's most widely accepted and easily negotiable medium of exchange.

Small denomination notes (outside the United States, pieces of paper money are referred to as "notes," not "bills") in local currencies are usually more useful and harder to find than larger notes, except in countries with collapsing currencies, where you may need a sack to carry US$20 worth of local bank notes. Moneychangers and banks usually give you your money in as few notes as possible. A rule of thumb for dealing with moneychangers: unless they hand you a huge pile of notes, hand back some of the notes they offer you and ask for smaller notes and more coins.

In a country where per capita income averages US$1 a day or less, changing a US$20 bill, or a local note of equivalent value, is like trying to change a US$100 bill at a corner store in the United States. It's possible, but it will clean out the till. Even black marketeers sometimes can't handle US$100 bills.

I'd start a lengthy around-the-world trip with at least US$100 in US$1 bills, preferably twice that many. In a pinch, you can pay for almost anything, anywhere in the world, directly in US$1 bills. You can pay in US$20 or US$100 bills too, but if that's all you have you may have to overpay grossly. If you arrive when the banks at the airport are closed, do you want to have pay US$20 for a cab ride from the airport to the city that should cost US$2?

Depending on my destinations, I'd bring perhaps US$500 more in US$5s, US$10s, and US$20s, and another US$1,000 in US$100 bills for places where the banks are particularly dysfunctional and dollars are used in parallel with the collapsed local currency.

Since 1996, the designs of USA paper money have been changing, with larger, off-center portraits and other changes to make notes harder to counterfeit. Further changes, including different colors for different denominations (the norm in other countries) are contemplated in coming years. All older designs of USA dollar notes remain in circulation and are equally valid, but in some countries banks and moneychangers may be reluctant to accept them. (There's a reason for their fears: in most countries old currency is "demonetized" and taken out of circulation, or declared worthless, when new currency designs are introduced.) Try to bring only notes in the latest design.

Wherever you are, and whatever currency you are using, insist on getting the cleanest, newest-looking notes you can. In some countries no one will accept old, torn, or dirty notes, and everyone will try to pass them off on foreigners.

It may feel strange at first to carry so much money. "I felt like a drug dealer when I first got here, walking around with all this money in my belt," the newly appointed chargé d'affaires at the USA embassy in Kazakhstan once told me. Obviously, you can't put 200 singles in a money belt. Wrap them well and disperse them through your luggage in several packets. Keep your money belt small enough not to be visible inside your clothes, and never open it in public if you can avoid doing so.

Reserve the limited space in your money belt for the real essentials that would be most difficult to replace: your passport, your immunization record ("yellow book"), your airline tickets (and any expensive rail or bus tickets), your ATM and credit card(s), a copy of your eyeglass and/or any other prescriptions, a few of your personal checks, and enough emergency cash (some in USA dollars and some in local currency) to tide you over if you are robbed of everything but your money belt.

I fold a US$100 bill up in each set of copies of my documents. After all, you should only need the copies of your documents if your money belt is stolen, in which case you will need money for at least a few days until you can get your documents replaced. For what it's worth, more people lose money belts—leaving them in hotel rooms or showers, for example—than have them stolen from under their clothes, or by robbers who strip them naked. I've never been robbed nor lost any of my tickets or essential documents. But a fair number of people have their pockets picked or have their wallets, cameras, belt packs, shoulder bags, luggage, or visible valuables stolen.

### Traveler's Checks

If you can afford to do so, bring a substantial reserve of traveler's checks in USA dollars, for places where you can't use your ATM card or the fees to use your ATM card are too high, and in case your ATM card is lost or stolen and can't be replaced until you get home.

You can get checks in major First World currencies, such as Euros or Japanese yen, but not in Third World currencies. If you will be in many countries, USA dollar checks are most widely accepted. Anywhere people know what money is worth, they know what US dollars are worth. That's not as true with any other currency, even Euros and British (UK) pounds ("sterling").

Bring primarily US$100 checks and just a few US$20 or US$50 checks. Cashing a check can be a tedious process that you won't want to do more often than necessary (it's not uncommon for it to take several hours, even at the main bank in a sizable provincial city), and many banks and money-changers charge per-check encashment fees. Thus US$20 checks are useful only if you will be in a country so briefly that you won't be spending close to US$100 before you would leave the country, which is really quite rare. In such cases it's usually easier just to change a US$20 bill than to bother with traveler's checks at all.

## MONEY TRANSFERS FROM HOME

If you have an ATM card or a credit card that can be used for a cash advance, it's easier than you may realize to have someone send you money from home. Anyone can deposit money into your bank account, and anyone can pay your credit card bill. (It's withdrawals from your account, not deposits or payments to your account, that require your signature.) It helps for the person making the deposit or payment to have a deposit slip or statement with the address and account details, but pre-pirinted deposit slips and payment coupons aren't essential. In a pinch, you can get all the necessary information by phone, and they can make a deposit or payment by mail. As soon as a deposit is cleared by your bank, you can withdraw it from any ATM worldwide with which your bank is linked. It's the cheapest (only the normal foreign-currency ATM charges) and fastest (as fast as your bank clears the deposit) way to have money transferred to yourself anywhere in the world.

Don't even think of trying to have money wired to yourself while you are traveling. Contrary to popular belief, wiring money is neither cheap nor fast nor reliable. Procedures vary enormously from place to place and bank to bank, too much so to give general advice other than not to attempt it. I've

# RISKS OF INTERNET MONEY MANAGEMENT

Internet banking, bill paying, and investment management sites offer a deceptively attractive alternative to personal assistance from a friend back home, but only at the price of bringing a computer with you or taking a serious risk by using public computers for money management.

All cybercafés and public terminals are inherently insecure, even when you're accessing a highly secure Web site. Everything you type, every mouse click, and everything you see on the screen can be, and often is, monitored and logged by the cybercafé proprietor or network administrator. Ignore anything the Web service or the cybercafé says about their security procedures. Because the data can be captured before it is encrypted for sending to the public Internet, local logging or remote monitoring over a LAN renders any Web site or browser security irrelevant. The capture of the data can be completely undetectable even to a computer security expert. Network administrators or hackers can install software to monitor other users on the LAN without the knowledge of the cybercafé.

Cybercafés, libraries, and the like install monitoring and logging software for a variety of reasons: to keep track of time online for billing; to log sites visited for market research or "data mining"; to assist in providing technical support to people who are having trouble using the computers; to prevent children from accessing adult sites; or to prevent hackers from using cybercafés as anonymous basis for attacking other computers. Or because they're bored and curious about what people are doing and want to snoop on their e-mail. Or because they are crooks.

seen too many stranded travelers whose money ran out or was stolen trying to eke out an existence in some travelers' ghetto, waiting for money to be wired from home

If you don't have an ATM, credit, or charge card, it is often faster and more reliable to have someone send you a bank check by air express (FedEx, DHL, or the like, or international postal Express Mail) than to try to have money wired. If your contact goes to a major bank or a foreign exchange broker, it's possible to get a check drawn on a bank in the country where you are, which you can cash with relative ease once you receive it. If not, the next best thing is a check in USA dollars, drawn on a major international bank whose name is likely to be recognized by banks in the country where you are. But this is a last resort, not a first one, and is still likely to take a week or more and cost a total of at least US$50 in courier charges and fees from the banks at both ends.

Suppose you were making US$1 an hour as a locally well-paid cybercafé system administrator, and noticed a traveler reviewing the US$10,000 balance in their online brokerage account. Would you be able to resist the temptation to take some of it for yourself.

If you sign in to an online banking, bill paying, or investment management site from a cybercafé, and someone later uses your password to transfer your life's savings to their account in Lithuania or Liberia, don't say I didn't warn you. Even if your password can only be used to pay a prearranged list of bills, a thief can charge things on your credit card, then use your password to pay your credit card bill before you have a chance to contest the unauthorized charges. (You lose most of your rights to contest a charge once you've paid the bill.)

It isn't easy to protect even your own computer against such "Trojan Horse" programs for remote monitoring of your online activity, but it is possible if you put the effort into it. Don't forget to guard against the risk that your computer itself will be stolen. If the thief is stupid, your computer will be fenced to someone who wants a cheap computer. If the thief is more knowledgeable, your computer will be fenced to someone who will try to use the data on it for "identity theft." Never store any financial passwords on your computer, or allow them to be stored as browser "cookies." (For more on what sort of computer to bring, and how to use it safely, see the "Practicalities" chapter of this book, and my companion volume in this series, *The Practical Nomad Guide to the Online Travel Marketplace*.)

Personally, I think the cost, weight, fragility, theft risk, complexity, and general nuisance value of lugging a laptop around the world (and having to replace it immediately if anything happens to it), far outweighs the difficulty of finding and fairly compensating a trustworthy real person to handle your essential affairs.

## CHANGING MONEY

Unless you've gotten local currency directly from an ATM, or have travelers checks in local currency, you'll need to exchange your USA dollars or other foreign currency for local currency. Usually this is necessary each time you cross an international border, although in a few "monetary unions" or "financial communities" the same currency is used in several neighboring countries. (Examples of this are the Euro and the two regional CFA Francs of Central and West Africa.)

Places to change money range from legal or illegal freelancers who approach you on the street brandishing calculators and whispering their only two words of English, "Change money?" to government and private banks and independent currency exchange offices or kiosks. Even in most English-speaking countries, signs for currency exchanges are more likely to use the French, Spanish, or Italian terms "Bureau de Change" or "Cambio" than the English "Money Exchange" or "Currency Exchange."

Don't waste too much time worrying about where and how to get the best exchange rate. While rates and fees will vary between banks, legal private moneychangers, and government agencies (I've been in at least one country where the best exchange rate was at the post office!), legal rates of exchange rarely vary by more than a few percent. Shop around a little if you don't like the first rate you are quoted, but don't get carried away. In my opinion, the differences in exchange rates are usually less important than the differences in convenience. Try to keep in mind how much money is really at stake. Is it really worth an hour's bus ride across town, or standing in lines for an extra hour, to save a dollar or two, or even 10?

The exchange rate published in the newspaper is usually the "interbank" rate used for electronic transactions involving hundreds of thousands or millions of dollars a at time. You'll never get this rate for cash, travelers check, credit or debit card, or ATM transactions. You can expect to pay 1.5 to 3 percent more than the interbank rate for credit, debit, or ATM transactions (plus any per-transaction fees from your bank for overseas or foreign-currency charges or withdrawals), and a minimum of about 4–5 percent above the interbank rate for cash or travelers check conversions. Worst-case retail rates for cash or travelers checks, especially with captive markets (e.g. when there is only one moneychanger at the airport or the border when you arrive) can be up to 10 percent above the interbank rate.

The difference between the interbank buying and selling rates is very small—the small percentage margin is made up for by the huge size of the transactions for which the interbank rate is used. So an easy way to figure out the margin being charged for cash or travelers check conversion is to divide the "spread" between the buying and selling rates in half. If the sign in the Cambio lists the "buying" rate for dollars at €1=USD0.950, and the "selling" rate at €1=USD1.050, you can assume that the interbank rate is halfway in between at 1.000. Thus the Cambio is making a reasonable 5 percent margin on both buying and selling transactions.

On the other hand, suppose the buying rate for dollars (USD) is US$1=5,100 Zambian Kwacha (ZMK), and the selling rate is 1,000 Kwacha=US$0.2325. If you don't know the interbank rate, how can you tell if this is a good rate? The selling rate, ZMK1000=USD0.2325, is equivalent to USD1=ZMK4300. So the interbank rate is presumably about USD1=ZMK(4,300+5,100)/2=ZMK4,700, and the moneychanger's margin is an unpleasant (4,700-4,300)/4,700=8.5 percent. Buy or sell your Kwacha elsewhere, if you can.

Simply put, the smaller the difference between the buying and selling rates (converted into the same terms), the smaller the moneychanger's margin and the better the deal. If the math seems confusing, practice until it becomes second nature, as this technique enables you to evaluate exchange-rate offers without knowing anything about the "official" or interbank rate.

The "black market," where one exists, is by definition illegal. The difference between the legal and black market exchange rates is directly proportional to the risks of black marketeering. The more money you stand to gain by changing money illegally, the more dangerous it is bound to be.

If the black market rate is only slightly better than the bank rate, that probably means that the black market is only nominally illegal, and fairly safe, although you can never complain to the police if you are shortchanged or defrauded by a black marketeer. In such cases the main issue is probably convenience or availability, rather than the small difference in rates. It isn't necessarily any easier to change money, much less cash a traveler's check, on the street than at a bank. I don't usually bother with the black market in places like this.

Where there's an extreme difference between the legal and black market rates, you can take it for granted that black marketeering is severely punished. In some countries you can get 100 times more local currency units for a dollar on the black market than at a bank, but it's a capital offense, for both the customer and the trader. On the other hand, such countries are frequently too expensive for budget travelers unless they change money on the black market. Police know this, of course, and foreign backpackers in such countries are under constant suspicion and scrutiny for black marketeering. Unscrupulous locals can also make good money in rewards from the police by informing on foreigners, even setting them up or framing them, for changing money illegally. Informing or entrapment may be more profitable and less risky than actual black marketeering. You have to be extremely careful and discreet, and if possible, avoid dealing with strangers.

Most countries fall at one or the other extreme. Least common is the situation where the black market rate is substantially but not inordinately higher than the legal rate, and black marketeering is only moderately risky (punishable only by a moderate fine, for example, rather than by imprisonment or flogging). Make your own decision, but at least be selective about who you deal with, and where, and be conscious of the risks and benefits at stake.

Expatriate foreigners who live in a country are often the best people to consult about whether to change money on the black market, how risky it is, or how to do it most safely. At least you can ask them about the black market with little risk that they will turn you in or set you up to be arrested or ripped off. If it is worth dealing with the black market, expats may be able to refer you to reliable contacts of theirs, such as local businesspeople, with whom you can change money much more safely than with strangers on the street. Failing any contacts with expats, ask at your hotel, or at a restaurant or shop where you have established a relationship, for advice on where and with whom to change money.

Banks and moneychangers generally only change paper notes (bills), not coins. Try not to have any coins left over when you leave a country, or you could be stuck with a pocket full of expensive souvenirs. The United States is extremely unusual in using paper money instead of coins for denominations as small as US$1. In the UK, for example, notes smaller than £10 (about US$16) are rarely seen, and £1 (US$1.60) and £2 (US$3.20) coins are common. Even many Third World countries have coins worth more than any coin in common use in the United States, and your pocket change can easily be worth US$20.

If you have coins left at the end of your stay in the country that you don't want to save for souvenirs or future visits, and that the money changers won't take, you can sometimes exchange them with travelers headed in the opposite direction. On the other hand, if you arrive in a country when all the money changers are closed, you can often find a departing traveler, or a returning local, to sell you enough local currency to tide you over until you get to a bank or currency exchange.

# MANAGING YOUR FINANCES WHILE YOU ARE ON THE ROAD

While you might wish to ignore what's happening back home, life, death, and taxes will all go on. If you are going away for more than a month, you'll do well to find someone to handle the essentials of your affairs while you're gone.

There are ways to take care of most things, if you have to, on your own. But none of them is really a substitute for a friend at home you can call on from time to time, or in an emergency—someone who can hold your mail for you, pay an occasional bill, send in a request for an extension of time to file your tax return (completed and signed in advance), or pass on messages in an emergency.

Most long-term travelers find someone to do these sorts of things for them, most often a parent, child, sibling, or other close friend. If there is anything this person might need to pay for on your behalf (there usually is), you'll need either to leave some blank signed checks, open a joint bank account, or give some sort of power of attorney. Signed blank checks are the most common method for trips of a couple of months; joint bank accounts are most often shared with an immediate family member and are most common for longer trips. You might also want to rent and give access to a safe deposit box with the documents such as your birth certificate, in case of emergency such as needing to replace all your identification papers if they are lost or stolen.

Try to make things as easy as possible for your contact and agent back home, and don't ask for any more than is really essential. Go over what you want done, and make sure you both understand clearly what is expected. Leave simple, clear, written instructions and lists. ("If such-and-such arrives in the mail, do this with it.") Make sure the contact knows where to find any papers or documents that might be necessary, such as your will or insurance policy. Leave a complete set of copies of your documents: tickets, passport, any visas, vaccination certificates, credit or charge cards, driver's license, international driver's license, traveler's check receipts, eyeglass prescription, and any pharmaceutical prescriptions. Leave complete information on anyone you might want contacted in an emergency. Leave as complete an itinerary and information on how you can be contacted as is possible.

If you rely primarily on e-mail, you may want to get an extra e-mail address for emergency use only, known only to your emergency contact and your travel agent. A burst of spam, an out-of-control mailing list loop or vacation-message error, a message with an oversized attachment, or a thief trying to delay your efforts to report the theft could fill up your regular e-mail box and prevent you from getting urgent new messages.

Most people who travel for six months or more do have to call someone back home for something at some point. (I know because, as a travel agent, I hear from travelers' parents, siblings, or friends, acting as intermediaries, every few days.) Most people underestimate the importance of a contact back home—I know I did on my first trip—and the pressure put on the contact in an emergency. Something always happens that you forgot to plan for or didn't anticipate. It might be small, but it's still essential. Be appreciative. Reward your contact. Ask before you leave what they might like brought back, and bring it. A dinner out— the best you can afford—before you go and when you get home is an excellent demonstration of gratitude. If you had to call on your friend's help, consider giving a weekend getaway as compensation. Without someone willing to help you out, you'll have a much harder time traveling for long periods of time.

# "Bon Voyage!"

## SOME PARTING ADVICE

This book may seem like an encyclopedia of potential pitfalls. To some extent it is. But it isn't meant to discourage, dissuade, or scare you. If I haven't written much about the fun components of this sort of travel, it's because they are the easy aspects, which come naturally.

No one needs to read a how-to book on the appropriate use of a US$3-a-day bungalow on a beautiful tropical beach, a US$5-a-night cabin in a secluded village at the foot of 7,500- meter (25,000 foot) mountains, or a US$10 suite in a grand old colonial hotel in the center of one of the world's biggest and most cosmopolitan cities. You only need help and advice with the hard parts.

Travel itself is the easy part. On the whole, most people find travel easier than they had expected. Most of the things they worry about don't turn out to be problems. The difficult part of many trips is the preparation for travel, rather than anything that happens once you hit the road. For a lot of people, including myself, the most difficult step toward taking a big trip is deciding to do it in the first place. Everything else is easy by comparison. You'll make mistakes, but so what? Every traveler does. Don't worry.

The biggest travel mistake you could make, in my opinion, would be not to travel around the world, at least once in your life, if you have a chance.

Similarly, if I've talked a lot about learning, that's because learning while traveling is so much easier than learning from afar, not because it's hard work. I learned more in my first three months of world travel than in three years of college at the University of Chicago. College was also more work and less fun, even for someone like me who liked school.

You'll learn the most, and have the best time, if you travel with an open mind. My goal for my first trip around the world was to learn the meaning of my ignorance. I wanted to find out just how much I could trust my own world view, how much was "truth" and how much the product of my perspective as an American. I still think it was a good approach.

It's better to think about questions to ask than to think about what answers you expect. You'll find out what's there when you get there; if you already knew what you'd find, you wouldn't need to travel to find it. There'll be time enough for evaluation and conclusions when you get home.

Those who neither ask questions nor listen to the answers pre-ordain themselves to learn nothing. I'm amazed by people who travel seeing only an image of the destination they formed well before their arrival, oblivious to anything inconsistent with their preconceptions.

I've sent thousands of people around the world, and met many more through my seminars and writing. A few had to cut short their planned trips because of injuries from car or bus crashes, family emergencies, or (more rarely) illness. But I can count on one hand those of my clients who came home early because they weren't having fun, or because they were overwhelmed by Third World travel. It's different —that's part of its interest—and it's impossible to know what it's like until you've experienced it. But most people who travel far afield find the process among the most enjoyable and rewarding experiences of their lives.

Finally, don't forget the obvious: travel is fun. Big fun. Travel to distant and different places is an enjoyable fantasy for almost everyone. If there's one thing that I hope you've learned from this book, it's that travel doesn't have to remain a fantasy. A trip around the world is not just a dream but one that becomes a reality for thousands of people every year. Whether your dream is a trip around the world, a first trip abroad, or any big trip, I hope reading this book will not be just an armchair journey but a step toward making your travel dreams come true.

*Bon voyage.*

"Let's go somewhere," Ben said one evening as they squatted by the river peacefully with the stars deepening overhead. "I'm tired of doing just chores all the time. I'm ready for something else…"

"There's too much work to do just now…"

"Well, I guess there's as much work here as anywhere. No more'n anywhere else."

"But how would you come to know about that? If you hadn't been other places?"

"You don't have to go off nowhere else to know you're going to have to work."

"Maybe some places you sit on the beach just waiting for coconuts to fall in your lap. Reading a book and just waiting."

"Reading's work, I guess, though. Most of it is, anyhow." Aidan adjusted his weight a little and hawked spit into the river.

"Well, anyway," he sighed. "That's the thing with work. You just pitch right in and do it."

—David Guterson, *East of the Mountains*

# "_Where_
## Do I Go from
### Here?"

# A RESOURCE
# GUIDE FOR
# T R A V E L
# PLANNING &
# PREPARATION

This is a selective and highly idiosyncratic list. I've gone further out of my way to include things I think you'll not find mentioned elsewhere than to include the things you'll probably have thought of, or heard of, already. Some of the suggested background reading may seem heavy and academic, but I've tried to pick resources accessible to general readers.

I've tried to list publications and writers from the regions described, rather than by outside observers. Lest there be any doubt, the editorial content of all of the publications listed below is in the English language, except in rare cases as noted; all addresses not otherwise identified by country are in the United States.

All books listed here, even those that are out of print, should be available through your local public library. If they don't have them, they can request them for you on inter-library loan. Independent bookstores can and will special-order any book in print, usually with no obligation. For out-of-print books, check with local independent used book stores, or the Advanced Book Exchange catalog of used books available from independent dealers worldwide at http://www.abebooks.com.

The current version of this resource guide is available on the *Practical Nomad* Web site at http://www.practicalnomad.com, so check there for updates if you can't find any of these resources at the addresses in this chapter. Your feedback on this list and your suggestions for additions, deletions, and changes for the next edition will be welcomed.

## GETTING TIME TO TRAVEL

*Redefining Corporate Sabbaticals for the 1990s* • **by Helen Axel**
ISBN 0-8237-0453-X • 1992, 44 pp • The Conference Board • 845 3rd Ave., New York, NY 10022-6679 • tel. +1-212-759-0900, fax +1-212-980-7014 • http://www.conference-board.org

Based on a survey of employers in the United States on their sabbatical and related employment-leave policies. Outlines a variety of types of formal and informal sabbatical programs, with examples. Also discusses the benefits to businesses of sabbatical programs. The Conference Board is a highly respected business membership organization, and this report may be just the sort of ammunition you need to help convince your employer to grant you time off.

*Six Months Off: How to Plan, Negotiate, and Take the Break You Need without Burning Bridges or Going Broke* • **by Hope Dlugozima, James Scott, and David Sharp** • ISBN 0-8050-3745-4 • 1996, 252 pp Henry Holt, New York

Equal parts empowerment, examples, and practical advice for sabbatical-takers. Especially good chapters on "Overcoming the Big Buts," "Negotiating for a Sabbatical," and "How to Use a Break to Jump-Start Your Career."

*Take Back Your Time: Fighting Overwork and Time Poverty in America*
**edited by John de Graaf** • ISBN 1-57675-254-3 • 2003, 258 pp
Berrett-Koehler Publishers, San Francisco • http://www.timeday.org

A wide-ranging anthology on what's wrong with our lack of vacation and rest, and what we can do about it. Contributors range from labor activists like Joe Robinson (see *Work to Live*, below) to environmentalists, psychologists, and exponents of voluntary simplicity. The emphasis is on collective political organizing to reclaim our time, and the demand for minimum guaranteed vacation. But there are also lots of suggestions for individual action as well as arguments and evidence to persuade your boss that workers who get enough time off—including longer vacations and sabbaticals—will be more productive. "Take back your time... because time is more than money."

*Time Off from Work: Using Sabbaticals to Enhance Your Life While Keeping Your Career on Track* • **by Lisa Angowski Rogak**
ISBN 0-471-31067-0 • 1994, 209 pp • John Wiley & Sons, New York

Includes lots of good stories and case studies from sabbatical-takers.

*Work to Live: The Guide to Getting a Life* • **by Joe Robinson**
ISBN 0-399-52850-4 • 2003, 318 pp • Perigee Books / Penguin Putnam, New York • http://www.timeday.org

Joe Robinson has done more than anyone else in the USA to call attention to the fact that "Europeans get six weeks off"—minimum, by law—"and we don't." What's more, he's trying to do something about it, through the "Work to Live" campaign for mandatory minimum vacation allowances which he began as publisher of a travel magazine and continues in this book. Best of all, he has loads of concrete advice on how to understand and overcome the fear and guilt that keep us from asking for, or simply taking, more time to do the things we really want to do—including travel. Insightful and empowering; possibly the most important book of the year for working people in the USA.

# BACKGROUND READING

## World Atlases

No single atlas is best for every purpose. Here are my recommendations for large format, one-volume atlases, for use in world travel planning. If you don't want to pay the price of the current edition, consider getting a heavily discounted copy of the previous edition from a used book store or library discard sale: a good 2-year-old large-format atlas can be more useful, and cheaper, than the current edition of a lesser atlas, or one less suitable for travel planning. Note that each of the publishers of the atlases listed below also publishes other atlases, usually in smaller formats, with confusingly similar titles.

*Oxford Atlas of the World* • ISBN 0195219198 (hardcover) • 10th edition
2002, 448 pp (38cm x 29cm, 15" x 11.5") • Oxford University Press, Oxford, UK

Possibly the best value for the money of any currently published one-volume English-language atlas. Eurocentric in coverage, but not inordinately so.

*DK Millennium World Atlas: A Portrait of the Earth in the Year 2000*
ISBN 0789446049 (hardcover) • 1999; 528 pp (49cm x 32cm, 19" x 12.5")
DK Publishing, New York

A strong alternative to the Oxford atlas for travel planning. Unlike most atlases, this one covers the Third World in the same detail as the First World. Easy to read, with excellent computer-generated depiction of landforms to help you visualize where you'll be going. Much weaker on place names, many of which appear to be taken from air navigation charts: often they are inconsistent with local or standard usage and spelling.

*National Geographic Atlas of the World* • ISBN 0-7922-7528-4
(paperback) • 7th Ed. 1999; 260 pp (46cm x 30cm, 18" x 12") • National
Geographic Society, Washington, DC

Extremely detailed, with the best gazetteer of any one-volume English-language atlas. But covers North America and Western Europe in much more detail than the rest of the world, and emphasizes political borders over physical geography. Probably better for reference than for travel planning. Discounts are often available to subscribers to *National Geographic* magazine.

(See also the map suppliers listed below under "Maps, Guidebooks, and Gear.")

## Global Surveys and References

*CIA World Factbook* • Central Intelligence Agency (United States)
http://www.odci.gov/cia/publications/factbook/

A few pages of factoids about each country of the world, as seen by the Central Intelligence Agency of the United States. You'll find lots of pointers to this on the Internet, but it's really too limited to be much use for developing understanding or making travel decisions. I guess any *real* intelligence is kept classified.

*Country Studies* and *Area Handbooks* • Federal Research Division, Library
of Congress (United States) • http://lcweb2.loc.gov/frd/cs

Book-length *Country Studies* for individual countries and *Area Handbooks* for regions of smaller countries were prepared and updated through 1998 by the Federal Research Division of the Library of Congress. Although they are no longer being maintained, these were— and for many regions still are—the most detailed unclassified world references available from any USA government agency. Full text of all titles published since 1986 is available on the

Internet; older volumes can be found in many libraries. "Most books in the series deal with a particular foreign country, describing and analyzing its political, economic, social, and national security systems and institutions, and examining the interrelationships of those systems and the ways they are shaped by cultural factors. Each study is written by a multidisciplinary team of social scientists [generally academics on government contracts]. The authors seek to provide a basic understanding of the observed society, striving for a dynamic rather than a static portrayal. Particular attention is devoted to the people who make up the society, their origins, dominant beliefs and values, their common interests and the issues on which they are divided, the nature and extent of their involvement with national institutions, and their attitudes toward each other and toward their social system and political order." These books provide an introduction to the political and economic status of the country and the background to current events (from the perspective, of course of the government and military of the United States) that is often conspicuously absent from most literature intended for tourists. Current academic texts on the country or region, though sometimes harder to find, are usually more informative and acknowledge more diverse points of view.

## Human Rights Watch

**United States** • 350 5th Ave., 34th Fl., New York, NY 10118-3299 • tel. +1-212-290-4700, fax +1-212-736-1300 • hrwatchnyc@hrw.org http://www.hrw.org

**UK** • 2nd Floor, 2–12 Pentonville Rd., London N1 9HF, UK • tel. +44-20-7713-1995, fax +44-20-7713-1800 • hrwatchuk@hrw.org

**EU** • Rue Van Campenhout 15, 1000 Brussels, Belgium • tel. +32-2-732-2009, fax +32-2-732-0471 • hrwatcheu@skynet.be

HRW publishes intermittent country and issue reports on human rights crises around the world, as well as an annual *World Report* summarizing general trends and issues and surveying countries with particular human rights problems. Politically biased, to be sure, but less so than, say, the USA government's annual *Country Reports on Human Rights*. A good starting point for information about human rights in countries you plan to visit.

## International Affairs Resources from the World Wide Web
**Virtual Library** • http://www.vlib.org/InternationalAffairs.html

The WWW Virtual Library is a nonprofit volunteer project that exemplifies the cooperative knowledge sharing of the early Internet. The International Affairs section is one of the best sources of links to academic sites about world regions, countries, and issues, many of them maintained as labors of love and/or teaching resources by academic experts on the respective places.

**Material World: A Global Family Portrait** • by **Peter Menzel**
ISBN 0-87156-437-8 (hardcover), ISBN 0-87156-430-0 (paperback) • 1994, 255 pp • Sierra Club Books, San Francisco

In each of 30 countries, an "average" family is photographed in front of their living space, with all of their material possessions spread out in view. Each of these "big pictures" is reproduced as a large, glossy color spread, accompanied by half a dozen pages of background notes, statistics, stories, and smaller photos of the family, their country, and the activities of their daily lives. Also available in a CD-ROM edition, but the photographs in the printed book convey much more beauty and detail than the video images on the CD-ROM. Recommended for all world travelers, even those who never leave their armchairs. Also available in the same spirit, although without the country-by-country format: *Women in the Material World*.

**Minority Rights Group International** • 379 Brixton Rd., London SW9 7DE, UK • tel. +44-20-7978-9498, fax +44-20-7738-6265 minorityrights@mrgmail.org • http://www.minorityrights.org • books distributed in the United States by Independent Publishers Group, 814 N. Franklin St., Chicago, IL 60610 • tel. 800-888-4741 (USA only) or +1-312-337-0747 • frontdesk@ipgbook.com • http://www.ipgbook.com

An international human rights organization and registered charity in the UK, Minority Rights Group International is primarily a publisher of topical books and reports on ethnic, linguistic, religious, and social minorities and on thematic issues such as refugees and indigenous peoples. What the tourist board won't tell you about whomever the government of a country you are going to doesn't like.

**The State of the World Atlas** • by **Dan Smith**
ISBN 0140514465 • 6th edition, 1999 • Viking Penguin, New York

World statistics, presented in easily read map form, on everything from population, language, and other demographics to economic resource flows and patterns of human rights abuses. Cheaper and easier to find than *The World Guide,* but not nearly as comprehensive or detailed. Check for the most recent edition.

**State of the World** • by the **Worldwatch Institute**
ISBN 0-393-05173-0 • 2003 edition, 241 pp • W.W. Norton, New York
Worldwatch Institute, 1776 Massachusetts Ave. NW, Washington, DC 20036 tel. 888-544-230 (publication orders from the United States only), +1-202-452-1999, fax +1-202-296-7365 • wwpub@worldwatch.org (publication orders) or worldwatch@worldwatch.org (general inquiries and correspondence) • http://www.worldwatch.org

Annual book-length collections of essays and research reports on regions and issues in "progress toward a sustainable society." Different topics are covered each year, and many of the articles are also available as separate pamphlets.

Worth browsing in a library; see the Web site, or write for a catalog of topical monographs.

**The Statesman's Yearbook: The Politics, Cultures, and Economies of the World** • ISBN 0-333-98096-4 • 139th edition, 2003, 2060 pp • Palgrave Macmillan, New York

The standard, and best, Northern reference work on the countries of the world. Authoritative-seeming but hopelessly Eurocentric and Northern in perspective and selection of details, despite some interesting statistics. Expensive. Not recommended except as a secondary reference to complement *The World Guide* (listed below), but it will tell you —if you don't know already—what, if any, significance a particular part of the South holds for the North.

**Tourism Offices Worldwide Directory** • http://www.towd.com

Not comprehensive, but a useful aid to finding government tourist information offices. The emphasis is on those located in the United States, and/or that have a presence on the Internet, but some others are listed as well. Just don't assume it doesn't exist if you don't find it here. Minimal advertising, and no commercial listing for travel agencies, tour operators, etc.—only government agencies.

**The World Guide** • ISBN 1-869847-72-5 • 10th English-language print edition, 2001–2002, 612 pp • 3rd multilingual (English/Spanish) CD-ROM edition, 2001-2002 • Instituto del Tercer Mundo, Montevideo, Uruguay http://www.guiadelmundo.org.uy/index_e.html • English-language edition distributed by New Internationalist Publications, London, UK • ni@newint.org http://www.newint.org

Earlier editions were entitled *The World: A Third World Guide*; the revised title reflects the reality that this is not just a guide to the South but a guide to the North as well, but as seen from the South. Compiled by a consortium of Third World journalists, this encyclopedia/almanac is the first place I turn for information on a country or place in the news with which I'm not familiar. The CD-ROM includes the complete text of the book, plus Amnesty International country reports on human rights, plus a graphical and cartographic interface for searching, analyzing, and displaying current and historical statistical data on the countries of the world. It's an invaluable learning tool, and belongs in every school with multimedia computers, but the book is more appropriate for most home users. (Don't expect any photos, sound, or multimedia on the CD-ROM.) Recent editions have gotten better and more affordable, and distribution of the World Guide has improved greatly. The book is the single best one-volume reference about the world; if you buy one expensive book, sight unseen, on the strength of my recommendation, make it this one.

**WorldSkip.com** • http://www.worldskip.com

A compendium of world news and information, including articles in English from local newspapers and other sources around the world. Parts of the Web site require a paid subscription, but much of it is still (as of this writing) free.

*World Travel Guide* • http://www.worldtravelguide.net • Columbus Press, London, UK • tel. +44-20-7417-0700, fax +44-20-7417-0710

The best of a bad lot of destination references for travel agents, this Web site can spare you collecting brochures to find out the most popular seasons to visit and things to see and do in different countries. It also has a useful (although not authoritative) compilation of visa and onward-ticket requirements for visitors to each country holding passports from the United States, Canada, UK, EU, Australia, and Japan. And its summary climate graphs are a model of clarity and ease of use. The print and CD-ROM editions, intended and priced for use by travel agents, also include listings and ads from local tour operators in other countries. But those most likely to be listed, or to advertise, are the largest and most expensive. See the Web site for other reference products for travel agents from Columbus Press.

## Southern Perspectives on the World

**Apex Press** • Council on International and Public Affairs • 777 United Nations Plaza, Suite 3C, New York, NY 10017 • tel./fax 800-316-2739 (United States only) or +1-914-271-6500 • cipany@igc.apc.org • http://www.cipa-apex.org

A nonprofit publisher, importer, and distributor of books on global issues from predominantly Southern perspectives. Well-annotated catalog on the Web site. Highly recommended.

*Asia and Western Dominance: A History of the Vasco da Gama Epoch of Asian History, 1498–1945* • by **K.M. Panikkar** • reprinted 1993, 350 pp • The Other Press, 607 Mutiara Majestic, 15 Jalan Othman, 46000 Petaling Jaya, Malaysia • tel. +60-3-7781-3197

Originally published in 1953 in London and reprinted in 1969 in the United States, this book was reissued most recently for the 500th anniversary of Vasco da Gama's arrival in Asia. A history, by an Indian scholar and diplomat, of the role of Europeans in Asia. The best starting point for Europeans traveling to Asia who want to understand how—in the context of the Europeans who have gone before them—they are likely to be viewed by the Asians they meet. Not currently in print in America or Europe (although there are some overseas distributors for the Malaysian edition), but you can probably find one of the older UK or USA editions in a used bookstore or in a library.

*Dark Victory: The United States, Structural Adjustment, and Global Poverty* by **Walden Bello**, with **Shea Cunningham** and **Bill Rau** ISBN 0-9350-2861-7 • 2nd edition, 1999, 160 pp • Institute for Food and

Development Policy ("Food First"), Oakland, CA • foodfirst@foodfirst.org
http://www.foodfirst.org

An overview of neocolonialism in the "post-Cold War" world. One of the first and most important books to articulate the critique of "globalization" that now dominates North-South discourse. Dr. Bello is a Philippine-American sociologist, activist, and journalist, and executive director of Food First, a research institute on hunger, democracy, and sustainable development. A concise introduction, though still somewhat academic. Those interested in more recent and detailed explorations of related themes may want to browse the rest of the Food First book catalog on their Web site.

### Glimpses of World History • by Jawaharlal Nehru
ISBN 19-561323-6 • first published 1934–35, Kitabistan, Allahabad, India
latest printing 1995, Jawaharlal Nehru Memorial Fund, 992 pp • distributed by
Oxford University Press, New Delhi, India (and other offices worldwide)

"Being further letters to his daughter, written in prison, and containing a rambling account of history for young people." Quite literally the text for a home-schooling course in world history (for Nehru's daughter, Indira Gandhi), and eminently suitable as such even today. Written from memory (and thus emphasizing themes, trends, and ideas rather than dates and details) by the greatest statesman of the 20th century, a Renaissance man and exceptional writer, and the person who, in founding the Non-Aligned Movement, first articulated the entitlement of the majority of the world's people to the dominant voice in world affairs. I could not imagine a better window into the Southern perspective on classical history. Best read in conjunction with Nehru's *The Discovery of India* and *The Unity of India* (a classic of anti-imperialism and anti-fascism) and his autobiography, *Toward Freedom*.

### Imperialism, the Highest Stage of Capitalism • by V.I. Lenin
Foreign Languages Publishing House, Moscow, Russia (and many other editions)

The failure of Stalinist government in Russia notwithstanding, Lenin's 1933 analysis of imperialism remains prevalent in most formerly colonized countries— which is to say, most of the world and its people. This may still be the single book by a Northerner that most influences Southern thought on North-South issues.

### Intermediate Technology Bookshop
http://www.developmentbookshop.com (online ordering, worldwide shipping)
http://www.developmentbookshop.com/retail.htm (Central London retail
storefront) • orders@itpubs.org.uk • 103-105 Southampton Row (tube stop:
Russell Square), London WC1B 4HL, UK • tel. +44-20-7436-9761, fax +44-
20-7436-2013

"Europe's leading development bookshop" offers a wide selection of books on

cultural, educational, environmental, economic, and political development—
not just technology.

**Modern Times Bookstore** • 888 Valencia St. (between 19th and 20th
Streets), San Francisco, CA 94110 • tel. +1-415-282-9246 • office
@moderntimesbookstore.com • http://www.moderntimesbookstore.com

Not just my favorite neighborhood bookstore but truly one of the most multicultural and international bookstores on the Left Coast of the United States.

*Neo-Colonialism, the Last Stage of Imperialism* • by **Kwame**
**Nkrumah** • first edition 1966, 280 pp • last reissued by International
Publishers, New York/Panaf Books, London, UK, 1974

By the leader of the independence movement and first prime minister of
independent Ghana, and one of the founders of Pan-Africanism and the
Non-Aligned Movement. A widely read analysis of how the former colonial
powers maintained their economic control even after the nominal political
independence of their former colonies—a key issue still throughout the
South, and especially in Africa.

*Non-Violent Resistance (Satyagraha)* and *Sarvodaya (The Welfare of All)*
by **M.K. Gandhi** • 1951 and 1954 • Navajivan Trust, Ahmedabad, India
(and other editions) • United States edition of Non-Violent Resistance (Satyagraha) published by Schocken Books, New York, 1961

Gandhi and Mao were the two great mass leaders of the world's two most
populous countries. India's government today is no more "Gandhian" than
China's is "Maoist," but Maoism and Gandhism remain the poles in relation
to which all other organizational theories of mass action and power are still
considered. More Northerners have heard of Satyagraha, but Gandhi considered the "constructive program" of Sarvodaya at least equally important.
Gandhi's advocacy of environmentalism (what would come to be known,
decades after his assassination, as "deep ecology"), appropriate technology,
and sustainability, long overlooked, has in recent years come to be seen as
prescient by more and more Northerners and Southerners alike. Essential to
an understanding of the dynamics of power and the theory of "development"
in the world today.

*Quotations from Chairman Mao Zedong* • by **Mao Zedong**
**(transliterated "Mao Tse-Tung" in earlier editions)**
ISBN 083512388X • Foreign Languages Press, Beijing, China (and many other
editions, most recently from China Books, San Francisco.)

Everyone has heard of this book, but few Northerners actually read it. Mao
may have fallen from grace in China, but his theories of tactics and organization have influenced the armies and national liberation movements that now
rule many countries.

**Revolution Books** • 9 West 19th St., New York, NY 10011
tel. +1-212-691-3345

Run by the Revolutionary Communist Party, and burdened with far too much Marx, Lenin, Mao Zedong, and Bob Avakian (don't ask) thought for my taste. But get beyond that, and this shop turns out to have one of the best selections in New York of literature from the Third and Fourth Worlds and about North-South issues.

### Transformation and Survival: In Search of Humane World Order
**by Rajni Kothari** • ISBN 81-202-0200-7 (Ajanta Publications, Delhi, India), ISBN 0-945257-17-1 (New Horizons Press, New York) • 1988, 220 pp

Rajni Kothari wrote the book on Indian politics—his *Politics In India* was long the standard academic text —but he is better known as one of the foremost Southern thinkers and writers on world affairs: founding fellow of the Centre for the Study of Developing Societies, the founding editor of the international journal *Alternatives*, and activist in the Lokayan group (recipient of the Right Livelihood Award or "Alternative Nobel Prize"). This collection of essays is an accessible but sophisticated analysis of the state of the world and its problems, as seen from the South. Influential and highly recommended, as are any of Kothari's works, especially the more recent ones such as *Poverty: Human Consciousness and the Amnesia of Development.*

### Upside Down: A Primer for the Looking-Glass World • by Eduardo
**Galeano (translated by Mark Fried)** • ISBN 0-312-42031-5 • paperback edition 2001, 358 pp • Picador USA, New York

An amusing, accessible, yet serious, "program of study" on the state of the world: North-South relations, globalization and imperialism, and the world as seen from South. (See below under "The Americas" for the same author's works on issues more specific to that region.)

### The West and the Rest of Us: White Predators, Black Slavers, and
**the African Elite • by Chinweizu** • ISBN 039-4480-51-1, 1st edition 1975, 520 pp, Random House, United States • ISBN 978-2651-00-1 (hardcover), ISBN 978-2651-01-X (paperback), 1987 revised edition, Pero Press, Lagos, Nigeria • printed in the UK and distributed outside Nigeria by SUNDOOR, BCM Box 4658, London WC1N 3XX, UK

One of the most thought-provoking treatises on North-South relations and neocolonialism from a Southern point of view. Chinweizu is a Nigerian journalist, poet, critic, and occidentalist. This is not a book about Africa, or the South generally, but about the self-described "West," from the perspective of what it has meant to the rest of the world. European, including European-American, readers may feel maligned and/or threatened by Chinweizu's blunt criticism, but his are views they will encounter often if they travel in the South. One of those books that's more widely talked about than actually read; a hard book to find, but one worth searching out. Polemical and focuses on the historical roots of current problems.

**Decolonising the African Mind** • by Chinweizu
ISBN 978-2651-03-6 (hardcover), ISBN 978-2651-02-8 (paperback) • 1987
Pero Press, Lagos, Nigeria

The sequel to *The West and Rest of Us*, this is a collection of more forward-looking essays on Africa's post-independence relationship with colonialism.

## The Ecology of Travel and Tourism

Travelers are not alone: we are part of the culture of tourism. We travel in isolation neither from each other nor from the places and peoples we visit. Understanding the patterns of tourism and its impacts on both physical and cultural ecologies, especially if we wish our travels to be responsible and sustainable, requires an essentially anthropological approach. Yet for the world's largest industry, and one that involves hundreds of millions of people, tourism is remarkably little studied as a sociological or anthropological phenomenon.

**Beyond the Beach: An Ethnography of Modern Travellers in Asia**
**by Klaus Westerhausen** • ISBN 974-4800-09-7• 2002, 272 pp • White Lotus Press, GPO Box 1141, Bangkok 10501, Thailand • ande@loxinfo.co.th
http://www.thailine.com/lotus • http://www.geocities.com/klaus_westerhausen

A field study by a long-term traveler turned anthropologist, but not academic in writing style. Focuses on the longest-term and lowest-budget of travelers, so not representative of all independent travelers. But remarkably successfully in depicting long-term travelers as a subculture with geographically scattered enclaves and ghettoes, and in putting forward the case for independent travel as potentially more sustainable and responsible than mass package tourism. Both the book and the author's Web site have excellent bibliographies of the limited academic literature on backpacker travel.

**Errant Journeys: Adventure Travel in a Modern Age** • by David Zurick
ISBN 0-292-79806-7 • 1995, 206 pp • University of Texas Press, Austin, TX

A low-key, contemplative, anecdote-laced reflection on the evolution of the "hippie trail" overland from Europe to Asia into today's phenomena of independent backpackers, adventure travel, and ecotourism.

**The Good Alternative Travel Guide: Exciting Holidays for Responsible Travellers** • by Mark Mann for Tourism Concern
ISBN 1-85383-8373 • 2nd edition, 2002, 246 pp • Earthscan Publications, London, UK • earthinfo@earthscan.co.uk • http://www.earthscan.co.uk

An overview and directory of tourism opportunities worldwide that involve local communities as participants, decision-makers, and stake-holders, not just servants or victims. Emphasizes locally directed tourism projects in the

Third and Fourth Worlds, and with indigenous peoples. Includes background material on the concept of community tourism, and an extremely good guide to resources for further research. Targeted at readers in the UK, but will be of value to others as well.

*Green-Travel* • **by Marcus Endicott** • http://www.green-travel.com

A huge and diverse collection of links related to "green" (ecological, sustainable, responsible, etc.) travel. Limited annotations, but if you surf around from here you're sure to find things of interest. Also includes the archives of the Green-Travel e-mail mailing list. You can subscribe to the mailing list from a link on the Web site.

**The International Ecotourism Society** • P.O. Box 755, Bennington, VT 05257 • tel. +1-802-447-2121 • fax +1-802-447-2122 ecomail@ecotourism.org • http://www.ecotourism.org

Despite the name, this is mainly a North American nonprofit membership organization. Founded in 1990 "to foster a true sense of synergy between outdoor travel entrepreneurs, researchers, and conservationists," TIES defines ecotourism as "responsible travel to natural areas that conserves the environment and sustains the well-being of local people." As the reference to "natural areas" suggests, the society has focused much more on physical than cultural ecology and impacts of tourism. Publishes resources and coordinates a global network of "ecotourism professionals."

**International Institute for Peace through Tourism**
http://www.iipt.org

Despite its name, IIPT has mainly been involved in work for sustainability and economic equity in tourism, rather than "peace tourism" or conflict resolution. "IIPT is a not-for-profit organization dedicated to fostering and facilitating tourism initiatives which contribute to international understanding and cooperation, an improved quality of environment, the preservation of heritage, and through these initiatives, helping to bring about a peaceful and sustainable world, [and] to mobilize the travel and tourism industry as a leading force for poverty reduction."

*Native Tours: The Anthropology of Travel and Tourism* • **by Erve Chambers** • ISBN 1-57766-089-7 • 2000, 137 pp • Waveland Press, Prospect Heights, IL http://www.waveland.com

A concise introduction to the range of issued raised by viewing travel and tourism through the lens of anthropology.

**Partners in Responsible Tourism** • info@pirt.org • http://www.pirt.org

A USA national (although mainly Northern Californian) membership organization and networking group within the travel industry, promoting responsible and sustainable tourism. Has sponsored consumer expos and public symposia on responsible travel.

## tourismanthropology
http://www.mailbase.ac.uk/lists/tourismanthropology

An Internet mailing list associated with the Tourism Commission of the International Congress of Anthropological and Ethnological Sciences, focusing on the anthropological issues of tourism. Low volume (averages about one message a day). Scholarly but not inaccessible. You can subscribe to the list or browse the archive of messages through the Web site.

*Tourism and Sustainability: Development and New Tourism in the Third World* • by Martin Mowforth and Ian Munt • ISBN 041527169X • 2nd edition, 2002, 376 pp • Routledge, London and New York

Not light reading—heavy and academic—but the single best survey available of the political, economic, cultural, and physical impacts of tourism. Lots of interesting case studies and references; outstanding bibliography.

*The Tourist City* • edited by Dennis R. Judd and Susan S. Fainstein
ISBN 0-300-07846-3 • 1999, 340 pp • Yale University Press, New Haven, CT

Independent travelers often spend more of their time in urban than rural areas, and tourism has become many cities' raison d'être. But ecotourism and sustainable tourism are often thought of in terms of wilderness and wildlife. With sections on "The Political Economy of Tourism," "Constructing Cities as Theme Parks," "Converting Cities into Tourist Sites," and "Tourism Strategies," this anthology includes contributions by anthropologists, sociologists, urban planners, architects, and scholars of tourism studies (a recognized academic discipline abroad, although only beginning to be recognized in the United States). An excellent survey of the impact of tourism on cities and the quest for sustainable, responsible city tourism. Lengthy bibliography, although its usefulness is limited by a lack of annotations.

*Tourism In Focus* • Tourism Concern
Stapleton House, 277-281 Holloway Road (tube stop: Holloway Road), London N7 8HN, UK • tel. +44-20-7753-3330, fax +44-20-7753 3331 info@tourismconcern.org.uk • http://www.tourismconcern.org.uk quarterly; annual membership (includes subscription) UK£24 (UK), UK£25, (elsewhere in Europe), UK£28 (rest of the world)

Tucked into some back rooms in a nondescript classroom building at the Univ. of North London, Tourism Concern is the world's foremost advocacy and research organization for ethics in tourism. "A membership network, information resource, and catalyst for change, promoting awareness of the impact of tourism on people and their environments." As an independent, nonprofit registered charity, it differs markedly from ecotourism organizations formed from within the travel industry, and has no direct counterpart in most other countries. Equally important, it's an open-minded organization that welcomes diversity and often devotes its magazine, *Tourism in Focus* to issues on which its membership differs. Focuses equally on tourism impacts on physical and cultural ecology, and on the political economics of tourism as the world's largest industry. Publishes a wide variety of literature, and has one of the world's best libraries of sustainable and responsible tourism resources. Call for an appointment before visiting, as the library is cramped and very heavily used by staff and researchers. My highest recommendation.

### *Tourists: How Our Fastest Growing Industry Is Changing the World*
**by Larry Krotz** • ISBN 0-571-19893-7 • 1996, 264 pp • Faber and Faber, Winchester, MA and London, UK

Extremely thoughtful, well-written, and honestly ambivalent exploration of such topics as, "Can tourism save the elephants?," "Traveling in a world of tourism," "The problem with tourists," "Can tourism be made responsible?" and "Can tourism save the world?."

### *Travel That Can Change Your Life: How to Create a Transformative Experience* • **by Jeffrey A. Kottler, Ph.D.** • ISBN 0-7879-0941-6
1997, 180 pp • Jossey-Bass, San Francisco

I could have listed this book in two or three other places in this resource guide. It's about educational travel, travel and personal growth, culture shock and cross-cultural interaction, and, as Kottler puts it, "traveling like an anthropologist." But Kottler is a clinical psychologist and therapist, and this book is above all an introduction to the psychological phenomena of travel and how they change the traveler. The focus is on what you can do to learn more and grow more through your travel experiences, without being taken by surprise by the changes in yourself. Highly recommended.

### *A Trip Too Far: Ecotourism, Politics, and Exploitation*
**by Rosaleen Duffy** • ISBN 1-85383-759-8 • 2002, 210 pp • Earthscan Publications, London, UK earthinfo@earthscan.co.uk • http://www.earthscan.co.uk

Based on an anthropological case study of ecotourism in Belize, but with lessons for other countries and regions. One of very few truly critical studies of the impact of ecotourism and its economic, social, and political context. Particularly interesting in its discussion of the marketing of ecotourism and its cultural consequences.

### World Ecotourism Summit • http://www.ecotourism2002.org
The World Ecotourism Summit in Québec, P.Q., Canada, in May 2002 was held in conjunction with the United Nations' designation of the year 2002 as

the "International Year of Ecotourism." As with many U.N. initiatives, the goals of the *Québec Declaration on Ecotourism* adopted at the summit are easier stated than achieved. But the declaration and the presentations and papers presented at the summit (all of which are available in full on the Web site), give an excellent picture of the state of official thinking around the world about tourism as a component of sustainable economic and cultural development.

## The World Information Order

If you wonder why so many of the resources listed here are so obscure, why we in the North hear so little about the South, and why even the terms "North" and "South"—so widely used in most of the world—are unfamiliar to most Northerners, here are some introductions to the politics of information: knowledge as power.

*Trends in World Communication: On Disempowerment and Self-Empowerment* • by Cees J. Hamelink
ISBN 983-9054-06-6 • 1995, 168 pp • Southbound/Third World Network, Penang, Malaysia • twn@igc.apc.org • http://twnside.org.sg • http://southside.org.sg

Hamelink is a Northerner, but this book from a leading Southern publisher is a cogent summary of contemporary Southern criticisms of the power politics of information and news. You'll encounter these arguments often—indeed, they are taken for granted on the opinion pages of many Southern newspapers—so this is a book you should be familiar with even if you aren't persuaded to agree with its author.

*The World News Prism: Changing Media of International Communications* • by William A. Hachten and Harva Hachten • ISBN 0813823196 • 5th edition, 1999, 272 pp • Iowa State University Press, Ames, IA

A surprisingly unbiased primer, by two American journalism instructors, on the differences between Northern and Southern perspectives on the news media and what is "newsworthy." An excellent introduction to why "the news" looks different from different parts of the world.

## Travel Narratives
### Stories and Advice from Fellow Travelers

One way to get an idea of what a place will be like for you is to read what other visitors say it was like for them. More and more travelers are posting their stories on the Internet, on these and other sites. Just remember that these are archives of unverified anecdotes and opinions, written by amateurs who often lack perspective on how different things may look to others. Your mileage may vary. Don't take anything you read in these places as authoritative, or rely on it alone.

Much information from fellow travelers is available on **Usenet newsgroups**. A Usenet newsgroup is a topical forum for free discussion, generally open to anyone on the Internet. Unlike in "chat rooms," people participating in Usenet newsgroups can read, post, and respond to newsgroup messages at their leisure, without having to be connected at the same time as the other participants. Imagine a bulletin board that's accessible to everyone on the Internet, not just subscribers to one commercial service such as AOL, or visitors to one specific Web site. Usenet newsgroups have the widest reach and most diverse participation of any online discussion forum. All good "newsreader" software will permit searches of the available newsgroups by name. There are many newsgroups in other categories that are useful for planning special-interest travel, or researching particular details, but the rec.travel.* and soc.culture.* hierarchies, especially the latter, are overwhelmingly the most useful for general destination research and travel planning. Some popular Usenet groups are:

**rec.travel.*** (rec.travel.asia, rec.travel.europe, rec.travel.air, rec.travel.budget.backpack, etc.)

**soc.culture.countryname or nationality** (soc.culture.indian, soc.culture.singapore, etc.)

## BootsnAll.com • http://www.bootsnall.com

A "community" site for independent, hostel-style independent travelers. The travel stories by members from around the world are the best feature of this site—the topical and destination guides are of erratic quality. More international in participation and perspective than most USA-based publications or Web sites.

## IgoUgo.com • http://www.igougo.com

"Real people sharing travel experiences." Includes a huge searchable database of trip reports (mostly quite brief) and reviews. Especially useful for hotel ratings.

## The Rec.Travel Library • http://www.travel-library.com

Archives of the Usenet newsgroups **rec.travel**, **rec.travel.air**, **rec.travel.budget.backpack**, **rec.travel.asia**, **rec.travel.europe**, etc; links to many other sites and databases; particularly valuable for its archive of trip reports originally posted to Usenet travel newsgroups.

## *Round-The-World Travel Guide* • by Marc Brosius
http://www.travel-library.com/rtw/html/faq.html

This guide evolved before, during, and after Marc Brosius' two-plus years of world wanderings. Especially valuable for giving a sense of how different travelers' experiences vary. Includes quotes from a variety of other travelers, including ones who give contradictory advice on the same issues. Very useful for finding out how other people have dealt with some of the logistical, practical, etc., issues in long-term, multicountry travel.

### The Thorn Tree • http://thorntree.lonelyplanet.com

Lonely Planet's Web site has the largest, best, and worst of travel bulletin boards: More true and more false information, more contradictory or obsolete advice, more touts, more myths and rumors. Plagued by posters with undisclosed commercial interests in the places and routes they are recommending.

### TripJournal.com • http://www.tripjournal.com

"A searchable online travel diary for global travelers." You can search these journal entries (posted by clients of AirTreks.com) by destination and/or keyword.

## Published Travelogues

I enjoy reading travel tales (and tall tales) for entertainment, but I have a low opinion of their value in preparing for travel or learning about possible destinations. Seeing how a place appears through the biases of travelers who have gone before you won't necessarily make travel easier, and may compromise your ability to see it on its own terms. Most travelogues emphasize the experience of the traveler rather than the lives of locals, focusing on the sensational and exotic. Frequently, the most widely read travelogues are out of date, reinforcing the tendency of travelers to look for the past and neither see nor be prepared for the present. On the whole, you'll be better off with contemporary newspapers, magazines, or novels from the places you plan to visit than with books or travelogues by foreigners. If you can't find books by locals, you may be better off with textbooks for classes in regional studies, or other works by foreign academics, than with travelogues by foreign travelers. I include here only a few examples of travelogues that transcend the usual limitations of this most common genre of travel literature, and that describe trips in fairly recent times.

### The American Kaleidoscope—A Chinese View • by Wang Tsomin
1986 • New World Press, Beijing (United States distribution by China Books, San Francisco, CA) • info@chinabooks.com • http://www.chinabooks.com

It's common for USA journalists posted in less-familiar countries to write books about them on their return. This book is a sort of *Inside China* in reverse. Ms. Wang's detailed account of her year of travels around the United States was a bestseller in China in the original edition in Chinese. This excellent English translation can reveal a great deal to USA (and other First World) readers about how our way of life appears to foreigners. As you travel, you will constantly be asked, "What's it like where you are from?" This book may help you figure out which to-you-mundane aspects of your life would be different or interesting to your questioners, and perhaps how to explain them.

### Danziger's Travels: Beyond Forbidden Frontiers • by Nick Danziger
ISBN 0586087060 • 1st edition 1987; reprinted 2002, 448 pp
HarperCollins, New York

What's most noteworthy about *Danziger's Travels* is that, despite his fixation on completing an overland journey across Asia (in which he succeeded), Danziger got deeply into the cultures and societies of west and central Asia. Much of that was the result of how he traveled: he had little money to set himself apart from the locals; bureaucratic delays forced him to travel slowly enough to learn local languages; and the only way for him to cross the war zones of Afghanistan was to walk, with an escort of guerrillas. Danziger shared everything with them, including being bombed and shot at, except that he didn't carry a gun to shoot back. Interesting regardless of what you think about which factions the United States was backing then in Afghanistan, or is now.

### In the Cities of the South: Scenes from a Developing World • by Jeremy Seabrook • ISBN 1-85984-081-7 • 1996, 303 pp • Verso, London and New York

An amazing book by an amazing writer. Jeremy Seabrook is one of the few Northern writers who chooses to write mainly for Southern publications, and he stands out for his empathy with the people he depicts. This may be the single best depiction of daily life for the majority of the world's urban peoples.

### A Malaysian Journey • by Rehman Rashid
ISBN 9-83998-190-0 • 3rd edition 2002 (1st ed. 1993), 287 pp • published by the author, Rehman Rashid, Kuala Kubu Baru, Hulu Selangor, Malaysia
rehman@pop.jaring.my

The most enlightening travel book I have yet read. Malaysia epitomizes multiculturalism and the world *problematique* of nationalism, ethnicity, and identity, in microcosm. Rashid—a journalist and newspaper columnist in Malaysia and several other countries—combines his own multiethnic autobiography with his travels in a journey of personal and national self-exploration and self-discovery. Unflinchingly honest and independent in voice, which is why it's self-published. Earlier editions were almost unobtainable outside Malaysia and neighboring countries, but "now that my book's longevity is pretty much proven," the author says he expects to have wider distribution for the 3rd edition.

### Peace Corps: The Great Adventure • "Volunteer Stories of Life Overseas" • ISBN 0-9644472-2-3 • 1997, 248 pp • Peace Corps, 1111 20th St., N.W., Washington, DC 20278-3741 • tel. 800-424-8580 (United States only) or +1-202-692-1200, fax +1-202-692-1201 • http://www.peacecorps.gov

An anthology of essays by returned Peace Corps volunteers, produced and distributed free by the Peace Corps as a recruiting tool. Excerpts are also available on the Peace Corps Web site.

### Red Odyssey: A Journey through the Soviet Republics • by Marat Akchurin • ISBN 0-06018-335-7 • 1992, 406 pp • HarperCollins, New York

By some miracle this narrative of a Tashkent-born Tartar's exploration of Central Asia and the trans-Caucasus —mostly by private car, uncommon as that was in what was then still the USSR—came to be published in English by a major USA publisher. A disconcerting but wonderful combination of the sensibilities of the American "road trip" with a distinctly Soviet pessimism and humor.

### The River's Tale: A Year on the Mekong • by Edward A. Gargan
ISBN 0375705597 • 2003, 352 pp • Vintage Books, New York

Journalists often use the books they write after completing an overseas assignment to tell the longer, more complex stories that didn't fit into newspaper articles written on daily deadlines. Gargan did something a bit different: he took leave of his job with *The New York Times* to spend a year traveling more slowly, so as to give himself time to see more deeply. A self-conscious, deliberate, and thoughtful case study of how long-term, slow-moving journeys differ from shorter, faster trips.

### The Size of the World • by Jeff Greenwald
ISBN 034540551X • 1997, 421 pp • Ballantine Books, New York

The true story of a trip around the world without leaving the surface (but with a laptop computer, until it was stolen, and a six-month deadline), as originally told in dispatches for the first Internet travel portal, the late lamented GNN (Global Network Navigator) Traveler's Center.

### Spokesongs: Bicycle Adventures on Three Continents • by Willie Weir
ISBN 1-891369-17-2 • 2nd enlarged edition 2000, 240 pp • Breakaway Books, P.O. Box 24, Halcottsville, NY 12438 • tel./fax 800-548-4348 (United States only) • orders@breakawaybooks.com • http://www.willieweir.com

India, South Africa, and the Balkans—by bicycle, and without reservations, support, or "sag wagon." Neither bicycling nor travel could have a more effective, enthusiastic, or sincere evangelist than Willie Weir. Read his book and, if you get a chance, try to see one of his presentations in person. What's best about this book, and Willie Weir's pitch for bicycle travel, is how clearly he communicates the effectiveness of bicycling in humbling travelers, immersing them in the lives of the places they pass through, and breaking through the barriers between travelers and hosts. My highest recommendation (although, being a bicyclist, I'm biased).

### Stranger in the Forest: On Foot Across Borneo • by Eric Hansen
ISBN 0375724958 • 1st edition 1988; reprinted 2000 • 288 pp • Vintage Departures, New York

Hansen truly immerses himself in the local way of life and is quite matter-of-fact about the privations and dangers that are entailed in places where the people are so poor. A good reality check on your expectations if you think you will truly live or travel "just like a local."

### Take Me With You: A Round-The-World Journey to Invite a Stranger Home • by Brad Newsham • ISBN 0345449126 • paperback edition with postscript 2002, 368 pp • Ballantine Books, New York (1st ed. 2000, Travelers' Tales, San Francisco)

A fascinating exploration of the differences in wealth and power between travelers and locals in the Third World. It was many years after the trip described in this book, and after the hardcover edition was published, before Newsham was able to follow through on his goal of inviting one of the people he met to visit him in the United States. The paperback edition contains a brief but worthwhile postscript on what happened when he did so.

# MAGAZINES FOR WORLD TRAVELERS

## General Magazines and Websites with Global Perspectives

### Cultural Survival Quarterly • 221 Prospect St., Cambridge MA 02139
tel. +1-617-441-5400, fax +1-617-441-5417 • csinc@cs.org or cultsurv@igc.apc.org • http://www.cs.org • annual membership (includes subscription) US$45

The best source of information in the United States on indigenous, endangered, and minority cultures, peoples, identities, and ways of life. *Cultural Survival Quarterly* covers issues you will never hear about anywhere else, or will hear about elsewhere only years later. Anthropological in perspective. *Cultural Survival Quarterly* has published several special issues and articles on the cultural impact of tourism and on the possibility of culturally responsible tourism and tourist development, including a good mix of pro-and anti-tourism views.

### InterPress Service • http://www.ips.org • http://www.ipsnews.net
individual subscriptions (US$30/year for Web access to current news and searchable archives) • http://globalinfo.org • Global Information Network, 146 West 29th St. #7E, New York, NY 10001 • tel. +1-212-244-3123, webmaster@globalinfo.org

What the Associated Press and Reuters are to world news from First World perspectives, the InterPress Service news agency is to news from the South. Global, regional, and topical news feeds in English from local journalists in more than 100 countries, as well as the *Service Francais Afrique* (French) and *América Latina* (Spanish). Current headline stories are available free on the IPS Web site; archives and regional news wires are available only by subscription through Globalinfo.org or other IPS subscriber publications.

**New Internationalist** • see Web site for worldwide subscription addresses, or to subscribe online • ni@newint.org • http://www.newint.org annual subscriptions UK£29 (UK), US$45 (United States), C$38.50 (Canada), A$70 (Australia), NZ$59 (Aotearoa/New Zealand), UK£35 /€44.25 (rest of the world, airmail)

Edited from the UK and Canada, with contributors worldywide, the *New Internationalist* is one of the most South-centered publications in the North. It has a strong focus on human development, North-South relations, and the reality of life for the people of the South. Publishes an unusual diversity of contributions from both Northern and Southern writers, with a healthy leavening of self-awareness that neither the editorial collective nor anyone else has complete information or the one right answer to any question.

**Third World Resurgence** • Third World Network • 228 Macalister Rd., 10400 Penang, Malaysia • tel. +60-4-226-6728 or 226-6159, fax +60-4-226-4505 • twn@igc.apc.org (alternate e-mail address twnet@po.jaring.my) http://www.twnside.org.sg (Third World Network) • http://www.southbound .com.my (Southbound publications) • Annual subscriptions for individuals in developed countries: US$30 surface mail, US$45 airmail (lower rates for Third World subscribers; higher rates for libraries and institutions; online subscriptions and publication orders accepted by credit card).

*Third World Resurgence* isn't everyone's cup of tea. It's usually dry, sometimes repetitious, plainly laid out and heavy on text, with a strong emphasis on international political economics. It's also one of the magazines I look forward to each month, bringing to my doorstep the perspectives of leading thinkers and grassroots activists from around the world. Unparalleled as a truly global vehicle for South-South exchange, with contributing editors in Ghana, India, and Uruguay and articles from every continent in every issue. (Selected excerpts from the magazine are also available on the Web.) The Third World Network and its associated publishing house, Southbound, also publish a growing list of books by leading Southern thinkers on globalization and other issues; see the complete catalogs on their Web sites.

**World Press Review** • **"News and Views from Around the World"** Stanley Foundation • editorial offices: 700 Broadway, 3rd floor, New York, NY 10003 • tel. +1-212-982-8880, fax +1-212-982-6968 • annual subscription US$27 (USA), US$35 (Canada), US$47 (rest of the world, airmail) letters@worldpress.org • http://www.worldpress.org

A monthly English-language magazine of excerpts, translations, and editorial cartoons from newspapers and magazines throughout the world; one of the oldest international publications in the United States. Extensive excerpts available free on the Web site. Especially useful for news in translation from countries where there are few English-language publications.

**WorldView** • National Peace Corps Association • 1900 L St., N.W., Suite 205, Washington, DC 20036 • tel. +1-202-293-7728, fax +1-202-293-7554 pubs@rpcv.org • http://www.worldviewmagazine.com (magazine), http://www.rpcv.org (organization) • 1 year (4 issues) US$25 (United States and Canada), US$35 (rest of the world)

*WorldView* is published by the principal independent association of returned Peace Corps volunteers. Little of the magazine is about the Peace Corps per se. But most of the writing is by Peace Corps veterans, and reflects the interests and sensibilities of past and present members of the Peace Corps: people who learn the language and live for long periods among the people, often in isolated and rural areas of Second, Third, and Fourth Worlds. Thoughtful, sensitive, often deeply perceptive.

## Travel Magazines for Independent World Travelers

Each of these magazines has its own target audience and definition of independent travel. For some it means customized tours or "bespoke holidays." For others it means extreme-sports expeditions feasible only for experts willing to risk their lives. Try to compare some sample copies before you subscribe.

**Backpacker** • "The World at Home and Abroad"
Netbackpacker Ltd., 3 Pembroke St., Dublin 2, Ireland • tel. +353-1-662-0083, fax +353-1-662-0098 • info@backpacker.ie • http://www.backpacker.ie • 1 year (12 issues) €25 (Rep. of Ireland), €35 (UK), €49 (rest of Europe)

The leading independent travel magazine from one of the world's leading nations of travelers. Available free at hostels, cybercafés, colleges and universities, and other backpacker hangouts in Ireland (and a few in London), or by mail subscription.

**Blue** • "The Adventure Lifestyle Magazine"
611 Broadway, Suite 405, New York, NY 10012 • tel. 877-BLUE-MAG (877-258-3624; United States only) or +1-386-447-6366, fax +1-212-777-0068 subscriptions@bluemagazine.com • http://www.bluemagazine.com 1 year (6 issues) US$20 (United States), US$25 (Canada), US$35 (rest of the world)

One of the places some of my shorter articles have appeared in print.

**Motionsickness** • 4117 SE Division St., Box 417, Portland, OR 97202-1646 editor@motionsickmag.com • http://www.motionsickmag.com • 1 year (6 issues) US$15 (United States), US$20 (Mexico/Canada), US$25 (rest of the world)

"Covering Globalization as seen through the lens of travel and tourism... the impact of international travel on regional cultures and environments; stories of discomfort; criticism of travel media; interviews with unknown travelers; profiles of people working in the travel industry; and everything else that doesn't fit into other travel magazines . . . . We hope to provide some balance by showing other perspectives of travel: the dirty, uncomfortable, economic, political, artistic, and even criminal side. None of this means that travel can't be or isn't exciting or deeply moving. But there's more to it than that, and we think that's it's just simply more interesting to look at all the facets of travel instead of just a few."

**National Geographic Adventure Magazine** • National Geographic Society, 1145-17th St., N.W., Washington, DC 20036-4688 subscriptions tel. 800-647-5463 (United States only) or +1-813-979-6845 http://www.nationalgeographic.com/adventure

Most mainstream travel magazines focus on luxury travel but rarely mention how expensive it is. But each issue of *National Geographic Adventure* features a "World on the Cheap" section, reporting the total cost (including transportation, accommodations, food, tours, and all incidentals) of an international trip from the United States. Frequent promotions for new subscribers (10 issues for US$12 in the United States, C$25 in Canada, when this book went to press), so there's no need to pay the newsstand price.

**Transitions Abroad** • **"Work-Study-Travel-Living"** • P.O. Box 1300, Amherst, MA 01004-1300 • tel. 800-293-0373 (United States only) or +1-413-256-3414, fax +1-413-256-0373 • info@transitionsabroad.com http://www.transitionsabroad.com • 1 year (6 issues) US$28(USA), US$32 (Canada); rest of the world US$46 (surface mail), US$56 (airmail)

A useful source of ideas for people planning long-term travel, especially those planning to live or work abroad. Emphasis on immersion and education. Loads of ads and references in each issue, especially for teaching, study, and volunteer programs. Also publishes several annual resource guides on work, study, and travel abroad; see the Web site for details.

**Wanderlust** • **"The Magazine for People with a Passion for Travel"** P.O. Box 1832, Windsor, Berks. SL4 6YP, UK • tel. +44-1753-620-426, fax +44-1753-620-474 • subs@wanderlust.co.uk • http://www.wanderlust.co.uk 1 year (6 issues) UK£17.50 (UK), UK£21 (rest of Europe, airmail), UK£21 (rest of the world, surface mail), UK£30 (rest of the world, airmail)

The largest and most established of UK magazines for independent travelers, with subscribers around the world.

# RESOURCES FOR SPECIFIC GROUPS OF TRAVELERS

The resources in this section address the special needs, interests, and concerns of particular groups of travelers. On the other hand, they aren't necessarily for independent travelers from those groups. On the whole, most of these resources are more oriented toward tours than independent travel.

## Older Travelers

**International Travel News** • editorial offices and correspondence: ITN, 2120 28th St., Sacramento, CA 95818, tel. +1-916-457-3643 subscriptions@intltravelnews.com • http://www.intltravelnews.com • subscriptions only: ITN, 2224 Beaumont St., Suite D, Sacramento, CA 95815 • tel. 800-486-4968 (United States only) or +1-916-457-3643 • 1 year (12 issues) US$18 (United States), US$28 (rest of the world)

The bulk of each 150-page-or-more issue of *ITN* is devoted to tips, advice, trip reports, reviews, queries, and replies from and by *ITN* readers. Zine-like format and lack of structure make it something of a grab-bag, although each issue has some good stuff. Those with access to the Internet will probably do better on Usenet newsgroups, but for others this is a good place to get suggestions and exchange ideas with fellow travelers. Just remember to make allowances for the diversity of the readership, and double-check advice and information before you rely on it. Best published source for reviews of tour operators by people who have been on their tours; less good for independent travelers. Nowhere explicitly labeled as being for older travelers, but most of the readership is over age 60.

**Marco Polo** • "The Magazine for Adventurous Travelers Over 50" 1299 Bayshore Blvd., Suite B, Dunedin, FL 34698-4246 • tel. +1-727-735-9455, fax +1-727-735-9534 • info@travelroads.com http://www.marcopolomagazine.com • 1 year (4 issues) US$10

Mostly oriented toward tours and travel packages, but does include some information for independent travelers.

## Women Travelers

**Go Girl! The Black Woman's Book of Travel Adventure** • **Elaine Lee, editor** • ISBN 0933377428 • 1997, 288 pp • Eighth Mountain Press, Portland, OR • laneybugg@aol.com • http://www.ugogurl.com • US$18 postpaid from Ugogurl Productions, P.O. Box 2603, Berkeley, CA 94702

Equal parts inspiration, entertainment, and advice. *Go Girl!* includes travel stories by Maya Angelou, Alice Walker, and dozens of less well-known but equally interesting black women, as well Elaine Lee's travel evangelism and advice. Includes lists of further resources for black women travelers. (If you're in the San Francisco Bay Area, catch Elaine Lee's travel show on KPFA and Pacifica Radio.)

*A Journey of One's Own: Uncommon Advice for the Independent Woman Traveler* • **by Thalia Zepatos** • ISBN 0-933377-52-5
3rd edition 2003, 288 pp • Eighth Mountain Press, Portland, OR

Combines the author's advice with stories from other women travelers. Includes a particularly good discussion of the pros and cons of traveling solo or with a partner.

**Journeywoman** • http://www.journeywoman.com

The leading portal site for women travelers of all types, from vacationers to businesswomen on the go.

*Passionfruit* • **"A Women's Travel Journal"** • 2917 Telegraph Ave. #136, Berkeley, CA 94705 • http://www.passionfruit.com • 1 year (4 issues) US$18

"Not a travel guide, *Passionfruit* is a forum where women can share journey tales and discuss global issues. This magazine is for women who recognize that a journey is more than a vacation; it is an opportunity to challenge our beliefs and expand our minds."

## Gay and Lesbian Travelers

*Our World* • **"The International Gay and Lesbian Travel Magazine"**
1104 North Nova Rd., Suite 251, Daytona Beach, FL 32117 • tel. +1-904-441-5367, fax +1-904-441-5604 • subscriptions@ourworldmag.com
http://www.ourworldmag.com • 1 year (10 issues) US$12 (online), US$35 (print edition in United States), US$45 (Canada), US$60 (rest of the world by airmail)

Comprehensive color glossy magazine for gay and lesbian travelers. The full contents of the print edition, and other features, are available to subscribers on the Web site.

*Out and About* • 350 Seventh Ave., Suite 1203, New York, NY 10001 • tel. +1-212-645-6922, fax +1-212-645-6785, TTY 800-929-2268 (United States only) • orders@outandabout.com • http://www.outandabout.com
Newsletter: 1 year (12 issues) US$20 (online), US$39 (print edition in United States), US$49 (Canada and Mexico), US$69 (rest of the world) • annual subscription to online databases and downloadable guides, including the newsletter online: US$49

In addition to the printed, advertising-free newsletter, *Out and About* operates an excellent Web site for gay and lesbian travelers. The most detailed information on specific cities and countries is available online only by subscription. But there's lots of stuff in the free areas, including ratings and reviews of airlines and other travel companies for their policies and treatment of gay and lesbian travelers and employees, directories of gay tour operators, and many other useful links and resources.

## Student Travelers

*Abroad View* • "Travel and Culture" • P.O. Box 745, Bennington, VT 05201-0745 • info@abroadview.com • http://www.abroadviewmagazine.com
Free on campuses; 2 years (4 issues) US$10 by mail

A magazine about the travel experiences and cultural perspectives of college students, alumni, and faculty. Dedicated to global education and cross-cultural understanding. Published by a foundation underwritten by sponsoring colleges; distributed to students involved in international education at more than 240 colleges throughout the United States. The Web site includes an archive, searchable by topic or destination, of past articles. *Abroad View* is a valuable publication even to non-academics for its emphasis on "the global education we actually receive when we uproot from our comfortable lives for study, travel or work in new environments . . . We publish contents that inform, challenge and expand the way we see and understand the world. The travelers who read *Abroad View* and write for it wander off the beaten path and explore new terrain in order to discover and educate themselves through direct experience." Highly recommended.

*Student Traveler* • 714 W. Olympic Blvd., Suite 724, Los Angeles, CA 90015
tel. 800-552-7157 (United States only) or +1-213-747-8612
info@swtmag.com • http://www.studenttravels.com • quarterly; distributed
free on college campuses; free sample copy mailed by request

Founded by students, "Designed to motivate and prepare students to travel around the world." Emphasizes practical advice and information for shoestring travel, including a strong international focus and advice on work, study, volunteering, and travel abroad. Extensive excerpts and other resources on the Web site.

## Travelers of Color

*Pathfinders Travel* • "The Travel Magazine for People of Color"
P.O. Box 29783, Elkins Park, PA 19027 • tel. 877-977-PATH (877-977-7284;
United States only) or +1-215-927-9950, fax +1-215-927-3359
subscribe@pathfinderstravel.com • http://www.pathfinderstravel.com • 1 year
(4 issues) US$15 (United States), US$27 (rest of the world, airmail)

A glossy magazine published since 1997 in association with a Black-owned travel agency, Pathfinders Travel Group. Heavy emphasis on travel within the United States, but some coverage of international travel.

*Travel Beyond Borders* • 408 13th St., #291, Oakland CA 94612 • tel. +1-510-234-6812, fax +1-510-234-6860 • staff@travelbeyond.org
http://www.travelbeyond.org • 1 year (4 issues) US$17.95 (e-mail/Web edition, or print edition in the United States), C$26.95 (e-mail/Web edition), C$46.95 (print edition in Canada), US$47.95 (print edition by airmail to the rest of the world)

"African Americans travel the globe in ways that no one else does and experience things that nobody else will." *Travel Beyond Borders* is, "The international travel magazine featuring world destinations from a 'colorful' perspective, showing you how to travel the world in a way relevant to people of African descent."

*Go Girl! The Black Woman's Book of Travel Adventure*

See the entry listed above under "Women Travelers"

## Travelers with Children

The biggest issue for many parents is whether taking children out of school to travel will interfere with their education. That's unfortunate, because travel—especially independent, international travel outside the First World— is one of the most valuable educational experiences a child (or anyone else) can have. Here are some resources which, while not specifically about travel, address the value of experimental learning. (You can also find travelogues by families including children who have traveled around the world together,, on the Web sites listed under "Stories and Advice from Fellow Travelers")

*Take the Kids Travelling: Survive and Enjoy!* • by Helen Truszkoska
ISBN 186011-950-6 • 2000, 224 pp • Cadogan Guides, London, UK
http://www.cadoganguides.com

Includes advice for a wide range of travel styles and children from toddlers to teens.

*Third Culture Kids: The Experience of Growing Up Among Worlds*
by David C. Pollock and Ruth E. Van Reken • ISBN 1-85788-295-4
2001, 351 pp • Intercultural Press, Yarmouth, ME; Nicholas Brealey, London, UK
http://www.interculturalpress.com • http://www.nbrealey-books.com

This is a pioneering and definitive reference on international and cross-cultural childhood living. Mainly oriented towards those who spend a significant part of childhood living abroad, but notes that as little as a year abroad as a child can have lifelong effects. On first glance, the book may seem to focus unduly on the problems of third culture kids, but that's not the authors' intent: if you aren't sure you *want* to travel around the world with your children, start with the chapter on "Why a Cross-Cultural Childhood Matters." Getting a childhood head start is crucial to cross-cultural learning, as it is for language learning. So it should be no surprise that "Third culture kids" (TCKs) or "global nomads"—including children of missionaries, military families, and other expatriates—have an influence on all aspects of international affairs—business, diplomacy, international organizations, etc.—far out of proportion to their numbers. Includes an excellent bibliography of further reading, resources, and support groups.

**Travel with Children** • by Cathy Lanigan • ISBN 0864427298
4th edition 2002, 280 pp • Lonely Planet, Footscray, Victoria, Australia

The first edition of *Travel with Children* was written by Lonely Planet co-founder Maureen Wheeler, and the current edition remains one of the best books in their catalog. Emphasis on Third and Fourth World travel.

**The Unschooling Handbook: How to Use the Whole World as Your Child's Classroom** • by Mary Griffith • ISBN 0-7615-1276-4 • 1998, 230 pp • Prima Publishing (div. of Random House), Rocklin, CA • http://www.primapublishing.com

This is not a book about travel, and not primarily about learning through travel. But it is about learning through experience as an alternative to classroom schooling or more structured "home schooling." As such, it might help give people planning to travel with children ideas about how to work with children and maximize the educational value of daily experience on the road. Also addresses issues in explaining the choice of experiential learning to others, and dealing with schools.

**The Whole World Guide to Culture Learning**
For resources on cultural education, see this book and the other listings below under "Cultural Awareness and Adaptation."

## Travelers with Disabilities or Special Needs
**Able to Travel** (USA title) • **Nothing Ventured** (UK title) • **"True Stories By and For People With Disabilities"** • ISBN 1-74710-208-2 • 1996, 560 pp • Rough Guides/Real Guides, London, UK

A wide-ranging anthology of personal narratives of world travel by people with disabilities. Not really a "how-to" book, but a book that may suggest possibilities you haven't thought of.

**Barrier-Free Travel: A Nuts and Bolts Guide for Wheelers and Slow Walkers** • by Candy Harrington • ISBN 1-4010-1964-1 (paperback), 1-4010-1965-X (eBook) • 2001, 230 pp • Xlibris, Philadelphia, PA • http://www.xlibris.com

By the founder of the *Emerging Horizons* magazine (see below).

**Emerging Horizons** • **"Accessible Travel News"** • C & C Creative Concepts, P.O. Box 278, Ripon, CA 95366 • tel. +1-209-599-9409,

fax +1-209-599-9482 • horizons@emerginghorizons.com
http://www.emerginghorizons.com • 1 year (4 issues) US$14.95 (United
States), US$19.95 (rest of the world)

A consumer-oriented magazine about accessible travel, primarily for people with mobility disabilities. Features unbiased information on foreign and domestic destinations, lodgings, travel tips, news and resources. Accepts no advertising and no paid listings. Distributed in your choice of format: in print by mail, online, as ASCII text by e-mail, or on floppy disk by mail

*Moving Violations: War Zones, Wheelchairs, and Declarations of Independence* • by John Hockenberry • ISBN 0-78686-078-2 • 1995, 371 pp • Hyperion Books, New York

Longtime National Public Radio foreign correspondent John Hockenberry details the personal, political, and technical issues of his Third World wheelchair travels. Not written specifically as a travel "how-to" book, but valuable as one, and worth reading even if you don't plan to visit any war zones and don't use a wheelchair. Highly recommended.

**WeMedia.com** • http://www.wemagazine.com

Formerly a print magazine for people with disabilities, their families, and friends; now a Web site and free e-mail newsletter covering travel as well as other issues.

# DESTINATION GUIDEBOOKS FOR INDEPENDENT TRAVELERS

## Avalon Travel Publishing

**Avalon Travel Publishing** • **"Because Travel Matters"** • 1400 65th Street, Suite 250, Emeryville, CA 94608 • tel. 800-345-5473 (United States only) or +1-510-595-3664, fax +1-510-595-4228 • info@travelmatters.com http://www.travelmatters.com

Avalon Travel Publishing (ATP) is the largest publisher in the United States of guidebooks for independent and active travelers. Bigger isn't necessarily better, of course, but ATP was my first choice of publishers when I wrote my first book, and I'm proud to be part of the Avalon Travel Publishing family. The focus on independent and active travel clearly distinguishes ATP from publishers whose guidebooks emphasize packages, guided tours, cruises, and resorts. Some of the ATP books and series most relevant to international travelers are listed below; see the Web site for the full catalog.

*Moon Handbooks* • http://www.moon.com

Moon Handbooks started in 1973 with Bill Dalton's *Indonesia Handbook*, which at one time was banned in Indonesia for saying too much, too truthfully, about Indonesian politics. Not surprisingly, Moon Handbooks continue, in general, to have more emphasis on politics and culture than do Lonely Planet or any other major competitor. My favorite Moon Handbooks are those to East and Southeast Asia, which I particularly recommend, having traveled with both, over Lonely Planet's guides to the same regions. Moon's booklist is especially strong on guides to North America, with comprehensive set of guides to individual states, provinces and regions of the United States, Canada, and Mexico, and growing coverage of Latin America and the Caribbean.

### Adapter Kit • http://www.adapterkit.com

Cultural and logistical country guides for longer-term stay and/or relocation, whether for work, study, volunteering, or retirement. "Passionately written by authors who have taken the plunge themselves."

### The People's Guide to Mexico • by Carl Franz; edited by Lorena Havens & Steve Rogers • ISBN 1-56691-434-5 • 12th edition (30th anniversary ed.) 2002, 583 pp • http://www.peoplesguide.com

Some of the best guidebooks, like this one, aren't part of any series. What's especially noteworthy about this, the best guide for independent travelers in Mexico, is that it has no lists whatsoever of specific hotels, restaurants, sites, or routes. The entire book is devoted to general advice about how to travel, including how to find destinations, places to stay, etc, on your own. I wish there were equally good books of this type for other countries or regions.

### Rick Steves' Guides • http://www.ricksteves.com

"Most guide books only tell you where to travel. Rick Steves teaches you how to travel." Deservedly the best-known guidebooks to Europe for Americans of all ages and budgets who don't want to be led around on tours. Just remember to take Rick's advice to heart: explore on your own, and don't limit yourself to considering only the places he mentions in his books.

### Road Trip USA • http://www.roadtripusa.com

The great American road trip isn't the only way to see America, but it is one of the best, and one of the most attractive for foreign visitors to the United States. Most American guidebooks emphasize the Interstate highways (multilane divided motorways or "dual carriageways"). Road Trip USA is about travel on the smaller roads that are much more interesting for anyone who isn't in quite so much of a hurry. Includes routes to follow in different regions, up and down and across the country, as well things to see and do along the way and background reading for the drive.

## Other Guidebook Publishers

*Guidebookwriters.com* • **"We Wrote the Books On It"**
http://www.guidebookwriters.com

Want to hire the person who wrote the book on your destination to spend an hour reviewing your proposed itinerary and suggesting improvements, or answering your questions about your plans? Guidebookwriters.com offers access to freelance authors of published guidebooks (including yours truly)—selected and screened for their expertise by a committee of their peers—for personal travel consulting and advice.

**Bradt Travel Guides** • 19 High St., Chalfont St. Peter, Bucks SL9 9QE, UK
tel. +1-44-1753-893-444, fax +44-1753-892-333 • enquiries
@bradt-travelguides.com • http://www.bradt-travelguides.com

Individualistic, often quite literary and very British, guidebooks focused on the needs of "the adventurous traveller who seeks out off-beat places and the dreamer who would like to travel there but perhaps never will."

**Cadogan Books Ltd.** • Network House, 1 Ariel Way, London W12 7SL,
UK • tel. +44-20-8600-3550, fax +44-20-8600-3599
http://www.cadoganguides.com • distributed in the United States by Globe
Pequot Press

An eclectic series of quite individualistic guidebooks, including some excellent ones.

**Footprint Handbooks** • 6 Riverside Court, Lower Bristol Rd., Bath BA2
3DZ, UK • tel. +44-1225-469-141, fax +44-1225-469-461
enquiries@footprintbooks.com • http://www.footprintbooks.com • distributed
in the United States by NTC, Lincolnwood, IL

A few of their titles have been around for decades, and have long been the standard English-language guides to their regions (the 2003 South American Handbook is the 79th annual edition). Now strong world rivals to Avalon Travel (Moon Handbooks), Rough Guides, and Lonely Planet. Written primarily for Europeans, who have much longer vacations than Americans. With less time pressure, Europeans are less likely to feel the need of a tour to ensure that they see what they came to see quickly, and are more likely to travel independently. Europeans are also more likely to have international travel experience than Americans, though, and the biggest shortcoming of the Footprint Handbooks vis-à-vis Moon Handbooks or Lonely Planet is a relative dearth of hand-holding and general information for first-time travelers. Many experienced travelers wanting compact guidebooks with up-to-date essentials on large regions swear by them, and I've found some of their guides to be the best available at particular times for particular places. (Note that it's easy to confuse Footprint Handbooks with Moon Handbooks, since both are often referred to simply as "the Handbook.")

**Let's Go Publications, Inc.** • 67 Mount Auburn St., Cambridge, MA
02138 • tel. +1-617-495-9659, fax 617-496-7070 • feedback@letsgo.com
http://www.letsgo.com • distributed by St. Martin's Press, New York
http://www.stmartins.com

A series of guidebooks written and revised annually by teams of Harvard
University students. Intended for students, and often dismissed by older
nonstudents. But while they may skimp on cultural background and overemphasize student ghettos and hangouts, the thorough annual updating
makes these some of the most up-to-date guides around when it comes to
details: names, addresses, phone numbers, schedules, and prices. They also
offer more detailed hand-holding and advice for first-time travelers than
some competing guidebooks, although as first-time travelers themselves the
writers have to re-invent the wheel every year, and don't always know
enough to give accurate or well-founded advice.

**Lonely Planet Publications** • http://www.lonelyplanet.com

Australia • 90 Maribyrnong St., Footscray, Victoria 3011, Australia • tel.
+61-3-8379-8000, fax +61-3-8379-8111 • talk2us@lonelyplanet.com.au

France • 1 rue du Dahomey, 75011 Paris, France • tel. +33-1-5525-3300,
fax +33-1-5525-3301 • bip@lonelyplanet.fr

UK • 10a Spring Place, London NW5 3BH, UK • tel. +44-20-7428-4800,
fax +44-20-7428-4828 • go@lonelyplanet.co.uk

United States • Embarcadero West, 150 Linden St., Oakland, CA 94607-
2538 • tel. 800-275-8555 (United States only) or +1-510-893-8555, fax +1-
510-893-8563 • info@lonelyplanet.com

Lonely Planet Publications started with Tony and Maureen Wheeler's "how to"
guide to crossing Asia by land. Today, LP publishes guides to more places than
anyone else, with an emphasis on the nitty-gritty details of how to get around,
and a correspondingly lesser emphasis on culture, politics, and interpretation
of what you'll see when you get there than many competing books from other
publishers. LP is great on things like how to make reservations and buy train
tickets in a place where doing so requires standing in six different lines in succession. But they also go to great lengths to tell you how to find beer in places
where drinking alcohol is a sin, a crime, or both; the "accepted" local protocol
for sex tourists to follow in negotiating prices with prostitutes; and other such
ill-considered advice. LP writers are paid a flat one-time fee for their work, so
they get no royalties and don't necessarily have a long-term commitment to
keeping their books up to date. Frequently, successive editions are updated by
different writers, or sections are compiled from different books by different LP
writers, giving most LP guidebooks a more uniform look and tone than the
more individualistic voices of the writers for competing series. As the Wheelers
have gotten older and wealthier, they have targeted their books at a gradually
older and wealthier audience. LP publishes guidebooks to more places than

anyone else, but their quality is especially erratic, particularly in the guides to places where there is no other guidebook, so they are under no competitive pressure. Some LP guides are superb, but I've seen more than one LP guidebook that was so misleading as to be worse than useless. Some recommended titles: India, Pakistan, Russia, Karakoram Highway. Not recommended: Vietnam, Southeast Asia, West Asia.

**Rough Guides** • http://travel.roughguides.com
UK • 80 Strand, London WC2R 0RL, UK
United States • 345 Hudson St., 14th floor, New York, NY 10014 •
distributed in the United States by Penguin Putnam

Like the Footprint Handbooks, Rough Guides cover a wider range of budgets for their European primary market. One of the special strengths of the Rough Guides is their attention to contemporary popular culture in the countries they cover. Check out the *Rough Guide to World Music*, for example, for a global survey of musical genres and artists that might help prepare you for some of what you'll hear on boom boxes and buses as you travel. Warning: Rough Guides give less nitty-gritty advice on logistics and often fail to note which of their advice is specifically intended for European citizens, even where visa requirements or optimal routes may be very different for North Americans.

**Vacation Work Publications** • 9 Park End St., Oxford OX1 1HJ, UK
tel. +44-1865-241-978, fax +44-1865-790-885 • sales@vactionwork.co.uk
http://www.vactionwork.co.uk

From Susan Griffith's flagship *Work Your Way Around the World*, Vacation Work has expanded its line to include a wide range of specialized titles on different occupations and types of work abroad and on specific countries, as well as general travel guides. I probably wouldn't choose the general guidebooks to specific destinations over those from competing series. But the guides to work abroad continue to be the best in the field.

**Whereabouts Press** • 1111 8th St., Suite D, Berkeley, CA 94710-1455 •
+1-510-527-8280, fax +1-510-527-8780 • mail@whereaboutspress.com •
http://www.whereaboutspress.com • UK and Europe distribution: Gazelle
Book Services, Falcon House, Queen Square, Lancaster LA1 1RN, UK, +44-
1524-68765, fax +44-+44-1524-63232, sales@gazellebooks.co.uk,
http://www.gazellebooks.co.uk • Australia distribution: Wakefield Publishing,
+61-8-8362-8800, fax +61-8-8362-7592, info@wakefield.com.au

Most literary guides for travelers emphasize travelogues by foreigners, often those from long in the past. Not these. The "Traveler's Literary Companions" from Whereabouts Press consist of contemporary writing about the countries by people in those countries. Most of the editors are from the subject countries, and many of the works included are by leading local writers. Some material originally in English; other pieces appear in these books for the first time anywhere in English translation. These are exactly what literary anthologies for travelers should be. I just hope the series survives and expands to cover more of the world with the same quality.

# REGIONAL AND COUNTRY-SPECIFIC RESOURCES

Most prospective travelers read mainly travel-specific books and literature. But many of the resources I find most useful in preparing myself for travel to a country or region tend not to be intended primarily for travelers.

## Abroad At Home

A great way to find information about travel destinations is through immigrants from those places, and resources directed at immigrants such as publications with news from and about their homelands. There are immigrant neighborhoods, cultural centers, newspapers and magazines, video rental shops, restaurants, and travel agencies specializing in even obscure parts of the world in multicultural mega-cities like London, New York, and Los Angeles. Here are a few directories to help you find them.

*Discover Los Angeles: An Informed Guide to L.A.'s Rich and Varied Cultural Life* • by **Letitia Burns O'Connor** • ISBN 0-89236-479-3 • 2nd revised printing 1997, 288 pp • J. Paul Getty Trust, P.O. Box 49659, Los Angeles CA 90049-0659 • tel. 800-223-3431 (United States and Canada only) or +1-818-778-6943, fax +1-818-779-0051 • http://www.getty.edu

Available in L.A. at the Getty Museuem bookstore, or online; hard to find in other bookstores. Limited and poorly indexed, but the best guidebook I've found to the cultures and community institutions of the majority of Angelenos, who don't trace their ancestry primarily to Western Europe.

*Passport's Guide to Ethnic New York* • by **Mark Leeds** ISBN 0844296333 • 2nd edition 1995, 407 pp • Passport Books, NTC Publishing Group, Lincolnwood, IL

Getting slightly dated, but still the best available guide to the diversity of New York City. Especially valuable for the many ethnic neighborhoods and resources in the boroughs outside Manhattan. Part of a discontinued guidebook series (still readily available second hand) that also included *Ethnic London*, *Ethnic Chicago*, *Ethnic Toronto*, and *Ethnic Montreal*.

*Global Journeys in Metro Detroit: A Multicultural Guide to the Motor City* • edited and published by **Marica Danner, Helen B. Love, and Patricia Banker Peart** • ISBN 0967337909 1999, 504 pp • New Detroit, Inc., 3011 West Grand Blvd., Suite 1200, Detroit, MI 48202-3013 • http://www.newdetroit.org

Produced by a consortium of business and civic organizations underwritten by the Ford Motor Company and other Detroit-area commercial, nonprofit, and government entities. Includes descriptions of ethnic, national, and religious cultures; how they came to the Detroit area, and where their communities are located; and directories of cultural and community organizations, institutions, media, events, and businesses. Each section is written by contributors from that cultural community. The model for what similar guidebooks to other places should be like.

*Global London: Where to Find Almost Everything Ethnic and Cultural in the Multilingual Capital* • http://www.global-london.com • by Philip Baker and Jeehoon Kim • ISBN 1903292093 • 2002, 224 pp • Battlebridge Publications, Box 421, 37 Store St., London WC1E 7QF, UK • +44-20-7278-1246, fax +44-20-7636-5550 • battlebridge@talk21.com • http://www.battlebridge.com • distributed in the United States by Independent Publishers Group, 814 North Franklin St., Chicago, IL 60610, 800-888-4741 (United States only) or +1-312-337-0747, fax +1-312-337-5985, frontdesk@ipgbook.com, http://www.ipgbook.com

Not a guidebook, but an extraordinarily comprehensive directory of about 10,000 listings: art galleries, cultural associations, religious centers, news media, language institutes, restaurants, shops, travel agencies, etc. The version on the Web is searchable by language/nationality/ethnicity and category, and includes phone numbers, addresses, and links to locator maps, but doesn't (yet) include e-mail addresses or URL's.

## Africa

AllAfrica.com • http://allafrica.com

Incorporates the nonprofit Africa News Service, which for decades was the foremost independent United States source of news about Africa. AllAfrica.com has offices in Nigeria, Senegal, South Africa, and Mauritius, as well as in the United States, and handles electronic distribution on behalf of the Panafrican News Agency (PANA, Africa's largest continent-wide news organization) and dozens of other African regional and national newspapers and news service. Truly the one-stop Web portal for news from and about Africa in both English and French.

*The Africans: A Triple Heritage* • by Ali A. Mazrui
ISBN 0-316-55200-3 • 1986, 336 pp • Little, Brown, and Co., Boston

As the companion volume to a PBS/BBC television series, this could easily be mistaken for no more than a coffee-table book. But this may be the best introduction to the relationship of Africa's past, present, and future available in English from an African perspective, with particular emphasis on culture and identity.

**Africa Book Centre** • 38 King St. (tube stop: Covent Garden), London
WC2E 8JT, UK • tel. 0845-458-1581 (from the UK only) or +44-20-7240-
6649, fax +44-20-7497-0309 • info@africabookcentre.com
http://www.africabookcentre.com

Possibly the best selection outside Africa of publications from Africa; the
periodical and pamphlet collections are especially interesting. Storefront sales
and worldwide mail order. Located in the African Cultural Centre, which
also hosts events about Africa and has a fine public library of Africana.

**Africa Book Centre Book Review** • **Africa Book Centre (see above)**
• single copy UK£2; 4 issues UK£12 (UK), UK£18 (rest of the world)

Includes a well-annotated catalog of newly available fiction and nonfiction,
divided into books from Africa and books from elsewhere about Africa. Most
are in English but some are in French.

**The African Book Mart** • 2440 Durant (at Telegraph), P.O. Box 3268,
Berkeley, CA 94703-0268 • tel. +1-510-843-3088

Run by a Nigerian-American social scientist, this small shop is one of the few
USA importers of books from Africa. The limited selection nonetheless includes
some hard-to-find gems as well as the standard works of modern African fiction
and nonfiction. Call or write for information on ordering by mail.

**Africa Today** • Suite 6, Third Floor, AMC House, 12 Cumberland Avenue,
London NW10 7QL, UK • tel. +44-20-8838-5900, fax +44-20-8838-3700
publisher@africatoday-uk.com • http://www.africatoday.com
http://www.africatoday.co.uk

Nigerian-owned, with a major bureau in Lagos and especially good coverage
of Nigeria, Africa's most populous country. A fresh voice. One year (12
issues) US$45, in print by mail or on the Web. (*Africa Today* is also the name
of an older, unrelated, highly respected and recommended, but scholarly and
somewhat less accessible academic journal about African affairs, with contributors worldwide. For this other *Africa Today*, see http://iupjournals.org/
africatoday.)

**Books from Africa (MEA Books)** • 1 Theodore Rd., Ladysmith, QC J0X
2A0 Canada • tel. +1-819-647-9927, fax +1-819-647-9928
info@meabooks.com • http://www.meabooks.com

Imported books published in dozens of countries throughout Africa—possibly the largest selection from any retailer in North America. Most in English
or French, but some in other languages; heavy emphasis on academic, government, and some NGO publications.

***New African*** • Head office and subscription department • IC Publications
Ltd., 7 Coldbath Square, London EC1R 4LQ, UK • tel. +44-20-7713-7711, fax
+44-20-7713-7898 • icpubs@africasia.com • http://www.africasia.com/newafrican
Paris office • IC Publications, 10 rue Vineuse, 75784 Paris CEDEX 16, France
tel. +33-1-44-30-81-00, fax +33-1-44-30-81-11

A monthly publication since 1966; correspondents throughout Africa; one of
the few publications to cover both anglophone and francophone Africa. Annual
subscription UK£36 (UK), US$90 (United States), UK£50 (rest of the world).
Check the Web site for discounted prices for new subscribers. IC Publications
also publishes the *New African Yearbook* and *The Middle East* (see below under
"The Islamic World and the Middle East"). For the parallel French-language
publications from the Africa Press Group, including the flagship francophone
African magazine, *Jeune Afrique*, see http://www.jeuneafrique.com or
http://www.lintelligent.com

***West Africa*** • **"The Pan-African Weekly"** • Afrimedia International
Ltd., Allenby House, 1a Temple Rd., London NW2 6PJ, UK • tel. +44-20-8450-
4848, fax +44-20-8450-3868 • http://www.westafricamagazine.com

Weekly since 1917. Emphasizes Western and sub-Saharan Africa (despite the
subtitle), and the African diaspora in Europe. 1 Year UK£75 (UK), €92
(Europe, airmail), US$139 (United States/Canada, airmail), UK£83 (rest of the
world, airmail).

## The Americas

*Américas* • **Organization of American States (O.A.S.)**
19th St. and Constitution Ave., Washington, DC 20077-7512 • tel. 800-222-
5405 (United States only) • http://www.oas.org • Published in both English
and Spanish-language editions. 1 year (6 issues) subscription to either edition
US$18 (United States); rates vary by country for subscriptions elsewhere.

Published by the O.A.S.—"a regional international organization of the Western Hemisphere,"—*Américas* is boosterish but errs more by omission (no bad
news, pessimism, controversy, or criticism of O.A.S. member governments)
than by commission. What it does choose to print gives an accurate, if relent-
lessly upbeat, picture of aspects of contemporary American life and culture
that guidebooks focusing on the "traditional" often overlook. Particularly
interesting for its depiction of the South American urban middle classes and
of contemporary Central and South American art and culture, and for its
placement of the United States in its regional context as part of "the Americas." And, of course, there are the slick color photos. Just keep in mind that
it's a magazine of government propaganda.

***Born in Blood and Fire: a Concise History of Latin America*** • **by John Charles Chasteen** • ISBN 0-393-97613-0 • 2001, 352 pp • W.W. Norton, New York

A highly readable overview of the broad patterns of continental history, from the first encounters with foreign invaders to contemporary neoliberalism.

***Brazzil*** • P.O. Box 50536 (2039 N. Ave. 52), Los Angeles, CA 90050-0536 editorial tel. +1-323-255-8062, fax +1-213-257-3487 • brazzil@brazzil.com http://www.brazzil.com

One year (12 issues) US$3 (to cover postage only) in the United States, US$18 by surface mail to the rest of the world; also available free at many Brazilian-American restaurants, music and dance clubs, record stores, travel agencies, etc. Monthly since 1989. This black and white, text-heavy, newsprint monthly could all too easily be mistaken for nothing more than a newsletter of community events and/or a vehicle for advertising to the Brazilian-American community. In fact, I've found it to be among the most intellectually sophisticated, yet accessible, of readily available English-language immigrant publications in the United States. Many articles are of interest to travelers. All nonfiction editorial content is in English; some poetry is in both English and Portuguese; each issue includes a short story or novel excerpt in Portuguese. Noteworthy for its no-holds-barred commentary on Brazilian current affairs, culture, and politics, *Brazzil* is unusually successful in addressing itself to the interests both of immigrants from Brazil to the United States and of visitors from the USA to Brazil (and neighboring countries).

**Interhemispheric Resource Center** • P.O. Box 4506, Albuquerque, NM 87196-4506 • tel. +1-505-842-8288 (orders and subscriptions), +1-505-388-0208 (main office), fax +1-505-388.0619 • irc@irc-online.org http://www.irc-online.org

A nonprofit research center that produces books, periodicals, and reports on countries and policy issues in the Americas, including a series on selected individual countries of Central and South America. Catalog of publications free on request, or on the Web site.

***Memory of Fire*** • **by Eduardo Galeano** • **English translation by Cedric Belfrage** • 3-volume series: ISBN 0-393318079 (vol. 1, *Genesis*), ISBN 0-393318060 (vol. 2, *Faces and Masks*), ISBN 0 393317730 (vol. 3, *Century of the Wind*) • first published 1985, latest edition 1998, W.W. Norton, New York

***Open Veins of Latin America: Five Centuries of the Pillage of a Continent*** • **by Eduardo Galeano** • English translation by Cedric Belfrage • ISBN 0-85345-9916 • first published 1973, 25th anniversary edition, 1998, 360 pp • Monthly Review Press, New York

Chronicles of Central and South American history by a renowned Uruguayan journalist, novelist, and poet. The *Memory of Fire* trilogy is a history of the Americas written in literary form, combining storytelling, fiction, poetry, autobiographies, and historical documents to present the points of view of the indigenous peoples of the Americas and the underclasses through the centuries. Some people find it too literary and fragmented; others find it far more moving than conventional historical writing. *Open Veins of Latin America* is more concise, analytical, and conventional polemically, though still eloquent, treatment of many of the same issues. Readers who like the style of one may not like the other, and vice versa. But try to read one or the other: these are narratives with which all travelers in Central and South America should be familiar.

**NACLA Report on the Americas** • nacla@nacla.org • http://www.nacla.org • annual subscription (6 issues) US$32 (United States), C$50 Canada), UK£25 (UK), US$42 (elsewhere in the world)

USA editorial offices and subscriptions • North American Congress on Latin America • 38 Greene St., 4th Floor, New York, NY 10013 • tel. +1-646-613-1440, fax +1-646-613-1443

Canadian subscriptions • Social Justice Committee • 1857 de Maisonneuve ouest, Suite 320, Montréal, QC H3H 1J9, Canada • tel. +1-514-933-6797, fax +1-514-933-9517 • sjc@web.ca • http://www.s-j-c.net

UK subscriptions• Latin American Bureau • 1 Amwell St., London EC1R 1UL, UK • tel. +44-20-7278-2829, fax +44-20-7278-0165 • info@lab.org.uk http://www.lab.org.uk

An independent, nonprofit, English-language source of news and analysis of Central and South America since 1966.

**The Nine Nations of North America** • by Joel Garreau
ISBN 0-380-57885-9 • 1982, 427 pp • Avon Books, New York

A bestseller in the United States when it was first published, this is dated but remains valuable as an introduction to regional cultural and economic geography for visitors to North America. Many North Americans would—and did—argue with Garreau's details, or about the significance of the differences between regions, but few would dispute the basic accuracy of his descriptions. North Americans might also find contemplating the diversity of their own countries— and thinking about how much, or how little, of that diversity would be apparent to a casual foreign tourist, particularly one who didn't speak the language—good preparation for looking for, and appreciating, the regional variations within truly multicultural countries like India, Indonesia, Russia, Nigeria, or Brazil.

**Planeta.com** • "Eco-Travels in Latin America" • ISSN 1089-8395 • http://www.planeta.com

Planeta.com is the premier Web site for English-language travel and general information from and about South and Central America, Mexico, and the Caribbean. A labor of love and remarkable accomplishment for publisher/webmaster Ron Mader. Includes news, excerpts, directories, and links to Web sites where available, of English-language publications from and about Mexico, Central America, and South America (see under "Journalism"), as well as a popular directory of Spanish language schools. There's a huge amount of material on and linked from this site, from extremely diverse sources. So it takes some time to find your way around the site, and you need to pay careful attention to the source of each specific item.

**South American Explorers Club** • 126 Indian Creek Rd., Ithaca, NY 14850 • tel. 800-274-0568 (United States only) or +1-607-277-0488, fax +1-607-277-6122 • explorer@saexplorers.org • http://www.samexplo.org US$50/year individual, US$80/year couple (United States); additional postage US$7 (Canada), US$10 (rest of the world)

Despite the impossibly antiquated-sounding name, this is actually a rather funky association of budget backpackers of all ages and interests. For almost 20 years, the South American Explorers Club has provided a networking center, information exchange, and facilities for independent travelers, primarily in Andean and northwestern South America. Membership gets you a quarterly zine-like magazine; use of the "clubhouses" and libraries of trip reports in Quito, Cusco (Cuzco), and Lima; and the assistance of the club staff in planning your trips and answering your questions.

## Asia

*The Asian Age* • Dolphin Media House, Spring Villa Road, Edgeware, Middlesex HA8 7EB, UK • tel. +44-20-8951-4878, fax +44-20-8951-4839 asianage@asianage.com • http://www.asianage.com

Edited from India under the direction of acclaimed journalist M.J. Akbar, and published simultaneously from London and six cities in India. The London edition makes this one of the few newspapers from South Asia that's available in print outside the region without paying high air-shipping charges. The Web site includes particularly interesting local content from the editions for each Indian city.

**The Asia Society** • 725 Park Ave. (at 70th St.), New York, NY 10021 tel. +1-212-327-9217, fax +1-212-517-8315 • asiastore@asiasoc.org (publication orders) • http://www.asiasociety.org (organizational information, events, programs, exhibits, and publications) • http://www.asiasource.org (information, links, and resources from and about Asia)

A long-established think-tank and resource center for the study of Asia and the promotion of understanding of Asia in the United States. The bookstore includes both the Asia Society's own publications and a variety of other hard-to-find books about Asia. The AsiaSource.org portal includes an eclectic selection of resources and links, including opinion pieces on current issues from varied Asian points of view.

**Asia Times Online** • http://www.atimes.com

A daily online newspaper produced in Hong Kong and Bangkok, with news and views about East, Southeast, South, and Central Asia. "We look at these issues from an Asian perspective; this distinguishes us from the mainstream English-language media, whose reporting on Asian matters is generally by Westerners, for Westerners." Especially valuable for the editorials and news analysis and the reporting on less-known regions of Asia.

***Asian Express*** • 211 Piccadilly, London W1J 9HF, UK • tel. +44-20-7439-8985, fax +44-20-7537-2141 • http://www.asianexpressnewspaper.com info@asianexpressnewspaper.com

The UK's daily "Asian"—which in British usage means mainly South Asian—newspaper since 1973. General British and world news from an Asian slant, as well as news of the subcontinent and the Asian community in Britain. Readily available, as most British newsstands are run by South Asians.

**Books N Bits** • 11829 Artesia Blvd. (Artesia Center mall), Artesia, CA 90701 • tel. +1-562-809-9110, fax +1-562-809-0084 http://www.booksandbits.com • booksnbits@earthlink.net or bksnbts@aol.com

Very small but promising importer and distributor of books and periodicals from South Asia. Noteworthy for having books from and about both India and Pakistan. Located on a strip of South Asian-American businesses in Artesia at the heart of the largest "Little India" on the west coast of the United States. Worth the 15-km (10-mile) detour if you're at Disneyland, or flying jetBlue to or from Long Beach airport, and are interested in South Asia, especially if you can't get to the larger overseas South Asian neighborhoods in New York, Toronto, Vancouver, or the UK.

**China Books and Periodicals** • 2929-24th St., San Francisco, CA 94110 tel. +1-415-282-2994, fax +1-415-282-0994 • info@chinabooks.com http://www.chinabooks.com

China Books is the primary USA importer and distributor of books, periodicals, audio tapes, and films in English from the People's Republic of China, including everything from newspapers and magazines to reference books, travel guides, maps, and a comprehensive line of English-Chinese language learning aids. China Books also distributes books about China from other countries, and has itself become a major publisher of books about China.

**East-West Center** • 1601 East-West Rd., Honolulu, HI 96848-1601
tel. +1-808-944-7111, fax +1-808-944-7376 • ewcinfo@eastwestcenter.org
http://www.eastwestcenter.org

The East-West Center is a think tank dedicated to promoting understanding between the United States and the peoples and nations of Asia and the Pacific. Largely funded by the United States and other Asia-Pacific governments, but nonetheless widely respected throughout the region. Especially noteworthy for its monographs on often-overlooked public issues and parts of the region, such as the Asian parts of Russia and the former USSR and the smaller Pacific nations and colonies. Well-researched but intended to be accessible to lay readers. Check out their bookstore on the University of Hawai'i's Manoa Campus, just across the freeway *mauka* (inland) from Waikiki.

*Far Eastern Economic Review* • GPO Box 160, Hong Kong SAR, China
tel. 800-522-2714 (from the United States only) or +852-2508-4338 • fax +852-2503-1549 • subscription@feer.com • http://www.feer.com • annual subscription (51 weekly issues) UK£140 (UK), €250 (EU), C$220 (Canada), A$260 (Australia), NZ$270 (Aotearoa/New Zealand), US$215 (United States and the rest of the world except Asia)

Although it is owned by Dow Jones, the stock brokerage, this is actually a more general newsmagazine than its subtitle, "Asia's Business Newsweekly," would imply. Excellent writing, with correspondents throughout the continent. Its major weakness is its political and editorial bias, one that will be familiar to readers of Dow Jones's principal publication in the United States, the *Wall Street Journal*. Excerpts available free on the Web site.

**Hollym International Corp.** • 18 Donald Place, Elizabeth, NJ 07208
tel. +1-908-353-1655, fax +1-908-353-0255 • hollym2@optonline.net
http://www.hollym.com • http://www.hollym.co.kr

The leading publisher and distributor of books in English on Korea-related topics, including Korean language textbooks and dictionaries; Korean culture and history; and living, working, and traveling in Korea. Editorial and distribution offices in both Korea and the United States.

*The Idea of India* • by Sunil Khilnani • ISBN 0-374-52591-9 • revised paperback edition 1999, 208 pp • Farrar, Straus, and Giroux, New York

The best book to come out of the wave of national self-examination that marked the 50th anniversary of India's independence. Beautifully written, with a superb annotated bibliography. Essential reading if you want to understand India today.

**India-West** • 933 MacArthur Blvd., San Leandro, CA 94577 • tel. +1-510-383-1140, fax +1-510-383-1155 • info@indiawest.com http://www.indiawest.com • annual subscription (51 issues) US$30

More than 100 pages weekly of news and views from, for, and about South Asia (not just India) and the South Asian community in the United States, especially the western United States. Particularly interesting for its general world news and commentaries (from its own correspondents in the United States and the subcontinent, as well as reprinted by arrangement with Indian journals) on world affairs as seen from India and by Indians. My personal favorite of USA publications with Third World points of view. Headlines and selected full stories available on the Web site.

**Indo-US Books** • 37–46 74th St., Jackson Heights, Queens, NY 11372 tel. +1-718-899-5590, fax +1-718-899-7889 • service@indousbooks.com http://www.indousbooks.com

Books, magazines, and newspapers from India. In the heart of New York's "Little India," only a block from the 74th St.-Broadway and Roosevelt Ave.-Jackson Heights subway stops, a short train ride from Manhattan and a mile from La Guardia airport. Definitely worth a detour if you're in New York. They offer mail order, if you know exactly what you want, but most of their stock isn't cataloged and you're more likely to find what you want by browsing in person. Especially good stock of current magazines: news, Bollywood gossip, fashion, etc.

**Middle EurAsian Books** • 1 Theodore Rd., Ladysmith, QC J0X 2A0 Canada • tel. +1-819-647-9927, fax +1-819-647-9928 • info@meabooks.com http://www.meabooks.com

A unique source of books and periodicals from the Caucasus, Trans-Caucasia, Central Asia, Kazakhstan, Moldova, Byelorussia and Russia (particularly its Asian regions and ethnic republics). Occasionally has publications from these places in English.

*Night Market: Sexual Cultures and the Thai Economic Miracle* by **Ryan Bishop and Lillian S. Robinson** • ISBN 0-415-91429-9 1998, 278 pp • Routledge, New York and London

Combines perspectives from anthropology, cultural studies, political economics, and feminism. Much of what can be learned from this book about tourism marketing, and about tourists' and "hosts'" images of each other, is applicable to much more than sex tourism and in many more places than Thailand.

**Other India Bookstore** • Above Mapusa Clinic, Mapusa 403 507 Goa, India • +91-832-263306, fax +91-832-263305 • oibs@bom2.vsnl.net.in or admin@oibs.ilbom.ernet.in • http://www.goacom.com/books •

Publishers and distributors (by mail order) of books that you won't find else-where: "The other India generates its own literature, celebrates its own wisdom and practice, documents its own insights and has its own marketplace. The Other India Bookstore does not keep any title from Europe or America! More than 1000 titles can be found here, all published from either Asia, Africa or Latin America. The Other India Press, the publishing arm of the Other India Bookstore, is the only Indian publishing house that is wholly devoted to prop-agating alternatives to conventional ways of perceiving and doing things."

***Patpong Sisters: An American Woman's View of the Bangkok Sex World*** • by **Cleo Odzer** • ISBN 1-55970-3725 • first published 1994, paperback edition 1997, Arcade Publishing / Blue Moon Books, New York

Field notes from an American woman's immersion in Thailand's culture and industry of sex tourism while researching her doctoral dissertation in anthro-pology. Anthropologists are expected to maintain an impossible double stan-dard of observational immersion with objectivity; this book is exceptional for the writer's openness and honesty about the contradictions and moral dilem-mas facing herself, one that a wider range of tourists are not usually willing to admit. Many of her observations about the dynamics of power between First and Third World people apply to nonsexual relationships as well. Very readable; not strident, academic, or preachy.

**Rediff.com** • http://www.rediff.com

The leading India-based news and information portal Web site, and one of the largest English-language news sites in the Third World, as well as sites in Hindi and Gujarati and a special English site for Indians in the United States. Just as dot-coms in the United States were able to buy print publishers, Red-iff.com now owns the oldest and largest print publication for Non-Resident Indians (i.e. those not residing in India), the weekly tabloid *India Abroad*. But you can get much more, for free, on the Web site.

**South Asia Books** • P.O. Box 502, Columbia, MO 65205 • tel. +1-573-474-0116, fax +1-573-474-8124 • sabooks@southasiabooks.com http://www.southasiabooks.com

Primarily a distributor to libraries and universities, but offers substantial discounts from list price to retail customers, even on single-copy orders. Huge selection, including books on all topics from India (mostly), Pakistan, and a few from other South Asian countries. The catalog could be better organized, but they can special-order virtually anything in *Indian Books in Print* for inclusion with their next regular bulk shipment from the subconti-nent. No storefront; mail order only. Catalog free on request; the Web site has only a partial catalog.

RESOURCE GUIDE

**ThingsAsian.com** • http://www.thingsasian.com

An outgrowth of what was originally a print magazine called *Destination: Vietnam*, ThingsAsian.com is now an Internet-only magazine about East, South, and Southeast Asia. Targeted toward independent budget travelers, with articles like a backpacker's "Honeymoon in Vietnam" (an excellent recommendation, in my opinion; my partner and I spent our 20th anniversary in Hanoi) and photographs that capture the scenery and the romance of Asia while giving a realistic picture of travel and daily life.

***Travels in the Skin Trade: Tourism and the Sex Industry*** • **by Jeremy Seabrook** • ISBN 0745317561 • 2nd edition 2001, 192 pp • Pluto Press, London and Chicago • http://www.plutobooks.com

Interviews focusing on the "demand side" of the sex industry: male visitors to Bangkok. Also includes interviews with sex workers. If you want to know who supports and perpetuates the sex-tourism industry, read this book.

## Europe

**European Book Co.** • 925 Larkin St. (between Geary St. and Post St.), San Francisco, CA 94109 • tel. 877-746-3666 (United States only) or +1-415-474-0626, fax +1-415-474-0630 • info@europeanbook.com http://www.europeanbook.com

The USA West Coast's largest importer of contemporary books and periodicals in European languages other than English. Emphasis on publications in French, German, and Spanish, but also carries some books and language learning materials in other European languages. Will special order from European publishers.

**Rick Steves' Europe Through the Back Door** • 120-4th Ave. North, P.O. Box 2009, Edmonds, WA 98020-2009 • tel. +1-425-771-8303, fax +1-425-771-0833 • customerservice@ricksteves.com • http://www.ricksteves.com

Rick Steves now hosts a public television show about travel and organizes and leads group tours, but his company and Web site still offer the advice for independent, do-it-yourself travelers that made him and his guidebooks famous in the first place. Includes a comprehensive set of answers to frequently asked questions, detailed information and advice for choosing Eurailpasses, and overall the single best collection of resources for planning travel from the United States to Europe. Organized topically and by country within Europe.

**Schoenhof's Foreign Books**

See the listing below under "Languages and Communication."

## The Islamic World and the "Middle East"

**Al Hoda Bookshop** • 76–78 Charing Cross Rd. (tube stop: Leicester Square), London WC2H OBB, UK • tel. +44-20-7240-8381, fax +44-20-7497-0180 • sales@alhodanet.com • http://www.alhodanet.com

Stocks a wide selection of books about Islam and Muslims as well as books from and about the Islamic world. Especially good for secular, English-language works on non-Arab parts of the Islamic world that are usually overlooked by non-Muslim sources.

**Books International** • P.O. Box 1950, Eilat 88000, Israel • 1204/1 Grofit Street (Commercial Center), Eilat, Israel • tel. +972-8-633-0205 • fax +972-8-633-0204 • info@booksinternational.com • http://www.booksinternational.com/

"The No. 1 source for books published in Israel." Storefront and mail order distributor of many books in English (and a few in other European languages, especially Russian), in addition to books in Hebrew and Arabic.

**Islamic Horizons** • Islamic Society of North America (ISNA) • P.O. Box 38, Plainfield, IN 46168-0038 • tel. +1-317-839-8157, fax +1 317-839-1840 horizons@isna.net • http://www.isna.net/horizons • annual subscription (6 issues) US$24 (United States), US$30 (Canada), US$60 (rest of the world, airmail)

In addition to religious and organizational news of ISNA, *Islamic Horizons* contains an impressive amount of secular news and analysis of events in the Islamic world that doesn't get reported elsewhere, including features on Islamic peoples and regions that are scarcely ever mentioned in mainstream journals. I'm an atheist but read it regularly, learn from it, and have been warmly welcomed and respected by the staff.

**Islamic Publications International** • P.O. Box 705, Oneonta, NY 13820 tel. 800-568-9814 (United States only) or +1-607-432-7138, fax 800-466-6111 (United States only) or +1-607-432-7240 • islampub@islampub.com http://www.islampub.com

Catalog free on request or on the Web. No storefront; worldwide mail order only. Much of this catalog, unsurprisingly, is on explicitly religious subjects and of limited interest to those who are neither believers nor students of Islam. But IPI also distributes secular works, mainly in English, on the peoples, politics, history, societies, and current events of the Islamic world, including places that are often overlooked.

**The Middle East** • IC Publications Ltd., 7 Coldbath Square, London EC1R 4LQ, UK • tel. +44-20-7713-7711, fax +44-20-7713-7898 icpubs@africasia.com • http://www.africasia.com/themiddleeast

Monthly since 1974, covering current events, business, and culture. Annual subscription UK£36 (UK), US$90 (United States), UK£50 (rest of the world).

Check the Web site for discounted prices for new subscribers. IC Publications also publishes *New African*. (See above under "Africa.")

**Middle East Report** • Middle East Research and Information Project
(MERIP) • 1500 Massachusetts Ave. NW, Suite 119, Washington, DC 20005
admin@merip.org (general info) • merip@nb.net (subscriptions)
http://www.merip.org • annual subscription (6 issues) US$37 (United States),
US$42 (Canada, Mexico), US$55 (airmail to the rest of the world)

Published since 1971, *Middle East Report* is a truly independent forum for all viewpoints—national, religious, secular, and otherwise—on one of the world's most factionalized regions. Also publishes special reports on countries, topics, and issues; see the Web site for recommended books and links for further information about the region.

## Worldwide List of Islamic Booksellers
http://www.msa-natl.org/resources/Bookstores.html

Compiled by the Muslim Students Association of the United States and Canada, this is "a list of publishers, organizations and booksellers that deal in books on Islam or the Middle East," including many secular resources on the region. Well-organized and linked.

## Oceania
**South Pacific Organizer** • http://www.southpacific.org

Web portal maintained by David Stanley, author of the definitive *Moon Handbooks South Pacific*. Includes an exceptionally comprehensive directory of books, films, music, and links to Web resources from and about even the smallest and most obscure islands of the Pacific.

### From a Native Daughter: Colonialism and Sovereignty in Hawai'i
**by Haunani-Kay Trask** • ISBN 0824820592 • 2nd revised edition 1999,
240 pp • University of Hawai'i Press, Honolulu, HI • 1st ed. 1993, Common
Courage Press, Monroe, ME

Of all the areas incorporated into the United States, Hawai'i is the one most shaped by, and economically dependant on, tourism. Much debated and enormously influential (throughout Oceania, not just in Hawai'i), this collection of speeches and essays is still the definitive statement of the argument for Hawaiian sovereignty and the critique of contemporary colonialism in the islands. Particularly trenchant on the relationship between tourism, cultural imperialism, indigenous peoples, and national identity. See especially the introduction and the chapter on "Corporate Tourism and the Prostitution of Hawaian Culture." Must reading for any visitor to Hawai'i, and with many lessons for travelers elsewhere in the region and the world.

# ACCOMMODATIONS

## Home Exchanges

Home exchange services have proliferated in recent years. Most let you preview their listings on their Web sites. Before you join, check to see that they have listings for the types of homes, in the types of places, that you'd like to (and be able to) exchange for your own home. Keep in mind that these are only listing services: you're responsible for making your own arrangements once you find someone who's interested in an exchange.

Some services allow only members to respond to listings. Others have "open listings" of members' homes available for exchange, with a mechanism to contact them through the Web site, even if you aren't a member, without revealing their e-mail address to you unless they choose to respond to your offer.

**Digsville.com** • 1100 Valley Brook Ave., Lyndhurst, NJ 07071 • tel. 800-856-9059 (United States and Canada only) or +1-201-964-9044, fax +1-201-964-9047 • membersupport@digsville.com • http://www.digsville.com

Digsville.com is the most sophisticated home exchange service Web site. You can have them e-mail you automatically, for example, whenever someone lists a home available for exchange that matches your criteria of location, date, etc. Listings include ratings of each host by the people they've previously exchanged with. About 4,000 members and growing, although a higher percentage of members are in the United States than for some other services. Open listings.

**ExchangeHomes.com** • 16654 Soledad Canyon Rd., Suite 214, Santa Clarita, CA 91387 • tel. 800-848-7927 (United States only) or +1-661-298-0376, fax +1-661-298-057 • Anne@exchangehomes.com http://www.exchangehomes.com

Closed listings.

## First Home Exchange Alliance (FHEA)

FHEA is a consortium of home exchange services based in the United States, UK, and France (each of which has members in many other countries). Participants in any one of the FHEA services have access to the combined listings for all of the services, so there's no need to join more than one.

**United States: The Invented City** • 41 Sutter St., Suite 1090, San Francisco, CA 94104, United States • tel. +1-415-252-1141 • info@invented-city.com • http://www.invented-city.com

**UK: Homebase Holidays** • 7 Park Ave., London N13 5PG, UK • tel. +44-20-8886-8752, fax +44-20-8482-4258 • info@homebase-hols.com • http://www.homebase-hols.com

**@ home around the world** • P.O. Box 19518, London SW11 6WF, UK
+44-20-7564-3739 • london@homearoundtheworld.com
http://www.homearoundtheworld.com

Gay-owned and operated international lesbian and gay home and hospitality exchange service. Listings can only be viewed by members, and anonymous message forwarding is available for those who prefer not to list their contact onformation.

**HomeExchange.com** • P.O. Box 30085, Santa Barbara, CA 93130
tel. 800-877-8723 (United States only), +1-310-798-3864, fax +1-310-798-3865
http://www.homeexchange.com

5,500 members. Open listings.

**Homelink International** • http://www.homelink.org

Over 11,000 listings, with local representatives in 23 countries and listings in more—see the Web site for contacts in countries other than those listed below. Closed listings.

**Homelink Australia** • 1st Floor Bldg. A, 9 Oakdale Rd., Gateshead,
NSW, Australia 2290 • tel. +61-2-4944-4245, fax +61-2-4920-9144
australia@homelink.org

**Homelink Canada** • 1707 Platt Crescent, North Vancouver, BC, V7J 1X9,
Canada • tel. +1-604-987-3262 • exchange@homelink.ca

**Homelink Great Britain** • Linfield House, Gorse Hill Rd, Virginia Water,
Surrey GU25 4AS, UK • tel. +44-1344-842-642, fax +44-1344-842-642
great-britain@homelink.org.uk

**Homelink Ireland** • 95 Bracken Drive, Portmarnock, Co. Dublin, Rep. of
Ireland • tel. +353-1-846-2598, fax +353-1-846-0305 • ireland@homelink.org

**Homelink New Zealand** • 383 Redoubt Road, R.D.1 Papatoetoe,
Auckland, Aotearoa/New Zealand • tel./fax +64-9-263-9677
newzealand@homelink.org

**Homelink South Africa** • P.O. Box 23188, Claremont, Cape Town 7735,
South Africa • tel. +27-21-794-3433, fax +27-21-794-3433

**Homelink USA** • P.O. Box 47747, Tampa, FL 33647 • tel. 800-638-3841
(United States only) or +1-813-975-9825 • usa@homelink.org

**International Home Exchange Network (IHEN)** • 118 Flamingo Ave., Daytona Beach, FL 32118 • tel. +1-386-238-3633, fax +1-386-254-3425 • http://www.homexchange.com

The first and one of the least expensive, but one of the smaller, of Internet-based home exchange services.

**Intervac** • http://www.intervac.com

11,000 listings in 50+ countries. See the Web site for contacts in countries other than those listed below.

**Intervac Australia** • Kareela Rd., Cremorne Point NSW 2090 tel. +61-2-8904-1016, fax +61-2-8904-1016

**Intervac Canada** • 606 Alexander Crescent N.W.T2M 4T3 Calgary, Canada • tel. +1-403-284-3747, fax +1-403-284-3747 • sc@intervac.ca http://www.intervac.ca

**Intervac Great Britain** • Coxes Hill Barn, North Wraxall SN14 7AD Chippenham, Wiltshire, UK • tel. +44-1225-892-011, fax +44-1225-892-011 holiday@intervac.co.uk • http://www.intervac.co.uk

**Intervac Ireland** • Phillipstown, Ballymakenny Rd., Drogheda, Co. Louth, Rep. of Ireland • +353-41-9830930, fax +353-41-9870225 • fkelly@intervac.ie http://www.intervac.org/ireland

**Intervac Israel** • Communication Center Neve Ilan, Room 316, MP Harei Yehuda 90850, Israel • tel. +972-2534-4351, fax +972-2579-0508

**Intervac New Zealand** • 54 McKinley Crescent, Wellington 6002, Aotearoa/New Zealand • tel. +64-0-4934-4258, fax +64-4934-4259 intervacnz@paradise.net.nz

**Intervac US** • 30 Corte San Fernando, Tiburon, CA 94920 • tel. 800-756-4663 (United States only), fax +1-415-435-7440 • info@intervacUS.com http://www.intervacUS.com

**Intervac South Africa** • P.O. Box 623, 1747 Muldersdrift, South Africa tel. +27-11-957-2594, fax +27-11-957-2594 • intervacza@icon.co.za

## Hospitality Exchanges

Note that many of the home exchange services listed above also list hospitality exchanges.

**Free-Stay.com** • http://www.free-stay.com

US$35/year fee, despite the name, for listing in membership directory on the Web.

**Hospitality Club** • http://www.hospitalityclub.org

Large, free, extremely diverse. Web only.

**Hospitality Exchange** • http://www.goldray.com/hospitality

US$20/year for listing in semiannual printed directories distributed to members; listings are *not* (yet) available on the Web.

**Servas International** • helpdesk@servas.org • http://www.servas.org

Not intended primarily as way to arrange free places to stay, "Servas is an international, non-governmental, interracial peace association run in over 100 countries by volunteers. Founded in 1949 as a peace movement, Servas International is working to build understanding, tolerance and world peace. Servas encourages travellers to experience other societies more deeply and with more understanding than they would be likely to do as `just plain tourists.' Through Servas, travellers have opportunities to meet hosts, their families and friends and join in their everyday life. Where convenient, hosts may offer two nights' accommodation and invite travellers to share a meal." See the Web site for contacts in countries other than those listed below.

**Britain** • 4 Southfield Rd, Burley-in-Wharfedale, Ilkley LS29 7PA, UK tel. +44-20-8444-7778 • servas@servasbritain.u-net.com http://www.servasbritain.u-net.com

**United States** • 11 John St., Room 505, New York, NY 10038-4009 • tel. +1-212 267-0252, fax +1-212-267-0292 • info@usservas.org http://www.usservas.org

**Stay4Free** • http://www.stay4free.com

Founded by a musician looking for places to stay while touring, so the members include a lot of musicians and artists. Free Web-only membership directory.

**Travelhoo International Hospitality Exchange**
http://www.travelhoo.com

More than 3000 members from 110 countries. Free; Web-only.

**Women Welcome Women Wordwide** • 88 Easton St., High Wycombe, Bucks HP11 1LT, UK • tel./fax +44-1494-465-441 http://www.womenwelcomewomen.org.uk

Operated by a nonprofit trust with an international board of trustees. "There are few rules, the most important being the confidentiality of the list" of members. Membership fee (donation) is optional, to facilitate participation by women from poorer countries.

## Hostelling International (HI)

**International Youth Hostel Federation (IYHF)** • 9 Guessons Rd., Welwyn Garden City, Hertfordshire AL8 6QW, UK • http://www.iyhf.org

Hostelling International is the brand name of IYHF. (There are also many private and unaffiliated dormitories, hotels, and guest houses calling themselves "hostels"; the name "hostel," in itself, is no guarantee of anything.) IYHF publishes two annual directories of Hostelling International hostels: *Volume 1: Europe and the Mediterranean* and *Volume 2: Africa, Americas, Asia and the Pacific*. The directories are available from national HI affiliates, as well as at many hostels. The complete worldwide hostel directories are available on the IYHF Web site, along with links to many national IYHF affiliates. IYHF also coordinates a computerized International Booking Network for immediate confirmation of advance reservations (usually guaranteed by credit card) at certain hostels, mainly in international gateway cities. For information on IYHF memberships, or for hostel reservations, contact the nearest HI national affiliate, a few of which (in some, though by no means all, of the countries where HI hostels are useful) are listed below. Many HI national affiliates operate storefront travel stores and information centers—check their Web sites for details. Check the main IYHF Web site at http://www.iyhf.org for affiliates in other countries.

**Australian Youth Hostels Association** • Level 3, 10 Mallett St., Camperdown, NSW 2050, Australia • tel. +61-2-9565-1699, fax +61-2-9565-1325 • yha@yha.org.au • http://www.yha.org.au

**Hostelling International Canada** • 400-205 Catherine St., Ottawa, ON K2P 1C3, Canada • tel. +1-613-237-7884, fax +1-613-237-7868 credit-card bookings tel. 800-663-5777 (from within Canada only) info@hihostels.ca http://www.hihostels.ca

**Youth Hostel Association (YHA) England and Wales** • Trevelyan House, Dimple Road, Matlock, Derbyshire, DE4 3YH, UK • tel. 0870 770 8868 (from within UK only) or +44-1629-592-700, fax 0870-770-6127 (from within UK only) or +44-1629-592-627 • customerservices@yha.org.uk http://www.yha.org.uk/

**Irish Youth Hostel Association, An Óige** • 61 Mountjoy St., Dublin 7, Rep. of Ireland • tel. +353-1-830-4555, fax +353-1-830-5808 mailbox@anoige.ie • http://www.anoige.ie

**Hong Kong Youth Hostels Association** • Rm. 225-227, Block 19, Shek Kip Mei Estate, Sham Shui Po, Kowloon, Hong Kong SAR, China • tel. +852-2788-1638, fax +852-2788-3105 • info@yha.org.hk http://www.yha.org.hk

**Israel Youth Hostel Association** • Binyanei Ha'mah, P.O. Box 6001, Jerusalem 91060, Israel • tel. +972-2-655-8400, fax +972-2-655-8432 iyha@iyha.org.il • http://www.iyha.org.il

**Japan Youth Hostels** • Suidobashi Nishiguchi Kaikan, 2-20-7 Misaki-cho, Chiyoda-ku, Tokyo 100-0006, Japan • tel. +81-3-3288-1417, fax +81-3-3288-1248 • http://www.jyh.or.jp

**Youth Hostels Association of New Zealand** • 193 Cashel St., 3rd Floor Union House, P.O. Box 436, Christchurch, Aotearoa/New Zealand tel. +64-3-379-9970, fax +64-3-365-4476 • http://www.yha.org.nz

**Northern Ireland Youth Hostel Association** • 22 Donegall Rd., Belfast BT12 5JN, UK • tel. +44-1232-324-733, fax +44-1232-439-699 info@hini.org.uk

**Scottish Youth Hostels Association** • 7 Glebe Crescent, Stirling FK8 2JA, UK • tel. +44-1786-451-181, fax +44-1786-891-333 http://www.syha.org.uk

---

**Hostels Association of South Africa** • 3rd Floor, St. Georges House, 73 St. Georges Mall, P.O. Box 4402, Cape Town 8000, South Africa • tel. +27-21-424-2511, fax +27-21-424-4119 • http://www.hisa.org.za

**Hostelling International—USA (formerly American Youth Hostels)** • 8401 Colesville Rd., Suite 600, Silver Spring, MD 20910• tel. +1-202-783-6161, fax +1-202-783-6171 • credit-card bookings tel. +1-301-495-1240, fax +1-301-495-6697 • http://www.hiusa.org • hostels@hiusa.org

In addition to its hostels, HI-USA operates regional Travel Centers that sell HI memberships, European rail passes and tickets, guidebooks, luggage and accessories, and International Student Identity Cards. HI-USA also runs periodic "World Travel 101" workshops and extremely useful "International Travel Day" travel fairs. See their Web site, or contact the local chapter in your area, for current workshops and other events.

**Russian Youth Hostel Association** • http://www.hostel.ru/ryha.htm

**St. Petersburg International Hostel** • 3rd Sovetskaya Ulitsa, 28, St. Petersburg 193036, Russia • mailing address (via more secure and reliable Finnish post): St. Petersburg International Hostel, P.O. Box 8, SF-53501,

Lappeenranta, Finland • tel. +7-812-329-8018, fax +7-812-329-8019
ryh@ryh.ru • http://www.ryh.ru

**Traveller's Guest House** • 50, Ulitsa Bolshaya Pereyaslavskaya, 10th
Floor, Moscow 129041, Russia • tel. +7-095-971-4059, fax +7-095-280-7686
http://www.tgh.ru • info@tgh.ru

Both the Traveller's Guest House (Moscow) and the St. Petersburg International Hostel provide safe, clean, reliable, budget accommodations in dormitories and some private rooms; sponsorship for visas to Russia and some other former Soviet republics; and assistance with domestic, inter-republican, and international train tickets from St. Petersburg and Moscow respectively. Reservations should be made well in advance (several months if at all possible), specifying all cities in Russia to be visited and the total range of dates in Russia (which must be listed on the invitation), in order to have time to obtain invitations and visas. Russian hostels are good places to meet other foreign independent travelers, who are a rarity in most places in Russia.

## Private Hostels and Backpacker Accommodations

**Hostels.com** • http://www.hostels.com

This Web site lists more hostels than any other, including some (not all) Hostelling International hostels and many private and independent hostels. The emphasis, however, is overwhelmingly on non-HI hostels. Hostels.com provides descriptions and links to Web sites for non-HI hostels, but has only perfunctory listings and rarely links to Web sites for HI-affiliated hostels. Consider this site a complement to, not a substitute for, the HI Web site (see above).

**Hostelworld.com** • http://www.hostelworld.com

A Web booking service for private hostels, owned by the same company in Ireland that supplies the reservation system for the HI Web site. Lists fewer hostels than Hostels.com, but accepts guaranteed online bookings, with immediate confirmation, for every hostel listed, and lists a wider range of budget accommodations, campsites, etc., including some in places where there are no hostels.

***Australia Accommodation Directory*** • http://www.australia.com • click on
"Advanced Search," then "Accommodation Search"

Many government tourism offices and directories rate only upscale hotels, but the Australian Tourist Commission inspects, rates, and lists even hostels and backpacker dormitory accommodations. Searchable by category (even by rating category within the hostel/backpacker listings!) and location. Includes ratings, facilities and services, locator maps, and Web and e-mail addresses.

***The Hostel Handbook for the US and Canada*** • **by Jim Williams** •
722 St. Nicholas Ave., Dept. HHB, New York, NY 10031 • tel. +1-212-926-
7030, fax +1-212-283-0108 • editor@hostelhandbook.com
http://www.hostelhandbook.com • single copy US$5 (United States and
Canada, postpaid); US$10 (rest of the world, postpaid); payment by check
payable to Jim Williams; credit card orders through Amazon.com

This small but invaluable pamphlet and the associated Web site list not just
most Hostelling International hostels but a large number of private and unaffiliated hostels, mainly catering to foreign backpackers. Most of these places
are a bit more expensive than HI hostels and don't necessarily meet HI standards. But many of them are in places popular with hostelers where HI hostels are short of space and most hotel prices are prohibitive. Most of these
places aren't listed anywhere else in print; you'd have to find them by word
of mouth or on the Web site, which may not be available when you're walking the streets looking for a bed. Highly recommended.

# TRANSPORTATION

## By Air

*Airline Ticket Consolidators and Bucket Shops FAQ* • **by Edward
Hasbrouck** • http://hasbrouck.org/faq

My answers to frequently asked questions about international airline ticket
discounts, posted monthly since 1991 on the Usenet newsgroup
"rec.travel.air." This book goes into much more detail, but check my FAQ for
important updates and changes, since book went to press, to the information, advice, and strategies in the "Air Transportation" chapter.

**AirTreks.com** • 442 Post St., 4th Floor, San Francisco, CA 94102 • tel.
877-AIR-TREKS (877-247-8735, from the United States and Canada only) or
+1-415-912-5600, fax +1-415-912-5606 • nomad@airtreks-inc.com
http://airtreks.com

Where I work as a travel consultant—when I'm not playing, traveling, writing books, giving travel seminars, or trying to change the world.
AirTreks.com (founded in 1987 as High Adventure Travel) is the oldest and
largest travel agency in the Americas specializing exclusively in around-the-
world, circle-the-Pacific, and other multistop international air tickets. The
AirTreks.com Web site has some sample routes and (best-case, low season)
prices to help you get an idea of what tickets might cost, a modular "Trip
Planner" you can use to customize a route and get an instant online estimate,
and many other unique travel planning tools, resources, and services.

*Passenger Air Tariff* • published jointly by the International Air Transport
Association (IATA) and the Société Internationale de Télécommunications
Aéronautiques (SITA) • distributed by IATA Netherlands Data Publications

P.O. Box 49, 1170 AA Badhoevedorp, The Netherlands • tel. +31-20-403-7991, fax ++31-20-403-7978 • pat.indp@iata.org
http://www.passengerairtariff.com

"Is there a list of all the published RTW fares and routes?" is such a frequently asked question that I feel obliged to give the answer, if only to try to dissuade you from pursuing such a do-it-yourself approach. The *Passenger Air Tariff* is a set of telephone-book sized volumes, updated monthly, constituting, the "single authoritative reference source of worldwide industry and carrier passenger airline fares and rules in printed form." This is *not* a reference for the lay reader; most travel agents don't even subscribe to the *Passenger Air Tariff* and wouldn't know what to do with it if they did. If you want to buy an RTW or Circle-Pacific ticket at a published fare, and don't want to pay a travel agent to research them for you, you have to be prepared to read through and learn to interpret more than 100 pages of technical jargon in seven-point type describing more than 150 different RTW and Circle-Pacific fares.

## By Rail

***Thomas Cook Overseas Timetable*** • Thomas Cook Publishing • P.O. Box 227, Thorpe Wood, Peterborough PE3 6PU, UK • tel. +44-1733-503-571, fax +44-1733-503-596 • publishing-sales@thomascook.com
http://www.thomascooktimetables.com/ • single copy UK£8.55 (UK) plus shipping, direct from the publisher; also available from Map Link (see "Maps" under "Logistics") and many other map dealers

"Overseas" means everywhere in the world except Europe, including the Americas and the former USSR east of Moscow. Includes limited information on bus and ferry routes as well as detailed train timetables. The compressed format, peppered with footnotes, cross-references, and cryptic symbols, is notoriously difficult to read. But there is no readily available alternative source of train schedules and route maps for most countries, either in print or on the Web. The regular subscription edition of the *Overseas Timetable* is published every other month. (In the alternate months Thomas Cook publishes a companion volume, the *European Timetable*, but it's much less essential as there are better sources of rail information for most of Europe.) If you can find it, get the quarterly "Independent Travellers Edition," which includes supplemental information on rail passes and on seasonal variations in schedules. Most mainline schedules for a given route and season change little from year to year. Even a copy a year or two old is adequate for most people's advance planning. Schedules from the most recent edition have to be verified locally, when you buy your tickets, anyway.

**Amtrak** • 60 Massachusetts Ave. NE, Washington, DC 20002 • from the United States only tel. 800-USA-RAIL (800-872-7245) • from Canada only tel. 800-4-AMTRAK (800-426-8725) • from the rest of the world you can call any of the following local numbers: +1-312-558-1075 (Chicago, IL); +1-212-582-6875 (New York, NY); +1-213-624-0171 (Los Angeles, CA); +1-617-482-3660 (Boston, MA); +1-215-824-1600 (Philadelphia, PA); +1-202-484-7540 (Washington, DC) • International sales support (not a reservation office, but can help you locate the nearest Amtrak agency): tel. +1-215-856-7954, fax +1-215-856-7805 • service@sales.amtrak.com • http://www.amtrak.com

Amtrak (the National Railroad Passenger Corp.) operates almost all interstate passenger trains in the United States. Free complete system timetable and fares information mailed on request; information on USA Rail Passes for foreign visitors generally must be obtained by phone, from the Web site, or through overseas Amtrak sales agents.

**National Association of Railway Passengers (NARP)** • 900 2nd St. NW, Suite 308, Washington, DC 20002-3557 • tel. +1-202-408-8362, fax +1-202-408-8287 • narp@narprail.org • http://www.narprail.org

NARP is a lobbying group for the interests of railway passengers in the United States, working to protect the small fraction of government funding for transportation that goes to Amtrak and other railroads. (Most transportation funding goes to build roads and to subsidize cars, trucks, and barges.) They also lobby the railroads for better service. A tiny but extremely knowledgeable organization, NARP has earned the respect of rail companies and politicians alike, and Amtrak listens more and more to NARP's advice. Support for NARP is crucial to the preservation, much less expansion or modernization, of long-distance rail transportation in the United States. Regular membership dues US$30/year, US$38/family (two people). NARP members get 10 percent off all Amtrak fares, including already-discounted fares, so NARP membership can pay for itself on a single transcontinental ticket. NARP's useful introductory pamphlet, *Amtrak Travel Tips*, is available free by request, and on the NARP Web site at http://www.narprail.org/tips.htm.

**VIA Rail Canada** • P.O. Box 8116, Station "A," Montréal, QC H3C 3N3, Canada • from Canada tel. 888-VIA-RAIL (888-842-7245) • from the United States tel. 800-561-3949 • from the rest of the world tel. +1-416-366-8411 (Toronto) or +1-514-989-2626 (Montréal) • service@viarail.ca http://www.viarail.ca

VIA Rail Canada operates all transcontinental passenger trains and most, but not all, other long-distance passenger trains in Canada. Free complete system timetable and fares guide—including prices and rules for Canrail passes— mailed on request. The excellent multilingual VIA Web site includes a complete directory of overseas VIA ticket agents and permits you to make reservations or request schedules, fares, and literature directly over the Web.

**Eurail** • http://www.eurail.com

General information about Eurailpasses and Europasses, including a directory of sales agents worldwide. No online sales. For much more information, and for pass sales in the United States and Canada, see the Rail Europe entry below. An excellent summary of train schedules between main Western European cities is supposed to be given to all Eurailpass buyers, although it is often in short supply.

**Rail Europe** • Westchester One, 44 S. Broadway, White Plains, NY 10601 from the United States only tel. 800-4-EURAIL (800-438-7245) • from Canada only tel. 800-361-RAIL (800-361-7245) • fax from the United States only 800-432-1FAX (800-432-1329) • info@raileurope.com http://www.raileurope.com

Provides Eurailpasses, regional and country-specific rail passes, and tickets for all passenger trains in Western Europe. Rail Europe represents Eurailpass and Britrail pass participants as well as the Eurotunnel, although each of the three requires separate tickets or passes. The Rail Europe Web site is one of the best sources of information on point-to-point European rail schedules and fares, which aren't available on most Eurail pass sites.

**Eurotunnel/Eurostar** • P.O. Box 2000, Folkestone, Kent CT18 8XY, UK tel. +44-345-881-881 (Eurostar), tel. +44-8705-35-35-35 (Eurotunnel) callcentre@eurotunnel.com • http://www.eurostar.com http://www.eurotunnel.com

The Eurotunnel consortium operates the Channel Tunnel, or "Chunnel" as it is popularly known. Three types of trains are run: Eurostar trains for walk-on passengers only, using French TGV technology; Eurotunnel trains carrying motor vehicles on drive-on, drive-off rail cars; and freight trains carrying cargo containers and trucks on special cars. Bicycles are also transported on Eurotunnel trains, but can't be booked on the Web site; contact Eurotunnel reservations by phone or e-mail for cyclist reservation and ticket information and procedures.

**Rail Australia** • P.O. Box 445, Marleston Business Centre, Marleston SA 5033, Australia • tel. +61-8-8213-4592, fax +61-8-8213-4490 ausrail@gsr.com.au • http://www.railaustralia.com.au

Rail Australia is the joint marketing association of all the government-owned regional railway companies in Australia. Rail Australia can provide schedule information and referrals to sales agents for Australian rail passes and tickets. The Web site includes details on pass options and prices, as well as a list of sales agents outside Australia. You can also buy most passes on arrival in Australia (unlike Eurailpasses or many other visitor passes).

**JR (Japan Rail) Group** • http://www.japanrailpass.net

Information on Japan Rail Passes in English, Japanese, and other languages. Includes pass prices and rules, and a worldwide directory of pass sales agents.

### Worldwide Passenger Rail Links (Trainweb)
http://www.passengerrail.com

The Web's largest directory of passenger rail links. Not all passenger railroads have Web sites, but if they do, this site probably lists them. Keep in mind, however, that this site includes links to secondary and unofficial sources of widely varying accuracy, reliability, and timeliness. Whenever possible, verify services and schedules locally.

### Worldwide Railfan Links (Trainweb) • http://www.trainweb.com

An extremely diverse collection of links to information by and for railroad aficionados ("railfans" in North American usage, "trainspotters" in British usage). Some railfans may seem obsessed with their hobby (I sometimes thought that my father was, and some people might think it of my own interest in passenger trains!), but on the whole they are remarkably generous and helpful in answering questions and tracking down information about what train services are available.

## By Water

### Complete Folding Kayaker • *by Ralph Diaz* • ISBN 0071408096
2nd edition 2003, 256 pp • Ragged Mountain Press/McGraw-Hill, Camden, ME

The definitive book on the only seaworthy portable boats. Diaz also edits a newsletter, *Folding Kayaker* (P.O. Box 754, New York, NY 10054; +1-212-724-5069), in which parts of the book first appeared. But the book is a better introduction to the topic and includes references to many other sources of information, boats, and equipment. Opinionated, but acknowledges other points of view. Diaz is a regular participant in the rec.boats.paddle newsgroup on the Internet. If you have questions about his book or his regular postings of answers to frequently asked questions don't answer, he'll answer them in the newsgroup or by e-mail at rdiaz@ix.netcom.com.

### Folbot (USA) Inc. • 4209 Pace St., Charleston, SC, 29405 • tel. 800-533-5099 (United States only) or +1-843-744-3483, fax +1-843-744-7783
folbot1@aol.com • http://www.folbot.com

Manufacturers of sturdy, affordable, seaworthy folding kayaks. Made in the United States, but they have sales agents in Canada, Australia, Japan, and the UK, and their boats pack small enough to be shipped worldwide as parcels or checked as airline luggage. My personal endorsement and recommendation (as a satisfied repeat customer who paid list price) for outstanding value and customer service.

**Cruise & Freighter Travel Association** • P.O. Box 580188, Flushing,
NY 11358 • tel. 1-800-872-8584 (from the United States and Canada only)
info@travltips.com • http://www.travltips.com

Although they call themselves a membership association, this is mainly a
travel agency specializing in passenger travel on oceangoing freighter ships.
The Web site includes a directory of transoceanic and other large freighters
that carry paying passengers, including routes and approximate trip durations and prices (starting from approximately US$75 per person per day), at
http://www.travltips.com/freighterdirectory.html.

**Freighter World Cruises** • 180 South Lake Ave., Suite 335, Pasadena,
CA 91101 • tel. 800-531-7774 (United States only) or +1-626-449-3106
info@freighterworld.com • http://www.freighterworld.com

Claims to be "the largest travel agency in the world dedicated to freighter cruising." Web directory by world region of passenger-carrying freighter services,
routes, and prices (including some on odd routes or at short notice for as little
as US$50 per person per day), as well general information on freighter travel.

# LOGISTICS

## Cultural Awareness and Adaptation

*American Ways: A Guide for Foreigners in the United States*
**by Gary Althen** • ISBN 1-877864-99-4 • 2nd edition 2002, 328 pp
Intercultural Press, Yarmouth, ME • http://www.interculturalpress.com

Often used as a textbook about USA cultural attitudes in English as a Second
Language classes, this book can also help prepare people from the United
States for travel abroad by giving them a sense of how they may appear from
other cultural perspectives—which of the things they take for granted are
actually culturally determined, and what aspects of their culture and behavior may seem strange to "foreigners" in places they visit.

*The Art of Coming Home* • **by Craig Storti** • ISBN 1-85788-297-0
2001, 216 pp • Intercultural Press, Yarmouth, ME/Nicholas Brealey, London, UK
http://www.interculturalpress.com • http://www.nbrealey-books.com

Most people have more difficulty dealing with "reentry shock" when they
return from abroad than they do with culture shock en route. This practical
book is worth reading even before you leave, so that you can have a better
idea what to expect.

*The Art of Crossing Cultures* • **by Craig Storti** • ISBN 1-85788-296-2
2nd edition 2001, 171 pp • Intercultural Press, Yarmouth, ME/Nicholas Brealey,
London, UK • http://www.interculturalpress.com • http://www.nbrealey-books.com

Lessons in how to deal with country and culture shock, including many examples of cross-cultural misunderstandings, how they occur, how to avoid them, and how to deal with them.

**The Global Soul: Jet Lag, Shopping Malls, and the Search for Home**
**by Pico Iyer** • ISBN 0-679-77611-7 • paperback 2001 (hardcover 2000),
303 pp • Vintage Departures, New York

Iyer's books are often pigeonholed as travelogues, but this is a far more profound essay than that characterization might imply. *The Global Soul* doesn't lack for insightful description of travel experiences and how they affect the external world, but its focus is on the internal changes being brought about through increased world travel, migration, multiculturalism and "globalization": changes in our conceptions of ourselves, our identities, our places in the world, and the meaning of "home." Necessary reading.

**Intercultural Press** • 374 U.S. Route One, P.O. Box 700, Yarmouth, ME 04096 • tel. 800-370-2665 (United States only) or +1-207-846-5168, fax +1-207-846-5181 • books@interculturalpress.com • http://www .interculturalpress.com • UK distribution and co-publication of selected titles by Nicholas Brealey Publishing • 3-5 Spafield St., Clerkenwell, London EC1R 4QB, UK • tel. +44-20-7239-0360, fax +44-20-7239-0370 http://www.nbrealey-books.com

The leading publisher and distributor in the United States of books and other materials for intercultural training. For people going abroad from the United States and for people coming from abroad to the USA, its catalog includes books (and some videos and other materials) for foreign students, businesspeople, and other types of visitors and residents; materials and training exercises for developing an awareness of one's own cultural perspective and an understanding of how others' perspectives might differ; and theoretical works on various types of cross-cultural interactions, communications, and exchanges. I've listed only a few of the specific titles of the most general value to travelers. Complete catalog free on request, and on the Web site.

**Living Overseas: A Book of Preparations** • **by Ted Ward**
ISBN 0-02-933960-X, ISBN 0-02-933940-5 (paperback) • 1984, 358 pp
The Free Press, New York/McMillan, London, UK)

Once the definitive book on the topic. Now dated but still with much useful advice. Out of print but still readily available secondhand or in libraries.

**Survival Kit for Overseas Living** • **by L. Robert Kohls**
ISBN 1-85788-292-X • 4th edition 2001, 181 pp • Intercultural Press,
Yarmouth, ME/Nicholas Brealey, London, UK • http://www.interculturalpress.com
http://www.nbrealey-books.com

Intended for people planning to live and work abroad, but also includes a chapter specifically for travelers and other short-term visitors to other countries and cultures. Emphasizes cultural rather than logistical issues.

*Trans-Cultural Study Guide* • by Volunteers in Asia • first published 1975, 2nd edition 1987, 155 pp • Volunteers in Asia Press • Haas Center for Public Service, 3rd Floor, P.O. Box 20266, Stanford, CA 94309 • tel. +1-650-723-3228, fax +1-650-725-1805 • info@viaprograms.org http://www.volasia.org

This book gives no answers, only questions: it's a pocket-sized primer of questions to ask oneself, and local people, to help understand why and how things in a "strange" (i.e., different) place are the way they are. Excellent food for thought.

*The Whole World Guide to Culture Learning* • by J. Daniel Hess
ISBN 1-877864-19-6 • 1994, 280 pp • Intercultural Press, Yarmouth, ME http://www.interculturalpress.com

A guide to learning about world cultures, filled with case studies, examples, and practical advice on experiential learning methods and the learning process. Intended mainly for older students, but will also be valuable for those who want to use international travel with children as an opportunity for on-the-road "home schooling" in world cultures and diversity. (A shorter version is also available from the same publisher as *Studying Abroad/Learning Abroad: An Abridged Edition of The Whole World Guide to Culture Learning.*)

(See also the listings above under "The Ecology of Travel and Tourism," and below under "Employment, Living, Schooling, and Volunteering Abroad.")

## Maps, Guidebooks, and Gear
### The BookWire Index: Travel Booksellers
http://www.bookwire.com/bookwire/booksellers/Travel-Booksellers.html

An industry directory of links to Web sites for bookstores in the United States self-identified as specializing in travel.

### Independent Travel Stores Association (ITSA)
http://www.travelstores.org

A nationwide (USA) trade association of specialty stores selling guidebooks, travel literature, maps, language materials, and travel accessories. See the Web site for a directory and links to members' individual Web sites.

### International Map Trade Association (IMTA) • 2629 Manhattan
Avenue, PMB 281, Hermosa Beach, CA 90254-2447 • tel. +1-310-376-7731, fax +1-310-376-7287 • imta@maptrade.org • http://www.maptrade.org

An international trade association. "IMTA members are the companies that create and sell the maps, atlases, globes and map-related products you use." See the Web site for an excellent hyperlinked worldwide directory of specialty map retailers (many of which also sell guidebooks and other products for travelers) and map production companies.

**International Travel Maps and Books (ITMB Publishing)** • mail order and retail: 530 West Broadway (at Cambie St.), Vancouver, BC, V5Z 1E9, Canada • downtown retail store: 539 West Pender, Vancouver, BC, Canada tel. +1-604 879-3621, fax +1-604 879-4521 • itmb@itmb.com http://www.itmb.com

North America's leading publisher of maps for international travel, and a leading distributor of maps from other publishers. First-rate cartography and production.

**Map Link** • 30 South La Patera Lane, Unit 5, Santa Barbara, CA 93117 • tel. 800-962-1394 (United States only) or +1-805-692-6777, fax 800-627-7768 (United States only) or +1-805-692-6787 • custserv@maplink.com http://www.maplink.com

The best map dealer I know of. Mostly a wholesaler, but happily accepts retail orders. Tell them where you are going and what you'll be doing and they'll give you expert advice on which maps will be best. Map Link has fewer maps on display in their retail storefront than Stanford's in London, but offers by far the most comprehensive and best-organized catalog, most helpful and knowledgeable staff, and best mail-order service. The better-known Rand McNally map stores actually get most of their imported maps through Map Link. Phone, fax, e-mail, or mail ordering; prompt and efficient worldwide shipping. My highest recommendation.

**Mountain Equipment Co-Op (MEC)** • 130 West Broadway (between Manitoba St and Columbia St), Vancouver, BC, V5Y 1P3, Canada • tel. 800-661-7399 (Canada and United States only) or +1-604-876-8650, fax 800-722-1960 (Canada and United States only) or +1-604-876-6590 • info@mei.ca http://www.mei.ca

Like the REI coop in the United States, MEC is a nonprofit, member-owned consumer cooperative. It's also one of Canada's largest suppliers of outdoor and travel gear and clothing, with stores from Vancouver to Halifax as well as mail, phone, and web ordering. See the Web site, or call, for store locations. Sales to members only, but for C$5 you can buy a share and become a member for life.

**Recreational Equipment, Inc. (REI)** • 222 Yale Ave. North, Seattle, WA 98109-5429 • tel. 800-426-4840 (United States and Canada only), +1-253-891-2500 • service@rei.coop • http://www.rei.coop

Founded in 1938, REI is a nonprofit consumer cooperative (the largest in the United States), entirely owned by the members and run by a member-elected board of directors. Lifetime membership is US$15; any "profits" are distributed to the members, in proportion to their purchases, at the end of each year. Dozens of stores throughout the United States as well as mail and Internet ordering. Facilitates workshops and clinics at stores for members to share their knowledge, skills, and experience. REI emphasizes equipment for active outdoor recreation, but has one of the largest selections of travel gear in the United States, including travel packs and many brands and models of water purifiers. Check out their helpful evaluation guides and comparative specification sheets for different types of gear, available online or in the their stores.

**Stanfords Maps and Travel Books** • 12–14 Long Acre (tube stops: Covent Garden or Leicester Square), London WC2E 9LP, UK • storefront shop tel. +44-20-7836-836-1915 • mail and phone orders tel. +44-20-7836-1321, fax +44-20-7836-0189 • http://www.stanfords.co.uk

Stanfords probably has more maps and guidebooks on display than any other store. Perhaps most useful to travelers from the United States as a place to browse through the many English-language guidebooks that aren't distributed in the United States.

**U.S. Geological Survey (USGS)** • tel. 888-ASK-USGS (888-275-8747; from the United States only), faxback service +1-703-648-4888 http://www.usgs.gov

**USGS National Center** • 12201 Sunrise Valley Dr., Reston, VA 20192 (near Washington Dulles International Airport) • tel. +1-703-648-4000

**U.S. Geological Survey** • Box 25046, Denver Federal Center (ask for directions to the map store at the Federal Center gatehouse), Denver, CO 80225 • tel +1-303-236-5900

**U.S. Geological Survey** • 345 Middlefield Rd., Menlo Park, CA 94025 tel. +1-650-853-8300

The best starting point, although not the only mapping agency or map source, for worldwide maps published by the USGS itself and many other USA government agencies. Extremely helpful and user-friendly. Over-the-counter retail sales only at the three locations listed above. Distributed elsewhere by Map Link (the largest and most comprehensive stock), ITMB (Canada), Stanfords (UK), and other map stores.

## Weather, Climate, and When to Go

**World Weather Guide** • by E.A. Pearce and C. Gordon Smith

**Hutchinson World Weather Guide** • ISBN 1859863426 • revised edition 2000, 480 pp • Helicon Publishing, Oxford, UK

**Fodor's World Weather Guide** • ISBN 0-375-70349-7 • 1998 edition, 456 pp • Random House, New York

**Times Books World Weather Guide** • ISBN 0812918819 •
revised edition 1990, 480 pp • Times Books, New York

Notwithstanding the different titles, these are all essentially the same book. Notwithstanding being out of print under all three titles, this is by far the best climate reference for world travelers. Get a second-hand copy of whichever edition you can find. (I have one on my desk at the office, and another at home.) Fortunately, climate change is slow enough and small enough that old copies aren't out of date: a change of a fraction of a degree in average temperature can be critical to the ecology, but doesn't affect the tables or descriptions in a book like this. Includes average daily maximum and minimum temperatures, rainfall, and humidity for each month of the year, as well as descriptions of typical weather, for hundreds of locations in even obscure and little-touristed countries around the world. Comprehensive, detailed, and invaluable.

### WorldClimate • http://www.worldclimate.com

It's easy to find information on current weather— what the conditions are today, or what they are expected to be tomorrow. But what travelers need is different, and much harder to find: information on climate—what the typical conditions are at a particular time of year. This no-frills Web site has charts and tables of temperature, humidity, and precipitation from a variety of public domain (mostly government) sources.

### World Travel Guide Online • http://www.wtgonline.com

Pick a country, then choose "Climate," for exceptionally easy-to-understand graphs of month-by-month patterns of temperature, precipitation, humidity, and sunshine.

### The Worldwide Holiday and Festival Site •
http://www.holidayfestival.com

No one can keep track of every holiday and festival in the world—not even the "official" public holidays. But this site comes closer than any other source. Searchable by date (with links to holidays on that date around the world), country, or religion, with predictions for moveable and floating holidays for about five years into the future.

### Solar Eclipse Information • http://umbra.gsfc.nasa.gov/eclipse

Compiled by eclipse researchers from NASA, with help from scientists and amateur eclipse followers around the world, the bulletins on this site are the definitive resource for would-be eclipse observers. A detailed bulletin is produced a year or more before each total eclipse of the sun, mapping the eclipse path and other data and giving details on likely observing conditions and chances of seeing the eclipse at each point.

## Employment, Living, Schooling, and Volunteering Abroad

*Alternatives to the Peace Corps: A Directory of Third World and U.S. Custom Opportunities* • **edited by Joan Powell** • ISBN 0-935028-83-8 9th edition, 2001, 128 pp • Food First Books • Institute for Food and Development Policy / Food First • 398 60th St., Oakland, CA 94618 • tel. 800-274-7826 (United States only) or +1-510-654-4400, fax +1-510-654-4551 • foodfirst@foodfirst.org • http://www.foodfirst.org

An excellent directory of USA-based domestic and international volunteer programs; also includes a few listings of programs based in the Third World, and a good bibliography of other resources.

*Alternative Travel Directory: The Complete Guide to Work, Study, and Travel Overseas* • **edited by Clayton A. Hubbs** ISBN 1-886732-02-7 4th edition 2002, 262 pp • Transitions Abroad • P.O. Box 1300, Amherst, MA 01004-1300 • tel. 800-293-0373 (United States only) or +1-413-256-3414, fax +1-413-256-0373 • info@transitionsabroad.com http://www.transitionsabroad.com

Mainly a guide to organized programs—tours, study programs, jobs, volunteer opportunities, etc.—rather than independent travel. Especially noteworthy for the diversity of organizations whose programs are listed: academic, governmental, charitable, and commercial. Mainly USA-based programs, but includes some programs based in other countries. Lots of ideas and resources for further research.

**Escape Artist** • http://www.escapeartist.com

Website by the publishers of the *Escape from America* e-mail newsletter. Huge and diverse collection of links (some good, some bad) and advertisements related to all aspects of expatriate and international life, including retirement abroad. Could be better organized and more selective, but there's lots of good stuff here.

**ExpatExchange.com** • http://www.expatexchange.com

Community Web site for expats around the world. A useful place to connect with foreigners already living in a place you are thinking of moving.

*The Expert Expatriate: Your Guide to Successful Relocation Abroad* • **by Melissa Breyer Hess and Patricia Linderman** • ISBN 1-85788-320-9 • 2002, 274 pp • Intercultural Press, Yarmouth, ME/Nicholas Brealey, London, UK • http://www.interculturalpress.com • http://www.nbrealey-books.com • excerpts online at http://www.expatguide.info

Primarily a logistical rather than a cultural guide. Written mainly for families relocating abroad with a prearranged job for at least one member of the family, and with a sponsoring organization (usually that employer) to assist them.

*The Global Citizen: A Guide to Creating an International Life and Career* • by **Elizabeth Kruempelmann** • ISBN 1-58008-352-8 • 2002, 384 pp • Ten Speed Press, Berkeley, CA

International career planning and job search advice from the former moderator of the international job message board on Monster.com. Sometimes overly optimistic, and relatively uncritical in its reviews of programs and organizations, but has lots of good suggestions on job-search tactics.

**Global Exchange** • P.O. Box 852, Newcastle NSW 2300, Australia • tel. +61-2-4929-4688, fax +61-2-4929-4727 • info@globalexchange.com.au http://www.globalexchange.com.au

Publishers of guides for Australians and Aotearoa/New Zealanders living, working, volunteering, or studying overseas, and for foreigners living or working in Australia. Many of these work opportunities are based on reciprocal working holiday schemes, in which the United States doesn't participate. (No relation to Global Exchange in the United States listed below.)

**GoAbroad.com** • http://www.goabroad.com

Website for students from the United States considering or planning work, study, or volunteering abroad.

*How to Live Your Dream of Volunteering Overseas* • by **Joseph Collin, Stefano DeZeraga, and Zahara Heckscher** • ISBN 0-14-200071-X • 2002, 468 pp • Penguin Putnam, New York

A suberb book, destined to become the standard reference on the topic. Other books on volunteering abroad are mostly compilations of organizational self-descriptions. In contrast, the descriptions of specific programs in this book are based on visits to their work sites abroad and interviews with current and former participants, giving honest, critical pros and cons. Even more valuable are the sections on how to define your own goals for volunteering, find a program (or create your own) that suits them, prepare for your overseas experience, and follow through after you return. Includes a discussion of independent travel as an alternative to organized or prearranged volunteer programs. If you are thinking of volunteering abroad, start with this book.

**iAgora.com** • http://www.iagora.com

Mainly a forum for international students, but also includes other expatriates.

**International Volunteer Programs Association (IVPA)** • 71 W. 23rd Street, 17th Floor, New York, NY 10010-4102 http://www.volunteerinternational.org

"IVPA is an alliance of nonprofit, non-governmental organizations based in

North America, that are involved in international volunteer and internship exchanges." The Web site includes a database of programs searchable by country or world region, program type, and duration.

### Peace Brigades International (PBI)

**International Office** • Unit 5, 89–93 Fonthill Rd., London N4 3HT, UK • tel. +44-20-7561-9141, fax 44-20-7281-3181 • info@peacebrigades.org • http://www.peacebrigades.org

**PBI-United States** • 428 8th St. SE, 2nd Floor, Washington, DC 20003 • tel. +1-202-544-3765, fax +1-202-544-3766 • info@pbiusa.org • http://www.peacebrigades.org/usa.html

PBI volunteers from around the world provide nonviolent escort services and assistance in conflict resolution in areas of violence. PBI goes only where it is invited and works primarily to support indigenous organizations seeking to resolve conflicts nonviolently. For those seeking an alternative to "conflict resolution" through military intervention or other use of force, or to acquiescence in war and repression, and willing to make a serious commitment to peace work, PBI provides an excellent opportunity to work for peace while learning about the world.

### *The Peace Corps and More: 175 Ways to Work, Study and Travel in the Third World* • by Medea Benjamin

• ISBN 0-9711443-1-1 • 4rd edition 2003, 200 pp • Global Exchange (USA) • 2017 Mission St., Room 303, San Francisco, CA 94110 • tel. 800-497-1994 (United States only) or +1-415-255-7296, fax +1-415-255-7498 • info@globalexchange.org http://www.globalexchange.org

A selective but useful directory mainly of USA-based nongovernmental organizations that offer structured volunteer work opportunities in the Third and Fourth Worlds. Also lists a few government programs and some socially responsible education and tour programs. Includes a good but equally selective bibliography. Global Exchange is an operator of "Reality Tours" from the United States, with an explicit preference, reflected in this and their other books, toward escorted group travel rather than independent "do it yourself" travel. (No relation to Global Exchange in Australia, listed above.)

### Volunteers for Peace (VFP)

• 1034 Tiffany Rd., Belmont, VT 05730-0202 tel. +1-802-259-2759, fax +1-802-259-2922 • vfp@vfp.org • http://www.vfp.org

VFP organizes multinational groups of volunteers for constructive projects around the world, mostly for a few weeks at a time. VFP workcamps are an excellent way to extend one's stay in a country, meet people from other countries, and learn more about local life than is possible for most tourist travelers. Call, write, fax, e-mail, or check their Web site for a schedule of forthcoming workcamps.

## VIA (formerly Volunteers in Asia and Trans-Pacific Exchange)

Haas Center for Public Service, 3rd Floor • P.O. Box 20266, Stanford, CA 94309 • tel. +1-650-723-3228, fax +1-650-725-1805 • info@viaprograms.org
http://www.volasia.org • http://www.viaprograms.org

One of the most culturally sensitive and politically responsible USA-based volunteer organizations, VIA sends volunteers from the United States to teach English in several countries in Asia for periods ranging from a few months to two years, as well as operating some shorter-term educational and exchange programs. Exceptionally good pre-departure preparation program.

## *Work Abroad: The Complete Guide to Finding a Job Overseas* • edited by Clayton A. Hubbs • ISBN 1886732116 • 4th edition 2002

Transitions Abroad • P.O. Box 1300, Amherst, MA 01004-1300 • tel. 800-293-0373 (United States only) or +1-413-256-3414, fax +1-413-256-0373
info@transitionsabroad.com • http://www.transitionsabroad.com

## *Work Your Way Around the World* • by Susan Griffith

ISBN 1-85458-251-8 • 10th edition 2001, 546 pp • Vacation Work, Oxford, UK
http://www.vacationwork.co.uk

The British emphasis of this book reflects the reality that UK and Irish citizens—with special reciprocal employment privileges in both EU (Western Europe) and Commonwealth (most former British colonies) countries—have by far the easiest time finding legal employment outside their home countries. But recent editions have been more careful to distinguish the different employment rules for citizens of other countries. Griffith is optimistic but not totally unrealistic about what sorts of jobs, and at what wages, you can expect to find, and gives particularly apt warnings about the poor job prospects for Northern visitors in Southern countries. Read this book before you plan to finance your trip by working along the way.

(See also the listings above under "Cultural Awareness and Adaptation." For those planning to live abroad with children, see *Third Culture Kids*, listed above under "Travelers with Children.")

## Languages and Communication

### Bay Foreign Language Books • Unit 3(B) Frith Business Centre, Frith Rd., Aldington, Ashford, Kent TN25 7HJ, UK • +44-1233-720-020, fax +44-1233-721-272 • http://www.baylanguagebooks.co.uk/

Suppliers of language learning material in almost 500 languages. Mainly a distributor to bookstores, government agencies, educational institutions, and libraries, but also sells directly to the public worldwide by mail order.

### Foreign Languages for Travelers • http://www.travlang.com/languages

Basic travel vocabulary and pronunciation guides for several dozen languages, with online audio clips. Very useful in learning to pronounce a few key words in each language ("yes," "no," "please," "thank you," "toilet," etc.).

**Grant and Cuttler** • 55-57 Great Marlborough St. (tube stop: Oxford Circus), London W1F 7AY, England • tel. +44-20-7734 2012, fax +44-20-7734-9272 contactus@grantandcutler.com • http://www.grantandcutler.com

The UK's largest foreign language booksellers. Language learning materials as well as fiction and nonfiction books, periodicals, and films from around the world.

**Internet Language Company** • mail order: 1309 NE Ravenna Blvd., Seattle, WA 98105 • storefront: 1205 E. Pike St. (Capitol Hill), Seattle, WA 98105 • tel. 800-218-2737 (from the United States only) or +1-206-328-7922, fax +1-206-770-6449 • info@multilingualbooks.com http://multilingualbooks.com

Language learning and translations books (dictionaries, grammars, phrasebooks, references, textbooks, literature readers), tapes, CDs and software for more than 100 languages.

**Kwikpoint International Translators** • Gaia Communications, Inc. 48 S. Early St., Alexandria, VA 22304-6307, • tel. 888-KWIKPOINT (888-594-5764; United States only) or +1-703-370-5527, fax +1-703-370-5526 info@kwikpoint.com • http://www.kwikpoint.com

Pocket, wallet, and passport-sized laminated cards with pictographs illustrating basic travel concepts for use in communication by pointing. Remarkably well-designed and functional.

**Language Book Centre** • 131 York St., Sydney NSW, Australia tel. 1-800-802-432 (free call outside Sydney and within Australia only) or +61-2-9267-1397, fax +61-2-9264-8993 • language@abbeys.com.au http://www.languagebooks.com.au

This division of Abbeys Bookshop offers the largest range in Australia of language learning and foreign language books and materials.

**LCL International Booksellers** • 104-106 Judd St. (tube stops: King's Cross and St. Pancras), London WC1H 9NT, UK • tel. +44-20-7837-0486, fax +44-20-7833-9452 • sales.lcl@btinternet.com • http://www.lclib.com

Specialists in dictionaries, textbooks, grammmars, and other resources for learning a wide range of languages.

*Merriam-Webster's Guide to International Business Communications* **by Toby D. Atkinson** • ISBN 0-87779-608-4 • 2nd edition 1999, 400 pp Merriam-Webster, Inc., Springfield, MA

When you need help figuring out how to dial a phone number in another country, what goes on which lines of an address, or how to find the physical location in a foreign city corresponding to a mailing address, this is the book to look for in the library. I wish I had read this book sooner. By the time I found it, I didn't need it, having learned its lessons by sometimes-painful and costly experience. Be sure to read the introductory chapters on "How to Get Phone Calls and Faxes Through" and "How to Make Your English More Understandable" to nonnative speakers, before you leave home. Gives detailed information on address, telephone, etc. formats only for selected countries, mostly First World, but notes correctly that, "An awareness of the terminology and practices in these countries will help you understand those in many others." I hope that future editions will expand coverage of the more populous countries or often-visited countries in the rest of the world. Most travelers probably won't find it worth buying, but every library and every office that ever does international business should have a copy. If yours doesn't, get them to buy it.

**The Other Tongue: English Across Cultures** • **edited by Braj B. Kachru**
ISBN 0-252062000, 2nd edition 1992, 384 pp, • University of Illinois Press,
Urbana, IL, • ISBN 0-564067-5, 2nd edition 1996, 384 pp, • Oxford University
Press, New Delhi, India, (distributed in the United States by South Asia Books)

That it is possible to travel the world speaking only English is due to the unique role of English as an international language. Today most people in the world who use English are not native speakers of English, were taught by nonnative speakers of English, and use English primarily to communicate with other nonnative speakers. If native speakers of English, especially monolingual ones, want to use English effectively for international communication, we need to understand and accept the variety of English dialects that have evolved and, in many cases, sunk deep local roots around the world: West African English, South Asian English, Malaysian/Singaporean English, etc. This book is a thought-provoking introduction to these issues. Academic, but quite accessible, and deliberately structured to introduce and survey the topic. Especially recommended to anyone interested in teaching English, it contains valuable insights for anyone seeking to communicate in English with nonnative speakers or speakers of other English dialects.

**Schoenhof's Foreign Books** • 76A Mt. Auburn St., Cambridge, MA
02138 • tel. +1-617-547-8855, fax +1-617-547-8551 • info@schoenhofs.com
http://www.schoenhofs.com

A fixture in Harvard Square for almost 150 years, Schoenhof's offers "the largest selection of foreign-language books in North America," including language-learning material for over 700 languages and dialects, as well as fiction and nonfiction in 50 languages. Strong emphasis on Europe and European languages, but does cover the world.

## Computers and Internet Connectivity

**alt.cybercafes FAQ** • http://cybercaptive.com/faq.shtml

Includes updated links to directories of cybercafés.

**The Cybercafe Search Engine** • http://www.cybercaptive.com

**CyberCafes** • **http://www.cybercafe.com**
http://www.cybercafes.com

**Curious Cat CyberCafe Connections** • http://www.curiouscat.com/
travel/cybercafe.cfm

Useful searchable databases of thousands of cybercafés worldwide. Each lists only a small fraction of the world's cybercafés, especially in the Third World, so don't worry if few or none are listed in the place you are going: where there's a city, there's a cybercafé.

**GRIC (Global Roaming Internet Consortium)** • http://www.gric.com

**GRIC dial-up access locations and phone numbers**
http://pbs.gric.com/html/popfinder.html

**GRIC member ISP's** • http://www.gric.com/network/isp_locator.htmlz

**iPass** • http://ipass.com

**iPass dial-up access locations** • http://ipass.com/pcgi/poplookup.php

**iPass providers (if your ISP doesn't offer iPass)**
http://ipass.com/?Order/Order_iPass

GRIC and iPass are each a consortium of Internet service providers (ISP's) who have joined together to offer each others' subscribers reciprocal access through their local dial-up numbers. GRIC and iPass each include member ISP's with thousands of dial-up Internet access numbers in more than 150 countries each—far more than any single ISP. Charges vary depending on both your ISP and the one whose access number you use, but are almost always less than making an international call to your own ISP's access number in your home country. Check with your ISP (or with those you are considering subscribing to while traveling) to see if they already belong to GRIC or iPass. If not, you can sign up through a consortium member, or directly. Check for the current status of wireless and broadband roaming access.

**Dynamism.com** • sales@dynamism.com • tel. 800-711-6277 (United States and Canada only) or +1-312-587-0402, fax +1-312-587-0270
http://www.dynamism.com

Many of the subnotebook and palmtop computers most suitable for travelers are sold only in Japan. Dynamism.com adapts them for United States and international use (substituting the English-langauge versions of the operating system, user interface, etc. for the Japanese ones) and distributes and supports them worldwide. If "Small is beautiful" and "Size matters" are your computer mantras, this is the place to find your fantasy.

**Infotec-Travel** • edited by Marcus Endicott • http://www.infotec-travel.com

One of the largest collections of travel-related links on the Internet, emphasizing technological issues. Also includes the archives of the *Infotec-Travel* e-mail mailing list on "information technology in travel and tourism."

**Safeware** • 6500 Busch Blvd., Suite 233, Columbus, OH 43229 • tel. 800-800-1492 (toll-free in the United States only) or +1-614-781-1492, fax +1-614-781-0559 • service@safeware.com • http://www.safeware.com

Laptop computers are fragile magnets for theft. Airlines won't accept liability for laptops or other electronic equipment, and even most travel insurance excludes them or limits coverage to a few hundred dollars. Safeware is the only major company providing affordable insurance for laptop computers against loss, theft, breakage, and other damage. At about US$100 a year for worldwide coverage, at full replacement cost, for a typical laptop computer and peripherals, insurance is a bargain. If you insure your laptop with Safeware, they'll also insure your camera and/or other electronic gadgets.

For a much more extensive guide to Internet access while traveling, whether or not you bring a computer with you, see the chapter on "Using the Internet While Traveling" in *The Practical Nomad Guide to the Online Travel Marketplace,* and the resource guide on the *Practical Nomad* Web site at http://hasbrouck.org/links, which lists cybercafés and many other places to find public Internet access terminals, dial-up roaming Internet access providers, and wired and wireless connectivity providers for travelers.)

## Telephones and Electronic Equipment

**Steve Kropla's Help For World Travelers** • http://www.kropla.com

A compendium of information on telephone, television, and electrical systems worldwide. Compiled as a labor of love and service to fellow travelers by corporate jet-setter and road warrior *par excellence* Steve Kropla, with the assistance of volunteer contributors around the world.

**TeleAdapt Inc.** • http://www.teleadapt.com

**TeleAdapt Asia** • Unit 711-712, 7/F Peninsula Tower, 538 Castle Peak Rd., Cheung Sha Wan, Kowloon, Hong Kong SAR, China • tel. +852-2780-9020, fax +852-2780-9019 • info@hk.teleadapt.com • http://www.teleadapt.com.hk

**TeleAdapt UK** • The Technology Park, Colindeep Lane, London NW9 6TA, UK • tel. +44-20-8233-3000, fax +44-20-8233-3132 contact@teleadapt.com • http://www.teleadapt.co.uk

**TeleAdapt USA** • 1762 Technology Dr., Suite 223, San Jose, CA 95110 tel. 877-TELEADAPT (877-835-3232; United States and Canada only) or +1-408-350-1440, fax +1-408-350-0160 • info@us.teleadapt.com http://www.teleadaptusa.com

TeleAdapt supplies a comprehensive range of power and telephone adapters, plugs, and converters. They maintain an incredible database of which frequencies, voltages, power plugs, telephone connectors, ringing signals, etc., are in use in which countries. Their Web site has a wealth of pointers for using a portable computer with a modem while traveling. Top-notch customer service; they are accustomed to dealing with traveling laptop-toting executives of noncomputer businesses, and their staff won't put you down for being a computer novice. Highly recommended.

**Telestial** • 1804 Garnet Ave., Suite 385, San Diego CA 92109 tel. +1-858-274-2686, fax +1-858-274-2757 • moreinfo@telestial.com http://www.telestial.com

Cell phones and prepaid SIMs for world travel, including both single-country SIMs (the cheapest choice for use within those specific countries), and SIMs with more expensive per-minute rates that can be used anywhere in the world (useful to have one of as a backup, even if you buy single-country SIMs in places where you stay a while).

**GSM World—the GSM Association** • http://www.gsmworld.com

Coverage maps, roaming agreements, and listings and links for local mobile (cellular) phone operators worldwide. The place to go to find out which of the international-standard GSM band(s) are in use in each of the countries you plan to visit, so you know whether you need a dual-or a tri-band phone to cover them all. (Warning: listings of new networks on GSMworld.com are sometimes premature. Always click through to the Web site for the local operator to verify the current status of their service.)

# PASSPORTS

## USA Passports

### National Passport Information Center • Passport Services Agency
U.S. Department of State • tel. 877-4USA-PPT(877-487-2778; toll-free from the United States only) • http://travel.state.gov/passport_services.html npic@state.gov

Local Passport Agency phone numbers give information only on scheduling appointments. Information concerning passport applications is also available on the Internet or from offices that accept passport applications, including many post offices and offices of county clerks.

**National Passport Center** • 31 Rochester Ave. Portsmouth, NH 03801-2900 • tel. +1-603-334-0500 • npic@state.gov

Applications accepted by mail only; no walk-in service at the addresses above. The Passport Agency urges you to apply for your passport by mail, not in person, which is fine as long as you have enough time (at least a month, preferably two or three months) before you plan to leave. Do not mail an application to the passport center without first taking the application, in an unsealed envelope, together with the originals of your proof of identity and citizenship (typically a driver's license or other state photo ID card and your birth certificate, for people born in the United States) to a post office or county clerk's office that accepts passport applications. They must inspect your documents and certify that you have proven your identity and citizenship before your application can be forwarded to the Passport Center. Applications can be sent by regular mail, but from the experiences of my clients and other travelers I very strongly recommend that passports and passport (and visa) applications be sent exclusively by Express Mail (not Priority Mail, registered mail, or certified mail) or by private overnight delivery services, and returned the same way, no matter how much time you have before your intended departure.

Walk-in applications at the Passport Agency offices listed below are accepted only on payment of rush charges and with evidence of impending departure, such as tickets or an itinerary on travel agency letterhead or forms. Most offices require appointments. Call ahead to verify current requirements and hours. (Note, however, that the phone numbers listed below are for appointment scheduling only. For information and advice about how to apply, you have to pay to contact the national Passport Information Center.) Walk-in applications are processed in order of priority of departure, and can be issued the same day if truly necessary.

**Boston Passport Agency** • Thomas P. O'Neill Federal Bldg. 10 Causeway St., Suite 247, Boston, MA 02222-1094 tel. +1-617-878-0900

**Chicago Passport Agency** • Kluczynski Federal Bldg. 230 S. Dearborn St., 18th Floor, Chicago, IL 60604-1564 tel. +1-312-341-6020

**Connecticut Passport Agency** • 50 Washington St., Norwalk, CT 06854 tel. +1-203-299-5443

**Honolulu Passport Agency** • Prince Kuhio Federal Bldg., 300 Ala Moana Blvd., Suite 1-330 Honolulu, HI 96850 tel. +1-808-522-8283

**Houston Passport Agency** • Mickey Leland Federal Bldg., 1919 Smith St., Suite 1400 Houston, TX 77002-8049 tel. +1-713-751-0294

**Los Angeles Passport Agency** • Federal Bldg., 11000 Wilshire Blvd., Suite 1000 Los Angeles, CA 90024-3615 tel. +1-310-575-5700

**Miami Passport Agency** • Claude Pepper Federal Office Bldg., 51 SW First Ave., 3rd Floor, Miami, FL 33130-1680 tel. +1-305-539-3600

**New Orleans Passport Agency** • One Canal Place (corner of Canal and N. Peters Sts.) 365 Canal St., Suite 1300, New Orleans, LA 70130-6508 tel. +1-504-412-2600

**New York Passport Agency** • 376 Hudson Street, New York, NY 10014 tel. +1-212-206-3500

**Philadelphia Passport Agency** • U.S. Custom House, 200 Chestnut St., Room 103, Philadelphia, PA 19106-2970 tel. +1-215-418-5937

**San Francisco Passport Agency** • 95 Hawthorne St., 5th Floor, San Francisco, CA 94105-3901 tel. +1-415-538-2700

**Seattle Passport Agency** • Henry Jackson Federal Bldg., 915 Second Ave., Suite 992, Seattle, WA 98174-1091 tel. +1-206-808-5700

**Washington Passport Agency** • 1111 19th St., N.W., Washington, D.C. 20524 tel. +1-202-647-0518

## Canadian Passports

**Passport Office** • Department of Foreign Affairs and International Trade, Government of Canada, Ottawa, ON K1A 0G3, Canada • tel. 800-567-6868 (toll-free from Canada only) • +1-819-994-3500 (Ottawa-Hull area) • +1-514-283-2152 (Montréal area) • +1-416-973-3251 (Toronto area) • +1-604-586-5200 (Vancouver area) • +1-819-994-3500 (Canadians living in the United States) • +1-819-994-3560 (TTY) • http://www.ppt.gc.ca

The Canadian Passport Office recommends that Canadian citizens apply for passports in person at one of the passport offices listed below, if possible, rather than by mail. (Note that this is the opposite of the preference of the United States government for USA citizens.) Application forms and instructions are available at Passport Offices, from some travel agencies and retail stores in northern areas of Canada, on the Internet, or by mail from the Ottawa address above.

Harry Hays Bldg., 220 4th Ave. S.E., Suite 254, Calgary, AB

Canada Place Bldg., 9700 Jasper Ave., Suite 160, Edmonton, AB

8011 Saba Rd., Suite 135, Richmond, BC

13401-108th Ave., Suite 900, Surrey, BC

Sinclair Centre 757 Hastings St. West, Suite 200, Vancouver, BC

Scotiabank Bldg. 747 Fort Street, 5th Floor, Victoria, BC

433 Main St., Suite 400, Winnipeg, MB

77 Westmorland St., Suite 430, Fredericton, NB

TD Place 140 Water St., Suite 702, St. John's, NF

Maritime Centre, 1505 Barrington Street, Suite 1508, Halifax, NS

Standard Life Bldg., 120 King St. W., Suite 330, Hamilton, ON

The Galleria, 101 Frederick St., Suite 630, Kitchener, ON

400 York St., Suite 201, London, ON

Central Parkway Mall 377, Burnhamthorpe Rd. E., 2nd Floor, Suite 116, Mississauga, ON

Joseph Shepard Bldg., 4900 Yonge St., Suite 380, North York, ON

C.D. Howe Bldg., 240 Sparks St., Level C, East Tower, Ottawa, ON

200 Town Centre Court, Suite 210, Scarborough, ON

Landmark Bldg. 43 Church St., Suite 600, St. Catharines, ON

979 Alloy Dr., 2nd Floor, Thunder Bay, ON

74 Victoria St., Suite 300, Toronto, ON

CIBC Bldg., 100 Ouellette Ave., Suite 1010 Windsor, ON

Place du Centre, 200 Promenade du Portage Commercial, Level 2, Gatineau (Hull sector), QC

Immeuble Saint-Michel, 3885 Harvey Blvd., Suite 408, Saguenay, QC

3 Place Laval, Suite 500, Laval, QC

Complexe Guy-Favreau, 200 René-Lévesque Boulevard W., Suite 803, West Tower, Montréal, QC

Belle Cour Tower, Place de la Cité, 2600 Laurier Boulevard, Suite 2410, 4th Floor Québec, QC

3300 Chemin Côte Vertu, Suite 112, Saint-Laurent, QC

1870 Albert St., Suite 500, Regina, SK

Federal Bldg., 101 22nd St. E., Suite 405, Saskatoon, SK

## UK Passports
### UK Passport Agency (an executive agency of the Home Office)
tel. +44-870-521-0410 (nationwide) • http://www.ukpa.gov.uk

You can start the application process for a UK passport by completing a form on their Web site. A printed application will then be mailed to you to sign and return with your photographs, payment, and documentation. Average processing time is less than a week in the off-season, but the Passport Office recommends that you apply for a passport at least a month before your intended departure, preferably longer, especially in the spring and early summer when the largest numbers of people apply for passports for summer holiday travel. If you're in a hurry, applications are accepted in person, for an additional charge, at the Passport Offices listed below. Most Passport Offices accept walk-in applications by appointment only, so call the national passport advice line (+44-870-521-0410) for an appointment before going to a Passport Office.

**Durham Passport Office** • Millburngate House, Durham, DH97, 1PA England

**Liverpool Passport Office** • India Buildings, 5th Floor, Water St., Liverpool L2 0QZ England

**London Passport Office** • Globe House, 89 Eccleston Square, London, SW1V 1PN, England

**Peterborough Passport Office** • Aragon Court, Northminster Rd. Peterborough PE1 1QG, England

**Belfast Passport Office** • Hampton House, 47–53 High St., Belfast BT1 2QS, Northern Ireland

**Glascow Passport Office** • 3 Northgate, 96 Milton St., Cowcaddens Glascow G4 0BT, Scotland

**Newport Passport Office** • Olympia House, Upper Dock St., Newport, Gwent NP20 1XA, Wales

## Irish Passports
**Passport Office** • Republic of Ireland • Dept. of Foreign Affairs • http://www.irlgov.ie/iveagh/services/passports

Irish citizens can obtain and submit passport application forms at the Passport Offices listed below, or through most post offices and Garda stations in Ireland or Irish embassies and consulates abroad.

Setanta Centre, Molesworth St., Dublin 2, tel. +353-671-1633

Irish Life Building, 1a South Mall, Cork, tel. +353-21-272-525 0r +353-21-276-964 (applications from counties Clare, Cork, Kerry, Limerick, Tipperary, and Waterford only)

## Australian Passports

**Passports Australia** • Department of Foreign Affairs and Trade • tel. 131-232 (toll-free from anywhere in Australia only) • passports.australia@dfat.gov.au http://www.passports.gov.au

Australian citizens can apply for a passport in person at most post offices in Australia. Post offices may require advance appointments for passport application interviews, so call in advance. Normal processing time is supposedly 10 working days; expedited processing is available for an additional charge on proof of imminent departure. Application forms and instructions are available at most post offices, or from Passports Australia. Applications are accepted directly at passport offices, rather than through post offices, only in special circumstances.

Sydney Passport Office, Level 7, Gateway House, Henry Deane Place, 26 Lee St., Sydney, NSW, Australia

## Aotearoa/New Zealand Passports

**Aotearoa/New Zealand Passport Office** • Dept. of Internal Affairs, P.O. Box 10-526, Wellington, Aotearoa/New Zealand • tel. 0800-22-50-50 (toll free within Aotearoa/New Zealand only) • +64-4-474-8100 • fax +64-4-474-8010 • passports@dia.govt.nz • http://www.passports.govt.nz

Aotearoa/New Zealand citizens can request passport application forms by phone or download them from the Web site listed above. Completed applications can be mailed to the Passport Office, or submitted through an Aotearoa/New Zealand Embassy, High Commission or Consulate abroad. Rush service through Passport Offices is available for an extra charge.

**Wellington Passport Office** • Level 3, Boulcott House, 47 Boulcott St. Wellington

**Auckland Passport Office** • Department of Internal Affairs, P.O. Box 6147 Wellesley St. Auckland

**Manukau Passport Office** • Department of Internal Affairs Hodgetts Bldg. (corner of Amersham and Osterley Ways), P.O. Box 76-222, Manukau, Auckland

**Christchurch Passport Office** • Department of Internal Affairs, 48 Peterborough St., P.O. Box 25-211, Christchurch

# VISAS

## Worldwide Visa and Entry Requirements

*Travel Information Manual* • TIM/TIMATIC B.V. • P.O. Box 49, 1170 AA Badhoevedorp, Netherlands • tel. +31-20-4037944, fax +31-20-4037984 info@timaticweb.com • http://www.timaticweb.com

This is the reference used by airlines in deciding whether you will be admitted to your destination (and thus whether to let you on the plane). Unlike most sources that list requirements only for citizens of a particular country, the *Travel Information Manual* includes information on visa, entry, and transit requirements for citizens of all countries. It's useful, but should never be relied on without double-checking with each country's embassy or consulate. Ask to look at a copy of the printed TIM at an airline office, or ask a travel agent to print out or e-mail the relevant pages from the electronic edition (TIMATIC), which is available through computerized reservation systems. The Web site is for paid subscribers only, but you may be able to get a brief free trial, which would suffice for one-time use to check the database for all the countries you plan to visit on a big trip.

## Visa Requirements for USA Citizens Traveling Abroad
## U.S. Department of State

Because visa requirements are determined by the government of the country you want to visit, the starting point in determining the entry requirements for another country is finding the nearest embassy or consulate of that country. Because all agents of foreign governments in the United States must register with the U.S. Department of State, lists of foreign diplomatic offices and officers found here are complete and definitive except in the case of governments not recognized by the United States, or of changes since the last (usually annual) update. Visa and entry requirements, however, can be changed without notice to the USA government, so the U.S. Department of State summaries of foreign entry requirements are only informational, not authoritative.

Some of this information is also available in print, but it changes sufficiently often that I can't recommend relying on the print versions. Get the latest revisions available on the Internet, and double-check them with the relevant embassies or consulates.

*Diplomatic List* • http://www.state.gov/s/cpr/rls/dpl

*Foreign Consular Offices in the United States* •
http://www.state.gov/s/cpr/rls/fco

The Diplomatic List covers foreign embassies in Washington, DC. Foreign Consular Offices covers all foreign consulates and other diplomatic offices elsewhere in the United States. Both include contact information (including URL's for many consular and embassy Web sites) and complete staff directories of all accredited diplomats, with titles.

### Foreign Entry Requirements •
http://travel.state.gov/foreignentryreqs.html

### HIV Testing Requirements for Entry into Foreign Countries
http://travel.state.gov/HIVtestingreqs.html

Please don't rely on these; verify everything with each country's own authorities. But these publications are useful as a starting point when contacting foreign embassies or consulates. There are two annual summaries by the U.S. State Department listing other countries' entry requirements for USA citizens. *Foreign Entry Requirements* covers general requirements; *HIV Testing Requirements for Entry into Foreign Countries* catalogs other countries' requirements for HIV testing, generally for long-term residents.

### U.S. Department of the Treasury, Office of Foreign Assets
Controls • http://www.treas.gov/ofac
http://www.treas.gov/offices/enforcement/ofac

This site contains current regulations for trade embargoes that restrict travel and tourism spending and/or imports by USA citizens from, in, or with listed countries and entities. Most USA government restrictions on travel come from this office, not the State Department; many of these rules affect visitors to the United States from other countries (if they have previously visited embargoed countries), not just citizens of the United States. The Web site includes a summary of current tourism and travel-related OFAC rules. Many travelers from the United States to countries like Cuba violate these rules, and/or consider them to be unconstitutional, but it's worth knowing whether the USA government might object to what you are doing.

### Embassy.org

The U.S. State Department list of foreign embassies in the United States is authoritative and comprehensive, but doesn't necessarily list their Web sites. Not all embassies have Web sites, of course, but this unofficial, commercial, Web site has the best available collection of links to those that do. Note that it lists only embassies in Washington, DC; there's no information here on consulates (or their Web sites) in the rest of the United States, or the rest of the world.

## Visa Requirements for Foreign Visitors to the United States
Visa Office • U.S. Department of State • tel. +1-202-663-1225
http://travel.state.gov/visa_services.html

Outside the United States, information on travel to the USA can be obtained from any USA embassy or consulate, but be prepared to wait in very long lines. This Web site has details on requirements for each type of visa as well as downloadable application forms and contact information for all USA embassies and consulates abroad.

## Visa Requirements for Foreign Visitors to Europe
Schengen Visa Information • http://www.eurovisa.info

A "Schengen visa" is a common visa valid throughout a large group of European countries that have abolished internal borders controls and established common entrance requirements. If you need a visa to any of the Schengen visa countries, you need to get a Schengen visa from the consulate or embassy of the first such country you will enter; you don't need to get separate visas for any further travel within or between participating countries. (Citizens of the USA, Canada, Australia, New Zealand, or of course the European Union generally don't need visas for short visits as tourists to any of the Schengen countries.)

# SAFETY AND HEALTH

## Government Health Advice and Information
Centers for Disease Control and Prevention • Traveler's Health Hotline • tel. 877-FYI-TRIP (877-394-8747; from the United States only) faxback service 888-CDC-FAXX (888-232-3299; from the United States only) http://www.cdc.gov/travel

Official USA inoculation and health recommendations for international travelers, general and by country and region. Available only by phone, fax, or on the Internet; no longer distributed in print.

*World Health Organization* • http://www.who.int
  *International Travel and Health* • http://www.who.int/ith
  *International Travel Health News* • http://www.who.int/health_topics/travel

The WHO is the UN-affiliated coordinating body for international public health efforts, disease prevention, and response to disease outbreaks. The WHO Web site includes the complete text of the WHO reference manual, *International Travel and Health*, as well as bulletins and advice on health issues for travelers in each country and region of the world.

## Government Political and Safety Advice and Information
*Bureau of Consular Affairs, U.S. Department of State*
http://travel.state.gov

I'm normally no fan of the U.S. State Department. But the Web site of the Bureau of Consular Affairs is a model of clarity and ease of use—despite getting little support from the rest of the State Department, and almost no funding. Links to all the most important USA government information for travelers, even when it comes from completely different departments and agencies (a rarity in the federal government world of bureaucratic compartmentalization).

**Consular Information Sheets** (all countries)
**Tips for Travelers** (selected countries and regions)
**Travel Warnings** (included with the Consular Information Sheet whenever a Travel Warning is in effect) • http://travel.state.gov/travel_warnings.html

These useful, if biased, publications from the U.S. Department of State are available on the Internet, at U.S. Passport Agency offices (see listing under "Passports"), and at USA consulates and embassies abroad.

**Background Notes** (all countries) • by the U.S. Department of State
http://www.state.gov/r/pa/ei/bgn

Not specifically for travelers, but give a broader overview than the Dept. of State's travel publications. A less statistical, more descriptive, and often more enlightening (if equally opinionated) source of USA government information about other countries than the better-known *CIA World Fact Book*.

**Consular Affairs Bureau** • Department of Foreign Affairs and International Trade, Government of Canada • 125 Sussex Dr., Ottawa, ON, KIA 0G2, Canada • tel. 800-267-6788 (toll-free from Canada and the United States only) or +1-613-944-6788, TTY +1-613-944-1310
voyage@dfait-maeci.gc.ca • http://www.voyage.gc.ca

Canada's DFAIT publishes perhaps the most comprehensive set of country-specific government travel advisories other than those from the government of the United States.

**Travel Advice Unit, Consular Division** • UK Foreign & Commonwealth Office • Old Admiralty Bldg., London SWIA 2PA, UK • tel. +44-20-7008-0232, fax +44-20-7008-0155 • consular.fco@gtnet.gov.uk
http://www.fco.gov.uk/travel

The UK Foreign and Commonwealth Office provides travel advice pamphlets of "dos and don'ts" for the countries with the largest numbers of visitors from the UK, as well as advisories on selected countries considered to have special risks. The Web site also has a lot of other good information, including contact details for all UK diplomatic posts abroad and downloadable application forms for visas to the UK.

**Consular Travel Advice** • Department of Foreign Affairs and Trade (DFAT) R.G. Casey Bldg., John McEwen Crescent, Barton, ACT 0221, Australia • tel. +61-2-6261-1111, fax +61-2-6261-3111
http://www.dfat.gov.au/consular/advice/advices_mnu.html

The Australian DFAT issues consular advice for visitors to a particular country only when they perceive real cause for concern. Even for citizens of the

United States or other countries, consular advice bulletins from the Australian government—or the absence thereof—can provide a useful "reality check" on the often more exaggerated or alarmist warnings from the USA government.

## Other Travel Health and Safety References

**Association for Safe International Road Travel (ASIRT)** • 11769 Gainsborough Rd., Potomac, MD 20854 • tel.+1-301-983-5252, fax +1-301-983-3663 • asirt@erols.com • http://www.asirt.org

Founded by the mother of an American medical student who was killed, with 21 other people, in a (typical) Third World bus crash, ASIRT compiles country-by-country reports on road travel safety, and works to increase awareness of road travel as the most dangerous aspect of travel. Among its other accomplishments, ASIRT is responsible for the addition of road safety information to the U.S. State Department's *Consular Information Sheets* ("Travel Advisories"). Most ASIRT *Road Travel Reports* say essentially the same thing: "Road travel is dangerous. Outside the First World, never travel by road at night." So it isn't necessary to get them for every country you plan to visit, although they are extremely useful if you actually plan to drive yourself. There's lots of other good general info on the Web site, including a pocket guide to how to say "Please drive more slowly" and similar things in many languages, and a checklist of seasonal road hazards (roads washed out by rain, blocked by snow, impassably muddy, etc.) in different parts of the world.

*Landmine Monitor* • **by the International Campaign to Ban Landmines** • ISBN 1-56432-277-7 • 2002 edition, 922 pp. • lm@icbl.org http://www.icbl.org/lm

Available in print form or in full text as an online database of annual country reports on the extent of mining, mine casualties, and mine clearance. A must-read for anyone contemplating travel in mined areas.

*Landmines: A Deadly Legacy* • **by the Arms Project of Human Rights Watch and Physicians for Human Rights** • ISBN 1-56432-113-4 • 1993, 548 pp • Human Rights Watch • http://www.hrw.org

Available from the Publications Department of Human Rights Watch; see "Global Surveys and References" under "Background Reading." Includes both general information and country case studies on several of the countries with the most severe problems, such as Cambodia. *Landmine Monitor* (see above) provides more current information on mine hazards in specific countries, but this book still gives a better overview of the dangers mines can pose to travelers, even decades after wars have ended.

*Staying Healthy in Asia, Africa, and Latin America* • by Dirk G.
Schroeder, Sc.D., M.P.H. • Avalon Travel Publishing • ISBN 1-56691-
133-8 • 5th edition 2000, 230 pp

Developed by Volunteers in Asia (see above under "Employment, Living,
Schooling, and Volunteering Abroad") for its own volunteers and training
programs, this book covers what to do before you go, immunization and
other requirements, what to bring, what to do to avoid getting sick, and what
to do if you do get sick. When your mind is dulled by sickness and you're
isolated in a place where no one speaks your language and/or there is no
doctor, and you need to figure out what to do, this is the book you want to
have in your backpack. Don't leave home without a copy. Proceeds from the
sale of *Staying Healthy* help support nonprofit programs in cross-cultural
education and village health care. My highest recommendation.

*Wide Awake at 3:00 a.m.* • by Richard M. Coleman, Ph.D. • ISBN
0-7167-1796-4 (paperback), ISBN 0-7167-1795-6 (hardcover) • 1986, 195 pp
W.H. Freeman & Co., New York

The best book on jet lag, what causes it, and how to deal with it. Jet lag is
a disturbance of the body's normal daily cycles of alertness, sleepiness,
and other functions. Coleman is an expert on those cycles: a former director of the Stanford University Sleep Disorders Clinic and a consultant on
shift-work, scheduling, and jet lag to businesses, traveling athletes, and
others. Honest and practical; not a "miracle cure" book, as there is no
"cure" for jet lag. Clearly and entertainingly written for a lay audience.
Highly recommended.

## Travel Medicine and Immunization Clinics

This is a selective list of some specialized travel health and immunization
clinics I know of, have used, or have had recommended to me by others. If
you have an ongoing relationship with a doctor, health care service, or health
maintenance organization, you may want to consult them first. I particularly
encourage readers who have had good experiences with travel clinics not
listed here, particularly those in cities and countries not listed, to let me
know so that I can include them in future editions.

This list is not intended to be exhaustive, and mergers and acquisitions in
the health care "industry" make it impossible to keep up to date. For travel
clinics in other areas, see your regular health care provider, or the worldwide
directories in the following section.

Most of these clinics fall into two categories: inexpensive drop-in immunization clinics (the cheapest option if you just need immunizations, sometimes located near ports and airports to serve travelers and ships and airline
crews) and more expensive specialized clinics, usually associated with teaching hospitals, that offer much more extensive (and expensive) physician con-
sultations, advice, and background reference information.

## United States

*Fear of Flying Clinic (FOFC)* • 1777 Borel Place, San Mateo, CA 94402
tel. +1-650-341-1595 • office@fofc.com • http://www.fofc.com

The FOFC is a nonprofit, public service agency that draws upon the expertise of professionals from the Federal Aviation Administration and major airlines. Instructors include a pilot, flight attendant, airline mechanic, and air traffic controller, who explain all aspects of air flight safety procedures and airplane control systems as well as basic principles of aerodynamics. Classes include instruction (evenings or weekends) by professionals in the field of aviation including a tour of a major airline's maintenance facility as well as an air traffic control tower. The clinic employs a licensed behavioral therapist who works closely with fearful fliers in developing techniques to conquer their anxieties. Based at San Francisco International Airport, but has a branch in Seattle and gives classes in other areas on sufficient demand.

**Airport Medical Clinic** • St. Mary's Medical Center, Catholic Healthcare West • Terminal 2 (former international terminal), Lower Level • San Francisco International Airport • tel. +1-650-821-5601, fax +1-650-821-5662 • http://www.stmarysmedicalcenter.com/index.asp?pg=SFOClinic • http://www.flysfo.com/guide_nonflash/airportinfo/medical.htm

Services are available 24 hours a day, but an additional after-hours charge applies outside normal clinic business hours.

**Travel Clinic** • Beth Israel Deaconess Medical Center • Kennedy Bldg., 6th Floor/West Campus • One Autumn St. ("T" stop: Longwood), Boston, MA • tel. +1-617-632-7740

Services by appointment only.

**Centinela Hospital Airport Medical Clinic** • 9601 S. Sepulveda Blvd., Los Angeles, CA 90045 • tel. +1-310-215-6020, fax +1-310-215-6034

Open 24 hours a day, 7 days a week.

**Travel Immunization Center** • Northwestern University Memorial Hospital • 201 E. Huron St., Galter Pavilion -9th Floor, Suite 240, Chicago, IL 60611 • tel. +1-312-926-3155 • http://www.nmh.org/services/outpatient_services/travel_immunization/travel_immunization_index.html

Walk-in immunizations sometimes possible, but appointments strongly recommended.

**Overseas Medical Center** • 49 Drumm St., 1st Floor, San Francisco, CA 94111 (opposite the Hyatt Embarcadero, near Embarcadero BART/Muni Metro station and the California St. cable-car turnaround) • tel. +1-415-982-8380

No appointment is necessary during drop-in hours, but call ahead to confirm current hours and availability of vaccines. Charges only for immunizations administered or prescribed; no per-visit charges.

**University of California at Los Angeles** • Travel and Tropical Medicine Clinic • 200 UCLA Medical Plaza-Medical Specialty Suites, 10833 Le Conte Ave., Los Angeles, CA 90095 • tel. +1-310-206-7663, fax +1-310-825-3632 • http://www.healthcare.ucla.edu/Handbook/program.asp?version=5619&progra mid=285

Immuninizations by appointment only.

## Canada

**Canadian Society for International Health** • 1 Nicholas St., Suite 1105 Ottawa, ON, K1N 7B7, Canada • tel. +1-613-241-5785, fax +1-613-241-3845 • csih@csih.org • http://www.csih.org • http://www.csih.org/trav_inf.html (Traveler Health Centres Directory)

The Canadian Society for International Health (CSIH) is a national non-governmental organization with members committed to the promotion of international health and development. The Web site includes a nationwide directory of public and private travel clinics and immunization facilities.

## United Kingdom

**British Airways Travel Clinics** • http://www.britishairways.com/travelclinics • +44-870-606-2782

**Central London (West End)** • 156 Regent St., London W1R 5TA, UK tel. +44-20-7439-9584 • Walk-in service Mon.-Fri. 0930-1715, Saturday 1000-1600

**City of London** • 101 Cheapside, London EC2V 6DT, UK • tel. +44-20-7606-2977 • Services by appointment only

British Airways travel clinics offer travel health advice and immunizations; some also sell travel health care products such as mosquito repellants and water purification units. No advice given over the phone.

## Worldwide

**American Society of Tropical Medicine and Hygiene (ASTMH)** 60 Revere Dr., Suite 500, Northbrook, IL 60062 • tel. +1-847-480-9592, fax +1-847-480-9282 • astmh@astmh.org • http://www.astmh.org http://www.astmh.org/scripts/clinindex.asp (Travel Clinic Directory)

The American Society of Tropical Medicine and Hygiene (ASTMH) is a professional organization for specialists in tropical medicine, hygiene, and related disciplines, mainly in the United States and Canada, but including some in other countries. A directory of all those members worldwide who wish to be listed (presumably excluding military doctors and others not providing services to the general public) is available on the ASTMH Web site. Some members are in individual practices, but many work at specialty travel clinics. Unfortunately, the directory listings are for individual physicians, not for clinics.

### International Association for Medical Assistance to Travelers (IAMAT) • info@iamat.org • http://www.iamat.org

United States • 417 Center St., Lewiston, NY 14092 • tel. +1-716-754-4883

Canada • 40 Regal Rd., Guelph, ON, N1K 1B5 • tel. +1-519-836-0102, fax +1-519-836-3412

Canada (alternate) • 1287 St. Clair Ave. West, Suite #1, Toronto, ON, M6E 1B8 tel. +1-416 652 0137

Aotearoa/New Zealand • P.O. Box 5049, Christchurch 5

Europe • 57, chemin des Voirets, 1212 Grand-Lancy, Geneva, Switzerland

IAMAT coordinates a referral network of bilingual and multilingual (mainly English-speaking) doctors around the world who have agreed to a standard schedule of fees, in USA dollars, for office visits and hotel or house calls for travelers. IAMAT membership and the IAMAT referral directory are free on request, but donations are encouraged. Many travelers find that it allays their fears to carry the portions of the IAMAT directory for the places they plan to visit. But it's rarely that hard to find an English-speaking doctor in the sort of big city where most IAMAT doctors practice, and in the South IAMAT rates are often higher than the prices IAMAT doctors, or equally qualified English-speaking doctors who treat foreign travelers, charge patients who don't mention IAMAT.

### International Society of Travel Medicine (ISTM) • P.O. Box 871089, Stone Mountain, GA 30087-0028 • tel. +1-770-736-7060, fax +1-770-736-6732 istm@istm.org • http://www.istm.org

A professional organization of travel medicine specialists with more than 1,200 members in 53 countries. The Web site includes a worldwide directory of clinics, hospitals, and private practices with which members are affiliated.

# TRAVEL INSURANCE

Some regular insurance agents handle travel insurance, especially long-term comprehensive travel medical insurance. You can also get travel insurance from travel insurance companies, direct providers of medevac and travel emergency services, and independent travel insurance brokers and agencies that can help you compare the offerings of different insurers. Following are some of those I know of, with the types of coverage or services they offer.

These listings are not intended as endorsements, but are just to help you get started on your own research. I've heard good and bad things about almost all of these companies.

**Medical Information for Americans Traveling Abroad** • by the
Bureau of Consular Affairs, U.S. Department of State
http://travel.state.gov/medical.html

Includes informational listings (not to be taken as an indication of government endorsement, accreditation, or approval) of USA-based and foreign-based companies providing air ambulance, emergency medical evacuation, and travel insurance services.

## Travel Insurance Companies

**International Medical Group (IMG)** • 407 Fulton St., Indianapolis, IN
46202 • tel. 866-368-3724 (toll-free in the United States only) or +1-317-655-4500, fax +1-317-655-4505 • insurance@imglobal.com
http://www.imglobal.com

Coverage: Comprehensive travel medical insurance. Expensive but genuinely comprehensive coverage. IMG is the primary provider of medical insurance for Peace Corps volunteers, and a leading insurer of missionaries and other USA expatriates living and travelling in the Second, Third, and Fourth Worlds.

**Travelex** • info@travelex-insurance.com • http://www.travelex-insurance.com

Coverage: Emergency medical, medevac, trip cancellation and interruption, supplier default. In addition to travel insurance, Travelex operates currency exchange and travel service offices in each major world region. (In 2001, Travelex purchased the financial services and insurance division of Thomas Cook.) So if you want a company with regional staff to help you if things go wrong, or if you want coverage for the default of any airline or travel supplier, consider the offerings from Travelex.

**Travel Guard International** • 1145 Clark St., Stevens Point, WI 54481
tel. 800-826-4919 (United States only) • http://www.travelguard.com

Coverage: Emergency medical, medevac, and trip cancellation and interruption. Travel Guard voluntarily covered those travelers who had purchased their insurance, and whose travel plans were disrupted after 11 September 2001, even though their insurance didn't cover war and terrorism and they could legally have refused to pay. Ask about supplies default coverage.

**CSA Travel Protection** • P.O. Box 939057, San Diego, CA 92193-9057
tel. 800-336-6409 (United States only) or +1-858-810-2428
csa@csatravelprotection.com • http://www.csatravelprotection.com

Coverage: Emergency medical, medevac, and trip cancellation and interruption. Ask about supplies default coverage.

**Specialty Risk International, Inc. (SRI)** • 9200 Keystone Crossing, Suite
300, Indianapolis, IN 46240 • tel. 800-335-0611 (United States only) or +1-

317-575-2652, fax +1-317-575-2659 • info@specialtyrisk.com
http://www.specialtyrisk.com

Coverage: Emergency medical, medevac, and trip cancellation and interruption. No supplier default coverage.

**Highway To Health** • Radnor Corporate Center, 100 Matsonford Rd.,
Bldg. 1, Suite 100, Radnor, PA 19087 • tel. +1-610-254-8700, fax +1-610-293-3529 http://www.highway2health.com

Coverage: Emergency medical, medevac, and trip cancellation and interruption. No supplier default coverage.

**Access America** • P.O. Box 90315, Richmond, VA 23286-4991 • tel. 866-807-3982 (United States only), fax 800-346-9265 (United States only) • service@accessamerica.com • http://www.accessamerica.com

Coverage: Emergency medical, medevac, and trip cancellation and interruption. Supplier default coverage is limited to a few selected airlines and tour operators, mainly the largest and most expensive, and excludes all companies that aren't specifically listed as covered.

## Prepaid Emergency Services Providers

**MEDJET Assistance** • 4900 69th St. North, Birmingham, AL 35206 • tel. 800-963-3538 (from the USA only) or +1-205-595-6626, fax +1-205-595-6658 • www.medjetassistance.com

Services: Emergency medical transportation. For a fixed annual fee, MEDJET Assistance will provide air ambulance transportation to the hospital of your choice, worldwide, if you are hospitalized. That's much more generous than typical travel insurance, which only covers transportation to the nearest hospital they deem suitable—not necessarily the one nearest your home—and only if *their* doctors decide it's essential. A subscription to MEDJET Assistance will get you home if you're hospitalized. Period. If you have insurance, but it doesn't provide for medical evacuation, this may be the way to go. (Note, however, that the standard MEDJET Assistance plan doesn't cover you if you are out of your home country for more than 90 days at a time. You have to pay a higher "expatriate" rate for coverage for longer stays abroad.)

## Independent Travel Insurance Brokers

Each of these brokers offers a selection of travel insurance policies from multiple issuers.

**Worldtravelcenter.com** • 1630 Duke St., 3rd Floor, Alexandria, VA 22314
tel. 800-786-5566 (United States only) or +1-402-397-3311 •
info@worldtravelcenter.com • http://www.worldtravelcenter.com

**InsureMyTrip.com** • 50 Motor Pkwy., Commack, NY 11725-5410 • tel. 800-487-4722 (United States only) or +1-860-290-4850, fax +1-860-282-6158 • info@insuremytrip.com • http://www.insuremytrip.com

**Travel Insurance Services** • 2950 Camino Diablo, Suite 300, Walnut Creek, CA 94597-3991 • tel. 800-937-1387 (United States only) or +1-925-932-1387 • info@travelinsure.com • http://www.travelinsure.com

# MONEY MATTERS

## Foreign Exchange and Currency Conversion

While you are traveling, it's generally best to think in local currency, rather than to try to convert every price or transaction. But exchange rate tables and conversion tools can be useful in travel planning, especially if you are trying to interpret or compare prices that are specified in different currencies. The exchange rate tables in most newspapers list only a few, First World currencies, and don't include many of the Third World currencies likely to be of interest to world travelers. Here are a couple of sources for exchange rates and conversions for a wider range of world currencies.

**Pacific Exchange Rate Service** • http://pacific.commerce.ubc.ca/xr

A database of currency exchange rates for about 200 currencies maintained by the business school at the University of British Columbia, Canada. The rates are all listed on a single Web page, so it's easy to save and/or print for offline reference.

**The Currency Site** • http://www.oanda.com

Available only while you are online; no databases or tools designed to be downloaded or used while offline. Most other Internet travel sites use "private label" versions of the OANDA.com currency converter.

## ATM Locators

All of the major credit, debit, charge, and ATM card networks have Web directories of locations worldwide where their cards can (supposedly) be used to get cash, if everything is working. Keep in mind, though, that these directories are not necessarily complete or up to date.

**American Express** • tel. 800-CashNow (United States only) or +1-336-393-1111 (collect from outside the United States)
http://maps.americanexpress.com/expresscash/mqinterconnect?link=home

**Co-op Network (credit unions and cooperatives)** • http://www.co-opnetwork.org/public/find_atm/index.cfm

**Discover Card** • http://go.vicinity.com/discoverd

**MasterCard/Cirrus/Maestro** • http://www.mastercard.com/
cardholderservices/atm

**STAR System** • http://star.infonow.net/bin/findNow?CLIENT_ID=STAR

**VISA/Plus/Electron** • http://www.visa.com/pd/atm •
http://visaatm.infonow.net/bin/findNow?CLIENT_ID=VISA

# CONSUMER PROTECTION

**American Society of Travel Agents** • Consumer Affairs Division
1101 King St., Suite 200, Alexandria, VA 22314 • tel. +1-703-739-2782, fax +1-703-684-8319 • consumeraffairs@astahq.com • http://www.astanet.com

Keeps records of complaints against members and offers informal assistance in mediating disputes between travelers and members. Requires members to subscribe to its code of professional ethics, and can expel members who fail to comply with its rules, fail to respond to complaints, or have too many unresolved complaints. Limited, but more effective than most industry self-regulation schemes.

**Air Travel Organiser's Licence (ATOL) Section** • Consumer
Protection Group, Civil Aviation Authority • K3 CAA House, 45–49 Kingsway, London WC2B 6TE, UK • tel. +1-44-20-7453-6430, fax +44-20-7453-6431
http://www.atol.org.uk

Most sales of discounted air tickets in the UK are covered by the ATOL consumer protection scheme. Travel agents selling tickets or packages requiring an ATOL must include their ATOL number in all advertisements and brochures; you can call either of the numbers above to verify an advertised ATOL number. ATOL licensees are required to post a bond to cover reimbursement of its customers if the agency, tour operator, airline, or other supplier of covered travel services defaults or goes out of business; ATOL fees also support a trust fund that makes up the difference in the cases where liabilities exceed the bonds. As the CAA puts it to UK travelers, "If it hasn't got an ATOL, don't book it at all." Note, however, that rules for purchases across borders, especially on the Internet, are still ambiguous in many cases.

## U.S. Department of Transportation (DOT)

The Department of Transportation, which is supposed to enforce federal laws affecting airlines, gives out one address for consumer complaints and another for enforcement requests, as follows.

**Aviation Consumer Protection Division (C-75)** • U.S. Department

of Transportation • 400 7th St., SW, Room 4107, Washington, DC 20590
tel. +1-202-366-2220 • airconsumer@ost.dot.gov http://airconsumer.ost.dot.gov

DOT's Aviation Consumer Protection Division operates a "complaint handling system for consumers who experience air travel service problems." Your letter to this office "will be reviewed and, in most cases, will be forwarded to an airline official for further consideration." Sounds like a big help, doesn't it? To be fair, I should note that they at least count the letters before they forward them, and publish monthly reports as to the numbers and general nature of complaints against each airline. It's mostly a system for monitoring quality-of-service issues rather than real enforcement, although in theory the complaint records can be used as a basis for rulemaking. I don't know anyone who's gotten a satisfactory response to a letter to this office.

### Office of Aviation Enforcement and Proceedings (C-70)
Office of the General Counsel • U.S. Department of Transportation
400 Seventh St., SW, Washington, DC 20590 • tel. +1-202-366-9342
http://www.dot.gov/ost/ogc/org/aviation

Requests for enforcement action by the Department of Transportation, as opposed to requests for resolution of individual disputes with the airlines, should be directed to the Office of Aviation Enforcement and Proceedings. This is the office, for example, to which to send complaints of such fraudulent and deceptive airline practices as code sharing and labeling of "change of equipment" flights as "direct," or reports of violations by the airlines of federal truth-in-advertising laws by advertising of "half roundtrip" prices or "one-way fares based on roundtrip travel." Airlines in the United States are exempt from most state and local consumer-protection and truth-in-advertising laws, so unless DOT takes action these practices will continue indefinitely. Be sure to make clear that you are not asking for your letter to be passed on to the offending airline for a formulaic reply from their customer-relations department, but making a legal request that the DOT initiate an investigation and consider whether enforcement proceedings against the airline are warranted for the violation or practice in question. Enough sacks of mail, dear readers, and maybe DOT will get the message.

### Califormia Seller of Seller of Travel Registration Unit • State of
California, Office of the Attorney General • 300 S. Spring St., Los Angeles, CA
90013 • tel. +1-213-897-8065, fax +1-213-897-8846 http://caag.state.ca.us/travel

### Travel Consumer Restitution Corp. (TCRC) • P.O. Box 6001,
Larkspur, CA 94977-6001 • fax +1-415-924-2033

The jurisdiction of the California Seller of Travel Law (Business and Professions Code Section 17550) and the TCRC is limited to purchases of travel services by California residents from sellers of travel located in California and registered with the state government. Registered sellers of travel must list their CST registration number in all advertisements and promotional materials; you can verify a CST registration number on the CST Web site. "Sellers of travel" include travel agents and tour operators. Cruise lines and USA airlines had the lobbying clout to have themselves exempted from the registration requirement and the restitution fund, so the law provides no protection against air or cruise line bankruptcy or other default. Non-USA airlines are clearly subject to the CST law but have thus far ignored it. It's unclear what would happen were a Californian to make a complaint against a foreign airline under the law; were foreign airlines directly to challenge the special exemption for USA airlines; or were anyone to challenge the law's application to sales of international tickets as infringing the exclusive jurisdiction of the federal government over international trade. It's typical of USA provincialism that this law was written without regard for its international implications.

# ADDITIONAL INTERNET RESOURCES

**Edward Hasbrouck** • http://hasbrouck.org

My home page, with archives of my e-mail newsletter, other articles, some information about who I am (other than a traveler, travel writer, and travel consultant), and what I do when I'm not traveling or writing about travel.

*The Practical Nomad* • http://www.practicalnomad.com

The Web site for this series of books. Look here for links to a much lengthier hypertext guide to Internet resources that supplement the printed books, as well as other updates, supplementary material, and announcements of new titles and editions.

*The Practical Nomad Guide to the Online Travel Marketplace*
**by Edward Hasbrouck** • ISBN 1-56691-250-4 • 2001, 440 pp.
Avalon Travel Publishing, Emeryville, CA

The companion and successor to this book in my *Practical Nomad* series of travel how-to books. Tips, references, and consumer advice on using the Internet for travel research, planning, reservations, purchasing, and while traveling.

# PUBLICATIONS INDEX

# URL INDEX

# GENERAL INDEX

e-tickets, 256–257

Eurail, 557

Europe: passports, 577; rail passes and tickets, 73–75, 473; rail transportation, 57–58, 68–69, 557; resources, 507, 510, 518, 544; road transportation, 91, 100, 101; timetables, rail, 68–69

European Book Co., 544

Eurotunnel/Eurostar, 557

evacuation insurance, medical, 371–372

exchange rates, 491–494

exotic diseases, 361

ExpatExchange.com, 565

expeditions, overland, 415–416

expenses: advance, 470–472; daily living, 476–478; long-distance transportation, 472–476; see also costs

**F**

family passports, 294–295

Far East, 26

faxes, 454–455

fear of flying, 354–356, 585

fees, see costs

ferries, seagoing, 136–138

ferries and ships, coastal, 138–139

film, see camera equipment

finances, managing while traveling, 494–495

first aid kits, 367–368

First Home Exchange Alliance (FHEA), 547–549

First World, 24

flashlights, 403

flexibility, 239–240

Fodor's World Weather Guide, 563

Folbot (USA) Inc., 558

food expenses, 477–478

Footprint Handbooks, 530

Foreign Languages for Travelers, 568–569

Fourth World, 25

freighters, 134–135

Freighter World Cruises, 559

frequent-flyer mileage, 263–264

**G**

gay: issues, 463–464; resources, 524–525

gifts for hosts, 479

Global Exchange, 566

GoAbroad.com, 566

government offices, 42–44, 573–574, 579–582, 591–593; foreign, 40–42

Grant and Cuttler, 569

Green-Travel, 511

GRIC (Global Roaming Internet Consortium), 571

GSM phones, 452–454, 573

guest houses, 422–423

guidebooks: budgeting for, 471–472; climate, 563–565; general information, 46–47, 420; independent travelers, 424–427; published travelogues, 516–519

**H**

Hasbrouck, Edward, 593

health and safety: air travel, 352–359; first aid kits, 367–368; general information, 348–349; information resources, 581–587; medical clinics, 584–587; resource information, 581–587; supplies to pack,

367–368, 470–471; surface transportation, 350–351; travel illnesses and other medical issues, 359–363; *see also* crime; immunizations

health inspections, 343

hiring drivers/chauffers, 104–107hitchhiking, 130–131

Hollym International Corp., 541

home exchanges, 417–418, 479, 547–549

Homelink International, 548

homestays, 419, 479

Hospitality Club, 550

hospitality exchanges, 418–419, 479, 549–551

hostels, 417, 551–554

hostile and problem countries, 289–292

hotels, 419–420

Human Rights Watch, 503

Hutchinson World Weather Guide, 563

hygiene, *see* health and safety

**I**

iAgora.com, 566

IgoUgo.com, 515

immigration, 331–333, 465–467

immunizations: clinics and travel medicine, 584–587; and health supplies, 470–471; needed shots, 366; reasons for, 343; where to get them, 366–367; *see also* health and safety

imported and immigrant publications, 47–50

independent travelers, 7–10

Independent Traveller's World, 51

Independent Travel Stores Association

(ITSA), 561

India: border with Pakistan, 305; rail transportation, 63–64; resources, 507, 508, 509, 518; timetables, rail, 69

Indonesia, rail transportation, 65

Indo-US Books, 542

information sources, *see* resources

Infotec-Travel, 572

insurance: companies, 587–590; comprehensive travel medical, 369–370; emergency travel medical, 370–371; general information, 368–369; independent brokers, 589–590; medical evacuation, 371–372; supplier default, 373; trip cancellation and interruption, 372–373

insurance companies, travel, 588–589

Intercultural Press, 560

Interhemispheric Resource Center, 537

Intermediate Technology Bookshop, 507–508

International Affairs Resources, 503

International Air Transport Association (IATA), 161–163, 164

International Campaign to Ban Landmines, 365, 583

International Civil Aviation Organization (ICAO), 162

International Congress of Anthropological and Ethnological Sciences, 512

International Ecotourism Society, The, 511

International Institute for Peace through Tourism, 511

International Map Trade Association (IMTA), 561

International Travel Maps and Books (ITMB Publishing), 562

489–490; traveler's checks, 489

Moon Handbooks, 528–529

mopeds, scooters, and motorcycles, 107–110

Mountain Equipment Co-op (MEC), 562

Myanmar/Burma, rail transportation, 65

myths about airline prices and routes, 145–152

**N**

NACLA Report on the Americas, 538

National Association of Railroad Passengers, 99, 556

Nepal, trekking, 337

New Internationalist, 520

newsgroups, 51–52

newspapers, 539, 540, 540

New Zealand: passports, 578; road transportation, 100

North, 26–27

North America: rail passes and tickets, 76–78, 473; rail transportation, 60–61, 65–66, 67–68; road transportation, 89, 100–101; timetables, rail, 67–68

numbers/numerals, 436–443

**O**

Office of Aviation Enforcement and Proceedings, 592

offices of foreign governments, 40–42

online services, see internet

open jaws, air travel, 216–217

open tickets, 244–247, 248

Organization of the Islamic Conference, 304

Other India Bookstore, 542

overland expeditions, 415–416

**P**

Pacific Exchange Rate Service, 590

packing suggestions, 367–368, 386–404

Pakistan: border with India, 305 ; rail transportation, 65

Partners in Responsible Tourism, 511–512

passports: advice and general information, 284–286; applying for, 287–289; Australia, 578; Canada, 575–576; costs/fees, 470; Cuba, 290–291; dual citizenship, 293–294; duplicates, 292–293; entry/exit stamps, 292; family documents, 294–295; Iran, 290; Ireland, 577; loose-leaf visas, 292; lost or stolen, 295–297; New Zealand, 578; North Korea, 289–290; problem and hostile countries, 289–292; resources for, 573–578; United Kingdom, 577; US, 286–289, 573–575

Passport Services, 286

paying for tickets, 254–255, 258–259

Peace Brigades International (PBI), 567

Peace Corps, 567

photography, see camera equipment

pickpockets, 386

plants and animals, 379–380

population centers, 31

postal mail, 404–406, 448–449

poverty and beggars, 462–463

Practical Nomad publications, 593

price estimates, 240–242

problem countries, 289–292

propaganda, 33–35

## R

racism, 371–372

Rail Australia, 557

Rail Europe, 557

rail transportation, 55–87; within countries and regions, 63–66; distances, 474; information resources, 555–558; international trains, 86–87; passes, tickets, and reservations, 71–83; resource information, 555–558; safety, 351; ticket prices, 83–84, 472–475; timetables, Thomas Cook, 66–71; transcontinental train routes, 57–62

rape, *see* sexual (assaults)

Recreational Equipment, Inc. (REI), 562–563

Rec.Travel Library, 515

refunds, airline tickets, 274–275

religion, visa applications, 311

religious calendars, 435–436

reservations: air travel, 243–254; cancelling or changing en route, 264–266; hotel, 419–420; reconfirming, 259–264

resources, 499–593; accommodations, 547–554; Africa, 508, 509–510, 518, 534–536; African-Americans, 525–526; Americas, the, 536–539; Asia, 506, 507, 510, 517, 518, 539–544; bicycling, 518; children, 526–527; climate, 506, 563–565; cultural awareness and adaptation, 559–561; disabilities or special needs, 527–528; document requirements, 506, 573–581; ecology, 510–514; employment abroad, 565–568; Europe, 507, 510, 518, 544; gays, 524–525; gear, 561–563; global surveys and references, 502–506; guidebooks, 528–546, 561–563; human rights,

504; India, 507, 508, 509, 518; Islamic World/Middle East, 545–546; language and communications, 568–570; lesbians, 524–525; living abroad, 565–568; maps, 561–563; Oceania, 546; passports, 506, 573–578; safety and health, 581–587; schooling abroad, 565–568; seniors, 523; Southern perspectives on the world, 506–510; students, 525; telephones and electronic equipment, 572–573; ticket requirements, 506; tourism, 505, 511–514; transportation, 554–559; for travel agents, 506; travel narratives, 514–516; travelogues, 516–519; visas, 506, 578–581; volunteering abroad, 565–568; weather, 506, 563–565

Revolution Books, 509

Rick Steves' guides, 529, 544

road transportation: animals/animal-drawn carts, 130; Association for Safe International Road Travel (ASIRT), 583; automobile and bus, 87–111, 123–129; bicycles, 111–123; buying or renting at your destination, 98–103; hiring a car and driver, 103–107; hitchhiking, 130–131; import duties and *carnets de passage*, 94–95; insurance, 93–94; licenses and permits, 92–93; mopeds, scooters, and motorcycles, 107–110; safety, 350–351; taxis, 128, 129–130; walking, 132–133

Road Trip guides, 529

Roth IRAs, 474–475

Rough Guides, 532

## S

sabbaticals, 474–475

# HELP MAKE THIS A BETTER BOOK

I travel as much as I can to keep my books up to date. The year 2002 began for me in Vietnam, and ended over Amazonia—three times, as my New Year's Eve red-eye flight from Argentina to the USA crossed from one time zone another for successive midnights—with stops on four continents in between. All details in this book were reviewed, and facts and prices verified to the best of my ability, in 2004 before this third edition went to press. However, all things change, and I welcome your assistance in keeping this book current.

Significant changes between going to press and the publication of the next edition of this book will be noted on the *Practical Nomad* Web site at http://www.practicalnomad.com. Internet references are themselves especially ephemeral, so check the *Practical Nomad* site, or let me know by e-mail, if any of the Internet or other resources in this book are no longer at the same addresses.

The information in this book is as accurate as was possible at the time it was written. In an effort to be helpful, I give opinions on many matters on which others would disagree; realize that these are only my opinions. Don't take anything you read here as gospel. Be as skeptical of what you read here as you would be of any other advice. If you think I'm wrong, please write and tell me so. If something is unclear or I've left something out that you'd like explained or think should be said, or if there is something you found especially useful, and want to be sure is retained, please let me know.

Please send all contributions, corrections, anecdotes, and suggestions to:

Edward Hasbrouck
c/o Avalon Travel Publishing
1400 65th Street, Suite 250
Emeryville, CA 94608 USA
e-mail: nomad@hasbrouck.org
http://hasbrouck.org

# DISCLAIMER

It's customary for reputable travel books to contain a disclaimer to the effect that the author accepted no "freebies" or discounts from suppliers of travel services mentioned in the work. The assumption is that free or reduced-rate transportation or other travel services for travel writers are given in exchange for implicit or explicit promotional consideration.

Because I can't say I received no discounts or wrote about nothing in which I have a financial interest, here's a full disclosure:

Writing doesn't (yet) pay my rent. In my "day job" as a travel consultant, I work at AirTreks.com. I also offer my consulting services through Guidebookwriters.com. I mention both of these companies and their websites in this book. After long and thoughtful consideration, I decided that the value of their services to you, the reader, should be more important than my fear of appearing self-serving. Feel free to ignore what I say about them if you think it motivated solely by self interest.

As a travel agent, I have received free and reduced-rate transportation (although far less than most people might think) on various airlines, more as partial compensation for having sold tickets on those airlines than in any expectation that I'll give them a favorable write-up in this book or elsewhere. I don't feel compromised: this book isn't a comparative review of airlines, and I'll let you make your own judgments about which ones to fly with. I personally choose based upon price. Were I to make recommendations, I'd pan some airlines that have given me free tickets and praise some others that I'd have to pay to fly.

I occasionally get discounts on hotels, almost always at upscale places where I wouldn't otherwise stay. I've also occasionally gotten free beds in hostels where I've been giving travel seminars—but where I would have stayed, and which I would recommend, anyway. I still recommend local hostelries of the sort that don't give discounts, or pay commissions, to travel agents.

Finally, a few publishers gave me complimentary copies of books listed in the resource guide, slightly reducing the amount I spent on compiling my library of travel references. I haven't listed any resources that I wouldn't be willing to pay for; I don't list some that I was sent for free; and my highest recommendation goes to some of those that are most expensive and for which I paid full price.

# ACKNOWLEDGMENTS

Thanks to all the fellow travelers who've shared their experiences with me over the years, first and foremost Ruth Radetsky, my companion in travel, life, and love for the last 22 years and, I hope, for the rest of my life.

I've learned much from my present and former colleagues at the travel agencies where I have worked, including Michael Sukhenko, W. Alexander Hagen, and J.-P. Whitecloud. At AirTreks.com, thanks to Bob Leppo, Lee Marona, Jim Pilaar, Tom Michelson, Jesse Walker-Shaw, Aimée Barile, Susan Samarasinghe, Cat MacLeod, Lorin Kalisky, John Taylor, Dan Gamber, David Derrick, Joe Roma, Cristy Dieterich, Nai Piangjai, Matt Radack, Glenn Talken, Xan Grayson, and all the rest of the team.

Holly Ridenour, Nancy Hale, Raba Gunasekara, Kay Burns, Stacy Hoffinger, Lija Ozols, Joy Kessler, Barbara Marré, Barbara Wein, and all the rest of the staff at Hostelling International in San Francisco have been unfailingly supportive; this book has benefited greatly from their feedback and that of participants in my seminars. Of the many other hostel volunteers and staff around the country and abroad who have been my friends and hosts, Travis Major and Peter Leblanc deserve special thanks. Melissa Dennison (REI and Adventure 16), Polly Bolling (REI), other REI staff and fellow members, Audrey Berger at Easy Going in Berkeley, Harriet Carrier at the Globe Corner Bookstores in Cambridge and Boston, Sandye Wexler at the Savvy Traveler in Chicago, Brenda O'Sullivan and the rest of the Modern Times collective in San Francisco, all my friends at Book Passage in Marin and Kepler's in Menlo Park, and others too numerous to list at hostels, bookstores, and travel stores have been equally helpful in organizing and hosting my seminars.

My e-mail correspondents, participants in "rec.travel.air" and other Internet newsgroups and mailing lists, and readers of my writings in diverse publications have been a helpful sounding board and source of ideas, questions, and issues needing to be addressed. Brian Lucas first made portions of what eventually became this book available online in the rec.travel archives, now at Travel-Library.com. Technical assistance has come from the unsung heroes of the "rtfm.mit.edu" faq-maintainers team, the "faq-maintainers" mailing list, and John A. Fotheringham of JafSoft.com. Marguerite Helen (the finest copyeditor I could hope to have for a mother), Alan Wald, Stephanie Tang, Rowan Sherwood, Ruth Radetsky, Henry Radetsky, Roger Karraker, Eric Kettunen, Aífe Murray, Steve Homer, Elizabeth Davidson, Hermine Craven, Kay Burns, Marc Brosius, and Tom Borden read and commented on all or parts of the manuscript at various stages. They have corrected many of my errors, and I am solely to blame for those that remain.

Assistance, suggestions, and answers to my queries on particular points came from Steve White, Maureen Karpan, Scott Leonard, Robert Ferguson, Helen Simpson, David Clover, Patricia Barnett, Wally Doerge, Robert Raymer, Sayyid M. Syeed, David Wright, Joseph Witherspoon, Dirk Schroeder, Jeffrey Perk, Matt Meyer, Dorothy McDonald, Michael Wm. McColl, John Lindsay-Poland, Matthew Lawrence, Tina Lassen, Steve Lantos, Dylan Hiroms, Carol Hahn, Jorge Gordillo, Robert Ferguson, Marcus Endicott, Hermine Craven, Ronald Boyer, Sheila Bostick, Perry and Joseph, Josh Standig, and Don Stevens. Susan Black and Henry Harteveldt of the Travel Commerce Expo and eTravelworld, Phillip C. Wolf and company of PhoCusWright, and Tim Gunstone and Simon Carkeek of Eye For Travel graciously facilitated my access to travel executives for interviews, and tolerated my critical questioning of other attendees at their events.

Bob Shurtleff, the Front Porch Salon, Aífe Murray, Tom Brosnahan, Don George, Wendy Grossman, Chris Baker, Carl Parkes, the late Paul Grimes, and my fellow members of the Bay Area Travel Writers and the guidebook writers e-mail list have provided personal and professional support and encouragement in my writing life.

Avalon Travel Publishing (ATP) continues to justify, in their relationship with me, their longstanding reputation as a writer's publisher. Thanks for the special contributions of Bill Newlin, Pauli Galin, Erin Van Rheenen, Angelique Clarke, Kevin McLain, Dave Hurst, Donna Galassi, Valerie Sellers Blanton, Patricia Reilly, Amanda Bleakley, Mary Beth Pugh (my rock star of a publicist), Rosie Levy, Krista Rafanello, and Stacy Johnson. Thanks also to the people in production and operations, and at PGW, who've helped to move this book from my hands (microphone, actually) to your hands.

The hospitality of Zeth Ajemian, Steve Homer, Steve Chalem, Ruth McKay, Peter Henry, Kevin Grendon, Lynn Fitz-Hugh, Joey Johnson, Joel and Claudia Kavenagh, Matt Meyer, Meg Starr, Kay and Al Forsyth, and Bob and Barbara Lewis helped enable me to afford to travel as widely as I have to spread the message of *The Practical Nomad*. I owe a special debt of gratitude to all those other hosts over the years whom I have failed to thank properly for their hospitality. Whether or not I ever get the chance to return your favors, may you all receive as warm welcomes, wherever you go, as so many of you have given me.

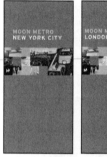

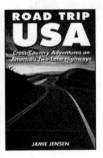

# U.S. ~ Metric Conversion

1 inch = 2.54 centimeters (cm)
1 foot = .304 meters (m)
1 yard = 0.914 meters
1 mile = 1.6093 kilometers (km)
1 km = .6214 miles
1 fathom = 1.8288 m
1 chain = 20.1168 m
1 furlong = 201.168 m
1 acre = .4047 hectares
1 sq km = 100 hectares
1 sq mile = 2.59 square km
1 ounce = 28.35 grams
1 pound = .4536 kilograms
1 short ton = .90718 metric ton
1 short ton = 2000 pounds
1 long ton = 1.016 metric tons
1 long ton = 2240 pounds
1 metric ton = 1000 kilograms
1 quart = .94635 liters
1 US gallon = 3.7854 liters
1 Imperial gallon = 4.5459 liters
1 nautical mile = 1.852 km

To compute Celsius temperatures, subtract 32 from Fahrenheit and divide by 1.8. To go the other way, multiply Celsius by 1.8 and add 32.

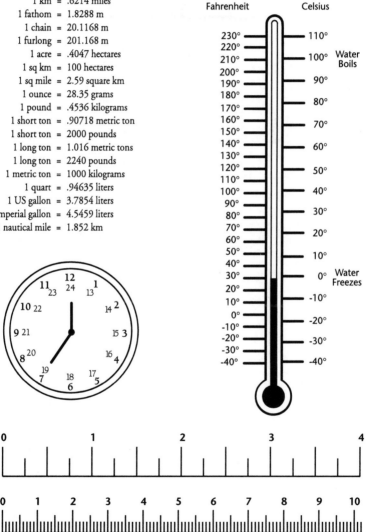

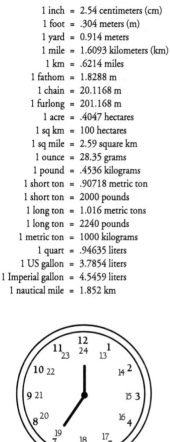